W9-AEK-607

FRIEDRICH SCHILLER

On the
Aesthetic Education
of Man

IN A SERIES OF LETTERS

Oxford University Press, Ely House, London W. 1

GLASGOW NEW YORK TORONTO MELBOURNE WELLINGTON
CAPE TOWN SALISBURY IBADAN NAIROBI LUSAKA ADDIS ABABA
BOMBAY CALCUTTA MADRAS KARACHI LAHORE DACCA
KUALA LUMPUR HONG KONG TOKYO

FRIEDRICH SCHILLER

On the
Aesthetic Education
of Man

IN A SERIES OF LETTERS

Edited and Translated with an Introduction
Commentary and Glossary of Terms

BY

ELIZABETH M. WILKINSON

AND

L. A. WILLOUGHBY

OXFORD
AT THE CLARENDON PRESS
1967

202203

BH
183
S25
1968

© OXFORD UNIVERSITY PRESS 1967

PRINTED IN GREAT BRITAIN
AT THE UNIVERSITY PRESS, OXFORD
BY VIVIAN RIDLER
PRINTER TO THE UNIVERSITY

In grateful memory of

ROBERT LEROUX

1885-1961

*Professor of German
in the
University of Strasbourg*

PREFACE

IT has long been our belief that Schiller's treatise *On Aesthetic Education* ought to be more widely known and more intensively studied. The lack of an edition oriented to English-speaking students prompted us to try to produce one for the Bicentenary of 1959. But as we proceeded with the task of elucidating this very difficult text we began to ask ourselves whether the best commentary of all would not perhaps be a translation more faithful to both the letter and the spirit of the original than those already available. Yet as we proceeded with this alternative project we were again led to wonder whether even the most faithful translation can at this juncture stand on its own feet without benefit of commentary.

This is not just because philosophy is—in Schiller's view even should be—difficult. We ought, he tells us in one of those unwieldy footnotes into which he packed some of his most trenchant observations, to be as suspicious of philosophers whose mode of argumentation is as facile as a fireside chat as of those whose conclusions are at odds with common sense. Nor is it just because of Schiller's own peculiar manner of philosophizing. Though not—like some recent philosophy we can think of—largely dependent for its validity upon the forms of the German language, it is yet informed throughout by his avowed intention of engaging heart as well as mind, and to this end leans so heavily on the figures of rhetoric that the translator is forced tó consider whether a version which is to be faithful to the spirit of the original ought not to reflect something of the shape and rhythm of its periods however unfashionably these may fall upon modern ears. But the real objection to abandoning critical apparatus, or sacrificing fidelity to readability, is that there are still too many cruxes of 'meaning' in the narrower sense of this word; cruxes requiring for their solution, not just knowledge of eighteenth-century German, but knowledge of eighteenth-century optics, animal psychology, and political theory, alchemy, emblematics, and gemmology—to say nothing of theology, philosophy, and aesthetics.

There may one day be a case for dispensing with editorial aids altogether, and trying to put Schiller's 'message' across through the kind of free rendering into a contemporary idiom adopted by the most recent translator of Aristotle's *Poetics*. But in our view the time is not yet ripe for it. Aristotle's text has, after all, been subjected to centuries of exegesis. Before such a frankly interpretative rendering of the *Aesthetic Letters* can be undertaken, not only the general tenor of Schiller's thesis, but the details of his argument and the peculiarities of his method, need to be exposed to the critical debate of scholars in many fields—and not just of those trained in the German tradition either.

For these reasons, and at the risk of falling between several stools, we finally decided on a bilingual edition which places at their disposal such linguistic and historical knowledge as we ourselves possess, and by pinpointing the manifold difficulties challenges them to find better solutions of their own. For the forthright tone we have adopted with earlier critics and translators springs from no illusion that we ourselves have always found the right one: the careful reader will discover that we have already had to modify the interpretation of an ambiguous passage for which we had earlier argued in print. It springs rather from the conviction that a too-modest tentativeness is less likely to uncover the issue at stake and provoke to further, and fruitful, disagreement. We realize that by including the German text at all, let alone the controversies and apparatus of scholarship, we may well have defeated, for the time being at least, our one aim of making Schiller's work more widely known—though we hope that we have so arranged the various sections of our edition that any reader can see at a glance what is likely to interest him and what he will undoubtedly want to skip. And we certainly hope that by including a translation *en face* we have not defeated our other aim of providing an edition for the university student. The time is surely past when he is likely to regard this as a crib enabling him to by-pass the original. If language has been presented to him as the exciting phenomenon it is, our chief means of thought as well as our normal medium of communication, he will be aware that all translation is interpretation, a challenge to deepen his understanding of both the foreign language and his own. It was with the—

wholly Schillerian—intention of setting his mind free for such independent operations that we finally decided for a close analysis of the form of the treatise, and against a summary of Schiller's argument. Those who feel the need for this latter are referred to the last chapter of S. S. Kerry's recent book on Schiller's aesthetics, or to the résumés with which R. Leroux prefaces his translation of each Letter.

The delay involved in turning our alternative projects into a single whole has had the great advantage—though it has inevitably involved further delays—of enabling us to benefit from much of the literature inspired by the Bicentenary. Not, unfortunately, from Professor von Wiese's apparatus and commentary in the *National-ausgabe*, which was not yet available when we went to press. We take comfort from the thought that ours makes no pretence of being a 'critical' edition in the strict sense of the term. It is in all respects a translator's edition—in its commentary, and large tracts of the introduction, no less than in its glossary of terms. If we have included an account of the German text and its story, it is only because, feeling unable to reprint any existing text exactly as it stands, we thought it proper—unlike many of its modern editors— to state our editorial principles, and give reasons for our omissions, inclusions, and modifications.

We are indebted to many friends and colleagues for information of various kinds: to Stuart Atkins, Heinz Bluhm, John Ellis, M. H. Fisch, W. B. Gallie, H. B. Garland, Lilian Haddakin, Stuart Hampshire, Heidi Heimann, Trevor Jones, S. S. Kerry, W. F. Mainland, Cecily de Monchaux, Roger Nicholls, Robert Pick, F. P. Pickering, Hans Reiss, Victoria Rippere, Hugh Sacker, Jenny Schwarz, F. J. Stopp, Eric Turner; to Marie-Luise Waldeck for valuable criticism of our translation, and Nelly Brunswick for arduous proof-reading; above all to Joyce Crick and Ann Weaver for help, information, and stimulus too manifold to define. Mrs. Weaver is also responsible for the Index. But perhaps our chief thanks are due to the translators who have preceded us, outspoken though we may have been in stressing our points of divergence. And quite especially to Robert Leroux, who proved the most reliable guide of all through the labyrinth of Schiller's thought.

We have sometimes, in moments of discouragement, doubted whether the style of his thought can be made accessible to our own day and age. But at the end of our labours we remain convinced that any attempt to do so is well worth the time and trouble involved. For Schiller's treatise is not just one of the greatest works in the German language. It is one of the few works in world literature which seriously explores the relation between art and politics. And one of the very few which offers both a pertinent analysis of a pressing problem of our modern age and valid pointers to the part aesthetic activity might play in resolving it.

E. M. W.

L. A. W.

University College London
10 November 1965

CONTENTS

REFERENCES AND ABBREVIATIONS

TEXT and translation are referred to throughout by Letter (Roman numeral) and paragraph (Arabic numeral), Schiller's own footnotes by an immediately following fn.—e.g., XIII. 4fn.—the notes in our own Commentary by Note; works listed in the Bibliography, including earlier translations, normally by author, or editor, alone; Schiller's letters, except where very long (e.g., the *Kallias* letters), by date alone. To avoid confusion, we have referred to early numbers of the *Deutsche Rundschau* by *Jahrgang* and *Heft*, since numbering by volume was only introduced retrospectively.

Goedeke	Hist.-krit. Ausgabe	⎫
SA	Säkular-Ausgabe	⎬ of Schiller's Works
NA	Nationalausgabe	⎭
Jonas	Complete edition of Schiller's letters	
Horen	The first version of the *Aesthetic Letters* as published in the *Horen* and reprinted in Goedeke	
JA	Jubiläums-Ausgabe of Goethe's Works	

EG	*Études Germaniques*
Euph	*Euphorion*
GLL	*German Life and Letters*
GQ	*German Quarterly*
GR	*Germanic Review*
GRM	*Germanisch-romanische Monatsschrift*
JEGP	*Journal of English and Germanic Philology*
MLR	*Modern Language Review*
PEGS	*Publications of the English Goethe Society*
RG	*Revue Germanique*
ZfdA	*Zeitschrift für deutsches Altertum*

INTRODUCTION

FOR a book proclaiming the virtue of aesthetic education Schiller's has surprisingly little to say about the concrete particulars of art: a reference in passing to the poetry of Anacreon and Catullus; an evocation, memorable but very likely misplaced, of the wondrous blend of womanhood and divinity in a late Roman Juno now thought not to be the statue of a goddess at all. Nor is there much more about the arts in general: Schiller's review of the relations between them, of the tendency of each to transcend its inherent limitations and aspire to the condition of one of the others, though seminal, is brief—a bare page; his hints on how to appreciate art, even briefer—a bare paragraph. And there is nothing very precise about the making of art either: nothing to compare in vividness or immediacy with that passage[1] in one of the poet's private letters (which so intrigued Freud that he reverted to it more than once) on the power of creative minds to relax censorship at the threshold of consciousness, to 'withdraw the sentinels from the gates and let images and ideas rush in pêle-mêle' before scrutinizing their relevance and value. Even the word 'aesthetic' itself is not defined by reference to a work of art, but to a thing—any thing—and to a person—a living one, not a figure of paint or stone; while the central concept of the treatise, the play-impulse, is no sooner identified as the fount of all art than it is also claimed as the foundation of 'the much more difficult art of living', and illustrated by an example drawn from life, from the life of personal relationship: love is defined as the ability to 'play' with its two concomitants, attraction and esteem. And when at the end we come to Schiller's vision of an Aesthetic State we find there no select company of aesthetes lost in idle contemplation of music and statuary, or regaling each other with their latest poems, but a community of people, scientists, scholars, artisans, citizens, going about their ordinary affairs—but with a different quality in their attitude both to the job in hand and to each other.

The reader will find here nothing about education through art in a sense familiar to us today—nothing like Herder's anticipation of modern kindergarten methods when he invites us into the 'Spielkammer des Kindes' and urges the importance of giving him clay or wax to play with;[2] indeed nothing about children at all—Schiller's profound reflections on the likeness, and difference, between their naïvety and the highest form of genius were reserved for his later essay *On Naïve and Sentimental*

[1] Translated and discussed in our Note to XXVII. 4fn.

[2] *Plastik* [1778]; *Werke*, ed. cit. viii. 7, 61, 72.

Poetry. He will find nothing about the practice of art as an outlet for man's creative urge, a means of relieving frustration or fostering self-expression; and little, apart from a few cautionary remarks and one crucial distinction, about that faculty so freely invoked by modern educationists, namely Imagination.

What he will find—has he but the staying-power to press on through what Carlyle called 'the Night of Kantism' and discover those 'passages that show like bright verdant islands in the misty sea of metaphysics'[1]— is an impassioned analysis of the cultural predicament of modern man: the evils of specialization, whether of knowledge or skill, or of one function of the psyche at the expense of the others; the dissociation of what once was united—sensibility and thought, feeling and morality, body and mind; the cleavage between different branches of learning, between the sciences and the arts, between the development of the individual and the welfare of the community, between those who are too exhausted by the struggle for existence to think for themselves and those who are too indolent to make creative use of their leisure; the reduction of man to a mere cog in the wheel of an over-developed society; the de-humanization of the citizen in a State where he is valued for the function he performs rather than the being that he is, treated as a classifiable abstraction and administered by laws which seem irrelevant to him as person. An analysis, in short, of problems which have become the stock talking-points of cultural Jeremiahs in our own day and age.

But he will also find—has he but the knack of recognizing familiar issues when they come in unfamiliar terms—a sober exploration of problems which have become the focus of serious inquiry in the human sciences today, in those borderlands where physiology, psychology, philosophy, and aesthetics meet, and in education where all must be brought to bear: the nature of insight and of perception; the degree of mental activity—abstraction, analysis, inference, synthesis—involved in the apparently involuntary, and seemingly so simple, operations of seeing, hearing, touching, &c.; the extent to which our higher intellectual and moral insights, if they are to be effective for action, must grow out of earlier insights gained through bodily exploration of the physical environment; the processes involved in the emergence of a persistent experiencing self, a self which can say 'I', out of that undifferentiated state—a state which Lévy-Bruhl was to call 'participation mystique'—in which we are more or less identified with the impacts the world makes upon us; the extent to which the stable and distinct forms we construe out of the vague and unified flux around us are dependent upon the experience we bring to their construing; the role played by identification and projection in

---

[1] *Life of Schiller* [1825]; *Collected Works*, London, 1869, pp. 134, 136.

this unceasing commerce between self and not-self, whether in our knowledge of objects or in our conduct with persons—Schiller's anticipation
of an anti-libidinal super-ego, which having made itself a tyrant within
the psyche inevitably projects its tyrannous demands upon others, is as
striking as his shrewd observations about the way reason is constantly
impressed into rationalizing our less reputable motives.

In other words, the issues raised here are as topical as a television broad-
cast or Third Programme talk—and as old as Plato and Aristotle. They
turn on the question posed in the *Nicomachean Ethics*: What is the relation of insight to action? Will understanding of virtue necessarily make
me virtuous? And on the question implied by *The Republic*: What is the
relation of art to politics? Is there any room for such a dubious phenomenon in the ideal State? These two questions form the double axis of the
Aesthetic Letters. And Schiller's chief contention is that they are not unconnected. Is it not possible that objects which are at once illusive yet
true, supremely playful yet profoundly serious, might be indispensable
both to individual sanity and to social order? Not just because they are
illusions necessary for survival amid the discontents of civilization, offering us consolation in a life inevitably frustrating, refreshment in a world
made abstract and dry by science and bureaucracy, an excuse for living
in a universe which tends all too easily to dissolve into the chaotic and
absurd—though Schiller is neither so unrealistic as to deny that they do,
nor so harshly inhumane as to argue that they should not. But because
of the part they might play in fostering the ordered growth of the mind
and furthering our sense of reality. For what could be more fitted to
mediate between the perceptions of sense and the insights of reason, or
between the insights of reason and the will to put them into effect, or
between the world within and the world without, than the objects we call
art? They alone present abstractions—but which are in sensuous form;
analyse our stock perceptions of reality—but by offering us new integra-
tions; project inner needs in terms of the outer world—but in such a way
that both are clarified; figure forth patterns in which confusion may well
be enacted—but is thereby bridled and tamed; allow us to identify ourselves with them completely—yet through their sublime self-sufficiency
free us from all compulsion to covet or control. They alone might enable
us to solve such perennial problems of education as how to make extensity
of knowledge compatible with intensity of understanding, richness of
experience with our ingrained need for order; how to promote a receptivity which is not passive and an activity which is not aggressive; how to
encourage a free interplay between the spontaneous processes of mind and
its deliberately purposive activities; how to develop a sense of form which
is still related to feeling and life. They more than anything else provide
a reason for doing what Schiller says we must do: extend the concept of

mind to include irrational processes of perceiving and thinking. They more than anything else offer us proof of what is perhaps the most provocative of all his contentions: that the clue to the whole history of human freedom is to be found in the fact that we are creatures of sense before we become creatures of reason.

What makes Schiller's treatment of these issues more urgently relevant than those of the Ancients is the moment at which he chose to raise them again. It was a moment when despair over increasing fragmentation and the demand for complete personalities, though not yet the clichés they have become in our time, were already acute, and when the contrast between Greeks and Moderns, to the disadvantage of the latter, was already something of a commonplace. But it was a moment, too, when the Greeks could be—and were by Schiller himself[1]—unfavourably compared with the Moderns on other grounds; when the democratic ideal, by which we still live in theory if not in practice, the right of every man to liberty, equality, and fraternity, not just in the spiritual but in the political sphere too, had not only been promulgated but asserted by force. What Schiller is demanding is the restoration of the wholeness and harmony characteristic of the individual Greek—but without the loss of those advantages which specialization and increase of knowledge have brought to the race. It is this determination to have the best of both worlds, to reconcile apparent incompatibles, which largely accounts for the difficulty of Schiller's treatise: for all the casuistries and *longueurs*, the seemingly pedantic qualifications, the barren wastes of abstraction. De Quincey, writing on a similar theme some thirty years later,[2] was content to draw the contrast between Greeks and Moderns and leave it at that: we have lost something they had; but we have something they had not. When, having completed his piece, he chanced on the *Aesthetic Letters*, he hailed the coincidence of Schiller's cultural analysis with his own—but rejected his educational aim. In his view, wholeness of personality was no longer a viable ideal, except for the odd individual in his purely private capacity. But what Schiller is advocating is a programme of education for Man—can it be right, he asks at the end of Letter VI, that *any* man should miss himself for the sake of progress either present or future?—a programme for the achievement of culture, not by return to those smaller, more primitive, communities in which it once flourished, but within the highly organized modern State with all its unavoidable differentiation of faculty and function. In other words, what he has to say about those two ancient questions is written out of a forward-looking belief in the value of specialization and the rightness of democracy, as well as out of acute awareness of the manifold problems they engender.

[1] See our Note to VI. 2.
[2] See below, p. 338.

THE MAN AND THE MOMENT

POLITICAL

It is often said that the *Aesthetic Letters* were born of a mood of disenchantment with the course the French Revolution had taken, with the degeneration of ideals into disorder and violence, the failure of successive governments to put principles into practice.[1] Such an over-simplification of Schiller's response to the changing political scene has the major drawback of leading us to evade the unique challenge of his treatise, to prejudge it as a recoil into the timeless world of beauty, an apolitical retreat into the ivory tower of aestheticism.[2] Like all historical interpretations this one reflects the bias of the interpreter. But it reflects too the traditional view of Schiller as an out-and-out idealist: in his youth a revolutionary enthusiast, impatiently eager to translate humanitarian ideals into political reality; in later years a withdrawn philosopher, resignedly content to seek their realization in more sublimated form. This is to ignore his continuing concern with the common weal and to exaggerate the radical propensities of his early plays. There was of course enough of revolutionary aggression in them to justify the election of 'le sieur Gilles, publiciste allemand' to honorary citizenship of the French Republic. But there is more of rhetoric in their alleged *Tyrannenhass* than is usually admitted[3]—the motto *in tyrannos* was in all probability affixed to *Die Räuber* by a later hand.[4] And in no one of them is the overthrow of monarchy presented as a successful, or even desirable, solution: the archrepublican, Verrina, in the end prefers the patriarchal despotism of hereditary princes to that of a flagrant demagogue such as Fiesco; for all its denunciation of the vices of princely absolutism, *Kabale und Liebe* envisages social reform proceeding from above, from the humane beneficence of an enlightened aristocracy rather than from the demands of an insurgent *bourgeoisie*; Posa's 'daring vision' in *Don Carlos* is of a State graciously conceded by a liberalized monarch rather than of one extorted by force. Even *Die Räuber* is an attack on the abuses of a social system rather than on the system itself.[5]

Nor was there any change in Schiller's attitude when the system had in

[1] For details of composition and publication see Appendix I.
[2] This is the view of the Marxist, Georg Lukács, amongst others, in *Goethe und seine Zeit*, ed. cit., p. 109. Cf. too 'Erklärung des Schiller-Komitees der Deutschen Demokratischen Republik 1959' in *Friedrich Schiller 1759–1959*, ed. cit., p. 14.
[3] Cf. W. Müller-Seidel, *Schillers Briefe 1772-85*; NA xxiii. 198.
[4] Cf. H. Stubenrauch, *Die Räuber*; NA iii. 342 f.
[5] Cf. Witte, loc. cit. (2), p. 290, who also points out that, according to modern historians, the French Revolution itself was an uprising against the corruption of the *ancien régime* rather than against the *régime* itself.

fact been overthrown in France. He was prepared to be as critical of republics as he had been of monarchies. Comparing the constitution of Lycurgus with that of Solon in his university lectures of August 1789, he praised Athens but condemned Sparta, and in a passage which reads like an anticipation of his *Aesthetic Letters* proclaimed as his ideal State that which—whatever its outward form—fosters the development of all its citizens. It is the liberal State of his friend, Wilhelm von Humboldt, a State interfering as little as possible with the freedom of individuals, but providing the protective framework within which they can flourish. To exalt the idea of the State as Lycurgus did is to confuse ends with means:

> The State is never an end in itself. It is of importance only in being a necessary condition for the achievement of man's proper end, which is nothing less than the cultivation of all his powers. . . . If a Constitution prevents this, if it hinders the progress of man's mind, it is to be rejected as harmful, however well thought out and perfect of its kind.[1]

Schiller still maintained his right to criticize the policies and abuses of government when the principles of free speech and a free press were threatened by censorship during the war with France. Whether he is himself thinking of undertaking a defence of Louis XVI, or encouraging his friend Körner to write an account of Cromwell's revolution, the reasons he gives are the same: either of these two seemingly opposed enterprises would permit the saying of things that ought to be said to and against governments without advocating the overthrow of any particular form of government.[2] Throughout this period, when the French were inevitably coming in for hostile criticism, he kept a watchful eye and an open mind. Sharing Körner's dislike of tub-thumping, of the tendency to settle large issues by the facile commonplace,[3] seizing avidly on the reports of travellers in an attempt to provide himself with first-hand information, he remained cautious, sceptical, hopeful, striving always for philosophical balance. It is wholly characteristic of him to say that his regular reading of *Le Moniteur*, the official gazette of the French Government, had raised his hopes of the French by opening his eyes to both their strength and their weakness.[4] As late as November 1792 he could still say

---

[1] SA xiii. 79. It is significant that the Geschwister Scholl in their revolt against Hitler should have made use of Schiller's manifesto, which had been reprinted at St. Gallen (Tschudy Verlag) in 1940 by E. Korrodi as a separate pamphlet entitled *Lykurg und Solon. Eine zeitgemässe Vorlesung*, and is quoted by Inge Scholl in *Die weisse Rose* (Fischerbücherei, 88, Fft. a. M., 1952; trsl. as *Six against Tyranny* by C. Brooks, London, 1955). Cf. J. P. Stern, 'The white rose', *GLL* xi (1957/8), 81 ff.

[2] To Körner, 21.xii.1792; 6.xi.1792.

[3] Körner to Schiller, 24.x.1789.

[4] To Körner, 26.xi.1792. Cf. Droz, op. cit., p. 174.

that he was by no means averse to seeking his fortune in France were
he prevented from finding it in Germany.

And even the Terror when it came could not shake his conviction that
it is a prime task of the philosopher to distinguish between principles and
practice and to investigate the relations between them. This is not to say
that he was not appalled by the atrocities. 'I haven't been able to look at
the papers for the last fortnight', he wrote on 8 February 1793, after the
execution of Louis XVI; 'I feel so sickened by these abominable butchers.'
And six months later, in the long letter to his patron which contains the
political substance of his *Aesthetic Letters*: 'The [revolutionary] attempt
of the French people . . . has plunged, not only that unhappy people
itself, but a considerable part of Europe and a whole century, back into
barbarism and slavery.'[1] Yet in the very same sentence human rights
themselves are described as 'sacred', and the goal of political freedom
presented as desirable, however unworthy of it men have proved in their
boldest attempt to attain it. The picture he paints of the unworthiness
of these 'wild beasts', whether in that letter or in Letter V of his published
treatise, is sombre indeed. But his realization of the historical importance
of the issues raised by the Revolution remains undimmed:

A matter which formerly would have been decided by the right of might, or
by mere opportunism, is now being brought before the judgement-seat of *pure
reason*, and at least makes some pretence of being decided according to *principles*.[2]

He saw no reason to change the matter of this sentence when he polished
its manner for publication in 1795. It is still there in the revised version
of 1801.[3] And it reflects unchanged the temper in which most of Schiller's
enlightened contemporaries—including his Danish patron, the Duke
of Augustenburg—had responded to the Declaration of the Rights of
Man of 1789. It had seemed to them the realization in practical politics
of all that the *philosophes* of the Enlightenment had stood for. Georg
Forster's reaction was typical: 'How splendid to see what philosophy has
brought to fruition in the minds of men and now realized in practice in
the State.'[4] So was that of von Gentz: 'For me', he wrote in 1790, 'the
failure of the Revolution would be one of the greatest disasters ever to

---

[1] 13.vii.1793; Jonas, iii. 333.
[2] Ibid., p. 331. Schiller's italics.
[3] II. 4. The contention of Snell (op. cit., p. 4), among others, that Schiller's radical
sympathies are more obvious in the original letters to his patron than in the published
version, and that his subsequent change of heart is due to what 'had happened in the
two intervening years', is supported neither by a comparison of the two texts nor by the
dates. The September massacres had taken place, and the King had been executed,
before he started writing the original letters. He went on writing them during the
Terror.
[4] Cited by J. Hoffmeister, 'Goethe und die französische Revolution', *Goethe. Vier-
monatsschrift d. Goethe-Gesellschaft*, vi (1941), 139.

befall the human race. For it represents the first practical triumph of philosophy, the first example of a form of government based on principles, and on a coherent logical system.'[1] But whereas von Gentz's recoil from its 'failure', from the subsequent disorder and violence, led him—via a translation of Burke's *Reflections on the Revolution in France*—to an unenviable notoriety as a supporter of Metternich's reactionary policies, Schiller remained faithful to its liberal principles. His way of doing so may not have been that of a Fichte who, undeterred by the violent turn of events, sprang to the defence of the Revolutionaries in a pamphlet that earned him the name of Jacobin and cost him his Chair in Jena.[2] It was perhaps more akin to that of the aged Kant who, having earlier gone so far as to deny categorically the subject's right to rebel,[3] now felt it timely, when the forces of reaction threatened a new obscurantism, to make a stand for freedom of thought, and in a treatise on religion published in 1793[4] went out of his way to defend political liberty too, countering the argument that the French were not ripe for freedom with the axiom that men only become ripe for freedom once they are set free. Their first attempts will naturally be crude, even dangerous; but 'we must be free in order to learn how to use our powers wisely in freedom'. What Schiller's way certainly was not, was the way of a political quietist. 'In circumstances such as these', he had written at the end of 1792,[5] 'one has no right to remain indolent and inactive. If every liberal mind had kept silent, no step would ever have been taken towards reform. There are times when one must speak out . . .'. And in July 1793[6] he is still prepared to invoke 'the law of the wise Solon' against any citizen who in a rebellion refuses to take sides.

The *Aesthetic Letters* are his way of taking sides. In them, he said,[7] he had 'made his profession of political faith'; and this embraces not only his 'true and sincere opinions . . . on the wretchedness of the actual political situation'[8] but his abiding belief in the political ideal from which this was a grievous falling away, an unshaken conviction that true political freedom remains the greatest good (VIII. 1) and its achievement the most perfect work man can ever hope to fashion (II. 1). But if he was convinced

---

[1] Hoffmeister, op. cit., p. 139.

[2] *Attempt to Put the Public Right about the French Revolution* [1793]. The ostensible charge preferred against him was atheism.

[3] Cf. H. S. Reiss, 'Kant and the Right of Rebellion', *Journal of the History of Ideas*, xvii (1956), 185.

[4] *Ges. Schriften*. Akademie Ausg., Berlin, 1907, vi. 188 fn. Cf. G. P. Gooch, 'German Views of the State' in *The German Mind and Outlook*, London, 1945, p. 16.

[5] To Körner, 21.xii.1792.

[6] To the Duke of Augustenburg, 13.vii.1793; Jonas, iii. 330.

[7] To Garve, 25.i.1795.

[8] To Goethe, 20.x.1794.

that 'this profession of faith would prove not entirely superfluous',[1] it was surely because his *Aesthetic Letters* are at the same time much more than this: not only an attempt to discover a perspective sufficiently unclouded by day to day events to reveal the momentous significance of the changes taking place in an age to which he gave his unreserved assent (II. 2), but also an attempt to discern in the changefulness of human affairs the unchanging needs and attributes of human nature. This shift, or rather extension, of interest was born of no sudden revulsion at the violent turn of events. It goes back beyond the Terror, beyond the execution of the King, to the autumn of 1792—just after the September massacres in fact—when he was urging Körner[2] to translate Mirabeau's *Sur l'éducation publique* (1791). What had so impressed him about it was 'the author's concern, even amid the very tumult of the birth-throes of the French Constitution, to endue it with the seed of permanence by making suitable provision for education'. To Schiller this was evidence of his 'solid' sense of reality; and it was in terms that recall this impression that, some two years later, he announced to the public the aims of the Journal[3] in which his own treatise on education was about to appear: in the very midst of the political tumult it would be concerned neither with party spirit, nor with the petty interests of the passing moment, but with bringing together individual traits of that ideal of humanity which it is given to our reason to conceive but which in actual experience is so easily lost sight of; it would inquire of history concerning the past and of philosophy concerning the future, and be actively engaged in the unobtrusive cultivation of those better insights, clearer principles, nobler morals, on which any improvement of our social condition must ultimately depend.

And if the organ in which his treatise on education appeared was called *The Graces* and not the *Europäische Staatenzeitung*, a political journal he had also thought of editing, this does not betoken any 'recoil' into the world of beauty either. The contracts for both journals were discussed at the same time, in the spring of 1794.[4] Again the dates are important: this was long after the events which are sometimes alleged to have driven Schiller to his aesthetic 'retreat'. And if in the summer of that same year[5] he felt compelled to abandon the political venture, it was partly because his lack of experience in practical politics made him doubt whether he would be able to keep to the publisher's schedule; but also because

---

[1] Ibid.   [2] 15.x.1792.

[3] *Ankündigung der Horen* (SA xvi. 151 ff.), 'that glorious piece of prose', as Thomas Mann calls it in *Friedrich Schiller*. An Oration pronounced at Stuttgart on 8 May 1955. Trsl. by E. M. Wilkinson, *GLL* ix (1955), 11. (This is a shorter version of the *Versuch über Schiller* listed in our Bibliography.)

[4] Cf. letter to Cotta of 19.v.1794, enclosing the signed contracts; Jonas, iii. 441 ff.

[5] To Cotta, 14.vi.1794.

increasingly precarious health made him want to devote what time he had left to projects offering scope for the rare combination of gifts with which he had been endowed—those of philosopher-poet.

Far from being a flight from political reality the *Aesthetic Letters* are Schiller's attempt to engage it in the way he felt most competent to do. The drive behind them is his belief that any reform which is to endure can only proceed from a change in man's whole way of thinking.[1] But what kind of thinking would it have to be in order to issue in action? The course the French Revolution had taken was after all but one example, if an outstanding one, of a failure to put principle into practice which he beheld everywhere around him even after a century of intellectual Enlightenment. Where philosophers alone had not succeeded, a poet-philosopher might perhaps prove of avail. Education through art, improbable as it may sound, seemed to Schiller the only way of closing the gap between insight and action in public politics as in private virtue.

AESTHETIC

At no earlier point in history could Schiller have thought of assigning to art the precise educational function he did. The systematic study of art, of its nature, effects, and its function as a distinctive value in human life, was not yet fifty years old. It had been started by A. G. Baumgarten when he founded what he called a new 'science' and christened it *Aesthetica* (1750). From the very beginning the name[2] gave rise to misconceptions; and the author's choice of Latin terms, together with the misleading German renderings they promptly received, has often caused his aims to be misunderstood and his achievement to be underrated.[3] What he wanted to investigate was neither mere taste—individual likes and dislikes—nor mere sensations—the feeling registered by a subject in response to a stimulus—but a mode of knowledge. His rationalist teachers, Leibniz and Wolff, had distinguished two kinds of knowledge: that which gives us 'clear ideas' of things, sufficiently clear, that is, for all practical purposes, enabling us to distinguish one thing from another and orientate ourselves in our perceptual environment; and that which gives us 'distinct ideas', distinct because, by breaking things down into their component parts, we understand their why and wherefore and thus come nearer to the truth which lies behind appearances. Baumgarten accepts this distinction, as he accepts their division of the human psyche into 'upper' and 'lower' functions. But he turns his attention to a kind of knowledge which is mediate between the two: to a mode of perception in which wholes are neither cursorily recognized for practical purposes

---

[1] To the Duke of Augustenburg, 13.vii.1793; Jonas, iii. 335.
[2] See Glossary under *ästhetisch*.
[3] Cf. Nivelle, op. cit., pp. 21 ff.

and as cursorily dismissed, nor yet subjected to the analytical procedures of science or philosophy, but dwelt on in all their sensible and undivided appearance for the sake of the insight and delight such contemplation may afford. If he terms this mode of perception 'confused', it is not because objects thus contemplated do not stand as clearly before our eyes as the 'clear ideas' of everyday life; on the contrary, they stand there in all that radiant *claritas* traditionally attributed to art. It is because in this mode of knowledge the object remains unanalysed. Its individual elements, however manifold and rich, are not to be isolated from the totality of the intuition. *Confusa* is to be taken in its strict etymological sense, not as 'disorder', but as a 'confluence', or 'fusing together', of elements.[1] What, Baumgarten is in effect asking, are the mental operations involved in grasping promptly and undividedly, as wholes, the complex structures of the sensible world? Might it not be possible to discover in the 'dark', involuntary, processes of sense-perception, imagination, intuition, laws not indeed identical with those governing the rational processes of mind but analogous to them? Is there not perhaps a logic of the imagination? And do its products in art and poetry not betray features of an order as severe as that of science, but more difficult to track down because it is, in Coleridge's words, 'more subtle, more complex, and dependent upon more, and more fugitive, causes'?[2]

The impulse to explore the workings of these 'inferior' faculties sprang from Baumgarten's first-hand experience of the limitations inherent in formal logic of which he was an acknowledged master. But his was no romantic revolution: he had no intention of trying to understand the nature of intuition by means of intuition itself. True, the objects of perception were not themselves to be subjected to analysis: that would have been to reduce the mode of knowledge now to be investigated to a mode of knowledge already well understood. But it was still reason which was to be brought to bear upon the processes involved in their prompt apprehension as wholes. In other words, methods of rational analysis were now to be extended to mental processes not themselves analytical or easily accessible to rational inspection. Baumgarten's achievement thus has a double face. In his choice of a field of inquiry he represents a reaction against rationalism, and could lead a Herder to say that he had 'looked down into the abyss of the human psyche to the point where the feelings of the animal turn into the feelings of the human being'.[3] In his method, however, he represents an integral part of Enlightenment, pushing back the frontiers of reasoned inquiry and shedding light on activities of the mind hitherto thought beneath rational concern. And in his ultimate aim

[1] Cf. E. Cassirer, *The Philosophy of the Enlightenment*, ed. cit., p. 346.
[2] *Biographia Literaria*, ch. i.
[3] *Werke*, ed. cit. xxxii. 186.

too. For although the inferior powers of the psyche were to be legitimized, this was not to be done by exalting them above reason: their role was seen rather as that of mediator from the 'darkness of unknowing' to the 'noon-light of distinct thought'.[1] And although reason was now firmly told that her rule must never degenerate into tyranny, for Baumgarten she still remained queen of the faculties.[2]

From the start, then, aesthetics was rooted in psychology. And in those branches of it which have to do with perception and epistemology, a con-nexion which has persisted down to the present day.[3] Not always with the happiest results. For where modern experimental aesthetics has not pro-ceeded as though it were engaged in what might more appropriately be called 'apolaustics', or the study of pleasure and displeasure,[4] it has tended to investigate aesthetic perception as though it were no different from any other kind of sense-perception, thus evading the precise object of the inquiry.[5] The Father of Aesthetics would no doubt have reminded his progeny that scientific experiments are always devised on the basis of assumptions, implicit or explicit, concerning the field of inquiry, and that questions put to a subject will inevitably be framed in the light of hypo-theses, conscious or unconscious, concerning the object to which he is asked to respond. In other words, the proper study of aesthetics must go hand in hand with an adequately developing theory of art. Schiller knew this as well as Baumgarten. And as a practising artist himself he had, as it were, a built-in control at the production-end for any expectations he might entertain concerning appropriate responses at the receiving-end. With this added equipment he was able to develop even further the notion of aesthetic perception as a mediating influence. And, as might be expected from one writing at a time when intellectual Enlightenment had come under massive attack from many sides, he was impelled to give the idea a new slant. Art, for him, was to have the role of mediating not just from sense-perception to Truth, to those intellectual insights which had been the chief concern of rationalist thinkers, but also from sense-perception to Virtue, to those moral feelings and dispositions which are the mainspring of reasoned and reasonable action.

But although Schiller did not dream of starting his treatise on aesthetic education without first coming to terms with Baumgarten,[6] it was not he

---

[1] *Aesthetica*, § 7. Cf. Gilbert & Kuhn, op. cit., p. 290.

[2] *Aesthetica*, § 12. Cf. E. Cassirer, *Enlightenment*, ed. cit., p. 347.

[3] A. Ames, f.i., who has made such significant contributions to our understanding of how we learn to see, started out from aesthetics. Cf. Johnson Abercrombie, op. cit., p. 41.

[4] The point was made as long ago as 1859 by Sir William Hamilton when discussing Baumgarten in his *Lectures on Metaphysics and Logic*, I. vii. 124.

[5] Cf. E. Bullough's critique of experimental aesthetics in *Brit. J. Psych.*, ii (1906–8) and xii (1921). [6] Cf. letter to Körner, 25.v.1792.

who presented him with a challenge. It was Kant. And not just his aesthetics but his moral philosophy too. What Kant had attempted here was in its way as revolutionary as the 'Copernican revolution' he had claimed for his theory of knowledge. If he had there deflected philosophical attention away from the question of what we know to the question of how we know it, arguing that human knowledge of the universe we inhabit cannot but conform to the faculties and functions of the human mind, so here he had tried to deflect it from its traditional preoccupation with the content of particular duties, and the problem of reconciling them, to the very form of Duty itself, arguing that the criterion of a moral act is to be sought not in its effects but only in its motive, that it is one prompted by no motive whatsoever except the categorical imperative to act in accordance with Duty. His aesthetics represent no comparable revolution. Nor did he imagine they did.[1] In this sphere the 'turn' to the subjective had already been accomplished by earlier thinkers, and was reflected in a growing recognition that beauty is in the eye of the beholder. All Kant had to do here was to bring this insight into line with the rest of his philosophical system, to transpose it from an expression of individual taste into the form of a universal judgement by subjecting it to the rigour of his 'transcendental' method. A pure aesthetic judgement, he concluded, is one that is as free of 'interest' as the pure moral act is free of 'motive', is one characterized by disinterested pleasure even as the other is characterized by disinterested duty.

No one could have been more appreciative of the rigour of Kant's distinctions than Schiller. By means of them he had firmly distinguished the beautiful from things with which it had often been confused, not only from the good and the perfect but from the merely pleasant or agreeable too, thus freeing art from its ancient subservience to extraneous ends, whether religious, didactic, or hedonistic, and securing for it an autonomy of its own. At a time when the 'fine' arts had at last been differentiated from all other products of human skill and ingenuity, Kant had, by defining beauty in terms of the kind of judgement it inspires, provided at least a subjective criterion for 'art' in this new and narrower sense.[2] At the same time he had crowned what Baumgarten had begun by widening the field of aesthetics to embrace far more than art itself; to embrace not only the beauties of nature but even such phenomena as human conduct, thus opening up possibilities which Schiller was to explore and exploit to the full for his idea of aesthetic education. If Kant's achievement still left him unsatisfied, he was always ready to concede that this might well be due to its method rather than its intention: that it was certainly not in the spirit of his 'transcendental' philosophy to empty forms of content

---

[1] Cf. Nivelle, op. cit., pp. 293 ff. and 357 ff.
[2] Cf. Glossary under *Kunst*.

and concepts of life, though this was probably there in the letter of it.[1] And in the long run, as he told Goethe,[2] this had had the effect of reducing the word 'beauty' to a hollow and empty sound. Was it not time for someone to take the risk of replacing it by 'truth' in an attempt to restore to the underlying concept its life-deriving and life-giving significance?

In thus reverting to Shaftesbury's identification of beauty with truth, Schiller was not of course suggesting that art gives us 'knowledge', empirical or ultimate, or can ever be a surrogate for science, philosophy, or religion; not trying to go back behind distinctions so painstakingly established by Kant. But were these as they stood really adequate to account for the nature and effect of an art such as literature, whose very medium is already weighty with meanings? It was easy enough to say that beauty consists in form alone, or to define a pure aesthetic response as 'disinterested' pleasure, if you took as your model, as Kant had done, an arabesque.[3] But what of the representational arts, which draw so heavily for their materials on what Goethe was to call 'höhere Lebens-interessen'?[4] What of tragedy, with its ancient and perennial enactment of such urgent 'life-interests' as sacrifice, death, and rebirth, an art whose materials are rarely pleasurable, but on the contrary engage man's deepest fears and taboos no less than the highest hopes and strivings of his moral sense? Kant's demand that in aesthetic experience the psyche should delight in the free play of all its faculties was all very right and proper. But was such free play only to be achieved in the *absence* of vital, or even disturbing, interests? The scales of a balance, as Schiller remarks when developing his own theory of play,[5] certainly stand level when they are empty; but they also stand level when they contain equal weights. Was it not possible for the desired equilibrium of the psyche to be induced by a form which balances these life-interests one against another in such a way that we are not the victim of any one of them but free to give ourselves to all? A form designed to ensure that instead of succumbing to their pressures, as we do in the course of our daily life, we are briefly enabled to contemplate the significant pattern of their stresses and strains? In other words, the 'truth' Schiller demands of art is that it shall be truly

[1] XIII. 2fn. § 2. Cf. XVIII. 4; but also XV. 5fn.

[2] 7.vii.1797. The point is made apropos their joint efforts to correct the one-sided, 'Apolline', image of Greek art and literature which was the legacy of Winckelmann and Lessing.

[3] Letter to Körner, 25.i.1793.

[4] To Eckermann, 2.v.1824: 'Religion stands in precisely the same relation to art as any other of life's higher interests. It is to be considered purely as material, having equal rights with all the other materials life affords.'

[5] XX. 3. Cf. his use of the same image in his essay *On the Use of the Chorus in Tragedy* (SA xvi. 125).

expressive of life as it is felt and thought, in all its concrete uniqueness and irreducibility to categories and abstractions. And his plea is for an aesthetic which admits the need for coming to terms with this vital content, as well as with the purely formal properties, of art.

Such a plea was of course essential to the thesis of his *Aesthetic Letters*. For if art was to educate, it had, surely, to make connexion with the chaos it claimed to conquer, not remain aloof from it. Forms, however 'beautiful', which touch our sentient life only at its periphery, could not hope to tame the passions or refine the drives which are the natural basis of will. Had not Kant, for the sake of a scrupulous definition, sacrificed the profound connexion of art with life? And was not a similar impoverishment implied in his definition of a pure moral act? An impoverishment of the concrete complexity of individual behaviour, with its mixture of motives, for the sake of a pure but unrealizable abstraction? Again, there was no question of going back on Kant's hard-won definition of a categorical imperative. But like Coleridge—who yielded to none in his admiration of Kant's philosophical integrity—Schiller was moved to ask: What, then, becomes of grace and graciousness, of those moral deeds in which the joy in the doing makes 'the whole man move together'[1] rather than with clenched rigidity and à contre-cœur? Moved to ask, as Coleridge was to ask when working through the *Metaphysic of Morals*: What then becomes of love—love, not as the mere beneficence to which Kant seems to reduce it, but love as a spontaneously outflowing sympathy? And Schiller would surely have endorsed his impatient dismissal of Kant and all of his school as 'wretched psychologists'.[2] For the very idea of education implies, not necessarily a denial of theoretical abstractions or unrealizable ideals as guiding lights, but a general orientation towards the practical and the possible and the intractably contingent. And in the realm of practical possibility was it not a question of transformation rather than of inhibition or repression? Transformation of our more primitive self-regarding motives in the cause of interests which transcend the purely personal? Even as in the aesthetic sphere it was a question of the artist transforming the materials, ordinary or extraordinary, which life affords him, and through the form he thus creates transmuting the interests of the beholder—his interests social and sublime, the perilously threatening as well as the pleasantly peripheral, the subterraneously repressed no less than the civilized and acceptable.

Above all Schiller was dissatisfied with the subjectivist bias of Kant's aesthetics. Like Goethe[3] he felt that from it one could learn much about

---

[1] As Steele had required he should: *Spectator*, vi; 7.iii.1711.

[2] *Notebooks*, ed. cit. i. 1705, 1710, and 1717. For a marginal note in the same strain, and a discussion of the similarity between Coleridge's reaction and Schiller's, see E. M. Wilkinson's note to 1705 [*p*].

[3] Cf. their correspondence of 18–19.ii.1795.

man but all too little about art and beauty. It had concentrated exclusively on statements of the type 'this rose is beautiful'. Was it not possible to say anything at all about statements of the type 'this is a beautiful rose'? Yet again, there was no question of returning to a tradition with which Kant had broken, of trying to discover such 'objective' properties of beauty as the golden section or any other hidden, but ultimately demonstrable, concordance of number or proportion. Schiller knew very well that beauty is only to be defined in terms of a relation. But was it not possible to say anything at all in terms of the objective pole of that relation? Not possible to find philosophical justification for Lord Kames's more balanced formulation[1] that 'beauty, which for its existence, depends upon the percipient *as much as upon the object perceived*, cannot be an inherent property of either'? In the field of art at least this must surely be possible. For although not even an acknowledged masterpiece can compel a particular individual to an aesthetic response, compel him to feel that it is beautiful *for him*, this is nevertheless the kind of response that works of art are pre-eminently designed to call forth. Surely it must be possible to point to features which set them apart as objects of pure semblance, having no other function than to serve as symbols expressive of the felt life within.

The points at which Schiller felt compelled to take issue with Kant—the vital import of art-forms (*Gehalt*), the transformation of life-materials into semblance (*Schein*), and of life-interests into a kind of play which yet has its own seriousness (*ein ernstes Spiel*)—were no doubt dictated by his inside knowledge of the particular art he practised. But in doing so, he was also drawing on almost a century's discussion of problems which Kant's aesthetics had not so much failed to solve as neglected to raise. If art was not to be tested by the rules of reason, was it then purely a matter of feeling? If so, how exactly did feeling come into it? Was a work of art to be thought of as a stimulus to the feelings of the beholder? Or as an overflow of the feelings of the artist, a symptom, analogous to tears, a sigh or a cry? Was it to be measured by the intensity of the passion it inspired, as Dubos thought? Or by the intensity of the passion that inspired it? Or was it not a stimulus or a symptom at all, but a symbol —a symbol articulated by the mind of the artist as he works on a medium, whether natural or, as in the case of language, artificial, kneading and shaping it until (as Herder taught the young Goethe[2]) it becomes a vehicle for expressing the otherwise inarticulate life of feeling, ours no less than his? If this was the case, then art could be thought of as a conceptualization of feeling, and there was a possibility of reconciling ancient theories

---

[1] *Elements of Criticism*, ch. iii; ed. cit. i. 261 (our italics). Cf. our Note to X. 7.

[2] Cf. E. M. Wilkinson and L. A. Willoughby, 'The Blind Man and the Poet' in *German Studies Presented to W. H. Bruford*, London, 1962, esp. p. 33.

of art as knowledge with more recent theories of art as an expression of feeling.

Much of this theorizing—and this is of immense importance for Schiller's thesis of education through art—had taken place within the wider context of investigations, empirical and speculative, into the natural history of the human mind. However much they may have differed on points of detail, or even in their basic convictions, Diderot and the *philosophes*, Hume, Rousseau, and Herder, German psychologists and logicians such as Tetens and Lambert who, in the wake of Leibniz, took the creation of art as a paradigm of the general formative activity of the human mind—they all in their several ways helped to replace the picture of the psyche as a collection of discrete faculties by a picture of the psyche as a unity and continuity.[1] In no single one of its acts is there any separating feeling from intellect, or cognition from conation: what we perceive is governed, not only by what we are sensorially and intellectually equipped to perceive, but also by what we expect, and need, and are eager, to perceive. And from the simplest and most involuntary acts of sense-perception to the highest abstractions and constructions of which man is capable, mind is involved in an imperceptible but continuous growth. It was a picture in which the passions were seen less and less as 'perturbations of the mind', having mere nuisance-value, and more and more as indispensable to its fruitful operations. Without their co-operation, as Hume put it, reason cannot take a single step forward. Or, in Diderot's words, the true power of the soul springs not from their destruction but from their harmonious balance.[2]

It was in such a climate of thought that Schiller had started to come to terms with the basic problems of aesthetics. In a review of Bürger's poetry (1791) he had argued that the poet's passion, however strongly felt, must—if his poem is to be more than a personal document, if it is to speak to, and speak for, the feeling of others—have become so alien to him, or distanced from him, through the new excitement of form that he can treat it as material to be fashioned 'in recollection' by the shaping power of his mind. In two essays on tragedy (1791–2) he had treated, not altogether successfully, of the difference between our pleasure in the tragic events of real life and the cathartic effect of the art of tragedy. In the drafts for a treatise, to be entitled *Kallias*,[3] he had sought a criterion of beauty within the subject–object relation, and—transposing Kant's notion of moral freedom into aesthetic terms—concluded that an object strikes us as beautiful when it seems to be determined by its own nature: when, though having a law within it, it yet appears free from every law;

---

[1] Cf. E. Cassirer, *Enlightenment*, ed. cit., ch. iii.   [2] Ibid., pp. 105 ff.
[3] Never completed, but preserved in the form of letters to his friend Körner, January–March 1793.

though subject to the physical laws of the universe, it yet appears to transcend them; though having a function outside itself, it yet appears to have subordinated function to form; when, in other words, it gives the impression of freedom made manifest to the senses, or of 'Freiheit in der Erscheinung'. In an essay *On Grace and Dignity* (1793) he had asked whether there is not a morality of being as well as a morality of doing, and attempted to reconcile Kant's freedom of the spirit, to be achieved only through self-abnegation, with Shaftesbury's freedom of the whole psyche, to be achieved when duty happily coincides with inclination. And in an extensive, and seminal, review of Matthisson's poems (1794) he had broached such fundamental issues as the distinction between the discursive aspect of poetry and what he called its 'musical' aspect, by which term he designated, not its aural properties alone, but the power—shared in some measure by all the arts but possessed in supreme degree by music —of 'symbolizing through analogical outer movements the inner movements of the psyche'; such issues as 'the symbolic operations' by means of which poet and painter alike are able to make the forms they borrow from the outer world expressive of the world within; such issues as the apparent contradiction between the concrete particularity of poetic utterance, on the one hand, and its universality of appeal, on the other.

All these interests reappear in the *Aesthetic Letters*, unified and transformed by the dominant intention of presenting art as an educative power. Transformed too by Schiller's evident desire to write not just a treatise on aesthetics but an aesthetic treatise. In attempting this he was responding to Baumgarten's demands that the new discipline should be 'the art of thinking beautifully' as well as 'the science of the beautiful'—an ambiguity which has dogged the subject down to the present day—and that the aesthetician himself should be 'a whole man', not thinking himself above the gifts of intuition and imagination, but endeavouring to integrate these with the 'rational' processes of inference and deduction. Herder, for all his admiration of Baumgarten as a pioneer in 'anthropology',[1] a thinker who in the precision of his distinctions might rank as 'the true Aristotle of our time',[2] had been quick to argue that if the one demand was ambiguous the other was superfluous. Aesthetics, if it was to make a genuine contribution to our understanding of human nature, would have to be frankly and unambiguously a science; in its higher manifestations of course it might, like any other science, partake of the grace of art, but this could be no part of its initial definition.[3] As for the aesthetician himself, why single him out for special exhortation to 'wholeness'?[4] The proper execution of his task would inevitably demand of him,

---

[1] *Werke*, ed. cit. iv. 15 and 25.
[2] Ibid. xxxii. 83. Cf. iv. 16.
[3] Ibid. iv. 22 ff.   [4] Ibid. iv. 25.

as of any other scientist, the fullest possible use of all his combined powers.

Schiller, when charting the future course of aesthetics in Letter XVIII, clearly had this kind of objection in mind. Hence his repudiation of 'intuitive' aesthetics, with its obsessive attachment to 'wholes'. But was it necessary to confuse if one also had a strong impulse to unite? Was it not possible to start with the most scrupulous distinctions, and yet not stop short of the most complete synthesis? And was it not possible to discover a manner which, while convincing the reader by the cogency of its argumentation, might yet *at the same time* delight him through the beauty of its form?

PERSONAL

If Schiller felt a special call to these tasks, it was because he saw himself as something of a 'hermaphrodite',[1] a cross between poet and philosopher.[2] Not that he was consistently enamoured of this hybrid condition. On the contrary, he wavered between moments of high confidence, when he felt it to be an asset, and moods of gnawing despair, when the pull in two directions seemed a handicap to excellence in either; when the influx of imagination seemed to disturb abstract thinking, and the invasions of cold reason to inhibit creative inspiration. In such moods he would complain[3] that when he was trying to write poetry the philosopher got in the way, and when he was supposed to be philosophizing the poet caught him unawares.

Such ambivalence towards the hybrid character of his creative activity was but one symptom of a dichotomy which tormented him for the greater part of his life and was, if we are to believe his own testimony, never entirely healed even at the end of it. What makes his self-diagnosis plausible is the cumulative weight of the evidence rather than any single piece of it. His addiction to the figure of antithesis, for example, might reasonably be held to betray the stylist rather than the man. But to such linguistic clash and conflict must be added the clash and conflict of opposed pairs of characters in his plays, and his sharp division of the psyche into two hostile camps in his aesthetic writings. Those 'inferior' forces which it was his avowed aim to rehabilitate he once described in a private letter[4] as 'sleeping lions, whom it were often best not to awaken since they are not so easily silenced again'. And even in

---

[1] He had used the Greek term of Körner's hybrid intellectual powers in a letter of 1.xii.1788; to Goethe, 31.viii.1794, he uses the German word, *Zwitterart*, of his own.

[2] After the appearance of the first nine of his *Aesthetic Letters*, he was actually called to a chair of philosophy in Tübingen, but declined. Cf. letter to Voigt, 26.iii.1795.

[3] To Goethe, 31.viii.1794.

[4] To Körner, 10.vi.1792.

those parts of his published work where the overt tenor of the argument is to rescue them from the repressive rigour of our intellectual and moral principles, they are referred to as an 'enemy', an enemy whom it were indeed wiser to reconcile than to overthrow, but an enemy all the same.[1] The image betrays him. Or, rather, it betrays a characteristic feature of his thinking. To dismiss him as a Kantian dualist has been a recurrent failing of Schiller scholarship: it has obscured his life-long inclination to think of the psyche as an organic unity. But to attempt to correct this by denying his evident dualism altogether is to fall into an error almost as unfortunate. For it is to miss his most characteristic, and his most valuable, contribution to our understanding of human nature: his insight into the dynamic interplay—and interstrife[2]—of opposing forces in the life of the psyche. In order to throw the Schillerian view of it into sharp relief, we have only to compare one of his many descriptions of its activities with one of Goethe's rare excursions into Kantian terminology.[3] Goethe sees the collaboration of the faculties as mutual aid: all is interrelation and overlapping of function, as between members of a family; they are brothers and sisters, needing each other, helping each other out, synthesizing, permeating, and so completing 'the at once absolutely closed, yet infinitely open, cycle of our states and conditions'. For Schiller, a fruitful 'collaboration' is only to be achieved through hostile forces holding each other in check: all is antagonism and arrogation of authority, the maintenance of a strict watch over frontiers and the invocation of immutable laws against trespassers. We find precisely the same contrast in their hopes for the kind of collaboration their own friendship might bring.[4] Schiller saw it in terms of a dramatic encounter between two diametrically opposed types, meeting each other exactly half-way, and modifying each other by exactly proportional concessions and approximations. Goethe saw it in terms of two different 'cycles of feeling, thought, and activity, which in part coincide, in part remain tangential'; it was for him not so much a question of *altering* the other as of bringing out the best that was in him, and warning him when he showed signs of becoming too one-sided.

The very violence with which Schiller tries to heal the dichotomy of modern man is further evidence of the reality of his own. It exceeds the element of compulsion which is perhaps inherent in the pedagogic situation itself and which can, if the aim is education to freedom, be productive of a curious paradox. This was an issue Rousseau had had to face if his

---

[1] e.g., XIII. 4fn. § 3. Cf. *Anmut und Würde*; SA xi. 218.

[2] Cf. XXIII. 8 and our Note thereto.

[3] e.g., that in VI. 12 with the behaviour of the Kantian faculties as seen through Goethe's eyes in a letter to the Erbgrossherzogin Maria Paulowna, 3.i.1817.

[4] Schiller to Goethe, 23.viii.1794; Goethe to Schiller, 1–19.x.1794.

social contract was to be anything more than a dead letter: having agreed that to deprive a man of his freedom is to deprive him of his essential nature, he was nevertheless forced to conclude that if he should refuse to obey the general will 'he must be *forced* to be free'.[1] And Fichte was frank enough to incorporate the element of pedagogic pressure into the subtitle of a popular exposition of his own philosophy: 'An Attempt to *Force the Public to Understanding*'.[2] In Schiller such 'normal' pressure is intensified by the habitual aggressiveness of his language. When he and Goethe first embarked on their joint cultural campaign, Goethe spoke of finding 'vehicles and masks' by means of which they might 'put over' their ideas to the public. Schiller, characteristically, had recourse to images of 'offensive and defensive weapons'.[3] And the violence is even there at the heart of his aesthetic *credo*: at the very point where he is intent on establishing that in the moment of aesthetic contemplation 'the psyche must remain completely free and inviolate', he will nevertheless speak of the artist not only overcoming and subduing his materials—which is perfectly legitimate—but of his achieving dominion over the beholder—which is far more questionable.[4]

The circumstances of his life and education did nothing to mitigate such a dualistic view of the world. He had wanted to be a preacher, dedicated to the cure of souls. He found himself instead impressed into training as an army doctor and responsible for the cure of bodies. Though not of bodies alone. Medical studies at the Duke of Württemberg's Military Academy[5] were oriented to those frontiers where physiology and psychology meet; and Schiller's report on one of his first cases[6] faithfully reflects the required psycho-somatic approach. The philosophical theories to which he was exposed did little to solve the problems this engendered. Here, as elsewhere in the Academy, the principles of enlightened liberalism held sway, and the pupils were confronted with maximum diversity: with the traditional deductive method of Descartes and Leibniz, on the one hand, and with the inductive empiricism of the *philosophes*, or the common-sense school of Reid and Ferguson, on the other. An ardent advocate of this 'reasoning from experience' was Schiller's favourite professor, J. F. Abel, who had prefaced the *theses*

---

[1] *Contrat Social*, I. vii; Vaughan, op. cit. ii. 36. Our italics.

[2] *Sonnenklarer Bericht an das grössere Publicum über das eigentliche Wesen der neuesten Philosophie. Ein Versuch die Leser zum Verstehen zu zwingen* [1801]; *Werke*, ed. cit. ii. 323 ff.

[3] Goethe to Schiller, 1.x.1794; Schiller to Goethe, 20.x.1794.

[4] XXII. 5. All this supports Goethe's remarks to Eckermann (18.i. 1825; 19.ii.1829) that Schiller had a violent, and even cruel, streak in him.

[5] Cf. R. Uhland, *Geschichte der Hohen Carlsschule*, Stuttgart, 1953. See also *Katalog der Ausstellung 'Die Hohe Carlsschule'*, ed. cit.

[6] SA xvi. 324 ff.

philosophicae his pupils were to 'dispute' during the session 1776 with the axiom: 'Vera philosophia est philosophia sensus communis quam e.g. Reid pluresque Angli sequuntur.' But even within this empirical approach Schiller found himself faced with conflicting doctrines of human nature. The view of it as a machine he was soon to deride in his first play (though he retained a curious partiality for mechanical images even as late as the *Aesthetic Letters*). The view of it as an animal was more difficult to dispose of. The chief problem involved here had been clearly posed by the translator and popularizer of Ferguson's *Moral Philosophy*, Christian Garve (whose influence on Schiller was almost as great as that of Ferguson himself): How, without assuming a dual source of knowledge in man, the one natural, the other supernatural, are we to explain his power to determine his own thinking? How, without recourse to innate ideas, ensure his freedom to think and act as he chooses? The Scottish philosophers themselves, for all their insistence that the study of man must acknowledge no authority but experience, had been obliged to postulate common sense as a gift of nature 'which has the light of truth in itself'.[1] Was this really so different from the doctrine of 'inward light' preached by those Pietists of Schiller's native Swabia from whose influence Abel was endeavouring to 'enlighten' him?

This question of human freedom, in whatever form it might present itself, was for Schiller the crux, and remained so throughout his life. But unlike Garve he was not content to leave it without an answer. And in his first dissertation of 1779, *Philosophie der Physiologie*, we find him searching for the point within the reciprocal action of body upon mind, and mind upon body, which will 'save' the freedom of the will. He thought it was to be found in *Aufmerksamkeit*, the power of the psyche to attend to certain links in the chain of involuntary associations rather than to others.[2] This is an evident anticipation of the *Selbstbewusstsein*, or self-awareness, which at the end of Letter XIX he will postulate as an essential, if inexplicable, attribute of human personality, as much a 'given', in germ at least, as our psycho-physical organism, though clearly dependent upon this for its manifestation. And it is noteworthy that even at this early stage the related power of the psyche to reassemble the ideas thus selected for attention is designated as *erdichten*,[3] a word not indeed synonymous with poetry-making but cognate with it.[4] So that already we may discern the

---

[1] Cf. Glossary under *Gemeinsinn*.

[2] SA xi. 37 f. Cf. his letter to Körner of 7.v.1785, in which the freedom to 'play with' the clockwork regularity of the mechanism is likewise linked with the gift of awareness: 'den preise ich selig, dem es gegeben ward, der Mechanik seiner Natur nach Gefallen mitzuspielen, und das *Uhrwerk* empfinden zu lassen, dass ein *freier* Geist seine Räder treibt'. [3] SA xi. 38.

[4] Though the simplex *dichten* itself can also mean 'feign', 'fabricate', 'invent'; and it is, as H. W. Cassirer points out (op. cit., pp. 217 f.), Meredith's mistake to have taken

shape of things to come: the impulse to seek and find in the freedom of aesthetic creativity the source of man's power to make of himself what he will.

In his second dissertation of 1780, *On the Connexion of Man's Animal Nature with his Spiritual*, the streak of melancholy in Schiller breaks through the positive scientism of his formal argument—a melancholy which is responsible for the awesome splendour of his apocalyptic visions, even as his pedagogic optimism is responsible for his impassioned evocations of a New Jerusalem. Under pressure from his 'enlightened' patron and professors, he here abandons his search for a point of freedom in the 'mechanism' of the mind–body relation in order to concentrate on the influence of body upon mind and—with a cautious disavowal of current animist doctrines—of mind upon body. Even that serenity of spirit which enables a man to rise triumphant above bodily affliction, and to ask in uttermost extremity 'Death, where is thy sting?', is here dismissed as but an illusion of spiritual strength. In reality, it is to be explained as a symptom of bodily weakness, a diminution of physical sensitivity to stimuli.[1] True freedom of the spirit has to wait on that moment when final dissolution of the vital processes releases it from its physical 'instrument', and the soul can set forth on its voyage of further discovery. Yet the overt trend of this second dissertation is not to be dismissed as mere conformism. The notion of the human mind as an organic growth, reciprocally related to the physical organism, was and remained a genuine interest, as genuine as his unshakeable belief in the freedom of the human spirit. But as yet the two remained unresolved in his thinking, and were to remain so until his encounter with Kant. For the present they simply confronted each other—as they do in his *Philosophical Letters* of 1786 or in the dialogues at the end of his novel *Der Geisterseher* of 1789[2]—but without any conclusion being reached.

Meanwhile Schiller had turned from medicine and philosophy to drama, a turn which may be interpreted as an attempt to resolve through action a problem he could not yet solve in thought: to *make* forms which will engage 'both of man's natures', forms which embody mind in a medium and speak to spirit through sense. Certainly his first comments on the function of the theatre in civic life suggest that this is what he aimed at doing. Whereas in his philosophizing he had been unable to find a link between our two natures except by postulating a hypothetical entity, a middle-*force* (*Mittelkraft*),[3] he now takes a notable step forward by arguing man's need for a middle-*state*, i.e., for a condition which is

---

it to mean 'poetry-making' in his translation of Kant's *Critique of Judgement* (ed. cit., p. 86).   [1] SA xi. 70 f.
[2] Cf. Schiller's own dialogue with Körner on this subject in their letters of 4–9.iii.1789.
[3] SA xi. 23 ff.

observable, at least by introspection, and is to be brought about by phenomena which are demonstrably not to be appreciated except through the engagement of both mind and sense. Man, he insisted in *The Stage as a Moral Institution* (1784), cannot for long continue in a state of either pure animality or pure intellectuality. 'Our nature . . . demands a middle-state (*einen mittleren Zustand*) which unites these two opposed extremes, moderates the harsh tension between them, and facilitates the reciprocal transition from the one state to the other.'[1] To effect this is the function of the aesthetic sense. The stage, by offering nourishment to each and all of our psychic forces without overstraining any one of them, engages and forms heart as well as mind, restores the unity of the organism, and returns us, rejoicing in the full knowledge of what it means to be a human being—'ein Mensch zu sein'—strengthened and healed to our fellow creatures.[2]

But even as he wrote this ringing defence of the art he practised, the first fine flush of creative inspiration—three plays in as many years and another on the way—was beginning to flag. The reflective movement of his mind was taking over again. At first in the service of his craft: ponderings on the requirements of a new form, the poetic drama of ideas, and explorations into the historical background of the theme he had chosen for his first venture in this vein. But the slowing-up of the creative process was alarming: *Don Carlos* took four years to complete. And his study of history was succeeded by a return to philosophy, by a prolonged involvement with Kant.[3] Here, in this philosophy which asked 'what man must be in order to be a human being', Schiller—for all his reservations about its method—found an answer to his early questionings more satisfying than any proffered by the philosophers of his youth, found an intellectual temper more in tune with his own conviction that man—for all his membership of the kingdom where nature's laws obtain—is yet challenged by his specifically human nature to manifest his power to be free of them. By shifting the question from 'what is given to man' (*gegeben*) to 'what is enjoined upon man' (*aufgegeben*) Kant had reoriented the whole ethical problem. And in this notion of freedom as *Aufgabe*, a task to be achieved, Schiller—as is clear from the turn his argument takes in Letter XI—saw a great opportunity of demonstrating, to himself no less than to others, that art has an indispensable role to play in the education of complete human beings.

Such private and public demonstration of the importance of his artistic calling had by this time become a vital need. It was—or so it now seemed to him—the self-criticism induced by philosophical reflection which had been responsible for the drying-up of the wells of creativity. But was it not possible to force the Depriver into the role of Restorer? To recover

[1] SA xi. 89 f.　　[2] Ibid., p. 100.　　[3] Cf. to Körner: 1.i.1792; 15.x.1792.

through even deeper reflection the confidence of which reflection itself had robbed him? 'I am full of impatience to get back to poetry', he wrote to Körner on 25 May 1792:

> My pen has a veritable itch to start on *Wallenstein*. It is really only in art itself that I feel my full powers; in theorizing about it I always have to plague myself with principles. And I'm no more than an amateur there anyway. But for the sake of poetic practice I am very ready to philosophize about the theory of it. Criticism itself must now make good the damage it has done me. And it has indeed done me damage. For the boldness, the living fire, I felt before I was aware of any rules at all, has been absent for many a year. I now see myself creating and fashioning. I observe the play of inspiration, and my imagination behaves with less freedom since it feels itself no longer unobserved. Yet once I have got far enough for artistry to become as much nature to me as nurture is to the truly cultivated man, then my imagination will recover its former freedom and suffer no inhibitions except those it freely imposes upon itself.

This conviction—that the *self*-consciousness which is characteristic of human beings carries within it the possibility of transforming even our most highly reflective activities into a new kind of spontaneity—this conviction was the driving-force behind Schiller's major aesthetic essays. It was also responsible for the cultural theory which informs them: the theory that man's true destiny takes him from a first phase of unselfconsciousness, through a second phase of highly cerebral lucidity, on to a third phase which combines the virtues of both in what looks like a return but is in reality a progress.

* * *

It was out of this need, and out of profound ambivalence—ambivalence towards the philosopher in himself, towards the analytical methods of philosophy as it had developed in the West, towards the methods and doctrines of the philosopher to whom he felt most drawn—that Schiller first conceived the idea of a treatise on aesthetic education. Conceived it just at the time when he was throwing out his first challenge to Kant in his essay on *Anmut und Würde*,[1] an attempt to show that the senses must first have been nourished if the spirit is to be rich as well as pure, that feeling must first have been tended if the will is to be flexible as well as firm, that the ideal of moral 'Dignity' is more likely to be achieved if the 'Grace' of psychic harmony has first been cultivated. But the sign of his ambivalence is that this essay could, and can, be read quite differently. Goethe, for instance, took it as an attack upon himself rather than on Kant.[2] In parts of it—and even in those very parts which sought to

---

[1] This is how Schiller, and Kant himself, regarded the essay *On Grace and Dignity.* Cf. Schiller to Körner, 18.v.1794.

[2] 'Erste Bekanntschaft mit Schiller'; JA xxx. 389 f.

rehabilitate the natural man—Nature was treated with a harshness which betrayed one who had felt her burdens rather than her beneficence. And Goethe was of course right in sensing resentment against achievements won by virtue of her favour alone. In the original drafts of his *Aesthetic Letters*[1] Schiller had insisted, categorically and explicitly, that however much he might love and admire those possessed of natural moral feeling—and he would find it impossible to love anyone who wasn't—he yet found himself unable to regard their noble conduct as anything more than an exquisite natural accomplishment. In order to allow them any personal merit as moral beings he would first have to be convinced that the acts they now performed with joy would have been no less dutifully carried out if they had demanded self-denial and self-sacrifice.[2] And it would indeed have been strange if Schiller had not so thought and felt. For every time he managed to think, or write, or create, despite bodily affliction, he knew of his own knowledge the truth of Kant's doctrine concerning the freedom of the human spirit. Every time he was prevented from achieving such a moral triumph, however, whether by ill-health, financial worries, or the difficulties of his own unalterable temperament, he realized again how much man is the victim of circumstance and dependent upon the degree of his temperature or upon the state of his bowels.

And such realization was not made any easier to bear by the immediate proximity of a rival who seemed able to produce poetry effortlessly, by the sheer grace of nature, one whom he had long admired, but also envied, on occasion even hated, but as yet did not really know. Sometimes it was Goethe's philosophy that came in for criticism:

> It draws too much on the world of sense, whereas I draw on the psyche; his whole way of thinking is too sensuous and proceeds too much by touch for my taste.[3]

Sometimes it was his character:

> He is an egoist to an excessive degree. He possesses the gift of attracting people, and of making himself agreeable by kindnesses both great and small; but he always manages to keep himself free . . . like a god, without ever giving himself. . . . That's why I hate him, while at the same time loving his spirit with all my heart. . . . I think of him as a proud prude whom one must get with child in order to humiliate her in the eyes of the world.[4]

---

[1] To the Duke of Augustenburg, 11.xi.1793; Jonas, iii. 382.

[2] The passage was not retained in the published treatise—except perhaps as the germ of the complex argument in XXIII. 7fn. on the difference between noble and sublime conduct. In which case the transformation of the thought is so striking that it would support our contention that the decisive factor in the recasting of Schiller's letters to his patron was the growing intimacy with Goethe.

[3] To Körner, 1.xi.1790.

[4] Ibid. 2.ii.1789.

He writes poetry with an eye to Goethe's opinion. Yet he would not dream of putting himself in the same class:

> He has far more genius than I; and far more knowledge to boot; a more certain touch, and an aesthetic sense which has been clarified and refined through wide knowledge of art of all kinds.[1]

Sometimes Schiller's lucidity about his own ambivalence is staggering:

> It is a curious mixture of hate and love he has aroused in me, a feeling not unlike that which Cassius and Brutus must have felt for Caesar. I could murder his spirit, and again love it with all my heart.[2]

Sometimes it is so courageous that it commands respect as well as wonder:

> I have to laugh when I think of all I have written to you about Goethe. You really *will* have seen me in all my weakness. . . . But never mind. . . . The long and the short of it is that this man, this Goethe, is in my way, and a constant reminder that fate has treated me harshly. How lightly was h i s genius borne along by his fate, and how hard have I had to struggle right up to this very moment.[3]

This feeling of being Nature's stepchild[4] was not to be assuaged until to such knowledge of Self was added knowledge of the Other. Until, emboldened by a conversation on art and aesthetics which revealed unexpected agreement on fundamental issues,[5] he dispatched that now famous letter of 23 August 1794, in which he 'drew the sum of Goethe's existence'—and received a reply acknowledging how truly it was drawn. Thus was inaugurated a day-by-day commerce of minds which lasted unbroken until Schiller's death in 1805. And in exchanging an interior dialogue with a projected image for the give-and-take of actual relationship, Schiller discovered that this darling of the gods, who from the outside and to all appearances seemed his very opposite, had far more in common with him than he had ever dreamed. Far from relying always on 'the mighty visitation unimplor'd', this poet by Nature and by Grace had, from his early twenties, been wont to reflect on the manner of his creating and to transform his reflections into 'second' nature.[6] He was as familiar as Schiller himself with that 'inward observer' of his own

---

[1] Ibid. 25.ii.1789.   [2] Ibid. 2.ii.1789.
[3] Ibid. 9.iii.1789.
[4] The image Goethe used, many years later, when describing the early stages of their relationship: 'er war [in *Anmut und Würde*] undankbar gegen die grosse Mutter, die ihn gewiss nicht stiefmütterlich behandelte' (JA xxx. 390). Schiller's ambivalence about the whole complex—Nature/Fortune/Inspiration/Goethe—is vividly evoked in Thomas Mann's short story, *Schwere Stunde*.
[5] Cf. his letter to Körner, 1.ix.1794.
[6] Cf. Goethe to Herder, July 1772, and our commentary thereon in GLL xv (1961), 110 ff.

creative processes—though far from fearing his intrusion he welcomed it as the source of man's power to shape his ends, moral and artistic, and as early as his thirtieth year had entrusted to his diary[1] the firm resolve to discover the periodic cycle of his own moods and states in order to make the best possible use of his natural rhythms. He too, if for different reasons, had felt the springs of creativity dry up within him, and had sought to renew them by contact with the soil of classical antiquity—by a flight to Magna Graecia which was the physical counterpart to Schiller's imaginative flight into such poems as *The Gods of Greece* and *The Artists*. Nor was Goethe as averse to philosophical ponderings on the nature of art as Schiller had imagined. On the contrary; though they might, as he now told Körner,[2] start from different angles and proceed by quite different paths, 'each was able to give the other something he lacked, and receive something in exchange'. And at this very moment, when he was starting to recast those letters to his patron into a publishable treatise, he received from Goethe the draft of an essay[3] bearing a title which might easily have stemmed from Schiller himself—*How far can the Idea that Beauty is Perfection allied with Freedom be applied to Living Organisms?*— and raised such questions as the following: What is the role of subordination and co-ordination in the organization of the higher animals? How, without impairing the free play of all the forces of an organism, is limitation for a particular action, determination to a specific end, to be achieved? How, without leaving the sphere of beauty, are *characters* to be developed? Do such questions not reflect the central problem of aesthetic education as Schiller finally posed it? How, without loss of moral fibre, is man to be made aesthetic? How, without destroying his power to act, is he to be made whole? Or, in the more broadly cultural terms of Letter VI: How, without forgoing the advantages of modern specialization, are we to educate complete human beings? No wonder that within three weeks of this *rapprochement* Schiller could write to his wife[4] that his 'correspondence' with the Duke of Augustenburg was 'acquiring a completely new look', and that he was eager to see 'what new things would be developed within him by these closer contacts with Goethe'.

Of Goethe's presence in the *Aesthetic Letters* there has never been any doubt. Schiller told him that he would find his portrait there when he sent him the first instalment a few weeks later.[5] And he has been variously identified as the ideal artist of Letter IX,[6] the natural scientist

---

[1] 26.iii.1780.   [2] 1.ix.1794.
[3] Enclosed in a letter of 30.viii.1794, but only recently discovered among Schiller's papers and published in *Goethe. Jb. d. Goethe-Gesellschaft*, xiv–xv (1952/53), 143 ff. Cf. *Goethes Werke*, Hamb. Ausg., xiii. 564.
[4] 12.ix.1794. Cf. letter to Körner of the same date.   [5] 20.x.1794.
[6] Though this has been questioned by Lutz (op. cit., p. 190) who sees it as a self-portrait.

of Letter XIII,[1] and the poetic counter-image of those martyrs to philosophical truth in Letter VI who, like Kant, have been forced to sacrifice wholeness of being to one-sided specialization of the analytical faculty. But there is a case for seeing him as the presiding genius of the whole treatise, and more responsible for the final form of its argumentation than is usually realized. If there is any single factor which might account for the difference between those adumbrations of aesthetic education which Schiller sent to his patron in 1793 and the work he published in 1795, it would have to be sought, not in any events of the political world, nor yet in any attempt to work the whole thing over in terms of transcendental philosophy,[2] but in the effect of closer acquaintance with one who seemed the living embodiment of all he was trying to advocate in theory—one who, in his own person, seemed to offer proof that the combination of Greek wholeness with Modern differentiation was a viable mode of existence.

For 'knowledge by acquaintance' forced Schiller to revise many of the simple antitheses which had dominated both his thinking and his creating. Here after all was one who was poet as well as philosopher, and not just naïve poet, but reflective poet too; one who swung easily between analysis and synthesis, thought and action, and accepted such opposites as a natural polarity; one who cultivated his personality and was yet a man of affairs, pursued the arts, yet never in the direction of the ivory-tower, but always with an eye to the public good—thus vindicating Schiller's youthful ideal that it is the function of art to restore us, strengthened and refreshed, to our fellow creatures; one who seemed to move *with* his nature rather than against it, and yet was undoubtedly possessed of moral fibre—thus forcing him to think through yet again the Kantian antithesis of nature versus freedom. Above all he was forced to revise his concept of 'wholeness' of personality; to recognize that in modern man at least this cannot be conceived as something static. Here was someone who might justifiably be said to be a fully rounded and well integrated human being. Yet he was at the same time a highly specialized individual, a poet, enjoying wholeness—in the sense of the perfectly co-ordinated play of all his forces —only in the brief moment of aesthetic contemplation, but for the rest subordinating them to the dominant needs of an exacting craft. For him, no less than for his fellows, the ideal of wholeness was only to be achieved as a changing pattern in time, a constantly shifting hierarchy of interests and values and powers, in which the dominant was properly determined by the requirements of the immediate situation.

All this is not to say that from now on Schiller became like Goethe, even in his thinking. Certainly under his influence he learned to appreciate that

---

[1] See our Note to XIII. 4fn. § 2.
[2] The contention of Lutz, op. cit., p. 223.

'tactile' way of thinking he had formerly criticized.[1] Certainly he struggled for closer contact with the outside world, longing for Goethe's presence because 'you always manage to make me turn outwards . . . when I'm alone I sink into myself'.[2] Certainly he acknowledged with more grateful spirit how dependent we are for our moods upon the forces of nature: 'I have been positively quickened', he wrote to Goethe[3] when sending him the second, most abstract and difficult, instalment of the *Aesthetic Letters*, 'by this promise of spring. It has poured new life into my present occupations, which were sorely in need of it.'

How tied we are, for all our vaunted independence, to the forces of Nature! And of what avail is our will if Nature leaves us in the lurch? What I have been fruitlessly brooding over for the last five weeks has been released within me by a warm ray of sunshine within three days. True, my earlier perseverance may have prepared this further phase, but the warming sun certainly played its part in actually bringing it about.

And certainly in revising his image of the Other he learnt to revise the image of his own Self, learnt to appraise himself more justly, and more kindly. No longer did he need to feel the shame he had once confessed to Körner[4] on account of the unpoetic—i.e., highly conscious and deliberately reflective—processes which had produced some of his most successful poetry. He now came to accept the fact that these are as proper to the making of poetry as to the making of philosophy—and that inspiration may have a part to play in both. Indeed under the beneficence of Goethe's appreciation of 'the singular blend of intuition and abstraction which is part of your nature',[5] he got to the point of looking more hopefully on his own 'hybrid' condition; of seeing that clearly defined thought is not necessarily the enemy of poetry, and does not necessarily impede the flow of inspiration. He even grew confident enough to believe that each of his two talents might be made to serve the other, that by 'a constant movement within himself he might be able to maintain these two heterogeneous elements in a kind of solution', and felt, as he wrote to Goethe,[6] that this had in fact been achieved in some of his philosophical poems. In a quite different way, but not to a lesser degree, it was also achieved in his *Aesthetic Letters*.

Yet there are limits set to our power to modify our 'type', as the author of *Naïve and Sentimental Poetry* very well knew.[7] Despite reassurance,

---

[1] Letters to Goethe, 17.xii.1795 and 18.xi.1796. Cf. p. xxxvi and fn. 3, above.
[2] Ibid. 23.vii.1799.
[3] 27.ii.1795.   [4] 25.v.1792.
[5] Letter to Schiller, 6.x.1795.   [6] 16.x.1795.
[7] Without this closer contact with Goethe one can scarcely imagine the 'complication' of the typology in that essay: the way the simple antithesis naïve/sentimental gradually makes way for types in which both are present, but the one subordinated to the other.

encouragement and success, periods of self-doubt recurred. In that very same letter to Goethe he confessed that for one hour of courage and confidence there were ten in which he did not know what to make of himself. He has only to receive an instalment of Goethe's new novel while he himself is in the throes of a philosophical work to feel that 'the poet is the only true human being, and the best of philosophers a mere caricature by comparison';[1] or that it is time for him to 'shut up his philosophical shop for a while and satisfy the yearning of his heart for objects that can be touched and felt'.[2] And when he does finally shut it up, it is with a bang! With a rather bitter distich[3] ruefully regretting all the time he has spent on Kant and his works:

> Zwei Jahrzehnte kostest du mir: zehn Jahre verlor ich
> Dich zu begreifen, und zehn, mich zu befreien von dir.

Such bitterness is a sign of continuing conflict. And, indeed, that side of Schiller's nature for which Kant and his doctrine of moral freedom had served as image and focus remained one element, and an important element, of both his poetic and his philosophic work. Fortunately so. For it was his fate, and his achievement, to illuminate out of the urgency of a felt conflict tensions which do in fact exist between beauty and virtue, grace and merit, the aesthetic and the moral; between that which is 'right' by nature and that which is 'only' made right by effort—by man's power to effect limited transformations in himself, and to be, in some measure, master of his destiny. Schiller may have felt drawn to those whose achievement, aesthetic or moral, seemed to flow with ease out of what they were. But the feeling that this had not been granted to *him* made him raise, and raise again, on behalf of the heavy-laden and afflicted, the relative merits of nature and effort, the beautiful and the sublime. He is the poet who sings—and sings in the best of his philosophical prose too— of a grace and beauty which is recognized as 'right', but longed for rather than possessed: this is what lends the accents of melancholy and nostalgia to even the most positive of his pedagogic exhortations or Utopian dreams. But he is also the poet of right conduct: and this is what lends the sting to his tragedies and the fibre to his pleas for an aesthetic education. It was perhaps only in lyric poetry, where ambiguity of language favours and fosters the simultaneous expression of opposing values, that he ever managed to reconcile what was and remained for him a basic conflict. In a poem such as *Das Glück*—a transparent tribute to Goethe and moving testimony to his own readiness to recognize the superiority

---

[1] Letter to Goethe, 7.i.1795. It is a feeling reflected in the 'alas!' of Letter I. 4, concerning analytical techniques. See our Note thereto.

[2] Letter to Goethe, 17.xii.1795.

[3] Written for *Xenien* of 1796, but not published until 1893 by E. Schmidt and B. Suphan as no. 382 of their complete edition (*Schriften d. Goethe-Gesellschaft*, viii).

of a type and a fate not his own—he can extol beauty and fortune, grace and happiness, the effortless and the gratuitous, and yet contrive, by the miracle of his verse, to compel our respect and sympathy for those virtues of effort and striving which he has overtly relegated to second place. In his essays, by contrast, he was constrained by the nature of discursive language, by the philosopher's 'sad dependence upon time', to present such conflicting values in succession, one after the other. Thus three months after the last instalment of his passionate plea for aesthetic education, there appeared in the same Journal an essay *On the Necessary Limits of the Beautiful, especially in the Presentation of Philosophical Truths*. And three months after that, one *On the Dangers of Aesthetic Manners and Morals*. Yet another three months and, still in the same Journal, came the exact counterpart of this: *On the Moral Value of Aesthetic Manners and Morals*. And all the time he was brooding on the old theme of the sublime, which he had first adumbrated in an essay published just at the time when he was starting work on his *Aesthetic Letters*, and which was, some have thought,[1] to have found a place there in a section entitled 'Energetic Beauty' which never in fact materialized. His essay *On the Sublime*, in praise of moral freedom and man's power to rise above nature, was not finally completed and published until 1801; and it constitutes his last word on these matters. But who can say that because, as a matter of historical fact, it was his *last* word, it was therefore also his *final* word?[2] Who can say that, but for his premature death, he would not again have come round to praising the beauty of grace, and illuminating still further facets of a problem which throughout his life he had found endlessly fascinating and tantalizingly impossible to solve?

THE FORM OF THE TREATISE

STRATEGY AND STRUCTURE

One obvious advantage of presenting Schiller's treatise as a highly personal document is that it helps to explain the singular exaltation of his manner: the ardour which sustains him through even the most 'barren wastes of abstraction', the accents of almost religious fervour in which he elevates Beauty to the 'perfect symbol' of our dual nature, 'triumphant proof' that it is man's bounden duty, indeed his very destiny, to reconcile sense and spirit in a union both joyous and blessed.[3]

The disadvantages of so presenting it are more obvious still. There is first of all the danger of fostering the reductive fallacy: of seeming to

---

[1] The identity of energetic beauty and the sublime was refuted by Böhm (op. cit., pp. 116 ff. and p. 189) as early as 1927. But Miller (op. cit., p. 110) still maintains that the former is a disguised form of the latter.

[2] David (loc. cit., p. 24), among others, argues that it was.

[3] Cf. XXIV. 3 and our Note thereto.

suggest that the significance of the work can be reduced to its significance for him, that because it *is* a personal document, it is this and nothing more. But, as C. G. Jung observed,[1] although it happens to be true that it was Schiller's own dichotomy which gave him such uncanny insight into the dissociation of modern man, this does not mean that his diagnosis was therefore beside the mark. Another 'type' would inevitably have diagnosed the dilemma differently; but this is not to say that what Schiller saw was not there to be seen, or that the cure he proposed is not worth considering just because it is so evidently a piece of special pleading for his own artistic vocation. It is a mark of his genius that he was able to find in the cultural situation of his day an objective correlative for his own problems, and to transform the purely personal into an issue of general concern.

A second danger is that of fostering the genetic fallacy: of seeming to suggest that an account of its origins is of necessity a reliable guide to the structure and significance of the work. The existence of earlier drafts is always conducive to this kind of assumption; and from the time they first came to light, attempts were made to find the key to Schiller's intentions in those letters he originally wrote to the Duke of Augustenburg. The scholar who offers the most detailed structural analysis of the finished treatise, Hans Lutz,[2] denies that he himself ever succumbed to this genetic temptation. An examination of the published work alone, so he insists, forced him to the conclusion that there are in it two completely unreconciled, and irreconcilable, strata of thought. In the one—discernible in Letters II, III, V, VIII, X, and XVI—Schiller is operating with a three-phase theory of cultural development: man's progress is from the physical through the aesthetic to the moral. In the other—discernible in Letters IV, VI, VII, XI–XV, and XVII–XXVII—he is operating with a synthesis theory: the physical and the moral are to be reconciled in the aesthetic. Schiller, it is said, continually oscillates between the two, and—what is worse—seems totally unaware that he is doing so. Hence the innumerable self-contradictions; hence the intermingling of the two theories in, for instance, Letter IX; hence our growing feeling as we read that the work was conceived according to the first theory and revised in the light of the second. It is high time, Lutz concludes, that we stopped trying to find unity in this educational treatise and read it rather as a vertical section through successive layers of Schiller's intellectual development.

[1] Op. cit. (1), pp. 101, 103 ff. Jung's view is supported, from a different angle and in a different context—a discussion of *Naïve and Sentimental Poetry*—by G. Lukács ('Schriftsteller und Kritiker' in *Essays über Realismus*, Berlin, 1948, p. 243): 'Der Ausgangspunkt Schillers war also eine persönliche Lebensfrage, die Antwort jedoch der Abriss einer Geschichtsphilosophie der Kunst, die der Ästhetik eine neue Wendung gab . . .'.
[2] Op. cit., pp. 169–233. Cf. esp. p. 223.

Once we do this, so he claims, most of the problems on which scholars have expended their ingenuity fall into place: in such 'geological' perspective, and only in this, can we hope to understand why the aesthetic is presented now as means, now as end; why 'freedom' connotes now moral freedom of the spirit (Kant), now aesthetic freedom of the whole personality (Shaftesbury); why Enlightenment is at one moment elevated to an ideal (Kant), at another decried for having produced a race of barbarians (Rousseau); why we are left with the impression that Schiller is forever starting off on a new tack without any clear idea of where he is going.

If this is not an example of the genetic fallacy, one wonders what is. By whatever method he may have reached it, Lutz's conclusion is that the *Letters on the Aesthetic Education of Man* are not a public utterance at all, but rather a private document testifying to their author's philosophical progress. The issue is important in itself. Either Schiller's work, whatever its shortcomings, offers us, as Professor Stuart Hampshire recently claimed,[1] a coherent theory—and a theory, he added, is what we need—concerning the place of art in the modern State, a serious answer to Plato's challenge, and based on knowledge at least as intimate as Plato's of the danger as well as the power of art. Or it is, as Lutz would have it, a thing of shreds and patches, containing amid the dross of philosophical confusion ingots of pure gold, but not worth considering as an educational manifesto of abiding relevance. The choice is clear cut. And the issue is important, too, because Lutz's thesis has been offered to English readers, as an accepted and acceptable view of the structure of the *Aesthetic Letters*, by both their latest translator and the author of the most recent book on the culture and society of Classical Weimar.[2] It might therefore be well, before offering our own counter-view, to examine his methodological credentials. There could scarcely be a better way of introducing the reader to Schiller's own characteristic methods and procedures—or, indeed, to the general tenor and import of his treatise.

Consider the following instance of Lutz's 'method' of exposing alleged illogicality. He takes two of Schiller's statements—that the majority of men are now demanding restitution of their inalienable human rights, and that the *physical* opportunity afforded by the historical moment has found an unreceptive generation (V. 2)—and confronts them with the severity of his own superior logic: 'If the majority is *for* the rational State, it follows that it must also be receptive *to* it.'[3] But does it follow? Only in a paraphrase so wholly inadequate to Schiller's main concerns: the

---

[1] 'The Conflict between Art and Politics', ed. cit.

[2] Bruford, op. cit., p. 278, frankly acknowledges Lutz's analysis. Snell's analysis, op. cit., p. 15, is clearly a résumé of Lutz, op. cit., pp. 221 ff.

[3] Op. cit., pp. 179 f. Our italics.

difficulty of actually living up to rights we have legitimately fought for and won; the difference between enlightened *principles*—entertained by, and acceptable to, the mind—and enlightened *dispositions*—involving our whole being, and capable of moving us to appropriate action. Lutz seems totally unaware of the fact that Schiller is here circling round a theme which he will not name until Letter VIII: the mysterious nature of Wisdom. That he is thinking through again, in terms appropriate to his own age, the ancient and perennial problem of how to transform intellectual into moral virtues. A preoccupation which goes back, through Renaissance and medieval distinctions between *scientia* and *sapientia*, to the classical ideal of Prudence which, according to Aristotle, does not consist only in knowing what is right, but also in doing it.[1] And—despite his claim to greater 'philological' exactitude than most of his predecessors —he seems totally unaware, too, of the peculiar nature of a poet's linguistic exactitude; an exactitude which consists, not in *ex*cluding connotations by means of definition, but in *in*cluding the maximum amount of meaning that is compatible with the particular context. If Schiller uses *unempfäng-lich* here, he expects his readers to be alive to the implications of *con*-ceiving as well as *re*-ceiving; to the fact that the seed so prodigally spent by Enlightenment and Revolution has found a generation unable, or unwilling, to receive it in the sense of being fructified by it, letting it ripen in the womb of personality until it issues as a new way of life. There is no question in passages such as these of Schiller being *against* Enlightenment. He is trying to find ways of making men enlightened at levels deeper than that of intellectual attitudes.

This tendency to blur what Schiller himself keeps distinct is a recurrent feature of Lutz's analysis. One of the worst instances of it is his attempt to convict Schiller of confused political thinking. Why, he asks, does he speak of the Natural State being undermined by the forces of Revolution (V. 2) when what he obviously has in mind is the Positive State? It is, he maintains, a typical example of his loose use of terms. But, in fact, this is one of the cases—and there are far more of them than one might expect —where Schiller is proceeding strictly according to his own definition: the one he made in III. 3, where the *Naturstaat* (or the *Notstaat*, as he had called it in III. 2) was defined as 'any political body whose organization derives from forces and not from laws', a definition which makes it perfectly clear that what he means by it *is* the Positive State. Even as the context makes it clear why he prefers the term 'Natural State':[2] viz. in

---

[1] *Nic. Eth.* VII. x. 2 ff. Cf. E. F. Rice, *The Renaissance Idea of Wisdom*, Cambridge, Mass., 1958.

[2] Cf. Glossary under *Natur* 3 (*c*). Not that Schiller has any objection to the term 'positive' in other contexts. He uses it of society (VI. 9), of conventions (IX. 3) and of laws (XXIV. 7).

order to draw attention to the fact that States which have arisen haphazardly, in the course of time, are the products of natural needs and forces rather than of planning according to the laws of reason. At no point in this treatise does Schiller use the term 'Natural State' in any other sense than this. But Lutz chooses to ignore his definition, and to explain his alleged terminological inexactitude as the outward and visible sign of confused thought. Haunting Schiller's mind, so he avers, is a schema derived from two distinct, and completely irreconcilable, sources: the 'cultural pessimism' of Rousseau and the 'progressive enlightenment' of Kant. It runs, he maintains,[1] like this: In the beginning was the state of nature (*Urstand*), i.e., the normative Natural=Rational State (*Natur=Vernunftstaat*), from which the Positive State of so-called civilized man is a lamentable falling-away into decadence and barbarism—though the return of that Rational=Natural State is nevertheless an ideal towards which man must strive.

But the equations and identifications on which this schema is based are of Lutz's making, not Schiller's. At no point in this treatise does Schiller entertain the notion of a normative Natural State located in the past (*Ur=Naturstaat*). He was far too schooled in Rousseau ever to dream of doing so. And Lutz is only able to attribute it to him by ignoring his consistently maintained distinction between the word *Staat* (= political State) and the word *Stand* (= condition). What Rousseau, and Schiller following him, do postulate, as a model which may guide men in planning the Rational State of the future, is not a State but a state (not a *Staat* but a *Stand*), not a body politic of any kind, but an age of individual freedom in which men were unfettered by any social or political constraints whatsoever. Such a state, Rousseau had insisted, was a pure invention, a piece of hypothetical reasoning 'not unlike those our physicists are in the habit of making every day'.[2] But it was a useful hypothesis, since by means of it men might discover what freedoms they must reasonably expect to forgo when entering voluntarily into the social contracts of the Rational State of the future. In following this train of thought in Letter III, Schiller may use terms more reminiscent of Kant's regulative ideas than of Rousseau's scientific hypotheses. But this is immaterial; for on this issue, as on many another, Kant and Rousseau are at one, and there can be no question of Schiller hovering uncertainly between them.

Nor is Lutz on firmer linguistic ground when he tries to expose Schiller's misuse of Kantian concepts. He seizes, for instance, on the last paragraph of Letter III, where Schiller first postulates the need for a 'third character' compounded of both man's natures, his physical and his moral, and adumbrates the process by which it is to be brought into being.

---

[1] Op. cit., pp. 179 f.
[2] *De l'inégalité*; Vaughan, op. cit. i. 141.

The first stage of this operation is the abstraction (*absondern*) from his physical character of its arbitrariness, and from his moral character of its freedom; the former is then to be brought into conformity with laws, the latter made dependent upon sense-impressions; the former removed further away from matter, the latter brought closer to it. What Lutz does is to stop short at the first stage of this process, paraphrase *absondern* (= isolate, secrete, abstract) first by *ausschalten* (= eliminate), then by *unterdrücken* (= suppress), and ask triumphantly: 'But what remains of a moral character when it is deprived of its freedom?'[1] What indeed! But again it is only possible for him to ask such a question in respect of his own inadmissible paraphrase. It is he who has introduced the notion of suppression, not Schiller; he who has failed to spot this early instance of a mode of synthesizing which Schiller will call by name in Letter XIII, and of which he will give an outstanding example in Letter XIV, when he lets the play-drive emerge out of the 'reciprocal subordination' of man's two basic drives. It is Lutz who is not alive to the chemical-alchemical image lurking in this use of *absondern*, i.e., 'abstract' in the sense of 'extract';[2] Lutz who fails to realize that Schiller's concern is precisely to avoid the *confusion* of man's two natures, their tendency to trespass on each other's preserves, and that to this end he introduces a complex process of synthesis in which a certain element of the one is modified by entering into relation with a dominant quality of the other. Such transmutations can of course only be brought about if the elements to be thus worked upon are first of all set free, detached from the compounds in which they normally find themselves.

What confidence can we have in any conclusion arrived at by such methodological malpractices? By ignoring Schiller's definitions, blurring his distinctions, attributing to him mental schemas he never entertained, and subjecting his language to the most cavalier treatment imaginable? But method apart, Lutz's conclusions are demonstrably false. Consider the two Letters on which his whole two-strata thesis is based. How can he pretend that Letter III is dominated exclusively by a three-phase theory of human progress when its last paragraph is devoted to adumbrating Schiller's most characteristic mode of synthesis? And how can he say

---

[1] Op. cit., pp. 170–2. Cf. p. 343, below.

[2] The metaphor of plastic surgery with which Kerry (op. cit. [2], p. 116) attempts to elucidate this difficult passage only obscures it. And not just because it is an anachronism. The interest of alchemy for the educationally minded eighteenth century resided, as Goethe clearly discerned, in its esoteric implications for the health of the psyche. That equipoise of psychic forces achieved, according to Schiller, in aesthetic contemplation, is described by Goethe in the section of his *Geschichte der Farbenlehre* entitled 'Alchimisten' (JA xl. 180 f.) as the supreme achievement of education: 'Ja diese Wünsche müssen leidenschaftlich in der menschlichen Natur gleichsam wüten und können nur durch die höchste Bildung ins Gleichgewicht gebracht werden.'

that Letter IV is dominated exclusively by a synthesis theory when one of its main ideas is the progressive 'ennobling' (again we note the latent alchemical image)[1] of empirical man in the direction of ideal man? The fact is of course that there are traces of both theories in both Letters—as indeed in most of the others. And, for all his protestations to the contrary, one can scarcely escape the impression that Lutz's division of them into two distinct strata must, wittingly or unwittingly, have been influenced by genetic considerations from the start. The confirmation of his structural analysis by 'subsequent' comparison with the original drafts[2] comes as suspiciously welcome; and it is—from his point of view—unfortunate that it is not more complete. For, as his own schema makes clear, there is nothing in the original drafts we possess that corresponds either to Letter III or to Letter IV. So that in this case—a crucial case—external evidence can provide no corroboration of two successive and irreconcilable strata of thought. Indeed one could just as plausibly argue that both these Letters were written at the revision stage and made to conform to an already existing, and consciously accepted, pattern of alternative theories of human development.

* * *

If there is anything to be learned from this close scrutiny of an earlier critic, it is that there is more of rigour in the construction of the *Aesthetic Letters* than is often supposed. This would seem to support Schiller's own claim that the structure *as a whole* was unassailable. He spoke repeatedly[3] of its unity, simplicity, and severity, of its inner consistency and the soundness of its foundations, of his conviction that it was 'all of a piece', and of his confidence that no objection which might be raised against it could henceforth 'overthrow the whole', since 'the rigour governing its organization would itself secure him against individual errors of application, much as the mathematician is warned of possible errors of calculation by the very form of the calculation he has to make'.[4]

An author is not necessarily a reliable judge of his own work. But the experience of translator and glossary-maker certainly confirms a high degree of complexity and 'closeness' in its organization. Whether the appropriate analogy is with any kind of mathematical structure may for the time being remain an open question. But some highly organized system of relations, with its own built-in controls, is certainly there. Perhaps because his task is not primarily to test the validity of Schiller's inferences or deductions but to establish meaning—whether the meaning of an individual word by comparing its incidence in a variety of contexts,

---

[1] Cf. the connexion between *veredeln* and *steigern* discussed in Glossary under *Idee*, &c.   [2] Op. cit., pp. 223 f.
[3] e.g., to Körner: 3.ii.1794; 10.xi.1794; 29.xii.1794; 5.i.1795; to Goethe, 29.xi.1794.
[4] To Goethe, 27.ii.1795.

or the meaning of a difficult crux by relating it to cognate thoughts and arguments elsewhere in the text—the translator rapidly acquires the habit of looking backwards and forwards, and backwards again, in search of illumination. In so doing he has to keep his mind open to a number of relations other than the logical: to simple recurrence, and recurrence through modification; to similarities and parallels, whether of thought or of position; to varying degrees of contrast, from simple antithesis to the most subtle forms of inversion; to telescoping, contraction, and condensation. And he cannot for long pursue this comparative activity without becoming aware that Schiller's treatise abounds in contradictions far more flagrant than any hitherto observed.

In the first paragraph of Letter VI it is said that man has to fall away from nature by the abuse of reason before he can return to her by the use of reason. In the last paragraph this same dual role is transferred to art: it is up to man to restore by means of a higher art the totality of human nature which art itself has destroyed.[1] As late as Letter XVII the source of man's freedom and of his will is said to be reason. From Letter XIX onwards it is said to be nature.[2] In XXV. 4 we are told that it is not in human nature to make a 'leap' from mere life to pure form. In XXVII. 4 we not only hear of the 'leap' that man makes from 'the purely material play' involved in the free association of ideas to 'the aesthetic play' involved when he first ventures on a free form, but even have the point underlined for us by the phrase 'a leap it must be called'. At the beginning of Letter III it is said that what makes man man is that he does not stop short at what nature made of him but has the power of raising himself, by his free choice, from physical necessity to moral necessity, i.e., of transforming nature into morality. At the beginning of Letter IV we hear what sounds like the exact opposite: it is enjoined upon man to ensure that his moral behaviour can be counted on with the certainty that we count on natural laws, i.e., he is to transform morality into nature. Can Schiller really have forgotten from one Letter to the next? Or from the first paragraph to the last? It seems unlikely. Such contraries are so frequent, so flagrant, and often so symmetrically placed, that it would seem far more plausible to assume that they are of the order of deliberate paradox rather than of inadvertent self-contradiction.

Just as striking, and an even more obvious pointer to the form of the total structure, is the number of times Schiller comes round—always at significant, and again often at symmetrically placed, points—to a similar postulate or demand, or to the fulfilment of an expectation created much earlier. Consider the notion of the 'common' sense (in the double meaning of this term).[3] It first appears in Letter I with reference to his own

---

[1] Cf. Glossary under *Kunst*.   [2] Cf. Glossary under *Natur*.
[3] Cf. Glossary under *Gemein*.

method: in Western philosophy the truths of common human reason have become clothed in the modes of analytical thought; this may be inevitable, even desirable; but they need to be recurrently divested of these technicalities and made available again to common human feeling. We encounter the notion a second time towards the end of Letter VI, where the 'common' sense is contrasted with the 'antagonism' of faculty and function which had to ensue if science and philosophy were to develop beyond the 'maximum' attained by the Greeks. It occurs a third time at the end of Letter XVIII apropos the relation of common human feeling to the analytical techniques of aesthetics. And finally, at the very end of the treatise, we are shown the role of the aesthetic in communicating the results of even the most esoteric methods of science and philosophy to the 'common' sense of the whole community. This idea of the 'common' and the 'open' thus provides a framework for the treatise as regards both its form and its content. And it turns up again at its two main axes: the demand for a cultural ideal which shall transcend the antithesis between Greek harmony and Modern differentiation; and the demand for an aesthetic which shall transcend the antithesis between intuitive impressionism and rational analysis.

Or take the challenging statement in XV. 9 that 'man is only fully a human being when he plays'. It is frankly presented as a paradox, the full significance of which will only become apparent when it has been applied to 'the twofold earnestness of duty and of destiny'. This, critics have complained, is never in fact accomplished. Moreover it is introduced here *ad hoc* as an intention for which we have not been prepared. Neither objection can be sustained. We were prepared for it as early as IV. 3, where a double criterion of human behaviour was proposed—'the one-sided moral' and 'the complete anthropological'. Nor will the expectations now aroused be disappointed. In the important footnote to Letter XXIII[1] the moral criteria of a dutiful act are sternly safeguarded, but we are also shown the double role that the aesthetic may legitimately play in its performance: a subordinate role, in educating men to be *able* to perform it; and what one might call a supererogatory role—the endowing of a moral act with a 'superfluous' grace. At the end of Letter XXVII, by contrast, we are shown both the co-ordinate and the dominant role that the aesthetic is to play in man's larger cultural destiny:[2] co-ordinate, because it is here ranged alongside the other modes of human activity—the practical and the scientific, the moral and the philosophic—and ranks equal with them; dominant, because it alone possesses the power of informing all other modes, whether of perception, knowledge, or communication, with a new quality without altering their essential character.

[1] For further elucidation of these difficult passages the reader is referred to our Notes.
[2] Not, as Böhm (op. cit., p. 30) suggests, the co-ordinate role alone.

But by far the most striking of all Schiller's goings around and about is the way he returns, nine times, at almost perfectly regular intervals of three, to the demand for a 'third thing'. In Letter III it is a 'third character' which shall combine the virtues of both man's natures, his animal and his rational. In VI it becomes clear that this third character will have to be something different from the wholeness and harmony of the Greeks. In IX Schiller exposes the circularity of his argument and the need for a third term if the dilemma is to be solved. In XII he starts the argument for a 'third drive' born of the reciprocal subordination of the two basic drives, the material and the formal. In XV beauty is defined as the objective correlative of this third drive, as a third quality resulting from the synthesis of life and form. In XVIII it is a third state that is postulated, a 'middle condition' mediating between passivity and activity and combining the advantages of each. In XXI this third state is at last named: it is the aesthetic mode of the psyche, defined as a 'Null' which is nevertheless infinitely fruitful. In XXIV we embark on the complex relation of this third state to each of the three phases through which both individual and race must pass if they are to complete 'the cycle of their destiny'. Finally, in XXVII, Schiller gathers together all these 'thirds' in his vision of a 'Third State', a community of individuals who, by fostering within themselves a 'third character', have restored totality of being without forfeiting either differentiation of faculty or specialization of function. It is a community which forms a State within the State (an Aesthetic State within the Positive State) and so fulfils the function assigned to the 'third character' in Letter III: to ensure the survival of the social community pending the reform of the political State. But it fulfils too that other function first demanded of it in Letter VII: to guarantee the existential reality of the Rational State of the future should it ever emerge.

Our aim in stressing this symmetry was not to provoke speculation concerning the significance of number-symbolism in an aesthetic treatise, fascinating as that might prove. Rather to draw attention to the overall movement of Schiller's strategy, which is not linear but circular. This is not to say that within the several parts he does not sometimes pursue the more familiar course of a line of argument leading straight to a conclusion. But he often pursues a kind of delaying tactics too, and not primarily to create suspense. Thus the paradox of Letter VI, in which one and the same cultural task was assigned now to reason and now to art, will indeed be resolved—but not until Schiller has looked at the relation between them from various angles and uncovered aspects of it which are not immediately apparent. Only then, in Letter XXIII, when he has shown that all the more abstract operations of reason are engaged in the aesthetic mode, *but engaged concretely*, in and through the objects of feeling and sense-perception, only then can he with a good conscience advocate art as the great healer of our cultural ills. For only then will he have presented it, not as a substitute for reason, but as an activity in which reason is already involved. And only then can he make his audacious claim that it is 'in the indifferent sphere of physical life' that man's moral education must begin. For only then will he have established the connexion between 'indifferency' and the aesthetic, and shown that it is out of this as yet 'undifferentiated' nexus of psycho-physical being that all man's modes of thinking and doing must evolve. It is on this basis that the wise educator will begin to develop the higher activities of reason, whether intellectual or moral. In so doing he will be carrying out the task enjoined upon man in IV.1: laying the foundations of his morality so firmly within the life of bodily feeling that he may be able to count on it with the certainty that we count on natural laws. But in deciding to educate in this way at all he will also be exercising the prerogative ascribed to man in III.1: taking thought about his history and his destiny, 'retracing by means of Reason the steps Nature took on his behalf', and modifying, or even reversing, a course hitherto followed unreflectingly.

Letter XXIII thus brings the resolution of yet another of the paradoxes we noted earlier. As indeed of many—and not just of those which precede it. From the perspective reached in this Letter it will be possible to say without self-contradiction that it both is, and is not, in human nature to make a 'leap'. For the leap Schiller is repudiating, as fact and as educational policy, is the rationalist assumption that the abstractions of reason spring fully fledged from the head of one who was but yesterday little more than an animal. In repudiating this, he was subscribing to the belief of those thinkers of the Enlightenment who studied the life of the mind as a continuous growth from its earliest beginnings in sense-perception.[1] Yet for Schiller some discontinuity between what he often calls the 'blind' life of feeling and the higher life of the mind was not to be denied (since a human being can obviously live the one without ever developing the other). For him, however, this discontinuity manifests itself much earlier, and not in the form of pure abstractions at all. His 'leap' comes with the first dawn of self-awareness and the creative impulse to form. This is the 'given'. Its origins, so he insists at the end of Letter XIX, are shrouded in mists impenetrable to metaphysicist and physicist alike. Its appearance is not our merit, nor its non-appearance our fault. Once given, however, responsibility for developing it is given too. For it contains within it the seeds of freedom; and it is in this sense that he can say that the aesthetic is the condition of the will and not vice versa.[2]

It is not difficult to see why Letter XXIII should provide the solvent for so many paradoxes; above all for the major one which attributes man's freedom now to reason and now to nature. For it is at this point that

[1] Cf. above, p. xxvii.   [2] XXIII. 5. Cf. XIX. 11.

Schiller turns from an examination of the structure of the psyche, its faculties, its drives and its modalities, to an exploration of their emergence in the individual and in the race. What, from the structural point of view, could properly be regarded as attributes or activities of one of the 'superior' functions (whether called 'reason' or the 'form-drive'), can now, from the genetic point of view, also be seen as 'a gift of nature' and in some measure dependent upon 'the favour of fortune'.[1] For it is in the nature of genetic inquiry to press back towards a 'given', to a point where the notion of simple causality seems to have reached the limits of its usefulness. And it is not surprising that in this part of Schiller's treatise we should so often be reminded of that pioneer of the genetic method, J. G. Herder. Not only of his notion of *Besonnenheit*, or his reiterated contention that concepts which are to be of real use in intellectual, aesthetic, or moral life must have been born of the child's haptic exploration of his environment,[2] but also of his conviction that it is idle in pondering the problem of faulty education to probe after a 'first' cause in the child, since what we are always faced with is a cycle, from generation unto generation:

The trouble starts early, often enough in our mother's womb. As we are, so are our children. No one can give to posterity anything better than *himself*.[3]

This is Schiller's position too, the characteristic position of pedagogue and therapist: Accept the nature and start on the nurture. Yet without any suggestion of postponing the educational process until one can start from scratch, *ab ovo*. It is up to each of us to start upon himself here and now, not just because—as Schiller argues at the end of Letter VI—it cannot be right that any man shall 'miss himself' for the sake of future generations, but because in working upon *himself* he will at the same time be working *for* future generations.

But it is not surprising either that this genetic section should have proved difficult to interpret. For in it Schiller retains for the embryonic manifestations of aesthetic, intellectual, and moral activity, as they appear in the undifferentiated life of childhood or primitive man, the same terms as he has hitherto used—and will use again—for the fully differentiated modes as they appear in adult life or sophisticated society. Not without justification; since—once this initial 'leap' is established—what he is out to stress is continuity. If then, in Letter XXIII, he exhorts man to start laying the foundations of his moral life within the aesthetic, or to start 'applying the law of his will even to his inclinations', he is not, as has been thought,[4] reintroducing into the aesthetic sphere moral criteria from

---

[1] XXVI. 1. Cf. XX. 1 and XIX. 11.
[2] In his *Plastik*. Cf. above, p. xi and fn. 2.
[3] *Vom Erkennen und Empfinden der menschlichen Seele* [1778]; *Werke*, ed. cit. viii. 214.
[4] e.g., by Böhm, op. cit., p. 94, and Wernly, op. cit., p. 199. Cf. our Notes to XXIII. 8.

which he has just been at such pains to free it, nor unaccountably reverting to the Kantian conflict between inclination and duty. Quite the reverse. He is not talking about the exercise of any fully developed moral sense at all. He is talking about the early awakening of such a sense, and of the power to act on it, as these first make themselves known in the 'seeing'— as opposed to the 'blind'—exercise of drives or satisfaction of instincts: in our first delight in forms for their own sake as well as for their function; in our first preference for performing one and the same life-preserving or life-perpetuating act in this way rather than that. And if he urges the cultivation of these seeds of insight and choice within our physical life, it is precisely in order to *avoid* a too frequent conflict between inclination and duty: in order to ensure that bodily feeling is enlisted from the start as an ally, instead of being left as a repressed slave or hidden foe ready to revolt at the first opportunity against moral abstractions, however enlightened, which have been imposed as an alien authority.

Schiller's strategy might in fact be called an 'uncovering' strategy. He starts with what looks like a fairly simple problem: as the events of the Terror show, man has proved unworthy of the political opportunity; enlightenment of head has apparently left him a savage at heart; it looks as though Truth needs a Drive to be her advocate in practice, as though it were high time to start educating the repressed or neglected aspects of the psyche; for in the words of his motto from *La Nouvelle Héloïse*, if it is reason that makes man, it is feeling that guides him.

But it turns out not to be a simple problem at all. The 'savagery' itself is soon revealed as twofold in nature and origin: there are those who are still savages because Enlightenment has passed them by, and those whom Enlightenment should have taught to know better. These latter are barbarians. Nor, we soon learn, is it simply a question of educating feeling so that insights won independently, by way of reason, can be made to work in practice. Insights which are to work in practice must themselves have been born out of feeling, although—a further complexity—feeling is itself dependent for its development upon a measure of insight. Schiller uncovers their mutual interdependence to a point where the *Discours sur l'inégalité* might have furnished a more suitable text:

Quoi qu'en disent les moralistes, l'entendement humain doit beaucoup aux passions, qui, d'un commun aveu, lui doivent beaucoup aussi.[1]

And it is not just the problem that turns out to be complex. So, and recurrently, do the solutions proposed. The amalgam of reason and feeling proposed in III turns out in XIII to be a very complex process indeed, a process of 'reciprocal subordination'. And it is only out of this complexity that that 'drive' can be born which, when we first heard of it in

[1] Vaughan, op. cit. i. 150.

VIII, seemed to be there for the seeking among the 'inferior' forces of the psyche. By now, too, it has become clear that it is by no means just a question of redressing an imbalance between the arrogant head and the atrophied heart. Our cultural dilemma is due rather to the tendency of each and all of the faculties to trespass on the preserves of another and usurp its function. So that it is a question of discovering how they are to be properly related in the various activities and spheres of life—which is to be dominant when, and how the rest are to be subordinated. Once these notions have been made explicit in Letter XIII, we realize, of course, that they were implicitly there much earlier if only we had had eyes to see them: reciprocal subordination, as we already noted,[1] was implied in the latent alchemical image of III. 5; while the notion of trespassing, elaborated with examples from science and psychology in XIII, from religion and philosophy in XXIV, and still resounding in XXVI and beyond, was announced without being named as early as V. 5, and taken up again in VI. 12. If, of course, some of these Letters have been *a priori* assigned to a different stratum from others, this uncovering strategy is unlikely to become apparent.

It will not, for instance, become apparent if VI has been assigned to a different stratum from X. In the former it might have seemed as though the culture of the Greeks were, with some reservations, a viable ideal for modern man. But only because their political history was there tacitly ignored.[2] Once this issue is raised, the reservations are multiplied. And in Letter X it *has* to be raised, because here Schiller's own solution of our cultural dilemma is brought before the bar of history—and found wanting. Past experience tells us that taste and beauty were often bought at the cost of moral rectitude, aesthetic culture at the price of political effeteness. If the claims made for art are to be sustained, they will have to be argued before a court other than experience. To suggest, as does Lutz,[3] that Schiller could have settled his doubts about the enervating effects of art by introducing his concept of 'energetic beauty' at this stage, is to miss the extent to which this concept depends upon the outcome of the psycho-ontological inquiry into human nature still to be undertaken—and the extent to which the decision to undertake this inquiry at all depends upon the conviction expressed in III that man is not tied to his past but has the power of reversing the course upon which history has set him.

Above all it is to miss Schiller's characteristic strategy. It is to expect him to have interrupted what is essentially a concentric approach by prematurely introducing a final and unambiguous solution in a way only suited to a frontal attack on the problem. This would not only be premature; it would be altogether out of style. For Schiller's whole purpose

---

[1] p. xlvii, above.   [2] Cf. p. xiv and fn. 1, above.
[3] Op. cit., p. 191.

is not to fix the mind, but to keep it moving. And to keep it moving by changing the viewpoint. He takes his reader by the hand and leads him around and around, bringing him now up against a deadlock which will not be resolved until he reaches a different point on the same or on another circle, now to a solution which, as he moves still further round, will reveal within itself problems of even greater complexity. He thus leaves him at the end with an impression, not only of a myriad-faceted problem, but of the multi-dimensionality of the solution he is offering. So that it is to miss his strategy again to imagine that he has reached his goal, and could have stopped, once he has satisfied himself that art can stiffen as well as refine, invigorate as well as integrate—once he has defined the mode in which a genuine work of art should leave us as 'lofty equanimity and freedom of spirit *combined with power and vigour*'.[1] As the history of aestheticism was to show, this 'solution' opens up a whole host of new problems, and all Schiller's subsequent Letters are designed to uncover the dangers lurking in the assumption that because art can liberate and re-create, it can also provide criteria for the right use of the freedom and vigour it affords—designed to safeguard the frontiers between art, knowledge, and morality, without restricting the unceasing traffic between them. Hence the much criticized distinctions between optical, intellectual, and aesthetic illusion in XXVI; hence the hair-splitting between noble and sublime conduct in the footnote to XXIII (with its warning against the disastrous consequences of mistaking aesthetic transcendence of duty for something which does not really exist, namely, moral transcendence of duty); hence the complex interrelatings of semblance and reality in XXVII. Once this strategy is recognized, it seems idle to expect that because our moral nature is initially presented as freedom, and our physical nature as constraint, we shall never have uncovered for us[2] the iron hand beneath the former or the liberating potentialities within the latter. Or that because, by XV. 3, Schiller has evolved out of a synthesis of 'life' and 'form' a definition of beauty as 'living form', he will never again confront us with situations in which form—and precisely in this sense of living form—will have to be opposed to life in the sense of mere, or real, or earnest, existence (XXVI. 8–11). Or that because—crowning illogicality according to Lutz[3]—the aesthetic is treated throughout as both the means of education and its goal, we shall not at some time have to be brought up against the hard fact that the germ of it has nevertheless to be 'given'; against that irreducible basis of natural endowment without which even the best of education is of no avail.

But perhaps such expectations imply not so much a mistaking of

---

[1] XXII. 3. Our italics.
[2] As in Letters XX–XXV; XX. 2 is especially important in this connexion.
[3] Op. cit., p. 210.

Schiller's strategy as a denial that he had any strategy at all. Criticism of his *Aesthetic Letters* too often reads as though he were making them up as he went along, victim of his own confusion to the very moment of going to press. The symmetry of the structure he finally contrived should tell us that at some point the shaping impulse must have taken over, and pre-occupation with the 'what' been absorbed into concern with the 'how'. No doubt the reader *is* being led through hesitations and uncertainties Schiller himself had experienced—but not necessarily along identical paths. A labyrinth[1] has been devised for leading him to the centre and out again, not only in the most convincing and persuasive way, but in a way that has been determined by the conclusions meanwhile reached by the author. Everything gets transformed by this act of composition: personal letters into a treatise couched in the epistolary form of long tradition; the august addressee into a fictional patron with whom the general reader can identify;[2] the empirical 'I' of the author into the fictional 'I' of the rhetor. And if this 'I' says 'but my imagination has carried me on too fast' (XXV. 4), it is naïve to respond by trying to catch Schiller out in an error of judgement.[3] This is a traditional gambit of the rhetor for deploying his argument, for letting his reader share the headlong sweep towards a con-clusion which has o'erleapt the major obstacle. As far as the public orientation of the treatise is concerned, it is totally irrelevant that only a couple of months after its publication the author should, in a private letter,[4] have stated that 'in the literal sense of the word' he did not really '*live* in his century'. All that matters to the reader, of his or any other century, is that in the treatise itself he is being addressed by a rhetor who, in confessing his allegiance to the age in which he happens to live (II. 2), commends a like commitment to others. Even the dropping of the motto when the treatise was revised need not mean that Schiller had now turned his back on Rousseau. It is much more likely to be due to artistic con-siderations concerning the suitability of so simple a formulation for a thesis of such immense complexity.[5]

Strategy is the notion we need if we would relate the structure of this work to its genesis without falling into confusions of this kind. Unlike

---

[1] To adopt the term Schiller uses of aesthetics in general (XVIII. 3), not (as Böhm, op. cit., p. 83 implies) of his own aesthetics in particular.

[2] Schiller implied as much in the first footnote of the *Horen* version, later omitted. On the artistic possibilities of fictitious letters cf. Hugo v. Hofmannsthal's views, especially as presented by H. S. Schultz in 'Hofmannsthal and Bacon: The Sources of the "Chandos Letter" ', *Comparative Literature*, xiii (1961), 4 ff.

[3] As Lutz (op. cit., p. 208) appears to do.

[4] To Reichardt, 3.viii.1795. Cf. Geneviève Bianquis, 'En marge de la querelle des Xénies: Schiller et Reichardt', *EG* xiv (1959), 327.

[5] Hence our own hesitations about retaining it (cf. p. 336, below)—and our final decision to do so.

'intention'—whether stated by the author or postulated by his critics—it implies what is realized, however imperfectly, in the language of the work itself, and recognizable by readers without reference to earlier drafts or versions. It requires us to treat the finished work as self-existent—but not by denying ourselves the illumination to be derived from a study of the mind which produced it. It allows us to accept what this tells us of uncertainties and revisions—full of gaps as such biographical evidence is bound to be—but preserves us from giving the unwarranted impression that these will necessarily be reflected in the final linguistic gesture. To think that they must, is to run the risk of seeing flaws which are not there —and mistaking the significance of those which are.

These are obvious enough. We may dismiss as a mere slip Schiller's reference (XXI. 1) to 'the last Letter' when what he clearly has in mind is the last but one. Not so his apparent vacillation about tragedy which, being 'in the service of the pathetic', is first relegated to the 'not entirely free arts'—only to be brought back into the aesthetic fold with the statement that even works of this class are, 'by true connoisseurs', deemed the more perfect the more they succeed in preserving the freedom of the psyche even amid the most violent storm of passion.[1] And not so the major flaw at the beginning of Letter XVIII, where beauty *tout court* tacitly takes over the functions just assigned to 'melting beauty'—and nothing more is heard of this latter, or of its counterpart 'energetic beauty' either.[2]

The treatise thus has the shape of a torso. A torso with one arm missing if, with some scholars, we assume that Letters XVIII–XXVII are, despite the missing adjective, really about melting beauty, and that Schiller at some point decided that energetic beauty, being identical with the sublime, was best treated—according to tradition—as a distinct 'genus', rather than as a 'species' of the beautiful.[3] Or a torso with two arms missing if, with other scholars, we deny the identity of the energetic and the sublime, argue that the last Letters treat of beauty as genus, and that both the species—melting beauty and energetic beauty—were destined for a 'system' of aesthetics which never in fact materialized.[4]

In either case we are left with the impression of a fragment. Schiller's treatise is far less than a complete theory of art and the arts. But it is also far more. Such unity as it possesses is to be sought in its theory of

[1] On Schiller's general uncertainty about the aesthetics of the art he himself practised see our Note to XXII. 5.

[2] Cf. p. 335, below, and our Note to XVI. 5.

[3] On Schiller's own use of the word *Species* see our Note to XVI. 4.

[4] A letter written when he was revising the treatise for his collected works (to Süvern, 26.vii.1800) might seem to support the former view. For Schiller there discusses tragedy in terms of the typology of Letters XVI and XVII, but using the term *erhaben* instead of *energisch*. Cf. Lieselotte Blumenthal's comments in NA xxx. 390.

education. Such imperfections as mar it lie, not in any rift running hori-
zontally throughout its whole length, but on its outer surface. They
spring, not from some uncertainty at the heart of his conception of the
vital role to be played by the aesthetic in the life of the modern individual
and the modern State, but from a subsequent indecision as to what to
include here and what to put elsewhere.[1]
    For all the closeness of its organization this is not really a 'closed'
structure at all. The circle of the argument is open at point after point.
And the footnotes are the outward and visible sign of it. Schiller attached
such importance to them that he gave emphatic instructions for them to
be printed in such a way that the reader is not tempted to skip them.[2] They
often function like windows opening on to a world of psychic reality
which refuses to be confined within any system of thought. A world of
swift-changing movement, in which the relation between states and dispositions just established in theory may well be reversed in practice,
either because the situation has changed, or because we have changed the
point of view from which the relation is to be judged. It is to miss this
function of the footnotes altogether to argue that the sublime only intrudes
into one of them, as a mode of conduct 'we rate incomparably higher'
than the aesthetic,[3] because Kant's moral freedom was an ideal that still
had Schiller in its grip, and would not let him go even after he had 'progressed' beyond it: to miss it through subordinating structural evidence
to biographical. But it is to miss it in another—and more dangerous—
way to argue[4] that 'rate incomparably higher' is here a purely aesthetic
judgement, and that moral categories have at last been properly subordinated to the aesthetic. For this is to ascribe to Schiller's advocacy
of aesthetic freedom a static superiority it does not in fact possess.
    Of course this is a treatise in praise of aesthetic education. But at no
point is it ever suggested that aesthetic freedom is an ideal to be pursued
to the exclusion of all else. Or that a man who has achieved the grace of
aesthetic harmony will never again be involved in the stresses and strains
of moral choice. From first to last the two ideals of freedom, the aesthetic
and the moral, are presented as two possibilities of the human psyche,
constantly interacting, the relation between them never fixed. The
aesthetic has to contribute to the development of the moral; and the
moral then in turn take its place within an overall aesthetic 'tone' which
may serve as an ideal for all normal occasions of private and public life.

----

[1] This impression is confirmed by Schiller's letter to Cotta, 12.vi.1795, explaining
that he was disinclined to publish 'any more of his *Aesthetic Letters* in the *Horen*' because
readers of his planned book would want more than a mere reprint of what had already
appeared in periodicals. See also letter to Körner, 12.ix.1794.
[2] To Cotta, 19.i.1795: 'zwar mit Notenschrift aber weitauseinander gedruckt . . .'.
[3] XXIII. 7fn. § 3.
[4] As Böhm, f.i., does, op. cit., p. 93.

But Schiller knows very well that crisis situations will always arise in which the only appropriate response, if we are to maintain our human dignity, is that narrowing down (XXIII. 5) of the free play of all our psychic forces to a moral choice which involves the denial of some of them: a sacrifice of the totality of self in the interests of something larger than self. It was his conviction that we are more likely to rise with a good grace to the rare sublimity of self-sacrifice for the sake of others, if we have not passed our days practising self-denial through repression of aspects of our own self.

The context in which Schiller finally placed his *Aesthetic Letters*[1]—a context not preserved by any of his editors—lends support to this view of their structure. And it is a tacit rebuke to those who, resting their case on genetic evidence alone, maintain that *On the Sublime* represents his final word on the subject of human freedom.[2] For what he did was to reverse the order of composition—if not of inception—placing this latest, and hitherto unpublished, essay first, the *Aesthetic Letters* next, and completing the trilogy with an essay on tragedy *Über das Pathetische*, which had been written and published when they were scarcely begun.[3] Read in this context, their 'fragmentary' impression is mitigated. Though not entirely removed. One can imagine other contexts which would mitigate it in a different way: if they were, for instance, flanked by those essays on the limitations and dangers of the aesthetic mode announced in XXVI. 5. Placed as they are by Schiller, however, they present aesthetic education as an activity mediating without cease between constraint and freedom, freedom and constraint. And, not least, between that sublime freedom, born of moral constraint, which men do on occasion actually achieve in real life, and the aesthetic freedom which is offered to us by the art of tragedy—that art in which all constraint, whether imposed by passion or by sublimity, is made bearable through beauty, and redeemed through the power of form. Thus did the tragedian assert himself without abdicating the role of educationist.

METHOD AND MANNER

Schiller's philosophical affiliations and affinities are still a subject of controversy. At the one extreme there are those who—in view of his preferred terminology, his many tributes to the 'critical' method, his testimony that on the cardinal point of ethics he is at one with Kant[4]—take him for a Kantian of more or less orthodox persuasion. At the other, those

---

[1] See below, p. 335.   [2] Cf. above, p. xlii and fn. 2.

[3] An interesting analogy is afforded by Goethe's reversal of the order of composition in his cycle of poems entitled *Trilogy of Passion*. The first of the three to be written—on reconciliation, or catharsis—was, very fittingly, finally placed last.

[4] To the Duke of Augustenburg, 3.xii.1793; Jonas, iii. 398 f.

who deny that he is any sort of Idealist at all—or are even able to discover in him an Existentialist before his time.[1] But there are also those who would exempt him from methodological examination altogether. Being a poet, some of these imply, he is unlikely to be concerned with, even if capable of, philosophical rigour or consistency. While others appear to imagine that descriptive exactitude has been furthered if they affix the label 'poetic' to the method and manner of his writings on aesthetics.

A good deal of this philosophical debate has been carried on—at least as far as its public presentation is concerned—in considerable remoteness from the language of Schiller's text; so that it is rarely possible to see on what actual readings conclusions have been based. A notable exception in this respect, as in others, is Wilhelm Böhm, who in the mid-twenties of this century decided that the time had come to turn from philosophical generalities to textual particulars—and to stop making special allowances. Schiller's excursions into philosophy ought to be judged by criteria appropriate to philosophy, not by appeal to his standing as poet or his stature as person. In this legitimate cause he subjected his treatise *On Aesthetic Education* to rigorous analysis, Letter by Letter, and almost paragraph by paragraph, disentangling the eighteenth-century methods available to him, putting his finger on points where he finds him slipping inadvertently from one to another or hovering uncertainly between them, and stressing the importance of little-known anticipations of phenomenology for a proper understanding of Schiller's thought in this particular treatise. At the end of his investigation of the text Böhm added a section in which he comes to terms with the more important of his predecessors, followed by a short list of his own conclusions—a double, and increasingly rare, service to his successors.

By an odd coincidence this searching analysis of the method of the *Aesthetic Letters* appeared while Lutz's equally searching analysis of their structure was in the press. And in many ways the two studies are very different: Böhm confining himself to the finished work, Lutz exploring its genesis; Lutz concluding that its many self-contradictions are only to be understood in the light of earlier drafts, Böhm discovering that despite apparent inconsistencies and methodological flaws the published treatise has a meaningful unity of its own. But, for all their differences, what these two critics have in common is that they offer an unusually close reading of the text itself. And, by another curious coincidence— since they are clearly independent of each other—the points at which they misread it are often the same. A plausible explanation would be that these represent genuine cruxes, points at which Schiller's language is so obscure as to be ambiguous. But this is by no means the case. Indeed at such

---

[1] Cf. Käte Hamburger's rigorous examination of the problem of Schiller's philosophical idealism in 'Schiller und Sartre', ed. cit.

crucial points neither of them offers much help to the translator. A truer explanation might be sought in the fact that several of their misreadings of linguistic particulars touch on aspects of Schiller's thesis which have been generally misunderstood, or totally ignored. For there has been a marked tendency to play down his concern for science and politics in this particular work, if not elsewhere, and—though to a lesser extent perhaps —his concern for reason and morality too.[1] With critics who confine themselves to generalities it is impossible to verify what one suspects may often have been the case: that expectations concerning the nature of the aesthetic, or the role likely to be assigned to it in a treatise of this title, have led to misreading of individual passages, and these misreadings then in turn provided support for conclusions which answer to the initial expectations. With Böhm and Lutz, who committed themselves to more detailed interpretation, the circularity of this procedure is often fully exposed. Which accounts for our detailed criticism of some of their detail. For though linguistic analysis may not be the end of philosophy, it is an indispensable beginning. And failure to recognize the meaning and function of words in a context not only makes a shaky foundation for criticizing the methods of another philosopher (whether he happens to be a poet or not); it can give rise to theories which are redundant, and to legends which obscure.

Böhm, for instance, must take some responsibility for the legend that Schiller excluded science and philosophy from his ideal of culture. True, he does not, like Lutz,[2] actually introduce into his critique of Letter IX a section headed 'The Suppression of Science'. But by offering an even more detailed analysis of the offending paragraph he lends the authority of a native German philosopher to what is in fact a gross misinterpretation of Schiller's language. For it is not the case that in IX. 3 'science, as fellow-swimmer [*sic*], is pushed off the drifting raft' so that Schiller may be free to concentrate exclusively upon art until the penultimate paragraph of his treatise. And Böhm is only able to say that this is so because he refers a demonstrative pronoun to the wrong antecedent.[3] The contrast— sustained throughout the paragraph—is not between art and science at all. It is between the frailty, wickedness, or perversion of human beings —whether persecutors, patrons, or practitioners—and the astonishing survival-power of the arts and sciences themselves. It is artists, no less then scientists, philosophers, or legislators, who are accused of having on occasion plunged truth and beauty into the depths of human degradation.

[1] There have been welcome hints of late that his concern for politics might be played up again. See, f.i., the Bicentenary pamphlet written by Benno v. Wiese for Inter Nationes, and obviously aimed at the widest foreign circles: *Schiller 1759–1959*, Bonn (in the English version, pp. 7 and 22).

[2] Op. cit., p. 190.

[3] Op. cit., p. 30. Cf. p. 343, below.

INTRODUCTION   lxiii

It is truth, no less than beauty, that is said to have risen triumphantly to
the surface despite all such betrayals. Only on the basis of his own misreading is Böhm able to conclude that such 'ad hoc invention [sic] of an
empirical proposition . . . says more for Schiller's instinct for methodological self-preservation than for his logic'—thus convicting him of a
methodological misdemeanour he has not in fact perpetrated.¹ And it is
worth mention in passing, since it is a not uncommon feature of Schiller
scholarship, that his formulation of this alleged misdemeanour—to say
nothing of his gratuitous galvanizing into inept life of a metaphor that
is three-quarters dead, and not meant to be anything more—betrays a
distinct tendency towards that 'hypostasization' and 'dramatic exaggeration' he is so quick to censure in Schiller's own philosophical style.

Böhm's treatment of the political issue in Letter III is if anything even
more confused and confusing than Lutz's. Whether because of the ingrained conviction he shares with many scholars that the Golden Age of
individual freedom was a reality to which Rousseau looked back with
romantic nostalgia; or because he too takes Schiller's 'Notstaat' to be a
primitive State instead of any positive State—those of his own age
included—which is based on power rather than on principles;² or because
—from an evident wish to justify the 'conservative' State—he simply does
not follow Schiller's compressed version of the mental operations claimed
as man's moral right and duty once he begins to reason about his political
situation: whatever the cause, Böhm is so anxious to manœuvre Schiller
into the position of boosting the aesthetic at all costs that he manœuvres
himself into the position of asking the ridiculous, and entirely redundant,
question: Does 'state of independence', as Schiller uses it here, really
connote Rousseau's original state of natural man? Or has it not perhaps
become imperceptibly identified with that 'sheer insight and free resolve'
with which he is said to have exchanged it for a state of social contracts?
In which case, Böhm triumphantly concludes, we should have a strategic
anticipation of that 'middle state', later called aesthetic, through which
man must pass on his way to freedom and morality! Schiller's treatise is
indeed full of anticipations—if that is the right term.³ But this is not one

¹ Lutz's criticism of Schiller's logic at this point—for which he finds gratuitous
extenuation in his 'Künstlerblut'—is even more inept than Böhm's. 'Logically speaking',
he argues, Schiller should have looked to scholars as well as artists for that 'third
character' which is to heal our cultural ills. Like Kant, in Was ist Aufklärung?, he should
have proclaimed science and learning as the shield and refuge of free thought. One is
at a loss to understand how the tenor of a whole thesis can be so mistaken. But in the
name of 'logic' one is entitled to ask why, because Schiller claims a unique function for
art, it should therefore be inferred that he must be claiming an exclusive one.

² The inconsistency that he—like Lutz—discerns (op. cit., p. 12) in Schiller's use
of Rousseau's ideas derives solely from his own confusion of the 'Notstaat' (= 'Naturstaat') with the hypothetical 'Naturstand'. Cf. above, pp. xlv f.

³ Our own view, elaborated above, pp. li–lvii, is that they are not so much

of them. At this point (III. 2) he is operating with borrowed political ideas—Hobbes, Rousseau, Kant—taking what he needs for his own purposes, but contributing nothing of his own. He is no more insinuating aesthetic ideas into what purports to be a purely political context than he is in II. 1, where—by attributing to the word 'art' aesthetic connotations it does not, as yet, necessarily possess—Böhm also imagines he can detect an 'inadvertent' anticipation of the main thesis in Schiller's designation of true political freedom as 'the most perfect of all the works to be achieved by the art of man'.[1]

The preconception that Schiller must be out to elevate the aesthetic above all other considerations quite clearly colours Böhm's view of his attitude to Kantian methods and assumptions. Thus in his discussion of Letter XIV he observes—and with evident regret—that the concept of culture just evolved 'now gets completely submerged again'; for that reconciliation of our two natures, which in Letter XIII had been proclaimed as the task of culture, is here presented 'merely' as a task of reason.[2] He consoles us with the thought that despite this 'lapse' an advance has in fact been made; for 'reason' in this instance can signify 'nothing less' (*sic*) than 'aesthetic ideal'. But such a thought is only possible either through mistaking the tenor of Schiller's thesis as a whole, or—and the two are obviously not unrelated—through ignoring the different meaning of the word 'task', and the different function of the genitive, in these particular contexts. In XIII. 2 *Aufgabe* is used in its ordinary sense of a task which may or may not be capable of realization. And the function of the genitive is twofold: culture, or education (since the word signifies process as well as result), is at once the goal of the task and the means of carrying it out. In XIV. 2, by contrast, *Aufgabe* is used as a technical term, weighted with, and limited by, the Kantian distinction between *auf-gegeben* and *gegeben*.[3] And the genitive has a quite different function: reason is not the goal of the task, but its source—the source of our knowledge concerning its nature, and our duty to achieve it. This represents no 'relapse' into Kantian ways of thinking; it is simply a reminder that the perfectly reciprocal sub- and co-ordination of our two natures, being an 'idea' of reason, is—like any other ideal—strictly speaking impossible of realization. There can be no question, either here or elsewhere, of 'reason' being synonymous with 'aesthetic', or with any other, ideal. For Schiller, as for Kant, it is the 'inward light', the 'still

anticipations—let alone inadvertent ones—as the deliberate adumbration of notions which are to be further explored at a later stage.

[1] Op. cit., p. 8. Cf. Glossary under *Kunst* and Wilkinson, loc. cit. (3), p. 58.

[2] The quotation marks round *bloss* are Böhm's own (op. cit., p. 44), and presumably imply irony. But the function of the word here (cf. Glossary) is purely distinctive, not derogatory at all.

[3] Cf. above, p. xxxiv.

small voice', to which all our ideas and ideals must constantly be referred. In the first published version of his treatise he had in fact used it—and at a later point of this same Letter XIV—interchangeably with 'conscience'.[1] An even more striking example of circular argumentation—since it leads directly to one of his major conclusions—is afforded by Böhm's summing up of Letter XXIII as 'the incorporation [*Hineinbildung*] of the aesthetic into the physical by moral means'.[2] This may well be intended as a purely methodological statement. But it is one of many instances where it is no easier to determine in Böhm's language than it is in Schiller's whether a statement has methodological or phenomenological reference, or both. This one has the major misfortune of obscuring one of the most seminal points of the whole treatise by reversing the process which is the object of Schiller's educational concern: the emergence in physical life of aesthetic activities which can serve as a basis for developing our more abstract intellectual and moral activities.[3] But read as a purely methodological statement it is unfortunate too. For it contrives to make it sound as though Schiller has yet again been guilty of a deplorable lapse. No more than Kant, we are told,[4] has he really succeeded in freeing himself from the dead hand of the Enlightenment, and treating of matters aesthetic in aesthetic rather than moral terms. Or, as Böhm puts it in his final conclusions:[5] Schiller never succeeds in defining the logic of the imagination as organ of artistic culture.

The short answer to this is that he wasn't trying to. But it merits expansion. We are unlikely to grasp what Schiller was after if we suppose that 'artistic culture' is an adequate rendering of 'aesthetic education'. This latter was to begin far earlier than the contemplation or creation of works of art; it was also to extend far beyond it. To explore the manifold and complex intervolvement of the aesthetic with intellectual and moral activities on both the hither, and the further, side of art proper was a manifest part of his intention. Manifest in the treatise itself; confirmed by his statements elsewhere. In one of the more often quoted of these[6] he said that his aim was to secure the sphere of beauty against any alien claims or demands that might henceforth be made upon it. But he also said, and on the same occasion, that his aim was to investigate and remove confused notions and prejudices concerning the nature of the aesthetic and 'the limits of its use in our thinking and doing, thus clarifying a topic which has been as one-sidedly defended as one-sidedly attacked'.

Nor are we likely to grasp the nature of his aim if we suppose that 'the aesthetic' for him is synonymous with 'imagination'. Böhm is so sure of it

[1] *Horen*, XIV. 5.   [2] Op. cit., pp. 89, 94.
[3] Cf. above, pp. li ff., and Note to XXIII. 8.
[4] Op. cit., p. 114.   [5] Ibid., p. 189.
[6] Letter to Körner, 3.ii.1794; Jonas, iii. 419.

that he attributes the identification, not only to Schiller himself,[1] but to the scholar whose work, as he readily acknowledges, represents a milestone in the interpretation of the *Aesthetic Letters*. Not, he admits,[2] that Gneisse actually uses the word *Einbildungskraft*; but that, quite obviously, is what he must have meant! But that precisely is what he did *not* mean. Whether because his eyes were sharpened by the new science of psychology[3]—he was writing at the end of the last century—or simply because he attended to what is actually said in the definition of *ästhetisch* appended to Letter XX, Gneisse's great virtue is to have seen that the aesthetic as Schiller understands it is a modality of the total psyche, not a function of any one of its faculties. It is, moreover, as becomes clear in subsequent Letters, a modulation which can intervene when we are engaged in any kind of activity whatsoever, from the most physical to the most abstract, the most trivial to the most portentous—including, of course, imaginative activity. This distinction between the faculties of the psyche and its modalities is fundamental to Schiller's conception of aesthetic education. And it is only in contexts where he assumes that such aesthetic modulation has already taken place, where he is treating of the products of a specifically *artistic* imagination, and exhorting us to respond to them in an *aesthetically* imaginative way, that we find him deploring our failure to recognize that the imagination has its own laws (XXVI. 14), or making 'the insubstantial realm of the imagination' synonymous with the world of aesthetic semblance (XXVI. 10). Elsewhere, when he is treating of imagination in general,[4] he shows it for what it is, a two-edged sword: a faculty infinitely productive, but essentially wayward; indispensable in all intellectual pursuits, as in practical and personal life, but —without the irremissive, though gentle, and often unnoticed, control of the understanding and the will[5]—capable of leading to self-dissipation or even to self-destruction. As for the logic of the artistic imagination in particular, he expressly disclaims all intention of exploring it further in the context of this treatise (XXVI. 7). Had he done so, he would have distinguished between those aspects of the creative process which are susceptible of conscious direction and those which are inaccessible to the inspection of even the most self-observant of artists. He would have reminded us that it is only in the finished products that these latter find their full articulation; that we may, therefore, by comparison of works

---

[1] Op. cit., *passim*, esp. pp. 94, 105 ff., 189.

[2] Ibid., p. 148.

[3] Böhm rightly insists (ibid., p. 148) that, for all its psychological insights, Schiller's treatise is not conceived or constructed as a work of psychology. But it nevertheless remains true that psychologists have proved more alive to his intention than have systematic philosophers.

[4] Cf. Glossary under *Einbildungskraft*.

[5] To borrow Coleridge's formulation from ch. xiv of *Biographia Literaria*.

of art themselves, hope to discover the laws of the imagination, though we shall always be precluded by the very inventiveness of genius from using them either to prescribe or to predict. And he would certainly have told us, and from personal experience, more than he did in his review of Bürger's poems[1] about that special gift which, in the artist, fosters the transition from the most urgently personal to the most purely formal passion: his preoccupation with his medium and the activities of his craft. All this is abundantly clear from his correspondence.[2] What is no less clear from the treatise itself is that he eventually decided to confine himself, within this wider context of aesthetic education, to establishing the one condition that is common to both artistic creation and aesthetic contemplation: viz., the aesthetic modulation of imaginative activity. Without the intervention of what in XXVII. 4 he will call 'an independent shaping power', a 'leap' from the free association of fantasies and ideas—whether triggered off by some external stimulus, or pursued at the dictates of conscious or unconscious needs and desires—to that freedom of aesthetic play which lifts us beyond the confines of our personal-practical self, no work of art will be conceived by the artist, nor any appropriate response to it be forthcoming from the beholder.

Above all we are unlikely to understand Schiller's method and manner, let alone his message, if we start out with stock preconceptions about either the Enlightenment itself or his attitude towards it. If Lutz finds this ambivalent, Böhm—clearly operating with a cliché of German literary historians—assumes that he was out to 'overcome' it but did not always succeed. C. G. Jung, probing deeper, diagnoses an unconscious affinity with its overweening rationalism. He rests his case in part on a sustained period in Letter VIII, which opens with the assertion 'Our age is enlightened . . .', goes on to list its positive achievements, only to reach its close with the challenging revocation 'Why, then, are we still barbarians?' Deaf, apparently, to the traditional figures of rhetoric—*enumeratio*, *inversio*, *reversio*—Jung brings up heavy irony to demolish Schiller's own: 'What strange overvaluation of the intellect . . . what rationalism!'[3] And on the basis of this misreading he then proceeds to class him as a 'type' in which intellect predominates over feeling. For this there may or may not be good linguistic evidence. This particular passage is no part of it.[4] And, whatever his alleged type, what Schiller will do in

---

[1] Cf. p. xxvii, above.

[2] See esp. the letter to Körner of 3.ii.1794, which contains a detailed account of the scope he originally intended to give his treatise.

[3] *Psychological Types*, ed. cit., pp. 101 f. (*Ges. Werke*, vi. 83).

[4] Jung's treatment of it affords a classic example of the hazards ahead of those who would psychoanalyse the dead. Without the reciprocity which is so essential a feature of the therapeutic process, it is imperative to be alert to the *modes* of language and to the *forms* of art, and not only to their content.

later parts of his treatise, is to develop precisely those arguments which Jung—mistaking his method no less than his manner—here adduces in evidence against him. He will plead for the education of feeling, not just for its own sake, but as a means of ensuring the better operation of reason. In so doing he will be developing insights which—though they may have been overlooked or undervalued by the more superficial of its rationalist philosophers—were an integral part of the Enlightenment, and *pace* Jung of the French Enlightenment too.[1]

* * *

It is a pity that Böhm should so often have mistaken Schiller's meaning. For with his talk of 'polar opposites being extended by means of homonyms' he came very close indeed to uncovering the principle which governs Schiller's use of terms. Though his account of it is not always as clear as it might be. By 'homonyms' we are to understand, not words of like formation,[2] but a series of antithetical word-pairs in which the *relation* between each pair is of identical form. Nor does he seem to have grasped either the point of the exercise or the way it works out in practice. Otherwise he could scarcely have offered the following series as an example of the kind Schiller builds: *Person/Zustand, Realität/Formalität, Sachtrieb/Formtrieb, Stofftrieb/Sachtrieb, Leiden/Tätigkeit*.[3] For, in the first place, *Stofftrieb* and *Sachtrieb* are not antonyms at all; they are synonyms. The latter does not even occur in the final version of the treatise; it was replaced by the former.[4] And, in the second place, the subsequent word-pairs do not exhibit the relation obtaining in the first, since the terms—where not synonyms—have been placed in reverse order. So that instead of ab, ab, ab, &c., we have ab, ba, ba, bb, ba. In other words, 'formality' and 'activity' have strayed over on to the wrong side. They belong with 'person' in a series which can be extended thus: reason, understanding, thought, form, freedom, will, law, necessity, infinity, the absolute. While 'reality' and 'passivity' belong with 'condition' in the antithetical series: sense, sensation, feeling, matter, nature, arbitrariness, compulsion, need, time, limitation.

It is, of course, perfectly true that these terms do on occasion change sides. But not without rhyme or reason. The reason varies. And so does the way in which Schiller makes them cross over. By far the most obvious is through inverting the second of two antitheses in order to turn them into a chiasmus. A period may be dominated by antithesis or by chiasmus; or the two may alternate. But, however long and complicated the period,

[1] Cf. Wilkinson, loc. cit. (4).
[2] As his formulations on pp. 56, 57, 63—by contrast with that on p. 190—would imply.
[3] We have telescoped the examples Böhm gives on pp. 56, 63, without, we believe, misrepresenting him.
[4] Or by its other synonym, *sinnlicher Trieb*.

Schiller never gets the terms of his two primary series inadvertently confused. The following passage affords a typical example of one dominated
by chiasmus.

Once you postulate a primary, and therefore necessary, antagonism between
these two drives, there is, of course, no other means of maintaining unity in
man than by unconditionally subordinating the sensuous drive to the rational.
From this, however, only uniformity can result, never harmony, and man goes
on for ever being divided. Subordination there must, of course, be; but it must
be reciprocal. For even though it is true that *limitation* can never be the source
of the *absolute*, and hence *freedom* never be dependent upon *time*, it is no less
certain that the *absolute* can of itself never be the source of *limitation*, or *a
condition in time* be dependent upon *freedom*. Both principles are, therefore, at
once subordinated to each other and co-ordinated with each other, that is to say,
they stand in reciprocal relation to one another: *without form no matter, without
matter no form*. How things stand with the *person* in the realm of ideas we
frankly do not know; but that it can never become manifest in the realm of time
without taking on *matter*, of that we are certain. In this realm, therefore, *matter*
will have some say, and not merely in a role subordinate to *form*, but also
co-ordinate with it and independently of it. Necessary as it may be, therefore,
that *feeling* should have no say in the realm of *reason*, it is no less necessary that
reason should not presume to have a say in the realm of *feeling*. Just by assigning
to each of them its own sphere, we are by that very fact excluding the other from
it, and setting bounds to each, bounds which can only be transgressed at the
risk of detriment to both.[1]

The paradigmatic chiasmus here appears, undisguised, at the centre:
without *form* no *matter*, without *matter* no *form*. But it is both preceded
and followed by structures which are no less strictly chiastic, though they
may not appear to be so at first sight. This is partly because they are more
extended; but chiefly because Schiller rings the changes by substituting
other terms. Instead of simply reversing *limitation . . . the absolute*, he lets
freedom and *time* stand in for them. This whole chiasmus is then repeated,
but in reverse order—and with the expansion of *time* to *condition in time*—
so that we get a double chiasmus within a chiasmus. *Condition* serves to
connect *time* with *limitation*; but also to connect the chiasmus preceding
the paradigm with that which follows it. For its true opposite is *person*;
and if our expectations are disappointed when they fail to appear together,
we are immediately compensated by the new perspectives opened up
when *person* makes a brief encounter with *matter*—only to relinquish it
immediately as its steady partner, *form*, hastens to reclaim it. The dance
of concepts comes to a close with a second undisguised chiasmus in terms
of the more familiar *feeling* and *reason*. The perfect symmetry of this
period becomes immediately apparent if we let *a* stand for terms drawn

[1] XIII. 2fn. § 1. We have used italics in order to throw the operative terms into
relief.

from the first of the above series, *b* for terms from the second, and transcribe thus:

ba ab : ab ba : *ab ba* : ab ba : ba ab

What Schiller is patently trying to do in passages such as these is to exhibit the dynamics of the psyche, rather than analyse or describe them. To this end he borrows from philosophers whose model of it may be quite different from his own—from Kant, Fichte, Reinhold—terms which will serve to express its fundamental duality. He then, combining tautology with the figures of antithesis and chiasmus, proceeds to play a kind of language game. The tautology serves to deflect attention from the substantival entities themselves to the relations between them; antithesis to express the tensions which pull the psyche apart; while chiasmus has various functions. In the above passage it appears as the perfect linguistic analogue of the principle of reciprocal sub- and co-ordination, enabling Schiller to reflect the manifold pull and thrust of opposites within the psyche while yet preserving its integrity. Enabling him to show forth by the very structure of his period the basic convictions enunciated at the beginning and the end of it: the antagonism of sense and spirit is not, in his view, primary; not an inevitable result of our being creatures of two worlds, but only a result of our mismanagement of the 'mixed nature' which is our human condition. Elsewhere the mirror quality of this rhetorical figure will be exploited, and made to serve as an analogue of that reciprocal relation between self and world which marks the dawn of reflection in man (Schiller actually uses the word 'reflection' in its double sense). And in one sustained period—whose complex, but perfectly symmetrical, structure we have tried to exhibit diagrammatically in Appendix III—antithesis and chiasmus combine to bring to birth in language, as it were, that 'third thing', the play-drive, which is to be brought to birth in reality through the complex interaction of the two fundamental, and opposed, drives of the psyche.

If—to resort to metaphor—we think of the two aspects of the psyche as two branches of a single house now divided against itself, then we may say that Schiller is not, like Kant, interested in defining the internal relations between the inhabitants of either household, nor in assigning to any one of them his proper function in its economy, but only in the prevailing tension, the frequent clash and conflict, the never-ceasing possibility of reconciliation, either between the two houses as a whole, or between any single pair which sallies forth to do battle on behalf of the rest. Or—to change the metaphor—we may think of a dance whose figures are executed, now by the whole *ensemble*, now by a single pair. And just as in such a dance it is, on the whole, the movements that engage us more than the individual performance of the several dancers, so in passages such as these, where Schiller is trying to show forth by means of his rhetoric the interstrife and interplay within the psyche, the terms are interchangeable in the sense that one couple can stand in for another so long as the measures of the dance prevail, and the rules of the language game are obeyed.[1] But only in this sense. And only in this kind of passage. It will not do to conclude that because Schiller sometimes takes over distinctions ready-made, instead of re-establishing them himself,[2] he does not therefore observe them when it is important to do so.[3] Or that because he sometimes 'plays' with borrowed terms in this way he must therefore be using them loosely. It will not, for instance, do at all to replace the term 'reason' by 'freedom', as Böhm does,[4] in XXIV. 4–8, even though they do both belong to the same series. For here Schiller is not trying to create linguistic analogues, or emblems; he is arguing a point, a point which he thinks—and expressly says—has never, for all its importance, been adequately explored. It turns on the distinction he had made, in the footnote to Letter XIX, between two kinds of freedom: that which is inherent in man as intelligent being, implanted in him with the light of reason; and that which he himself achieves when he learns how to manage his 'mixed', his sensuo-rational, nature. Only with the second does he reach his full stature as a human being. The first may well, paradoxically enough, only increase his servitude, making of him no more than a rational animal ('ein vernünftiges Tier'), a creature having over the animals themselves the highly questionable advantage of a power which leaves him a constant prey to care and anxiety. For reason, no more immune than any other faculty from the temptation to mistake its proper object and sphere of operation, is quite capable of putting its lofty insights concerning infinity and necessity, the unconditional and the absolute, at the service of what is—despite all disguise of ingenious rationalization—neither more nor less than our instinctual drive towards unlimited material well-being. It is with such trespassings and aberrations that Schiller is concerned in these paragraphs. And he discusses them, not by reference to 'the aesthetically false', as Böhm asserts[5] (again the word 'imagination' leads him to drag in the aesthetic where it has no right to be), but by reference to science

---

[1] There is a good example at the end of XVIII. 2, where *Empfinden/Denken* do duty for the three couples in the middle of the paragraph. And Schiller himself, when revising from the *Horen*, actually dropped the couple *Tätigkeit/Leiden*, without any apparent damage to the thought.

[2] Cf. letter to Körner, 10.xi.1794, and Glossary, p. 302.

[3] e.g., in XXIV. 6, where the distinction between *Vernunft* and *Verstand* is vital; or in XXVII. 7 (see our Note thereto), where the passage is meaningless unless we realize that *Wille* is being used in its strictly Kantian sense.

[4] Op. cit., p. 97.

[5] Ibid. Such aberrations of *taste* are not, in fact, dealt with until XXVII. 4.

and philosophy, politics and religion: to the arguments we evolve, whether about first and final causes, or about no-cause at all; to the utopias we construct, whether private or public, of this world or the next. If we tamper with Schiller's terms in a passage such as this—imagining, perhaps, that his equivalences are identical with those of Kant—we obscure the growing-point of his whole thesis, the point at which he was moved to take issue with Kant, and are in consequence tempted to seek their divergence in areas where they are in perfect accord.

It is in order to bring out this notion of 'trespassing' that Schiller sometimes makes terms 'change sides' in a way quite different from that described above. Not by a reversal of *position*, as in the figure of chiasmus, but by a reversal of *value*, achieved through exploiting the lability of word-meanings. Freud's remarks on the curious correspondence between the antithetical meaning of primal words and the freedom of dreams to represent any element by its wishful contrary are not irrelevant here.[1] Though in recommending psychiatrists to learn more about the development of language he was thinking about its primitive beginnings in the past, whereas Schiller's mind was running on the possibility of exciting new developments for the future. He was making a calculated, and highly sophisticated, bid to extend the scope of philosophy by experimenting with the power of language to offer analogical as well as analytical projections. It was all part of his hope that it might not prove impossible to supplement analysis by synthesis, to make philosophy reflect at least something of the living dynamics of the phenomena it is primarily concerned to dissect. We know of these hopes and aims from statements Schiller made both in this text and elsewhere.[2] But they can be inferred without difficulty from his practice. His reversals of word-meaning are frequently as pointed and precise as his reversals of word-position, and should make us suspect that what we are here faced with is not a loose use of terms, but a shrewd awareness of the connexion between the ambiguity of language and the ambivalence of thought before it is cast into the Either/Or strait jacket of logical discourse. Thus the word 'free' may suddenly forswear its normal allegiance to either moral or aesthetic values, and appear in the opposite camp as a synonym of 'unrestrained', 'lawless', 'arbitrary', or even 'wanton'. But if this had been inadvertent, would Schiller on one occasion have juxtaposed these opposed meanings in one and the same sentence (XXVII. 4)? Or further underlined his point by the use of spaced type? And if 'form' suddenly leaves the party to which we had thought it irrevocably pledged, and appears—disconcertingly enough—as indistinguishable from 'substance'

[1] 'Über den Gegensinn der Urworte' [1910]. *Ges. Schriften*, Leipzig, 1924— [in progress], x. 221–8 (*Complete Psychological Works*, xi. 153–61).
[2] These are discussed in their historical perspective on pp. xcvii ff., below.

(XXVI. 14), the reason is not really so very far to seek. By divesting the word completely of its previously established associations with 'living form'—that dynamic but precarious balance of opposing forces holding each other in check—and placing it in a context of 'soundness' and 'solidity' and static attachment to traditional manners and customs, Schiller reminds us how easily the forms of social intercourse can harden into convention, can forfeit their life and movement and freedom of spirit, and become in their unchanging rigidity as opaque as any substance.

Notoriously fickle in its allegiance is of course the word 'nature', and to complain of its ambiguity has become one of the overworked commonplaces of Schiller criticism. The philosopher Eduard Spranger[1] at least draws our attention to the positive aspect of such 'tiresome indeterminacy'. Like *Existenz* in our own day, he observes, 'nature' was for Schiller's age a concept of dynamic centrality, too pregnant with living significance to admit of precise definition. This is true enough. But it does not follow that there is therefore no 'law' to be discovered in a particular author's use of either word. Close examination may reveal such significant relations between its various meanings that we are forced to assume a mode of conceptual organization less obvious, perhaps, but not therefore less coherent than that which may be achieved through verbal definition. And in this treatise at any rate, as we have tried to show in our Glossary, Schiller exploits the multiple meanings of the word available to him in order to mirror the manifold perplexity of man's felt involvement with nature: a part of it, yet in some sense set over against it; caught in its inexorable laws, yet to some extent able to modify them; and, where not able to do so, capable—in some measure at least—of rising above them by adopting a different stance in his unavoidable acceptance of their ultimate power.

* * *

Schiller's treatment of the ideas and methods he takes over is not unlike his use of borrowed terms. To say that he is an eclectic is to state the obvious. And scholars have not been slow to point out his indebtedness to Shaftesbury or the Scottish philosophers, to Hemsterhuis or Wilhelm von Humboldt, and—more recently and most illuminatingly—to Quintilian,[2]

---

[1] In the *Nachwort* to his edition of *Naive und sentimentalische Dichtung*. Turmhahn Bücherei, 15/17, Marbach a. Neckar, 1953, p. 144.

[2] In his pioneer article on Schiller's philosophical rhetoric, Meyer (loc. cit., pp. 331 f.) points out that his reading of Quintilian coincided with the birth of his eldest son, whom he intended to bring up on the lines of 'des trefflichen Römers herrliche Grundsätze über die Erziehung'. Nor is it without relevance that in the letter to his publisher (5.vii.1793) requesting Quintilian's work, Schiller should have expressed pleasure at the proposal of his colleague, C. G. Schütz, Professor of Rhetoric in Jena, to translate *Anmut und Würde* into Ciceronian Latin.

whom he admired, not only for his handling of the techniques of language, but for his doctrine that right speaking is important for right living, and that rhetoric is therefore a means of educating the whole man and the good man: one who possesses all imaginable excellences of both mind and heart, a *virtuoso* in the sense that Shaftesbury still uses this term. Schiller himself made no secret of his manifold indebtedness. For his university lectures of 1790 he may have disclaimed all intention of reading a single book on aesthetics.[1] But it was a different matter once his Danish patron had provided him with the leisure to prepare a treatise on the subject. And his letters between 1792 and 1794 are full of requests for books, or references to his reading:[2] names still remembered—such as Baumgarten, Winckelmann, Mendelssohn and Kant, Karl Philip Moritz, Burke, Home and Hogarth, Batteux, Mirabeau, and Pestalozzi—others long forgotten except by the scholar—such as Heydenreich, Maimon, Rehberg, Webb, Wood, Sulzer, and Theodor von Dalberg. Nor does Schiller make any attempt to hide traces of his borrowings in the treatise itself. The authors he actually mentions by name may be few—Kant, Fichte, Burke, Mengs, and (in the *Horen* version) Herder. But he could take it for granted that the presence of many others would be recognized: writers, both ancient and modern, who had concerned themselves with the good life and the good State, from Plato and Aristotle, and even St. Augustine, down to Rousseau, Wieland, Klopstock, and Lessing—to say nothing of Goethe, or of that most German of French thinkers, Diderot, and other contributors to the *Encyclopédie*.[3]

But there are eclectics and eclectics. And the question is how these manifold appropriations function in the treatise itself. Few, if any, of them as echoes, conscious or unconscious, let alone as surreptitious purloinings. Schiller is quite content to rest such claims to originality as he may have on his main thesis—the unanswerable case for aesthetic education in modern society—and to derive whatever help he can for arguing it even from those with whom he may otherwise disagree. Some of his borrowings, then, and not the least important, function rather as allusions, overt or covert, to predecessors who have provoked him into defining his own position. Such is obviously the case with Plato's *Republic* or Rousseau's indictment of the arts and sciences. And such, surely, is the case too with his oblique reference (VIII. 6) to other renderings of that slogan of the *Aufklärung*, the Horatian tag, *sapere aude*. This has recently been identified as 'a hidden borrowing' from Kant's *Answer to the Question:*

---

[1] To Körner, 16.v.1790.

[2] See esp. the long list in his letter to Körner of 11.i.1793.

[3] The general indebtedness of the German classics to the French Enlightenment merits further investigation, and is receiving it in East Germany in the ambitious project of the Berlin Akademie for a *Schriftenreihe zur Geschichte der deutschen und französischen Aufklärung* (Akademie-Verlag).

What is Enlightenment? And no doubt the borrowing—if such it may be called—did remain hidden from scholars until it was spotted by Herman Meyer.[1] But scarcely from Schiller's contemporaries. The external circumstances alone make this unlikely. Professor Meyer himself points out that this essay of 1784 had just been reprinted in no less than two separate collections of Kant's shorter works.[2] It was, as he puts it, no doubt ringing in Schiller's ears, if not lying on his desk. By the same token, of course, in other ears, or on other desks, too! And Kant's was probably not the only rendering of *sapere aude* that was 'ringing in Schiller's ears' either. At least not by the time he came to cast his original letters to his patron into a treatise for publication. In the former he had improved on Kant's version, 'Habe Mut, *dich* deines *eigenen* Verstandes zu bedienen', by translating: 'Ermanne dich, weise zu sein'. In the latter, this was emended to 'Erkühne dich, weise zu sein'—a change which is not without interest.[3] For the turn, 'Erkühne dich . . .', had been put into circulation as early as 1740, and in a context which—in view of Schiller's prompt reference to his favourite myth of Minerva springing fully armed from the head of Jupiter—might seem to be decisive. This was in J. D. Köhler's numismatic compendium, *Historische Münzbelustigung*, which ran as a weekly for over twenty years in the middle of the century and was reprinted, complete with index volume, in 1764–5.[4] Volume xii reproduced the medal struck in 1736 for the Society of Alethophiles, or Lovers of Truth. It depicted a bust of an armed Minerva bearing on her plumed helmet the heads of Leibniz and Wolff, the whole encircled by the legend *sapere aude*, which Köhler, in his full and interesting commentary, translated as 'Erkühne dich vernünfftig zu seyn'.[5]

---

[1] 'Eine versteckte Entlehnung' is the sub-title of the first section of his article on Schiller's philosophical rhetoric referred to above.

[2] Meyer, loc. cit., p. 316: Kant's *Kleine Schriften*, Neuwied, 1793; Kant's *Zerstreute Aufsätze*, Frankfurt u. Leipzig, 1793.

[3] Meyer makes no reference to this change. There is perhaps no reason why he should. Though one wonders whether, in a study based on the contrast between Schiller's philosophical style and Kant's, it would not have been more appropriate to choose the published version, with its evident rhetorical polishing, rather than the original private letter of 11.xi.1793 (Jonas, iii. 370 f.).

[4] It was, incidentally, in Goethe's library (cf. *Goethes Bibliothek: Katalog*, ed. H. Ruppert, Weimar, 1958, item 2472), and was apparently, according to Goethe's diary, a subject of discussion with Schiller and others on 21.viii.1803.

[5] Our attention was drawn to this medal, and to Köhler's translation of its motto, by Franco Venturi: 'Was ist Aufklärung? Sapere aude!', *Rivista Storica Italiana*, lxxi (1959), 119 ff. This valuable article, which traces the vicissitudes through which the quotation from Horace passed on its way to becoming an international slogan, only came to our notice after our Commentary had gone to press. Venturi makes no mention of Schiller; critics and commentators of the *Aesthetic Letters* make no mention of the medal. Yet the connexion might be worth pursuing, especially in view of the well-known interest of Weimar circles in numismatics and dactyliography (cf. our Notes to IX. 5, XXV. 3, and

But if external evidence makes it unlikely that such verbal and visual associations were ever intended to be anything other than tacit allusion, the internal evidence makes it virtually impossible. For their placing is both strategic and pivotal. Schiller introduced them just before what was, when his *Letters* appeared in serial form, the end of the first instalment; at a point where—with the unerring instinct of the publicist—he was about to leave his readers in suspense with an open question, 'to be answered in our next'. And the question is a crucial one, on which the whole of his subsequent argument turns: the obscure relation between character and understanding, virtue and wisdom. The *closeness* of the relation was a commonplace: it was implied, for instance, by Dacier when, in his bilingual edition of Horace (1727), he translated *sapere aude* by 'ayez le courage d'être vertueux', but glossed this with the note, 'pour aspirer à la sagesse, il faut du courage'. As Professor Franco Venturi points out,[1] it was only under the influence of the Alethophiles that the saying became more associated with the diffusion of light and enlightenment than with the attainment of virtue and wisdom. But it was left for Schiller to bring out into the open the apparent *circularity* of the relation: to question whether the conative factor, so firmly identified by Kant as the prerequisite of enlightenment, really has psychological priority. Courage may indeed be the condition of enlightenment. But is enlightenment not also a condition of the courage for it? Is the relation between them not one of reciprocal causality? To the educationist—as distinct from the rationalist, or even from the transcendental, philosopher—this is a question of supreme importance. Where is he to start? With the will? Or with the understanding? It is because the answer, as he frankly admits, seems to be leading him round in 'a circle' that Schiller feels justified in reiterating his claims for art as a *third* term capable of mediating between such pairs of interdependent factors. This does not mean that he is simply indulging in repetition for purposes of persuasion. He may have come round to the same point again; but in stating it in these terms, and in bringing out their circular causality, he has also carried his argument a significant stage further. For when he argued the case for a third, or middle, state in Letter III it was in the technical terms of a particular system of philosophy. And when he demanded it again in Letter VI, it was in terms of the current myth about the vanished wholeness of the Greeks. But now, in Letter IX, it is divested of terms reminiscent of either the system or the myth. The problem of personal and political education is here posed in plain language, as immediately intelligible to his own day as it had been to

XXVII. 11). For some of the rewards of approaching the literature of the German classics via visual emblems see F. P. Pickering's illuminating study, 'Der zierlichen Bilder Verknüpfung. Goethes "Alexis und Dora"—1796', *Euph.* lii (1958).

[1] Loc. cit., p. 124.

antiquity—or would be to the future. And in posing the problem thus he commits himself to offering his own solution of it in terms no less general, and no less fundamental. To continuing the argument to the point where *his third term, the aesthetic, is revealed as a matrix of psychic activity in which will and understanding are both involved, even if in as yet undifferentiated form*; as a state of being, therefore, which is as conducive to the formation of character as to the development of insight, capable of being used to foster virtue no less than to promote wisdom.

What Schiller is plainly doing here is defining more closely the challenge he had thrown out—to later centuries as well as his own—at the end of Letter VII. This is not, it must be emphasized, a challenge to desist from the task of enlightenment just because it may often appear to have failed. It is a challenge to take this same task yet a stage further by re-examining its basic assumption. For to turn the light of reasoned inquiry on to the paradox inherent in the ancient saying which had been raised to a modern battle-cry, was automatically to turn it on to a point in the cycle of human behaviour which still, after centuries of discussion, remained shrouded in obscurity. And had not been made any less obscure by the transcendental 'turn' introduced into philosophy by Kant! It is at this point of Schiller's treatise that the issue between them lies closest to the surface. And there would be a case for arguing that, when he turned from the mere postulation of an anti-Kantian ideal of conduct, as presented in his essay *On Grace and Dignity*, to the far more difficult problem of how this was to be achieved in practice, it was Kant's brief but stern reminder of the moral commitment involved in *Aufklärung*, rather than any of his three *Critiques*, which precipitated the old issue in new terms, and terms peculiarly appropriate to an educational enterprise.

But Schiller does not always treat his sources in this way. Sometimes he frankly makes use of borrowed material for his own purposes. Not because he necessarily agrees with it in every particular, but because he has not the space, or does not see the need, to come to terms with it in this present context. Such is the case with the myth of Greek wholeness,[1] Rousseau's political theories, or Herder's account of man's emergence out of a homogeneous state of nature into the subject–object dichotomy. The case, too, with his adoption of the method, common in his day, of using historical modes of description for non-historical purposes.[2] And such, surely, is the case with his use of the transcendental method. In reply to the charge that he was asking too much of his readers in this respect, he argued that

---

[1] On his political reservations about Wilhelm von Humboldt's presentation of this see our Note to VI. 2 and pp. xiv, lv, above.

[2] For presenting purely theoretical distinctions, for example. Though he may not debate its validity here, Schiller takes care (XXV. 1fn.) to show that he is fully aware of the nature of this procedure.

may be he was; but that, had he been forced to offer formal proof for all the Kantian ideas he was postulating, he could never have managed to treat in so small a space 'a subject which does, after all, encompass the whole of man'.[1] In a frequently quoted statement on the way he had used Kantian method in this particular treatise, he himself laid exclusive emphasis on its 'critical' function:

> Whenever it is a question of merely demolishing, or of attacking other people's dogmas, I have proceeded on strictly Kantian lines. Only where I am concerned to build something new of my own do I find myself in opposition to him.[2]

This is true enough. Schiller does indeed invoke Kant here as an antidote to dogmatic confusion. He will continue to do so—and Goethe too for that matter—whenever a new obscurantism threatens.[3] But it is scarcely the whole truth. However 'destructive' in intent, the effect on the conduct of his own argument is very constructive indeed. How, without the turn from the historical to the transcendental viewpoint, could he ever have progressed beyond Letter X?[4] How, without the model of Kant's ethical imperative, ever have arrived at his own aesthetic injunction 'Let there be beauty!' in Letter XV?[5] Or how, without the transcendental repudiation of metaphysical questions about the why and wherefore of things, ever have defended his decision at the end of Letter XIX to *assume* self-awareness as a basic human drive instead of speculating about its origins (a passage with which the aged Kant felt sufficiently in sympathy to incorporate it into one of his own works)?[6]

But however varied their function, and however disparate the sources on which he drew, the net result of Schiller's borrowings is not a loose agglomeration of discrete or incompatible elements. His eclecticism here is of the order Goethe must have had in mind when—taking biological formation as his model—he defined an eclectic as 'anyone who assimilates from his environment, and the activities that go on there, whatever is commen-

---

[1] To Körner, 10.xi.1794.

[2] To F. H. Jacobi, 29.vi.1795.

[3] Cf. their joint reaction, cited in our Note to I. 4, to the anti-Kantian aims of Goethe's brother-in-law, J. G. Schlosser; Goethe's linguistic objections to Hamann's demand that man should always act 'as a whole' (JA xxiv. 81); or his strictures on Heinroth's transgression of the proper limits of anthropology (JA xxxviii. 263).

[4] One has only to compare Lessing's critique of Rousseau (*Neuestes aus dem Reiche des Witzes*, 1751) to see the benefits that accrued to Schiller from his use of Kantian method. Lessing is content to counter Rousseau's indictment of art by adducing different historical facts, or a different interpretation of the same facts. Schiller, by contrast, makes a methodological volte-face, replacing the question 'What has art done for man in the past?' by the question 'What ought it to do in the future?'

[5] Cf. his letter to Körner, 25.x.1794: 'Das Schöne ist kein Erfahrungsbegriff, sondern vielmehr ein Imperatif.'

[6] Published posthumously. For details see our Note to XIX. 9.

surate with his own nature'.[1] Because Schiller handles his sources with sovereign freedom, it does not follow that he treats them cavalierly. It is a question, not of deformation, but of transformation; a transformation not unlike that which physical elements undergo when they become incorporated into an entirely different system of relations. If we attend too closely to the way individual elements functioned in the systems from which he borrowed them, we run the risk—it is a risk that Schiller scholarship has constantly run—of not seeing that he has a system of his own at all, or of not identifying the principles which govern either his selection of elements or his mode of transforming them.

Consider, for example, what happens when he confronts that bugbear of the eighteenth century, the *Schwärmer*, or Enthusiast, with the principle of reciprocal causality which, as he tells us in Letter XIII, he had just found admirably expounded in Fichte's *Wissenschaftslehre*. The psychology of this cautionary type had been endlessly analysed, and what Schiller himself has to say about it in Letter IX is little more than an application to the artist of the general strictures Lessing had passed on religious *Schwärmer* in his *Education of the Human Race*.[2] But in his play, *Nathan der Weise*, Lessing had also isolated a particular aspect of their behaviour-pattern: the disastrous exchange which ensues when head is driven to play the role of heart, and heart the role of head.

> ... Schwärmer,
> Bei welchen bald der Kopf das Herz und bald
> Das Herz den Kopf muss spielen. — Schlimmer Tausch! —
>
> (I. i. 136 f.)

Here, in this *locus classicus*—and in the form of a chiasmus too!—was the germ of that principle of usurpation which Schiller was to elaborate into the negative pole of his thesis. And as its positive counterpart, a paradigm of the *right* kind of relation between the forces of the psyche, he now elaborates, out of the principle of reciprocal causality, a dynamic and highly complex behaviour-pattern: reciprocal sub- and co-ordination. At first sight the two patterns are deceptively alike. In both it is a question of now one faculty, now another, gaining the upper hand. Both patterns, therefore, might seem to manifest a laudably flexible response to the demands of the ever-changing environment. In fact, the difference between them is radical. In the one case, a faculty achieves dominance through mistaking the nature of the objective situation: a man thinks when he should be feeling and feels when he should be thinking. In the other, he knows when to do which: each faculty sticks to its own job, but achieves

---

[1] *Maximen und Reflexionen*; JA xxxviii. 271.
[2] Cf. our Note to IX. 5. The distinctions Lessing and others made between *Schwärmerei* and *Enthusiasmus* are irrelevant here.

dominance, as and when necessary, by subordinating (*not* suppressing)[1] all the rest. It is a question here, not of an exchange or usurpation of functions, but of a changing hierarchy of functions. And the change is determined by a just appraisal of the total situation, without as well as within. In this case we have genuine flexibility, and a flexibility which is by no means incompatible with a formed personality. In the case of the *Schwärmer*, by contrast, the flexibility is bogus, concealing a personality as flabby and formless as that of the other is firmly defined. If he nevertheless presents a recognizable type, to which the eighteenth century could give a serio-comic name, it is because his responses—being prompted solely from within, by his own compulsive needs—rapidly become predictable. For his counterpart there can be no name; and Schiller does not give him one here either. Understandably, since this dynamic principle of behaviour can give rise to no 'type.'[2] The responses in this case—being governed, not by compulsive pressure from within, but by a readiness for creative encounters with the world without—will have as their only predictable feature a flexible appropriateness to the particular situation. Reciprocal sub- and co-ordination is, in fact, nothing more—though this in itself is much—than an ideal paradigm, the concrete realization of which, by different individuals in different contexts, cannot but give rise to an infinite variety of human behaviour.

Neither of these two elements—neither the logical principle nor the psychological type—is original with Schiller. Out of their confrontation, however, he achieves something entirely characteristic: an ideal behaviour-pattern with its own built-in warning system. Not just the obligatory philosophical warning that we can never do more than approximate to the ideal; but the typically Schillerian warning that we may well deceive both ourselves and others into believing that we are approximating to it when all we are really doing is indulging in its opposite. Human behaviour, he reminds us here as elsewhere, is—even at its best—profoundly ambiguous. The originality of his procedure lies not in his analysis of the concrete case (less evident here than in other treatises), or the psychological penetration (impressive enough even here) with which he unmasks the devious self-deception lurking beneath men's loftiest 'enthusiasms', moral, spiritual, and intellectual. It lies rather in the abstract rigour with which he demonstrates the nature of the connexion between the ideal prototype and its cautionary counterpart, exposing by the sheer formality of his procedure the fatal flaw which accounts for the radical difference

---

[1] As Lutz has it. Cf. p. xlvii, above.

[2] The term 'der ästhetisch gestimmte Mensch' (XXIII. 5) clearly denotes a modality of the psyche rather than a type; 'edle Seele' appears only in a footnote (XXIII. 7). Both are far more dynamically charged (see Glossary under *edel* and *Stimmung*) than the earlier prototype 'schöne Seele'.

underlying any deceptive similarity: viz. the lack of reciprocity between self and world. To adopt his own favourite method of stating relations in terms of direct and inverse ratio, we might reduce his conclusions to the following schema:

The more reciprocity between self and world, the more likelihood of reciprocal sub- and co-ordination between the forces within the self—and vice versa.

The less reciprocity between self and world, the more likelihood of usurpation and trespassing between the forces within the self—and vice versa.

The doctrine of indirection is not original with him either. The paradox that in order to go forward it may well be necessary to take a step backwards is, after all, enshrined in the French proverb not infrequently quoted by C. G. Jung to express the creative significance of regression: *reculer pour mieux sauter*. It is unlikely that Schiller was simply elaborating on this. But his immediate source, even if it were to be discovered (among the Pietist mystics, for example),[1] is less relevant in our present context than the possibility of once again comparing the use made of this same idea by Lessing. And again at the end of his own treatise on education, where he adduces it in order to contrast the headlong impatience of religious *Schwärmer* with the slow, indirect, workings of Providence.[2] But whereas for Lessing it is no more than an aside which could be dropped without harm to his thesis, Schiller makes it into the king-pin of his argument. He does this by first of all tying it in with other paradoxical, and equally unoriginal, notions. With something strangely akin to that *nisus indifferens*, or primal indifference of indeterminate forces, of which his Swabian compatriot, the Pietist F. C. Oetinger,[3] had written in a discussion of Newton's alleged indebtedness to Jakob Böhme for his arguments concerning space—*spatium est sensorium Deo*—and the motion of

---

[1] Before postulating a collective unconscious, or any other form of polygenesis, to explain the similarity between some of Schiller's doctrines and those of the East (cf. *Psychological Types*, ed. cit., p. 152), it would be necessary to explore all possible channels of transmission, early and late, not forgetting those *Lettres édifiantes et curieuses* (Paris, 1707–73) written by the Jesuits from their foreign missions.

[2] For details see our Note to XX. 3.

[3] *Sämmtliche Schriften*, hrsg. v. K.C.E. Ehmann, Stuttgart, 1852–64, i. 327–31. In an Appendix urging caution upon readers of theosophico-mystical writings, Oetinger observes that 'Law, an Englishman not unknown in the Journals', had maintained that Newton was reluctant to quote Böhme as his source because he was the object of general calumny. 'Law' is of course William Law, Anglican divine and author of the famous *Serious Call* (1728), whose predilection for Böhme's heresies subsequently caused him to leave the Church and sow the seeds of Methodism. This back and forth between religion and science, heresy and orthodoxy, throws an interesting light on the so-called secularization of ideas. In this case it looks as though the process had already gone a long way before the 'enlightened' humanist, Schiller, added his own aesthetico-psychological slant.

determinate objects. Or with the *coincidentia oppositorum* manifested by the 'abnormal' numbers zero and infinity, conceivable but not knowable, hence an apt paradigm of the intersection of the determinate with the indeterminate (as Kant had found when seeking a basis for those border-line cases of his epistemological system, ideas with purely regulative function).[1] Out of a whole complex of such paradoxes Schiller evolves his own doctrine of creative regression; of the inescapable need, if integration is to be achieved and the health of the psyche maintained, for a recurrent retreat into aesthetic determinability: a state of sheer nullity as regards any of our specific goal-directed pursuits, but a nullity which is infinitely fruitful for the potentiality of the psyche as a whole; a state of pure indifference in that it lacks all bias to any particular kind of activity, but an indifference which yet has a distinct *nisus* towards activation in general.[2] This doctrine is then built so firmly into his own system that without it the case for aesthetic education as he understands it falls to the ground. Without it he laid himself open to the charge of offering as a rival ideal to Kant's moral activism a Nirvana-like passivity; to his logically incongruous, but eminently robust, doctrine of freedom through self-frustration, a no doubt more seductive, but psychologically just as untenable, doctrine of freedom through self-fulfilment; to his presenta-tion of morality as the one-sided repression of man's lower nature by his higher, a less rigoristic, but in the last analysis no less static, notion of organic wholeness; to his hope of progress through more enlightened thinking in science, philosophy, and politics, an aesthete's vision of a world made better through refinement of taste.

This was the last thing he wanted to do. The last thing he wished to imply was that taste, however cultivated, can of itself ever furnish us with directives for either knowledge or conduct; or that in putting the case for aesthetic education as a necessary cause of true morality he was also proposing it as a sufficient cause. On this he may have been more plain spoken—because less rhetorical—in the original exchange of letters with his patron:

Taste cannot increase our knowledge, or correct our concepts. . . . When I say that the education of taste is the most effective means of correcting the faults and failings of our age, I am far from implying that I consider it the only means, or overlooking the immense part which a firmly based natural science, together with a pragmatic philosophy, must play in the education of the human race.[3]

[1] Cf. Kroner, op. cit., pp. 88 f. and our Note to XXI. 4. Kant's criticism of the misuse of regulative ideas in speculative cosmology (*Critique of Pure Reason*: 'The Antinomy of Pure Reason', Sect. 9) has clearly left its mark on XXIV. 5–7.

[2] It cannot be sufficiently emphasized that the *nisus* is towards activity rather than passivity, life rather than death, but not, of itself, towards good rather than evil. With the doctrine of aesthetic indifference as set forth in XXI. 4–6, cf. XV. 9, XXII. 3–5, XXIII. 8.   [3] 11.xi.1793; Jonas, iii. 374.

But there is nothing in his published treatise to suggest he had changed his mind.[1] Nor had he ever wished to imply that the ultimate aim of aesthetic education was a collection of self-sufficient individuals, however beautifully integrated and harmonious. His vision from start to finish was of a better society of interrelated human beings. Indeed, the very concept of a harmonious, integrated, individual no longer seemed as simple as when he had worked it out in terms of the 'schöne Seele'. For all the insights provoked by his analogy with the grace of bodily movement, he had not then really come to grips with the dynamics of human behaviour. The radical change of viewpoint is reflected in his changed handling of the 'enemy' metaphor.[2] In *Anmut und Würde* it had been:

> Only when they flow out of his total personality, as the combined action of both principles, i.e., only when they have become second nature to him, are his moral attitudes really secure; for as long as the moral spirit continues to employ violence against it, the natural drive is bound to retaliate with force. An enemy who is merely *overthrown* can rise again, but an enemy *reconciled* is truly overcome.[3]

In the *Aesthetic Letters* this becomes:

> Since it costs effort to remain true to one's principles when feeling is easily stirred, we take the easier way out and try to make character secure by blunting feeling. For it is, of course, infinitely easier to have peace and quiet from an adversary you have disarmed than to master a spirited and active foe.[4]

Out of context this might suggest a reaction in favour of sterner, more Kantian, ways of dealing with our recalcitrant instincts and passions. In context, the more robust tone is clearly the result of a decisive advance in his own ways of thinking. If the 'enemy' now remains an enemy, never completely reconciled—and not with his fangs drawn either—it is because Schiller has seen that a high degree of imbalance can still represent a stable situation, and that a harmony which is to be life-tending must involve constant adjustment between balance and imbalance. If feeling is now to be mastered as well as fostered, it is because in the light of his new principle of reciprocal subordination he can envisage it as, now dominant, now subordinate, as occasion requires. The change of viewpoint in fact reflects a complete—and, in view of his educational aims, very necessary—rethinking of his long cherished conception of the psyche as organism. For, though there had never been any danger of his replacing Kant's moral tyrant by a lusty barbarian in bondage to sense and passion, there had been a danger of his replacing one-sided repressiveness—whether from above or from below—by a concept of wholeness

---

[1] Unless, of course, one misreads it. Cf. above, pp. lxii f.
[2] Cf. above, pp. xxix f.   [3] SA xi. 217 f.
[4] XIII. 4fn. §3.

that was soft at the centre. Soft, not in the way of the *Schwärmer* described above, dupe of the high-minded posturings of his unconscious drives, but soft through lack of any adequate drive at all: a 'schöne Seele' tending towards *Schwärmerei* through addiction to an ideal of harmony which is totally unviable. If the former was inclined to make inappropriate response to challenge, the latter would be inclined to avoid it altogether, to linger inappropriately in an equilibrium that must in the long run become spurious. Wholeness of personality, Schiller has now seen, must be reconceived as a changing pattern of behaviour in time. And if the analogy of an organism is to be invoked at all, then it can no longer be in terms of the simple antithesis, common enough in his day, between a mechanical 'aggregate of elements' and a living 'organized whole'—not even with the added rider 'in which part and whole are reciprocally means and end'.[1] It had to include notions of imbalance, asymmetry, dominant principle, and hierarchical subordination, all of them characteristic of living forms, and becoming increasingly marked with increasing differentiation.

And all of them, as he well realized, at odds with the equipoise and stasis of aesthetic determinability. Yet the regenerative possibilities of this latter were too valuable to let go. By means of his doctrine of indirection Schiller was able to 'save' both ideals: contemplation and activity, right being and right doing, the integration of the individual within himself and his integration within society. And to save them in a way which left them not just as alternative possibilities—whether co-existent, as *vita contemplativa* and *vita activa*, in different individuals, or diachronic, as alternating modes in the same individual—but firmly related as means to end. Wholeness of personality, in the sense of the perfect equipoise of all the forces of the psyche, is now presented as a state to which man briefly returns in order to recreate himself. Rarely, if ever, achieved in its purity, and but precariously maintained even in its approximations, it can—if manifested out of context or adhered to out of season—all too easily result in a harmony which is illusory or an indifference which is inhuman. The test of its genuineness is that we emerge from it with no inclination to one kind of activity rather than another, but ready to meet any immediate challenge that life may present: to engage in relationships which commit us, actions which define us, and even to suffer that severe retrenchment of potentiality involved in choice, judgement, or decision. This is a doctrine based on a dual conviction: that experience of aesthetic

[1] It was in these terms that Körner, for instance, had written to Schiller (6.xii.1790) of his own indebtedness to Kant and Goethe in working out a 'new aesthetic credo' based on the concepts of life and harmony. It seems plausible to assume that Schiller himself owed some debt to Goethe for the more complex and dynamic view of organic life reflected in the *Aesthetic Letters*. For it was in these years that the latter was preoccupied with those studies in comparative morphology in which concepts of asymmetry, hierarchy, and reciprocity between organism and environment, figure so prominently.

determinability may enable us to perform such determinate actions with sensibility refined, feeling quickened, imagination enriched, and understanding enlarged; and that experience of such determinate actions will in turn ensure that the formative principle, so powerfully activated in aesthetic contemplation, has sufficiently rich and varied material on which to work. It is a conviction which accounts for Schiller's insistence[1] that education must not only provide for both extensity and intensity, but also see to it that they are brought into the right kind of relation with each other.

Yet those scholars who protest that the aesthetic is presented not as means but as goal are obviously not being just blind or perverse. Ambiguity, it has been pointed out,[2] is there in the very title of the work, which can imply either education *through* the aesthetic or education *to* the aesthetic. In the light of its contents we should want to insist that it not only can, but must, imply both—and more: education *from* the aesthetic through the aesthetic to the aesthetic. We would go even further and suggest that this is not as incompatible with the contention that the goal is *moral* harmony as some have thought. In order to reconcile the two views we have to go beyond our own earlier conclusion that the open *structure* of the work precludes our regarding any state—whether moral or aesthetic, harmony or disharmony—as final, and recognize that Schiller's *method* itself is in fact directed towards relating symmetrical and asymmetrical structures within a process of growth,[3] i.e., a one-way process which is irreversible except in the finality of death. And we have to go beyond Böhm's conclusion[4]—one of the more important of his insights—that in this treatise Schiller seems as interested in preserving antitheses as in achieving syntheses, and realize that he is in fact operating with more than one type of synthesis (illustrated by means of triangles in Appendix III).[5] This was indispensable to his purpose. For if he was to show the aesthetic as a state which—for all its closed symmetry—is not sealed off from our other states and activities, but is constantly feeding and being fed by them, in different ways and at different levels, then he needed more than an alternating pattern of achieved synthesis being broken down into new antitheses. He needed some kind of open-ended category which would allow him to relate these in a way that reflected a measure of continuity in the dialectical pattern. And this he does in fact provide with his binary-type syntheses.

[1] XIII. 2–4; for the practical pedagogue one of the most challenging passages of the whole work.

[2] By von Wiese in his paperback edition, p. 115.

[3] If Lutz had perceived this (cf. above, pp. xliii f.) he need not have concluded that the work is marred by a rift running through the whole length of its structure.

[4] Op. cit., p. 127.

[5] This seems not to have been observed, though with its realization many of the alleged inconsistencies of thought and terminology become meaningful.

Unlike the more familiar type this involves the use of only two terms: the synthesis bears the same name as one of the antitheses, and thus represents, not only a higher concept, but a concept with a bias in favour of one of the opposites it embraces.[1] Schiller exploits this asymmetry to more than one end. It enables him, for instance, to support the essential perspectivism of his strategy[2] by presenting the same state of affairs from more than one angle. Thus man is said to have fallen away from Nature by the abuse of Reason. If the task then enjoined upon him is to heal the nature-reason dichotomy in his fallen nature by a return to Nature, the process may be regarded in two different ways. If we think chiefly of the state of harmony in which he would find himself once he had achieved it, then Nature must be raised to the synthesis. If, however, we dwell on all the effort of reason that must go to its achievement, then Reason must be shifted to the apex of the triangle in order to emphasize the triumph of the human spirit which is involved in learning how to live in accordance with our true nature. It might, of course, be objected that it would have been less confusing to use a different term to distinguish the higher concept from the lower, e.g., Wisdom as opposed to mere intelligence.[3] And Schiller on occasion does.[4] But his more usual practice of retaining the same word for both nevertheless has point. It enables him to reflect his conviction that improvement of our human condition will ultimately depend, not on the discovery of any new faculty in human nature, but on the right use of those we already possess. And by raising, now the one, now the other, antithesis to the synthesis he can also express his belief that the return is in reality a progress: that in trying by means of reason to discover what man's true nature is, we shall at the same time discover the destination towards which he should go.

Used to this end, these asymmetrical syntheses do no more than assimilate to his own method and manner convictions he shared with his master, Rousseau. Used to chart the manifold contributions the aesthetic could

---

[1] The type had long been familiar to us from Goethe's thought (see Appendix III). While working on the *Aesthetic Letters* we also came across it in an account of Zen Buddhism by the French psychiatrist, H. Benoit (*The Supreme Doctrine*, London, 1955, p. 81; cf. pp. 6 ff.). We did not then (Wilkinson, loc. cit. [3], p. 72) sufficiently stress the different use to which it is there put. The common feature is only the asymmetry of the synthesis.

[2] Cf. above, pp. lv ff.

[3] And Schiller scholars have often felt the need to transpose his terms on these lines. Cf., for instance, Boucher's attempt (loc. cit., p. 335) to dispose of his alleged inconsistency of thought by opposing 'les raisons' to 'la Raison' (= 'la Sagesse'), 'le rationnel' to 'le raisonnable'.

[4] e.g., *Vernunft* as opposed to *Vernünftelei* in VI. 1. It was only in the light of the general principles governing his terminology, and especially his discussion of the aberrations of reason in XXIV. 4–8, that we felt justified in translating these as 'use of reason' and 'abuse of reason'.

make to the fabric of modern living, they serve to express convictions entirely his own. And here there could be no question of using a different term to distinguish the higher concept from the lower: it would have obscured the unity underlying the variety of its manifestations in the physical-moral continuum. For if—in order to implement his old contention that moral conduct will only be secure if it springs from our whole being—he now proposed to argue that education must begin with the aesthetic cultivation of the 'indifferent' (though not mindless) sphere of physical life, then all that he needed was a familiar ternary-type synthesis uniting the physical and the moral in the aesthetic.[1] But since he also proposed to argue that—powerful as it may be in activating our total potential—the aesthetic is powerless to furnish directives for moral conduct, then he had to show it interacting with the moral in the narrower sense, i.e., with received precepts and principles, to produce Moral harmony, i.e., a Morality which is backed by the full force of personal assent. And for this he needed, not a resolution of the former synthesis into two new antitheses, but a binary synthesis into which it enters as one of the antitheses. Nor could the process stop here. For moral harmony —if it is to remain genuine and vital—must, as we have seen, be subject to the self-renewal characteristic of all growth. And a powerful challenge to the complacency of moral harmony is the aesthetic in its most differentiated, and most radically subversive form, viz. the kind of art in which the reality-principle vies for supremacy with the pleasure-principle. Art which takes as its material the ideas and values of our cultural life, and—with superb irreverence for the authority of the contexts from which they are drawn—transmutes them into forms which challenge us to re-shape even our most cherished attitudes in the light of a newly stretched imagination. Here we have the Aesthetic exercising its disruptive-formative influence on Moral harmony to produce a still higher MORALITY. But this is not the only possible interaction at this level. Moral harmony, however perfect, and however self-renewing, is bound—as we also saw—to involve a one-sided retrenchment of potential whenever it issues as determinate action. And it is on such determinate actions that Schiller envisages the aesthetic—whether writ large or small—exercising an influence of another kind: an influence which affects their modality without altering their structure; which lends to their performance a grace which, though superfluous as regards their strictly moral value, allows them to partake of the harmony of beauty. In this case, AESTHETIC would be the dominant of a binary synthesis.

---

[1] Just how complex was the process of reciprocal subordination by which he envisaged even this type of synthesis being achieved we have endeavoured to illustrate in Appendix III. 1. Cf. our Note to XIV. 4, and pp. xlvi f., above.

It is possible to construct a schema which reflects something of this progressive refinement, or ennoblement (*Veredlung*),[1] of human behaviour: a scale ascending step-wise, working outwards from, and back into, some aesthetic node, each synthesis open-ended into the one above it. Like all schemas, this one is inadequate to the living complexity it represents. On each step of the ladder we really need a horizontal extension of binary syntheses side by side, reflecting those countless situations in which— without any perceptible 'progress', but at the instance of appropriateness to the particular context—now the aesthetic, now the moral, becomes dominant. And in each case 'moral' could be replaced by 'intellectual',[2] and provoke a salutary corrective to loose thinking about the role of beauty in abstract thought. Especially in an age which, distressed by the divergence of art and science, seeks at all costs to demonstrate an underlying identity. Schiller, as always, points to the more difficult task of discovering connexions without obliterating differences. The aesthetic, he would say, undoubtedly plays a vital part in intellectual activity: whether contributory, as in the processes resulting in an elegant theory, or supererogatory, as in the elegant presentation of intellectual findings. But in neither case is the product that indissoluble fusion of sense and spirit, mind and medium, that we call beauty in art. Or, as he puts it in XXV. 5: in the case of intellectual truth, the beauty can be removed without the truth being thereby invalidated; in the case of art, it can not.

If we now ask whether the aesthetic rates higher than the moral, we can without fear of equivocation answer both yes and no. 'No', if by aesthetic we mean the often unrecognized contributions made by the aesthetic sense to intellectual and moral life. For its role here is subordinate, though none the less important for that. But the answer must also—though perhaps less obviously—be 'no', if we mean the differentiated mode of aesthetic contemplation. For here the criterion of value is appropriateness of response in a given context. And by this criterion the aesthetic can rate as no more than *co*-ordinate with any of our other activities—even the practical. There are times when a practical gesture betrays a more imaginative response to need than even the most imaginatively aware formulation of the total significance of all that is involved. And there can be no doubt that a moral deed springing from true moral harmony would— since it involves relatedness to others—rate higher in Schiller's hierarchy of values than even the most deeply satisfying aesthetic experience. If, however, we take 'aesthetic' to mean that extra dimension of graciousness with which all our conduct—physical, intellectual, and moral—may be endowed, then the answer must be an unequivocal 'yes'. And in this

[1] See Glossary under *edel*.
[2] As has been observed—most recently by Sayce, loc. cit., p. 153—the former frequently subsumes the latter.

sense—though in this sense only—is it true to say that he presents the aesthetic as the goal as well as the means of education.

It is this firm distinction between the structure of an act and its modality, together with his implicit criterion of appropriateness, that makes for the flexibility of Schiller's hierarchy of values. He is no absolutist in the rigid sense. But no mere relativist either. Even in a treatise designed to advocate the aesthetic education of all our being and doing, he could—as we saw—break the closeness of his design in order to safeguard the structure of a mode of conduct profoundly at odds with aesthetic harmony, but one which we none the less 'rate incomparably higher', viz. the sublime.[1] By no means all scholars are misled by such statements into the belief that his faith in aesthetic education sometimes wavered. But none seems prepared to suggest that he conceived of any interaction between these two incompatibly structured modes. The most they will allow is that the aesthetic and the sublime remained for him two highly valued possibilities of the human psyche which he never managed to reconcile in a higher unity.[2] But is this not because the unity they seek would have to bear a name which was different from either? Would have to show the form of a ternary, rather than a binary, synthesis? Our examination of his strategy and structure alone inclined us to the conclusion that the aesthetic might have a contributory role to play in the achievement of a sublime act. Does not our examination of his method and manner justify the conclusion that it might conceivably play a dominant role too? Does not the logic of his hierarchy of syntheses carry us under its own momentum towards the notion of an aesthetic modality of the sublime? And not just in the art of tragedy, but in real life too? If any act, including the moral, is susceptible of a qualitative modulation which leaves its distinctive structure unaltered, are we not justified in extrapolating to the most supremely moral act of all? Is not a doctrine of aesthetic education, based—as this one is—on the distinction between form and substance, bound to include the possibility of a man giving his life for another with a grace that is purely gratuitous? Could not even this act, which in substance involves a repudiation of the bodily life of sense, yet draw sustenance for the form of its enactment from a lifelong delight in the sensuous life of beauty?

It is from the vantage-point of such ultimate intersection of symmetry and asymmetry—life and death, stasis and process, death as renewal, the relation of art to all of these—that we might perhaps most profitably

---

[1] XXIII. 7fn. Cf. above, p. lix.

[2] Thus the Japanese scholar, Otokozawa, who—according to his German résumé (loc. cit., p. 14)—exhorts us to seek in the totality of his life and works the synthesis which Schiller himself failed to find. We prefer to rest our case on the system of relations established in this particular treatise.

re-examine Schiller's profound, and endlessly debated, difference with Kant on the dual issue of the unity and freedom of the human personality. The issue on which he was, paradoxically, most profoundly indebted to him. To deny the debt is almost inevitably to mistake the nature of the difference. If in his *Aesthetic Letters* there is—superficial linguistic appearances to the contrary—no trace of the psycho–physical parallelism of his youth, it is because, as we saw,[1] the transcendental method had reassured him that, in theory at least, nothing need be feared for the freedom of the human spirit by regarding man as—wholly and completely, and in all his aspects—a natural phenomenon. His earlier conception of the psyche as an organism analogous to the physical organism, and either determined by it or reciprocally dependent upon it, has now been replaced by a model entirely different: a creature of flesh and blood, whose observable behaviour may be conveniently classified as, among other things, physical or mental, and who may indeed be disposed to experience in terms of opposites[2]—some of which, though by no means all, coincide with a physical–mental dichotomy[3]—but who is himself no longer thought of as a bipartite structure compounded of a body and a mind. Inasmuch as this unified creature still manifests a dual personality, it is not as a *physis* and a *psyche*, but as a denizen of Kant's two worlds, nature and freedom: of the former by his constitution, of the latter by his calling.

But here the resemblance with Kant's own model ends. And for the very good reason that Schiller made a sharp distinction between the principles of the transcendental method and the implications of the transcendental manner. The former he to some extent assimilated; the latter

[1] p. xxxiv, above. Graham's contention (loc. cit. [3], pp. 131 ff.) that his youthful 'conception of the human psyche as an organism on the analogy of a biological organism . . . recurs with unbroken continuity throughout his theoretical writings' obscures the radical nature of the change which resulted from his involvement with the philosophy of Kant. The metaphors she adduces from Letters VI and VII offer no support for 'the interdependence of body and soul'; and the concept of *Wechselwirkung*—first introduced in Letter XIII and not, as the German version of her article has it (*Jb. d. dt. Schiller Ges.*, iv. 293), in Letter VII—is treated in terms which normally cut right across the body–mind antithesis. In thus obscuring Schiller's genius for change and development through creative encounters with a number of different minds, she also deflects attention from the true nature of his originality in his treatise on aesthetic education.

[2] Kerry's assertion (op. cit. [2], p. 78) that Schiller 'is compelled to isolate and oppose, in the dualistic attitude, elements of the psyche which intuitively he sees as a unity' may or may not be true. Applied to the *Aesthetic Letters*, however, it would have the major disadvantage of reducing to a statement about Schiller's own mind what surely has public value as a diagnosis of Western modes of feeling and thinking.

[3] As the series of antitheses he builds (cf. above pp. lxviii f.) amply prove. In XIX. 9 he states explicitly that *both* drives—the *physischer* and the *moralischer*, the material and the formal—are *within the mind*. It should be evident that such terms have a range of meaning which coincides exactly neither with modern usage nor with Schiller's own youthful dichotomies.

he entirely repudiated. He must have been among the first to bring to bear upon a philosophical system the sort of linguistic and psychological criticism[1] which has become familiar enough in our post-Freudian age.[2] But more charitable—and more realistic—than some who probe beneath the surface of ostensive demonstration, he gives due weight to the *cultural* determinants of Kant's rigoristic scrupulosity (which is why, in VI. 13, he classes him among the martyrs in philosophy's crusade against error). Nor does he underrate the value of his *conscious* aims: it is not—contrary to modern expectations—the spirit of Kant's philosophy he attacks, but the letter.[3] How, he asks in effect, can freedom be expressed in the imperative mood? Has the moral man, as Kant presents him, 'any more freedom of choice between self-respect and self-rejection than the sensual slave between pleasure and pain'? Is he not in bondage to a built-in compulsion of pure reason and the pure will? It is sometimes said that Schiller had failed to grasp Kant's distinction between regulative principles and constitutive ideas.[4] It might be truer to say that he was shrewd enough to discern Kant's own propensity to make the former sound like the latter. Shrewd enough to detect that even he was not immune from the temptation to reify abstractions, or to endow concepts evolved in the interests of philosophical clarification with the force of psychological drives. Shrewd enough to suspect that the hidden model with which he actually operated, as distinct from the unified being he overtly proposed, was a creature sharply, and indeed disastrously, divided.

For he was divided in a way which is as alien to life as it is to freedom. What Schiller objected to in the Kantian model was not only its lack of grace and graciousness. Not even just its illogicality—an idea of freedom which is tantamount to successful self-coercion. It was its rigidity—a conception of moral life which, in the stasis of its unchanging behaviour-pattern, is at odds with the change and process of all other forms of life; its destructiveness—the risk of fostering a will so aggressive that it either emasculates natural impulse or provokes from it a counter-aggression of the most primitive kind; above all, perhaps, its impracticability— an ideal of human conduct which lies outside the realm of genuine possibility because it is, in the last analysis, incompatible with human nature in its phenomenal existence.

---

[1] Coleridge's Kant criticism started some ten years later and was influenced by Schiller's (see above, p. xxv and fn. 2).

[2] Is, for instance, R. Tucker's analysis of Kant's model of human being and behaving (*Philosophy and Myth in Karl Marx*, Cambridge, 1961, pp. 36 ff.) any more discerning?

[3] XIII. 2fn. §2. Cf. his fuller analysis in *Anmut u. Würde* (SA xi. 217 ff.) of the implications lurking behind Kant's 'harsh' mode of presentation (*Darstellung*).

[4] His use of this latter term in XIII. 4fn. §2, no less than his readiness to adduce imperatives in a purely regulative capacity himself (see above p. lxxxii and fn. 1), suggests the contrary.

Schiller's ideal is, of course, unrealizable too. But only because any ideal is beyond our complete attaining, not because its content implies that an aspect of our nature is, at best, unnecessary to the attempt, at worst, a liability rather than an asset.[1] In terms of the Christian theology his turn of phrase so often recalls, we might say that for Schiller the Fall lies, not in our having been cursed with a 'mixed nature', but in the knowledge that it is open to us either to manage it or mismanage it. Our task, therefore, is both 'theoretical' and 'practical': to discover the Way, and to decide to tread it. And though the Goal can, as he says (XI. 7), never be reached, there is—as he also says (IX. 6)—a sense in which it has already been reached from the moment we choose to take the Way. For the progress of a man's life is never to be dismissed as mere means: it is always, and at the same time, both means and end. Hence Schiller's interest in the beginnings of the Way, in the order in which the fundamental aspects of our nature first manifest themselves. If Kant leaves us with the impression of an order imposed from above, by a Will which springs to life fully armed, as it were, to carry out injunctions received by Reason from some noumenal realm, Schiller states expressly that he is concerned with the emergence of an order from below, with the phenomenal antecedents of reasoning and willing.[2] For him, the key to the right management of the personality, and hence to its true freedom, lies in the fact that the sensuous drive—the life of sense, and feeling, and natural impulse—develops first, has 'priority in time'.[3] Only thereafter does that other fundamental, and distinctively human, 'drive', viz. awareness of self, make its appearance. And only out of the interaction of both drives can the will be developed or freedom fostered.[4] Awareness of self is thus —as he states unambiguously in XIX. 11—the condition of the will, and not vice versa. From those in whom it has not yet dawned—as from those

[1] His awareness of the difference between his own ideal and Kant's emerges most clearly in XXV. 6 (cf. our Notes thereto) where the possibility of an actual, if momentary, realization of his own ideal is also envisaged. That this possibility coexisted in his mind with a complete grasp of the importance of Kant's theoretical distinction is borne out by his use of *Aufgabe* in both its ordinary and its transcendental sense (cf. above, p. lxiv) and by the strictly untranscendental 'usually' of his letter to Körner, 25.x.1794, where—having stated that beauty is not an empirical concept but an 'imperative'—he goes on: 'in der wirklichen Erfahrung aber bleibt [diese Aufgabe] *gewöhnlich* unerfüllt . . .' (our italics).

[2] Cf. above, pp. lii ff. Schiller's interest in the genetic, as distinct from—but related to—the structural, aspects of the psyche has never received the attention it deserves.

[3] XX. 2. Cf. VII. 2; XII. 3; XIX. 6; XXIII. 8. As we indicated above, p. xiv, he goes so far as to claim that this priority affords 'the clue to the whole history of human freedom'.

[4] It is essential to the understanding of Schiller's thought to realize that he does not derive self-awareness from the life of sense: it is, as we stressed above, p. liii, a 'given'. But it is equally essential to realize that it cannot operate except in and through the life of sense.

who, through forces beyond their control, have been permanently or temporarily deprived of it (XII. 2fn.)—we have no right to demand either moral responsibility or that freedom which is at once the condition and the sign of an integrated personality.

Freedom is thus the product of two opposed drives. A typical ternary synthesis—though with something of a bias toward process, since the one antithesis emerges later than the other. Time is of the essence; and in visual depiction the base of the triangle should not, strictly, be horizontal. And from this point onwards asymmetry takes over completely. Freedom, our sense of a shaping consciousness, interacts with spontaneous, involuntary experience in such a way that it transposes it, as it were, into a new key—and is, at the same time, itself intensified and enhanced. This notion of transposition pervades the whole treatise. It is through awareness of this freedom in ourselves and in the beloved that lust is transformed into love (XXVII. 7). Through its agency too— and not just through artistic skill[1]—that the brute contingency of a physical medium (IV. 4), the involuntary play of associations (XXVII. 4fn.), or the resources of cultural material (XXII. 5), are shaped into a semblance which is expressive of felt life. The natural impulse to play is transposed thereby into aesthetic play (XXVII. 4), optical illusion into aesthetic illusion (XXVI. 6), material superfluity into that gratuitous and purposeless superabundance which is the mark of beauty (XXVII. 2). In each case, Schiller argues, nature provides the substructure without which the superstructure would be impossible. But, as he sees it, the latter is not simply a development out of the former through continuous differentiation. There is an element of discontinuity too. As he puts it when making the distinction between material superfluity and aesthetic superfluity: until the free, the shaping power of his imagination comes into play, man 'enjoys more, but he does not enjoy differently'.

Again it would be possible to construct a schema illustrating the progressive 'ennoblement', or refinement, of the total personality as Schiller conceives it: a rising scale of binary syntheses, in which, now freedom, now the particular experience with which it interacts, is raised to the synthesis. In a sense, the process is reminiscent of the mystical doctrines of his Pietist compatriot, Oetinger:[2] of his concept of *Geistleiblichkeit*, of the personality as a spirit-body continuum, the spirit only

---

[1] Cf. the distinction implied in both IV. 4 and XXII. 4 between the physical laws governing the plastic arts and their aesthetic properties. Knowledge of the former may be indispensable to the creation of the latter, but they are not identical.

[2] *Swedenborgs und anderer irdische und himmlische Philosophie*, Frankfurt u. Leipzig, 1765, ii. 335 ff. Cf. C. A. Auberlen, *Die Theosophie F. C. Oetingers nach ihren Grundzügen*, Tübingen, 1847, pp. 147 ff., and the section 'Geist-leibliche Totalität' in W.-A. Hauck, *Das Geheimnis des Lebens. Naturanschauung und Gottesauffassung F. C. Oetingers*, Heidelberg, 1947, pp. 84 ff.

able to become perfect—as it is only able to become manifest—through body; the spirit, therefore, developing as a continuous purification out of this 'mixed' unity. But it is more reminiscent still of Goethe's theory of polarity and *Steigerung* (progressive intensification and refinement), and precisely because this so explicitly accommodates both asymmetry and discontinuity.[1] This is nowhere more clearly apparent than when for the last time, just before his death,[2] Goethe brought this theory to bear on the further 'cohobation', as he also called it, of his own personality. Of the polar opposites he there lists—conscious/unconscious, theory/practice, spontaneity/reflection, success/failure, support/resistance, the inborn/the acquired—only one is singled out for double mention, thus making the series lop-sided, and indicating that this is at once a term within the series and a term which transcends it. This odd term out is 'reflection': the power which enables us to manage all the others, including as it were itself; the power which, through such exercise, grows into what he elsewhere called 'a conscious unconsciousness'.[3]

Schiller's concept of the freedom of the personality is not at all unlike this. It is not a function of any one faculty, neither of reason nor the will. Nor—at least not when it is fully developed—of any one aspect of the psyche, such as conscious as opposed to unconscious. It is rather the still, and the seeing, centre to which all our activities, even those of reason, must be referred for their ultimate reasonableness; a point which is identical with no one of our manifestations, but where all our manifestations meet. Lineal descendant of that silent observer within himself, whose presence he had at first feared might be destructive of his best creative efforts,[4] it has now been raised to the central tenet of his doctrine of education. Contemplative rather than analytical—of what goes on both within and without[5]—self-awareness can, Schiller now tells us, turn all who will let it into artists of life, enabling them to discover form in the unceasing flux, and convert merely contingent events into significant experience. The freedom it thus engenders is not freedom from passion, but freedom to do more than just passively suffer the brute impact of passion; not immunity from prejudice, aberration, even hallucination, but the possibility of not being blindly identified with any one of these our conditions. Above all, it is not freedom from 'engagement'. Its ultimate goal may be non-

---

[1] We are by no means implying that the influence here was all in one direction. Recently discovered material (R. Matthaei, 'Neue Funde zu Schillers Anteil an Goethes Farbenlehre', *Goethe. Jb. d. Goethe-Gesellschaft*, xx [1958], 155 ff.) suggests that Schiller's participation in Goethe's theory of colour bore precisely on the concepts of *Veredlung Steigerung, Intension,* and *Harmonie.*

[2] Letter to Wilhelm v. Humboldt, 17.iii.1832.

[3] In a review of F. Rochlitz, *Für Freunde der Tonkunst* (1824); JA xxxvii. 282.

[4] See above, pp. xxxv and xxxvii f.

[5] See our Notes to XXVII. 4fn.

attachment, but never detachment. For Schiller, genuine awareness of
self can only grow with and through awareness of others. And can only
grow together with that other, no less dubious, gift: the power of communicating with others, and sustaining a silent dialogue between me and myself.[1]
Dubious, because the use of these gifts, as of all others, is up to us. And,
like all others, self-awareness contains within itself the cure of the malaise
of which it is the source. Born of distance, difference, isolation—of the
shattering realization that I am an 'I' separate from all other 'I's—it
nevertheless enables us, if we will, to find in the mirror of art a measure
of freedom from the terrors of alienation through the shared universality
of the forms of experience.

*   *   *

Continuity which accommodates discontinuity, identical structures
with changing modalities, the interaction of symmetrical and asymmetrical
patterns, shifting hierarchies and open-ended categories, annulled hypotheses and built-in warnings—these are the modes of thought we
would identify as Schiller's own. Not in the sense that they are peculiar
to him, but in the sense that it is these which determine what he takes
and what he makes. Their 'openness' may not be conducive to systematic
philosophy; but it is by no means incompatible with a coherent structure
of conceptual relations.[2] For such modes of thought are congruent with
each other. They are congruent with his manner—chiasmus, for instance,
lends itself to the reflection of partial no less than of perfect symmetry.
And they are congruent with his strategy and structure: with the delayed
solution of problems, the uncovering of snags in the solutions proposed;
with the subordination of linear argument to an overall encircling movement; with the breaking of this circle to open up other perspectives, or
remind us of the unfinished reality which eludes even the most open of
systems.

It is these open modes of thought which govern Schiller's attitude to
his sources, leaving him unabashed by the authority of traditional and
contemporary thought alike. For the great paradoxes handed down by
the perennial philosophy of East and West he has a wise regard. For he
knows very well that there is a logic which obeys rules other than those of
consecutive, Aristotelian, logic, and that there is a substratum of truth in
such sayings as 'the Goal is the Way', or 'the Direction is the Destination';
that there is a regress which is a progress, or a sense in which we can only
seek what we have already found. But he also knows that such traditional
wisdom, if it is to become fruitful for modern man, has to be opened to the
inspection of new methods, and thought through again. He is just as little

---

[1] XXVI. 2 and Note.

[2] Böhm, op. cit., p. 190 (cf. below, p. cxxiv and fn. 4) acknowledges the resultant
unity, but without—in our view—identifying the modes of thought which make for it.

overawed by either the technicalities or the 'systems' of contemporary philosophy. He takes from them—whether for his epistemology or his ethics, his theory of perception or his theory of psychological drives— just what he needs, and no more. For all his transcendental appearance, he remains a child of the pragmatic spirit in which he had been schooled by his first Duke, and of which he was now firmly reminded by the no less 'enlightened' patron[1] to whom he addressed his own mature thoughts on education. Thus his central concept, the play-drive, may—when first announced as 'a completely unthinkable concept'—have an unmis- takably mystical ring about it: it would not, from a purely structural point of view, be at all inapt to compare it—a 'third drive' which can be brought to birth within us, and is yet not a new drive at all, but a new quality in those we already possess—to, say, the opening of the 'Third Eye' in Zen Buddhism. But Schiller's subsequent treatment of this 'birth' is not mystical at all. It is informed by the empirical psychology of his day, and invites further translation into terms of ours. And it is a similarly curious and open attention that he extends to the loaded words, or the insufficiently examined assumptions, of his own 'enlightened' age. Mistrustful of a simplistic linear causality, he did not, as we saw, hesitate to uncover the circularity lurking in its chosen watchword. But he was not, as we also saw, content to treat this as an impasse beyond which it was idle for analytical thought to attempt to press. He himself did not rest until, with his novel handling of the lately advanced concept of the aesthetic, he had opened up possibilities of relating *sapere* to *aude*, en- lightenment to character, at a stage of human growth where insight and will are still susceptible of a common education.

Long after *Aufklärung* and the reactions against it had run their course, in an aphorism whose scarcely veiled allusion to Schiller seems to have been missed (though it starts with the identical quotation from *Nathan der Weise* which he had taken as his point of departure in his essay *On the Sublime*), Goethe offered a brief, but precise, appraisal of Schiller's educa- tional endeavour in historical perspective.[2] Lessing, he says, had felt the force of circumstance too keenly to be able to allow that any man need be forced to act under compulsion: hence he makes his Jewish hero say 'Kein Mensch muss müssen'. But along came a second (surely Kant with his categorical imperative) who pointed out that 'he who truly wills is in fact under obligation to act'. Finally a third—'freilich ein Gebildeter' (and obviously Schiller with his message of 'ästhetische Bildung')—went

---

[1] In his letter to Schiller, 2.ix.1793 (Hans Schulz, op. cit., p. 80).
[2] *Wilhelm Meisters Wanderjahre*, ii. 11: 'Betrachtungen im Sinne der Wanderer', no. 103 (also in *Maximen und Reflexionen*; JA iv. 233). The same thoughts occur in his correspondence with Zelter, 4–21.i.1826. But private origins and allusions clearly do not preclude the public connotations we discern in the published aphorism.

further still, and argued that he who truly understands is thereby moved to act: 'wer einsieht, der will auch.' With this, Goethe observes, we would seem to have described the full circle of human conduct: understand/will/must. And yet, he implies, also opened it. For men do on the whole act according to the measure of their understanding (which is why, he concludes, nothing is more appalling than to see ignorance in action). And understanding, after all, differs from either *wollen* or *müssen* in being the point of intersection between individual and race. Here we do not start from scratch; nor are we simply caught in the unrepeatable cycle of our own personal conduct. We are also heirs of the cumulative understanding of both the past and the present.

'Wer einsieht, der will auch.' True insight has motive power. There could scarcely be a better short statement of the content of Schiller's treatise. And it is the legacy of his method no less than of his message. Unlike some Romantics and post-Romantics, he did not, because Reason had failed to supply all the answers, feel tempted to suppose that some other faculty might of itself do better. He tells us, it is true, that man has need, if he is to understand himself and the world, of nothing less than his total equipment: sense, feeling, imagination, intuition. But he also tells us that Reason—not as the source of Absolute Truth, but as our ability to reason and be reasonable—is still an indispensable assessor of the material they severally and jointly provide. It may not be an infallible guide; but it is still, if it is not puffed up and disdainful of their co-operation, the most reliable guide we have. To his own work on education he brought all the manifold gifts he possessed, thus by practice no less than by precept exhorting later workers in the field to do likewise. And to do more. To bring out into the open their metaphysical premises and their hidden models; to become methodologically self-conscious without thereby losing the courage to think constructively; above all, perhaps, to see that the whole point of evolving a theory as 'closed' as he tried to make his own is not to put an end to further investigation, but precisely to provide a key which may open up new fields of inquiry. If *sapere aude* was his point of departure, it is also the challenge he bequeathed to posterity.

THE FUNCTION OF THE FORM

We argued above[1] that at some points of this treatise Schiller raises his discourse to a higher power by devising a linguistic analogue of the dynamics of the psyche. Now, at the end of our analysis, we suggest that the treatise as a whole implies an attempt to devise a form which matches its theme. For is not education concerned precisely with what Goethe was to call the absolutely closed, yet infinitely open, cycle of our

[1] pp. lxx f.

states and conditions?[1] Concerned with it in theory, because without some blue-print of human nature and its normal stages of development it cannot begin to allow for the innumerable deviations from the norm in individual personality? Concerned with it in practice, because the form stamped in each individual by inheritance is indeed unalterably closed—yet infinitely open, not only to the influences of formal and informal training, but to the unpredictable happenings of fate and fortune?[2] The manifold intersection of the closed circle by linear progress was something of which Schiller had been acutely aware ever since those assignments in the practice of psychotherapy which had been part of his training as an army doctor. And it finds reflection in his educational treatise when he speaks of the cycle of man's animal behaviour being 'opened' by his awareness of form, so that he finds himself set upon 'a path to which there is no end' (XXVII. 1). Or when he exploits the double orientation of the word *Bestimmung*:[3] backwards to man's point of departure, to his basic equipment for carrying out the task to which he is destined; forwards to his destination, and the never finished work he must put in on himself if he is to grow in the direction of that for which he was designed.

If our suggestion is correct, then aspects of this work which have often been construed as a sign of Schiller's own uncertainty would have to be reassessed as part of an attempt to reflect in its form the element of uncertainty in education itself. But are we not, in making such a suggestion, offering the most plausible reason of all for calling his work poetic, a designation we have elsewhere in this edition[4] strongly resisted? More plausible by far than that implied by scholars who hail his every turn to the empirical as proof of the poet in him (as though the empirical had no place in philosophy). Or—a nice irony this—than that advanced by C. G. Jung[5] who, taking precisely the opposite line, sees his turn to the transcendental at the end of Letter X as a sign of the poet taking over (which would make Lord Kames and Immanuel Kant into poets too). And more cogent than several other reasons commonly advanced which might on the face of it seem plausible enough: the fervour with which he pleads the cause of beauty (as though belief in its power were identical with its creation); the alleged vagueness or irrationality of his thought (a romantic heresy about poetry to which Schiller himself would not have subscribed);[6] the dactylic rhythms of his prose (as though the garb of

---

[1] See above, p. xxx and fn. 3.

[2] Which is why Lutz's strictures on the role assigned by Schiller to the 'Gunst der Zufälle' strike the thoughtful pedagogue as naïve: 'that would be the end of all education' is his comment (loc. cit., p. 210) on the opening of Letter XXVI.

[3] See Glossary.   [4] pp. lxi and 301, fn. 3.

[5] *Psychological Types*, ed. cit., p. 111.

[6] As William Empson recently emphasized ('Argufying in Poetry', *The Listener*, 22.viii.1963), such an anti-intellectual view constitutes a relatively brief interruption of

verse were a necessary criterion of 'poetic' discourse);[1] his employment of metaphors (as though these were notably absent from the language of either philosophy or science—any more than concepts and argumentation are absent from a great deal of the world's poetry). By contrast with these, features we ourselves have isolated in Schiller's treatise[2] are features which have been recurrently advanced by thoughtful critics and aestheticians as 'efficient causes' of poetry in the broadest sense of this term: a tendency to exploit the sound-look of words as well as their meaning; to control the number of relevant meanings co-present in any particular occurrence of a word by other aspects of the linguistic structure; to make linguistic structures into analogues of the life of 'felt thought'; to pursue a circular, looped movement which turns back upon itself rather than linear progress towards a fixed conclusion; to make the form as a whole a reflection of the content. Even so, the presence of such features within a work does not make that work as a whole poetic, since all of them, severally or jointly, can be used to other ends. It is by now, one would have thought, firmly enough established—even if we have forgotten that the late eighteenth century established it before us—that the difference between poetry and prose lies, not in the presence or absence of any linguistic element or elements, but in the principle which governs their total organization. Or—as Coleridge had it[3] when warning us that images, however beautiful, do not of themselves characterize the poet—in the 'predominant passion' which modifies them in accordance with the purpose of the whole.

But it is not just for a frequent lack of cogency in the supporting arguments that we deplore the tendency to call this treatise 'poetic'—whether the intention be appreciative or dismissive—but for the results to which it can lead. Used in the habitual way, as a vague blanket term, it serves as an alibi for not according serious linguistic and philosophical attention to Schiller's method and manner. Used with greater precision, and pressed to its logical conclusion, it is bound to involve a denial that he was out to convey a message.[4] This unusual step was in fact taken recently by

tradition; while the leading article in that same number draws attention to a contemporary group of poets who regularly meet to analyse their poetry.

[1] See below, p. 343. Since *Dichtung*, unlike 'poetry', often includes fictional and dramatic works in prose, the argument from metre to 'poetic' is even weaker when advanced by German scholars than by English.

[2] In various sections of this edition and, earlier, in Wilkinson, loc. cit. (3) and (5).

[3] *Biographia Literaria*, ch. xv. On his German antecedents in this connexion see Wilkinson's note to entry 406 in *Notebooks*, ed. cit. i.

[4] This contention holds even though we know—and know that Schiller knew (see above p. lxxxvii)—that it is a function of poetry, as of all art, to move men to re-fashion themselves. But not so to move them by means of a 'message'—unless this word be taken in a sense so extended that it becomes useless as a term of linguistics or aesthetics.

W. Rasch,[1] and we applaud his consistency even though we cannot approve his conclusion. Starting from the common, but highly debatable, assumption that conceptual precision must be synonymous with a one-to-one equation between word and sense,[2] he draws the plausible, but by no means proven, inference that since this is lacking Schiller cannot be writing legitimate philosophy. From this he infers that he must therefore be 'merely playing' with the forms of argumentation. And from this leaps to the wholly unwarranted conclusion that since, in Schiller's view, it is the function of all art to induce the free play of all our psychic forces, this must be the end to which his treatise itself is designed. Far from having a message of whose truth he is concerned to convince or persuade us, his purpose is to create that 'pure disponibility' whose educative function he so eloquently pleads. But this, surely, is to confuse the form of the treatise with its content: why should its function be identical with that of the phenomena of which it treats? It is to leave us without a theoretical explanation of the palpable difference between this treatise and Schiller's philosophical poetry on the same sort of theme. It is to imply that there has never been any philosophical tradition of 'playing' with hypotheses and argumentation—and to highly serious as well as not so serious purpose.[3] Above all it is to ignore distinctions Schiller himself was at great pains to establish. Rasch very properly cites in support of his claim a passage from one of Schiller's reviews[4] to the effect that a moral treatise no less than a household utensil can be raised, by the treatment it receives from author or craftsman, to the status of a 'free' work of art. But to give such a statement the philosophical underpinning it requires, it should have been glossed by the distinctions he makes in XXV. 5[5] between beauty in art on the one hand, in science or philosophy on the other;[6] it should

---

[1] Loc. cit. In fn. 9 Rasch welcomes our isolation of genuinely poetic features, but deplores our subsequent refusal to call the treatise poetic, and our attempt to place it instead in the long tradition of works concerned with the cure of souls and society (Wilkinson, loc. cit. [3], pp. 76 ff.). We readily concede that research still to be done may lead to its being differently placed; but we remain unrepentant in our belief that the treatise has a message, and that there is some tradition in which to place both the message itself and the method and manner of conveying it.

[2] Such precision as Schiller exhibits was obviously not of this kind. But he is not alone among philosophers in this. Nor, as we have shown in our Glossary, does it necessarily mean that he exercises no sort of control over the meanings of words.

[3] See below, p. cxxv. [4] *Über Matthissons Gedichte*; SA xvi. 252.

[5] Cf. above, p. lxxxviii.

[6] Instead of which Rasch glosses it with a passage from the same review which bears on the curious and, at first sight, incongruous relation between the extreme particularity of poetry on the one hand and the universality of its appeal on the other (cf. our Notes to XVIII. 4 and XXII. 4). This is a problem profoundly interesting in itself, and one which has become topical again of late. But it is a different problem altogether from that with which Schiller was concerned when he talked of raising a didactic treatise to the aesthetic power; or from that with which Rasch was concerned when he set himself to examine the

have been related to his observations on the differing relation between thought and expression in poetry on the one hand, rhetoric on the other;[1] and it should have been firmly placed in the context of his theory that the form of a work is the organization of all its elements towards a specific end.[2] It might then have become apparent that what Schiller had in mind was not the annulling, or even alteration, of the primary didactic or—in the case of a household utensil—practical function, but its assimilation *intact* into a form with a 'higher' end, and hence governed by a different principle of organization, viz. the aesthetic.[3]

It is difficult to say which is the more unfortunate at the present juncture: to deflect attention from Schiller's method or to deny that he had a message. For if his message speaks urgently to a generation whose task is to educate for a society committed to specialization in what may well be an age of plenty, and hence faced with the promise—or, as some might feel, the threat—of increasing leisure, his method throws out a challenge to all who are concerned with keeping the lines of communication open between what has misleadingly been called 'the two cultures' but is in reality a whole diversity of cultures. Since this was an essential part of aesthetic education as Schiller conceived it, and since his own treatise was an attempt at *haute vulgarisation* through the aesthetic communication of abstract ideas, it is undeniable that his method was most intimately intervolved with his message. But this does not mean that they cannot be theoretically distinguished. Indeed it is imperative that they should be. Imperative, too, to distinguish his stated aims concerning the aesthetic presentation of science or philosophy from his own attempt to put them into practice, since the former might prove suggestive even if the latter were judged unsuccessful. Above all it is imperative, if he is not to seem at once more idiosyncratic and less original than he really was, to place his endeavour in relevant contexts and traditions.

Schiller's efforts on behalf of *haute vulgarisation*, like the whole of his joint campaign with Goethe to improve public taste, have suffered from a species of reasoning not uncommon in historical judgement: because they proved unsuccessful they must therefore have been invalid (why not perhaps premature?). And they have suffered too, perhaps even more than his ideas on aesthetics and aesthetic education, from being appraised

manner and function of Schiller's own treatise on aesthetic education. The scholar's business, when faced with such prodigality of seminal ideas as Schiller permitted himself in his reviews, is surely to disentangle them from each other, and relate them to those parts of his more extended works where they received substantiation.

[1] As in his Jena lectures on aesthetics (1792–3); SA xii. 338 f. 'Rhetoric' here, of course, in the sense of the arts of eloquence and persuasion (*Beredsamkeit*), not—as in antiquity—of the art and science of all modes of language.

[2] A succinct formulation of this in *Über die tragische Kunst* (1792); SA xi. 178.

[3] On the relativity of 'higher' see above, pp. lxxxviii f.

almost exclusively in one or both of two, often irrelevant, sometimes inappropriate, and never entirely adequate, contexts: 1. that of his own psychological motivation—the acutely felt and memorably voiced tension between his divergent talents, or the personal motives behind his controversy with Fichte; 2. that of German philosophy in the late eighteenth century—and the narrowly systematic philosophy at that. We have only to extend the perspectives backwards to antiquity to see how much his concern for making the 'mysteries' of learning accessible to the *sensus communis* through a sophisticated exploitation of all the modes of language was part of the long tradition of classical rhetoric.[1] Just as we have only to extend them forwards to our own age to realize how much, like others among his contemporaries, he was revitalizing that venerable tradition through new linguistic, psychological, and sociological awareness; turning it already in the direction of present-day debates between those who are so convinced of the cultural value of science that they believe its transmission to non-scientists to be merely a matter of improving techniques of communication, and those who, less disquieted perhaps by the cultural gap, insist that its abstruse 'languages' have become so inseparable from its results that any attempt to translate these into other terms is bound to involve, not only a watering-down, but an actual distortion, of its truth.

But even if we remain within the eighteenth century itself, and simply widen the context beyond that of systematic philosophy, it soon becomes apparent that preoccupation with the increasing discrepancy between technical terms and the common language, between the analytical abstractions of science and the concrete uniqueness of art, between the existential wholeness of life as it is lived and the separating distinctions that have to be made as soon as we begin to philosophize about it, was not a symptom of some psychological disturbance peculiar to Schiller, but a problem which came to a head in his age and has still not been solved in our own. This is not to say that psychology is not involved or does not merit attention. It *is* to say that the psychological interest resides in the differing reactions of distinguished minds to different aspects of a problem which existed. A Hamann and a Blake were content to denounce analysis and abstraction; a Herder and a Goethe could take them in their stride as an inevitable concomitant of modern consciousness; a Coleridge and a Schiller, each in his own way, agonized over the problem—and in agonizing illuminated many a subtlety.[2] Only a few years before Schiller

---

[1] Meyer (cf. above, pp. lxxiii f.) discovers parallels in both Cicero and Quintilian with Schiller's train of thought in XXVII. 11 (see our Note).

[2] Cf. above, p. lxxviii, fn. 3; Wilkinson and Willoughby, *Goethe, Poet and Thinker*, London, 1962, pp. 142 f.; and Wilkinson, 'The Inexpressible and the Un-speakable', *GLL* xvi (1963), 313 ff.

—frustrated by his long-drawn-out excursions into philosophy—was nostalgically insisting that 'the poet is the only true *human being*',[1] Blake had included in one of his etchings the same thought in almost identical words: 'the Poetic Genius is the true Man, and the body or outward form of Man is derived from the Poetic Genius.'[2] And only a few years after Schiller—committed, whatever his sense of personal frustration, to the need for analytical procedures—had publicly declared himself no less suspicious of philosophers whose *methods* are in tune with common human feeling than with those whose *results* are out of touch with it (XVIII. 4fn.), we find Coleridge casting similar thoughts into a private piece of self-exhortation in one of his Notebooks.[3] Ruminating on the recurrent endeavour of philosophers, ancient and modern, to reduce distinguishable operations of mind—feeling, perceiving, imagining, thinking, willing—to a single process, he repudiates all such attempts at 'explaining [the many] into one', and concludes:

My *Faith* is with Fichte, but never let me lose my reverence for [such] *distinctions*. . . . So doing I may combine & harmonize Philosophy and Common Sense.

But it was not just poets who were anxious to 'combine and harmonize Philosophy and Common Sense'. It was philosophers too. And even if we confine ourselves to Kant, but extend our gaze beyond the confines of his three *Critiques*, Schiller's aims look far less idiosyncratic than they have usually been made to appear. For had not the master himself, in a 'popular' treatise on religion that we know Schiller knew and admired,[4] set the seal of his approval on the non-bindingness of technical terms outside of 'the Schools'? It seems never to have been observed that in contending that Kantian ideas have only to be 'divested of their technical form' to stand revealed as 'the immemorial pronouncements of Common Reason' (I. 4), Schiller was saying no more than Kant himself had said in his Preface to the second edition of that work,[5] when he rebutted a charge that by using technical terms from his *Critiques* he had created a barrier for the common reader. For anyone genuinely interested in religion, he there argued, 'would find *the matter itself* contained, even if *in other words,*

---

[1] As in the letter to Goethe of 7.i.1795 (cited in our Note to I. 4) or that of 29.viii. 1795: 'For philosophizing half the man will do, while the other half can relax; whereas the Muses drain one's very life-blood away.' Cf. above pp. xxix and xli.

[2] In 'All Religions are One' (etched about 1788); *The Complete Writings of William Blake*, ed. G. Keynes, London, 1957, p. 98.

[3] Ed. cit. ii. 2382. Cf. Wilkinson, loc. cit. (5), pp. 31 f.

[4] See Note to XXVI. 14.

[5] This appeared just when Schiller was starting to recast his letters to his patron (see Note to I. 2) and carried Kant's appreciation of his *Anmut und Würde*: 'Er spricht mit grosser Achtung von meiner Schrift und nennt sie das Werk einer Meisterhand' (letter to Körner, 18.v.1794).

in the most popular of sermons or a children's catechism'.[1] And was not this protest entirely in the spirit of his own master, Rousseau, who had concluded his famous indictment of the arts and sciences with an invocation to virtue, 'science sublime des âmes simples', in which he asked whether so much 'technical apparatus' is really necessary in order to recognize the laws which are engraved in every human heart—whether it is not enough to hearken, amid the silence of the passions, to the still voice of conscience?[2] But it was also in the spirit of those who had reminded their contemporaries that 'the voice of conscience' was itself, in part at least, a linguistic phenomenon. Of Moses Mendelssohn, for instance, who—in a work which was also on religion and also recently republished[3] —had pointed to the unrecognized expenditure of linguistic effort which has gone into the evolving of those quite simple truths we now take for granted.

This is the property of all moral truths. As soon as they are brought to the light of day, they become so amalgamated with the language of everyday life, and so combined with the everyday notions of ordinary men, that they seem self-evident to common human understanding. So that henceforth we cannot help marvelling how men could ever have managed to stumble along a path which to us now seems perfectly straight. We forget all the effort it must have cost to clear so straight a path through the surrounding wilderness.

Extending the perspectives thus reminds us how strong still was the faith that the widening gap between specialist thinking and common understanding not only must, but could, be bridged. But it reminds us too that such faith did not simply depend on the observable fact that 'what was born and christened in the Schools passes by degrees into the world at large, and becomes the property of the market and the tea-table'.[4] It was sustained by the conviction that, indisputable as it may be that language is a cardinal determinant of thought, it is also true that an identical thought can be transposed into different language, that the

---

[1] Our italics, in order to point the contrast with which Kant, no less than Schiller, was concerned. Scholars have made heavy weather of Schiller's ambivalence towards the technicalities of philosophy. In view of Kant's own words on the subject, some of the explanations they have devised seem superfluous, if not far-fetched. Thus Böhm explains it at one point (op. cit., pp. 123 f.) by an unwillingness to come into open conflict with Kant; at another (ibid., p. 65) by Schiller's 'instinct for philosophical self-preservation'—a locution to which he seems unduly addicted (see above, p. lxiii); at yet another (ibid., p. 8) by his conviction of the 'methodological [sic!] inadequacy of all philosophizing'.

[2] Premier Discours; Havens, op. cit., p. 162.

[3] Jerusalem, oder über religiöse Macht und Judentum (1783, 1791²); ed. cit. iii. 260. The passage quoted here was transcribed, with comments, by Coleridge in Notebook 50, entries 61, 62 (due to appear in Notebooks, ed. cit. iii), and may well be reflected in the footnote on language and common sense at the end of ch. iv of Biographia Literaria.

[4] Biogr. Lit. iv. fn.

spirit will remain constant though the letter may vary; or, as Kant had it, that 'the matter itself' is the same even when expressed 'in other words'. To claim otherwise, Herder had declared some thirty years before,[1] would spell the death of philosophy. In the modern, scientific, age each mode of discourse had its differentiated function to perform, and the function of philosophy was precisely to disentangle thought from the language which gave it birth: to take the speech of everyday life, which almost seems to do our thinking for us, and go on transposing and retransposing it into alternative terms until 'the everyday notions of ordinary men' have been distinguished as concepts whose nature and relationships are clear to the mind in whatever language they may be couched. True, he went on, there is one mode of discourse—and one mode only—of which one may justifiably assert and demand that a thought differently expressed is a different thought. This is the poetic mode. Its unique function of expressing the inner life as it is lived—the movements of thinking as it is actually thought, with all the accompaniments of bodily feeling—requires that here thought *should* 'cleave to the precise mode of expression' as soul does to body; remain implicit in the particular linguistic form, and never wholly to be explicated out of it by either paraphrase or translation. But to postulate such 'conglutination' as a desideratum for philosophy—to reverse the post-Baconian way of analysis and be content 'to think the thought *implicite* with its particular form of expression', let the tenor be as it were 'swallowed up' in the vehicle—this, Herder concluded, could only result in a 'Philosophie der Faulen'.

This is yet another context which has been curiously neglected by Schiller scholars.[2] Curiously—and unfortunately, since it throws into sharper relief than any other the originality and subtlety of his insight into the problems of popularization. The last thing Schiller wanted to foster was a 'Philosophie der Faulen': existential murkiness, confusion of modes and frontiers, avoidance of differentiation and 'the way of analysis', were as abhorrent to him as they were to Herder.[3] He was as sharply

---

[1] In his *Fragmente über die neuere deutsche Literatur*. Dritte Sammlung, i. 6–12. The most important points of the argument summarized here are on pp. 394–7 and 415–21 of *Werke*, ed. cit. i.

[2] Even by the two who have contributed most to our understanding of Schiller's attitude to language and the problems of popularization: by Meyer (loc. cit., p. 350), presumably, because he deemed Herder's passion for distinctions less relevant than the demand for 'totality' which he shared with Hamann; by Jolles (loc. cit., pp. 92 ff.), presumably, because he was more intent on Schiller's disagreement with Herder's later theories on the rejuvenation of language. As Wilkinson (*GLL* xvi [1963], 310 f.) has pointed out, Jolles's interpretation of what Schiller meant by the living 'body' of language as opposed to the 'dead letter' (see below, pp. cvi f.) would have benefited greatly by reference to Herder's seminal ideas of thirty years before, which had become part and parcel of contemporary thinking.

[3] See above, p. lxxviii and fn. 3.

aware as anyone of our ingrained resistance to the breaking-down of cherished wholes, especially in art and aesthetics. But his suggestion for overcoming it, as he makes clear in XVIII. 4, was through the eventual presentation of new wholes achieved by uniting what has first been scrupulously distinguished. We suggested above[1] that this conception of the proper task of aesthetics might well be regarded as a response to the challenge of Herder's objection that Baumgarten had prejudiced its future from the start by assigning it a privileged position, as a cross between an art and a science. We now suggest that Schiller's proposals for raising this, or any other science, to the status of an art through the manner of its linguistic presentation might also be regarded as an attempt to reconcile what Herder had distinguished as two apparently irreconcilable modes of discourse. Might it not be possible, Schiller seems to have asked himself, to preserve intact the principle of translatability required of analytical discourse, and yet *at the same time* embody it in a form owing some allegiance to the principle of untranslatability which governs poetic discourse?

But there is a further reason why it is unfortunate to neglect the context of Herder's early distinctions between the various modes of language. For it is there[2] that we find a classic account of the situation which Schiller takes as his point of departure when considering the problem of popularization: the 'roundabout way' that has to be taken by anyone wishing to address himself to the *feeling* of an audience through the medium of the *written* word. Rarely can the dilemma of the modern poet have been evoked with such dramatic gusto. Unlike the bard of old, says Herder, he has to renounce the *natural* expression of feeling, which is through the sign-language of the body. Nor can he simply let his tears fall on to the page until the ink runs. He has to convey his whole soul through the dead letter of an abstract symbolism. And this he will not achieve by simply emulating the sensuous and natural speech of everyday life; for there we merely fumble and adumbrate when trying to express what we feel, and fall back, in a fret of frustration at our own inarticulacy, on the sigh, or the cry, or the phrase helplessly broken off. The poet, by contrast, has to make feeling fully articulate in language itself. And this he can only do by taking as his model the Platonic myth of the body as the mirror of the soul: recognizing that the outward forms of language—its sound and its look, the length and shape of the word, the sentence, the period—can be made to take on the contours of his thought, and become as much

[1] pp. xxviii f.

[2] *Fragmente*, ed. cit., pp. 394 f. For a fuller discussion of the influence of Herder's ideas see Wilkinson and Willoughby, 'The Blind Man and the Poet', *German Studies Presented to W. H. Bruford*, London, 1962, pp. 47–51, and Wilkinson, 'The Inexpressible and the Un-speakable', *GLL* xvi (1963), 308 ff.

part of the total significance of his 'Sinn-bild' as does the paraphrasable meaning of his discourse.

When Schiller speaks of the poet's task[1] we find the same insistence on the 'very long way round' that the poet must take if he would make 'the dead letter' of his abstract, generalizing, medium take on the breath of individual life; the same paradox that the miracle of transparency will only be achieved by a master who loves the opaqueness of his medium—a paradox precipitated (less cryptically than in Blake's etching) in those twin distichs entitled *Language* and *To the Poet*,[2] in which he first laments the barriers to full communion which are erected by speech, and then exhorts the poet to overcome them by engaging in a love-affair with language: exploiting its outward forms as a lover explores the body of his beloved. All this is no more than Herder had said. Schiller's whole originality lies in the extension of this line of inquiry to the art of the popularizer. This kind of writer has a seemingly impossible task. For his prime function is to convey information, or treat of theory and argument, as objectively as possible. Yet if he would make it meaningful, and fruitful, for the non-expert he must address himself to more than his intellect. He must somehow contrive to engage his total personality. And it is as regards this aspect of his task that he finds himself in the same dilemma as the poet. His whole difficulty, wrote Schiller,[3] arises from the circuitous route he must take:

from the quite peculiar circumstance that the writer is as it were invisible, and has to work upon his reader from a distance; that he is denied the advantage of affecting the psyche directly through the living expression of speech to the ac-companiment of gestures; that he can only address feeling indirectly, through abstract signs, hence through the medium of the understanding . . . .

But this disadvantage was balanced by advantages of which Schiller was no less clearly aware. Physical distance, he went on, enables the writer to leave the recipient of his discourse with 'a greater measure of *psychical* freedom than is ever possible during communication in the living pre-sence'. And it seemed to him that from an inquiry into the cultural impli-cations of the medium of the printed word—one of the more important features, as he said, distinguishing the modern world from the ancient[4]— certain rules or principles might emerge for the writer in general and the

---

[1] In, for instance, an unpublished essay *Das Schöne der Kunst* (enclosed in a letter to Körner, 28.ii.1793; Jonas, iii. 291 ff., esp. 297–9); or *Über naive und sentimentalische Dichtung* (SA xii. 175 f.). The fact that Schiller operates with the theory of art as an imitation of nature, or with a theory of language that differs in some respects from Herder's, is irrelevant here: the cultural situation with which they are preoccupied is the same.

[2] Which first appeared over the initials G[oethe] u. S[chiller] in the *Musenalmanach* for 1797; SA i. 149.

[3] To Garve, 25.i.1795. [4] Ibid.

popularizer in particular. In letters to friends from whom he hoped to elicit an article on the subject he indicated the chief points to which he would direct his attention if he were undertaking it himself. On the one hand, to the linguistic techniques of the writer: the means whereby he might breathe the life of his own individuality into scientific discourse without prejudice to the objectivity of his subject-matter.[1] On the other hand, to the psychology of the reader: the difficulty of appealing to the individual psyche without confining the appeal to purely private and peculiar aspects of it.

In trying to evolve an ideal of popularization, I would take particular account of the relation between *objectivity* and *subjectivity*, for it is on this that everything seems to turn. In living exchanges everything objective becomes subjectivized, since the whole individual is involved in the utterance, and the whole effect is made *upon an individual*. In communication through the printed word, the aim is to address the *genus*, and this can only happen through appeal to the genus. Yet at the same time each individual is to be affected as such, and that can only happen through appeal to the individual. The requirement therefore is *generalized individuality*. . . . But the matter is infinitely more complex than this, as you yourself will discover.[2]

It has been said that Schiller's ideas on this subject are 'of a startling modernity'.[3] And in a sense this is true. But perhaps the reason for their abiding relevance only comes clearly into focus if we first realize just how *un*-modern they are. He, after all, was tackling the problem in an age dominated by the printed word.[4] We have just moved out of it. The invention of audio-visual media has opened up possibilities unimagined by him— among them the likelihood of whole sections of the population reverting to oral communities as in the pre-Gutenberg era. He was preoccupied with the implications of a medium which imposes physical distance between communicator and recipient; his counterpart today[5] is faced with the implications of media capable of exposing us to the total impact of the speakers' physical presence. A major difficulty for the writer, according to Schiller, is to engage feeling at all; since before a reader can appreciate what is being expressed he must first be able to construe an abstract symbolism—the linguistic shorthand for experience—and this involves an operation of the understanding. The danger of the newer

[1] To Garve, 25.i.1795. [2] Letter to Körner, 10.xi.1794.
[3] By Meyer, loc. cit., p. 340.
[4] For his repeated emphasis on the cultural implications of this see his letters to Körner and Garve of 1.ix and 1.x.1794, as well as those already quoted.
[5] The most thought-provoking, if also the most sensational, of these is Marshall McLuhan. His always exciting, if sometimes exasperating, books (*The Mechanical Bride*, 1951, *The Gutenberg Galaxy*, 1962, *Understanding Media*, 1964) bring home to us the full extent of the sociological, psychological, even physiological, differences between our own cultural situation and that of the eighteenth century.

media is that understanding may easily go into abeyance altogether while viewers are immersed in the undifferentiated sense-experience of events that can now be reproduced simultaneously with their occurrence. The writer's corresponding major risk, as Schiller saw it, is that in 'personalizing' his discourse—as he must if he is to engage the personality of his reader—he may well drive him even further into the isolation which is characteristic of the reading situation, imprisoning him within the subjective limitations of his individual viewpoint instead of speaking to what Coleridge called the 'all in each and all of us'. The risk with the newer media is exactly the reverse: by their intrusion on personal privacy they tend to turn us into collective participants, making us move, not in the direction of that 'generalisierte Individualität' which was Schiller's ideal, but towards a 'general cosmic consciousness'[1] which is something very different indeed.

If, despite these profound cultural differences, what he has to say continues to have relevance, it is not just because the printed word still prevails alongside newer media: because among those who only look and listen there are still those who also read. It is because he cut right through the mere technicalities of that particular medium to the 'inner significance' of the reciprocal relation between writer and public. Because he saw so clearly that effects, desirable or undesirable, never ensue automatically from the nature of the medium itself—any medium—but that all depends on the use of it. Because—as a result of this insight—he maintained uncompromisingly that problems of human communication, though they have to be worked out *in terms of* a particular medium, can never be *solved* except in and through the socio-psychodynamics of human relations. Because he conceived the investigation of the whole problem in broad 'anthropological' terms (not excluding the economic). Because he faced the fact that any investigation of it is unlikely to yield either valid or useful results unless we take into account, not only what men are, but also what we should like them to be.

In this present age, when such a large proportion of the public derive their education through *reading*, and another not inconsiderable proportion make it their business and livelihood to provide such education through writing, it would, so it seems to me, be both interesting and useful to uncover the *hidden implications* of this reciprocal relation; to investigate *on anthropological lines* the consequences it has for both parties; and, by evolving an ideal of what it could and should be for them both, contribute as far as possible to purifying and ennobling it.[2]

But perhaps the overriding reason for his continuing relevance is that he was led—as much by the accidents of temperament and talent as by the political situation in which he happened to find himself—to envisage the

---

[1] The term is McLuhan's.   [2] To Garve, 1.x.1794.

hazards of popularization in an open society. No less convinced than Kant,[1] or his friend Wilhelm von Humboldt, that 'the first and indispensable condition' of mass-education is political freedom,[2] this was for him, quite literally, the 'first' condition and not the last. His devastatingly disturbing insights into the dynamics of power and freedom—whether within the individual psyche, in inter-personal, or in broadly social and cultural relations—impelled him to go on from there and ask: How do we make the individual think for himself, how do we activate the freedom of his psyche, once that 'first and indispensable' freedom is guaranteed and permissiveness prevails? The economic aspect of the crux is apparent in a letter to his publisher declaring his editorial policy in face of the public's —not, even to him, surprising—reaction to the first two numbers of the *Horen*:

> . . . but if the Journal is to remain good, and become even better, we ought to neglect such isolated opinions and go our own way with unfaltering steps. Then we shall see *whether the public is to force us, or we are to force the public. Thinking for many people means really hard work.* But we must somehow contrive to make those who can't think ashamed to admit it, and become willy-nilly our eulogists in order to appear what they are not.[3]

But, as so often happens in such editorial predicament, circumstances proved his master. The frailty and fallibility of contributors forced him to accept, out of consideration for his publisher, articles which not only offended his taste but ran counter to the advertised aims of his Journal. And long before there were any signs of Cotta himself becoming uneasy, Schiller was privately voicing his forebodings about the inevitable outcome:

> . . . at the present time it is out of the question for any one periodical—whether good, bad, or indifferent—to achieve widespread success in Germany. The public no longer possesses that uniformity of taste which is characteristic of the childhood of man; still less the sort of unity which is to be expected at the highest level of culture. It is at a stage somewhere between the two. For bad authors that is a splendid time. But for those who are not only out to make money, that much the worse.[4]

This is almost a paradigm of the dilemma which is bound to arise in a

---

[1] Cf. above, p. xviii.

[2] Cf. above, p. xvi, and W. H. Bruford, 'The Idea of "Bildung" in Wilhelm von Humboldt's Letters' in *The Era of Goethe*. Essays presented to James Boyd, Oxford, 1959, p. 34.

[3] To Cotta, 2.iii.1795; our italics. Another reference to 'forcing the public' in a later letter to Cotta, 11.v.1795.

[4] In a letter to Goethe, reporting a conversation with Wilhelm von Humboldt, 15.v.1795.

free society, whether the medium of mass-communication be print or television. And the question it raises is not the relatively simple: *Do* you—
whether by law or economic necessity—deprive the individual conscience
of responsibility? but the more complex: What exactly is the nature of
the responsibility that you leave to the individual conscience—whether
of pedagogue or publicist, of popularizer or public-relations man? Do
you give people what they want (or you presume to imagine they want)?
Or do you try to raise them to what they could be (or you imagine they
could be)? If you do the former, may you not be guilty of withhold-
ing what they really need? If you do the latter, are you not—more
obviously than in the former case, though not necessarily with more
justice—exposed to the charge of forcing them into your own image of
what men could or should be? And if that image happens to include the
concept of inner freedom, may you not find yourself committed to the
paradox of trying to force them to be free?[1] Yet if you renounce this as
being even more unworthy than it is illogical, are you not in imminent
danger of becoming the victim of a seductive illusion? Is the teacher who
prides himself on exerting no influence not deceiving himself about the
whole nature of the pedagogic situation? Or the popularizer who professes
to be simply giving the facts 'straight' not labouring under a false conception of objectivity? Is the principle of 'negative' freedom—i.e., non-
interference with the liberty of the individual except when it threatens
the liberty of others—ever an adequate concept outside the sphere of law
(even if there)? Do human beings not have to be prodded into thinking
for themselves? Have they not a boundless proclivity for inertia and submission? Is their need for freedom stronger than their desire to be en-
slaved? And was Plato not perhaps right in maintaining that anyone who
is good at setting them free is also good at enslaving them? Yet even if
he was, can the answer lie in abdication from power? Must it not rather
lie in learning more about the proper use of power? The whole enterprise
of education, private or public, is beset with pitfalls, self-deception, and
recurrent disillusion. But is that any reason for abandoning it in despair?

Such are the perplexities and questionings Schiller prompts us to
pursue. His own most mature—by no means simple and not altogether
comfortable—answers to some of them are to be found in the essay on
popularization he had failed to elicit from his friends: *On the Necessary
Limits of the Beautiful, especially in the Presentation of Scientific and
Philosophic Truths.*[2] But before he could give them this final formulation he
first had to come to terms with serious charges against his own practice

---

[1] The connexion with Schiller's own psychology is patent (see above pp. xxix ff). But
this should not blind us to the objective reality of the questions he raises.

[2] One of the two essays—later amalgamated—referred to at the end of XXVI. 5.
See Note thereto and pp. xlii, lx, above.

in this difficult art—charges levelled by his 'friend Fichte'[1] in the course of an acrimonious exchange of letters following on Schiller's refusal to publish his treatise *Über Geist und Buchstab in der Philosophie. In einer Reihe von Briefen.* Like most such disputes this is a sorry tale, often told,[2] and we do not propose to add to the list of conjectured personal motives behind the reasons Schiller gave for his editorial decision. We shall confine ourselves to issues which are of theoretical or historical interest.

What the title announced by Fichte had led him to expect was an inquiry into the relation between the spirit and the letter in philosophy. What he actually got, as a lengthy first instalment, was a disquisition on the relation between the spirit and the letter in poetry and the fine arts. In other words, a contribution which—as Schiller pointed out to him[3]—covered much the same ground as his own *Aesthetic Letters* (which had scarcely ceased running) and was moreover couched in the same epistolary form. A situation calculated to embarrass any editor (from which it does not necessarily follow that his refusal to publish was justifiable). And the contents were even less calculated to commend themselves to a thinker of Schiller's persuasion who also happened to be a practising poet. For the implications of Fichte's first instalment—explicitly confirmed in his reply[4] to Schiller's protest—was that, in the last analysis, the relation between letter and spirit in poetry and art is no different from their relation in philosophy. How could anyone, who shared Herder's conviction that the future of philosophy depended on keeping its mode of discourse clearly distinct from that of poetry, not protest against the idea that the relation between thought and expression is virtually identical in both? Or who knew—from inside knowledge of making it—that poetry, like all art, has its roots in bodily life, not be sceptical of the idealist proposition that here, no less than in philosophy, *Geist* is ultimately all? Or who was so preoccupied with the need, in the age of the printed word, to make language itself do what voice and gesture can do for the rhetor, not feel impatient of Fichte's claim that if only his periods were declaimed—preferably by himself—

---

[1] As Schiller had called him when making public acknowledgement of his indebtedness in the footnotes to IV. 2 and XIII. 2.

[2] Never with greater understanding for the acrimony on both sides, or a firmer grasp of the supra-personal issues involved, than by Meyer, loc. cit., pp. 344 ff. The additional issues we discern throw those on which we are agreed into slightly different perspective. For the relevant literature on the dispute see Günter Schulz (*Jb. d. Goethe-Gesellschaft,* xvii [1955], 114 ff.), who published recently discovered transcripts of Fichte's essay made by Schiller before he returned the MS., adding a further conjecture of his own for Schiller's refusal to publish: rivalry with Fichte for the friendship of Goethe.

[3] In a letter of 23–24.vi.1795, which took him no less than four drafts to compose. These are extant (Jonas, iv. 191 ff.), though not the letter itself; but an attempt has been made to reconstruct it by Günter Schulz in NA xxvii. 200 ff.; cf. 365 ff. Fichte replied at length on 27.vi.[1795]; see *J. G. Fichtes Briefwechsel,* hrsg. v. Hans Schulz, i (Leipzig, 1930²), 470 ff.   [4] Ibid., p. 470.

they would at once lose their alleged stiffness?[1] Is it likely that a writer as sophisticated as Schiller, who had on the one hand insisted that his *Künstler* was not philosophy in verse but a *poem*,[2] and yet on the other described the first nine of his *Aesthetic Letters* as a philosophical elaboration of the subject-matter of that same poem,[3] would not know—and again from inside knowledge—that he had been handling language quite differently in each case? And not, therefore, understandable that he should have been inclined to dismiss out of hand Fichte's charge[4] that, whereas good writers—himself included—had always used figurative language merely to *supplement* their philosophical abstractions, he (Schiller) tended to make images into a *substitute* for concepts, thus depriving imagination of its inherent and inalienable freedom by 'trying to force it to *think*'?

What Fichte could presumably not have known is that Schiller had himself come to terms with a very similar-sounding problem when first outlining his theory of popularization to his patron a couple of years earlier. Arguing that the function of this kind of writer is to address himself to the understanding when it is operating, not 'logically', but rather 'aesthetically, as a kind of tact . . . [or as] Common Sense', he had been prompt to add the caveat: 'Not that there is any question of sense itself ever being able to *think* . . .'.[5] At first sight the difference from Fichte's later accusation might seem merely verbal; or at most a matter of alternative classification within an anyhow outmoded faculty psychology: the power *he* was denying to the imagination, Schiller had denied to the aesthetic sense. In fact, the difference is fundamental. For what Schiller is concerned with at this point is not—as he sometimes obviously is—the tendency of any particular faculty to mistake its own function and usurp

[1] Ibid., pp. 473 f. Meyer (loc. cit., pp. 342, 346) surely obscures two important distinctions by saying that Schiller himself had made this same point when he told Körner (19.i.1795) of the favourable impression he had made on Goethe by reading the first nine of his *Aesthetic Letters* aloud. For whereas Fichte was concerned with the *aesthetic* effect of his periods, Schiller was pleased that the *sense* of his treatise could be grasped even by non-Kantians. And whereas Fichte was making the aesthetic effect dependent on the actual physical act of reading aloud, Schiller's whole theory and practice of popularization turned on the question of how to assimilate rhetorical effects into the printed word without benefit of declamation.

[2] To Körner, 9.iii.1789.

[3] To Körner, 3.ii.1794.

[4] 27.vi.[1795]; ed. cit., p. 473 (our italics). Schiller replied in a letter which again took him three drafts to compose (3–4.viii.1795; Jonas, iv. 220 ff.) and was never in fact dispatched.

[5] 21.xi.1793; Jonas, iii. 396 (our italics). Cf. Glossary under *Sinn* (2) and—for the double meaning of 'common' here—also under *Gemeinsinn*. In support of his 'synonymization' of *ästhetisch/Takt/Gemeinsinn* Schiller invokes linguistic usage (cf. XII. 2fn. and Note). The fact that all (*sic*) languages have adopted the term 'common *sense*' for this type of mental operation reflects, he implies, an awareness that understanding can—and in the majority of cases does—work in and through sense-perception.

that of another, but the possibility of the psyche *as a whole* being able to think in two entirely different ways. In the one, when the understanding is operating 'logically'—which is, he says, relatively rare—it is clearly aware of the principles governing its own operations, and the other functions of the psyche, though not necessarily in complete abeyance, are strictly subordinated to this self-conscious discursive activity.[1] In the other, by contrast—which, he says, is what goes on most of the time—there is no such awareness and no such subordination. The psyche as a whole grasps what is presented as a whole—and 'before it has had time to become its own spectator as it were, and to take cognizance of its own processes,[2] our inner sense is affected . . . and thinking passes over into feeling'. When he came to publish his essay on popularization, Schiller gave a name to this latter type of thinking: *darstellend denken* (thinking presentationally).[3] Here in this early letter to his patron, it had as yet no name. We have to take the meaning of *denken* from the context.[4] And this makes unambiguously clear two things that are essential for understanding what Schiller is about:
1. one of the models of the psyche with which he is here operating is the Herderian one of a single entity involved in different kinds of activities;
2. in postulating a type of thinking other than 'logical' he is making no concessions to irrational notions of apprehension by 'feeling' or some vaguely mysterious 'intuition'. Understanding is at work in presentational thinking no less than in discursive thought: 'der Verstand wirkt hier ebenso gut, als bei dem schulgerechten Denker . . .'.[5] Without this assumption, as we saw,[6] his theory of aesthetic education falls to the ground. And so does his theory of popularization.[7] It was an assumption made before he read Fichte's work, and it remained unaffected by Fichte's criticism of his own.

If this nevertheless went home it was, then, not because Schiller had ever been tempted to claim that the aesthetic or the 'common' sense can

---

[1] This latter point is only implicit in the letter to his patron. He will make it explicit later on, e.g., in XXV. 5.

[2] The same idea as in his much earlier letter to Körner quoted by Freud, and by us in our Notes to XXVII. 4fn.

[3] SA xii. 134.

[4] As of course we do in Fichte's letter to him, where it obviously signifies discursive thinking.

[5] Susanne K. Langer's chapter on discursive and presentational forms (*Philosophy in a New Key*, Pelican Books, 25, New York, 1948, pp. 63 ff.)—which must itself owe much, however mediately, to this eighteenth-century distinction—throws interesting light on some of its implications.

[6] pp. li f., above.

[7] Which is why we cannot agree with Meyer (loc. cit., p. 350) that the subsequently discarded motto from Rousseau is the perfect short description of Schiller's theory—or practice—of popularization, any more than it is of his treatise on education (see above, p. liv).

think 'logically', or that the imagination, of itself, can 'think' at all. And perhaps not even—or not only—because of any doubts it cast on the validity of work he had already published. It went home chiefly because of what still stood before him. For now, just when he was on the point of rounding off his theory of aesthetic education by casting into publishable form his thoughts on popularization, he was forced to re-think the role he had formerly assigned to imagination. Its function, he had then written to his patron,[1] was to liberate the psyche from the constraint imposed upon it by scientific or philosophical subject-matter. And this it was to do by casting a pleasing veil of arbitrariness or freedom over the logical rigour and technical apparatus. A master in this art must, therefore, be able to 'transform what has been achieved by abstraction into material for the imagination to work on, transposing concepts into images, and resolving deductions into feeling...'. This would not in any case have been able to stand, in view of the far more subtle theory of imagination meanwhile evolved in his already published *Aesthetic Letters*. The merely 'natural', or 'negative', freedom of the imagination, he had here argued, needs the constant control of understanding and reason in scientific and moral activity; otherwise it all too easily degenerates into arbitrariness. As it does too in the artistic sphere, unless it is raised to a freely shaping power by the aesthetic modulation of the total psyche.[2] So that he is unlikely to have been impressed by the reasoning behind Fichte's charge: 'You yourself put fetters on the imagination, *which can never be other than free.*' What this does, however, seem to have provoked is a quite different—and far more characteristically Schillerian—question: whether the much vaunted freedom of the imagination may not have precisely the opposite of a liberating effect upon the psyche. Whether images—no less than facts, concepts, or argumentation—may not curtail its freedom, not only by disposing it in one direction rather than another, but by taking such powerful hold upon it that the abstractions they were designed merely to illustrate become obscured rather than clarified. In a similar way, Fichte's charge that he had tried to make images do the work of concepts—even though he did not accept it—seems to have goaded him into taking a sharper look at his somewhat nebulous notions of '*transposing* concepts into images' and '*resolving* deductions into feeling'. Indeed at the whole relation he was postulating between abstraction and concretion, the discursive 'message' and the aesthetic form—between the liberating engagement of the total psyche and the advancement of understanding he believed this might effect.

Nowhere is this more clearly apparent than in the most frequently quoted passage of his undispatched reply to Fichte:[3]

[1] Jonas, iii. 395 ff.   [2] See pp. lxvi, lxxxviii, and xciii.
[3] Jonas, iv. 221. Our italics,

Nor can I, in respect of philosophical style, allow any comparison of my own manner with that of another, least of all anyone who is a didactic writer and nothing more. It is my constant endeavour, *alongside* the inquiry itself, to engage the whole ensemble of psychic forces, and as far as possible to work on all of them at once. I am not therefore content with just making my thoughts clear to the reader. I want *at the same time* to entrust my whole soul to him, and to work upon his powers of sense and feeling no less than upon those of mind and spirit. This presentation of my whole nature, even when treating of the sort of abstract matters in which man is normally wont to speak purely as genus, demands for the appraisal of my manner an entirely different standpoint. . . .

This has seemed conclusive evidence alike to those who would claim for him a privileged position among philosophers as to those who allege that this is what he claimed for himself. But of course he is claiming nothing of the sort. He is simply claiming the right to be accounted among those who are judged by their effect upon individuals, as distinct from any contribution they may or may not have made to the progress of thought— and who therefore continue to be *read* where others need only be cited.[1] If he rejects comparison with 'didactic writers pure and simple', it is not because he regards them as of less value than himself: the mention of Aristotle—if not of Home—is enough to preclude this.[2] It is because the highly 'individualized' style that such writing implies is not susceptible of judgement by criteria automatically transferable from one author to another: the word 'genus' alone should be enough to remind Schiller scholars that his thoughts are still turning round that concept of 'generalisierte Individualität' which is the key to his theory of *haute vulgarisation*. Just as the fact that, only a few days before receiving Fichte's letter, he had expressed[3] his admiration of Herder's—after all, profoundly different— manner of popularization in terms strikingly similar to those here used of his own, should have warned them that this was no ideal invented *ad hoc* in order to justify himself in the face of adverse criticism:

And this precisely is what makes them [*Briefe zu Beförderung der Humanität*] so distinctive—and is of course what the predicate 'humanity' [in your title] really implies—that you do not tackle your theme with *isolated* functions of the psyche: that you do not merely *think*, merely *perceive*, or merely *feel*; but that you feel, think, and perceive at one and the same time; i.e., grasp and assimilate with the totality of your human nature.

Nevertheless, the difference between the two passages is more significant than their likeness, and points the direction his thought was taking. In the earlier one, to Herder, he is content to speak of co-ordination alone: of a single whole thinking presentationally. In the later, to Fichte, things have become much more complicated: discursive thinking, which itself involves

[1] Jonas, iv. 230.   [2] Ibid., pp. 221, 226.
[3] In a letter to Herder of 12.vi.1795.

considerable subordination of the other functions of the psyche, is now said to take place *at the same time* as the co-ordinated response of the total psyche. We insisted some years ago[1] that the operative words in the later passage are 'at the same time' (*zugleich*) and 'alongside' (*neben*). We should now be inclined to describe these as shorthand terms for a relationship more complex than mere juxtaposition or simultaneity. Terms no less in need of expansion than the hyphen in that much-quoted description of his projected *Aesthetic Letters*: 'meine philosophisch-poetische Visionen'[2] —which, as it stands, could equally well apply to his philosophical poetry. What he obviously needed to do, if he was to avoid the charge of himself fostering confusion, was to spell out the relation such hieroglyphs implied. To clarify the difference between a mode of discourse which, whether in prose or in verse, involves only co-ordination of the linguistic elements, and one which, by function and intent, involves both sub- and co-ordination in reciprocal relation.

And it is indeed with these, and other modes of thought familiar to us from his *Aesthetic Letters*, that we find him operating in his essay on popularization. The change from his earlier views on the subject could scarcely be more radical. Formerly he had been content with two categories of discourse: 'didactic'—addressed to the specialist and designed merely to inform and instruct—as opposed to 'aesthetic'—addressed to a wider public and designed, through a liberal use of imagination, to educate the whole personality. Now, as a result of his further brooding on the relation between imaginative activity and the freedom of the psyche, this bi-partite classification is replaced by a tri-partite one. The second of the two earlier categories has obviously been subdivided: into *populär* on the one hand, 'aesthetic' on the other. But the surprising—and important— thing is that the 'popular', instead of retaining its earlier aesthetic affiliations, moves over and is classed, along with strictly scientific discourse, as a sub-category of the 'didactic'.[3] The reason is not far to seek: neither of them does more than instruct. The 'popular' may do it more concretely. But concretion is here enlisted in the service of purely intellectual understanding, tied as illustration to particular abstractions. The imagination of the reader merely reproduces 'received impressions', his psyche is not freed for any spontaneous productivity of its own.[4] To achieve this latter end is the function of the 'aesthetic', in the much stricter sense meanwhile established in his *Aesthetic Letters*; a sense based not—or not primarily— on the antithesis abstraction/concretion, but on the antithesis *Stoff/Form*.

---

[1] Wilkinson, loc. cit. (3), p. 77.

[2] Letter to the Duke of Augustenburg, 9.ii.1793; Jonas, iii. 251.

[3] SA xii. 126.

[4] For the antecedents of this contrast between the 'reproductive' and the 'productive' activity of the imagination see XXVII. 4fn.

The mark of this mode of discourse is not the presence or absence of imaginative *material* but the organization of the total *form*. An organization which manifests itself as 'freedom of movement' in the disposition of the total structure, and as 'sensuousness' in the total linguistic expression[1] ('sensuous' here clearly—as Herder used it[2]—not with reference to the objects of sense that language may evoke, but to the outward forms, or 'bodiliness', of language itself).

But it is with the establishment of this third category that the characteristically Schillerian problems begin—and are tackled in a characteristically Schillerian way. For the first thing he now does is to play down the aesthetic in favour of rigorously scientific discourse, warning us of the dangers of fine writing in general and of the deleterious effect it may have on youthful minds in particular. This has been called a brilliant tactical manœuvre, designed to put himself in a stronger position for defending it 'once the tables have been turned'.[3] But it is far more than that. It is part of a strategy which arises of necessity out of the very structure of his thinking. For in the first place it has to be shown that aesthetic discourse—like aesthetic education in general—though indispensable, is no substitute for the scientific or the moral. Its function is indeed unique; but not therefore exclusive or even, except in a strictly qualified sense, predominant.[4] Warnings of the dangers which are inseparable from its inherent power for good have therefore to be built into the theory itself, not just included as a rhetorical device for achieving a persuasive presentation of it. And in the second place, the mode of aesthetic discourse he subsequently swings round to defend is not identical with that he had criticized, even if it does bear the same name (*schöner Vortrag*). This latter is AESTHETIC DISCOURSE raised to a higher power; and it results from a union of aesthetic discourse with scientific discourse.[5] A typical binary synthesis. Unless we realize this, his argument is bound to appear confused. And is almost bound to foster the idea that the organization he requires of this mode of discourse is identical with the use made of scientific or philosophical material in a novel, a play, or a poem. A mistaken idea. For in these latter, as Schiller had already observed in his Jena lectures of 1792/3,[6] all such material—the forms of argumentation no less than abstractions and generalizations—are merely 'eingebildet': 'played' with in order to create a fiction, or semblance. Once amalgamated with all the other linguistic materials which have gone to its making, they are no longer to be abstracted out as 'message'

[1] SA xii. 126.
[2] See above, pp. cv ff.
[3] Meyer, loc. cit., p. 347.   [4] See above, pp. lxiii, fn. 1 and lxxxviii ff.
[5] SA xii. 133 f. Cf. above pp. lxxxv ff. Meyer, loc. cit., p. 348, identifies this as the crux of Schiller's theory, without however remarking on the type of synthesis it represents or its occurrence elsewhere in his work.
[6] SA xii. 338 f.

or argument. They remain implicit within the total symbol, which shares the end of all art: to 'make a raid on the inarticulate', as T. S. Eliot has it; or, in the language of the eighteenth century, to express the otherwise inexpressible dynamics of the inner life.[1] In the sort of *haute vulgarisation* Schiller has in mind this is not the case at all. The end here is not primarily expressive, but communicative: to bring the 'mysteries' of specialization out into the open and make them accessible to the common man. The scientific or philosophical material may indeed be 'played' with; but it is not merely 'borrowed' for the ulterior end of creating a fictional semblance. Nor is it so completely fused with other kinds of linguistic material that it can no longer be abstracted out. On the contrary; the union here is of a quite different, a subordinative, order. One kind of structure—what Schiller calls the 'logical'—is assimilated unimpaired, as he insists,[2] without mitigation of its own sort of rigour, into a 'higher' (because more complex) mode of linguistic organization, viz. the aesthetic. And, as we saw before,[3] either of the two antitheses, scientific or aesthetic, can be raised to the synthesis according to context or perspective. If, for instance, we chiefly have regard to function and intent at the time of writing, when such discourse is put at the service of popularization, then we may be inclined to think of it as SCIENTIFIC DISCOURSE raised to a higher power. If, on the other hand, we have regard to its function of engaging more than intellectual understanding—and this might well be the case if it continues to be read after the scientific method or results have been proved invalid or become outdated[4]—then the aesthetic component would predominate and go to the apex of one of our illustrative triangles.

These same modes of thought must also be implied in the term he uses of the reader's psychological response: presentational thinking. For if, as he had stated earlier,[5] and as he undoubtedly still held—this is the kind of thinking that goes on in most of us most of the time—then he cannot possibly be assuming that it goes on in precisely the same way in all types of situation. Otherwise his statement here[6] that a writer can count on few readers who think at all, on fewer still who 'can think presentationally', makes no sense. It only makes sense if we assume that in the work of a

---

[1] Cf. Glossary under *Inhalt*, &c.

[2] SA xii. 133. [3] p. lxxxviii, above.

[4] Nothing in the above argument implies that the ideational material used in fiction *cannot* be tested for its scientific or philosophical validity. Schiller himself can speak of having changed his mind about some of the aesthetic ideas in his poem *Die Künstler* (letter to Körner, 27.v.1793)—but without any suggestion that this necessarily diminishes its value as poetry. What the argument *does* imply is that the distinction between philosophical 'poetry'—in the widest sense of this term—and the kind of aesthetic discourse Schiller has in mind when he treats of popularization, turns not on the question of validation at all but on the mode of linguistic organization.

[5] See above, p. cxiv. [6] SA xii. 134.

more overtly systematic thinker PRESENTATIONAL THINKING would here have to be writ large, since it implies a synthesis of presentational and discursive thought. And only if we assume that he is still, as he was in his treatise on *Aesthetic Education*, operating with the notion of modalities, as well as structures, of the psyche.[1] Presentational thinking may be no less active in those motor activities which are most efficiently performed when performed as it were 'unthinkingly' than in that prompt appraisal of a complex configuration of moral issues which expresses itself as a value-judgement. But it is not at work in the same way because the one response is governed by practical needs, the other by moral purposes. And in neither is it at work in the same way as in aesthetic contemplation, with its brief release from needs and purposes altogether. Here it must, on Schiller's own showing, have a purely co-ordinate role in that free play of all the psychic forces which manifests itself as a perfect if precarious equipoise. In the response he is now postulating to aesthetic popularization this cannot be the case—despite the fact that here too the total psyche is to be engaged and freed. And despite the fact that, as he shrewdly observes,[2] the more important repercussions may well be long delayed—one sign that the process has been educative as distinct from merely instructive. For in 'pure' aesthetic contemplation the immediate result is 'pure disponibility'; and a sure sign of its being achieved, as we had been told in XXII. 3, is that it leaves us not more inclined to one kind of activity rather than another, but re-created and 'empowered' for any and all. A piece of *haute vulgarisation*, by contrast, is to free us through its aesthetic form for productive activity *on the specific intellectual material* it presents. So that here we have to assume reciprocal action between co-ordination and subordination, an aesthetic modality as distinct from an aesthetic structure of the psyche—in short, an analogy in the intellectual sphere with that notion of aesthetic supererogation that Schiller had earlier postulated for the moral.[3]

This seems to be borne out by his use of the term which mediates between the linguistic object and the psychological response to it: the term 'translation'. For what makes Schiller's complex argument more complex still is that—in his theory of communication as in his theory of art—he wants to treat not only of both poles, the objective and the subjective, but of the relation between them. Nor is this all: he tries to make his theory allow for failures at either end. More even than this: for failures of two opposite kinds. Thus a work of popularization may fail in its effect either because the writer has not succeeded in subordinating his discursive material to his aesthetic form, or because he has allowed form to usurp the

---

[1] As defined in XXI. 4. Cf. pp. lxxxvii ff., above.
[2] SA xii. 131, 136.
[3] See p. lxxxviii, above and our translation of XXIII. 7fn. §2.

function of substance, beauty to trespass upon the territory of truth. But even if he has avoided both of these pitfalls, the reader himself may still fail in his response. And in two precisely corresponding ways: he may indulge the presumptions of imagination and delight in form to the neglect of substance; or, lacking form in himself, he may insist on abstracting the discursive 'message' and translating it into other terms.[1] But whereas if this happens *vis-à-vis* a work of art there is no 'message' there to be abstracted out—and to invent one the reader has to perform the act of destruction Schiller had described in XXII. 6—here there *is*—and Schiller says so quite unambiguously.[2] It *need* not be abstracted and translated; and in an ideal response it will not be. But it *can* be, and legitimately so. In other words: Schiller is here doing more than treat of an inappropriate response to a mode of discourse which is by its nature strictly untranslatable. He is postulating a mode of discourse which is at one and the same time untranslatable and translatable. And if this is not to be dismissed as cheating, we have no option but to conclude that he is again operating with a binary synthesis, with the schema of UNTRANSLATABILITY as a higher concept embracing both itself and its opposite. In other words, he is putting the case for a kind of linguistic structure which—no less distinct from the purely 'poetic' than it is from the purely 'scientific'—may serve as a vehicle for disseminating knowledge, or even for making a contribution to knowledge, but whose function is not exhausted by either.

*   *   *

There is no mistaking the edge in Schiller's remarks about those who feel the need to translate such discourse into other terms. Of a 'commoner cast of mind', they are like a child who 'has to spell out the words before he has learnt to read'[3] (a more exact analogy might have been a foreign language before one has made the 'leap' to understanding without construing). And there is no harm at all in taking them as a dig at Fichte, who had complained that he always had to translate Schiller into other terms before he could understand him.[4] No harm at all—as long as we are not content with reducing their significance to such biographical interest. For, as we have seen, Schiller's impulse to unite—without confusing—two apparently irreconcilable modes of discourse also had its roots in contemporary theories of language and philosophy, still has relevance to such theories today, and indeed—by extrapolation—to theories of popularization (if such develop) embracing media not purely linguistic. And no harm

---

[1] SA xii. 134. The parallel argument in his theory of art is in XXII. 3–6.

[2] SA xii. 133 f.

[3] Ibid. This obviously has nothing to do with intelligence, as his argument about the single common factor between 'höchste Stupidität' and 'höchster Verstand' in XXVI. 4–5 shows.

[4] Letter of 27.vi.[1795]; ed. cit., p. 473.

at all as long as we are not thereby led to overlook the pointer these remarks provide to his own practice in the *Aesthetic Letters*. For what else was he doing there but trying to relieve the reader of the need to translate for himself by doing some of the work of translation for him? And it would not be at all far-fetched to regard this as a response to a challenge unwittingly thrown out by Kant, who in giving authority for treating his own technical terms as non-binding[1] had left the common reader with a seemingly insoluble problem. For how can he simply *disregard* terms with which he is totally unfamiliar? Are they not bound to hang like a veil of opacity between him and the perennial truths they were designed to elucidate for the specialist? But if they could not just be ignored—as Kant, with his characteristic lack of linguistic and psychological insight, had implied—might there not perhaps be a way of making them less opaque? Might it not be possible to transpose and retranspose them into other—some of them more familiar—terms, until words altogether are transformed into the sort of veil which reveals rather than obscures? When through the activity of translating him into another language we first became aware that it was something of this sort that Schiller was doing in his own, we were content with saying that in some passages his terms and statements are *to some extent* interchangeable.[2] It was only later that we hit on tautology as a more exact description of what he is actually about than either 'interchangeability' or two other terms we had formerly welcomed: 'jeu de substitution' and 'kunstvolle Abwandlung'.[3] These certainly have the merit of counteracting earlier tendencies to over-emphasize the ponderousness of his philosophical style by drawing attention to its evident elements of 'artistry' and 'play', to the 'elegance' which it was his own expresssed wish to achieve.[4] But they have the disadvantage of possibly encouraging more recent tendencies to treat it all as 'purely' artistic play,[5] and of deflecting attention away from the profoundly serious linguistic preoccupations which lay behind this. Tautology, by contrast, does justice to both the *Ernst* and the *Spiel*. For by virtue of the uses to which it has historically been put, it leads us back to age-old speculations about the limits of discourse, and so helps us to see the point of what is in fact a genial adaptation of tradition.

Much has been made of Schiller's tendency to create confusion by using, not only the same word—e.g., Nature[6]—for a number of different concepts, but a number of different words for the same concept: no fewer than eight, it has been estimated,[7] for the Godhead. And much has been made, too, of his tendency to hypostasize and personify concepts, to carry even

---

[1] See above, pp. ciii f. [2] Wilkinson, loc. cit. (3), pp. 59–69.
[3] Hell, loc. cit., p. 348, and Meyer, loc. cit., p. 321.
[4] To Cotta, 12.vi.1795. [5] See above, pp. xcix ff.
[6] See above, p. lxxiii. [7] Snell, op. cit., p. 14.

further, for instance, Kant's own tendency to transform mental faculties into virtual entities.[1] The point that has not been made is that these two alleged 'faults' are functionally related: the purpose of the former is precisely to counteract the latter. Had not a traditional function of tautology been to counteract man's inveterate tendency to hypostasize—his tendency to represent the Invisible God by means of some image and to identify His essence with one particular Name? Hence the naming of the Unnameable by multiplying His names, the conceiving of the Inconceivable by enumerating His attributes—the endless attempts to give expression to that for which, in Schiller's own words (XV. 9), 'mind has no concept nor speech any name'. But is this not the ultimate paradox—whether asserted of the ineffably Divine Being or, as Schiller does here, of the ineffable within us: the inexpressible feelings and thoughts aroused in us by the beauteous image of a pagan divinity? At the very centre of a treatise designed to no other end than to define beauty and our response to it he denies the possibility of doing any such thing. Not the possibility of *his* being able to achieve it, but the possibility of language being able to do it at all. We should beware of dismissing this as an expression of personal despair over the inadequacy of language (he will, after all, pursue his enterprise to the end of this treatise and beyond). It is also—if not rather— a reflection of one more facet of the same tradition. Had it not been a function of the so-called 'Negative Theology' to make precisely the sort of denial that Schiller makes here? And if, by the form of its statements, this can be regarded as the very antithesis of the 'affirming', or *kataphatic*, theology, it can also, by its function, be regarded as the logical conclusion of its attempt to guard against idolatry of word or image by multiplying names and attributes. For if the mystical adherents of the 'negative way' were so often charged with heresy, it was not so much because they had misrepresented the truth about language, but because they had misinterpreted the implications to be drawn from it. Because they had let their zeal for avoiding idolatry of words lead them into the hybris of denying the value of words altogether. Again we should beware of dismissing either Schiller's 'denial' or his complementary 'affirmation' through tautology as but one more example of the eighteenth-century tendency to secularize theological modes of thought. It is unlikely that he was any less aware than his contemporaries[2] that the theological controversies about Names and Attributes had themselves been waged with weapons drawn from the secular linguistic theories of the Greeks, from a long-established 'science of names' which was, in Origen's words, 'both very profound and very subtle'. And had not that same Origen, of all the Church Fathers the one

---

[1] A view recently perpetuated in English by Kerry, op. cit. (2), p. 40 and *passim*.

[2] On Goethe's awareness of it see Wilkinson, 'The Theological Basis of Faust's *Credo*', GLL x (1957), 229 ff.

most congenial to the eighteenth century, made it unambiguously clear in a famous passage that the paradox of theology was rooted in the paradox of language itself?[1] That the powerlessness of words to represent the attributes of God was but one aspect of the powerlessness of words to convey the individual qualities of things in general? And had he not also, and in the same *locus classicus*, gone on to make it equally clear that this was no reason for not trying? For not using names 'to lead the inquirer by the hand, as it were, towards such knowledge as human faculties can attain'?

That Schiller knew just what he was about when he adapted such ancient tradition to the modern task of popularization is suggested, not only by the interest he showed in synonymy just about this time,[2] but by the fact that so many other features of his treatise serve the same end as the ubiquitous tautology of statement. Thus he is not, as we have seen, content with a single model of the psyche: the discrete entities of the Kantian model are counteracted by the more dynamic Herderian one of a unified entity functioning in a number of different ways; and both are thrown into different perspective by the fact that he also operates with the notion of changing modalities as well as changing structures and activities of the psyche. One function of this plurality is undoubtedly to convey to the reader that no one model is adequate to explain the complexity of human behaviour, and that an inevitable concomitant of the usefulness of any model is its inherent limitation. But it serves also to prevent his readers from confusing any or every model with the reality itself. And so does his plurality of methods.[3] If he covers the same ground several times, each time drawing on the terms and theories of a different thinker, it is partly to indicate that different purposes require different descriptions; but it is also to remind us that the reality at stake is something other than even the most conceivably adequate mode of describing it. Böhm was of the opinion that the unity of his own view prevailed despite such eclecticism.[4] We would rather say that the kind of unity he aimed at was achieved precisely because of it. One might even speak of a tautology of systems—had he not, after all, in his opening Letter, said that he would have failed in his task if the reader were to be reminded of any particular philosophical school? And it is, from then on, almost as if he were playing a game with philosophical techniques, using them as alternative conventions for talking about the same thing, tolerant of all but committed to none. Yet not merely offering them for entertainment by uncommitted minds. The 'play' has

---

[1] *Contra Celsum*, vi. 65. The passage was included in C. F. Rössler's *Bibliothek der Kirchen-Väter in Uebersezungen und Auszügen . . . sammt dem Original der Hauptstellen*, ii (1776), 250 f.

[2] See the references to F. A. Weisshuhn's 'Beiträge zur Synonymistik' in his correspondence with Goethe, 19–28.ii.1795 (cf. NA xxvii. 298, 333).

[3] Cf. Wilkinson, loc. cit. (3), p. 75 and (5), p. 19.

[4] Op. cit., pp. 61–63, 190.

serious intent. On the one hand, to encourage in the reader a syncretic power of discovering common ground in diverse systems. On the other, to prevent him succumbing to the tyranny of any system at all; to administer the kind of therapy Coleridge had in mind when he said that the writings of the Mystics had acted in no slight degree to prevent him from 'being imprisoned within the outline of any single dogmatic system, [and so] contributed to keep alive the *heart* in the *head* . . . '.[1] Nor does such tautologous play necessarily imply that all systems are held in equal esteem. Long before there was any sign of dissension, Schiller had contrasted the survival-value of Fichte's philosophy with that of Kant. Neither was immune from the mortality to which all method is heir. But whereas Kant's philosophy would survive long after its form was superseded because its fundaments were in tune with common reason,[2] Fichte's could not hope to do so because his inherent solipsism was at odds with it. 'According to [him] . . . all reality is in the *Ich*. The world he regards as but a ball thrown by the *Ich*, and caught by it again as reflection throws it back.'[3] What Schiller's tautologous play does imply is a sceptical reservation about all hypotheses, theories, explanations—his own included.[4] Again, the difference on which we are here at pains to insist has its antecedents in philosophical tradition. For whereas the Sophists had played with the technicalities of philosophy not just in order to doubt the truths they presented but in order to dismiss truth altogether, the Sceptics had put their doubting to serious purpose, refusing either to affirm or deny any position in order to show that—as Schiller puts it in I. 4—'in the account of the analytical thinker truth is bound to appear as a paradox'.[5] The sort of unity Schiller wanted to achieve was one which would make transparently clear to the reader that this was not always due to failure or perversity on the part of some individual thinker, but was inherent in the nature of analytical discourse itself. Not because he wanted to make him dispirited

---

[1] *Biographia Literaria*, ch. ix.   [2] Cf. our Note to I. 4.

[3] Letter to Goethe, 28.x.1794. They often referred to Fichte as 'das grosse Ich von Ossmanstedt'.

[4] Consider the reservation in XV. 3: 'this explanation, if such it can be called . . .'; or the irony of his frequent apologies for the 'fatigues' of the analytical journey through 'the wastes of abstraction'.

[5] We are much indebted here to Professor Rosalie L. Colie who first drew our attention to the role of paradox and tautology in the philosophical tradition of the West. Her many papers on the subject are now conveniently listed in her article 'The Rhetoric of Transcendence', *Philological Quarterly*, xliii (1964), 146. Our debt to Mr. M. O'C. Walshe, who first drew our attention to the use made of tautology in the ancient philosophy of the East, is recorded in Wilkinson, loc. cit. (3), p. 68, fn. 2, and (5), p. 18, fn. 2. His translations from the Ven. Nyanaponika Mahathera's Abhidhamma Studies (*The Middle Way. Journal of the Buddhist Society*, London, xxxiv, 1959) brought home to us the part tautology can play in counteracting the dangers of a purely analytical theory of psychology.

with the whole analytical enterprise, whether in science or in philosophy. On the contrary: the letter in which he resorts to the most extreme formulation of the tautological principle of his treatise—'Eins steht für alles und alles steht für Eins'[1]—is also the one in which he talks of forcing the reader to *think*, to interpret the parts by reference to the whole and the whole by reference to the parts. What he was trying to offer him was a rigorously coherent system of relations which nevertheless activated him to move freely—to carry on Schiller's work of substitution and transposition according to the state of knowledge arrived at in his own generation. Which is why we ourselves have spent so long trying to uncover the principles governing the form of his treatise, and the traditions from which they derived, instead of offering yet one more paraphrase of its substance in Schiller's own terms. And why we have not, on the other hand, hesitated from time to time to transpose into terms of our own age what he was saying in terms of his.

Just how difficult it is to find a single metaphor which will adequately characterize a form such as this must by now be evident. As the product of a dramatist, it has inevitably and frequently been termed 'dramatic'. And this certainly does justice to the clash and conflict of its perpetual antitheses, and to the dynamic conativeness of many of its verbs. But even on the most symbolic fringes of drama, character counts for something; and it is just this closer acquaintance with the individual protagonists who take part in his action that is precluded by Schiller's policy of substitution and synonymy. Even after our own over-long commerce with the text we do not feel that we have become any more familiar with *Empfindung*, or learnt to distinguish her on sight from *Gefühl*. Nor do we feel that this is really what matters. What *does* matter is, as we have argued above,[2] to be quite sure which of the two main families they belong to, and what, if they go visiting, is the point of their visit. Again, it has been said that Schiller makes a mythology, not only out of his borrowed concepts, but out of the methods he borrows too.[3] But myth is a form of cognition in which truths are inseparable from the particular form in which they are embodied; whereas the whole point of Schiller's tautology of methods and models is that it works in precisely the opposite direction from this. Music, on the other hand, a metaphor to which we ourselves have had recourse in our attempt to show that the clearly defined meaning of the substantives is less important than the relation between them[4]—and which is certainly not inapposite for those passages which exhibit the dynamics of the psyche as distinct from any of its contents[5]—goes too far in its suggestion that the

---

[1] To Körner, 10.xi.1794.
[2] pp. lxviii ff.
[3] By Böhm, op. cit., p. 189 and *passim*; a view now preserved in English by Kerry, op. cit. (2), pp. 8, 92, 110, and *passim*.
[4] Wilkinson, loc. cit. (3), p. 69.
[5] See pp. lxx f., above.

meaning of the concepts is of no importance whatsoever. And so too does mathematics, an analogy Schiller himself used,[1] and one which receives considerable support from Latzel's recent analysis of the *Kallias* letters. He there proceeds, so Latzel argues[2]—and suggests that it might well prove to be the case elsewhere—exactly as a mathematician does: first deriving his concepts by a strictly deductive method (and thereby evolving some that were wholly foreign to Kant), in order subsequently, like any scientist, to seek in the outside world empirical evidence which will confirm them. It is obvious that this analogy cannot hold at all points for a linguistic system, since semantic values are here always intrinsic if not always paramount. But, quite apart from this inherent limitation, it would only be applicable to the 'logical' structure of Schiller's treatise, and not to the 'aesthetic' form into which—according to his theory of popularization—this was to be assimilated.

And this of course is the trouble. An analogy which, whatever its inevitable limitation, holds well enough of the one structure, will not do at all for the other. Nor is it only in the choice of metaphors that this has been overlooked. In both analysis and description of the treatise scholars have either overlooked or forgotten the fact that Schiller is not just out to construct his own system of abstract relations; nor, as is more often alleged, out to engage the total psyche of the reader *rather than* construct any system of his own. He is out to do both things at once; and to do them, moreover, in such a way that the two heterogeneous systems, the abstract and the concrete, interlock without being irreducibly fused. One consequence of this oversight is that far too much attention has been paid to his imagery. Too much attention of a kind. For what one would still like to know—on the basis of a count as distinct from personal impression—is how the frequency of his images compares with that of other philosophers. Just as one would still like to know to what extent they are original, or to what extent they are to be regarded as pregnant. It is over thirty years ago now since Böhm showed that Fichte was wrong in alleging that Schiller tried to make images do duty for concepts. In this treatise, he concluded, they are never more than 'Zugabe',[3] a makeweight to the argument itself. This goes too far in its apparent denial of the fact that they nevertheless do in some way interact with the argument. In precisely what way we still do not know. Nor are we likely to know until more attention has been paid to those features of the treatise which act as a counterweight to the alleged substantiality of his imagery. His quite evident avoidance of the fallacy of 'misplaced concretion', for example: illustrations of any kind are as sparse here as he himself insisted they ought to be in all scientific and

[1] See p. xlviii, above.
[2] Loc. cit., pp. 38 f.
[3] Op. cit., p. 127.

philosophical discourse;[1] while Ruskinian or Paterian attempts to find an equivalent in words for the imaginative and mental impact of a work of art are—with one notable exception—entirely absent.[2] Or there is the recurrently symmetrical patterning of his periods (which is in such marked contrast to the original letters to his patron). This not only facilitates, it positively demands, the sort of rapid reading which precludes undue attention to any of the individual parts, and certainly ought to prevent exploratory lingering over the associative potentialities of any particular image.[3] And it is surely a fact of the greatest significance, even though it has received no attention at all, that the central concept of this treatise on education—the irreversible process of growth—is not catered for by imagery or illustration at all. The metaphors of organic growth are few, and not calculated either by their nature or by their position to carry the weight of a concept which is notoriously recalcitrant to theoretical treatment. It is accommodated instead by a system of asymmetrical syntheses which, though assimilated into the verbal texture and never made explicit as a schema, is none the less 'there' and abstractable by means of linguistic analysis.[4]

It is to the mode of this assimilation that further attention might profitably be directed. How did Schiller succeed in making his logical structure interlock with his aesthetic form? Or if he be deemed not to have succeeded, what pointers does his attempt offer as to how it might conceivably be done? What steps did he take to incorporate the forms of discourse appropriate to theoretical argument—conceptual, syntactical, consecutive—into the non-consecutive, asyntactical, sensuous particularity of poetic language without so obliterating the independent existence of the former that it can no longer be judged as theoretical argument in its

[1] See SA xii. 124 fn., where he supported his objection by arguing that illustrations are bound to militate against the general applicability of any proposition; and a later letter to Goethe (12.i.1798), where he supported it by arguing—conversely—that no proposition can be adequate to the concrete individuality of the illustration.

[2] Some might be content to explain this by his avowed lack of knowledge of, sense for —or even interest in—the plastic arts (see, for instance, his letter to Goethe, 1.x.1800, and to Wilhelm v. Humboldt, 17.ii.1803). But his avoidance of it here extends to all the arts; and this, combined with the fact that his single venture into this field *is* provoked by a statue, suggests that in this treatise at least it was a seduction deliberately eschewed rather than a task beyond his powers.

[3] The 'wearisome effect' of which Fichte complained (in his letter to Schiller of 27.vi.1795) is much more likely to have been due to his—as it might well be to our—lack of practice in grasping this type of rhetorical complex than to any alleged substitution of image for concept. And, as we have shown above (p. lxiii), Böhm's tendency to attend to imagery rather than to syntactical and rhetorical relations had at least one disastrous consequence.

[4] It is because this concept of growth is so firmly built into his abstractable system that it is possible, even imperative, for the interpreter to speak in terms of the early education of the child even though Schiller himself does not treat of it in so many words.

own right? Anticipating objections that there was too much abstraction, Schiller told Körner that he was ready to do whatever he could[1]—ready, interestingly enough, 'to replace a word or phrase by something more popular (mit etwas Vulgarerem)'—but that he felt he had more or less reached the limits of concretion: that to give the treatise more 'flesh and blood' would be to risk weakening the rigorous cogency of his 'system'. And it is noteworthy that out of all the available means of 'poetic' concretion so many of those chosen should serve a double function: in the logical structure and in the aesthetic form. Thus alliteration, assonance, play on prefixes or on the root-syllables of words, serve not only to give 'body' to the language but to point vital, if often widely separated, connexions in the argument.[2] Or—as we again discovered through the work of translation— the asyntactical pattern of the rhetorical figures, which is so often made to serve as an emblem of the invisible dynamics of the psyche, also serves as a guide to the syntax of both grammar and logic. And the figure of chiasmus in particular, which has so often served poets as an emblem of some mirror-relation—between God and the soul, for example[3]—serves him here, not only as an emblem of the reciprocal relation between self and world, or the reciprocal sub- and co-ordination of the forces of the psyche,[4] but as a means of arguing the highly abstract epistemological and psychological issues which are the corner-stone of his thesis. While if we take imagery in a wider sense than that in which it usually is taken, we may see how this principle of 'double function' is at work even in that aspect of language which is perhaps the most difficult of all to analyse: its rhythmical organization. Meyer has reminded us[5] that if Schiller often uses 'thus' and 'therefore', 'since 'and 'because', with rhetorical rather than logical function, he is working—consciously or unconsciously—in a tradition which goes back to Aristotle's distinction between demonstration by formal proof and demonstration which aims, not at proof, but only at plausibility. And Empson has recently reminded us[6] that 'argufying in poetry' is not only mental, but also *feels* muscular; that in the hands of a master the word 'therefore' is no more stale than the word 'dawn'; coming at the right place it has just as much imagery about it because 'it is like

---

[1] Letter of 5.i.1795. His actual words are: 'Ich will alles tun, was meine Menschheit erlaubt.' In the context this would seem to imply his human convictions as well as—if not rather than—his human limitations.

[2] See below, pp. 346 f.

[3] Wesley, for instance, who according to F. Baker (*Representative Verse of Charles Wesley*, London, 1962, pp. xxxvii f.) used the most formal instruments of rhetoric to give expression to an intensely charged personal faith, frequently made chiasmus into a verbal emblem of some of the great paradoxes of the Christian religion, e.g., the Incarnation: 'Let Earth and Heaven agree/Angels and Men be join'd.'

[4] See pp. lxx f., above.

[5] Loc. cit., p. 337.

[6] *The Listener*, 22.viii.1963.

giving the reader a bang on the nose'. So that there would be a case for considering whether these ubiquitous logical adverbs and conjunctions do not serve, both to sustain the plausibility of his argument, and also to embody it in that sensuous life of rhythmical language which remains the secret of his prose as of his verse, and is perhaps the chief source of its power. Just as there would be a case for considering whether the uncertain reference of some of his quite ordinary words is not also part of his overall attempt to make the treatise face in two directions at once. It may be tiresome for the translator to have to decide whether to make *Zirkel* refer to the virtuous circle of the process of education or to the apparently vicious circle of Schiller's argument about it;[1] whether *aufstellen* means to establish a proposition about reality or to establish the reality itself, *behaupten* to assert something in language or to maintain something in fact; whether *hervorgehen* refers to what has emerged from the course of the argument or to what is to emerge from the psychical processes discussed therein; whether *auf Seiten* is to be taken as a dead metaphor or— in a treatise whose theme is reconciliation of the two warring sides of human nature—should not be restored to life and rendered as 'on the side of'. But it is unlikely that Schiller was less aware than his contemporaries of the importance of distinguishing between words and things.[2] And his pointed synonymization of *Betrachtung* and *Reflexion* (XXV. 2) just at the point where he treats of the development of self-awareness through the mirroring of self in world[3] suggests the very opposite of linguistic naïveté. Suggests that he was out, on the one hand, to unmask the hidden metaphors in some of the most abstract words of 'speculative' thought and, on the other, to point to the ultimate paradox of epistemology: 'the mind reflecting on its own operation by means of its own operation'.[4]

But of all the devices used tautology is by far the most perfectly adapted to the task of knitting the two heterogeneous structures together by performing a function in each of them. For it had itself always been double-faced. A stylistic and philosophical vice when used inadvertently, it had nevertheless been made to serve the ends of both theological and philosophical virtue. A constant reminder of the dangers of mistaking the letter for the spirit, it had yet held out to the poet the hope of making spirit incarnate through love of the letter. A means of warning men that they cannot hope to 'see face to face', but only—as the Lutheran version has it—'through a mirror in a dark word',[5] it had also been one of the means whereby they

---

[1] See our Note to IX. 1.

[2] On Goethe's awareness of it see Willoughby, '"Name ist Schall und Rauch". On the Significance of Names for Goethe', *GLL* xvi (1963), 294 f., 306.

[3] See above, p. lxx.

[4] Colie, 'The Rhetoric of Transcendence', ed. cit., p. 147. She also calls this 'inevitable self-reference' of epistemology 'the fundamental tautology'.

[5] 1 Corinthians xiii. 12.

wove those dark words into a veil through which they might glimpse an
unseen reality. In Schiller's treatise this traditional two-faced stance is
galvanized into dynamic life. The two opposing tendencies of tautology,
towards abstraction and towards concretion, are turned into forces of such
equal intensity that they hold each other in precarious balance. For, as we
have seen, those very same periods which through recurrent translation of
word and statement serve to render language so transparent that it cannot
be confused with the realities of which it speaks, are also *at the same time*
made to serve as a veil which offers us a glimpse into the true nature of
psychic reality—serve as a reminder that this is not in the least like the
mosaic it inevitably has to become in the language of the analytical thinker
(and this holds whether he speaks in terms of faculties or forces, of processes or activities), but a perpetual motion of intricate overlapping and
interacting. More like a dance, in fact. And this—for Schiller himself the
perfect analogue, not only of the unceasing movement in both macrocosm
and microcosm, but also of the dynamics of social conduct in his Aesthetic
State[1]—remains perhaps the most apposite of all metaphors for the form
of his treatise.[2] Not just for the rhythms of his periods—for their involu-
tions and convolutions, their flow and recoil, the tensions sustained within
their outward harmony—but for the philosophic and aesthetic complexity
of the form as a whole. Partly because the manifest tautology of dance is a
paradigm of the essential tautology of all art: of its inherent tendency to
offer a hundred different treatments of the same subject, to find a thousand
different forms of expression for the thoughts and feelings common to all
men.[3] Partly because of its particular blend of abstraction and concretion,
especially in the figure-dance (which was what Schiller chiefly had in mind):
the perpetually repeated figures—so highly formalized that they can
easily be recorded in notation—admit of only as much individuality in
their successive execution by the different dancers as can be expressed
through the grace of bodily movement.[4] And finally because dance has so
often been used as illustration or analogue in connexion with a number of
different problems relevant to this treatise. By Pope for the apparent ease
of writing which comes only from having truly learnt one's craft.[5] By Paul
Valéry[6]—and apparently by Malherbe before him—to point the difference
between the purposeful, linear, forward-going movement of discursive
prose and the looped, or helical, movement of poetry which is a constant

---

[1] See our Notes to VI. 14 and XXVII. 12.

[2] Cf. Wilkinson, loc. cit. (5), pp. 19 ff.

[3] Cf. Goethe in conversation with Eckermann, 30.xii.1823.

[4] It was, interestingly enough, in his poem *Der Tanz* (written just after the completion
of his *Aesthetic Letters*) that Goethe thought Schiller had achieved the most perfect
balance of abstraction and concretion (see above p. xl and fn. 5).

[5] *Essay on Criticism*, ll. 362 f.

[6] 'Poésie et pensée abstraite', *Variété*, v. 149 f.

return upon itself. By Nietzsche for the smoothly articulated movements in the mind of a good philosopher.[1] By T. S. Eliot for the reconciling suspension of opposites in both aesthetic and mystical contemplation.[2] And by Valéry himself again, in *L'âme et la danse*,[3] for that state of grace and achievement which was Schiller's special concern: the second nature of true wisdom which, though indistinguishable from the spontaneous play of childhood's innocence, is reached only on the other side of knowledge, sophistication, and awareness of self.[4]

And it is precisely this kind of 'return', which is a progress and not a regress, that must never be lost sight of in any final assessment, whether of Schiller's educational theory or of his manner of presenting it. His attitude to language, science, and philosophy was one which, like Goethe's, did not stop short at analysis. But it was also one which—again like Goethe's—never repudiated it. It is of the utmost significance for their joint endeavour in every field that the distich in which they asserted their belief that all truths have ultimately to be 'shaped', and to be 'seen', should—by means of the caesura—have placed all the emphasis on the word 'ultimately'; and that it should moreover have been addressed, not to the poet, nor to just any kind of philosopher, but to the 'scientific genius'—that is, to one who, though he may start on the hither side and finish on the further side of it, would never deny the necessity of proceeding by way of analysis:

Wissenschaftliches Genie

Wird der Poet nur geboren? Der Philosoph wird's nicht minder,
Alle Wahrheit zuletzt wird nur gebildet, geschaut.[5]

---

[1] '. . . und ich wüsste nicht, was der Geist eines Philosophen mehr zu sein wünschte, als ein guter Tänzer' (*Die fröhliche Wissenschaft*, 5. Buch, § 381: 'Zur Frage der Verständlichkeit'. Cf. *Götzen-Dämmerung*: 'Was den Deutschen abgeht', § 7).

[2] *Four Quartets*, London, 1952, pp. 9, 40, 43, and *passim*.

[3] Trsl. by Dorothy Bussy as *Dance and the Soul*, London, 1951, esp. pp. 19, 33.

[4] In a brief poem entitled 'Because', sent to us when we first started publishing our thoughts on the form of Schiller's treatise, and now included in his *Weather and Season* (London, Longmans, 1963, p. 54), Mr. Michael Hamburger brings together a number of these related elements:

> . . . How mind abhors a circle! Let there be laws!
> A schoolboy knows effects must have a cause.
> All know it, but the wise man and the dancer,
> Tautologists who as they turn are still,
> Find every virtue in a vicious circle—
> The serpent's mouth that bites the serpent's tail—
> And are because they are because they are.
> (Quoted by kind permission of author and publishers.)

[5] *Xenien*, 51: SA ii.99; JA iv.161.

RECEPTION AND REPERCUSSIONS

The immediate reception of the *Aesthetic Letters* was as mixed as that of the Journal in which they appeared.[1] It is perhaps not surprising that Goethe—or anyone else—should have 'devoured' the first nine of them at one sitting.[2] They are by far the easiest to swallow. And the 'common reader' may still feel, as he did, 'heartened . . . to find what he had long recognized as right, what he had in part lived and in part wanted to live, expressed with such cogency and such nobility'. A second, more considered, reading left him convinced that this first instalment not only reflected his own way of thinking but confirmed him in his own way of doing.[3] But his judgement of the whole was positive too. Whatever initial resistance they might encounter, Schiller's ideas were bound, he wrote, to find eventual acceptance—adding with an irony which proved singularly prescient: 'They'll oppose him now, I'm afraid; but in a few years they'll be plundering him without acknowledgment.'[4] Nor is it surprising that Körner, who had held his hand through its long-drawn-out birthpangs, and made many a constructive criticism, should have expressed his faith in Schiller's educational theory by reference to the principle which, while indispensable to its efficacy, has proved one of the greatest stumbling-blocks to its acceptance, viz. the notion of an 'aesthetic imperative'.[5] Or that the future founder of the University of Berlin, Wilhelm von Humboldt, while fully aware of the comprehensive unitariness of the theory, should also have seized on individual points which are of particular interest to the practical educationist:[6] the psychological penetration of Schiller's remarks on the self-deceptions of rationalization; the subtle distinctions between noble and sublime conduct; the importance of the aesthetic for improving our intellectual insights as well as our moral disposition; the

---

[1] For published criticism up to 1805 see Fambach, op. cit. The editor of NA xxvii (*Schillers Briefe 1794-1795*), Günter Schulz, gives a survey of the reception of the first numbers of the *Horen* as expressed in private letters, together with a special section on the immediate reception of the *Aesthetic Letters* (pp. 232-40).

[2] Letter to Schiller, 26.x.1794.   [3] Ibid. 28.x.1794.

[4] Letter to W. v. Humboldt, 3.xii.1795. Cf. too their conversation dated 'early April' 1797, in which Goethe is reported to have said that 'never before had he found anyone with whom he could reach such close agreement on aesthetic principles [as with Schiller]'. This is confirmed by his latest published account of their 'collaboration' in his *Annalen* (written 1822-5, publ. 1830; JA xxx, 31, 38, 392 f.). A conversation with Eckermann of 14.xi.1823 is sometimes quoted as evidence that in later life he was inclined to repudiate it as 'useless' theorizing (a recent offender in this respect is R. Friedenthal, *Goethe — Sein Leben und seine Zeit*, München, 1963, p. 445, who not only runs Eckermann's words together with Goethe's in a single quotation, but entirely misrepresents Goethe's attitude to theory and analysis in general, and to Kant's philosophy in particular). In fact his sole concern in this latter conversation is with the inhibiting effect that philosophical speculation seemed to have had upon Schiller's dramatic creativity.

[5] Letter to Schiller, 7.xi.1794.   [6] Ibid., mid-July 1795.

necessity for *distinguishing* its various functions as well as recognizing its *unifying* quality. Even his single criticism goes to the heart of the matter. For it is on the distinction between two related kinds of freedom in the footnote to XIX. 12—whether, as he found, obscurely expressed or not—that the possibility of education in Schiller's sense turns.[1] Nor were all philosophers as critical as Fichte was almost bound to become after their unpleasant exchanges. Kant may not have kept his promise to comment at greater length on the *Letters* when the final instalment had appeared.[2] But when Schiller sent him the first two as a tribute to 'the fruits that a study of your writings has brought forth within me',[3] he not only acknowledged them as 'vortrefflich'[4] but—according to reliable reports[5]—took every opportunity of praising them to other people. While Hegel, whose own aesthetics were deeply indebted to Schiller on the crucial point of the dialectical reconciliation of opposites,[6] hailed them in a letter to Schelling as 'a masterpiece', underlining his judgement with hopeful prognostication: 'How happy Kant must be to see his labours bearing such early fruit in worthy successors. They will one day result in a glorious harvest.'[7]

But negative reactions outnumbered, even if they did not outweigh, the positive. 'The *Horen* is now being attacked from all sides', Schiller wrote to Körner on 2 November 1795, 'and my *Letters* in particular.' Klopstock apparently dismissed them as pretentious 'non sens',[8] Herder abhorred them as 'Kantische Sünden'.[9] Garve, whose influence as a popularizer of philosophical and aesthetic ideas can scarcely be over-estimated, and whose own style is as easy to read as it is evasive of difficulties, contented himself with a characteristic: 'Are they really worth all the praise they've received in the *Literatur-Zeitung*? I would have thought they made heavy weather of things that are in fact very simple.'[10] The art critic, F. W. B. Ramdohr, who in his own work on aesthetics, *Charis* (1793), had taken the first tentative steps towards a psychology of the unconscious, was more patronizing still: 'half-truths on poetical stilts, as in all Schiller's philosophical writings'.[11] Like others he was

---

[1] See above, pp. xcii ff. and Glossary under *Freiheit* (3).

[2] But for further repercussions of this latter in his work see our Note to XIX. 9 and p. lxxviii above.

[3] Enclosed in a letter of 1.iii.1795.   [4] Letter to Schiller, 30.iii.1795.

[5] Letter of David Veit to Rahel Levin, 11.x.1796 (cited Fambach, op. cit., p. 172). Cf. Schiller to Körner, 10.iv.1795, and to Jacobi, 29.vi.1795.

[6] See Glossary under *aufheben*.   [7] 16.iv.1795 (cited NA xxvii. 233).

[8] According to W. v. Humboldt's diaries (*Ges. Schriften*, hrsg. v. A. Leitzmann, Berlin, 1916 ff., xiv. 337).

[9] Schiller's letter to Körner, 7.xi.1794; cf. Goethe's to Schiller, 26.x.1794.

[10] Letter to C. F. Weisse, 8.iii.1795 (cited Fambach, op. cit., p. 168). The review in the *Allgemeine Literatur-Zeitung*, Jena u. Leipzig, 31.i.1795 (Fambach, op. cit., pp. 104-11), was by Schiller's Jena colleague, C. G. Schütz.

[11] Letter to Schütz, 28.ii.1795 (cited Fambach, op. cit., p. 115), criticizing his review in *ALZ* as too favourable. Cf. NA xxvii. 275.

astonished that an editor could so misjudge his public. He had after all, as the writer of an anonymous letter roundly informed him,[1] undertaken in the 'Advertisement' of his new Journal to present the results of 'science' in a simple and agreeable form for the benefit of the common reader, and—by contrast with Wieland, Mendelssohn, or the editor of *Der Philosoph für die Welt* (i.e., J. J. Engel), to say nothing of the English *Spectator*—failed miserably as both editor and author. It was on the manner of his writing, too, that leading *Aufklärer*—who must have felt personally arraigned by his indictment of the failure of purely intellectual enlightenment—brought their heaviest guns to bear. Nicolai was condescending enough to praise his educational theory as 'ein angenehmer Traum eines guten Kopfes'; but he devoted well over a hundred pages of his *Beschreibung einer Reise durch Deutschland und die Schweiz*[2] to castigating 'philosophische Querköpfe' in general and the 'für den gesunden Menschenverstand dunkle und unverständliche Schreibart' of contributors to the *Horen* in particular. Manso, in a long review in the *Neue Bibliothek der schönen Wissenschaften und der freyen Künste*,[3] also complained of the 'obscurity' of the style which had 'held him up on every page';[4] of Schiller's use of technical terms, and of his evident signs of strain in adapting his own style to that of an author as alien to him as Kant;[5] of a 'metaphysisch-ästhetische Sprache' which could lay claims to neither beauty nor clarity, but simply resulted in 'an uninterrupted and distasteful mixture of learned abstractions and fine phrasing, one long series of rhetorical sophistries and wearisome antitheses'.[6] Towards the end of his review Manso expressed the hope that some member of Campe's society for the purification of the German language might turn his attention to the barbarisms of the new 'critical' philosophy and perhaps even 'render some piece, whether by Hr. Schiller or his friend Hr. Fichte . . . into German'.[7] And in the very next month, W. F. A. Mackensen, professor of philosophy in Kiel, went a long way to doing just this,[8] vying with Manso himself in deflowering Schiller's rhetoric, and recasting phrase after phrase as it ought to have been written. Anyone attempting a critique of Schiller's language today might with profit first take a look at how these rationalist philologists tackled it before him. 'Was ist ein Grieche *voll* Form und *Fülle?*', asks Manso,[9] underlining the offending pleonasm—

---

[1] Cited Fambach, op. cit., pp. 221 f.

[2] Berlin u. Stettin, 1781–96, xi. 177–304. Cf. Fambach, op. cit., p. 180, and letters of W. v. Humboldt to Schiller, 23.x.1795 and 9.iv.1796.

[3] Leipzig, September 1795; Fambach, op. cit., pp. 126 ff.

[4] Ibid., p. 133.   [5] Ibid., p. 137.

[6] Ibid., p. 140.   [7] Ibid., p. 142.

[8] *Annalen der Philosophie u. des philosoph. Geistes* (hrsg. v. L. H. v. Jakob), Halle u. Leipzig, Oktober 1795; Fambach, op. cit., pp. 151 ff.

[9] Fambach, op. cit., p.141.

and misquoting his author in the process. For what Schiller actually wrote was 'voll Form und voll Fülle' (VI. 2), which by their standards may be even worse, but at least suggests that there might be rhetorical point to the apparant redundancy of meaning. While with an insensitivity to semantic change which augers ill for the lexicographical activities of Campe's society, Mackensen takes Schiller to task for ever having conceived the improbable notion of 'presenting' (*darstellen*) philosophical ideas.[1] True, Kant himself, normally so precise in his use of words, had indulged in the unfortunately vague term 'philosophische *Darstellung*', and been unwise enough to speak of David Hume's 'incomparable *Darstellungskunst*'. So it was not, perhaps, surprising that the author of *The Robbers* should have taken it into his riotously imaginative head to try to go one better, and present philosophical ideas in a totally different fashion from the eminently sane and sober Hume! Mackensen obviously has no inkling that in Schiller's context both *darstellen* and *Kunst* have been endowed with a quite specialized aesthetic sense which in Kant's they did not—and were not intended to—bear.[2] What he however does see, and say—and it remains true even though his own linguistic tools may have been inadequate for attempting the task—is that the only way of getting at Schiller's 'system' is through a better understanding of his idiom.[3]

But if Schiller got rough treatment from the Rationalists he fared no better at the hands of the up-and-coming Romantics. Jean Paul, who was soon to write a *Vorschule der Ästhetik* of his own (1804), attacked the *Letters* as formalistic and frivolous,[4] totally misunderstanding the play-concept—as of course did Hölderlin, who found it wholly incompatible with his own conception of the religious and prophetic character of the poet's mission.[5] Clemens Brentano found them 'somewhat wooden',[6] the eldest of the Schlegel brothers, Moritz, 'nothing but a brilliant display of concepts'.[7] Friedrich—characteristically—directed his acerbity *ad*

---

[1] Fambach, op. cit., p. 153.

[2] See above, pp. cxiv, cxix f., and Glossary under *Kunst*.

[3] Fambach, op. cit., p. 154.

[4] In his Preface to the second edition of *Quintus Fixlein*, 1796; *Sämtliche Werke*, hrsg. v. E. Berend, Weimar, v (1930), 21.

[5] His criticism of poetry as play is in two letters to his brother, 2.xi.1797 and 1.i.1799, in the first of which he invokes Klopstock in support. In neither does he actually mention the *Aesthetic Letters*; but both P. Bertaux (*Hölderlin. Essai de biographie intérieure*, Paris, 1936, p. 319) and M. B. Benn (*Hölderlin and Pindar*, 's Gravenhage, 1962, pp. 67 f.) take him to be referring to them. Bertaux concedes that Hölderlin had misunderstood the concept; and certainly what he has to say about the effect of poetry in the second of the two letters—a 'stillness, not empty but vibrant, a harmony in which all the forces of the psyche are active'—is indistinguishable from Schiller's position. On his indebtedness to VI. 7 see our Note thereto.

[6] Letter to his sister, mid-January 1802.

[7] Letter to A. W. Schlegel, 22.vi.1795.

hominem: Schiller had not digested his Kant, and must be suffering from biliousness and colic; what a contrast between his metaphysical fumblings and Fichte's inspired eloquence and complete mastery of the subject![1] August Wilhelm, whose review of the first few numbers of the *Horen* (he was himself then a contributor) studiously avoided precise reference to Schiller's treatise,[2] later spoke of the 'kalte abgezirkelte Eleganz' of Schiller's prose style, which 'in his Letters on Aesthetic Education turns into sheer deadness, and yet cannot fail to impress... because of a certain dignity and the *semblance* of philosophical profundity'.[3] This is one of those negative judgements which is based on such accurate observation that it provides useful pointers to more positive revaluation. And so too does the somewhat bewildered, but by no means inappropriate, reaction of a Kantian enthusiast which was reported to Schiller by Wilhelm von Humboldt[4] and ought not, in view of his theory of popularization, to have disconcerted him unduly. With Kant, this reader complained, one might have to worry over every sentence; but at least when one had struggled to the end one was quite clear about what one had read. With Schiller it was just the opposite. One took in each individual sentence with perfect ease, and thought one had grasped it all—only to find that, if one asked oneself afterwards what one had read, one was simply unable to put it into words. To which von Humboldt—putting his finger firmly on the importance of the manner for the assimilation of the message—commented:

This seems to me a basically correct judgement—only it says more about the reader than about [the author]. Of course the Kantian mode of presentation, like that of any purely didactic writer, can be learnt parrot-fashion (*nachplappern*). With yours there is nothing for it but to think it all through again for oneself (*nachdenken*).

It is no doubt inevitable that nearly all these contemporary reactions should have reflected more about the readers of Schiller's treatise than about the treatise itself. If Quintilian was on the one hand held up to him as a model he might have done well to follow,[5] he was on the other hand upbraided for having fallen into 'the abominable tone of a Seneca or Quintilian'.[6] If his style was unfavourably contrasted with 'the inspired eloquence' of a Fichte, it was also lumped together with Fichte's and contrasted with the 'heavenly simplicity' (*sic*) of Kant.[7] Perhaps more surprising is the fact that Körner's

---

[1] Letter to A. W. Schlegel, 17.viii.1795. Cf. below, p. 344.

[2] *ALZ*, January 1796; Fambach, op. cit., pp. 185 ff.

[3] In a footnote added for the 1828 edition of his critical writings (*Kritische Schriften*, Berlin, ii. 4) to his essay on Bürger of 1800. Böhm (op.cit., p. 127) rightly observes that what Schlegel takes to be arbitrary features are an integral part of the form.

[4] Letter of 15.viii.1795.

[5] By Manso; Fambach, op. cit., pp. 138 f.

[6] By J. J. Horner (cited NA xxvii. 238).

[7] By Mackensen (Fambach, op. cit., p. 153).

—and Schiller's own—fears that the chief obstacle to appreciation would be the high degree of abstraction proved unfounded (though obviously almost all the recorded impressions come from German intellectuals and are hence biased in favour of this). By far the more frequent objection is the so-called 'poetic' quality of his style (by which is of course usually meant his imagery). Thus his patron was of the opinion that 'our good Schiller is not cut out for a philosopher; he needs a translator to elaborate his fine phrases with philosophic precision, and to transpose him from the poetic into the philosophic mode'.[1] Most surprising of all—though, in view of the notorious indolence of human beings when faced with a challenge to change themselves rather than their environment, perhaps not so surprising—is the ubiquitous evasion of Schiller's message in order to concentrate on his manner. Mackensen even went so far as to say in so many words that anyone misled by the title into thinking there was something here for the educator would be sadly deluded.[2] And even such an ardent admirer as C. L. Fernow, then endeavouring to put German aesthetics across to artistic circles in Rome and hoping that the *Aesthetic Letters* might serve him as mediator, confessed[3] that he was having to 'stake all his faith' on an attempt to persuade his sceptical audience that the import of these 'hieroglyphs' was not just abstract nonsense, but something profoundly true and of vital concern. Moreover, though he himself found the style full of power and elegance, he had qualms about its possibly setting a new fashion in philosophizing:

. . . for all my aesthetic appreciation of it, there is a voice within me which protests that it would be highly undesirable if such a style were to become predominant in the language and manner of philosophy. Schiller himself is a bold and lofty spirit who, borne aloft on powerful wings, can swoop unerringly and rend the dark obscurity with the lightning of his genius. But this power is unique in him; and I would hope that his manner of presentation would remain unique to him too. What I'm afraid of is *imitators*. They will inundate us with a flood of flatulent philosophy.—May Heaven preserve us from it!

He need not have feared. When the 'flatulent philosophy' did appear, it was not because of any desire to copy Schiller! If his power was inimitable, his passion for combining it with scrupulous distinctions has always been highly unpopular. And the one feature of his method and manner which was least a question of personal 'style', and might with profit have been adapted by other writers to the task of popularization, namely tautology,

---

[1] Letter of the Duke of Augustenburg to his sister, end of February 1795; Hans Schulz, op. cit., p. 153. To Schiller himself (19.iii.1795; ibid., p. 155) the Duke merely complained of the many obscurities which would no doubt resolve themselves on further readings. In his reply of 5.iv.1795 Schiller—rightly—put some of the blame on the incapacity of the German language to serve as an organ of cultivated intercourse.

[2] Fambach, op. cit., p. 152.

[3] Letter to Wieland, 12.xi.1795 (cited NA xxvii. 239).

was not even noticed. Except by his friend, L. F. Huber, who was at that time concerned with the problem of how best to make Kant known to the French. His comments[1]—never, to our knowledge, quoted in accounts of the reception of Schiller's treatise—show that he had more than an inkling of the potentialities of the principle even if he does not use the actual word. Having observed that the first thing he would have to do before embarking on a translation (or a 'naturalization', as he in fact called it) was to compile a list of all possible German synonyms of Kant's technical terms, so as to be able to accommodate his thought to the genius of the French language through 'variants' and 'modifications', he goes on:

> I have now read your Letters on Aesthetic Education . . . and found precisely there a number of highly instructive linguistic amplifications which make me more than ever convinced of the need to gloss the whole of the Kantian philosophy by means of synonyms, paraphrasis, and exegesis, as you yourself have done, not *ex professo*, but in the course of your own argument.

Although available in print since 1896, these percipient remarks have had no repercussions on the study of Schiller's method and manner. Böhm's somewhat misleading conclusion in terms of 'homonyms' seems to have been reached without any historical awareness of the late eighteenth-century interest in synonymy and its possible relevance to popularization.[2] And we ourselves might not have been alive to their significance, had our eyes not been alerted through practical problems of translation not altogether dissimilar from Huber's own—though dissimilar of course, as he rightly implies, precisely because Schiller had himself offered valuable pointers towards possible means of naturalizing technical terms, not simply from one language into another, but from the language of specialization into the language of everyday. Just as we might never have seen the point of another rarely quoted reaction— von Humboldt's impression of the increasing 'rapidity' of Schiller's style, especially in the last instalment[3]—had the work of translation not already convinced us of the reciprocal relation between tautology and the kind of rapid reading we have recommended as appropriate for this text.[4]

After this initial spate of lively reactions, whether positive or negative, the *Aesthetic Letters* moved out of the mainstream of living controversy into the back-waters of academic history. They became a name rather than

---

[1] Letter to Schiller, 20.iv.1795 (in the Appendix to *Briefwechsel zwischen Schiller und Körner*, ed. cit., iv. 393 f.). It is not without interest that the work of Kant which Schiller recommended Huber to translate first (19.ii.1795; ibid., p. 390) should have been that popular treatise on religion whose second preface carried the authority for a liberal attitude to technical terms (see above, pp. ciii ff.).

[2] See above, pp. lxviii and cxxiv. [3] Letter to Schiller, mid-July 1795.

[4] p. cxxviii, above. Both Huber's and v. Humboldt's letter came as welcome confirmation of conclusions we had already published in Wilkinson, loc. cit. (3), pp. 61 f. and (5), pp. 17 f.

a reality and, if mentioned at all, then only with the perfunctory deference reserved for antiquated monuments of art and literature. As far as either their message or their manner was concerned, there descended upon them again that 'tiefes Stillschweigen' which von Humboldt had reported[1] from Berlin while the *Aufklärer* were sharpening their weapons for the attack. And C. G. Jung was surely right when he maintained in 1932 that they had lain dormant 'like a Sleeping Beauty of literature' for more than a century.[2] Schiller did indeed become, as Novalis had predicted,[3] 'the educator of the coming century'. But not, as Novalis—who was very ready to identify poetry with play[4]—had hoped, through a proper understanding of his aesthetic theory. Rather in his role of 'Moral-Trompeter von Säckingen', as Nietzsche aptly designated his public image.[5] That is to say, through the 'nachplappern' of quotable snatches of moral uplift, applied directly to moral conduct with complete disregard for that doctrine of indirection without which, as we have seen,[6] his theory of aesthetic education falls to the ground. From time to time, it is true, some lone voice would break the prevailing silence in order to invoke his concept of *Schein*; but as a principle of art rather than of life. Karl Th. v. Dalberg, brother of the Mannheim *Theaterintendant* who had produced Schiller's first play, had seized on this as the most important, and practically useful, doctrine for the artists of the future.[7] And Ferdinand Lassalle, founder of the first German labour party, even invoked it against Marx and Engels (who had advised him to 'Shakespearisieren' instead of 'Schillern') in defence of the fictional reality of his historical play *Franz von Sickingen*. Were they not, he asked, confusing two distinguishable worlds, that of *historischer Ernst* with that of *ästhetischer Schein*, and equating a work of art with a political document?[8] While Nietzsche made no secret of the fact that his own doctrine of the Apollonian principle in art was rooted in the concept of *schöner Schein*.[9]

But it was left for another poet to revive Novalis's conception of Schiller as a pioneer of education through art. Heine had already said as much

---

[1] Letter to Schiller, 15.viii.1795.

[2] In a lecture entitled 'Die Stimme des Innern', published as 'Vom Werden der Persönlichkeit' in *Wirklichkeit der Seele*, Zürich, 1934. This is the final chapter of *The Integration of the Personality* (ed. cit. pp. 281 f.).

[3] *Gesammelte Werke*, hrsg. v. C. Seelig, Zürich, 1945, v. 156.

[4] Ibid. iv. 167.

[5] *Götzen-Dämmerung*: 'Streifzüge eines Unzeitgemässen', § 1.

[6] pp. lxxxi f., above.

[7] Letter to Schiller, 25.vii.1795; cf. 2.ii.1795. Dalberg himself wrote an essay on 'Kunstschulen' for the *Horen* (1795; St. v).

[8] See P. Demetz, op. cit., pp. 147, 151 f.

[9] *Die Geburt der Tragödie aus dem Geiste der Musik*, §§ 1–4. He had, he tells us (*Autobiographisches aus den Jahren 1856 bis 1869*: 'Meine literarische Tätigkeit . . . 1862'), read the *Aesthetic Letters* while still at school.

when, in his posthumously published *Gedanken und Einfälle*,[1] he brought the central tenet of Schiller's theory of art into intimate connexion with the art of life:

> The visible work is the harmonious articulation of invisible thought; which is why the art of life, too, implies harmony of both action and the state of mind it expresses. . . . In art, form is everything; the material counts for nothing.

Among these same posthumous aphorisms Heine incidentally offers one of the most perspicacious descriptions of Schiller's style ever written:

> With Schiller, thought celebrates its orgies—the most sober concepts, garlanded with vine-leaves, brandish the thyrsis and dance like Bacchantes—drunken reflections.[2]

But it was a far more ardent apostle of 'pure form' than ever Heinrich Heine was, none other than Stefan George himself, who publicly proclaimed him again as the educator of the German people, and by virtue of this particular treatise. Even in the first edition of *Das Jahrhundert Goethes* (1902) he had acknowledged him as the 'most subtle of aestheticians' ('der feinste Schönheitslehrer'). In his Preface to the second edition of 1910 he went much further—at the same time radically readjusting the traditional emphasis in Schiller's claims to lasting renown. Arguing that any final appraisal would assign only historical importance to his plays, he locates his permanent value in his writings on aesthetic education:

> These remarks would have been unnecessary had Schiller not, as author of *Die Glocke, Die Jungfrau von Orleans* and *Maria Stuart* . . . been acclaimed as *the* German poet. But as aesthetician and educator, as author of the *Aesthetic Education of Man*, there is a Schiller who is still a stranger among his own people, who will presumably remain so for long years to come, but who will one day celebrate a glorious resurrection.[3]

The only resurrection he has so far celebrated was certainly not glorious, and—although deriving directly from his teaching—scarcely one of which George could have approved. For Hitler's future Minister of Propaganda, Joseph Goebbels, had during his student days in Heidelberg sat at the feet of Friedrich Gundolf, a member of the exclusive George circle and brilliant exponent of *Artistenkunst*. And in his novel *Michael. Ein deutsches Schicksal in Tagebuchblättern* (1929)[4] he plundered Schiller's aesthetics—while cunningly omitting Schiller's operative distinctions. A comparison of the following passage with IV. 4 and XXVII. 11 is highly instructive:

---

[1] *Sämtliche Werke*, hrsg. v. O. Walzel, Leipzig, x (1915), 249 f.

[2] Ibid., p. 252.

[3] *Deutsche Dichtung*, hrsg. u. eingel. v. Stefan George u. Karl Wolfskehl. Bd.iii: *Das Jahrhundert Goethes*, Berlin, 1910², p. 7. Cf. H. Stefan Schultz, 'Über das Verhältnis Stefan Georges zu Schiller' in *Deutsche Beiträge zur geistigen Überlieferung* [Chicago], iv (Friedrich Schiller 1759-1959), Bern, 1961, pp. 109 ff.

[4] München, 1933³, p. 21.

Art is an expression of feeling. The artist is distinguished from the non-artist by the fact that he has the power to give expression to what he feels. In some form or another: the one in images, a second in clay, a third in words, a fourth in marble—or even in historical forms. The statesman is an artist too. For him the people is neither more nor less than what stone is for the sculptor. The leader and the led ('Führer und Masse') presents no more of a problem than, say, painter and colour. Politics are the plastic art of the State, just as painting is the plastic art of colour. This is why politics without the people, or even against the people, is sheer nonsense. To shape a People out of the masses, and a State out of the People, this has always been the deepest intention of politics in the true sense.

What is missing here is not only Schiller's grasp of the principles of analogical thinking: his clear awareness of the limitations of the model of either craftsman or artist for a proper understanding of the role of states-man; his firm demarcation of the frontiers between the aesthetic State and the political State; his infallible insight—and instinct—that without the concept of *Schein* these two realms can be neither properly distinguished nor properly related. What is also missing is Schiller's unfailing reverence for the dignity of individual personality: the imperative always to treat a human being as end, and never to reduce him to the mere means of shaping a body politic, of whatever ideological persuasion. This ingrained respect for individual human beings, no less than his superior grasp of intellectual distinctions, was of course also absent from the weekly directives for the benefit of editors of periodicals which the Nazi Ministry of Propaganda began to issue in May 1939. That for the 180th anniversary of Schiller's birth reads:

Erzieherisch: Schiller als Erzieher seines Volkes ... Die Kunst Erzieherin des Menschen und Staatsbürgers bei Schiller. Lehre vom ästhetischen Staat. — Schillers Leben grösstes Vorbild (vgl. *Wallenstein*: 'Es ist der Geist, der sich den Körper baut').[1]

There is a triple irony here. For the quotation from *Wallenstein*—with its implication that mind has causal or chronological priority—garbles, almost to the point of reversing, the chief burden of Schiller's educational message: that we are creatures of sense before we become creatures of reason, and that it is therefore in the undifferentiated sphere of physical life that we must start work on the intellectual and the moral. Moreover, as G. Mathieu points out,[2] the official Marxist attitude as defined by the East German *Zentralkomitee* for the 150th anniversary of Schiller's death in 1955 is, curiously enough, reminiscent at point after point of those Nazi directives of fifteen years earlier, or of such notorious books as Hans Fabricius's *Schiller als Kampfgenosse Hitlers* of 1932. And there is a final

[1] See G. Mathieu, *GLL* vii (1954), 197.
[2] In a second article, *GLL* ix (1955), 42 f.

irony. For if extremes meet here, in the relatively recent present, they also meet—though in a different way—in the longer perspective of history. Until the Nazis saw the possibility of impressing him into the service of the totalitarian State, the post-Kantian Schiller had consistently been either commended by the extreme Right or condemned by the extreme Left as essentially a-political. Thus no sooner had his treatise appeared than his Jena colleague, C. G. Schütz, praised him for eschewing all references to 'political constitutions of our own time'[1]—with complete disregard for the unequivocal statement in II. 4 that every responsible citizen was doubly involved in the great Revolutionary issue: involved both as thinking human being, morally obliged to take part in the making of such decisions, and involved as interested party, practically subject thereafter to whatever decision was taken. In a similiar spirit the arch-reactionary von Gentz seized on his vivid evocation of the brutality which is bound to ensue once the traditional bonds of civic order are loosened (V. 4) as the last word that could be said on this unpleasant subject[2]—again with complete disregard for the no less unequivocal statement in VII. 3 that, though political salvation must ultimately depend on a radical change in men's whole way of thinking, he had no wish to deny that isolated attempts at political reform might meanwhile succeed. The revolutionary Left, on the other hand, did not make its reaction heard until the middle of the next century, when Engels's much quoted—often without reference and sometimes embroidered[3]—condemnation of Schiller's alleged 'flight' from political realities as 'die Vertauschung der platten mit der überschwenglichen Misère'[4] became and remained the stock party-line. It had, it is true, already been challenged in 1905 by the lapsed—or lapsing—Marxist, Franz Mehring, in *Schiller — Ein Lebensbild für deutsche Arbeiter*, an unsuccessful attempt to find among the giants of the German past a living exemplar for the German workers of the present. Unsuccessful, however, not just because of Mehring's political ambivalence.[5] Rather because, like critics of quite different persuasion, he relied on argument from the personality of the author instead of resting his case firmly on the

[1] *ALZ*, ed. cit.; Fambach, op. cit., p. 105.

[2] 'Über den Einfluss der Entdeckung von Amerika auf den Wohlstand und die Cultur des menschlichen Geschlechts' in *Neue Deutsche Monatsschrift*, ii (August 1795), 269-319; cited Fambach, op. cit., p. 222. Cf. letter of W. v. Humboldt to Schiller, 28.ix.1795.

[3] e.g., by Rohrmoser, loc. cit., p. 364. Lukács cites it briefly in *Goethe und seine Zeit*, ed. cit., p. 109, *in extenso* in *Karl Marx und Friedrich Engels als Literaturhistoriker*, Berlin, 1948, p. 81—both times without reference. Nor is it always made clear that this was no considered judgement on the *Aesthetic Letters*, but a brief aside, in a passage on Goethe, contrasting the 'universal, active, fleshly' nature of his genius with the transcedental idealism of Schiller.

[4] *Deutsch-Brüsseler Zeitung*, No. 95, 28.xi.1847; *Marx-Engels Gesamtausgabe*, Moskau, Leningrad, i. 6 (1933), 57.

[5] As Demetz (op. cit., p. 247) argues.

public implications of his educational treatise. In Mehring's hands 'the indirect way through the aesthetic' became no more than a psychological need inevitable in a poet of such idealist temperament, instead of—as Schiller himself had intended—an educational propaedeutic indispensable for all citizens who would cultivate what Henry James was to call 'the civic use of imagination'. For the editor of the *Stellungnahme des Zentralkomitees der Sozialistischen Einheitspartei Deutschlands* fifty years later the argument from biography was still good enough. But he had to be far more adroit in accommodating it to the orthodox Marxist view. In his hands, therefore, the doctrine of indirection became a temporary deviation from Schiller's psychological norm. And in a seemingly courageous bid not to gloss over Schiller's two major 'flaws'—his escape into the world of *schöner Schein* and his condemnation of the excesses of the French Revolution—he issued the directive that these were to be explained as grave, but pardonable, aberrations into which any philosopher under the influence of Kant might understandably be misled, and a consequence of Schiller's inevitable failure to appreciate the finer points of the 'form' of revolutionary activity.[1] It still remains for any German critic to see, or at least to say, that the political relevance of Schiller's educational theory stands or falls by an unreserved acceptance of *schöner Schein*, and a proper understanding of its relation to the concept of living form on the one hand and the doctrine of indirection on the other.

In neither France nor England—for obvious reasons of political history—did Schiller's treatise call forth this kind of partisan reaction: neither from Right nor from Left, neither as commendation nor as condemnation. Indeed until quite recently[2] it was not even realized that it has political implications at all: that in a world committed to universal suffrage and universal education both its basic assumptions and its sceptically hopeful conclusion represent a challenge to governments of whatever persuasion. Nor in either of those countries—and again for obvious reasons of linguistic development—was the poetic quality of Schiller's language a source of such profound misgivings. On the contrary; it was the purple passages—or, as Carlyle called them,[3] 'the bright verdant islands'—which were hailed with relief in 'the misty sea of metaphysics'. It was this sea itself that in countries other than Germany proved a hindrance to whole-hearted appreciation. To Madame de Staël, for example, who first put the *Aesthetic Letters* on the literary map of Europe. She had gone to Weimar in December 1803, armed with introductions and avid for information, and she stayed there until February 1804, absorbing the impressions which were to issue six years later in the book which has continued to shape the image of eighteenth-century German culture in the minds of most

---

[1] See Mathieu, loc. cit. (1955), pp. 45 f.
[2] By Hampshire, loc. cit. (1) and (2).   [3] See above, p. xii.

foreigners. Schiller's first impression of her[1] is worth recording in our present context, not so much for his shrewd insight into her individual psychology as for his sympathetic appraisal of the formative cultural influences which had made her what she was:

> Frau von Staël will strike you [i.e., Goethe] as being an exact replica of the image you have already formed of her *a priori*. She is all of a piece—not a single trait that is adventitious, false or pathological. This means that despite the immense divergence of temperament and ways of thinking one feels perfectly at ease with her, ready to hear all she has to say and to say anything to her in return. She represents the intellectual temper of the French in its purest form, and presents it in an extremely interesting light. In everything we call philosophy, hence in the last resort on all ultimate matters, one is completely at odds with her, and remains so however long one argues. Yet her natural temperament and feeling are better than her metaphysics, and her fine intelligence is raised to the power of genius. She insists on explaining, understanding, and taking a yardstick to everything. She will tolerate nothing vague, obscure or inaccessible: what she cannot illuminate with the torch she carries simply does not exist for her. Hence she has a horror of our Idealist Philosophy, which in her opinion can only lead to mysticism and superstition, a noisome atmosphere in which she cannot breathe. For what we call poetry, on the other hand, she has no sense whatsoever, and in works of this order is only capable of seizing on the passion, the rhetoric or the generalities. Yet she is unlikely to be misled into prizing what is spurious; it is rather a case of not always recognizing what is genuine.

This soon seems to have become the accepted view of her in Weimar circles. For only a few weeks later it reappears—in terms astonishingly similar to Schiller's own, though shorn of the finesse of his psychological and cultural distinctions—in a letter from that colporteur of German philosophical ideas, Henry Crabb Robinson, to his brother:[2]

> And tho' she unites all that alarms a Man—A most commanding eloquence, brilliant wit, a piercing observation . . . She is yet mistress of the art of putting every one at his ease . . . I was invited to her in order to be interrogated on the new Philosophy and saw clearly enough *that I was used* . . . [she] is one of those persons who with a most acute understanding & elegant wit—has nothing else. *She has not the least sense for poetry & is absolutely incapable of thinking a philosophical thought*—her Philosophy is only a map of observations connected together by a loose logic and Poetry is for her . . . only rhetorick in verse. She cannot perceive any thing in poetry more than *fine passages*!!! And what is an eternal bar to all her advances she does not suspect that there is anything above

---

[1] Letter to Goethe, 21.xii.1803.

[2] 30.i.1804; *Crabb Robinson in Germany 1800–1805*. Extracts from his Correspondence. Ed. Edith J. Morley, Oxford, 1929, pp. 132 ff. Cited also by Hertha Marquardt (*Henry Crabb Robinson und seine deutschen Freunde*; Bd. I bis zum Frühjahr 1811, *Palaestra*, 237, Göttingen, 1964, pp. 158 f.), who offers a critical review of all the earlier literature and draws on still unpublished material in Dr. Williams's Library.

her reach—Of course she cannot understand properly speaking, a syllable o
the new Philosophy.

This of course is the crux. In his enthusiasm for 'the new Philosophy'
Robinson was succumbing to a common German tendency to equate this
with philosophy itself—an identification which was to become the bane of
Schiller scholarship. It was not really a case, as Robinson asserted, of her
being 'absolutely incapable of thinking a philosophical thought' at all. On
the contrary; she had already published two works which were by no means
unrelated to Schiller's own philosophical concern—*De l'influence des
passions sur le bonheur des individus et des nations* (1796) and *De la littérature
considérée dans ses rapports avec les institutions sociales* (1800)—both of
which had appeared in German translation.[1] It was rather a case, as
Schiller himself had implied, of two entirely different ways of philosophizing: on the one hand, the empirical, sceptical spirit—whether of the
French or of the English—with which, from his student days, Schiller had
retained considerable sympathy; on the other, the new 'critical' philosophy,
inaugurated by Kant's 'Copernican revolution', to which both French and
English avant-gardistes were attracted in recoil from the pragmatic eclecticism of their home-products. These were, as Crabb Robinson put it
soon after his arrival in Germany, 'antipodes'.[2] And a year later he was
writing: 'I am confident only in my rejection of the English empirical
philosophy, & . . . waver between Kantianism and Schellingism.'[3] It was
this same impulse that had sent Coleridge to Germany in 1798—though
he soon developed a clearer awareness than Crabb Robinson, Benjamin
Constant, or certainly Mme de Staël ever had, of all that was entailed in
not distinguishing between Kant and Schelling. A distinction concerning
the importance of which neither Goethe nor Schiller entertained any
doubts whatsoever.[4] Faced with what Robinson called[5] Schelling's

new metaphysical theory of Aesthetick or the Philosophy of the Arts . . . compounded of the most profound abstraction and enthusiastick mysticism . . . a
Philosophy, in its *pretensions* more glorious than any publicly maintained since

---

[1] Her *Versuch über die Dichtungen*, in Goethe's translation, had already appeared in
Die Horen (1796, St. ii), in order—as he put it in his letter to Schiller of 6.x.1795—'den
Tanz der Horen auch in das umgeschaffne Frankreich hinüber zu leiten'.

[2] 15.ix.1802; Morley, ed. cit., p. 113. 'Yet Godwin', he added incidentally, 'is an
excellent bridge between the two Systems. He has after all as much of Kant as of
Mirabeau.'

[3] September 1803; omitted by Morley, but quoted by Marquardt, op. cit., p. 147.

[4] The appreciation of all three poet-thinkers of some aspects of Schelling's thought is
by no means irreconcilable with their common mistrust of his philosophical and scientific method. On the fundamental difference between Goethe's natural philosophy and
Schelling's see E. Cassirer, 'Goethe und die mathematische Physik. Eine erkenntnis-
theoretische Betrachtung' in *Idee und Gestalt*, Berlin, 1924², p. 74.

[5] Morley, ed. cit., pp. 117 f.

the days of Plato & his Commentators: a Philosophy equally inimical to Locke's Empiricism, Hume's Scepticism & Kant's Criticism . . .

—faced with 'mystical Metaphysicks'[1] of this or any other kind, the 'Aristotelian spirit' which was an important element in the complex cultural heritage of both poet-thinkers soon asserted itself, and they were capable of giving voice to a mistrust of 'the vague, obscure and inaccessible, . . . of mysticism and superstition' which, though differently based and differently argued, was no less decided than Mme de Staël's own. So that it is one of history's ironical twists that she of all people should have helped foreign *amateurs* of 'the new Idealist philosophy' to send Schiller down to posterity as 'a metaphysician', as Robinson labelled him after their first meeting,[2] and his educational treatise as a 'theory of art too full of metaphysics', as she herself described it in *De l'Allemagne*.[3] Probably none of them meant any more by the term than 'abstractions too subtle for communication to others', to quote another of her formulations. But it was nevertheless highly misleading, and on more than one score. For in the first place it ignores Schiller's repudiation of traditional 'metaphysics' in favour of the new 'critical' philosophy as expressed, for instance, in the passage approvingly appropriated by Kant at the end of Letter XIX:[4] he was not, he there insisted, concerned to explain the possibility of things, but content to establish the kind of knowledge which may enable us to understand experience. And in the second place Schiller's 'abstractions', subtle though they may be, are expressly designed to demonstrate the importance of giving due weight to the *physical* concomitants of the psycho-physical phenomena of which he treats. And in the third place they were fashioned, not into a system closed after the manner of metaphysical systems, but into a theory—a theory which, for all its close structural coherence, extended an open invitation to successive generations, not only to put it into practice by an act of pragmatic faith, but to subject it where possible to empirical test by the changing methods and abstractions of science.

And it is also ironical that it should have been through Mme de Staël—especially when we recall Schiller's own characterization of her—that the heritage of Enlightenment in his thought should have been so obscured, and that he should have gone down to posterity as a 'Romantic'. This,

---

[1] Ibid., p. 153.

[2] In a letter of 13.i.1802; Morley, ed. cit., p. 100.

[3] Pt. 2. ch. xxxi. Printed in Paris in 1810, her book was immediately suppressed by Napoleon's censor on the grounds that it was 'not French'. It was published in London in 1813, first in French, then in English. Crabb Robinson's own estimate of his share in the negotiations (*Diaries, Reminiscences, and Correspondence*, ed. T. Sadler, London 1869, i. 416, 422) is apparently much exaggerated. See D. G. Larg, 'H. C. Robinson and Mme de Staël', *Review of English Studies*, v (1929), 22–35.

[4] See our Note to XIX. 9 and p. lxxviii, above.

despite the German mentors who successively attended her—Wilhelm von Humboldt, the brothers Schlegel, Zacharias Werner—all of them in their different ways competent to make clear to her the temper of mind which distinguished the 'Classical' humanism of Weimar from that of the new Romantic School. And despite, too, the subsequent efforts of Heinrich Heine to revise and reverse the emphases in the cultural image she had created by writing a *De l'Allemagne* of his own (Paris, 1835). Yet for all its false emphases her image had the great virtue of making the mature Schiller known abroad. From her *salons*, as from her book, there went out vital information about his poetic works and his philosophical thought; and although the *Aesthetic Letters* themselves were not authoritatively translated until the centenary of 1859,[1] his aesthetic ideas were already being transmitted—along with those of Kant, Schelling, and Hegel—from 1818 onwards by Victor Cousin in his *Cours de philosophie* at the Sorbonne.[2] So that by 1831—thanks to the combined efforts of such Germanophiles (not forgetting contributors to *Le Globe*,[3] and the many German intellectuals resident in France)—Carlyle was able to declare in *Fraser's Magazine*:[4]

Among the French . . . Schiller is almost naturalized; translated, commented upon, by men of whom Constant is one; even brought upon the stage, and by a large class of critics vehemently extolled there. Indeed, to the Romanticist class, in all countries, Schiller is naturally the pattern man and great master; as it were, a sort of ambassador and mediator, were mediation possible, between the Old School and the New; pointing to his own Works, as to a glittering bridge, that will lead pleasantly from the Versailles gardening and artificial hydraulics of the one, into the true Ginnistan and Wonderland of the other.

The role here assigned to him as dramatist is no bad description of him as aesthetician either. But from being labelled mediator to 'the Romanticist class' it was but a step to being made a member of that class itself. And there—as far as the foreigner is concerned—Schiller has remained, despite recurrent efforts to dislodge him. In part, one could sometimes be tempted to suspect, because of a sheer phonetic accident: the formidable cluster of consonants with which so many eminent names of the early nineteenth century began—Schelling, Schlegel (two of these, just to make confusion worse), Schleiermacher, Schopenhauer! In reality, no doubt, because of inadequate knowledge of the full complexity of the eighteenth-century traditions from which he sprang, or because of failure to recognize the classical quality in the dynamic ideal of harmony at which he aimed.

[1] By Adolphe Régnier for the *Œuvres de Schiller*, Paris, 1859–62.

[2] Published in 1836 and again, in revised form, in his popular and frequently reprinted work *Du vrai, du beau et du bien* of 1853.

[3] For Goethe's high opinion of this Journal as an organ of international understanding and *Weltliteratur* see his conversations with Eckermann, 1.vi.1826, 3.x.1828, 17.x.1828.

[4] *Critical and Miscellaneous Essays*, 1869, iii. 94.

Carlyle's published verdict on the *Aesthetic Letters*—whether in the *Fraser's Magazine* article or in his earlier *Life of Schiller* (1825)—was on the whole favourable. And in some respects very discerning indeed. It may not have been the whole truth, but he certainly caught an important facet of it when he said that though 'cast in the mould of Kantism, or at least clothed in its garments', Schiller's native thought in its native form was 'recognizable even in its *masquerade*'.[1] He put his finger on the true significance of Schiller's manifold affiliations with traditional religion—affiliations which of late have been far too summarily disposed of under the convenient rubric 'secularization':

> These *Letters on Aesthetic Culture*, without the aid of anything which the most sceptical could designate as superstition, trace out and attempt to sanction for us a system of morality, in which the sublimest feelings of the Stoic and the Christian are represented but as stages in our progress to the pinnacle of true human grandeur; and man, isolated on this fragment of the universe, encompassed with the boundless desolate Unknown, at war with Fate, without help or the hope of help, is confidently called upon to rise into a calm cloudless height of internal activity and peace, and *be*, what he has fondly named himself, the god of this lower world.[2]

He realized quite clearly what John Stuart Mill was soon to isolate as 'the peculiarity of the Germano-Coleridgian school'—'that they saw beyond the immediate controversy, to the fundamental principles involved in all such controversies':[3]

> Whoever reads these treatises of Schiller with attention, will perceive that they depend on principles of an immensely higher and more complex character than our 'Essays on Taste', and our 'Inquiries concerning the Freedom of the Will'. . . . They do not teach us 'to judge of poetry and art as we judge of dinner', merely by observing the impressions it produced in us; and they *do* derive the duties and chief end of man from other grounds than the philosophy of Profit and Loss.[4]

Above all he recognized the 'compactness' of the reasoning[5] and the cosmopolitan character of Schiller's whole cast of mind.

> . . . of all German Writers . . . he has the least nationality: his character indeed is German, if German mean true, earnest, nobly-humane; but his mode of thought, and mode of utterance, all but the mere vocables of it, are European.[6]

---

[1] *Life of Schiller*; *Collected Works*, 1869, pp. 133 f. Our italics.

[2] Ibid., pp. 135 f.

[3] *Mill on Bentham and Coleridge*, ed. F. R. Leavis, London, 1950, p. 129.

[4] *Life of Schiller*, ed. cit., p. 135. The pungency here is not all Carlyle's own. The quotation is from *Wilhelm Meisters Lehrjahre* (Bk. viii. ch. 7; JA xviii. 351), which he had just been translating, and is in the same vein as Schiller's derision, in XXII. 6, of those who react to art or poetry as though it were either a sermon or an intoxicating drink.

[5] *Critical and Miscellaneous Essays*, ed. cit. iii. 140.

[6] Ibid., p. 94.

It was in this dual context of *Weltliteratur*, on the one hand, and aesthetics, on the other, that Goethe placed Carlyle's *Life* when discussing the state of German culture with Eckermann in 1827:[1]

> It is in the aesthetic sphere that we Germans are particularly weak at present, and it will be a long time before a man like Carlyle turns up amongst us. But it is pleasant to think that in view of the close intellectual commerce between English, French, and German we are now reaching a stage where we can mutually correct each other's views and opinions. That is the great benefit which will result from the idea of *Weltliteratur*, a benefit which will become more and more apparent as time goes on. Carlyle has now written a Life of Schiller, and achieved an over-all appraisal of a kind that no German will easily achieve.

But, for all the discernment and balance of his over-all appraisal, there were in Carlyle's account significant omissions and false emphases which can have played no small part in delaying appreciation of Schiller's educational theories in English-speaking countries. Nor, as his Journal shows and W. Witte has emphasized,[2] were these altogether due to lack of perception. It was rather a question of things glimpsed, but then deliberately repudiated. We may dismiss, as the sort of private petulance familiar to any author wearied by an exacting task, his explosive outburst: 'One is tired to death with his and Goethe's *palabra* about the nature of the fine arts'.[3] Not so the general tenor of the entry in which it is embedded:

> Did Shakespeare know anything of the aesthetic? Did Homer? . . . People made finer pieces of workmanship when there was not a critic among them, just as people did finer actions when there was no theory of the moral sentiments among them. Nature is the sure guide in all cases; and perhaps the only requisite is that we have judgement enough to apply the sentiment implanted in us *without an effort* to the more complex circumstances that will meet us more frequently as we advance in culture or move in a society more artificial.[4]

What Carlyle is doing here is, on the one hand, to appropriate and approve —though without saying so—Schiller's conclusions concerning the ideal of personal and social behaviour appropriate to complex and sophisticated societies, as set forth in the last of his *Aesthetic Letters* and illustrated by the image of an English figure-dance in one of his *Kallias* letters.[5] But even as he approves it Carlyle repudiates precisely that which, according to Schiller, alone could make it possible: the effort of self-awareness and

---

[1] 15 July. On Carlyle's pride and pleasure in Goethe's subsequent review of the *Life* see J. A. Froude, *Thomas Carlyle. A History of the first forty years of his Life, 1795–1835*, London, 1896², i. 262 f., 414 ff.

[2] 'Carlyle's "Conversion"' in *The Era of Goethe*. Essays presented to James Boyd, Oxford, 1959, pp. 190 f.

[3] May 1823. Cited Froude, ed. cit. i. 201.

[4] Ibid., pp. 201 f. Our italics.

[5] Translated in our Note to XXVII. 12.

reflective thought which must go to the achievement of such apparent spontaneity and effortless grace. Carlyle is content to invoke the Method of Nature: all we have to do is to acquire judgement enough to apply without effort the sentiment she implanted in us to the more complex situations of modern society. For Schiller this begs all the questions his educational treatise attempts to answer. How do we acquire that particular sort of judgement? And—for us in our post-Freudian age even more important—how do we learn to return what we have managed to raise to the light of consciousness to the twilight of the unconscious again? Learn how to interiorize and activate insights afforded by science— whether the science of ourselves or of the world—so that they become 'second' nature? So that they are transformed into felt dispositions which issue promptly and spontaneously in appropriate judgement or action?[1] Schiller's answer was that the Method of Nature could never be more than a model for the end-product. The process itself, as far as modern man was concerned, inevitably involved the Ordeal of Consciousness. And this of course meant that the end-product would be qualitatively different too. Would consist, not in the unconscious spontaneity of Nature, but in that 'conscious unconsciousness' which Goethe prized so highly.[2] Or, as Schiller himself argued in *On Naïve and Sentimental Poetry*, what we are exhorted to do is not to remain little children but to 'become *as* little children'; to recover their undismayed simplicity, but in the midst of our own knowledge and sophistication.

Carlyle's other important omission was no less deliberate, and even more detrimental to a proper understanding of all that Schiller meant by aesthetic education and the civic function he assigned to it. In the same entry of his Journal he wrote:

[Schiller] talks in some of his essays about the aesthetic being a necessary means of improvement among political societies. His efforts in this cause accordingly not only satisfied the restless activity, the desire of creating and working upon others which forms the great want of an elevated mind, but yielded a sort of balsam to his conscience. He viewed himself as an apostle of the Sublime. Pity that he had no better way of satisfying it.

Here, long before the more misguided disciples of Freud, is an attempt to reduce public endeavour to terms of private need, to explain it away as at best sublimation, at worst personal compensation.[3] And, in consequence, the political implications of Schiller's '*palabra* about the nature of the fine arts' were dismissed out of hand, and a theory of education which took as its point of departure the political situation at a crucial point in history,

---

[1] Cf. Wilkinson, *In Praise of Aesthetics.* An Inaugural Lecture delivered at University College London, 1962, pp. 7 ff.

[2] See above, p. xciv and fn. 3.

[3] On the drawbacks of such reductive thinking see above, pp. xlii f.

and had as its aim the betterment of the Common Weal, was presented to the English as though it were advocating a surrogate for religion, and a purely personal religion at that. No wonder Carlyle disapproved. For, as Witte has pointed out,[1] his own religious 'conversion' fell just at the time when he was wrestling with his *Life of Schiller*, and must have been a motivating influence. But, as so often, failure of will was inextricably bound up with failure of understanding. The image he repudiated was chiefly of his own making. And a little more patience with the *palabra* might conceivably have led him to see Schiller's treatise, not primarily as a contribution to art-theory, and still less as a piece of aesthetic or moral uplift, but as a perfectly sober and serious challenge to work out a type of education suited to a modern State in an increasingly scientific world. As it was, the first—and for long years to come authoritative—*Life* sent Schiller down to posterity as far more of a starry-eyed idealist than in fact he was, and with the link he wished to establish between aesthetic education and the Common Weal permanently severed. 'He has an intellectual vision, clear, wide, piercing, methodical; a truly philosophic eye', he conceded in the piece he wrote for *Fraser's Magazine*.[2] Yet, he went on:

he looks aloft rather than around. It is in high, far-seeing philosophic views that he delights; in speculations on Art, on the dignity and destiny of Man, rather than on the common doings and interests of Men. . . . For the most part, the Common is still to him the Common. . . . In speculation he is either altogether abstract and systematic, or he dwells on old conventionally-noble themes; never looking abroad, over the many-coloured stream of life, to elucidate and ennoble it; or only looking on it, so to speak, from a college window.

Neither here nor in the *Life* does one get the feel of that Schiller who dismissed with such down-to-earth contempt those who get their priorities wrong, and are for ever prating about the 'Dignity of Man' before they have seen to it that he is adequately fed, housed, and clothed:

Würde des Menschen
Nichts mehr davon, ich bitt' euch. Zu essen gebt ihm, zu wohnen;
Habt ihr die Blösse bedeckt, gibt sich die Würde von selbst.[3]

There may be nothing quite as pungent as this in the *Aesthetic Letters* themselves. But the order of priorities is made no less explicit. The political State is relieved of blame for having lost sight of the dignity of men as long as it was a question of ensuring their physical existence (V. 4). The trouble with idealists is said to be that, for the sake of their political reforms, they are often prepared to risk the physical existence 'which man

[1] 'Carlyle's "Conversion"', ed. cit., pp. 179 f.
[2] *Critical and Miscellaneous Essays*, ed. cit. iii. 124 ff.
[3] *Musenalmanach für 1797*; SA ii. 90.

actually possesses, and without which he possesses nothing' (III. 3). Indeed the 'priority' of man's physical needs—it is Schiller's own word—was for him, as we have already emphasized,[1] the key to the whole curious history of man's quest for human freedom and dignity (XX. 2). True, he was, as Carlyle admits, the first to acknowledge his own lack of empirical knowledge and rich experience of the world: he does so publicly in the opening paragraphs of this treatise.[2] And in this particular context, he would have argued, he had tried to make a virtue out of necessity and to ensure, by a deliberate avoidance of examples and illustrations, that 'universality' of application which Carlyle so sadly missed in his writings. The 'abstractness' of a theory is in any case no evidence that the abstractions did not have their origin in a loving observation of 'the complexities of what is at hand',[3] or are not destined to find their ultimate application in 'the common doings and interests of Men'. Concern for the human condition can take many forms. And though Schiller was never in any danger of confusing first things with last things he yields to no one, not even the most material of socialists, on the need to put first things first.[4]

One long-term effect of Carlyle's omissions is that no one to our knowledge has ever sought to establish, by comparison and contrast, the precise nature and extent of Schiller's influence on early English attempts to reconcile the demands of an expanding scientific, industrialized, ameliorative society with the need of the individual citizen to cultivate the harmonious development of his own personality; on such attempts as Carlyle's own *Signs of the Times* (1829), Coleridge's *On the Constitution of Church and State* (1830), or those essays on Bentham and Coleridge (1838–40) in which John Stuart Mill tried to mediate a synthesis between the English utilitarian tradition and the more humanizing tendencies of 'the Germano-Coleridgian school'. It is true that Schiller usually makes his appearance in any list of influences. But—in the wake of Carlyle's example—along with incompatibles as well as compatibles: with Schelling, Novalis, Jean Paul, writers whose social commitment, conception of art, attitude to science, or basic philosophical assumptions were entirely different from his own.[5] Such an alignment makes it appear as though Schiller's influence fell all on the side of preserving traditional values, on the individualist, artistic, even aristocratic, endeavour to remain personally human within an increasingly inhumane society ('aristocratic fastidiousness' was a trait

[1] p. xcii and fn. 3, above.   [2] See also our Note to I. 2.
[3] *Critical and Miscellaneous Essays*, ed. cit. iii. 125.
[4] Witte, who has made recurrent attempts to adjust the emphasis and present Schiller as a more down-to-earth realist, reminds us (loc. cit. [3], p. 6) of Thomas Mann's feigned horror at the evidence for 'socialist materialism' which might be elicited from his writings.
[5] Raymond Williams's important book on *Culture and Society 1780–1950* (London, 1958, p. 71) affords a typical example.

Carlyle thought he detected in him[1]), and that it was left for native thinkers to attempt the task of reconciling such values with mechanization, 'the cash-nexus', and social progress. But this, of course, is not the case at all. Or, if it is, then it is a case of a model imperfectly known or largely misunderstood. We have apparently no external evidence that Coleridge read Schiller's treatise *On Aesthetic Education*. But the internal evidence makes it seem more than likely that he knew this, just as he knew *Über Anmut und Würde* and *Über naive und sentimentalische Dichtung*.[2] The very title and—with qualifications—theme of his own essay *On the Constitution of Church and State* is reminiscent of its last paragraph, where Schiller drew an analogy between his Aesthetic State and 'the pure Church and the pure Republic', especially in the *Horen* version where he also promised to provide a Constitution for it.[3] What Coleridge certainly knew, and knew very well, were those many distichs in which Schiller precipitated the quintessence of his thought. He copied down or translated a number of those which appeared in the *Musenalmanach für 1797*, and not only on such themes as moral beauty and moral good, the poet and his public, the dead letter and the living spirit, or the language of general communication and the living speech of poetry,[4] but on more socially oriented topics such as class-distinctions, the best political constitution, the best form of religion, the historical moment.[5] One of them, on 'having' and 'being' (*Das Werte und Würdige*), he expanded into a note for Southey's *Omniana*.[6] His much-quoted conviction that 'all truth is a species of revelation'—from a letter to Poole of 23 March 1801, a year in which he was reading and re-reading a good deal of Schiller—sounds like a transcription of the distich on 'Scientific Genius' that we have quoted above,[7] but with the operative qualifications left out. Not that Coleridge would have disapproved of the qualifications. He is, as we have frequently emphasized,[8] at one with Schiller in endorsing the value of scientific analysis and philosophical distinctions, the function of abstract knowledge and abstract language for 'purposes of memory, arrangement, and general communication'.[9] The operative antithesis for him is not, as it has been for so many,[10] between 'thinking' and 'feeling' but rather, as it was for

[1] *Critical and Miscellaneous Essays*, ed. cit. iii. 126. It might seem confirmed by Goethe's self-defensive outburst to Eckermann (4.i.1824) on his own democratic sympathies.

[2] *Notebooks*, ed. cit. i. 451 ff. (Appendix A: 'Coleridge's Knowledge of German as Seen in the Early Notebooks').

[3] See our Note to XXVII. 12.

[4] See above, p. cvi and Wilkinson, *GLL* xvi (1963), 308 ff.

[5] *Notebooks*, ed. cit. i and ii; entries 1063, 3050, 3131, 3220, and notes thereto.

[6] London, 1812, i. 237. Cf. our Note to XXIV. 3.

[7] p. cxxxii.   [8] See especially, p. ciii.

[9] *The Friend* (1818), Section ii, Essay 11; London, 1837³, iii. 231.

[10] Cf. Raymond Williams, op. cit., p. 69.

Schiller, between different modes of both. He is like Schiller—and unlike John Stuart Mill (at least as Raymond Williams presents him[1])—in not making art and poetry into a mere refuge for the individual citizen, a purely personal 'source of inward joy', a last means of contact with 'the perennial sources of happiness'.[2] In other words Coleridge was as indebted to Schiller for the 'civilization' aspects of his thought as for the 'cultivation' aspects of it: for his social concern as much as for his concern with what Mill was to call 'the culture of the inward man'[3] (an echo—witting or unwitting, direct or indirect—of Schiller's 'Bearbeitung des innern . . . Menschen' in XIII. 4fn., §3[4]). But where Coleridge seems to us entirely unlike Schiller is in his transformation of the 'Third State' into an institution, a 'third estate' of the realm: in his call for a Clerisy, or National Church, comprehending 'the learned of all denominations; the sages and professors of . . . all the so-called liberal arts and sciences'.[5] It was in this idea of a nationally endowed class 'for the cultivation of learning, and for diffusing its results among the community . . .', that Mill found Coleridge so useful to him in his concern for the rights of the individual against public opinion, the democratic State, and a philosophy like Bentham's which can only 'teach the means of organizing and regulating the merely *business* part of the social arrangements'.[6] It was, he thought, a permanent benefit bequeathed to political science by 'the Conservative philosophers'. But it was an idea as remote from Schiller's conception as was Carlyle's 'Man-of-Letters Hero' or his call for an organic 'Literary Class'.[7] Remote from it in its suggestion for a distinct class, a cultured *élite*, as in its implication that this was only to be achieved by traditional types of book-learning. Remote from it, too, in the proposed connexions with Church and State. Schiller's reference to these was in the nature of analogy: in order to make the point that his Aesthetic State would exist—as they, in their pure form, had always existed—in the hearts of its members, invisible except in and through their conduct. Anyone might become a member of it, from the highest to the lowest, the most simple to the most sophisticated: lettered or unlettered, craftsman or tradesman, manager, administrator, or technologist. And none has special privilege or status there, neither sage nor artist—and certainly not professors! It may of course be argued that to bring this about through aesthetic education, in

[1] Ibid., pp. 66 ff.
[2] J. S. Mill's *Autobiography*; repr. in 'The World's Classics', no. 262, pp. 125, 113.
[3] *Mill on Bentham and Coleridge*, ed. cit., p. 132.
[4] On our difficulties in translating the various occurrences of 'der innere Mensch' see below, p. 346.
[5] *On the Constitution of Church and State*, ch. v; London, 1839[3], p. 49.
[6] *On Bentham and Coleridge*, ed. cit., pp. 148, 73.
[7] *On Heroes, Hero-Worship and the Heroic in History*; *Collected Works*, 1 869, pp. 184 ff. and 195 ff.

the broad but precise sense in which he conceived this, is bound to involve a measure of public planning. But this still seems to us different from the kind of State intervention Coleridge envisaged. And there would be a case for investigating whether Schiller's conception—the attempt to mark out within the positive State an area in which personal and social conduct is governed by criteria other than those of law, politics, or the received morality of public opinion; criteria which are distinct from these, yet freely interacting with them; on the one hand mitigating the effect of their stringency, on the other modifying them in the direction of the more enlightened and humane—whether such a conception is not more attuned to the needs of an 'open', democratic, and forward-looking society. Just as there might be a case for exploring whether such a complex and flexible art of life, the most valuable heritage of Weimar Classicism, did not perhaps after all find a more faithful reflection in the social and political theorizing of a John Stuart Mill than where it is usually sought: among those various high priests of aesthetic culture who did indeed make art into what Raymond Williams has called 'a saving clause in a bad treaty', 'a special reserve area in which feeling can be tended and organized'.[1]

For if it was Carlyle who severed the connexion Schiller had been concerned to establish between art and politics, it was they who got hopelessly crossed again the lines of communication between art and morality which he had been at such pains to disentangle. It has been said[2] that if Schiller had not started to *preach* education through art, 'there would have been no provocation for the modern acute disseverance of aesthetic and ethical values'. But this is to father on to him the homiletic sins of his progeny (several of whom—Ruskin, William Morris, Burne-Jones, Walter Pater—had, like him,[3] originally intended to take Holy Orders). What matters surely is not *that* they preached, irritating though this may prove to the unconverted, but *what* they preached. The text Schiller chose was of a complexity appropriate to the nature of the problem: 'Only connect— but on no account by confusing.' His followers usually seem content with one half of it or the other: 'Connect at all costs and never mind the confusion' or 'Keep things distinct and never mind the connexion'. They preached on either 'Art for Morality's sake': like Ruskin treating its works as 'sermons in stone', and naïvely assuming that a sense of beauty could not fail to further the performance of moral deeds; or, like William Morris, confusing art with craft, pleasure in labour with joy in contemplation, the social and religious function of art with its aesthetic function. Or else on 'Art for Art's sake': like Pater exhorting their flock, in a kind of inverted asceticism, to deny art any fruits at all beyond that of startling the spirit into a sharp and eager apprehension, and enabling the individual 'to burn

[1] Op. cit., p. 67.   [2] By Nolte, op. cit., p. 148.
[3] See above, p. xxxi.

always with a hard, gem-like flame';[1] or, like Wilde, insisting that 'the sphere of Art and the sphere of Ethics' are not only 'absolutely distinct' but 'absolutely *separate*'—with what disastrous consequences for both art and life he was bitterly to discover. But to whichever persuasion they belonged, none of them seemed to see what Lessing had stated with laconic simplicity when discussing Rousseau's indictment of the arts and sciences:[2] art is what we make of it; it is entirely up to us whether its effects on us are wholesome or harmful. And none of them was prepared, as Schiller was, to essay the hard labour or risk the philosophical tedium of demonstrating in theory how its indifferent and gratuitous potential might be put to whole-some rather than harmful effect. The moral caution is certainly there in the fate of Dorian Gray—but not in the theory implied by any of Wilde's essays. And when, horrified by this fictional acting-out of his doctrines, Pater felt it incumbent upon him to essay those tedious 'art-casuistries' in the light of which—as he had earlier admitted[3]—'a true appreciation of these things is alone possible', he proffered a defence of his creed which begs more than one crucial question:

A true Epicureanism aims at a complete though harmonious development of man's entire organism. To lose the moral sense, therefore, for instance, the sense of sin and righteousness, as Mr. Wilde's hero—his heroes are bent on doing as speedily, as completely as they can—is to lose, or lower, organisation, to become less complex, to pass from a higher to a lower degree of development.[4]

Here, with the familiar eighteenth-century analogy of biological organiza-tion is the concept of 'cultivation' as it had come down from Schiller through Coleridge, who had defined it, by contrast with 'civilization', as 'the harmonious development of those qualities and faculties that characterize our humanity'.[5] But, as we have shown above,[6] this was a position Schiller had reached in *Anmut und Würde*—and subsequently found inadequate for his treatise on education. Inadequate, because too static for the dyna-mics of human behaviour; hence too simplistic, however much one may reiterate the word 'complex'. Because, without 'changing hierarchy' and related concepts, the theory cannot do justice to the fact that man's psyche is, and must be, differently structured in response to different situations: cannot relate his 'being' to his 'doing'.

But whether, like Pater and Wilde, they drew heavily on him—directly

---

[1] In his famous 'Conclusion' to *The Renaissance*, which he felt it incumbent upon him to suppress in the second edition because of the unfortunate effect it had had upon im-mature minds—though he restored it again in the third.

[2] *Neuestes aus dem Reiche des Witzes*, 1751.

[3] At the beginning of 'The School of Giorgione'.

[4] In *The Bookman*, November 1891; *Uncollected Essays* by Walter Pater, Portland, Maine, 1903, p. 127.

[5] *On the Constitution of Church and State*, ch. v; ed. cit., p. 46.

[6] pp. lxxxii ff. and lxxxix ff.

or indirectly—or, like Ruskin, 'heartily disliked his writings'[1] and repudiated his doctrine without even bothering to understand it, the net result is pretty much the same. What he had tried to keep distinct, but yet related, they put asunder. 'It has been said by Schiller in his letters on aesthetic culture', wrote Ruskin in Part III of *Modern Painters*,[2] 'that the sense of beauty never farthered the performance of a single duty. What gross and inconceivable falsity!' For our understanding of the history of ideas it is immaterial whether Ruskin is quoting from memory, at second-hand, or from hearsay. What he does is typical; and his editors obscure the precise nature of it by assigning the quotation to Letter X instead of Letter XXI. For in the former Schiller is merely recapitulating the stock arguments against art as they had been put forward from Plato to Rousseau; he has not yet embarked on his own theory at all. In the latter he is at the heart of it: elaborating the doctrine of indirection which he had made into the pivot of it, and employing his characteristic strategy of first denying the various false claims that are commonly advanced on behalf of art, in order thereafter to throw sharply into relief all that it, and it alone, *can* do. What Ruskin does is to cut the theory clean in half, stop short with the 'Nought' (of XXI. 4) and ignore the complementary 'Infinite' (of XXI. 5), hence missing the doctrine of indirection altogether. He misses it because of his implicit belief in the direct action of beauty upon moral conduct. Pater, more philosophically sophisticated, nevertheless missed it too—and hence landed himself in the familiar position of running with the moral hares while hunting with the aesthetic hounds.

There can be little doubt that a major obstacle to the appreciation of Schiller's educational theory has been the word 'aesthetic' itself.[3] From the start, as he himself indicated, it had been open to misunderstanding and abuse. From Kant to Ruskin,[4] and beyond, its opponents have employed the argument from etymology. And from quite early on it invited irony and satire. From Heine, for instance, in his *Lyrisches Intermezzo* (no. 50):

> Sie sassen und tranken am Teetisch
> Und sprachen von Liebe viel.

[1] Letter to H. Schütz Wilson, 17.iii.1879; *Works*, London, 1903, xxxvii. 277. He had, he wrote (xiv. 274), 'the feeblest hold of facts and the dullest imagination'. But he was probably more indebted to him than he realized. And not only for his indictment of modern fragmentation, '. . . mere segments of men, broken into small fragments and crumbs of life' (x. 196), but for his general awareness of the artist's power to forge the qualities he abstracts from material reality into a new unity with an aesthetic consistency and reality of its own (cf. XXVI. 8 and our Note thereto).

[2] *Works*, ed. cit. iv. 215 and fn. 2. Cf. our Note to XXI. 4.

[3] See Glossary.

[4] *Works*, ed. cit. iv. 47 f. His objection is to the use of a word with this meaning for anything so abstract as 'theory'—an objection it is not difficult for either logician or philologist to dispose of.

Die Herren, die waren ästhetisch,
Die Damen von zartem Gefühl.

And a few years later from the Romantic poet, Eichendorff, who in his novel *Dichter und ihre Gesellen* mocked at the 'ästhetische Bärenhaut' on which sluggards idle away their time. In 1882, in his lecture on 'The English Renaissance of Art',[1] Wilde was able to tell his American audience that for 'nine-tenths of the British public' the word simply meant 'the French for affectation or the German for a dado'; for it had just received its final *coup de grâce* from Gilbert and Sullivan through their delicious parody in *Patience*, where it was made synonymous with 'idle chatter of a transcendental kind'. It has never really recovered from a tendency to apply it to purely surface qualities (Wilde himself had first used it in connexion with the clothes of a fellow undergraduate[2]), to sheer virtuosity, or even to mere techniques.[3] Rarely, if ever, has it been used with that fullness of meaning which Schiller accorded it: of the work of art as a whole—including the import implicit within the form as well as the form itself; and of the whole man in a mode of being characterized by the full and harmonious extension of all his potentialities.

But of course 'aesthetic' was not the only one of Schiller's terms that caused trouble. It did not in the least help matters that he attributed the production and appreciation of that sacred mystery called beauty to such a frivolous-sounding thing as the *Spieltrieb* (and here again Carlyle prejudiced the issue by rendering it, despite all Schiller's careful qualifications, as the 'sport-impulse'[4]). Nor that he made such an ambiguous sounding concept as *Schein*, with its overtones of dissembling and insincerity, central to his theory of education. Again his qualifications did not help.[5] It was lost on his readers, German and English alike, that it was essential to his theory that 'semblance' *should* be open to use or to abuse: otherwise he obscured the characteristic 'gratuitousness' of art and confused the frontiers between the aesthetic and the moral which Kant had been concerned to clarify. To the English, in any case, the hair-splitting

---

[1] *Essays and Lectures* (Methuen's Popular Edition, London, 1911³), p. 119.

[2] *The Letters of Oscar Wilde*, ed. Rupert Hart-Davis, London, 1962, p. 30; a few years later (ibid., p. 88) in connexion with his own.

[3] Cf. Bullough, *Aesthetics*, ed. cit., pp. xix–xxiii, and Wilkinson, *In Praise of Aesthetics*, ed. cit., pp. 5 f.

[4] *Critical and Miscellaneous Essays*, ed. cit. iii. 127.

[5] The Earl of Listowel, for instance, a pupil of Victor Basch at the Sorbonne, makes a not uncommon error when he says that for Schiller the artist is only concerned with the exterior and surface of objects, with their mere appearance, or *Schein*, rather than with their substantial reality (*A Critical History of Modern Aesthetics*, London, 1933, p. 32). Contrast Schiller's most explicit statement of his own position (SA xii. 139): 'To possess substance without form is indeed only half to possess. . . . To possess form without substance, on the other hand, is to possess but the shadow; and no amount of virtuosity in expression can avail him who has nothing to express.'

distinctions of Letter XXVI came through in the elegant but over-simplified version of a Pater, condensed into a single adverb in the last sentence of *The Renaissance*—'art comes to you proposing *frankly* to give nothing but the highest quality to your moments as they pass, and simply for those moments' sake'—or in the dazzling but disturbing paradoxes of a Wilde in his defence of *The Truth of Masks.*[1] If we add to these termino-logical factors the offence given to our native Puritanism by the tendency of some of his followers to raise art and the aesthetic to a surrogate for religion (which is what Wilde said[2] Pater had done in *Marius the Epicurean*), and the offence to our native spirit of empirical pragmatism by the appear-ance of metaphysical transcendence, then it is not difficult to see why, as the centenary of his death approached, and with the Wilde scandal still a vivid memory, Schiller's stock as aesthetician should have been at its lowest. Thus the American author of a still highly regarded *Life and Works*,[3] Calvin Thomas, deplored the 'logic-chopping' of the *Aesthetic Letters*—in the true tradition of William James, who asked 'Why does the *Ästhetik* of every German philosopher seem to the artist like the abo-mination of desolation?'[4]—and found their individual insights more satisfying than the work as a whole. And the doyen of English Germanists, J. G. Robertson, in a centenary appreciation,[5] though recognizing the vital importance of the work for the progress of German culture, saw in it a culmination of the magnificent humanism of the eighteenth century rather than a promise for the future, and—like Lukács (strange bedfellows, as Witte ironically observes[6])—was inclined to relegate Schiller to the age before the French Revolution. Wholly characteristic of this period is the summary dismissal of the *Letters* in a 'University Manual' on *The Philosophy of the Beautiful*[7] as 'very misty-margined indeed'.

By the twenties their stock was beginning to rise again. A sharp attack on Schiller as the inventor of the 'nightmare science' of aesthetics by that arch-classicist, Irving Babbitt (T. S. Eliot's teacher at Harvard), called forth a protest from A. O. Lovejoy, founder of 'the history of ideas', and

---

[1] How Wilde's theory of masks combined with the concept of *Schein* in the mind of Yeats—though he had it from *Wilhelm Meister* (JA xviii. 14) which he thought 'the wisest of all books'—and how he forced himself to acquire 'this necessary technique of seeming', was recorded some years ago in 'Reminiscences of W. B. Yeats' by L. A. G. Strong (*The Listener*, 22.iv.1954).

[2] *Letters*, ed. cit., p. 476.

[3] New York, 1901.

[4] Cited Elton, op. cit., p. 2. A number of linguistic philosophers have recently com-plained of the 'dreariness' of aesthetics and dismissed it as largely bogus. See, for instance, J. A. Passmore and W. E. Kennick in *Mind*, lx (1951), 318 and lxvii (1958), 334.

[5] *Schiller after a Century*, Edinburgh and London, 1905, pp. 85 and 90 f.

[6] Loc. cit. (3), pp. 6 f.

[7] By W. Knight, London, 1891 (1903²), p. 63.

the controversy ran through four numbers of *Modern Language Notes*.[1] About the same time, in their *Foundations of Aesthetics*,[2] Ogden, Richards, and Wood expressed surprise that Schiller's theory of 'living form' had not attracted more attention. Though their own reservations about it, like those of C. G. Jung,[3] seem to us to betray an inadequate appreciation of what one might broadly term the 'dialectics' of his thought:[4] of the tension of substantial opposites that he allows to persist within the formal equipoise of his dynamic concept of harmony; of all the inner as well as outer, unconscious as well as conscious, content that is implicitly subsumed under the concept he called 'life'. By the early forties the time was ripe for a recognition of the educational importance of the work—as distinct from its importance for aesthetics or art-theory. And Herbert Read, who a decade earlier[5] had been inclined to wonder whether 'the idealistic conception of art, developed on the basis of Kant's aesthetic by writers like Schiller, Fichte and Schelling, and given a more popular romantic expression by poets like Richter and Novalis, is worth the time that would be involved in mastering its mysteries', was evidently persuaded by Jung's lengthy analysis in *Psychological Types* that the 'mysteries' of Schiller's two major treatises at least might be worth the time after all, and were in any case not to be summarily disposed of under the category 'idealist theories of art'. In his influential *Education through Art* of 1943 he came out with praise for the *Aesthetic Letters* no less warm than Jung's own.[6]

Yet, as the bicentenary of Schiller's birth in 1959 plainly showed, the English have not become more markedly appreciative, or even more noticeably interested. Philip Toynbee hit the nail firmly on the head when he then wrote:[7] 'The English have never, I think, been very much interested in Schiller. . . . We know that he *must* be a great writer, but we find it hard to respond to his fervent sublimities.' In the case of his *Letters on Aesthetic Education* the obstacles to discovery are formidable enough before one even gets to the difficulties of the work itself. The accepted short titles—*Briefe über die ästhetische Erziehung* or, quite simply, *Ästhetische Briefe*—have led to confusion, not only with the personal

[1] xxxv and xxxvii (1920–2). See also Babbitt's essay 'Schiller as Aesthetic Theorist' in *On Being Creative, and other Essays*, ed. cit., and J. R. Frey, 'Schiller in Amerika', *Jb. d. deutschen Schillergesellschaft*, iii (1959), 358 ff.   [2] Ed. cit., pp. 81 ff.

[3] In *Psychological Types*, ed. cit., pp. 110 ff.

[4] Cf. E. L. Stahl ('Hölderlin's Idea of Poetry' in *The Era of Goethe. Essays Presented to James Boyd*, Oxford, 1959, p. 152), who seems to us to overstate the contrast between Hölderlin's view and Schiller's, and to underestimate Hegel's indebtedness to Schiller for the concept of *aufheben* (see Glossary) by not differentiating between the semantic content of the various occurrences of the word in Letter XVIII.

[5] In *Art Now*, London, 1933, p. 35.   [6] Cf. p. 339, below.

[7] In a review (*The Observer*, 26.iv.1959) of Thomas Mann's *Last Essays*, which includes his 1955 tribute to Schiller.

correspondence out of which he shaped his treatise on education, but with the *Kallias* letters, which were never shaped into a treatise at all, and were concerned with art-theory and nothing more—and even with his much earlier *Philosophische Briefe* of 1786, which were on a different theme altogether. The remedy in our view is not henceforth to avoid the short titles but to make their correct reference familiar—which is why we have, throughout this edition, used them both in German and in English interchangeably with the full title. But this full title itself has also put obstacles in the way of discovery. For, like the content of the treatise, it has—and inevitably—a double orientation which makes for difficulties of classification. Where ought it to be put? Under aesthetics and art-theory? Or under pedagogy, education, or perhaps even psychology? Those repositories of classified knowledge, the encyclopaedias, reflect something of the doubts and uncertainties about what is perhaps an insoluble problem. In the latest edition of the *Encyclopaedia Britannica* (1957) it is referred to in the article on 'Aesthetics' by E. F. Carritt (in the same article of the fourteenth edition—1929/32—Benedetto Croce had apparently not thought it appropriate for, or worthy of, mention there at all)—but only in order to make the point that neither Schiller nor Hegel added anything to Aristotle's theory of catharsis, though they might have interpreted it more liberally through seeing it as the externalization and contemplation of man's impulses. In the corresponding article of the *New Chambers* (1955) Herbert Read could raise none of the enthusiasm he had expressed when treating of the work in the context of psychology, education, and children's art, but—falling back once again on his earlier category of idealist art-theory—placed Schiller in the tradition which runs from Kant through Schelling and Hegel down to Croce. Perhaps the most striking evidence of ignorance and uncertainty—and at the same time a further obstacle to discovery—is to be found in our official home of learning, the British Museum, where the edition of Schiller's works chosen for the open shelves is one which states as a, perfectly legitimate, editorial principle that everything has been left out which is of merely historical interest[1]— but then proceeds to leave out his Letters *On the Aesthetic Education of Man.*

* * *

But as we have implied, and as René Wellek confirms in his *History of*

---

[1] *Schillers Werke*, hrsg. v. Paul Brandt mit einer Einleitung v. K. Heinemann, Leipzig, [1923]. It is in five volumes and the Introduction states: '[Diese Ausgabe] verzichtet auf alles, was in Schillers Werken nur noch ein geschichtliches oder literarhistorisches Interesse hat.' Since it includes *Über naive und sentimentalische Dichtung*, it is difficult to see just how these criteria have been applied. This has now been replaced on request by a more recent five-volume edition (*Sämtliche Werke*, hrsg. v. G. Fricke u. H. G. Göpfert in Verbindung mit H. Stubenrauch, München, 1962³) which does contain the *Aesthetic Letters*.

Modern Criticism, the full extent of Schiller's influence has never been adequately recognized.[1] And no account, however complete, of his actual reception, or of the rise and fall of his prestige,[2] could give an accurate picture either of the extent of the repercussions he has had or of their exact nature. This is chiefly because Goethe's prophecy was speedily fulfilled.[3] People did indeed start 'plundering' him, all too often 'without acknowledgment'. And they started in the very next year, when a 'System-programm des deutschen Idealismus' was drawn up—as some think by Hölderlin, but more likely by Schelling[4]—setting forth the new Romantic attitude to art, science, and philosophy: proclaiming the aesthetic act as 'the highest act of reason'; beauty, in the Platonic sense, as the idea embracing all other ideas; and poetry as 'what it was in the beginning—the teacher of mankind . . . which will supersede and outlive all the other arts and sciences'. This grandiose claim for the civilizing mission of art obviously owes much to Schiller's doctrine of aesthetic education. It no less obviously alters—one may with justice say that it distorts—its whole emphasis and intent. Gone are all his distinctions, vanished all his scruples. There is no hint here of the dangers of the aesthetic. And there is no trace, either, of Schiller's committedness to maximum differentiation. The kind of unity that was in the beginning is to prevail again at the end. What was primary is to have unqualified primacy.[5] No wonder Crabb Robinson could write home from Jena:[6]

Poetry & Mysticism these are the Idols worshipped here—Beauty & Truth are asserted to be one—Poetry is maintained to be nothing but esoterick philosophy and Philosophy esoteric poetry!!!

[1] Ed. cit. i. 254 f. Wellek himself briefly indicates the lines it followed in various countries.

[2] See F. Ewen, *The Prestige of Schiller in England, 1788–1859*, New York, 1932; R. Pick's Introduction to his Bibliography of *Schiller in England 1787–1960*, ed. cit.; and W. Schirmer, *Der Einfluss der deutschen Literatur auf die englische im 19. Jahrhundert*, Halle, 1947.

[3] See above, p. cxxxiii.

[4] On its disputed authorship see Wellek (op. cit. ii. 367 f.), who rightly observes (ibid., pp. 74 f.) that it in any case contains the gist of Schelling's published writings on this theme during the next decade.

[5] Lohner (loc. cit., p. 145) cites the following from Schiller's letter of 4.xi.1795 to the Gräfin Schimmelmann as evidence of the 'astonishingly exact congruity' between his thought and Schelling's: 'Die höchste Philosophie endigt in einer poetischen Idee, so die höchste Moralität, die höchste Politik. Der dichterische Geist ist es, der allen Dreien das Ideal vorzeichnet, welchem sich anzunähern ihre höchste Vollkommenheit ist.' We should be inclined to object that even in this private letter the difference is as discernible as the likeness: there is no suggestion that history, science, and philosophy will *disappear*, or that poetry can—or should—*take their place* (cf. our argument on p. cxxxii, above). But however that may be, in his published writings on aesthetic education the structure of his thought is fundamentally different from Schelling's.

[6] 17.x.1802; Morley, ed. cit., p. 114.

Not one of these 'mystical' equations could Schiller have endorsed without recourse to what some might call the 'casuistry' of his principle of reciprocal subordination.

And this brings us to a further, if related, difficulty in tracing the nature and extent of his influence: not just the fact of the purloining—with or without acknowledgment—but the manner of it. From the start his readers were a prey to the common human predilection for attending to the parts rather than to the whole. And once cut loose from their moorings within his own 'system'[1] his individual concepts proved, not unnaturally, susceptible to some curious affiliations. As, in the course of the nineteenth century, they drifted to France and England, and from both countries across the Atlantic and back again—to be reclaimed eventually for Germany, in their refurbished rather than their original guise, by Stefan George, Karl Wolfskehl, and Hugo von Hofmannsthal—as Romanticism turned into Symbolism and both became transformed into the doctrine of 'Art for Art's Sake', these ideas gradually began to reflect a temper of mind subtly, but nonetheless fundamentally, alien to Schiller's own. They merged imperceptibly not only with the metaphysical diffuseness of Schelling-type thinking—the assimilation of all mental activity to the aesthetic, of all linguistic utterances to the poetic, of all sorts and conditions of human creativity to the artistic—but also with trends that point in the very opposite direction from this: with the artist's increasing sense of alienation, his tendency to retreat from a hostile world into an ivory tower; with his impulse to recoil from well-meaning attempts to make art reflect this uncongenial world or serve its sociological purposes; with his consequent, often desperate, determination to mark off his own 'aesthetic' territory through insisting on a doctrine of 'pure' form; with his almost aggressive assertion of the distinctiveness of his own mode of utterance through making poetic language difficult of access—even to the point where it ceases to have relevance for the ordinary man. This is as much the opposite of Schiller's intention as Schelling's apparent ambition to make poets of us all. For Schiller, the poet was assuredly not to be the creature of his age. But he was not to be its high-priest either, still less remain an outsider remotely aloof from it. He was to serve his fellow men; admittedly after his own fashion, a fashion dictated by insights into his own art and craft—but dictated also by insight into the recesses of the human heart. If his form was to be 'purified', it was not, as yet, out of any self-defensively aggressive need to remind his fellow citizens what art is all about. It was in order to hold up a clarifying mirror to their obscure intimations, and thereby help them towards the realization of human potentialities of which they might as yet be but dimly aware. If the theory of popularization he evolved had as its corner-stone a concept of aesthetic

---

[1] A word he himself used of his treatise in a letter to Körner of 5.i.1795.

discourse, this implied disparagement neither of science and philosophy on the one hand nor of the Common Man on the other. Its formidable face was to present itself only to him who undertakes an enterprise as hazardous as this. Its public, and gracious, face was to further relatedness among human beings: on the one hand to make the Common Man at home in a world increasingly dependent on esoteric techniques; on the other hand to discourage him from renouncing his rightful claim to reasoned criticism of the specialist. The whole movement of his aesthetic education is towards openness and towards integration. It may have to proceed via indirection and through differentiation. But its ultimate aim is to bring a new kind of cultural—and civic—order into a rapidly changing society.

Few, if any, of those who have pursued the repercussions of Schiller's thought have been guided by a due awareness that his individual concepts can only be made to bear the projection of alien content, or be assimilated to alien attitudes and ends, if they are deprived of the controls they mutually exert upon each other within his own firmly structured theory. Just as few of those who have traced the history of poetics, aesthetics, and criticism have brought out clearly enough the complexity of the intellectual and artistic climate which prevailed in Germany at the end of the eighteenth century: the fact that tendencies which already threatened to fly wildly apart, and by the end of the nineteenth century were to harden into positions so widely divergent that reconciliation seemed impossible, were there, in a few minds of great genius, held together in a balance which was all the more fruitful for being so precarious. Thus it has been rare for anyone to point as firmly as did Oscar Wilde in the direction of one of Schiller's major achievements: the adjustment of 'the balance between form and feeling'.[1] Rarer still for anyone to do, as Susanne Langer did in her book *Feeling and Form*, and take Schiller's concept of aesthetic semblance as the starting-point for a modern theory of art—showing how, without it, such concepts as artistic 'creation' or 'living form', indeed the whole metaphorical apparatus of organism-aesthetics, cannot stand up to philosophical scrutiny. Rarest of all for anyone to remind us, as Stuart Hampshire has done,[2] that in re-examining the whole question of the relation between art and politics in the modern world we don't need to start absolutely from scratch, but can take our cues from the only serious attempt to devise a *theory* of the relation between them since Plato.

There is in consequence, despite the valuable work that has been done,

---

[1] 'The English Renaissance of Art'; *Essays and Lectures*, ed. cit., p. 126.
[2] Loc. cit. (1). It is, of course, not uncommon for writers to grope towards theories which are reminiscent of Schiller's without ever mentioning him. One recent example must serve for many: J. Bruce's 'Notes on Hampshire's "Thought and Action"', *Brit. Journal of Aesthetics*, iv (1964), 40 ff.

still a whole chapter to be written on the repercussions of Schiller's thought. And it would in our view have to take the form of a morphology of ideas: a comparative investigation of their content, constellation, and the ideological context in which they appear. But if structural considerations should be paramount, this does not mean that genetic considerations—questions of origin and influence, direct or indirect—need be left out of account. Not only because they are of biographical interest in tracing the growth of an individual mind, or of historical interest in bringing to light forgotten channels of transmission, but because they serve to focus attention on the conditions, if not the causes, of historical change. Thus it should no longer be possible to claim, as Sir Kenneth Clark does in his paper-back edition of *The Renaissance*,[1] that Pater was being in the least original in those arguments on the relations between the arts which culminate in his famous assertion: '*All art constantly aspires towards the condition of music.*' As his reference to the term *Andersstreben* used by 'German critics' clearly indicates, his source was German. What one wants to know at this point is which 'German critics' Pater had in mind. The term *Andersstreben* is not to our knowledge ever used by Schiller. But the argument, even down to the word 'obliterate' (an obvious rendering of *vertilgen*), is his—though Pater's elegantly turned, but elliptical, version has none of his circumspect qualifications and distinctions.[2] And just because of this, his elevation of music to the prototype of all art appears unfortunately categorical and unnecessarily provocative. What we should like to know is how much of this metamorphosis had been effected before it reached Pater—by the Romantics, by Schopenhauer, by Hegel—and just how much of it was his own. Above all, it would be interesting to see whether English critics—who are sometimes, and not unnaturally, provoked by Pater into retorting, in the spirit of Ezra Pound, that all *poetry* at least constantly aspires towards the condition of sculpture (Schiller himself had shown its tendency towards both)—might not, if they were referred to Pater's ultimate source,[3] find there a more acceptable version of the real point at issue: the still endlessly discussed question of the relation between form and content in art. More acceptable because—through a firm distinction between *Stoff* and *Gehalt*, and a consequent avoidance of the ambiguity of the word 'content'—it there becomes clear in just what sense music may serve as a prototype of all the arts, and in what respects it can never stand as model for them.

Nor should it any longer be possible to refer Wordsworth's equally

---

[1] Fontana Library, London, 1961, p. 21.

[2] Cf. our Notes to XXII. 4 and 5.

[3] Not only Letter XXII, but Schiller's essay on Matthisson's *Gedichte*—and even Goethe's aphorism on music (quoted in our Glossary under *Inhalt*, &c.) which may not have been without influence on Pater either.

famous, and even more influential, 'emotion recollected in tranquillity' simply to his own experience (though this may have confirmed, or been confirmed by, it) or even just to English anticipations of it in the earlier eighteenth century. His immediate source, as was pointed out some thirty years ago now,[1] was undoubtedly Schiller's 'aus der sanftern und fernenden Erinnerung mag er dichten'.[2] And the channel of transmission in this case was undoubtedly Coleridge, who—as evidence which has come to light through the publication of his *Notebooks* confirms[3]—had almost certainly read Schiller's review of Bürger's poems while in Göttingen (a review, as Carlyle was to observe,[4] 'so often descanted on'). The combination of different types of evidence here raises plausibility to the order of historical proof: the famous phrase did not occur in Wordsworth's first Advertisement of the *Lyrical Ballads* (1798), but only in the Preface of 1800 written after their visit to Germany; the sequence of his argument on the 'idealizing' process follows Schiller's exactly, and the crucial formulation is verbally reminiscent of it; Coleridge's own version of the same idea in Chapter xv of *Biographia Literaria*, where he takes issue with Wordsworth's Preface, is verbally reminiscent of other, related, points in Schiller's argument. But again, the establishment of influence is of less interest in itself than the opportunity it affords of observing an early stage in the transformation of an idea: from its appearance as the 'rule' of *éloignement* in classical poetics right down to its 'politicization' in the dramatic theory of Bertolt Brecht. In Schiller's account of the creative process the dominant idea is not 'recollection', nor even 'tranquillity'; it is 'distance'. Not necessarily temporal distance, nor yet—as it had often been in classical poetics—spatial distance, but 'psychical' distance. 'Recollection' is for him but one means of 'distancing' personally experienced 'passion' or emotion; and his transitive use of the still normally intransitive verb *fernen*[5] brings out very clearly that this was the only aspect of time's virtue that concerned him here. His analogy, and in some sense his model, is the actor's curious blend of identification with, and aloofness from, the role he is playing (which makes it seem plausible that he may well have read Diderot's *Paradoxe sur le comédien* in manuscript).[6]

---

[1] By Willoughby, 'Wordsworth and Germany', *German Studies Presented to H. G. Fiedler*, Oxford, 1938, pp. 443 f.   [2] SA xvi. 238 ff.

[3] Ed. cit. i, note to entry 787, and Appendix A, p. 453.

[4] *Critical and Miscellaneous Essays*, 1869, iii. 122.

[5] To take Schiller's use of it here as *intransitive*, as the most recent editor, Herbert Meyer, still does (NA xxii. 416; cf. Julius Petersen, SA xvi. 394) is to mistake the whole tenor of his thought—and to perpetuate the error of Grimm's *Wörterbuch* which offers the passage from *Über Bürgers Gedichte* as evidence of intransitive usage. Adelung (1775) records the intransitive use only; Campe (1808), the transitive use too—but only by poets after Klopstock.

[6] Cf. R. Mortier, *Diderot en Allemagne, 1750–1850*, Paris, 1954. On Wellek's juxtaposition of Wordsworth and Diderot rather than Wordsworth and Schiller (op. cit.

But like all good analogies and models this one is useful precisely by virtue of its limitations. The only thing the poet and the actor have in common is that neither achieves the necessary distance from his felt 'material' without the intervention of a purely 'formal' excitement deriving from preoccupation with his craft. This is the point that Schiller brings out in a way that Diderot does not. And he thereby establishes a relation of reciprocal causality between formal excitement and aesthetic distance—a relation which, in XXII. 5 and 6 of his *Aesthetic Letters*, he was to extend to aesthetic response as well as artistic creation, arguing that without such qualitative change of attitude we can never gain access to the import of the work as a whole, but remain content with the adventitious excitements of its subject-matter. It was a position that Edward Bullough had to recover all over again in 1912 in his now classic article on ' "Psychical Distance" as a Factor in Art and an Aesthetic Principle'[1] which, like all Bullough's work, owes a great deal to Schiller, though curiously enough he does not mention him by name. But he does not mention Oscar Wilde either, who had clearly shown his understanding of the principle by bringing together, in a brief but masterly survey, the names of Plato and Aristotle, and Leonardo da Vinci, of Goethe and Schiller, Keats and Wordsworth, Baudelaire, Gautier, and Edgar Allan Poe.[2] What Bullough succeeded in doing was to bring together, as reciprocally conditioning factors in a single, if complex, psychical state, responses which nineteenth-century aestheticians had come to envisage as an alternation: a successive alternation in time between empathy and detachment, involvement and alienation (or whatever antithetical terms one chooses). And this precisely is what Schiller had achieved *vis-à-vis* the earlier eighteenth century, which (still under the influence of the imitation theory) conceived of this same alternation in terms of illusion—and the breaking of the illusion through awareness of the formal qualities of the artist's medium.[3] In Wordsworth, by contrast, this whole notion of 'distance' is obscured: the precise relation between the 'tranquillity' in which the emotion is to be 'recollected' and the 'excitement' in which it is to be 're-created' is never made clear; and it almost sounds as though a lapse of time were an indispensable condition of the poetic formulation of personal experience —an implication which, from the evidence of many poets, we know not to be the case. In *Biographia Literaria* the notion of psychical distance comes to the fore again, especially—and influentially—in the following:

i. 56, 240) see Wilkinson, 'Coleridge und Deutschland' in *Forschungsprobleme der Vergleichenden Literaturgeschichte*, ii. Tübingen, 1958, pp. 20 f. It tends to obscure both the channels of transmission and the gradual metamorphosis of the basic idea.

[1] Reprinted in *Aesthetics*, ed. cit., pp. 91 ff.

[2] 'The English Renaissance', ed. cit., pp. 125 ff.

[3] The progress to Schiller's (and Goethe's) position was the main argument of Wilkinson's *Johann Elias Schlegel: A German Pioneer in Aesthetics*, ed. cit.

Hence it is, that from the perpetual activity of attention required on the part of the reader; from the rapid flow, the quick change, and the playful nature of the thoughts and images; and, above all, *from the alienation, and, if I may hazard such an expression, the utter aloofness of the poet's own feelings from those of which he is at once the painter and the analyst*; that though the very subject cannot but detract from the pleasure of a delicate mind, yet never was poem less dangerous on a moral account.[1]

Readers interested in the history of ideas may compare this, not only with Letter XXII, but with the following passage from *Über Bürgers Gedichte*:

> Selbst in Gedichten, von denen man zu sagen pflegt, dass die Liebe, die Freundschaft u.s.w. selbst dem Dichter den Pinsel dabei geführt habe, hatte er damit anfangen müssen, *sich selbst fremd zu werden, den Gegenstand seiner Begeisterung von seiner Individualität los zu wickeln, seine Leidenschaft aus einer mildernden Ferne anzuschauen.*[2]

'Alienation'—not of the self from the world, but within the psyche itself: 'sich selbst fremd werden'. Brecht would no doubt have denied it, for he repudiated the German classics in favour of Diderot. But we can hardly rule out the possibility that Schiller's use of the adjective *fremd* in this well-known aesthetic context may have had as much influence on his choice of the term *Verfremdungseffekt* as Hegel's philosophical term *Entfremdung*. In any case it is the verbal similarity that prompts us to bring them into relation at all, and to examine this latest modification in the history of a traditional idea; a modification so radical that some might say it is no longer the same idea. In fact, it is a throw-back to an earlier stage of its historical development. For with his naïve assumption that the spectator will necessarily be 'freer' if jerked out of emotional involvement into intellectual activity Brecht is denying all that we have learnt since Freud—and all that Schiller himself was already teaching: that we can be the slaves of our thinking no less than of our feeling. Indeed with his whole antithesis between intellect and emotion he reverts to a faculty psychology which, as we observed earlier,[3] was already outmoded by the end of the eighteenth century. Just as with his doctrine of an alternation between involvement and alienation he regresses to a position which is outdated in aesthetic theory, however dramatically effective it may be in his own theatrical practice.

In the above examples verbal similarity in the expression of a single idea was an important factor in establishing influence. Another type of evidence is the close proximity of a number of different, though related, ideas. This is what we find in the few pages surrounding Coleridge's

---

[1] Ch. xv. Our italics. [2] SA xvi. 239 f. Our italics.
[3] See above, p. cxiii.

well-known definition of poetic genius in terms of 'the balance or reconciliation of opposite or discordant qualities' at the end of Chapter xiv of
Biographia Literaria. There is a whole cluster of ideas here which are to
be found in Schiller too, and chiefly in his *Aesthetic Letters*.[1] Ever since
Sara Coleridge pointed to Schelling as the source of many of her father's
ideas, there has been a tendency to overestimate the influence of German
Idealist philosophy upon his thinking—with a corresponding counter-
tendency, among those who find evidence of similar ideas in his writing
before he ever read Schelling, to put a great deal of it down to 'genial
coincidence'. It seems to us that there is a case for considering whether
he did not find some of his most formative ideas (which would not, of
course, rule out 'genial coincidence' either) among the eighteenth-century
poets and thinkers he read while he was still learning German in Göttingen—not forgetting such influential popular philosophers as Garve.
Coleridge's much-quoted principle of 'the predominant passion', for
instance, to which all the parts of a poem—images, sounds, metre, rhythm
—must be 'subordinated' (it is the fundamental principle of his argument
against Wordsworth's Preface), may well have come straight from J. A.
Eberhard's article on 'Rhythm' published in 1795: he certainly borrowed
the Series in which it appeared from the University Library, and made
notes on other articles.[2] The 'balance of opposite or discordant qualities'
is as prominent a feature of Schiller's theory as it is of Schelling's (and
if Schelling termed the resultant state 'Indifference',[3] so after all did
Schiller—and Burke—before him).[4] The question that still needs to be
asked is whether the unity that Coleridge evolved for himself out of his
manifold borrowings, and on which he so clearly put the stamp of his own
mind, is not more akin to the aesthetic, psychological, practical temper of
a Schiller, whose passion for distinctions he certainly shared,[5] than to the
metaphysical system of a Schelling, with its profoundly a-psychological
—where not anti-psychological—bias. Crabb Robinson, for instance,
records Schelling's fulminations against the empirical spirit of the
English:[6]

[You should] hear something like his abuse of [Erasmus] Darwin last Wednes-
day, whose Conceit [from his poem *The Botanic Garden* of 1794] concerning the
influence of the breast in forming our Sensations of beauty he quoted 'only to

---

[1] Starting with Coleridge's observations on the office of philosophy and the privilege
of the philosopher, which are strikingly parallel to XVIII. 4 and fn.

[2] *Notebooks*, ed. cit. i, note to entry 406, and Appendix A, p. 452.

[3] A point made by Rose F. Egan, *The Genesis of the Theory of 'Art for Art's Sake' in
Germany and in England*, Pt. ii. Smith College Studies in Modern Languages, ii. 4
(1921) and v. 3 (1924), p. ix.

[4] See our Note to XV. 9.

[5] See above, p. ciii.

[6] Letter of 14.xi.1802; Morley, ed. cit., pp. 117 f.

show to what *bestialities* (the very words) the empirical philosophy of Locke leads, and how the Mind of Man is *brutalised* [when] unenlightened by Science'.

Coleridge, of course, would not have thought the breast-hypothesis at all improbable, let alone 'bestial'.[1] And neither would Schiller:[2] his injunction to start our intellectual and moral education in the 'indifferent' (aesthetic) sphere of physical life is not just an exhortation; it subsumes a statement of fact. But however the answers to questions of affinity or influence turn out, there is a further question to be asked. Is Coleridge's doctrine of imagination—which has been of such immense influence on English educational theory and practice as well as on English criticism—adequate for an understanding of the nature, the making, or the appreciation of art and poetry? Imagination, after all—and Coleridge knew this as well as Schiller, though his disciples have often seemed to ignore it—is at work in all our pursuits, in science and philosophy as well as in art and poetry, and in personal and practical life too. And in all of them it needs to be under the 'irremissive control' of the understanding and the will, as Coleridge has it. But what distinguishes its operations in poet or artist is not just that this 'irremissive control' is in them 'gentle and unnoticed',[3] but that —as Schiller makes far more explicit (XXVI. 7)—they combine 'a loving attachment to sheer semblance' with the power of creating semblance in a particular medium. As we have shown above,[4] this concept of *schöner Schein* is inseparable from Schiller's theory of poetic or artistic imagination. What part does it play in Coleridge's?

An even more teasing problem of affinity, and possible influence, arises in the case of Keats's 'Negative Capability', the quality which above all others, according to him, goes 'to form a Man of Achievement'.[5] For here it is a question, not of a cluster of ideas, but the juxtaposition of two ideas only. But they are ideas which would not normally be brought into relation at all, and which most people might consider mutually exclusive. 'Negative Capability' in itself—though a wonderfully expressive oxymoron for that state of aesthetic determinability which Schiller characterized as

---

[1] As is clear from Kathleen Coburn's article ('Reflections in a Coleridge Mirror' in *From Sensibility to Romanticism. Essays Presented to Frederick A. Pottle*, New York, 1965, pp. 422 ff.) on his frequent use of breast-mirror imagery, and his interest in the pictorial emblem of the breast-as-mirror.

[2] To say nothing of Goethe. His seemingly simple little nature poem of 1775, *Auf dem See*, is in reality a statement about the growth of the mind, from the breast situation onwards, through the reciprocal mirror-reflection of inner and outer world.

[3] *Biographia Literaria*, ch. xiv. Cf. above, p. lxvi.

[4] pp. lxv ff.; cf. p. xciii. The contrast Schiller draws, in XXVII. 4 and fn., between the free association of ideas in fantasy and the freely creative power of aesthetic imagination is, incidentally, not identical with Coleridge's distinction between Fancy and Imagination.

[5] Letter to George and Tom Keats, [27?].xii.1817. See our Note to XXI. 5fn.

Null—negative and unfruitful as regards any specific results, but infinitely fruitful through its restoration of our full potentiality[1]—would afford no evidence of influence. It could easily derive from a common source: as we have argued,[2] Schiller himself was probably drawing on more than one tradition, and his whole originality lies in the firmness with which he relates the negative fruitfulness of this infinite potentiality to the realized fruitfulness of our determinate states and conditions. And he does this most strikingly in the footnote to Letter XXI, where he maintains that men destined for great achievement are those capable of 'lingering in this state of aesthetic indetermination without pressing impatiently for some result'—a state beautifully described by Keats as 'when man is capable of being in uncertainties, Mysteries, doubts, without any irritable reaching after fact and reason'. Unlike Coleridge, Keats was not versed in German Idealism.[3] But he was apparently profoundly influenced towards his theory of negative capability—of the poet's loss or lack of personal identity—by Hazlitt's *Essay on the Principles of Human Action* (1805),[4] an essay which bore the sub-title 'Being an Argument in favour of the Natural Disinterestedness of the Human Mind', and which was only pursued and completed under the encouragement of Coleridge.[5] So that the possibility of German influence is not entirely ruled out. Yet even if it were to be established, it would be important to bring out the contrast as well as the likeness. For Keats, negative capability appears to be the only necessary condition of 'achievement'. For Schiller it is no less necessary that it should—and even in the poet—be combined with 'a sense of reality'.

Whether, then, we go into questions of historical influence or are, like Lohner,[6] frankly—and legitimately—ready to disregard these in the interests of demonstrating the close parallels between Schiller's views on art and those of modern poets, we ought in any future study to pay far more attention to problems of structural differences of thought within apparent, even verbal, likeness.[7] We ourselves, for example, are not at all sure that we are altogether right to have identified Schiller's *Gleichgültig-*

[1] XXI. 4 and 5. Cf. above, p. clviii.

[2] pp. lxxxi ff., esp. p. lxxxiv.

[3] And according to W. J. Bate (*John Keats*, Cambridge, Mass., 1963, pp. 238 f.), he caught very little of it from Coleridge.

[4] Ibid., pp. 256 and 260 f.

[5] *The Complete Works of William Hazlitt.* Centenary Edition by P. P. Howe, London, 1930, i: editor's note facing p. 1.

[6] Loc. cit., p. 148: 'Dabei spielt es keine Rolle, ob diese Dichter Schiller gekannt haben oder nicht.'

[7] Faced with the 'reciprocal subordination' of historical and structural considerations in Wilkinson, loc. cit. (2) and (4), Paulsen (loc. cit., pp. 444, 388) professes bewilderment 'vor dieser Art von Argumentierung' and discerns in it 'etwas Unverbindliches'. Perhaps because he didn't identify the method.

keit and *Bestimmbarkeit* with Valéry's *indifférence* and *disponibilité*.[1] But
the suggestion may provoke someone else to probe the precise nature of
the difference. Just as Lohner's admirable essay has provoked us to the
following reservations. He is probably right[2] to infer a similar structure
of thought underlying the astonishingly close verbal parallel between T. S.
Eliot's theory of the 'objective correlative' and a passage in Schiller's
well-known letter to Goethe of 27 March 1801:

> Anyone who is capable of objectifying a state of feeling in such a way that this
> object then compels me to enter into that same state of feeling, and in con-
> sequence works upon the life within me, I would call a poet, or maker.

Though Schiller's position is far more sharply defined in his essay *Über
Matthissons Gedichte*,[3] and it seems to us doubtful whether—at any rate in
the form it has there—it would, as Lohner surmises, be vulnerable to the
sort of objections that have been levelled against Eliot's formulation.
And Lohner is undoubtedly right, too, when he discerns[4] in that same
letter to Goethe an anticipation of the modern poet's attachment to the
idea of poetry as a deliberate making rather than an involuntary becoming
(*entstehen*): his preoccupation with the conscious aspects of the creative
process, as this has developed through Baudelaire and Poe, Flaubert and
Henry James, Mallarmé and Valéry—with their talk of poems as *études*
or *exercices*—down to Gottfried Benn's insistence on 'artistry' and critical
control, on the logic and mechanics of devices deliberately employed. But
here, surely, it would be important to explore far more thoroughly a
number of crucial differences. It might not, for instance, have been
inapposite to observe that Oscar Wilde, surveying this same development
in the nineteenth-century 'Renaissance' of poetry, traced the resurgence
of self-consciousness, not just to Goethe and Schiller, but right back to
the Greeks.[5] Or that Schiller himself in using the foreign word *Poet*, and
deliberately pointing its etymology, was acknowledging his own debt to
antiquity. And it would certainly have been relevant to bring out far
more strongly the extent to which—and in that same letter too—Schiller
emphasizes the indispensability of *un*-conscious processes in both the
making and the effect of poetry. Lohner does admittedly draw a contrast
with Poe, who denied all knowledge of chance, intuition, or any initial
obscure conception:[6] of that 'erste dunkle, aber mächtige Total-Idee'
which, according to Schiller, the poet fearfully hopes that he may, 'by the
most lucid awareness of his own mental operations, find realized with

---

[1] See our Note to XV. 9. We should feel even more hesitant about identifying them
with Gide's *disponibilité*.
[2] Loc. cit., pp. 135 f.   [3] See above, p. xxviii.
[4] Loc. cit., pp. 133 ff.   [5] See above, p. clxviii.
[6] 'The Philosophy of Composition' (1846); *Complete Works of Edgar Allan Poe*. Ed.
by J. A. Harrison, New York, 1902, xiv. 194 f.

undiminished power in his completed work'. What Lohner does not add is Schiller's insistence that 'without such an initial, obscure but powerful, conception of the whole, an intuition which precedes all the technical labour, no poetic work can come into being (*entstehen*) at all'. Nor does he quote his definition of poetry as 'the articulation and communication of that unconscious conception'. Or his precisely balanced contrast between two types of non-poet: the one who, no less than the poet, may be moved by a poetic idea but lacks the power to objectify it; the other who imagines that everything can be achieved by conscious artistry alone.

But the non-poet can also, no less than the poet, produce a work in full consciousness and with a logic of its own. Yet such a work will remain merely a product of reflection; for it does not take its origin in the unconscious, or find its end therein.

Above all it would have been illuminating to mention Schiller's point of departure in this exchange of letters with Goethe. It was their joint repudiation of Schelling's transcendental, and totally a-psychological, contention that art reverses nature's direction and proceeds from consciousness to unconsciousness. This ran counter to their own experience of the creative process, with its unceasing two-way traffic between unconscious and conscious.[1] The perfect balance of their position comes out in Schiller's conclusion that the mark of the true poet, as distinct from either type of non-poet, is the *interaction* of conscious with unconscious: 'Das Bewusstlose mit dem Besonnenen vereinigt macht den poetischen Künstler aus.' It is this balance—together with their 'zarte Empirie', their scrupulous respect for the realities of poetic experience where these controvert the propositions of Idealist philosophy—that marks them as 'classical': classical in temper and tradition—a temper not always absent from minds we might in other respects tend to class as 'romantic'. *Besonnenheit*, as we saw,[2] was one of Herder's key-terms. And the ancient paradox of the poet as a waking or rational dreamer, with which Schiller had operated some fifteen years earlier in a letter to Körner on a similar theme,[3] is also employed by such diverse thinkers as Moses Mendelssohn[4] and Coleridge.[5]

We emphasize this diversity in order to underline the limitations, as well as the usefulness, of all such categories. There has been a marked tendency in the many recent, and laudable, attempts to dislodge Schiller from his Olympian perch, and bring him closer to our own needs and problems, to replace 'classical' or 'romantic' by the category 'modern'.

[1] Cf. above, pp. xxxvii f. and cl f.
[2] See above, p. liii.
[3] Translated in our Note to XXVII. 4fn.
[4] Letter to Abbt, [*c.* August 1764]; *Ges. Schriften*, ed. cit. v. 330.
[5] *Notebooks*, ed. cit. ii, entry 2086.

One sometimes wonders whether there is not here some confusion between modernity and relevance—and a consequent risk of obscuring precisely those aspects of his thought which might have a special appeal to us today just because they distinguish him from the so-called 'moderns'. Neither Lohner nor Benno von Wiese[1]—who rightly sees in Schiller's principle of distance an anticipation of Gottfried Benn's or Thomas Mann's intimate knowledge of 'das kühle Laboratorium der Kunst'—really puts his finger on the precise nature of the radical change that occurred somewhere along the line of development from the one to the other. For the difference is not just one of degree. The poet's knowledge of his own mental processes did not simply get 'clearer' or 'cooler' as time went on. His mental 'model' of artistic creation underwent a complete change. If Poe says that 'poetry, in elevating, tranquillizes the *soul*. With the heart it has nothing to do';[2] or if Wilde gives this a characteristically challenging twist with the paradox 'all bad poetry springs from genuine feeling'[3]—they are not just *over*-stating their case. They have got the structure of Schiller's thought fundamentally out of true. For he faced up to the fact that a great deal of good poetry springs from genuine feeling too; and in his review of Bürger's poems stated explicitly that, *provided a poet can achieve the necessary distance from his passion*, then the more he has experienced in his own person the better it will be for his poetry.[4] What really happened in the course of the nineteenth century was the reduction of this subtle principle of 'psychical distance' to the simplistic notion of intellectual detachment; a change from dynamic thinking in terms of process to static thinking in terms of entities. Processes which in Schiller's view could still, though distinguishable, alternate or even coexist within the same mind, became hypostasized into two creatures within one skin: the Man and the Poet.[5] And the possibility, even the desirability, of commerce between the two was increasingly called in question, not only in accounts of the creative process but in the field of literary criticism too. Of late there have been clear signs of a strong reaction against the whole idea of such a dichotomy. Understandable, and prompted by a healthy instinct, it is nevertheless argued with little logic, a total lack of historical sense, and a marked tendency—not uncommon in reactions—to throw away valid positions won long ago but fouled up in the heat of more recent skirmishes. It would be irony indeed if principles of Schiller's strategy which might provide a

---

[1] *Friedrich Schiller*, ed. cit., pp. 433 f.

[2] *Works*, ed. cit. xiii. 131; cf. xiv. 197.

[3] 'The Critic as Artist'; *Intentions* (Methuen's Popular Edition, London, 1911[5]), p. 201.

[4] SA xvi. 239. The thought is retained in his contention at the end of XXII. 5 (see our Note) that there is certainly such a thing as an art of passion, but that a passionate art is a contradiction in terms.

[5] Cf. Wilkinson on 'Künstlerische Distanz', loc. cit. (2), esp. pp. 73 f., 79 f.

relevant, and even welcome, corrective to these reactionary tactics were to be eclipsed in the name of a modernity which is even now no longer modern.

And if this holds for his views on the making of art, it holds no less for the equally vexed question of the effect and function of art. Since he was probably not without influence on the rise of the aesthetic movement, and was certainly claimed as an ancestor by the high priests of 'pure form' and 'art for art's sake', it is perhaps not unnatural that these labels should have stuck. Chiefly on the evidence of a single much-quoted statement that in a true work of art the subject-matter (*Stoff*) will be entirely consumed (*vertilgt*) by the form (XXII. 5). Yet as Böhm pointed out long ago,[1] and as Wellek has since confirmed,[2] this does not at all warrant the conclusion that he was out to rob us of subject-matter altogether. Unfortunately the arguments they adduce in support of their basically correct judgement tend to obscure Schiller's position rather than illuminate it. Böhm's distinction between 'subjective' and 'objective' *Stoff* is superfluous, if not actually untenable; his identification of the latter with 'technical form' is impossible: Schiller never uses *Stoff* to mean *Form*, technical or otherwise.[3] Wellek, by identifying these two terms with the Kantian 'dualism between mere unorganized sense data and the categories of man's mind', shifts the discussion from an aesthetic to an epistemological context (a slip not uncommon in Schiller scholarship). All that *Stoff* can include when used by Goethe and Schiller we have set forth in our Glossary.[4] For them, anything that the world offers to the artist, whether unorganized or already highly organized, may legitimately be regarded by him as mere raw material for his own formative purposes. A major cause, one suspects, of much misinterpretation of the offending sentence is failure to recognize the hidden biological metaphor in the word *vertilgen*: the process of hierarchical organization, as the forms of whatever material is consumed are broken down and assimilated to the principle of a 'higher' form. To render the word by 'obliterate' (Pater),[5] or 'annihilate' (Wilde),[6] or 'erase' (Wellek),[7] does indeed make it sound as though Schiller wants to empty art of subject-matter if not of content.[8] In fact the subject-matter is still all there in the finished work—but completely transmuted, if the artist is a master at his job, by the formative principle which pervades its every detail. But in any case, within Schiller's system of thought—as a close student of his language must soon realize—the forms of art,

---

[1] Op. cit., p. 82.   [2] Op. cit. i. 233 f.
[3] The single, deliberate and meaningful, exception is discussed on pp. lxxii f., above.
[4] See under both *Inhalt* and *Materie*.
[5] *The Renaissance*, ed. cit., p. 129. Cf. above, p. clxvi.
[6] 'Lecture to Art Students'; *Essays and Lectures*, ed. cit., p. 212.
[7] Op. cit. i. 234.
[8] On the distinction see Glossary under *Gehalt*.

unlike those of logic or mathematics, are never 'pure'. They are always 'mixed': always 'living forms',[1] whether the adjective is actually there, or only implied by the context.

But if Schiller cannot with justice be held responsible for any sort of doctrine of pure form, can he be held responsible for any version of art for art's sake? The answer here is both yes and no: it all depends what is meant by it. Gilbert and Kuhn[2] repudiate Rose F. Egan's thesis that this 'was not an original creation of the group of French writers generally credited with it, but pre-existed in German philosophy and criticism', on the grounds that inquiries 'into the historical roots of any phenomenon [are] easily tempted into a derivation *ab ovo*'. Maybe! But temptation has an uncanny way of exerting its strongest pressures upon virtue. And the virtue of such inquiries is that they give us a sense of perspective, and preserve us from the heresy that originality is necessarily the enemy of tradition. One reviewer[3] of Louise Rosenblatt's later book on *L'Idée de l'art pour l'art* actually takes *her* to task for precisely the opposite failing: for not tracing its ancestry back far enough; for presenting it as a peculiar outgrowth of the nineteenth century, instead of showing that writers of the Renaissance, and their classical originals, have as much claim to be included in the tradition as Ruskin, Arnold, or the *fin-de-siècle* school. While E. H. Gombrich[4] points to what he believes to be the first clear enunciation of the principle in Lessing's *Laokoon* (1766), and tells us that the famous phrase itself—usually attributed to Gautier, but also claimed by Victor Hugo[5]—was actually used three years later by Herder in his *Kritische Wälder* (1769): 'Ein Kunstwerk ist der Kunst wegen da'. Gilbert and Kuhn rightly observe that the principle of the 'autonomy' of art means something utterly different in Winckelmann, Goethe, or Schlegel on the one hand, and in Flaubert or Wilde on the other. But that, surely, is the point. What exactly was the difference? And how and why did it come about? Did Thackeray, apparently the first to use the phrase in England, mean the same as Herder when he wrote in 1839:[6] 'Please God we shall begin, ere long, to love art for art's sake'? Or when he claimed that Carlyle—at first sight a highly improbable candidate for the honour

---

[1] Since making our point (in Glossary under *Form*) that this 'schema' represents a condensed chiasmus, we found interesting evidence of its classical origin in T. B. L. Webster's *Art and Literature in Fourth Century Athens*, London, 1956, p. 9: 'Thus both the two opposite tendencies [of Greek art and literature], the enlivening of the formal and the formalizing of the living, continue to operate in [the] fourth century . . .'.

[2] Op. cit., p. 485, fn.

[3] B. E. C. Davis, *MLR* xxvii (1932), 345 f.

[4] *Lessing*, Proceedings of the British Academy, xliii (1957), 141.

[5] Cf. G. Highet, *The Classical Tradition*, Oxford, 1949, p. 444.

[6] Letter to his mother. Cf. Anne Thackeray Ritchie, *Chapters from Some Memoirs*, London, 1894, p. 140.

—had 'worked more than any other to give it its independence'? Scarcely, if—as Miss Egan surmises[1]—he was using it in the restricted sense of 'freedom from service to political causes'. On the other hand, did he mean something wholly and irreconcilably different from Herder? Or from Baudelaire when he wrote:[2] 'La poésie ne peut pas, sous peine de mort ou de déchéance, s'assimiler à la science ou à la morale; elle n'a pas la Vérité pour objet; elle n'a qu'Elle-même'? Schiller would have been at one with any or all of them in maintaining that art is 'autonomous', in the sense of not being subservient to alien ends, whether political or social, ethical or intellectual. He was no less suspicious than Poe of 'the heresy of *The Didactic*',[3] the demand that every poem should communicate a truth or inculcate a moral: it was the butt of his irony at the end of Letter XXVI. And his firm distinction between subject-matter and function would have preserved him from that beguiling modern version of it which *will* have it that because a good deal of literature treats of moral choices, and hence of moral values, it cannot possibly be morally neutral in its effects. History and experience had taught him better. On the other hand, he could never have agreed with Poe that a poem is either written, or that it exists, 'solely for the poem's sake'.[4] This would have smacked to him of a confusion between form and function. And although in the scientific study of works of nature it has often proved of great advantage not to distinguish between these two, in both the theoretical and the critical study of works of art it is essential to do so. That self-sufficiency, which (in Letter XV) Schiller acclaimed as the mark of all great art, was for him a property of the *form*. He did not therefore conclude that this self-sufficient form had no *function*. It is not the *end* of poetry which turns back upon itself in self-stultifying sterility. It is the *language* of poetry which—in constant involution, like the motion of a serpent—turns back upon itself to achieve a self-sufficiency which is absent from the linear movement of discursive prose. Schiller's position is not that of Baudelaire and Poe at all—'elle n'a pas d'autre but qu'Elle-même'. It is more like that of Benjamin Constant: 'L'art pour l'art, et sans but; tout but dénature l'art. *Mais l'art atteint au but qu'il n'a pas.*'[5] Constant attributed this 'idée très ingénieuse' to Crabb Robinson's discussions of Kant's aesthetics. But he was seeing a good deal of Schiller at the time. And Schiller could certainly have told either of them, whether in conversation or through his published work, just what that further 'end' was. For it was this very issue between himself and Kant that had provoked

[1] Op. cit. i. 15.

[2] In 'Théophile Gautier' (1859); *Œuvres complètes*, Paris, 1961, p. 685.

[3] *Works*, ed. cit. xiv. 271.   [4] Ibid., p. 272.

[5] *Journaux intimes*, 11. ii. 1804; ed. A. Roulin and C. Roth, Paris, 1952, p. 58. Our italics.

him to produce a treatise on aesthetic education.[1] The immediate end of
art, according to him, was the articulation of the otherwise inexpressible
life within us. And it is for this reason that, though he might well have
endorsed Wilde's dictum that 'emotion for the sake of action is the aim of
life', he could never have endorsed his conclusion that 'emotion for the
sake of emotion is the aim of art'.[2] Its aim was *understanding*: the enlargement and deepening of insight into ourselves and others. And he would
without doubt have endorsed Pater's advocacy of the aesthetic transformation of daily life:[3] the elevation of even its 'trivialities'—the furniture of
our houses, dress, and fashion, 'gesture and speech, and the details of daily
intercourse'—into 'ends in themselves'. But for him this 'elevation into
ends in themselves' has a further end. It is to be done, not just because
these things thereby acquire 'a mysterious grace and attractiveness in the
doing of them', but because—as he argues in Letter XXIII—it is in this
'aesthetically free handling of common reality', in this 'indifferent sphere
of physical life', that man's *moral* life must begin. Again he would have
agreed with him that unless art is free of adventitious subterfuge it can
never work its own, unique and irreplaceable, effects; that it must come
to us 'proposing frankly to give nothing but the highest quality to [our]
moments as they pass'.[4] But he would never have gone along with him as
far as that final phrase of his famous Conclusion to *The Renaissance*: 'and
simply for those moments' sake'. For Pater, 'success in life'[5] lay in maintaining the ecstasy of these heightened 'moments as they pass'. For
Schiller, it lay in discovering 'form' in the whole variety of our moments,
ecstatic or otherwise. That is the felt conviction behind his rhetorical
device of converting a plurality of momentary experiences into a series
of singular abstractions at the end of XVI. 2.[6] This may well send our
thoughts in the direction of Paul Valéry's aphorism: 'Man is born in the
plural, he dies in the singular.' But for Valéry, as for Pater, this 'singu-
larity' results from our unfortunate tendency 'to form habits', to succumb
to the pressures of 'a stereotyped world'.[7] It implies loss of 'openness',
loss of 'freedom', loss of those innumerable possibilities with which we
started out in life. For Schiller, on the other hand, there is indeed a necessary, a philosophical, connexion between loss of infinite potential and the
limited 'form' of all realization. But between the discovery of our 'identity',
the shaping of a formed personality, and any loss of 'openness' or flexibility in ourselves there is none. This is a contingent, a psychological,
problem. And to combine 'openness' with 'form', 'extensity' with 'intensity',

---

[1] See above, pp. xxiv ff.
[2] 'The Critic as Artist'; *Intentions*, ed. cit., p. 169.
[3] *The Renaissance*, ed. cit., pp. 131 f.   [4] Ibid., p. 224.
[5] Ibid., p. 222.   [6] See our Note and pp. 345 f., below.
[7] *The Renaissance*, ed. cit., p. 222.

is in his eyes a psychological achievement. Hence he can see it as both a result of our freedom and a sure sign of our increasing freedom. And for him this more than compensates for the loss of that initial freedom of infinite possibility.[1] To Wilde's aphorism 'life is terribly deficient in form',[2] therefore, he might well have replied: it is our business to give it form. But he would have been profoundly suspicious of his consequent prognostication that 'as civilization progresses, and we become more highly organized, the elect spirits of each age, the critical and cultured spirits, will grow less and less interested in actual life, and *will seek to gain their impressions almost entirely from what Art has touched*'.[3] He would have thought it completely wrong-headed of them if they did! Just as he would almost certainly have disapproved of Coleridge's or Carlyle's intellectual *élite*.[4] For although he was too realistic not to admit (as indeed he does in the concluding paragraph of his treatise) that aesthetic education is, in the present state of society, the privilege of some few 'elect spirits', his *desideratum*—that 'task for more than *one* century' outlined in Letter VII —was the aesthetic education of the whole of society. And he never envisaged this coming about through the withdrawal of the 'elect', or through a neglect of 'actual life' in favour of impressions derived from art. All this—like Pater's 'not the fruit of experience but experience itself is the end', or Gide's 'culte du moi'—was bound, he would have thought (to judge from his strictures on the aestheticism of past ages), to result in the 'immoralism' we associate with Nietzsche's romanticizing of aesthetic grandeur, regardless of whether it be good or evil. It lacks that ethical and social awareness which Hofmannsthal, rightly or wrongly, held to be the great difference between the English and the French aesthetic movement—an issue on which he eventually came to differ strongly from Stefan George,[5] whose *Blätter für die Kunst* had been prefaced by the programmatic statement that they were intended 'der kunst besonders der dichtung und dem schrifttum dienen, alles staatliche und gesellschaftliche ausscheidend'. And it is precisely this civic concern which makes Hofmannsthal seem closer to Schiller than any advocate of 'pure form' could ever be—even George himself, for all his admiration of the *Aesthetic Letters* and his own efforts on behalf of aesthetic education.[6]

---

[1] Cf. our introductory Note to Letter XI.

[2] *Intentions*, ed. cit., p. 158.

[3] Ibid. Wilde's italics.   [4] See above, p. clv.

[5] Cf. Michael Hamburger, 'Hofmannsthal and England' in *Hofmannsthal. Studies in Commemoration*. University of London Institute of Germanic Studies, London, 1963, p. 15.

[6] It is for this reason that we remain finally unpersuaded by Melitta Gerhard's in many ways persuasive attempt to demonstrate the closeness of their educational ideal: 'Schillers Zielbild der ästhetischen Erziehung und das Wirken Stefan Georges', *Monatshefte*, li (1959), 275 ff.

Not form for form's sake, then; nor even art for art's sake; and certainly not—in the vein of Schopenhauer—art for death's sake, an escape from the tyrannous pressures of the Will into the Nirvana of pure contemplation. But art for life's sake—and for the sake of 'the even more difficult *art* of life' (XV. 9). And not just in the sense of the enhancement or enrichment of the life of the individual, but for the better ordering of the life of the community. Yet pervading all Schiller's faith in the efficacy of art, or his hope that men may become wise enough to know how to use it, is his realistic—and sometimes sceptical—insight that this will indeed depend on their wisdom. In other words, he was never under any illusion that the benefits of art will automatically proceed from the virtue inherent in it. On the contrary: they will depend on men's decisions about what sort of art they want, and what sort of function they expect it to perform. So that having never assigned unqualified primacy to aesthetic values, he never—like a Schelling or a Pater—found himself in the position of having to recant in favour of religion or morality. Nor was he guilty of the 'fallacy of the single factor'. So that while steadfastly maintaining that there is indeed something art alone can do, he never claimed that it can do everything. Hence he would have agreed with Poe that taste has a social function to perform in leading us 'gently back to Beauty, to Nature, and to Life'.[1] But he would have thought it was asking too much of taste to expect, as Poe did, that 'it alone' can do this. Indeed the astonishing thing about Schiller's theory, in view of the fact that he was himself a poet, is that he is as much concerned to keep art in its place[2] as to show forth its unique and inalienable power. The full realism—and the full scepticism—of his position is perhaps most succinctly, and most faithfully, reflected in Goethe's aphorism: 'There is no more certain way of escaping the world than through art, and there is no more certain way of connecting with it than through art.'[3]

*   *   *

The prime object of such an exercise in comparative morphology is not to enhance Schiller's prestige. Let alone by trying to claim 'originality' for him in the sense of establishing the 'priority' of his ideas—an enterprise which the eighteenth century was still inclined to view with profound, and very proper, suspicion.[4] It should be undertaken not for his

---

[1] 'The Colloquy of Monos and Una'; *Works*, ed. cit. iv. 204.

[2] This is an important point that Lohner (loc. cit., p. 151) fails to bring out when he draws parallels between Schiller's arguments in Letter XXVI and Baudelaire's separation of poetry, art, and beauty from truth, science, and morality. Schiller is concerned with their *mutual* trespassings, intrusions, and encroachments. His expressed intention —and in spaced type—is to safeguard the frontiers of truth and morality no less than the autonomy of art.

[3] *Die Wahlverwandtschaften*; JA xxi. 191.

[4] Witness the rejoinders to Louis Dutens' influential *Recherches sur l'origine des*

sake but for ours. And chiefly in order to show up where responsibility for misunderstanding him may reasonably be laid at his own door, and where it must be fairly and squarely placed upon the shoulders of his interpreters. But it would also, we suspect, confirm in a quite dramatic way—by demonstrating the sometimes disastrous consequences of wittingly or unwittingly fragmenting his theory—the systematic coherence revealed by close structural analysis of the text. A coherence which Fichte discerned as a 'felt unity' in Schiller's thought even before he had seen this particular treatise, and which, so he told Wilhelm von Humboldt,[1] only needed to be cast into the form of a system in order to prove 'epoch-making' (the fact that he did not much care for the manner of the systematization when he eventually saw it is another matter).[2] Above all we could imagine that such a comparative enterprise might well expose clearly to view the key-position occupied in Schiller's theory by the two related concepts which have proved the greatest stumbling-block of all to whole-hearted acceptance of Weimar aesthetics: semblance and play. Presumably because it is still felt by some that *Schein* can be cultivated only at the expense of *Sein*. By Max Bense, for instance, who in the first volume of his much-quoted *Aesthetica* (1954) repudiated 'semblance' (though attributing it to Hegel, not Schiller) in favour of the much 'richer, deeper, and more complex' concept of 'sign' or 'symbol' (*Zeichen*) because, as he opined, 'all suggestion of "unworthiness" is thereby avoided and the theme of Being more clearly and more impressively sounded'.[3] Whether symbol is a 'richer' or 'deeper' concept than semblance is hardly worth discussing: these are metaphors of immensely seductive, but not very luminous power. Whether it is more 'complex' is dubious. That it is far wider, on the other hand, is indisputable. So wide, in fact, as to be useless —unless associated with semblance. For otherwise we are left without any criterion for distinguishing the symbols of art from the whole variety of signs and symbols by which man lives, and makes sense of the world in which he lives. Finally, whether 'symbol' sounds the theme of 'Being' either more clearly, or more impressively, than 'semblance' is highly debatable. One would have thought that it was now fairly clear from that most recent—and most influential—of the human sciences, 'perception studies', how much we are dependent for our understanding of the 'being' of the world outside us upon semblances both false and true, upon our

découvertes attribuées aux modernes (1766), or Klopstock's ruminations on the difference between *Erfindung* and *Entdeckung*—from both of which Coleridge derived consolation when brooding on the problem of his own originality (*Notebooks*, ed. cit. i, entries 387, 930, 950, 1315, 1316, and notes thereto; cf. Wilkinson, 'Coleridge und Deutschland', ed. cit., pp. 21–23)—or Goethe's pronouncements on 'priority' and 'plagiarism'.

[1] Reported in von Humboldt's letter to Schiller of 22.ix.1794.

[2] See above, pp. cxii ff.

[3] *Aesthetica*, Stuttgart, 1954–60, i. 39 f. Cf. Wilkinson, loc. cit. (i), pp. 220, 226 f.

interpretations, appropriate and inappropriate, of the data it presents to our senses. This is something that Schiller, as a true son of the eighteenth century, understood very well indeed.[1] It is something that Lohner, despite his in many ways perceptive account of Schiller's *Schein*, does not perceive.[2] Otherwise he would scarcely insist that it makes no sense to take Schiller literally when, in an admittedly difficult passage of XXVI. 8, he talks of the artist 're-claiming' semblance from being, and asserting his undisputed rights of ownership by treating it according to laws of his own. The verb *zurücknehmen*, Lohner argues, must here be understood in the less usual sense of 'separate' or 'take away': it cannot possibly mean 'take back'. But this precisely is what it *does* mean. For since semblance is not a property of 'being' itself, but a product of the mind which construes it, man may indeed be said to be simply reclaiming what is his own when he starts treating it as an autonomous realm in the creation of works of art. Lohner's misunderstanding is but one among many examples of a failure to move, as rapidly—and with such certain dexterity—as Schiller himself, from the epistemological to the aesthetic sphere, and beyond that again to the moral.[3]

As for the relation of semblance to the 'being' of the world within us, to the gradual establishment of our own feeling of personal identity, we should have thought that the supplication of Goethe's Mignon,

So lasst mich scheinen bis ich werde,

had been more than amply borne out by both psychology and philosophy. We have only to think of all that we have learnt about the serious function (as distinct from any consciously serious intent) underlying the seemingly gratuitous play of children. Or of that interesting revival of 'the truth of masks',[4] Jung's doctrine of the *persona*: that semblance of personality, without which we cannot live or hope to grow into a true 'self' —to identify completely with which, however, is to abandon all hope of doing either. Our thoughts may very well be turned in this direction when we read what Schiller has to say about honest and dishonest, free and dependent, semblance in Letter XXVI: about those who turn courtesy into deceit by flattering for their own ends; or—more subtle still—those who take all forms of courtesy as an infallible sign of insincerity; or—and perhaps subtlest of all—those who are unsophisticated, and unfree, enough to expect more of the forms of courtesy and consideration than they are designed to offer. But these same passages may also turn our thoughts in a quite different direction: towards recent 'existential' ponderings on such problems of identity and identification. Towards Sartre's

---

[1] See our Notes to XXVI. 6, and p. xxvii, above.
[2] Loc. cit., pp. 138 f.
[3] For other examples see above, p. clxxvi, and our Note to XXVI. 7.
[4] See above, p. clx and fn. 1.

suspicion that we are all acting parts—the man who is a doctor, the part of a doctor; the man who is a waiter, the part of a waiter; he who mourns, the role of sadness; and he who is considerate, the role of concern—and that this cannot be otherwise, since a man has no pre-existent essence determining what he must be. Schiller's sense of the ambiguity of human life and human conduct was no less sharp, and in a way no less afflicted, than Sartre's: we can infer as much from his treatise; we know it, and often poignantly, from his poetry and his plays. What, then, preserved him from concluding, as Sartre does, that we must all be in a condition of *mauvaise foi*? That '*dis*-honest semblance' is the destiny thrust upon us? Or that the only escape we are offered from it is the marginal chance of an *acte gratuit*? How is it that he was able to accept the fact that semblance we have always with us, inseparable from our human condition, and yet treat it as neutral? More than that: believe that in honest semblance there lies the hope of transforming man's whole way of life? Is the difference between them a logical one? Is Sartre's trouble, as Alasdair MacIntyre has suggested,[1] that at a certain point of his argument he 'makes a false move'? That he 'proceeds to assimilate the (conceptual and necessary) facts that everybody has to comprehend themselves under descriptions, and by means of concepts, which they did not make, to the (psychological and contingent) facts that some people cannot identify with their roles, while others indulge in dramatization or pretence'? And would we be justified in concluding that on this, as on related issues,[2] Schiller did not thus confuse the logical with the psychological? Or are we to explain it differently, and say that he had more faith in man's power to adjust by conscious effort his unconscious preconceptions and prejudices, whether epistemological or ethical? Or are we to put it all down to a difference of temperament, conviction, or the prevailing *Zeitgeist*? The difference between Sartre's *acte gratuit*, for instance, and that quality of 'supererogatory' grace which Schiller thought might occasionally be observable even in those sublime acts of self-sacrifice in which a man achieves more than our moral experience would lead us to expect of him, is not only one of structure. It is also one of temper. For in Sartre the meagre possibility of escape from the conformity of habitual behaviour into an act of 'pure authenticity' has nothing to do with grace (in either sense of the word). The 'overplus' remains moral in character (one wonders—in view of his strictures in XXIII. 7fn.—what Schiller would have thought of such a dubious concept); and it is, moreover, only likely to be achieved by those who are committed in a particular political direction. In Schiller, by contrast, it has that gratuitous quality of grace abounding which inheres, parodoxically, in the concept of 'super-

---

[1] *The Listener*, 22.iii.1962.
[2] Cf. above, pp. clxxix f.

erogation';[1] and it may—contrary to all expectations, and against all possible predictions—be granted to any man, and of whatever persuasion.

With the word 'observable' we have touched on something that removes Schiller as far from the Existentialists as from the Kantians. For profoundly as these may otherwise differ, they have one thing in common: their emphasis is on the view from within, on what Heine called the 'invisible thought', as opposed to the 'visible work',[2] on the unseen 'purity' of will, or 'authenticity' of conviction, rather than on the articulation of these as they become manifest to others. Schiller is at least as interested in the view from without—yet another example of his equal concern with the subjective and objective poles of any activity. At first sight, his faith in form might tempt one to find an affinity with those Existentialists who maintain that in a moral act the content is nothing, the manner everything. But he would never have extrapolated thus from his theory of art to a theory of morals. In the first place he would have denied that the content is irrelevant. And in the second place he understood something different by 'manner'. For them, manner applies to the reality of belief *behind* the performance. For him, it also includes the manifest manner of the performance itself: all those overt bodily signs and symptoms whose significance an observer may indeed interpret so promptly and unconsciously that he could never give an account of them, but which are nevertheless there to be observed.

It is this concern with the manifest and the observable which in a way removes Schiller from philosophy altogether, and brings him within the orbit of the human sciences. Not just of psychology or perception studies, but of those schools of anthropology which, taking language as their model, have turned their attention to the whole field of cultural communication: to what has been called 'the silent language',[3] the manifold means whereby people 'talk' to each other without the use of words. In the light of such endeavour it might be well worth re-examining, not only Schiller's attitude to the vexed question of 'moral beauty', but also his attempt to find a criterion of beauty itself in the notion of 'freedom made manifest'. And it would certainly be worth re-examining his whole theory of play as a primary instinct which finds its highest human manifestation in aesthetic phenomena. For if some recent investigations of both human and animal play have revealed it as not just an excess of animal spirits, or a luxury product of the mind, but rather one of the primary message-systems, a

[1] Colin Smith (*Contemporary French Philosophy. A Study in Norms and Values*, London, 1964, p. 228) refers to A. MacIntyre's use of this theological parallel in 'What Morality is not', *Philosophy*, xxxii (1957). Our own use of the term 'supererogatory' in XXIII. 7fn. (cf. p. lxxxviii, above) was prompted by the theological overtones of Schiller's own language (see our Notes to XXIII. 7fn. §2 and XXIV. 3).

[2] See above, p. cxli.

[3] The title of a book by the anthropologist, Edward T. Hall (New York, 1959).

means of communication, other investigations—such as research into the painting activity of apes—seem to show that some form of aesthetic satisfaction may be a primary need even in animals, and not reducible to a mere secondary function of more 'primitive' instincts. Both sets of findings would be relevant to a better understanding of Schiller's 'play-drive'. And it is not inconceivable that his distinctions might, in return, prove relevant to the evaluation of these recent findings. But not, of course, until the original form of his theory has been unearthed from under the rubble of misconceptions that has overlaid it. Herbert Spencer may seem to have damned it with faint praise when, in the revised version of his *Principles of Psychology* (1870–2), he invoked in support of his own association of play with aesthetic activities 'the statement of a German author', whose name he could not remember, 'as being one which, if not literally true, is yet the adumbration of a truth'.[1] But at least Spencer did not distort Schiller's theory. Huizinga, in his 'Study of the Play-Element in Culture', *Homo Ludens* (1938), distorts it in a way that is only explicable on the assumption that he can have read little more of the treatise than the single Letter (XIV) to which he actually refers.[2] Schiller does not, as he alleges, attempt to explain 'style' in art by means of the 'play-instinct' alone. On the contrary, he expressly states that the making of art also involves 'the imitative formative drive' (*nachahmender Bildungstrieb*), together with urges and talents of which he does not propose to treat in his present context (XXVI. 7).[3] So that when Huizinga objects that 'it seems preposterous to ascribe the cave-paintings of Altamira, for instance, to mere doodling—which is what it amounts to if they are ascribed to the "play-instinct" ', and insists that the 'plastic urge' involves not only decoration, but construction and imitation too, he is merely saying what Schiller himself had said before him. When he suggests that Schiller applied his play-drive to the plastic arts alone, he is reducing the scope of his theory in a quite unwarrantable way: Schiller did not even apply it to art alone; like Huizinga himself, he was concerned with its manifold functioning in human culture as a whole. While when he equates it with 'mere doodling', he is simply creating a pseudo-object against which to direct his redundant criticism. What Huizinga in fact employs is the by no means untypical gambit of tilting at windmills he has first erected himself. And it has the unfortunate consequence of obscuring that very point in Schiller's theory which might prove of permanent value in any comprehensive study of the role of play in animal and human societies: his handling of differentiation within continuity. His establishment, on the one hand, of an unbroken continuity between even our highest forms of aesthetic activity and our biological inheritance—between art at its most

---

[1] ii. 627. [2] Ed. cit., pp. 168 f.
[3] See our Note thereto and pp. lxvi f., above.

sophisticated and what he called 'material' play, whether this occurs in animals or in humans. His insistence, on the other hand, that within this unbroken continuity there are, nevertheless, differences not just of degree but of kind.[1] When E. F. Carritt, in his *Theory of Beauty* (1914)[2], doubted whether anything was to be gained for aesthetic theory by a term which does such violence to linguistic usage, he was missing the first point: Schiller himself, after all, had confronted precisely the same sort of doubts, and decided that the continuity implied by the use of a single term outweighed any possible affront to normal usage.[3] When De Witt H. Parker, on the other hand, in his *Analysis of Art* (1926),[4] objected to 'Schiller's famous pronouncement that man is a whole man only when he plays' on the grounds that in games, even of the intellectual type, man 'is usually only a fragment of himself', he was missing the second point: Schiller's insistence on discontinuity within continuity. And he misses it, moreover, for precisely the same reason that Huizinga and others have missed it: because he takes issue with a single passage instead of with the theory as a whole. Hence, exactly like Huizinga—though with a greater show of sympathy—he counters 'the authority of Schiller's famous pronouncement' of XV. 9 with arguments he could well have derived from Schiller himself. 'Not in play but in art', he triumphantly concludes, 'is man a whole man'—which is what Schiller had already implied in XV. 8. And he appears to have overlooked completely the traditional rhetorical gambit of postponement with which the paradoxical sounding proposition, as Schiller himself calls it, is introduced: the warning that only after it has received subsequent elaboration and qualification will it prove capable of sustaining the whole edifice of both art itself, and the even more difficult art of life—a promise which by Letter XXVII will have been amply fulfilled.

Once such accretions have been cleared away, and the bare bones of Schiller's own argument exposed to view, it would be important, we should have thought, to discover in what respects his theory (as distinct from any of the somewhat perfunctory empirical evidence he adduced more to adorn than to support it) is validated or invalidated by recent research in a number of fields. For, as we have argued above,[5] the 'open form' of his treatise implies that such testing and re-testing was one of the challenges he threw out to posterity. On the other hand, we ought not to forget that the findings of scientific research are rarely presented as pure observation or experimentation. They are usually embedded in 'theory' in the sense that inferences have already been drawn from them, and interpretation—even evaluation—put upon them. This is peculiarly, and inescapably, the

---

[1] See our Notes to XXVII. 4fn., and pp. lxvii, xciii, above.
[2] London, 1949[5], p. 15.
[3] See Glossary under *Trieb*.
[4] Ed. cit., pp. 165f.
[5] pp. xcv ff. and cxxvi.

case in the human sciences; for here the conceptual framework chosen for describing and explaining human life is part of the reality to be described and explained. And it is at this point that we move back within the orbit of philosophy. For only a philosopher can tell us how Schiller's conceptual framework compares in appropriateness with some of the highly dubious concepts employed in sociology, anthropology, and related studies today. Can tell us, for instance, whether his attempt to accommodate discontinuity within continuity is logically viable. Or whether he successfully avoided the danger—evident in some otherwise extremely fruitful attempts[1] to apply the findings of perception studies to the visual arts—of reducing the problems of aesthetic perception in particular to those of sense-perception in general. Or whether the hope he shared with Goethe,[2] that all the many kinds and degrees of perception—'from the child's longing for an apple on the tree to the fall of same which is said to have inspired Newton to his theory'—will one day be analytically distinguished for us, was a forlorn hope. Or whether, faced with the plethora of recent discoveries about the painting of apes or the dancing of bees, the art of children or the art of machines, they would not—after taking due, and even excited, cognizance of it all—have been right to go on insisting (as we may infer from their work they would have gone on insisting) that we shall never fully understand the 'human use' of human art except within the specifically human context of human awareness and human choice.

But the sort of philosopher likely to be able to tell us such things is not one who is committed to any particular system, or interested in making Schiller over in his own image—whether Marxist or Existentialist, neo-Kantian or neo-Hegelian. Rather one who is intent on uncovering the method and the message by a critical examination of the language. Which is why one could regret that this was never undertaken by the Harvard philosopher, Charles Peirce. For he possessed the two prime qualifications necessary for the task: unusual feeling for the work itself, combined with the logical and linguistic bias which makes him the acknowledged precursor of contemporary linguistic philosophers. His philosophical reading had begun with Schiller's *Aesthetic Letters*.[3] They made a profound and indelible impression upon him, and—unlike Kant's *Critique of Pure Reason*, which he eventually came to see was in the main mistaken—this

---

[1] Such as M. L. Johnson Abercrombie's *Anatomy of Judgment*, ed. cit.; or E. H. Gombrich's *Art and Illusion*, ed. cit. (2).

[2] Letter to Schiller, 6.i.1798.

[3] See *Charles S. Peirce's Letters to Lady Welby*. Ed. by I. C. Lieb, New Haven, Conn., 1953, p. 27 (23.xii.1908). The 'oddly enough' with which W. B. Gallie (*Peirce and Pragmatism*, Penguin Books, no. A 254, 1952, p. 35) accompanies this piece of information is an oblique reflection on the status enjoyed by Schiller's treatise in English-speaking countries.

favourable impression lasted throughout his life. What Schiller had 'to say about the Spiel-Trieb' in particular, he wrote, 'made so much impression upon me as to have thoroughly soaked my notion of "play" to this day'.[1] It seems more than probable that the importance Peirce continued to attach to the work was not unconnected with the conclusion he eventually reached: that though 'aesthetics and logic seem, at first blush, to belong to different universes . . . that seeming is illusory, and that, on the contrary, logic needs the help of aesthetics'. Or again: 'When our logic shall have paid its *devoirs* to Aesthetics and [to] Ethics, it will be time for it to settle down to its regular business.'[2] The conclusion, in other words, though he never worked it out thoroughly in writing, that logic rested on ethics, and ethics on aesthetics.[3] We ourselves would be inclined to hazard a guess that, if he was influenced to these conclusions by any one part of Schiller's treatise rather than another, it must have been by those much-misunderstood passages of Letter XXIII in which Schiller derived the growth of ethical values and intellectual abstractions out of the undifferentiated sphere of aesthetic, or psycho-physical, life.[4] However that may be, it seems obvious that Peirce got Schiller's message far more clearly than, say, Schelling.[5] Here is no question of the assimilation of all modes of mental activity to the aesthetic. It is rather a question of a hierarchical structure very much akin to Schiller's own. Whether, if worked out, it would have had the flexibility of Schiller's changing hierarchies is another matter.[6]

We have left this particular repercussion until last because it seems to us the one most pregnant with possibilities for the immediate future. According to Herman Meyer[7] one of the most urgent tasks for Schiller scholarship is the re-examination of his style in the light of ancient rhetoric. And he is undoubtedly right—if only for the reason that to trace Schiller's heritage preserves us from the dual naïveté of finding him either idiosyncratic or original where he was merely being traditional, and hence throws the exact nature of his true originality into sharper relief. But because he was such a powerful transformer of tradition there are

---

[1] Letter to Lady Welby, 23.xii.1908; *Letters*, ed. cit., p. 27.

[2] *Collected Papers of Charles Sanders Peirce*. Ed. by C. Hartshorne and P. Weiss, Cambridge, Mass., 1932: vol. ii, *Elements of Logic*, §§ 197–200. Cf. vol. v. § 402, fn. 3.

[3] We are indebted to our former pupil John M. Ellis who, while still an undergraduate, drew our attention to Peirce's interest in Schiller's aesthetics; to Stuart Hampshire for putting us in touch with Max H. Fisch of the University of Illinois, who is engaged on a biography of Peirce; and quite especially to Professor Fisch himself for so promptly and readily supplying us with confirmation of Peirce's appreciation of Schiller's treatise from unpublished papers in the possession of Harvard University.

[4] See our Notes to XXIII. 8.   [5] See above, pp. clxiii f.

[6] See above, pp. lxxxix and xcv.

[7] Loc. cit., p. 349, fn. 119.

aspects of his language which are not fully illuminated by relating him only to the past. And it is here that recent linguistic philosophy might perform a useful service. This is often charged with having produced no constructive results of its own; with having been content to expose the pseudo-problems and tidy up the confusions of other philosophers. But a little 'nettoyage de la situation verbale', as Paul Valéry once put it,[1] would not come at all amiss in Schiller scholarship at the present juncture. And if when applied to his critics the results did often turn out to be merely negative, when applied to the text of his own treatise, a more sophisticated concern with the functioning of words in particular contexts, with the logical use of myths and fictions,[2] with the operation of metaphors and models—to say nothing of Wittgenstein's notion of language games— might well prove the kind of necessary propaedeutic which constitutes a positive contribution in itself. Before we can decide, for instance, whether the present tendency to strip him of his Kantian mask has not perhaps gone too far, we need to know rather more about his actual use of that tiresome little word 'ought'. For although he may not be the sort of Idealist we used to think he was, the fact remains that the pivot of his play-theory is in the form of an imperative (XV. 8). But is it a true 'categorical' imperative? Is it normative or prescriptive? Is it of the same order as the 'ought' in IX. 7, where he tells the poet in what situations he should treat men as 'they are', and in what situations he should treat them as 'they ought to be'? The *soll* of XV. 8 has the appearance at least of being purely transcendental in character. That of IX. 7, on the other hand, sounds as though it might have been in part historically derived, influenced by experience of 'the best that men have thought and done'. On the other hand again, there is no denying that Schiller attributes to the poet an intuitive insight into what men ought to be as well as into what they are. Is the relation between the 'is' and the 'ought' here not perhaps the same as that between the 'is' and the 'could be' in Goethe's definition of the function of art in *Wilhelm Meister*: to present man as 'was [er] sei und was er sein könne'?[3] And is Schiller not, like the heroine of Goethe's novel, prompted to this view by the pedagogic conviction that to treat men as they are is to make them worse than they are, whereas to treat them as they ought to be is to bring them nearer to the point of

---

[1] 'Poésie et pensée abstraite', *Variété*, v. 131.

[2] We have in mind the use of such myths as 'the state of nature' or 'the social contract', which was recently defended by G. H. von Wright in his Gifford Lectures: *The Varieties of Goodness*, London, 1963.

[3] JA xviii. 312. This is sometimes misquoted as 'was er sei und könne', an error derived from the *Registerband* of this edition (p. 202) which alters the meaning radically. It is not without interest that William Faulkner's definition of the function of literature, in his speech on receipt of the Nobel Prize in 1950, related the 'is' to the 'could be' in precisely the same way.

becoming so ?[1] Shall we not in the end have to recognize that norms and ideals are an integral part of Schiller's realism?

Or, again, it might be profitable before discussing the viability or non-viability of his Aesthetic State in general terms of idealism or scepticism, optimism or pessimism, to ascertain precisely with what models he was operating. To contrast his metaphor of statesman or pedagogue as artist, for instance, not only with such distortions as it underwent at the hands of a Goebbels[2] but also with the use made of it by Plato, for whom the distinction between craftsman and artist—which for Schiller's model is crucial—did not yet exist. We should find that we cannot give an accurate description of his model without recourse, not only to his concept of semblance, but to his distinction between honest and dishonest semblance, and to his firm repudiation of any automatic transference of the artist's attitude to that of either the pedagogue or the politician. And in order to understand the relation of his Aesthetic State to the Political State we would do well to investigate the sources of his model for it, which were—in part at least—religious. Like the Kingdom of God, it appears to have a triple location. As an ideal it is strictly unrealizable on earth. Yet it is also 'within us', as vision and as longing. And within the limits of earthly realization it also—'like the pure Church and the pure Republic' (XXVII. 12)—becomes manifest in the relations between some men. It is not, therefore, intended to become a substitute for the body politic (any more than the 'pure' Church was intended to be a substitute for the 'body' of the Church). It is to be the leaven within it, lightening its imperfections or inspiring us to improve on them—and at the same time reconciling us to the fact that the Political State can never, in the nature of the case, provide us with all that the Aesthetic State within it can offer and achieve.

Or, again—to remain within the area of secularization—which particular doctrine of the 'Fall' did he take as his model for the re-education of man? And did he simply take it over as it stood, or did he modify it? What is certainly crucial in the model with which he operated in this particular treatise is the fact that the cause of man's 'Fall' is identical with the source of his power to 'redeem' himself—to become fully human by learning, in full consciousness, how to manage the 'mixed nature' with which he is endowed, how to feel at home with himself and with the world in which he is destined to live. And, as always when dealing with Schiller's secularization of theological doctrine, we should not lose sight of the fact that this model is oriented to the future no less than to the past (just as it finds its parallels not only in religious doctrine of the West but also of the East). For it is the one with which all psychotherapy, implicitly or explicitly, operates. Without some norm of human being and human behaviour—which, at its best, is something different from a mere statistical

---

[1] JA xviii. 302.   [2] See above, pp. cxli f.

average—the work cannot begin. But the object of the endeavour is not
to move any individual towards 'change', in the sense of persuading him
to come into line with such a norm as a standard outside, and alien to,
himself. Rather towards 'change' in the sense of coming to terms with the
individual variant of that human norm that he happens to be. It is within
this dual perspective, so it seems to us, that one would have to determine
whether it is really justifiable to claim Schiller as the originator or precursor of later doctrines of 'alienation' such as those of Hegel or Marx.
And it is not only the precise structure of his model that would have to
be taken into account, but also the temper in which he writes of the dawn
of self-awareness: of that differentiation of subject from object, of self
from world,[1] which is—if we will only let it—to become our saving grace.
For these are some of the most radiant passages in the whole treatise. And
they stand under the sign of Goethe's *Iphigenie*, that dramatic treatment
of the ancient myth whose burden is our emancipation out of primal darkness into the light of full humanity through the reciprocal growth of
insight and love.

But there are more important things to do with Schiller's treatise than
merely to classify and categorize it. And we single out three problems
which seem to us of particular urgency and relevance at this present time.
Is it not, as we very much suspect, because he operates with two different
models of the Whole Man that he is more successful than most in dealing
with the problems of culture and society?[2] With that more common model
of wholeness as the harmonious co-ordination of all our forces and faculties which, however, according to him, we can only briefly achieve in the
state of aesthetic contemplation? And with that other, far more complex,
model—to which he was almost certainly influenced by Goethe—of wholeness as a pattern of changing responses in time: responses involving the
subordination of the rest of the psyche to the dominance of that force or
faculty which is appropriate to the demands of the particular situation?[3]
And is it not because of the way he relates the one model to the other that
he is able to accommodate to his ideal of a Whole Man, not only specialization of vocation or skill, but also that retrenchment of 'wholeness'
involved in civic responsibilities? To go along with Goethe who, in the
Pedagogic Province of *Wilhelm Meister* repudiated general culture, the
Renaissance ideal of *uomo universale* of which he himself was heir, and in
some sense a late example, in favour of the specialization which he felt
to be the mark and the need of our modern age? To avoid the doubts
expressed by Rousseau in his *Émile* as to whether it is any longer possible

---

[1] It should be obvious from what we have said above (pp. clxii ff.) that his use in
aesthetic contexts of a term which may be translated as 'alienation' proves nothing in
this respect.

[2] See above, pp. cliii ff.   [3] See above, pp. xxxix, lxxxiii ff. and clvii.

to educate someone to be at the same time both a man and a citizen? And is it not, again, because of this double model that he is able to avoid the amputation of culture from work, and to transcend some of the alternatives which are often presented as mutually exclusive: art for leisure or art for life; art as consolation, refuge, safety-valve, or art as the great destroyer and re-orderer—the enemy of stasis, inertia, and conservation, and yet at the same time an agent of new balance and increased health? He is able to allow—as some advocates of popular culture are not—for the high value placed by modern societies upon the contemplation of works of art, and yet to give the inescapable impression that he would judge of the 'culture' of a society not only by the number of its art galleries or its willingness to subsidize theatres and concerts, but by the manners of its people, their food, their buildings and their conversation.

The second of our two problems is not unrelated to this transcendence of the antithesis between culture and society, though it is by no means identical with it. It concerns a rift in our educational theory and practice which goes far deeper than the alleged split between the two cultures (though it is not unrelated to this either): the dichotomy between the sort of learning that involves abstraction and the sort of learning which involves what is normally termed self-expression. Schiller, it seems to us, avoids this divergence, which results—among other things—in the almost total lack of communication between educationists interested in the one or the other, in the parlous state of the teaching of mathematics, in the frequent failure to make the teaching of language anything more than either a mechanical and meaningless drill, on the one hand, or an idiosyncratic and undisciplined expression of the inner life on the other. To discover just how he avoids it is a challenge to the logician no less than to the educationist. We suspect that it has something to do with the fact that the aesthetic, as he conceives it, is a more appropriate concept for a unified education than the concept of imagination which has been so prominent in modern educational theory. But also with the fact that in the growth of the mind as he presents it—as a reciprocal mirroring of inner and outer world—knowledge is not divorced from feeling or values. And finally with the fact that he did not go along with the Romantic attitude as epitomized by, say, a Blake—art is the key to life, science the key to death—but rather with Goethe's attitude when he welcomed the new trend towards natural science in the universities with an apparent stricture on the humanities—'for almost a century now the humanities have ceased to humanize those who practise them'.[1] Goethe did not thereby mean to repudiate the humanistic traditions of the past from which he himself had drawn such sustenance. What he did mean, and Schiller would have agreed with him, is that art or learning which cuts itself off

[1] Letter to Karl von Knebel, 25.xi.1808.

from revitalizing contact with scientific inquiry is doomed to inwardness, stagnation, or the sort of self-sufficient arrogance which can only result in de-humanization.

Finally we come to the challenge thrown out to linguistician and linguistic philosopher alike by the form of Schiller's treatise when viewed within the context of his theory of popularization. For the problems it raises turn on nothing less than the limits of philosophy, on the one hand, and the possibility of aesthetic linguistic structures in addition to those we normally call literature, on the other. Is that assimilation of 'translatability' into 'untranslatability' to which he was provoked by Herder's linguistic doctrines theoretically possible or practically feasible?[1] Is there no other way of making abstractions concrete again except by creating the semblances and fictions of art? Is the only possible end-product of a refusal to over-simplify the dynamic complexity of life itself a poem, a play, or a novel? Schiller's apparent vacillation in response to such questions depended, as we have already shown,[2] less on changes of conviction than on the rise and fall of his own confidence. When it ran high he felt that he himself had perhaps done something to orient philosophy in the direction of a more dynamic account of human behaviour, towards the achievement of synthesis without sacrifice of analysis, towards a new style of concretizing the abstractions that philosophy is bound to make. He was, and remained, as acutely conscious as Heidegger of 'the infinite gap that yawns between life itself and reasoning about life'.[3] Sometimes he shared his view that it was a flaw peculiar to a certain type of philosophizing, the Kantian in particular, and that one might look forward to a different kind of philosophy altogether.[4] At others he felt that it was perhaps inherent in the nature of philosophy itself. But what he never contemplated was the sort of solution to the problem attempted, in their different ways, by either Hamann or Heidegger: an endeavour to by-pass analysis and make philosophy render the wholeness of existence directly.[5] Some of the most thought-provoking hints he ever gave of how it might be possible to bridge the gap from 'the reality of a given case' to the principles of reasoning about it—or, as he also put it, 'von der transzendentalen Philosophie zu dem wirklichen Faktum'—actually occur in the context of literary criticism.[6] But they have even wider application. And they turn, as we might expect from his theory of popularization, on the mutual interpenetration of 'philosophy' (here in the broad, eighteenth-century sense) and the aesthetic.[7]

It is within this context of his attitude to the limitations of some

---

[1] See above, pp. xxviii f. and cxx f. [2] See above, pp. xl f.
[3] Letter to Goethe, 7.i.1795. [4] Ibid., 28.x.1794.
[5] See letter to Goethe, 9.ii.1798, translated in our Note to I. 4.
[6] Letter to Goethe, 20.i.1802. [7] See above, pp. cxviii ff.

philosophies, and the possible limits of philosophy altogether, that it might be profitable to reconsider the problem which has teased most Schiller scholars: to what extent are his plays an illustration of his theories? Or—if 'illustration' suggests a far too naïve view of the indirections of the creative process—what, if any, is the relation between his theory and his practice? Here again a comparison with Sartre could well prove illuminating. For in his case it seems perfectly clear that his sense of the inadequacy of even the existential style of philosophizing drove him, not only to the inclusion of concrete cases within his theoretical work, but to the fictional supplementation of it in his novels and plays. Is Schiller's an analogous case? Or is it something entirely different? It has been both argued[1]—and disputed[2]—that in *Wilhelm Tell* he offers a concrete symbol of his Aesthetic State. According to some, through the form of the idyll, with the Swiss people themselves as an ideal community. In which case he was working in the same tradition as Rousseau, or as Wordsworth in his *Descriptive Sketches*—the tradition of 'the golden age of the Alps'. According to others it is not the community, but the titular hero himself who represents the living embodiment of aesthetic man as Schiller conceived him: who steps out of his individual isolation and, through the personal hazard of his heroic deed, accomplishes the general will. It has also been argued—with great subtlety and ingenuity in one of the most thought-provoking studies of the relation between Schiller's theory and practice[3]—that his tragedies may be seen as the reverse side of the medal: as examples of how aesthetic potential turns into false power if manifested in inappropriate situations. Others again have seen the poetic concretization of Schiller's ideas not in his own works but in Goethe's. In the vision of the aged and blinded Faust of a community of 'free people on a free soil', avoiding the dangers of complacency because still 'umrungen von Gefahr'.[4] Or in the interaction between the two 'drives' in Faust's 'psyche', which were apparently to have been reconciled in a never completed *Epilog* by presenting his 'perfection' (*Vollendung*) as a creative artist.[5] We ourselves incline to a different view, and would seek the most adequate fictional counterpart in the work that Schiller was receiving in

---

[1] By Melitta Gerhard, op. cit., F. Martini, loc. cit., and Ilse Appelbaum Graham, loc. cit. (2), among others.

[2] Especially by H. Cysarz, op. cit., pp. 368 ff.

[3] By Ilse Appelbaum Graham, op. cit. (1). One wonders, however, whether by concentrating on one single feature of the aesthetic state to the exclusion of others—its pure determinability, or infinite potentiality—Dr. Graham has not stretched the term aesthetic to the point where it is indistinguishable from vacillation, indecision, or the power-impulse; whether the more potentially interesting case is not that in which the *truly* aesthetic attitude becomes vitiated simply through being maintained out of season (see above, pp. lxxxiii ff.).   [4] Cf. G. C. L. Schuchard, loc. cit., pp. 533 ff.

[5] Cf. H. Bergenthal, 'Schillers Briefe "Über die Ästhetische Erziehung des Menschen" und Goethes "Faust". Einige Parallelen', *Monatshefte*, xxxii (1940), 305 ff.

instalments while actually engaged on his treatise, namely *Wilhelm Meister*. And we would suggest that some of the heart-burnings he experienced about the inferiority of philosophical activity[1] was due, not just to the fact that Goethe was being poetically productive while he himself was still struggling to complete the series of theoretical works provoked by his study of Kant, but by the actual content of Goethe's novel (and especially, perhaps, by the sixth Book, which presented all the virtues and limitations of a 'schöne Seele'). For here, in the expansiveness of the epic form, it was possible to present (*darstellen*), with all the concrete uniqueness of the individual case, a whole panorama of the relations between life and art, the aesthetic and the moral, between semblance true, false, and misplaced. We would even venture the hypothesis—unprovable, no doubt, but a possible stimulus to further investigation of this uniquely creative partnership—that the existence of Goethe's novel may have played its part in Schiller's decision not to furnish the promised 'Constitution' for his Aesthetic State[2] (after the manner of Klopstock's *Gelehrtenrepublik*), but to leave his readers free to ponder and elaborate for themselves the rich and subtle implications of his final Letter.

All this may sound as though we thought that the chief challenge of Schiller's treatise is to scholars of various kinds. This is, of course, not the case at all. Its challenge is to any person, parent, or pedagogue who can read its message aright. And there must be many who have read it aright and acted upon it. Acting upon it, moreover—whether successfully or unsuccessfully—is a very real factor in its right interpretation. For however Schiller may ultimately be classified, he is in one quite precise sense a pragmatist:[3] in the sense that, though not arrived at by purely empirical means, his propositions are to be tested operationally. We shall not know whether they are true until we have tried them out—and tried out exactly what Schiller meant by them, and not something we should like him to have meant. The task of the scholar, then, is far from being a purely 'academic' activity. It is directly, and reciprocally, related to the personal and public challenge. For each new interpretation provokes a new kind of testing, and each kind of testing works back upon interpretation. Schiller more than once voiced the opinion that these *Letters* were the best thing he had ever done, or was capable of doing, and that they would constitute his claim to immortality.[4] One is tempted to say that time alone will tell. But time alone will never prove their efficacy. The onus is upon us to ensure that the task he predicted would take more than one century does not take more than two!

---

[1] See especially his letter to Goethe, 7.i.1795.
[2] See our Note to XXVII. 12.   [3] Cf. above, p. lxxxii.
[4] See especially his letters to F. von Hoven, [21 ?] 22.xi.1794, to Cotta, 9.i.1795, and the draft of his letter to Fichte, 3.viii.1795; Jonas iv. 222 f.

FRIEDRICH SCHILLER

———

ÜBER
DIE ÄSTHETISCHE ERZIEHUNG
DES MENSCHEN
in einer Reihe von Briefen

Si c'est la raison, qui fait l'homme,
c'est le sentiment, qui le conduit.
ROUSSEAU

ERSTER BRIEF

1. SIE wollen mir also vergönnen, Ihnen die Resultate meiner Untersuchungen über das Schöne und die Kunst in einer Reihe von Briefen vorzulegen. Lebhaft empfinde ich das Gewicht, aber auch den Reiz und die Würde dieser Unternehmung. Ich werde von einem Gegenstande sprechen, der mit dem besten Teil unsrer Glückseligkeit in einer unmittelbaren, und mit dem moralischen Adel der menschlichen Natur in keiner sehr entfernten Verbindung steht. Ich werde die Sache der Schönheit vor einem Herzen führen, das ihre ganze Macht empfindet und ausübt und bei einer Untersuchung, wo man ebenso oft genötigt ist, sich auf Gefühle als auf Grundsätze zu berufen, den schwersten Teil meines Geschäfts auf sich nehmen wird.

2. Was ich mir als eine Gunst von Ihnen erbitten wollte, machen Sie grossmütigerweise mir zur Pflicht und lassen mir da den Schein eines Verdienstes, wo ich bloss meiner Neigung nachgebe. Die Freiheit des Ganges, welche Sie mir vorschreiben, ist kein Zwang, vielmehr ein Bedürfnis für mich. Wenig geübt im Gebrauche schulgerechter Formen, werde ich kaum in Gefahr sein, mich durch Missbrauch derselben an dem guten Geschmack zu versündigen. Meine Ideen, mehr aus dem einförmigen Umgange mit mir selbst als aus einer reichen Welterfahrung geschöpft oder durch Lektüre erworben, werden ihren Ursprung nicht verleugnen, werden sich eher jedes andern Fehlers als der Sektiererei schuldig machen und eher aus eigner Schwäche fallen, als durch Autorität und fremde Stärke sich aufrecht erhalten.

3. Zwar will ich Ihnen nicht verbergen, dass es grösstenteils Kantische Grundsätze sind, auf denen die nachfolgenden Behauptungen ruhen werden; aber meinem Unvermögen, nicht jenen Grundsätzen schreiben Sie es zu, wenn Sie im Lauf dieser Untersuchungen an irgend eine besondre philosophische Schule erinnert werden sollten. Nein, die Freiheit Ihres Geistes soll mir unverletzlich sein. Ihre eigne Empfindung wird mir die Tatsachen hergeben, auf die ich baue; Ihre eigene freie Denkkraft wird die Gesetze diktieren, nach welchen verfahren werden soll.

FIRST LETTER

1. I HAVE, then, your gracious permission to submit the results of my inquiry concerning Art and Beauty in the form of a series of letters. Sensible as I am of the gravity of such an undertaking, I am also alive to its attraction and its worth. I shall be treating of a subject which has a direct connexion with all that is best in human happiness, and no very distant connexion with what is noblest in our moral nature. I shall be pleading the cause of Beauty before a heart which is as fully sensible of her power as it is prompt to act upon it, a heart which, in an inquiry where one is bound to invoke feelings no less often than principles, will relieve me of the heaviest part of my labours.

2. What I would have asked of you as a favour, you in your largesse impose upon me as a duty, thus leaving me the appearance of merit where I am in fact only yielding to inclination. The free mode of procedure you prescribe implies for me no constraint; on the contrary, it answers to a need of my own. Little practised in the use of scholastic modes, I am scarcely in danger of offending against good taste by their abuse. My ideas, derived from constant communing with myself rather than from any rich experience of the world or from reading, will be unable to deny their origin: the last reproach they are likely to incur is that of sectarianism, and they are more liable to collapse out of inherent weakness than to maintain themselves with the support of authority and borrowed strength.

3. True, I shall not attempt to hide from you that it is for the most part Kantian principles on which the following theses will be based. But you must ascribe it to my ineptitude rather than to those principles if in the course of this inquiry you should be reminded of any particular philosophical school. No, the freedom of your mind shall, I can promise you, remain inviolable. Your own feeling will provide me with the material on which to build, your own free powers of thought dictate the laws according to which we are to proceed.

4. Über diejenigen Ideen, welche in dem praktischen Teil des Kantischen Systems die herrschenden sind, sind nur die Philosophen entzweit, aber die Menschen, ich getraue mir es zu beweisen, von jeher einig gewesen. Man befreie sie von ihrer technischen Form, und sie werden als die verjährten Aussprüche der gemeinen Vernunft und als Tatsachen des moralischen Instinktes erscheinen, den die weise Natur dem Menschen zum Vormund setzte, bis die helle Einsicht ihn mündig macht. Aber eben diese technische Form, welche die Wahrheit dem Verstande versichtbart, verbirgt sie wieder dem Gefühl; denn leider muss der Verstand das Objekt des innern Sinns erst zerstören, wenn er es s i c h zu eigen machen will. Wie der Scheidekünstler, so findet auch der Philosoph nur durch Auflösung die Verbindung und nur durch die Marter der Kunst das Werk der freiwilligen Natur. Um die flüchtige Erscheinung zu haschen, muss er sie in die Fesseln der Regel schlagen, ihren schönen Körper in Begriffe zerfleischen und in einem dürftigen Wortgerippe ihren lebendigen Geist aufbewahren. Ist es ein Wunder, wenn sich das natürliche Gefühl in einem solchen Abbild nicht wiederfindet und die Wahrheit in dem Berichte des Analysten als ein Paradoxon erscheint?

5. Lassen Sie daher auch mir einige Nachsicht zustatten kommen, wenn die nachfolgenden Untersuchungen ihren Gegenstand, indem sie ihn dem Verstande zu nähern suchen, den Sinnen entrücken sollten. Was dort von moralischen Erfahrungen gilt, muss in einem noch höhern Grade von der Erscheinung der Schönheit gelten. Die ganze Magie derselben beruht auf ihrem Geheimnis, und mit dem notwendigen Bund ihrer Elemente ist auch ihr Wesen aufgehoben.

4. Concerning those ideas which prevail in the Practical part of the Kantian system only the philosophers are at variance; the rest of mankind, I believe I can show, have always been agreed. Once divested of their technical form, they stand revealed as the immemorial pronouncements of Common Reason, and as data of that moral instinct which Nature in her wisdom appointed Man's guardian until, through the enlightenment of his understanding, he should have arrived at years of discretion. But it is precisely this technical form, whereby truth is made manifest to the intellect, which veils it again from our feeling. For alas! intellect must first destroy the object of Inner Sense if it would make it i t s o w n. Like the analytical chemist, the philosopher can only discover how things are combined by analysing them, only lay bare the workings of spontaneous Nature by subjecting them to the torment of his own techniques. In order to lay hold of the fleeting phenomenon, he must first bind it in the fetters of rule, tear its fair body to pieces by reducing it to concepts, and preserve its living spirit in a sorry skeleton of words. Is it any wonder that natural feeling cannot find itself again in such an image, or that in the account of the analytical thinker truth should appear as paradox?

5. I too, therefore, would crave some measure of forbearance if the following investigations, in trying to bring the subject of inquiry closer to the understanding, were to transport it beyond reach of the senses. What was asserted above of moral experience, must hold even more of the phenomenon we call Beauty. For its whole magic resides in its mystery, and in dissolving the essential amalgam of its elements we find we have dissolved its very Being.

ZWEITER BRIEF

1. ABER sollte ich von der Freiheit, die mir von Ihnen verstattet wird, nicht vielleicht einen bessern Gebrauch machen können, als Ihre Aufmerksamkeit auf dem Schauplatz der schönen Kunst zu beschäftigen? Ist es nicht wenigstens ausser der Zeit, sich nach einem Gesetzbuch für die ästhetische Welt umzusehen, da die Angelegenheiten der moralischen ein so viel näheres Interesse darbieten und der philosophische Untersuchungsgeist durch die Zeitumstände so nachdrücklich aufgefordert wird, sich mit dem vollkommensten aller Kunstwerke, mit dem Bau einer wahren politischen Freiheit zu beschäftigen?

2. Ich möchte nicht gern in einem andern Jahrhundert leben und für ein andres gearbeitet haben. Man ist ebenso gut Zeitbürger, als man Staatsbürger ist; und wenn es unschicklich, ja unerlaubt gefunden wird, sich von den Sitten und Gewohnheiten des Zirkels, in dem man lebt, auszuschliessen, warum sollte es weniger Pflicht sein, in der Wahl seines Wirkens dem Bedürfnis und dem Geschmack des Jahrhunderts eine Stimme einzuräumen?

3. Diese Stimme scheint aber keineswegs zum Vorteil der Kunst auszufallen; derjenigen wenigstens nicht, auf welche allein meine Untersuchungen gerichtet sein werden. Der Lauf der Begebenheiten hat dem Genius der Zeit eine Richtung gegeben, die ihn je mehr und mehr von der Kunst des Ideals zu entfernen droht. Diese muss die Wirklichkeit verlassen und sich mit anständiger Kühnheit über das Bedürfnis erheben; denn die Kunst ist eine Tochter der Freiheit, und von der Notwendigkeit der Geister, nicht von der Notdurft der Materie will sie ihre Vorschrift empfangen. Jetzt aber herrscht das Bedürfnis und beugt die gesunkene Menschheit unter sein tyrannisches Joch. Der Nutzen ist das grosse Idol der Zeit, dem alle Kräfte fronen und alle Talente huldigen sollen. Auf dieser groben Wage hat das geistige Verdienst der Kunst kein Gewicht, und, aller Aufmunterung beraubt, verschwindet sie von dem lärmenden Markt des Jahrhunderts. Selbst der philosophische Untersuchungsgeist entreisst der Einbildungskraft eine Provinz nach der andern, und die Grenzen der Kunst verengen sich, je mehr die Wissenschaft ihre Schranken erweitert.

SECOND LETTER

1. But should it not be possible to make better use of the freedom you accord me than by keeping your attention fixed upon the domain of the fine arts? Is it not, to say the least, untimely to be casting around for a code of laws for the aesthetic world at a moment when the affairs of the moral offer interest of so much more urgent concern, and when the spirit of philosophical inquiry is being expressly challenged by present circumstances to concern itself with that most perfect of all the works to be achieved by the art of man: the construction of true political freedom?

2. I would not wish to live in a century other than my own, or to have worked for any other. We are citizens of our own Age no less than of our own State. And if it is deemed unseemly, or even inadmissible, to exempt ourselves from the morals and customs of the circle in which we live, why should it be less of a duty to allow the needs and taste of our own epoch some voice in our choice of activity?

3. But the verdict of this epoch does not, by any means, seem to be going in favour of art, not at least of the kind of art to which alone my inquiry will be directed. The course of events has given the spirit of the age a direction which threatens to remove it ever further from the art of the Ideal. This kind of art must abandon actuality, and soar with becoming boldness above our wants and needs; for Art is a daughter of Freedom, and takes her orders from the necessity inherent in minds, not from the exigencies of matter. But at the present time material needs reign supreme and bend a degraded humanity beneath their tyrannical yoke. Utility is the great idol of our age, to which all powers are in thrall and to which all talent must pay homage. Weighed in this crude balance, the insubstantial merits of Art scarce tip the scale, and, bereft of all encouragement, she shuns the noisy market-place of our century. The spirit of philosophical inquiry itself is wresting from the imagination one province after another, and the frontiers of art contract the more the boundaries of science expand.

4. Erwartungsvoll sind die Blicke des Philosophen wie des Weltmanns auf den politischen Schauplatz geheftet, wo jetzt, wie man glaubt, das grosse Schicksal der Menschheit verhandelt wird. Verrät es nicht eine tadelnswerte Gleichgültigkeit gegen das Wohl der Gesellschaft, dieses allgemeine Gespräch nicht zu teilen? So nahe dieser grosse Rechtshandel, seines Inhalts und seiner Folgen wegen, jeden, der sich Mensch nennt, angeht, so sehr muss er, seiner Verhandlungsart wegen, jeden Selbstdenker insbesondere interessieren. Eine Frage, welche sonst nur durch das blinde Recht des Stärkern beantwortet wurde, ist nun, wie es scheint, vor dem Richterstuhle reiner Vernunft anhängig gemacht, und wer nur immer fähig ist, sich in das Zentrum des Ganzen zu versetzen und sein Individuum zur Gattung zu steigern, darf sich als einen Beisitzer jenes Vernunftgerichts betrachten, so wie er als Mensch und Weltbürger zugleich Partei ist und näher oder entfernter in den Erfolg sich verwickelt sieht. Es ist also nicht bloss seine eigene Sache, die in diesem grossen Rechtshandel zur Entscheidung kommt; es soll auch nach Gesetzen gesprochen werden, die er als vernünftiger Geist selbst zu diktieren fähig und berechtiget ist.

5. Wie anziehend müsste es für mich sein, einen solchen Gegenstand mit einem ebenso geistreichen Denker als liberalen Weltbürger in Untersuchung zu nehmen und einem Herzen, das mit schönem Enthusiasmus dem Wohl der Menschheit sich weiht, die Entscheidung heimzustellen! Wie angenehm überraschend, bei einer noch so grossen Verschiedenheit des Standorts und bei dem weiten Abstand, den die Verhältnisse in der wirklichen Welt nötig machen, Ihrem vorurteilfreien Geist auf dem Felde der Ideen in dem nämlichen Resultat zu begegnen! Dass ich dieser reizenden Versuchung widerstehe und die Schönheit der Freiheit vorangehen lasse, glaube ich nicht bloss mit meiner Neigung entschuldigen, sondern durch Grundsätze rechtfertigen zu können. Ich hoffe, Sie zu überzeugen, dass diese Materie weit weniger dem Bedürfnis als dem Geschmack des Zeitalters fremd ist, ja dass man, um jenes politische Problem in der Erfahrung zu lösen, durch das ästhetische den Weg nehmen muss, weil es die Schönheit ist, durch welche man zu der Freiheit wandert. Aber dieser Beweis kann nicht geführt werden, ohne dass ich Ihnen die Grundsätze in Erinnerung bringe, durch welche sich die Vernunft überhaupt bei einer politischen Gesetzgebung leitet.

4. Expectantly the gaze of philosopher and man of the world alike is fixed on the political scene, where now, so it is believed, the very fate of mankind is being debated. Does it not betray a culpable indifference to the common weal not to take part in this general debate? If this great action is, by reason of its cause and its consequences, of urgent concern to every one who calls himself man, it must, by virtue of its method of procedure, be of quite special interest to every one who has learnt to think for himself. For a question which has hitherto always been decided by the blind right of might, is now, so it seems, being brought before the tribunal of Pure Reason itself, and anyone who is at all capable of putting himself at the centre of things, and of raising himself from an individual into a representative of the species, may consider himself at once a member of this tribunal, and at the same time, in his capacity of human being and citizen of the world, an interested party who finds himself more or less closely involved in the outcome of the case. It is, therefore, not merely his own cause which is being decided in this great action; judgement is to be passed according to laws which he, as a reasonable being, is himself competent and entitled to dictate.

5. How tempting it would be for me to investigate such a subject in company with one who is as acute a thinker as he is a liberal citizen of the world! And to leave the decision to a heart which has dedicated itself with such noble enthusiasm to the weal of humanity. What an agreeable surprise if, despite all difference in station, and the vast distance which the circumstances of the actual world make inevitable, I were, in the realm of ideas, to find my conclusions identical with those of a mind as unprejudiced as your own! That I resist this seductive temptation, and put Beauty before Freedom, can, I believe, not only be excused on the score of personal inclination, but also justified on principle. I hope to convince you that the theme I have chosen is far less alien to the needs of our age than to its taste. More than this: if man is ever to solve that problem of politics in practice he will have to approach it through the problem of the aesthetic, because it is only through Beauty that man makes his way to Freedom. But this cannot be demonstrated without my first reminding you of the principles by which Reason is in any case guided in matters of political legislation.

DRITTER BRIEF

1. Die Natur fängt mit dem Menschen nicht besser an als mit ihren übrigen Werken: sie handelt für ihn, wo er als freie Intelligenz noch nicht selbst handeln kann. Aber eben das macht ihn zum Menschen, dass er bei dem nicht stille steht, was die blosse Natur aus ihm machte, sondern die Fähigkeit besitzt, die Schritte, welche jene mit ihm antizipierte, durch Vernunft wieder rückwärts zu tun, das Werk der Not in ein Werk seiner freien Wahl umzuschaffen und die physische Notwendigkeit zu einer moralischen zu erheben.

2. Er kommt zu sich aus seinem sinnlichen Schlummer, erkennt sich als Mensch, blickt um sich her und findet sich — in dem Staate. Der Zwang der Bedürfnisse warf ihn hinein, ehe er in seiner Freiheit diesen Stand wählen konnte; die Not richtete denselben nach blossen Naturgesetzen ein, ehe e r es nach Vernunftgesetzen konnte. Aber mit diesem Notstaat, der nur aus seiner Naturbestimmung hervorgegangen und auch nur auf diese berechnet war, konnte und kann er als moralische Person nicht zufrieden sein — und schlimm für ihn, wenn er es könnte! Er verlässt also, mit demselben Rechte, womit er Mensch ist, die Herrschaft einer blinden Notwendigkeit, wie er in so vielen andern Stücken durch seine Freiheit von ihr scheidet, wie er, um nur e i n Beispiel zu geben, den gemeinen Charakter, den das Bedürfnis der Geschlechtsliebe aufdrückte, durch Sittlichkeit auslöscht und durch Schönheit veredelt. So holt er, auf eine künstliche Weise, in seiner Volljährigkeit seine Kindheit nach, bildet sich einen N a t u r s t a n d in der Idee, der ihm zwar durch keine Erfahrung gegeben, aber durch seine Vernunftbestimmung notwendig gesetzt ist, leiht sich in diesem idealischen Stand einen Endzweck, den er in seinem wirklichen Naturstand nicht kannte, und eine Wahl, deren er damals nicht fähig war, und verfährt nun nicht anders, als ob er von vorn anfinge und den Stand der Unabhängigkeit aus heller Einsicht und freiem Entschluss mit dem Stand der Verträge vertauschte. Wie kunstreich und fest auch die blinde Willkür ihr Werk gegründet haben, wie anmassend sie es auch behaupten und mit welchem Scheine von Ehrwürdigkeit es

THIRD LETTER

1. NATURE deals no better with Man than with the rest of her works: she acts for him as long as he is as yet incapable of acting for himself as a free intelligence. But what makes him Man is precisely this: that he does not stop short at what Nature herself made of him, but has the power of retracing by means of Reason the steps she took on his behalf, of transforming the work of blind compulsion into a work of free choice, and of elevating physical necessity into moral necessity.

2. Out of the long slumber of the senses he awakens to consciousness and knows himself for a human being; he looks about him, and finds himself—in the State. The force of his needs threw him into this situation before he was as yet capable of exercising his freedom to choose it; compulsion organized it according to purely natural laws before h e could do so according to the laws of Reason. But with this State of compulsion, born of what Nature destined him to be, and designed to this end alone, he neither could nor can rest content as a Moral Being. And woe to him if he could! With that same right, therefore, by virtue of which he is Man, he withdraws from the dominion of blind necessity, even as in so many other respects he parts company from it by means of his freedom; even as, to take but o n e example, he obliterates by means of morality, and ennobles by means of beauty, the crude character imposed by physical need upon sexual love. And even thus does he, in his maturity, retrieve by means of a fiction the childhood of the race: he conceives, as idea, a s t a t e o f n a t u r e, a state not indeed given him by any experience, but a necessary result of what Reason destined him to be; attributes to himself in this idealized natural state a purpose of which in his actual natural state he was entirely ignorant, and a power of free choice of which he was at that time wholly incapable; and now proceeds exactly as if he were starting from scratch, and were, from sheer insight and free resolve, exchanging a state of complete independence for a state of social contracts. However skilfully, and however firmly, blind caprice may have laid the foundations of her work, however arrogantly she may maintain it, and with whatever appearance of venerability she may surround

umgeben mag — er darf es, bei dieser Operation, als völlig un-
geschehen betrachten; denn das Werk blinder Kräfte besitzt keine
Autorität, vor welcher die Freiheit sich zu beugen brauchte, und
alles muss sich dem höchsten Endzwecke fügen, den die Vernunft
in seiner Persönlichkeit aufstellt. Auf diese Art entsteht und rechtfertigt sich der Versuch eines mündig gewordenen Volks, seinen
Naturstaat in einen sittlichen umzuformen.

3. Dieser Naturstaat (wie jeder politische Körper heissen kann,
der seine Einrichtung ursprünglich von Kräften, nicht von Gesetzen
ableitet) widerspricht nun zwar dem moralischen Menschen, dem
die blosse Gesetzmässigkeit zum Gesetz dienen soll, aber er ist
doch gerade hinreichend für den physischen Menschen, der sich
nur darum Gesetze gibt, um sich mit Kräften abzufinden. Nun ist
aber der physische Mensch w i r k l i c h, und der sittliche nur p r o -
b l e m a t i s c h. Hebt also die Vernunft den Naturstaat auf, wie sie
notwendig muss, wenn sie den ihrigen an die Stelle setzen will, so
wagt sie den physischen und wirklichen Menschen an den proble-
matischen sittlichen, so wagt sie die Existenz der Gesellschaft an ein
bloss mögliches (wenn gleich moralisch notwendiges) Ideal von
Gesellschaft. Sie nimmt dem Menschen etwas, das er wirklich
besitzt, und ohne welches er nichts besitzt, und weist ihn dafür
an etwas an, das er besitzen könnte und sollte; und hätte sie zu viel
auf ihn gerechnet, so würde sie ihm für eine Menschheit, die ihm
noch mangelt und unbeschadet seiner Existenz mangeln kann, auch
selbst die Mittel zur Tierheit entrissen haben, die doch die Bedingung seiner Menschheit ist. Ehe er Zeit gehabt hätte, sich mit seinem
Willen an dem Gesetz fest zu halten, hätte sie unter seinen Füssen
die Leiter der Natur weggezogen.

4. Das grosse Bedenken also ist, dass die physische Gesellschaft
i n d e r Z e i t keinen Augenblick aufhören darf, indem die moralische i n d e r I d e e sich bildet, dass um der Würde des Menschen
willen seine Existenz nicht in Gefahr geraten darf. Wenn der Künstler an einem Uhrwerk zu bessern hat, so lässt er die Räder ablaufen;
aber das lebendige Uhrwerk des Staats muss gebessert werden, indem es schlägt, und hier gilt es, das rollende Rad während seines
Umschwunges auszutauschen. Man muss also für die Fortdauer der
Gesellschaft eine Stütze aufsuchen, die sie von dem Naturstaate,
den man auflösen will, unabhängig macht.

it—Man is fully entitled in the course of these operations to treat
it all as though it had never happened. For the work of blind forces
possesses no authority before which Freedom need bow, and everything must accommodate itself to the highest end which Reason
now decrees in him as Person. This is the origin and justification
of any attempt on the part of a people grown to maturity to transform its Natural State into a Moral one.

3.   This Natural State (as we may term any political body whose
organization derives originally from forces and not from laws) is,
it is true, at variance with man as moral being, for whom the only
Law should be to act in conformity with law. But it will just suffice
for man as physical being; for he only gives himself laws in order
to come to terms with forces. But physical man does in fact exist,
whereas the existence of moral man is as yet problematic. If,
then, Reason does away with the Natural State (as she of necessity
must if she would put her own in its place), she jeopardizes the
physical man who actually exists for the sake of a moral man who
is as yet problematic, risks the very existence of society for a merely
hypothetical (even though morally necessary) ideal of society. She
takes from man something he actually possesses, and without which
he possesses nothing, and refers him instead to something which he
could and should possess. And if in so doing she should have counted
on him for more than he can perform, then she would, for the sake
of a humanity which he still lacks—and can without prejudice to his
mere existence go on lacking—have deprived him of the means of
that animal existence which is the very condition of his being human
at all. Before he has had time to cleave unto the Law with the full
force of his moral will, she would have drawn from under his feet
the ladder of Nature.

4.   What we must chiefly bear in mind, then, is that physical
society in time must never for a moment cease to exist while moral
society as idea is in the process of being formed; that for the sake
of man's moral dignity his actual existence must never be jeopardized.
When the craftsman has a timepiece to repair, he can let its wheels
run down; but the living clockwork of the State must be repaired
while it is still striking, and it is a question of changing the revolving
wheel while it still revolves. For this reason a support must be
looked for which will ensure the continuance of society, and make it
independent of the Natural State which is to be abolished.

5. Diese Stütze findet sich nicht in dem natürlichen Charakter des Menschen, der, selbstsüchtig und gewalttätig, vielmehr auf Zerstörung als auf Erhaltung der Gesellschaft zielt; sie findet sich ebenso wenig in seinem sittlichen Charakter, der, nach der Voraussetzung, erst gebildet werden soll, und auf den, weil er frei ist und weil er nie erscheint, von dem Gesetzgeber nie gewirkt und nie mit Sicherheit gerechnet werden könnte. Es käme also darauf an, von dem physischen Charakter die Willkür und von dem moralischen die Freiheit abzusondern — es käme darauf an, den erstern mit Gesetzen übereinstimmend, den letztern von Eindrücken abhängig zu machen — es käme darauf an, jenen von der Materie etwas weiter zu entfernen, diesen ihr um etwas näher zu bringen — um einen dritten Charakter zu erzeugen, der, mit jenen beiden verwandt, von der Herrschaft blosser Kräfte zu der Herrschaft der Gesetze einen Übergang bahnte und, ohne den moralischen Charakter an seiner Entwicklung zu verhindern, vielmehr zu einem sinnlichen Pfand der unsichtbaren Sittlichkeit diente.

5. This support is not to be found in the natural character of man which, selfish and violent as it is, aims at the destruction of society rather than at its preservation. Neither is it to be found in his moral character which has, *ex hypothesi*, first to be fashioned, and upon which, just because it is free, and because it never becomes manifest, the lawgiver could never exert influence, nor with any certainty depend. It would, therefore, be a question of abstracting from man's physical character its arbitrariness, and from his moral character its freedom; of making the first conformable to laws, and the second dependent upon sense-impressions; of removing the former somewhat further from matter, and bringing the latter somewhat closer to it; and all this with the aim of bringing into being a third character which, kin to both the others, might prepare the way for a transition from the rule of mere force to the rule of law, and which, without in any way impeding the development of moral character, might on the contrary serve as a pledge in the sensible world of a morality as yet unseen.

VIERTER BRIEF

1. SOVIEL ist gewiss: nur das Übergewicht eines solchen Charakters bei einem Volk kann eine Staatsverwandlung nach moralischen Prinzipien unschädlich machen, und auch nur ein solcher Charakter kann ihre Dauer verbürgen. Bei Aufstellung eines moralischen Staats wird auf das Sittengesetz als auf eine wirkende Kraft gerechnet, und der freie Wille wird in das Reich der Ursachen gezogen, wo alles mit strenger Notwendigkeit und Stetigkeit aneinander hängt. Wir wissen aber, dass die Bestimmungen des menschlichen Willens immer zufällig bleiben, und dass nur bei dem absoluten Wesen die physische Notwendigkeit mit der moralischen zusammenfällt. Wenn also auf das sittliche Betragen des Menschen wie auf n a t ü r - l i c h e Erfolge gerechnet werden soll, so muss es Natur s e i n, und er muss schon durch seine Triebe zu einem solchen Verfahren geführt werden, als nur immer ein sittlicher Charakter zur Folge haben kann. Der Wille des Menschen steht aber vollkommen frei zwischen Pflicht und Neigung, und in dieses Majestätsrecht seiner Person kann und darf keine physische Nötigung greifen. Soll er also dieses Vermögen der Wahl beibehalten und nichtsdestoweniger ein zuverlässiges Glied in der Kausalverknüpfung der Kräfte sein, so kann dies nur dadurch bewerkstelligt werden, dass die Wirkungen jener beiden Triebfedern im Reich der Erscheinungen vollkommen gleich ausfallen und, bei aller Verschiedenheit in der Form, die Materie seines Wollens dieselbe bleibt; dass also seine Triebe mit seiner Vernunft übereinstimmend genug sind, um zu einer universellen Gesetzgebung zu taugen.

2. Jeder individuelle Mensch, kann man sagen, trägt, der Anlage und Bestimmung nach, einen reinen idealischen Menschen in sich, mit dessen unveränderlicher Einheit in allen seinen Abwechselungen übereinzustimmen die grosse Aufgabe seines Daseins ist.* Dieser reine Mensch, der sich mehr oder weniger deutlich in jedem Subjekt zu erkennen gibt, wird repräsentiert durch den S t a a t, die objektive und gleichsam kanonische Form, in der sich die

---

* Ich beziehe mich hier auf eine kürzlich erschienene Schrift: Vorlesungen über die Bestimmung des Gelehrten von meinem Freund Fichte, wo sich eine sehr lichtvolle und noch nie auf diesem Wege versuchte Ableitung dieses Satzes findet.

FOURTH LETTER

1. THIS much is certain: Only the predominance of such a character among a people makes it safe to undertake the transformation of a State in accordance with moral principles. And only such a character can guarantee that this transformation will endure. The setting up of a moral State involves being able to count on the moral law as an effective force, and free will is thereby drawn into the realm of cause and effect, where everything follows from everything else in a chain of strict necessity. But we know that the modes of determination of the human will must always remain contingent, and that it is only in Absolute Being that physical necessity coincides with moral necessity. If, therefore, we are to be able to count on man's moral behaviour with as much certainty as we do on natural effects, it will itself have to be nature, and he will have to be led by his very impulses to the kind of conduct which is bound to proceed from a moral character. But the will of man stands completely free between duty and inclination, and no physical compulsion can, or should, encroach upon this sovereign right of his personality. If, then, man is to retain his power of choice and yet, at the same time, be a reliable link in the chain of causality, this can only be brought about through both these motive forces, inclination and duty, producing completely identical results in the world of phenomena; through the content of his volition remaining the same whatever the difference in form; that is to say, through impulse being sufficiently in harmony with reason to qualify as universal legislator.

2. Every individual human being, one may say, carries within him, potentially and prescriptively, an ideal man, the archetype of a human being, and it is his life's task to be, through all his changing manifestations, in harmony with the unchanging unity of this ideal.* This archetype, which is to be discerned more or less clearly in every individual, is represented by the S t a t e, the objective and, as it were, canonical form in which all the diversity of individual

---

* I refer to a recent publication of my friend F i c h t e, *Lectures on the Vocation of a Scholar*, in which illuminating deductions are drawn from this proposition in a way not hitherto attempted.

Mannigfaltigkeit der Subjekte zu vereinigen trachtet. Nun lassen
sich aber zwei verschiedene Arten denken, wie der Mensch in der
Zeit mit dem Menschen in der Idee zusammentreffen, mithin ebenso
viele, wie der Staat in den Individuen sich behaupten kann: entweder dadurch, dass der reine Mensch den empirischen unterdrückt, dass der Staat die Individuen aufhebt; oder dadurch, dass
das Individuum Staat w i r d, dass der Mensch in der Zeit zum
Menschen in der Idee sich v e r e d e l t.

3. Zwar in der einseitigen moralischen Schätzung fällt dieser
Unterschied hinweg; denn die Vernunft ist befriedigt, wenn ihr
Gesetz nur ohne Bedingung gilt: aber in der vollständigen anthro-
pologischen Schätzung, wo mit der Form auch der Inhalt zählt und
die lebendige Empfindung zugleich eine Stimme hat, wird derselbe
desto mehr in Betrachtung kommen. Einheit fordert zwar die Vernunft, die Natur aber Mannigfaltigkeit, und von beiden Legisla-
tionen wird der Mensch in Anspruch genommen. Das Gesetz der
erstern ist ihm durch ein unbestechliches Bewusstsein, das Gesetz
der andern durch ein unvertilgbares Gefühl eingeprägt. Daher wird
es jederzeit von einer noch mangelhaften Bildung zeugen, wenn der
sittliche Charakter nur mit Aufopferung des natürlichen sich behaupten kann; und eine Staatsverfassung wird noch sehr unvollendet
sein, die nur durch Aufhebung der Mannigfaltigkeit Einheit zu
bewirken im Stand ist. Der Staat soll nicht bloss den objektiven und
generischen, er soll auch den subjektiven und spezifischen Charakter
in den Individuen ehren und, indem er das unsichtbare Reich der
Sitten ausbreitet, das Reich der Erscheinung nicht entvölkern.

4. Wenn der mechanische Künstler seine Hand an die gestaltlose
Masse legt, um ihr die Form seiner Zwecke zu geben, so trägt er
kein Bedenken, ihr Gewalt anzutun; denn die Natur, die er bearbeitet, verdient für sich selbst keine Achtung, und es liegt ihm nicht
an dem Ganzen um der Teile willen, sondern an den Teilen um
des Ganzen willen. Wenn der schöne Künstler seine Hand an die
nämliche Masse legt, so trägt er ebenso wenig Bedenken, ihr Gewalt
anzutun, nur vermeidet er, sie zu zeigen. Den Stoff, den er bearbeitet, respektiert er nicht im geringsten mehr als der mechanische
Künstler; aber das Auge, welches die Freiheit dieses Stoffes in
Schutz nimmt, wird er durch eine scheinbare Nachgiebigkeit gegen
denselben zu täuschen suchen. Ganz anders verhält es sich mit dem
pädagogischen und politischen Künstler, der den Menschen zugleich

subjects strive to unite. One can, however, imagine two different ways in which man existing in time can coincide with man as Idea, and, in consequence, just as many ways in which the State can assert itself in individuals: either by the ideal man suppressing empirical man, and the State annulling individuals; or else by the individual himself b e c o m i n g the State, and man in time being e n n o b l e d t o t h e s t a t u r e of man as Idea.

3.   It is true that from a one-sided moral point of view this difference disappears. For Reason is satisfied as long as her law obtains unconditionally. But in the complete anthropological view, where content counts no less than form, and living feeling too has a voice, the difference becomes all the more relevant. Reason does indeed demand unity; but Nature demands multiplicity; and both these kinds of law make their claim upon man. The law of Reason is imprinted upon him by an incorruptible consciousness; the law of Nature by an ineradicable feeling. Hence it will always argue a still defective education if the moral character is able to assert itself only by sacrificing the natural. And a political constitution will still be very imperfect if it is able to achieve unity only by suppressing variety. The State should not only respect the objective and generic character in its individual subjects; it should also honour their subjective and specific character, and in extending the invisible realm of morals take care not to depopulate the sensible realm of appearance.

4.   When the artisan lays hands upon the formless mass in order to shape it to his ends, he has no scruple in doing it violence; for the natural material he is working merits no respect for itself, and his concern is not with the whole for the sake of the parts, but with the parts for the sake of the whole. When the artist lays hands upon the same mass, he has just as little scruple in doing it violence; but he avoids showing it. For the material he is handling he has not a whit more respect than has the artisan; but the eye which would seek to protect the freedom of the material he will endeavour to deceive by a show of yielding to this latter. With the pedagogic or the political artist things are very different indeed. For him Man is at once the material on which he works and the goal towards which he strives. In this case the end turns back upon itself and becomes

zu seinem Material und zu seiner Aufgabe macht. Hier kehrt der
Zweck in den Stoff zurück, und nur weil das Ganze den Teilen dient,
dürfen sich die Teile dem Ganzen fügen. Mit einer ganz andern
Achtung, als diejenige ist, die der schöne Künstler gegen seine
Materie vorgibt, muss der Staatskünstler sich der seinigen nahen,
und nicht bloss subjektiv und für einen täuschenden Effekt in den
Sinnen, sondern objektiv und für das innre Wesen muss er ihrer
Eigentümlichkeit und Persönlichkeit schonen.

5.   Aber eben deswegen, weil der Staat eine Organisation sein
soll, die sich durch sich selbst und für sich selbst bildet, so kann er
auch nur insoferne wirklich werden, als sich die Teile zur Idee des
Ganzen hinauf gestimmt haben. Weil der Staat der reinen und
objektiven Menschheit in der Brust seiner Bürger zum Repräsentanten dient, so wird er gegen seine Bürger dasselbe Verhältnis zu
beobachten haben, in welchem sie zu sich selber stehen, und ihre
subjektive Menschheit auch nur in d e m Grade ehren können,
als sie zur objektiven veredelt ist. Ist der innere Mensch mit sich
einig, so wird er auch bei der höchsten Universalisierung seines
Betragens seine Eigentümlichkeit retten, und der Staat wird bloss
der Ausleger seines schönen Instinkts, die deutlichere Formel seiner
innern Gesetzgebung sein. Setzt sich hingegen in dem Charakter
eines Volks der subjektive Mensch dem objektiven noch so kon-
tradiktorisch entgegen, dass nur die Unterdrückung des erstern dem
letztern den Sieg verschaffen kann, so wird auch der Staat gegen
den Bürger den strengen Ernst des Gesetzes annehmen, und, um
nicht ihr Opfer zu sein, eine so feindselige Individualität ohne
Achtung darnieder treten müssen.

6.   Der Mensch kann sich aber auf eine doppelte Weise entgegen
gesetzt sein: entweder als Wilder, wenn seine Gefühle über seine
Grundsätze herrschen; oder als Barbar, wenn seine Grundsätze
seine Gefühle zerstören. Der Wilde verachtet die Kunst und erkennt die Natur als seinen unumschränkten Gebieter; der Barbar
verspottet und entehrt die Natur, aber verächtlicher als der Wilde
fährt er häufig genug fort, der Sklave seines Sklaven zu sein. Der
gebildete Mensch macht die Natur zu seinem Freund und ehrt ihre
Freiheit, indem er bloss ihre Willkür zügelt.

7.   Wenn also die Vernunft in die physische Gesellschaft ihre
moralische Einheit bringt, so darf sie die Mannigfaltigkeit der Natur

identical with the medium; and it is only inasmuch as the whole serves the parts that the parts are in any way bound to submit to the whole. The statesman-artist must approach his material with a quite different kind of respect from that which the maker of Beauty feigns towards his. The consideration he must accord to its uniqueness and individuality is not merely subjective, and aimed at creating an illusion for the senses, but objective and directed to its innermost being.

5. But just because the State is to be an organization formed by itself and for itself, it can only become a reality inasmuch as its parts have been tuned up to the idea of the whole. Because the State serves to represent that ideal and objective humanity which exists in the heart of each of its citizens, it will have to observe toward those citizens the same relationship as each has to himself, and will be able to honour their subjective humanity only to the extent that this has been ennobled in the direction of objective humanity. Once man is inwardly at one with himself, he will be able to preserve his individuality however much he may universalize his conduct, and the State will be merely the interpreter of his own finest instinct, a clearer formulation of his own sense of what is right. If, on the other hand, in the character of a whole people, subjective man sets his face against objective man with such vehemence of contradiction that the victory of the latter can only be ensured by the suppression of the former, then the State too will have to adopt towards its citizens the solemn rigour of the law, and ruthlessly trample underfoot such powerfully seditious individualism in order not to fall a victim to it.

6. But man can be at odds with himself in two ways: either as savage, when feeling predominates over principle; or as barbarian, when principle destroys feeling. The savage despises Civilization, and acknowledges Nature as his sovereign mistress. The barbarian derides and dishonours Nature, but, more contemptible than the savage, as often as not continues to be the slave of his slave. The man of Culture makes a friend of Nature, and honours her freedom whilst curbing only her caprice.

7. Consequently, whenever Reason starts to introduce the unity of the moral law into any actually existing society, she must beware

nicht verletzen. Wenn die Natur in dem moralischen Bau der Gesellschaft ihre Mannigfaltigkeit zu behaupten strebt, so darf der moralischen Einheit dadurch kein Abbruch geschehen; gleich weit von Einförmigkeit und Verwirrung ruht die siegende Form. T o t a l i t ä t des Charakters muss also bei dem Volke gefunden werden, welches fähig und würdig sein soll, den Staat der Not mit dem Staat der Freiheit zu vertauschen.

of damaging the variety of Nature. And whenever Nature en-
deavours to maintain her variety within the moral framework of
society, moral unity must not suffer any infringement thereby.
Removed alike from uniformity and from confusion, there abides
the triumph of form. W h o l e n e s s of character must therefore be
present in any people capable, and worthy, of exchanging a State
of compulsion for a State of freedom.

FÜNFTER BRIEF

1. Ist es dieser Charakter, den uns das jetzige Zeitalter, den die gegenwärtigen Ereignisse zeigen? Ich richte meine Aufmerksamkeit sogleich auf den hervorstechendsten Gegenstand in diesem weitläuftigen Gemälde.

2. Wahr ist es, das Ansehen der Meinung ist gefallen, die Willkür ist entlarvt, und, obgleich noch mit Macht bewaffnet, erschleicht sie doch keine Würde mehr; der Mensch ist aus seiner langen Indolenz und Selbsttäuschung aufgewacht, und mit nachdrücklicher Stimmenmehrheit fordert er die Wiederherstellung in seine unverlierbaren Rechte. Aber er fordert sie nicht bloss; jenseits und diesseits steht er auf, sich gewaltsam zu nehmen, was ihm nach seiner Meinung mit Unrecht verweigert wird. Das Gebäude des Naturstaates wankt, seine mürben Fundamente weichen, und eine physische Möglichkeit scheint gegeben, das Gesetz auf den Thron zu stellen, den Menschen endlich als Selbstzweck zu ehren und wahre Freiheit zur Grundlage der politischen Verbindung zu machen. Vergebliche Hoffnung! Die moralische Möglichkeit fehlt, und der freigebige Augenblick findet ein unempfängliches Geschlecht.

3. In seinen Taten malt sich der Mensch, und welche Gestalt ist es, die sich in dem Drama der jetzigen Zeit abbildet! Hier Verwilderung, dort Erschlaffung: die zwei Äussersten des menschlichen Verfalls, und beide in Einem Zeitraum vereinigt!

4. In den niedern und zahlreichern Klassen stellen sich uns rohe gesetzlose Triebe dar, die sich nach aufgelöstem Band der bürgerlichen Ordnung entfesseln und mit unlenksamer Wut zu ihrer tierischen Befriedigung eilen. Es mag also sein, dass die objektive Menschheit Ursache gehabt hätte, sich über den Staat zu beklagen; die subjektive muss seine Anstalten ehren. Darf man ihn tadeln, dass er die Würde der menschlichen Natur aus den Augen setzte, solange es noch galt, ihre Existenz zu verteidigen? Dass er eilte, durch die Schwerkraft zu scheiden und durch die Kohäsionskraft zu binden, wo an die bildende noch nicht zu denken war? Seine

FIFTH LETTER

1. Is this the character which the present age, which contemporary events present to us? Let me turn my attention at once to the object most in evidence on this enormous canvas.

2. True, the authority of received opinion has declined, arbitrary rule is unmasked and, though still armed with power, can no longer, even by devious means, maintain the appearance of dignity. Man has roused himself from his long indolence and self-deception and, by an impressive majority, is demanding restitution of his inalienable rights. But he is not just demanding this; over there, and over here, he is rising up to seize by force what, in his opinion, has been wrongfully denied him. The fabric of the natural State is tottering, its rotting foundations giving way, and there seems to be a p h y s i c a l possibility of setting law upon the throne, of honouring man at last as an end in himself, and making true freedom the basis of political associations. Vain hope! The m o r a l possibility is lacking, and a moment so prodigal of opportunity finds a generation unprepared to receive it.

3. Man portrays himself in his actions. And what a figure he cuts in the drama of the present time! On the one hand, a return to the savage state; on the other, to complete lethargy: in other words, to the two extremes of human depravity, and both united in a s i n g l e epoch!

4. Among the lower and more numerous classes we are confronted with crude, lawless instincts, unleashed with the loosening of the bonds of civil order, and hastening with ungovernable fury to their animal satisfactions. It may well be that objective humanity had cause for complaint against the State; subjective humanity must respect its institutions. Can the State be blamed for having disregarded the dignity of human beings as long as it was still a question of ensuring their very existence? Or for having hastened to divide and unite by the [mechanical] forces of gravity and cohesion, while there could as yet be no thought of any [organic] formative principle

Auflösung enthält seine Rechtfertigung. Die losgebundene Gesellschaft, anstatt aufwärts in das organische Leben zu eilen, fällt in das Elementarreich zurück.

5. Auf der andern Seite geben uns die zivilisierten Klassen den noch widrigern Anblick der Schlaffheit und einer Depravation des Charakters, die desto mehr empört, weil die Kultur selbst ihre Quelle ist. Ich erinnere mich nicht mehr, welcher alte oder neue Philosoph die Bemerkung machte, dass das Edlere in seiner Zerstörung das Abscheulichere sei; aber man wird sie auch im Moralischen wahr finden. Aus dem Natursohne wird, wenn er ausschweift, ein Rasender; aus dem Zögling der Kunst ein Nichtswürdiger. Die Aufklärung des Verstandes, deren sich die verfeinerten Stände nicht ganz mit Unrecht rühmen, zeigt im ganzen so wenig einen veredelnden Einfluss auf die Gesinnungen, dass sie vielmehr die Verderbnis durch Maximen befestigt. Wir verleugnen die Natur auf ihrem rechtmässigen Felde, um auf dem moralischen ihre Tyrannei zu erfahren, und indem wir ihren Eindrücken widerstreben, nehmen wir unsre Grundsätze von ihr an. Die affektierte Dezenz unsrer Sitten verweigert ihr die verzeihliche e r s t e Stimme, um ihr, in unsrer materialistischen Sittenlehre, die entscheidende l e t z t e einzuräumen. Mitten im Schosse der raffiniertesten Geselligkeit hat der Egoism sein System gegründet, und ohne ein geselliges Herz mit heraus zu bringen, erfahren wir alle Ansteckungen und alle Drangsale der Gesellschaft. Unser freies Urteil unterwerfen wir ihrer despotischen Meinung, unser Gefühl ihren bizarren Gebräuchen, unsern Willen ihren Verführungen; nur unsre Willkür behaupten wir gegen ihre heiligen Rechte. Stolze Selbstgenügsamkeit zieht das Herz des Weltmanns zusammen, das in dem rohen Naturmenschen noch oft sympathetisch schlägt, und wie aus einer brennenden Stadt sucht jeder nur sein elendes Eigentum aus der Verwüstung zu flüchten. Nur in einer völligen Abschwörung der Empfindsamkeit glaubt man gegen ihre Verirrungen Schutz zu finden, und der Spott, der den Schwärmer oft heilsam züchtigt, lästert mit gleich wenig Schonung das edelste Gefühl. Die Kultur, weit entfernt, uns in Freiheit zu setzen, entwickelt mit jeder Kraft, die sie in uns ausbildet, nur ein neues Bedürfnis; die Bande des Physischen schnüren sich immer beängstigender zu, so dass die Furcht, zu verlieren, selbst den feurigen Trieb nach Verbesserung erstickt und die Maxime des leidenden Gehorsams für die höchste

from within? Its very dissolution provides the justification of its existence. For society, released from its controls, is falling back into the kingdom of the elements, instead of hastening upwards into the realm of organic life.

5.   The cultivated classes, on the other hand, offer the even more repugnant spectacle of lethargy, and of a depravation of character which offends the more because culture itself is its source. I no longer recall which of the ancient or modern philosophers it was who remarked that the nobler a thing is, the more repulsive it is when it decays; but we shall find that this is no less true in the moral sphere. The child of Nature, when he breaks loose, turns into a madman; the creature of Civilization into a knave. That Enlightenment of the mind, which is the not altogether groundless boast of our refined classes, has had on the whole so little of an ennobling influence on feeling and character that it has tended rather to bolster up depravity by providing it with the support of precepts. We disown Nature in her rightful sphere only to submit to her tyranny in the moral, and while resisting the impact she makes upon our senses are content to take over her principles. The sham propriety of our manners refuses her the first say—which would be pardonable— only to concede to her in our materialistic ethics the final and decisive one. In the very bosom of the most exquisitely developed social life egotism has founded its system, and without ever acquiring therefrom a heart that is truly sociable, we suffer all the contagions and afflictions of society. We subject our free judgement to its despotic opinion, our feeling to its fantastic customs, our will to its seductions; only our caprice do we uphold against its sacred rights. Proud self-sufficiency contracts the heart of the man of the world, a heart which in natural man still often beats in sympathy; and as from a city in flames each man seeks only to save from the general destruction his own wretched belongings. Only by completely abjuring sensibility can we, so it is thought, be safe from its aberrations; and the ridicule which often acts as a salutary chastener of the enthusiast is equally unsparing in its desecration of the noblest feeling. Civilization, far from setting us free, in fact creates some new need with every new power it develops in us. The fetters of the physical tighten ever more alarmingly, so that fear of losing what we have stifles even the most burning impulse towards improvement, and the maxim of passive obedience passes for the

Weisheit des Lebens gilt. So sieht man den Geist der Zeit zwischen Verkehrtheit und Rohigkeit, zwischen Unnatur und blosser Natur, zwischen Superstition und moralischem Unglauben schwanken, und es ist bloss das Gleichgewicht des Schlimmen, was ihm zuweilen noch Grenzen setzt.

supreme wisdom of life. Thus do we see the spirit of the age waver-
ing between perversity and brutality, between unnaturalness and
mere nature, between superstition and moral unbelief; and it is only
through an equilibrium of evils that it is still sometimes kept within
bounds.

SECHSTER BRIEF

1. SOLLTE ich mit dieser Schilderung dem Zeitalter wohl zu viel getan haben? Ich erwarte diesen Einwurf nicht, eher einen andern: dass ich zu viel dadurch bewiesen habe. Dieses Gemälde, werden Sie mir sagen, gleicht zwar der gegenwärtigen Menschheit, aber es gleicht überhaupt allen Völkern, die in der Kultur begriffen sind, weil alle ohne Unterschied durch Vernünftelei von der Natur abfallen müssen, ehe sie durch Vernunft zu ihr zurückkehren können.

2. Aber bei einiger Aufmerksamkeit auf den Zeitcharakter muss uns der Kontrast in Verwunderung setzen, der zwischen der heutigen Form der Menschheit und zwischen der ehemaligen, besonders der griechischen, angetroffen wird. Der Ruhm der Ausbildung und Verfeinerung, den wir mit Recht gegen jede andre blosse Natur geltend machen, kann uns gegen die griechische Natur nicht zustatten kommen, die sich mit allen Reizen der Kunst und mit aller Würde der Weisheit vermählte, ohne doch, wie die unsrige, das Opfer derselben zu sein. Die Griechen beschämen uns nicht bloss durch eine Simplizität, die unserm Zeitalter fremd ist; sie sind zugleich unsre Nebenbuhler, ja oft unsre Muster in den nämlichen Vorzügen, mit denen wir uns über die Naturwidrigkeit unsrer Sitten zu trösten pflegen. Zugleich voll Form und voll Fülle, zugleich philosophierend und bildend, zugleich zart und energisch sehen wir sie die Jugend der Phantasie mit der Männlichkeit der Vernunft in einer herrlichen Menschheit vereinigen.

3. Damals, bei jenem schönen Erwachen der Geisteskräfte, hatten die Sinne und der Geist noch kein strenge geschiedenes Eigentum; denn noch hatte kein Zwiespalt sie gereizt, mit einander feindselig abzuteilen und ihre Markung zu bestimmen. Die Poesie hatte noch nicht mit dem Witze gebuhlt und die Spekulation sich noch nicht durch Spitzfindigkeit geschändet. Beide konnten im Notfall ihre Verrichtungen tauschen, weil jedes, nur auf seine eigene Weise, die Wahrheit ehrte. So hoch die Vernunft auch stieg, so zog sie doch immer die Materie liebend nach, und so fein und scharf sie auch trennte, so verstümmelte sie doch nie. Sie zerlegte zwar die menschliche Natur und warf sie in ihrem herrlichen Götterkreis

SIXTH LETTER

1. HAVE I not perhaps been too hard on our age in the picture I have just drawn? That is scarcely the reproach I anticipate. Rather a different one: that I have tried to make it prove too much. Such a portrait, you will tell me, does indeed resemble mankind as it is today; but does it not also resemble any people caught up in the process of civilization, since all of them, without exception, must fall away from Nature by the abuse of Reason before they can return to her by the use of Reason?

2. Closer attention to the character of our age will, however, reveal an astonishing contrast between contemporary forms of humanity and earlier ones, especially the Greek. The reputation for culture and refinement, on which we otherwise rightly pride ourselves *vis-à-vis* humanity in its m e r e l y natural state, can avail us nothing against the natural humanity of the Greeks. For they were wedded to all the delights of art and all the dignity of wisdom, without however, like us, falling a prey to their seduction. The Greeks put us to shame not only by a simplicity to which our age is a stranger; they are at the same time our rivals, indeed often our models, in those very excellences with which we are wont to console ourselves for the unnaturalness of our manners. In fullness of form no less than of content, at once philosophic and creative, sensitive and energetic, the Greeks combined the first youth of imagination with the manhood of reason in a glorious manifestation of humanity.

3. At that first fair awakening of the powers of the mind, sense and intellect did not as yet rule over strictly separate domains; for no dissension had as yet provoked them into hostile partition and mutual demarcation of their frontiers. Poetry had not as yet coquetted with wit, nor speculation prostituted itself to sophistry. Both of them could, when need arose, exchange functions, since each in its own fashion paid honour to truth. However high the mind might soar, it always drew matter lovingly along with it; and however fine and sharp the distinctions it might make, it never proceeded to mutilate. It did indeed divide human nature into its several aspects, and project these in magnified form into the divinities of its glorious

vergrössert auseinander, aber nicht dadurch, dass sie sie in Stücken riss, sondern dadurch, dass sie sie verschiedentlich mischte, denn die ganze Menschheit fehlte in keinem einzelnen Gott. Wie ganz anders bei uns Neuern! Auch bei uns ist das Bild der Gattung in den Individuen vergrössert auseinander geworfen — aber in Bruchstücken, nicht in veränderten Mischungen, dass man von Individuum zu Individuum herumfragen muss, um die Totalität der Gattung zusammenzulesen. Bei uns, möchte man fast versucht werden zu behaupten, äussern sich die Gemütskräfte auch in der Erfahrung so getrennt, wie der Psychologe sie in der Vorstellung scheidet, und wir sehen nicht bloss einzelne Subjekte, sondern ganze Klassen von Menschen nur einen Teil ihrer Anlagen entfalten, während dass die übrigen, wie bei verkrüppelten Gewächsen, kaum mit matter Spur angedeutet sind.

4.   Ich verkenne nicht die Vorzüge, welche das gegenwärtige Geschlecht, als Einheit betrachtet und auf der Wage des Verstandes, vor dem besten in der Vorwelt behaupten mag; aber in geschlossenen Gliedern muss es den Wettkampf beginnen und das Ganze mit dem Ganzen sich messen. Welcher einzelne Neuere tritt heraus, Mann gegen Mann mit dem einzelnen Athenienser um den Preis der Menschheit zu streiten?

5.   Woher wohl dieses nachteilige Verhältnis der Individuen bei allem Vorteil der Gattung? Warum qualifizierte sich der einzelne Grieche zum Repräsentanten seiner Zeit, und warum darf dies der einzelne Neuere nicht wagen? Weil jenem die alles vereinende Natur, diesem der alles trennende Verstand seine Formen erteilten.

6.   Die Kultur selbst war es, welche der neuern Menschheit diese Wunde schlug. Sobald auf der einen Seite die erweiterte Erfahrung und das bestimmtere Denken eine schärfere Scheidung der Wissenschaften, auf der andern das verwickeltere Uhrwerk der Staaten eine strengere Absonderung der Stände und Geschäfte notwendig machte, so zerriss auch der innere Bund der menschlichen Natur, und ein verderblicher Streit entzweite ihre harmonischen Kräfte. Der intuitive und der spekulative Verstand verteilten sich jetzt feindlich gesinnt auf ihren verschiedenen Feldern, deren Grenzen sie jetzt anfingen mit Misstrauen und Eifersucht zu bewachen, und mit der Sphäre, auf die man seine Wirksamkeit einschränkt, hat man sich auch in sich selbst einen Herrn gegeben, der nicht selten mit

pantheon; but not by tearing it to pieces; rather by combining its aspects in different proportions, for in no single one of their deities was humanity in its entirety ever lacking. How different with us Moderns! With us too the image of the human species is projected in magnified form into separate individuals—but as fragments, not in different combinations, with the result that one has to go the rounds from one individual to another in order to be able to piece together a complete image of the species. With us, one might almost be tempted to assert, the various faculties appear as separate in practice as they are distinguished by the psychologist in theory, and we see not merely individuals, but whole classes of men, developing but one part of their potentialities, while of the rest, as in stunted growths, only vestigial traces remain.

4. I do not underrate the advantages which the human race today, considered as a whole and weighed in the balance of intellect, can boast in the face of what is best in the ancient world. But it has to take up the challenge in serried ranks, and let whole measure itself against whole. What individual Modern could sally forth and engage, man against man, with an individual Athenian for the prize of humanity?

5. Whence this disadvantage among individuals when the species as a whole is at such an advantage? Why was the individual Greek qualified to be the representative of his age, and why can no single Modern venture as much? Because it was from all-unifying Nature that the former, and from the all-dividing Intellect that the latter, received their respective forms.

6. It was civilization itself which inflicted this wound upon modern man. Once the increase of empirical knowledge, and more exact modes of thought, made sharper divisions between the sciences inevitable, and once the increasingly complex machinery of State necessitated a more rigorous separation of ranks and occupations, then the inner unity of human nature was severed too, and a disastrous conflict set its harmonious powers at variance. The intuitive and the speculative understanding now withdrew in hostility to take up positions in their respective fields, whose frontiers they now began to guard with jealous mistrust; and with this confining of our activity to a particular sphere we have given ourselves a master within, who not infrequently ends by suppressing the rest of our

Unterdrückung der übrigen Anlagen zu endigen pflegt. Indem hier die luxurierende Einbildungskraft die mühsamen Pflanzungen des Verstandes verwüstet, verzehrt dort der Abstraktionsgeist das Feuer, an dem das Herz sich hätte wärmen und die Phantasie sich entzünden sollen.

7. Diese Zerrüttung, welche Kunst und Gelehrsamkeit in dem innern Menschen anfingen, machte der neue Geist der Regierung vollkommen und allgemein. Es war freilich nicht zu erwarten, dass die einfache Organisation der ersten Republiken die Einfalt der ersten Sitten und Verhältnisse überlebte; aber anstatt zu einem höhern animalischen Leben zu steigen, sank sie zu einer gemeinen und groben Mechanik herab. Jene Polypennatur der griechischen Staaten, wo jedes Individuum eines unabhängigen Lebens genoss und, wenn es not tat, zum Ganzen werden konnte, machte jetzt einem kunstreichen Uhrwerke Platz, wo aus der Zusammenstückelung unendlich vieler, aber lebloser Teile ein mechanisches Leben im Ganzen sich bildet. Auseinandergerissen wurden jetzt der Staat und die Kirche, die Gesetze und die Sitten; der Genuss wurde von der Arbeit, das Mittel vom Zweck, die Anstrengung von der Belohnung geschieden. Ewig nur an ein einzelnes kleines Bruchstück des Ganzen gefesselt, bildet sich der Mensch selbst nur als Bruchstück aus; ewig nur das eintönige Geräusch des Rades, das er umtreibt, im Ohre, entwickelt er nie die Harmonie seines Wesens, und anstatt die Menschheit in seiner Natur auszuprägen, wird er bloss zu einem Abdruck seines Geschäfts, seiner Wissenschaft. Aber selbst der karge fragmentarische Anteil, der die einzelnen Glieder noch an das Ganze knüpft, hängt nicht von Formen ab, die sie sich selbsttätig geben (denn wie dürfte man ihrer Freiheit ein so künstliches und lichtscheues Uhrwerk vertrauen?), sondern wird ihnen mit skrupulöser Strenge durch ein Formular vorgeschrieben, in welchem man ihre freie Einsicht gebunden hält. Der tote Buchstabe vertritt den lebendigen Verstand, und ein geübtes Gedächtnis leitet sicherer als Genie und Empfindung.

8. Wenn das gemeine Wesen das Amt zum Massstab des Mannes macht, wenn es an dem einen seiner Bürger nur die Memorie, an einem andern den tabellarischen Verstand, an einem dritten nur die mechanische Fertigkeit ehrt, wenn es hier, gleichgültig gegen den Charakter, nur auf Kenntnisse dringt, dort hingegen einem Geiste der Ordnung und einem gesetzlichen Verhalten die grösste

potentialities. While in the one a riotous imagination ravages the hard-won fruits of the intellect, in another the spirit of abstraction stifles the fire at which the heart should have warmed itself and the imagination been kindled.

7. This disorganization, which was first started within man by civilization and learning, was made complete and universal by the new spirit of government. It was scarcely to be expected that the simple organization of the early republics should have survived the simplicity of early manners and conditions; but instead of rising to a higher form of organic existence it degenerated into a crude and clumsy mechanism. That polypoid character of the Greek States, in which every individual enjoyed an independent existence but could, when need arose, grow into the whole organism, now made way for an ingenious clock-work, in which, out of the piecing together of innumerable but lifeless parts, a mechanical kind of collective life ensued. State and Church, laws and customs, were now torn asunder; enjoyment was divorced from labour, the means from the end, the effort from the reward. Everlastingly chained to a single little fragment of the Whole, man himself develops into nothing but a fragment; everlastingly in his ear the monotonous sound of the wheel that he turns, he never develops the harmony of his being, and instead of putting the stamp of humanity upon his own nature, he becomes nothing more than the imprint of his occupation or of his specialized knowledge. But even that meagre, fragmentary participation, by which individual members of the State are still linked to the Whole, does not depend upon forms which they spontaneously prescribe for themselves (for how could one entrust to their freedom of action a mechanism so intricate and so fearful of light and enlightenment?); it is dictated to them with meticulous exactitude by means of a formulary which inhibits all freedom of thought. The dead letter takes the place of living understanding, and a good memory is a safer guide than imagination and feeling.

8. When the community makes his office the measure of the man; when in one of its citizens it prizes nothing but memory, in another a mere tabularizing intelligence, in a third only mechanical skill; when, in the one case, indifferent to character, it insists exclusively on knowledge, yet is, in another, ready to condone any amount of obscurantist thinking as long as it is accompanied by a spirit of

Verfinsterung des Verstandes zu gut hält, wenn es zugleich diese einzelnen Fertigkeiten zu einer ebenso grossen Intensität will getrieben wissen, als es dem Subjekt an Extensität erlässt — darf es uns da wundern, dass die übrigen Anlagen des Gemüts vernachlässigt werden, um der einzigen, welche ehrt und lohnt, alle Pflege zuzuwenden? Zwar wissen wir, dass das kraftvolle Genie die Grenzen seines Geschäfts nicht zu Grenzen seiner Tätigkeit macht, aber das mittelmässige Talent verzehrt in dem Geschäfte, das ihm zum Anteil fiel, die ganze karge Summe seiner Kraft, und es muss schon kein gemeiner Kopf sein, um, unbeschadet seines Berufs, für Liebhabereien übrig zu behalten. Noch dazu ist es selten eine gute Empfehlung bei dem Staat, wenn die Kräfte die Aufträge übersteigen, oder wenn das höhere Geistesbedürfnis des Mannes von Genie seinem Amt einen Nebenbuhler gibt. So eifersüchtig ist der Staat auf den Alleinbesitz seiner Diener, dass er sich leichter dazu entschliessen wird (und wer kann ihm Unrecht geben?), seinen Mann mit einer Venus Cytherea als mit einer Venus Urania zu teilen.

9. Und so wird denn allmählich das einzelne konkrete Leben vertilgt, damit das Abstrakt des Ganzen sein dürftiges Dasein friste, und ewig bleibt der Staat seinen Bürgern fremd, weil ihn das Gefühl nirgends findet. Genötigt, sich die Mannigfaltigkeit seiner Bürger durch Klassifizierung zu erleichtern und die Menschheit nie anders als durch Repräsentation aus der zweiten Hand zu empfangen, verliert der regierende Teil sie zuletzt ganz und gar aus den Augen, indem er sie mit einem blossen Machwerk des Verstandes vermengt; und der regierte kann nicht anders als mit Kaltsinn die Gesetze empfangen, die an ihn selbst so wenig gerichtet sind. Endlich überdrüssig, ein Band zu unterhalten, das ihr von dem Staate so wenig erleichtert wird, fällt die positive Gesellschaft (wie schon längst das Schicksal der meisten europäischen Staaten ist) in einen moralischen Naturstand auseinander, wo die öffentliche Macht nur eine Partei m e h r ist, gehasst und hintergangen von dem, der sie nötig macht, und nur von dem, der sie entbehren kann, geachtet.

10. Konnte die Menschheit bei dieser doppelten Gewalt, die von innen und aussen auf sie drückte, wohl eine andere Richtung nehmen, als sie wirklich nahm? Indem der spekulative Geist im Ideenreich nach unverlierbaren Besitzungen strebte, musste er ein

order and law-abiding behaviour; when, moreover, it insists on special skills being developed with a degree of intensity which is only commensurate with its readiness to absolve the individual citizen from developing himself in extensity—can we wonder that the remaining aptitudes of the psyche are neglected in order to give undivided attention to the one which will bring honour and profit? True, we know that the outstanding individual will never let the limits of his occupation dictate the limits of his activity. But a mediocre talent will consume in the office assigned him the whole meagre sum of his powers, and a man has to have a mind above the ordinary if, without detriment to his calling, he is still to have time for the chosen pursuits of his leisure. Moreover, it is rarely a recommendation in the eyes of the State if a man's powers exceed the tasks he is set, or if the higher needs of the man of parts constitute a rival to the duties of his office. So jealously does the State insist on being the sole proprietor of its servants that it will more easily bring itself (and who can blame it?) to share its man with the Cytherean, than with the Uranian, Venus.

9.   Thus little by little the concrete life of the Individual is destroyed in order that the abstract idea of the Whole may drag out its sorry existence, and the State remains for ever a stranger to its citizens since at no point does it ever make contact with their feeling. Forced to resort to classification in order to cope with the variety of its citizens, and never to get an impression of humanity except through representation at second hand, the governing section ends up by losing sight of them altogether, confusing their concrete reality with a mere construct of the intellect; while the governed cannot but receive with indifference laws which are scarcely, if at all, directed to them as persons. Weary at last of sustaining bonds which the State does so little to facilitate, positive society begins (this has long been the fate of most European States) to disintegrate into a state of primitive morality, in which public authority has become but one party m o r e, to be hated and circumvented by those who make authority necessary, and only obeyed by such as are capable of doing without it.

10.   With this twofold pressure upon it, from within and from without, could humanity well have taken any other course than the one it actually took? In its striving after inalienable possessions in the realm of ideas, the spirit of speculation could do no other than

Fremdling in der Sinnenwelt werden und über der Form die Materie verlieren. Der Geschäftsgeist, in einen einförmigen Kreis von Objekten eingeschlossen und in diesem noch mehr durch Formeln eingeengt, musste das freie Ganze sich aus den Augen gerückt sehen und zugleich mit seiner Sphäre verarmen. So wie ersterer versucht wird, das Wirkliche nach dem Denkbaren zu modeln und die subjektiven Bedingungen seiner Vorstellungskraft zu konstitutiven Gesetzen für das Dasein der Dinge zu erheben, so stürzte letzterer in das entgegenstehende Extrem, alle Erfahrung überhaupt nach einem besondern Fragment von Erfahrung zu schätzen und die Regeln s e i n e s Geschäfts jedem Geschäft ohne Unterschied anpassen zu wollen. Der eine musste einer leeren Subtilität, der andre einer pedantischen Beschränktheit zum Raube werden, weil jener für das Einzelne zu hoch, dieser zu tief für das Ganze stand. Aber das Nachteilige dieser Geistesrichtung schränkte sich nicht bloss auf das Wissen und Hervorbringen ein; es erstreckte sich nicht weniger auf das Empfinden und Handeln. Wir wissen, dass die Sensibilität des Gemüts ihrem Grade nach von der Lebhaftigkeit, ihrem Umfange nach von dem Reichtum der Einbildungskraft abhängt. Nun muss aber das Übergewicht des analytischen Vermögens die Phantasie notwendig ihrer Kraft und ihres Feuers berauben und eine eingeschränktere Sphäre von Objekten ihren Reichtum vermindern. Der abstrakte Denker hat daher gar oft ein k a l t e s Herz, weil er die Eindrücke zergliedert, die doch nur als ein Ganzes die Seele rühren; der Geschäftsmann hat gar oft ein e n g e s Herz, weil seine Einbildungskraft, in den einförmigen Kreis seines Berufs eingeschlossen, sich zu fremder Vorstellungsart nicht erweitern kann.

11. Es lag auf meinem Wege, die nachteilige Richtung des Zeit-Charakters und ihre Quellen aufzudecken, nicht die Vorteile zu zeigen, wodurch die Natur sie vergütet. Gerne will ich Ihnen eingestehen, dass, so wenig es auch den Individuen bei dieser Zerstückelung ihres Wesens wohl werden kann, doch die Gattung auf keine andere Art hätte Fortschritte machen können. Die Erscheinung der griechischen Menschheit war unstreitig ein Maximum, das auf dieser Stufe weder verharren noch höher steigen konnte. Nicht verharren, weil der Verstand durch den Vorrat, den er schon hatte, unausbleiblich genötigt werden musste, sich von der Empfindung und Anschauung abzusondern und nach Deutlichkeit der Erkenntnis

become a stranger to the world of sense, and lose sight of matter for the sake of form. The practical spirit, by contrast, enclosed within a monotonous sphere of material objects, and within this uniformity still further confined by formulas, was bound to find the idea of an unconditioned Whole receding from sight, and to become just as impoverished as its own poor sphere of activity. If the former was tempted to model the actual world on a world conceivable by the mind, and to exalt the subjective conditions of its own perceptual and conceptual faculty into laws constitutive of the existence of things, the latter plunged into the opposite extreme of judging all experience whatsoever by one particular fragment of experience, and of wanting to make the rules of its o w n occupation apply indiscriminately to all others. The one was bound to become the victim of empty subtilities, the other of narrow pedantry; for the former stood too high to discern the particular, the latter too low to survey the Whole. But the damaging effects of the turn which mind thus took were not confined to knowledge and production; it affected feeling and action no less. We know that the sensibility of the psyche depends for its intensity upon the liveliness, for its scope upon the richness, of the imagination. The preponderance of the analytical faculty must, however, of necessity, deprive the imagination of its energy and warmth, while a more restricted sphere of objects must reduce its wealth. Hence the abstract thinker very often has a c o l d heart, since he dissects his impressions, and impressions can move the soul only as long as they remain whole; while the man of practical affairs often has a n a r r o w heart, since his imagination, imprisoned within the unvarying confines of his own calling, is incapable of extending itself to appreciate other ways of seeing and knowing.

11. It was part of my procedure to uncover the disadvantageous trends in the character of our age and the reasons for them, not to point out the advantages which Nature offers by way of compensation. I readily concede that, little as individuals might benefit from this fragmentation of their being, there was no other way in which the species as a whole could have progressed. With the Greeks, humanity undoubtedly reached a maximum of excellence, which could neither be maintained at that level nor rise any higher. Not maintained, because the intellect was unavoidably compelled by the store of knowledge it already possessed to dissociate itself

zu streben; auch nicht höher steigen, weil nur ein bestimmter Grad von Klarheit mit einer bestimmten Fülle und Wärme zusammen bestehen kann. Die Griechen hatten diesen Grad erreicht, und wenn sie zu einer höhern Ausbildung fortschreiten wollten, so mussten sie, wie wir, die Totalität ihres Wesens aufgeben und die Wahrheit auf getrennten Bahnen verfolgen.

12.   Die mannigfaltigen Anlagen im Menschen zu entwickeln, war kein anderes Mittel, als sie einander entgegen zu setzen. Dieser Antagonism der Kräfte ist das grosse Instrument der Kultur, aber auch nur das Instrument; denn solange derselbe dauert, ist man erst auf dem Wege zu dieser. Dadurch allein, dass in dem Menschen einzelne Kräfte sich isolieren und einer ausschliessenden Gesetzgebung anmassen, geraten sie in Widerstreit mit der Wahrheit der Dinge und nötigen den Gemeinsinn, der sonst mit träger Genügsamkeit auf der äussern Erscheinung ruht, in die Tiefen der Objekte zu dringen. Indem der reine Verstand eine Autorität in der Sinnenwelt usurpiert und der empirische beschäftigt ist, ihn den Bedingungen der Erfahrung zu unterwerfen, bilden beide Anlagen sich zu möglichster Reife aus und erschöpfen den ganzen Umfang ihrer Sphäre. Indem hier die Einbildungskraft durch ihre Willkür die Weltordnung aufzulösen wagt, nötiget sie dort die Vernunft, zu den obersten Quellen der Erkenntnis zu steigen und das Gesetz der Notwendigkeit gegen sie zu Hilfe zu rufen.

13.   Einseitigkeit in Übung der Kräfte führt zwar das Individuum unausbleiblich zum Irrtum, aber die Gattung zur Wahrheit. Dadurch allein, dass wir die ganze Energie unsers Geistes in Einem Brennpunkt versammeln und unser ganzes Wesen in eine einzige Kraft zusammenziehen, setzen wir dieser einzelnen Kraft gleichsam Flügel an und führen sie künstlicherweise weit über die Schranken hinaus, welche die Natur ihr gesetzt zu haben scheint. So gewiss es ist, dass alle menschliche Individuen, zusammen genommen, mit der Sehkraft, welche die Natur ihnen erteilt, nie dahin gekommen sein würden, einen Trabanten des Jupiter auszuspähn, den der Teleskop dem Astronomen entdeckt, ebenso ausgemacht ist es, dass die menschliche Denkkraft niemals eine Analysis des Unendlichen oder eine Kritik der reinen Vernunft würde aufgestellt haben, wenn nicht in einzelnen dazu berufnen Subjekten die Vernunft sich vereinzelt, von allem Stoff gleichsam losgewunden und durch die

from feeling and intuition in an attempt to arrive at exact discursive understanding; not rise any higher, because only a specific degree of clarity is compatible with a specific fullness and warmth. This degree the Greeks had attained; and had they wished to proceed to a higher stage of development, they would, like us, have had to surrender their wholeness of being and pursue truth along separate paths.

12.   If the manifold potentialities in man were ever to be developed, there was no other way but to pit them one against the other. This antagonism of faculties and functions is the great instrument of civilization—but it is only the instrument; for as long as it persists, we are only on the way to becoming civilized. Only through individual powers in man becoming isolated, and arrogating to themselves exclusive authority, do they come into conflict with the truth of things, and force the Common Sense, which is otherwise content to linger with indolent complacency on outward appearance, to penetrate phenomena in depth. By pure thought usurping authority in the world of sense, while empirical thought is concerned to subject the usurper to the conditions of experience, both these powers develop to their fullest potential, and exhaust the whole range of their proper sphere. And by the very boldness with which, in the one case, imagination allows her caprice to dissolve the existing world-order, she does, in the other, compel Reason to rise to the ultimate sources of knowing, and invoke the law of Necessity against her.

13.   One-sidedness in the exercise of his powers must, it is true, inevitably lead the individual into error; but the species as a whole to truth. Only by concentrating the whole energy of our mind into a s i n g l e focal point, contracting our whole being into a single power, do we, as it were, lend wings to this individual power and lead it, by artificial means, far beyond the limits which Nature seems to have assigned to it. Even as it is certain that all individuals taken together would never, with the powers of vision granted them by Nature alone, have managed to detect a satellite of Jupiter which the telescope reveals to the astronomer, so it is beyond question that human powers of reflection would never have produced an analysis of the Infinite or a Critique of Pure Reason, unless, in the individuals called to perform such feats, Reason had separated itself off, disentangled itself, as it were, from all matter, and by the most intense

angestrengteste Abstraktion ihren Blick ins Unbedingte bewaffnet hätte. Aber wird wohl ein solcher, in reinen Verstand und reine Anschauung gleichsam aufgelöster Geist dazu tüchtig sein, die strengen Fesseln der Logik mit dem freien Gange der Dichtungskraft zu vertauschen und die Individualität der Dinge mit treuem und keuschem Sinn zu ergreifen? Hier setzt die Natur auch dem Universalgenie eine Grenze, die es nicht überschreiten kann, und die Wahrheit wird so lange Märtyrer machen, als die Philosophie noch ihr vornehmstes Geschäft daraus machen muss, Anstalten gegen den Irrtum zu treffen.

14. Wie viel also auch für das Ganze der Welt durch diese getrennte Ausbildung der menschlichen Kräfte gewonnen werden mag, so ist nicht zu leugnen, dass die Individuen, welche sie trifft, unter dem Fluch dieses Weltzweckes leiden. Durch gymnastische Übungen bilden sich zwar athletische Körper aus, aber nur durch das freie und gleichförmige Spiel der Glieder die Schönheit. Ebenso kann die Anspannung einzelner Geisteskräfte zwar ausserordentliche, aber nur die gleichförmige Temperatur derselben glückliche und vollkommene Menschen erzeugen. Und in welchem Verhältnis stünden wir also zu dem vergangenen und kommenden Weltalter, wenn die Ausbildung der menschlichen Natur ein solches Opfer notwendig machte? Wir wären die Knechte der Menschheit gewesen, wir hätten einige Jahrtausende lang die Sklavenarbeit für sie getrieben und unsrer verstümmelten Natur die beschämenden Spuren dieser Dienstbarkeit eingedrückt — damit das spätere Geschlecht in einem seligen Müssiggange seiner moralischen Gesundheit warten und den freien Wuchs seiner Menschheit entwickeln könnte!

15. Kann aber wohl der Mensch dazu bestimmt sein, über irgend einem Zwecke sich selbst zu versäumen? Sollte uns die Natur durch ihre Zwecke eine Vollkommenheit rauben können, welche uns die Vernunft durch die ihrigen vorschreibt? Es muss also falsch sein, dass die Ausbildung der einzelnen Kräfte das Opfer ihrer Totalität notwendig macht; oder wenn auch das Gesetz der Natur noch so sehr dahin strebte, so muss es bei uns stehen, diese Totalität in unsrer Natur, welche die Kunst zerstört hat, durch eine höhere Kunst wieder herzustellen.

effort of abstraction armed their eyes with a glass for peering into the Absolute. But will such a mind, dissolved as it were into pure intellect and pure contemplation, ever be capable of exchanging the rigorous bonds of logic for the free movement of the poetic faculty, or of grasping the concrete individuality of things with a sense innocent of preconceptions and faithful to the object? At this point Nature sets limits even to the most universal genius, limits which he cannot transcend; and as long as philosophy has to make its prime business the provision of safeguards against error, truth will be bound to have its martyrs.

14. Thus, however much the world as a whole may benefit through this fragmentary specialization of human powers, it cannot be denied that the individuals affected by it suffer under the curse of this cosmic purpose. Athletic bodies can, it is true, be developed by gymnastic exercises; beauty only through the free and harmonious play of the limbs. In the same way the keying up of individual functions of the mind can indeed produce extraordinary human beings; but only the equal tempering of them all, happy and complete human beings. And in what kind of relation would we stand to either past or future ages, if the development of human nature were to make such sacrifice necessary? We would have been the serfs of mankind; for several millenia we would have done slaves' work for them, and our mutilated nature would bear impressed upon it the shameful marks of this servitude. And all this in order that a future generation might in blissful indolence attend to the care of its moral health, and foster the free growth of its humanity!

15. But can Man really be destined to miss himself for the sake of any purpose whatsoever? Should Nature, for the sake of her own purposes, be able to rob us of a completeness which Reason, for the sake of hers, enjoins upon us? It must, therefore, be wrong if the cultivation of individual powers involves the sacrifice of wholeness. Or rather, however much the law of Nature tends in that direction, it must be open to us to restore by means of a higher Art the totality of our nature which the arts themselves have destroyed.

SIEBENTER BRIEF

1. SOLLTE diese Wirkung vielleicht von dem Staat zu erwarten sein? Das ist nicht möglich, denn der Staat, wie er jetzt beschaffen ist, hat das Übel veranlasst, und der Staat, wie ihn die Vernunft in der Idee sich aufgibt, anstatt diese bessere Menschheit begründen zu können, müsste selbst erst darauf gegründet werden. Und so hätten mich denn die bisherigen Untersuchungen wieder auf den Punkt zurückgeführt, von dem sie mich eine Zeitlang entfernten. Das jetzige Zeitalter, weit entfernt, uns diejenige Form der Menschheit aufzuweisen, welche als notwendige Bedingung einer moralischen Staatsverbesserung erkannt worden ist, zeigt uns vielmehr das direkte Gegenteil davon. Sind also die von mir aufgestellten Grundsätze richtig, und bestätigt die Erfahrung mein Gemälde der Gegenwart, so muss man jeden Versuch einer solchen Staatsveränderung so lange für unzeitig und jede darauf gegründete Hoffnung so lange für schimärisch erklären, bis die Trennung in dem innern Menschen wieder aufgehoben und seine Natur vollständig genug entwickelt ist, um selbst die Künstlerin zu sein und der politischen Schöpfung der Vernunft ihre Realität zu verbürgen.

2. Die Natur zeichnet uns in ihrer physischen Schöpfung den Weg vor, den man in der moralischen zu wandeln hat. Nicht eher, als bis der Kampf elementarischer Kräfte in den niedrigern Organisationen besänftiget ist, erhebt sie sich zu der edeln Bildung des physischen Menschen. Ebenso muss der Elementenstreit in dem ethischen Menschen, der Konflikt blinder Triebe, fürs erste beruhigt sein, und die grobe Entgegensetzung muss in ihm aufgehört haben, ehe man es wagen darf, die Mannigfaltigkeit zu begünstigen. Auf der andern Seite muss die Selbständigkeit seines Charakters gesichert sein und die Unterwürfigkeit unter fremde despotische Formen einer anständigen Freiheit Platz gemacht haben, ehe man die Mannigfaltigkeit in ihm der Einheit des Ideals unterwerfen darf. Wo der Naturmensch seine Willkür noch so gesetzlos missbraucht, da darf man ihm seine Freiheit kaum zeigen; wo der künstliche Mensch seine Freiheit noch so wenig gebraucht, da darf man ihm seine Willkür nicht nehmen. Das Geschenk liberaler Grundsätze wird Verräterei an dem Ganzen, wenn es sich zu einer noch gärenden

SEVENTH LETTER

1. CAN we perhaps look for such action from the State? That is out of the question. For the State as at present constituted has been the cause of the evil, while the State as Reason conceives it, far from being able to lay the foundations of this better humanity, would itself have to be founded upon it. Thus the course of my inquiry would seem to have brought me back to the point from which for a time it had deflected me. The present age, far from exhibiting that form of humanity which we have recognized as the necessary condition of any moral reform of the State, shows us rather the exact opposite. If, therefore, the principles I have laid down are correct, and if experience confirms my portrayal of the present age, we must continue to regard every attempt at political reform as untimely, and every hope based upon it as chimerical, as long as the split within man is not healed, and his nature so restored to wholeness that it can itself become the artificer of the State, and guarantee the reality of this political creation of Reason.

2. Nature in her physical creation points the way we have to take in the moral. Not until the strife of elemental forces in the lower organisms has been assuaged does she turn to the nobler creation of physical man. In the same way, the strife of elements in moral man, the conflict of blind impulse, has first to be appeased, and crude antagonisms first have ceased within him, before we can take the risk of promoting diversity. On the other hand, the independence of his character must first have become secure, and submission to external forms of authority have given way to a becoming liberty, before the diversity within him can be subjected to any ideal unity. As long as natural man still makes a lawless misuse of his licence, one can scarcely run the risk of letting him glimpse his liberty; and as long as civilized man as yet makes so little use of his liberty, one can hardly deprive him of his licence. The gift of liberal principles becomes a betrayal of society as a whole when it allies itself with

Kraft gesellt und einer schon übermächtigen Natur Verstärkung zusendet; das Gesetz der Übereinstimmung wird Tyrannei gegen das Individuum, wenn es sich mit einer schon herrschenden Schwäche und physischen Beschränkung verknüpft und so den letzten glimmenden Funken von Selbsttätigkeit und Eigentum auslöscht.

3. Der Charakter der Zeit muss sich also von seiner tiefen Entwürdigung erst aufrichten, dort der blinden Gewalt der Natur sich entziehen, und hier zu ihrer Einfalt, Wahrheit und Fülle zurückkehren — eine Aufgabe für mehr als Ein Jahrhundert. Unterdessen gebe ich gerne zu, kann mancher Versuch im Einzelnen gelingen; aber am Ganzen wird dadurch nichts gebessert sein, und der Widerspruch des Betragens wird stets gegen die Einheit der Maximen beweisen. Man wird in andern Weltteilen in dem Neger die Menschheit ehren und in Europa sie in dem Denker schänden. Die alten Grundsätze werden bleiben, aber sie werden das Kleid des Jahrhunderts tragen, und zu einer Unterdrückung, welche sonst die Kirche autorisierte, wird die Philosophie ihren Namen leihen. Von der Freiheit erschreckt, die in ihren ersten Versuchen sich immer als Feindin ankündigt, wird man dort einer bequemen Knechtschaft sich in die Arme werfen und hier, von einer pedantischen Curatel zur Verzweiflung gebracht, in die wilde Ungebundenheit des Naturstands entspringen. Die Usurpation wird sich auf die Schwachheit der menschlichen Natur, die Insurrektion auf die Würde derselben berufen, bis endlich die grosse Beherrscherin aller menschlichen Dinge, die blinde Stärke, dazwischen tritt und den vorgeblichen Streit der Prinzipien wie einen gemeinen Faustkampf entscheidet.

forces still in ferment, and reinforces an already too powerful Nature. The law of conformity turns into tyranny *vis-à-vis* the individual when it is allied with an already prevailing weakness and physical limitation, and so extinguishes the last glimmering spark of independence and individuality.

3.   The character of the age must therefore first lift itself out of its deep degradation: on the one hand, emancipate itself from the blind forces of Nature; on the other, return to her simplicity, truth, and fullness—a task for more than o n e century. Meanwhile I readily admit that isolated attempts may succeed. But no improvement in the body politic as a whole will thereby ensue, and discrepancies in practice will continue to belie unanimity of precepts. In other continents we shall honour humanity in the negro; in Europe profane it in the thinker. The old principles will remain; but they will wear the dress of the century, and Philosophy now lend her name to a repression formerly authorized by the Church. Fearful of freedom, which in its first tentative ventures always comes in the guise of an enemy, we shall either cast ourselves into the arms of an easy servitude or, driven to despair by a pedantic tutelage, escape into the wild libertinism of the natural state. Usurpation will invoke the weakness of human nature, insurrection its dignity; until finally blind force, that great imperatrice of human affairs, steps in and decides this pretended conflict of principles as though it were a common brawl.

ACHTER BRIEF

1. SOLL sich also die Philosophie, mutlos und ohne Hoffnung, aus diesem Gebiete zurückziehen? Während dass sich die Herrschaft der Formen nach jeder andern Richtung erweitert, soll dieses wichtigste aller Güter dem gestaltlosen Zufall preisgegeben sein? Der Konflikt blinder Kräfte soll in der politischen Welt ewig dauern und das gesellige Gesetz nie über die feindselige Selbstsucht siegen?

2. Nichts weniger! Die Vernunft selbst wird zwar mit dieser rauhen Macht, die ihren Waffen widersteht, unmittelbar den Kampf nicht versuchen und so wenig als der Sohn des Saturns in der Ilias, selbsthandelnd auf den finstern Schauplatz heruntersteigen. Aber aus der Mitte der Streiter wählt sie sich den würdigsten aus, bekleidet ihn wie Zeus seinen Enkel mit göttlichen Waffen und bewirkt durch seine siegende Kraft die grosse Entscheidung.

3. Die Vernunft hat geleistet, was sie leisten kann, wenn sie das Gesetz findet und aufstellt; vollstrecken muss es der mutige Wille und das lebendige Gefühl. Wenn die Wahrheit im Streit mit Kräften den Sieg erhalten soll, so muss sie selbst erst zur Kraft werden und zu ihrem Sachführer im Reich der Erscheinungen einen Trieb aufstellen; denn Triebe sind die einzigen bewegenden Kräfte in der empfindenden Welt. Hat sie bis jetzt ihre siegende Kraft noch so wenig bewiesen, so liegt dies nicht an dem Verstande, der sie nicht zu entschleiern wusste, sondern an dem Herzen, das sich ihr verschloss, und an dem Triebe, der nicht für sie handelte.

4. Denn woher diese noch so allgemeine Herrschaft der Vorurteile und diese Verfinsterung der Köpfe bei allem Licht, das Philosophie und Erfahrung aufsteckten? Das Zeitalter ist aufgeklärt, das heisst die Kenntnisse sind gefunden und öffentlich preisgegeben, welche hinreichen würden, wenigstens unsre praktischen Grundsätze zu berichtigen. Der Geist der freien Untersuchung hat die Wahnbegriffe zerstreut, welche lange Zeit den Zugang zu der Wahrheit verwehrten, und den Grund unterwühlt, auf welchem Fanatismus und Betrug ihren Thron erbauten. Die Vernunft hat sich von den Täuschungen der Sinne und von einer betrüglichen Sophistik gereinigt, und die Philosophie selbst, welche uns zuerst von ihr

EIGHTH LETTER

1. Is Philosophy then to retire, dejected and despairing, from this field? While the dominion of forms is being extended in every other direction, is this, the most important good of all, to remain the prey of formless chance? Is the conflict of blind forces to endure for ever in the political world, and the law of sociality never to triumph over hostile self-interest?

2. By no means! Reason herself, it is true, will not join battle directly with this savage force which resists her weapons. No more than the son of Saturn in the *Iliad* will she descend to personal combat in this gloomy arena. But from the midst of the warriors she chooses the most worthy, equips him, as Zeus did his grandson, with divine weapons, and through his victorious strength decides the great issue.

3. Reason has accomplished all that she can accomplish by discovering the law and establishing it. Its execution demands a resolute will and ardour of feeling. If Truth is to be victorious in her conflict with forces, she must herself first become a f o r c e and appoint some d r i v e to be her champion in the realm of phenomena; for drives are the only motive forces in the sensible world. If she has hitherto displayed so little of her conquering power, this was due, not to the intellect which was powerless to unveil her, but to the heart which closed itself against her, and to the drive which refused to act on her behalf.

4. For whence comes this still so prevalent rule of prejudice, and this obscuring of minds in the face of all the light which philosophy and empirical science have kindled? Our Age is Enlightened; that is to say, such knowledge has been discovered and publicly disseminated as would suffice to correct at least our practical principles. The spirit of free inquiry has dissipated those false conceptions which for so long barred the approach to truth, and undermined the foundations upon which fanaticism and deception had raised their throne. Reason has purged herself of both the illusions of the senses and the delusions of sophistry, and philosophy itself, which first

abtrünnig machte, ruft uns laut und dringend in den Schoss der Natur zurück — woran liegt es, dass wir noch immer Barbaren sind?

5. Es muss also, weil es nicht in den Dingen liegt, in den Gemütern der Menschen etwas vorhanden sein, was der Aufnahme der Wahrheit, auch wenn sie noch so hell leuchtete, und der Annahme derselben, auch wenn sie noch so lebendig überzeugte, im Wege steht. Ein alter Weiser hat es empfunden, und es liegt in dem vielbedeutenden Ausdrucke versteckt: *sapere aude*.

6. Erkühne dich, weise zu sein. Energie des Muts gehört dazu, die Hindernisse zu bekämpfen, welche sowohl die Trägheit der Natur als die Feigheit des Herzens der Belehrung entgegensetzen. Nicht ohne Bedeutung lässt der alte Mythus die Göttin der Weisheit in voller Rüstung aus Jupiters Haupte steigen; denn schon ihre erste Verrichtung ist kriegerisch. Schon in der Geburt hat sie einen harten Kampf mit den Sinnen zu bestehen, die aus ihrer süssen Ruhe nicht gerissen sein wollen. Der zahlreichere Teil der Menschen wird durch den Kampf mit der Not viel zu sehr ermüdet und abgespannt, als dass er sich zu einem neuen und härtern Kampf mit dem Irrtum aufraffen sollte. Zufrieden, wenn er selbst der sauren Mühe des Denkens entgeht, lässt er andere gern über seine Begriffe die Vormundschaft führen, und geschieht es, dass sich höhere Bedürfnisse in ihm regen, so ergreift er mit durstigem Glauben die Formeln, welche der Staat und das Priestertum für diesen Fall in Bereitschaft halten. Wenn diese unglücklichen Menschen unser Mitleiden verdienen, so trifft unsre gerechte Verachtung die andern, die ein besseres Los von dem Joch der Bedürfnisse frei macht, aber eigene Wahl darunter beugt. Diese ziehen den Dämmerschein dunkler Begriffe, wo man lebhafter fühlt und die Phantasie sich nach eignem Belieben bequeme Gestalten bildet, den Strahlen der Wahrheit vor, die das angenehme Blendwerk ihrer Träume verjagen. Auf eben diese Täuschungen, die das feindselige Licht der Erkenntnis zerstreuen soll, haben sie den ganzen Bau ihres Glücks gegründet, und sie sollten eine Wahrheit so teuer kaufen, die damit anfängt, ihnen alles zu nehmen, was Wert für sie besitzt? Sie müssten schon weise sein, um die Weisheit zu lieben: eine Wahrheit, die derjenige schon fühlte, der der Philosophie ihren Namen gab.

seduced us from our allegiance to Nature, is now in loud and urgent tones calling us back to her bosom. How is it, then, that we still remain barbarians?

5.   There must, therefore, since the cause does not lie in things themselves, be something in the disposition of men which stands in the way of the acceptance of truth, however brightly it may shine, and of the adoption of truth, however forcibly it may convince. A Sage of old felt what it was, and it lies concealed in that pregnant utterance: *sapere aude.*

6.   Dare to be wise! It is energy and courage that are required to combat the obstacles which both indolence of nature and cowardice of heart put in the way of our true enlightenment. Not for nothing does the ancient myth make the goddess of wisdom emerge fully armed from the head of Jupiter. For her very first action is a warlike one. Even at birth she has to fight a hard battle with the senses, which are loath to be snatched from their sweet repose. The majority of men are far too wearied and exhausted by the struggle for existence to gird themselves for a new and harder struggle against error. Happy to escape the hard labour of thinking for themselves, they are only too glad to resign to others the guardianship of their thoughts. And if it should happen that higher promptings stir within them, they embrace with avid faith the formulas which State and Priesthood hold in readiness for such an event. If these unhappy men deserve our compassion, we are rightly contemptuous of those others whom a kindlier fate has freed from the yoke of physical needs, but who by their own choice continue to bow beneath it. Such people prefer the twilight of obscure ideas, where feeling is given full rein, and fancy can fashion at will convenient images, to the rays of truth which put to flight the fond delusions of their dreams. It is on precisely these illusions, which the unwelcome light of knowledge is meant to dissipate, that they have founded the whole edifice of their happiness—how can they be expected to pay so dearly for a truth which begins by depriving them of all they hold dear? They would first have to be wise in order to love wisdom: a truth already felt by him who gave philosophy her name.

7. Nicht genug also, dass alle Aufklärung des Verstandes nur insoferne Achtung verdient, als sie auf den Charakter zurückfliesst; sie
geht auch gewissermassen von dem Charakter aus, weil der Weg zu
dem Kopf durch das Herz muss geöffnet werden. Ausbildung des
Empfindungsvermögens ist also das dringendere Bedürfnis der Zeit,
nicht bloss weil sie ein Mittel wird, die verbesserte Einsicht für das
Leben wirksam zu machen, sondern selbst darum, weil sie zu Verbesserung der Einsicht erweckt.

7. It is not, then, enough to say that all enlightenment of the understanding is worthy of respect only inasmuch as it reacts upon character. To a certain extent it also proceeds from character, since the way to the head must be opened through the heart. The development of man's capacity for feeling is, therefore, the more urgent need of our age, not merely because it can be a means of making better insights effective for living, but precisely because it provides the impulse for bettering our insights.

NEUNTER BRIEF

1. ABER ist hier nicht vielleicht ein Zirkel? Die theoretische Kultur soll die praktische herbeiführen, und die praktische doch die Bedingung der theoretischen sein? Alle Verbesserung im Politischen soll von Veredlung des Charakters ausgehen — aber wie kann sich unter den Einflüssen einer barbarischen Staatsverfassung der Charakter veredeln? Man müsste also zu diesem Zwecke ein Werkzeug aufsuchen, welches der Staat nicht hergibt, und Quellen dazu eröffnen, die sich bei aller politischen Verderbnis rein und lauter erhalten.

2. Jetzt bin ich an dem Punkt angelangt, zu welchem alle meine bisherigen Betrachtungen hingestrebt haben. Dieses Werkzeug ist die schöne Kunst, diese Quellen öffnen sich in ihren unsterblichen Mustern.

3. Von allem, was positiv ist und was menschliche Konventionen einführten, ist die Kunst wie die Wissenschaft losgesprochen, und beide erfreuen sich einer absoluten Immunität von der Willkür der Menschen. Der politische Gesetzgeber kann ihr Gebiet sperren, aber darin herrschen kann er nicht. Er kann den Wahrheitsfreund ächten, aber die Wahrheit besteht; er kann den Künstler erniedrigen, aber die Kunst kann er nicht verfälschen. Zwar ist nichts gewöhnlicher, als dass beide, Wissenschaft und Kunst, dem Geist des Zeitalters huldigen und der hervorbringende Geschmack von dem beurteilenden das Gesetz empfängt. Wo der Charakter straff wird und sich verhärtet, da sehen wir die Wissenschaft streng ihre Grenzen bewachen und die Kunst in den schweren Fesseln der Regel gehn; wo der Charakter erschlafft und sich auflöst, da wird die Wissenschaft zu gefallen und die Kunst zu vergnügen streben. Ganze Jahrhunderte lang zeigen sich die Philosophen wie die Künstler geschäftig, Wahrheit und Schönheit in die Tiefen gemeiner Menschheit hinabzutauchen; jene gehen darin unter, aber mit eigner unzerstörbarer Lebenskraft ringen sich diese siegend empor.

4. Der Künstler ist zwar der Sohn seiner Zeit, aber schlimm für ihn, wenn er zugleich ihr Zögling oder gar noch ihr Günstling ist.

NINTH LETTER

1. But is this not, perhaps, to argue in a circle? Intellectual education is to bring about moral education, and yet moral education is to be the condition of intellectual education? All improvement in the political sphere is to proceed from the ennobling of character—but how under the influence of a barbarous constitution is character ever to become ennobled? To this end we should, presumably, have to seek out some instrument not provided by the State, and to open up living springs which, whatever the political corruption, would remain clear and pure.

2. I have now reached the point to which all my preceding reflections have been tending. This instrument is Fine Art; such living springs are opened up in its immortal exemplars.

3. Art, like Science, is absolved from all positive constraint and from all conventions introduced by man; both rejoice in absolute i m m u n i t y from human arbitrariness. The political legislator may put their territory out of bounds; he cannot rule within it. He can proscribe the lover of truth; Truth itself will prevail. He can humiliate the artist; but Art he cannot falsify. True, nothing is more common than for both, science as well as art, to pay homage to the spirit of the age, or for creative minds to accept the critical standards of prevailing taste. In epochs where character becomes rigid and obdurate, we find science keeping a strict watch over its frontiers, and art moving in the heavy shackles of rules; in those where it becomes enervated and flabby, science will strive to please, and art to gratify. For whole centuries thinkers and artists will do their best to submerge truth and beauty in the depths of a degraded humanity; it is they themselves who are drowned there, while truth and beauty, with their own indestructible vitality, struggle triumphantly to the surface.

4. The artist is indeed the child of his age; but woe to him if he is at the same time its ward or, worse still, its minion! Let some

Eine wohltätige Gottheit reisse den Säugling bei Zeiten von seiner Mutter Brust, nähre ihn mit der Milch eines bessern Alters und lasse ihn unter fernem griechischen Himmel zur Mündigkeit reifen. Wenn er dann Mann geworden ist, so kehre er, eine fremde Gestalt, in sein Jahrhundert zurück; aber nicht, um es mit seiner Erscheinung zu erfreuen, sondern furchtbar wie Agamemnons Sohn, um es zu reinigen. Den Stoff zwar wird er von der Gegenwart nehmen, aber die Form von einer edleren Zeit, ja jenseits aller Zeit, von der absoluten unwandelbaren Einheit seines Wesens entlehnen. Hier aus dem reinen Äther seiner dämonischen Natur rinnt die Quelle der Schönheit herab, unangesteckt von der Verderbnis der Geschlechter und Zeiten, welche tief unter ihr in trüben Strudeln sich wälzen. Seinen Stoff kann die Laune entehren, wie sie ihn geadelt hat, aber die keusche Form ist ihrem Wechsel entzogen. Der Römer des ersten Jahrhunderts hatte längst schon die Kniee vor seinen Kaisern gebeugt, als die Bildsäulen noch aufrecht standen; die Tempel blieben dem Auge heilig, als die Götter längst zum Gelächter dienten, und die Schandtaten eines N e r o und C o m m o d u s beschämte der edle Stil des Gebäudes, das seine Hülle dazu gab. Die Menschheit hat ihre Würde verloren, aber die Kunst hat sie gerettet und aufbewahrt in bedeutenden Steinen; die Wahrheit lebt in der Täuschung fort, und aus dem Nachbilde wird das Urbild wieder hergestellt werden. So wie die edle Kunst die edle Natur ü b e r l e b t e, so schreitet sie derselben auch in der Begeisterung, bildend und erweckend, voran. Ehe noch die Wahrheit ihr siegendes Licht in die Tiefen der Herzen sendet, fängt die Dichtungskraft ihre Strahlen auf, und die Gipfel der Menschheit werden glänzen, wenn noch feuchte Nacht in den Tälern liegt.

5. Wie verwahrt sich aber der Künstler vor den Verderbnissen seiner Zeit, die ihn von allen Seiten umfangen? Wenn er ihr Urteil verachtet. Er blicke aufwärts nach seiner Würde und dem Gesetz, nicht niederwärts nach dem Glück und nach dem Bedürfnis. Gleich frei von der eiteln Geschäftigkeit, die in den flüchtigen Augenblick gern ihre Spur drücken möchte, und von dem ungeduldigen Schwärmergeist, der auf die dürftige Geburt der Zeit den Massstab des Unbedingten anwendet, überlasse er dem Verstande, der hier einheimisch ist, die Sphäre des Wirklichen; er aber strebe, aus dem Bunde des Möglichen mit dem Notwendigen das Ideal zu erzeugen.

beneficent deity snatch the suckling betimes from his mother's breast, nourish him with the milk of a better age, and suffer him to come to maturity under a distant Grecian sky. Then, when he has become a man, let him return, a stranger, to his own century; not, however, to gladden it by his appearance, but rather, terrible like Agamemnon's son, to cleanse and to purify it. His theme he will, indeed, take from the present; but his form he will borrow from a nobler time, nay, from beyond time altogether, from the absolute, unchanging, unity of his being. Here, from the pure aether of his genius, the living source of beauty flows down, untainted by the corruption of the generations and ages wallowing in the dark eddies below. The theme of his work may be degraded by vagaries of the public mood, even as this has been known to ennoble it; but its form, inviolate, will remain immune from such vicissitudes. The Roman of the first century had long been bowing the knee before his emperors when statues still portrayed him erect; temples continued to be sacred to the eye long after the gods had become objects of derision; and the infamous crimes of a N e r o or a C o m m o d u s were put to shame by the noble style of the building whose frame lent them cover. Humanity has lost its dignity; but Art has rescued it and preserved it in significant stone. Truth lives on in the illusion of Art, and it is from this copy, or after-image, that the original image will once again be restored. Just as the nobility of Art s u r - v i v e d the nobility of Nature, so now Art goes before her, a voice rousing from slumber and preparing the shape of things to come. Even before Truth's triumphant light can penetrate the recesses of the human heart, the poet's imagination will intercept its rays, and the peaks of humanity will be radiant while the dews of night still linger in the valley.

5.   But how is the artist to protect himself against the corruption of the age which besets him on all sides? By disdaining its opinion. Let him direct his gaze upwards, to the dignity of his calling and the universal Law, not downwards towards Fortune and the needs of daily life. Free alike from the futile busyness which would fain set its mark upon the fleeting moment, and from the impatient spirit of enthusiasm which applies the measure of the Absolute to the sorry products of Time, let him leave the sphere of the actual to the intellect, which is at home there, whilst he strives to produce the Ideal out of the union of what is possible with what is necessary. Let

Dieses präge er aus in Täuschung und Wahrheit, präge es in die Spiele seiner Einbildungskraft und in den Ernst seiner Taten, präge es aus in allen sinnlichen und geistigen Formen und werfe es schweigend in die unendliche Zeit.

6. Aber nicht jedem, dem dieses Ideal in der Seele glüht, wurde die schöpferische Ruhe und der grosse geduldige Sinn verliehen, es in den verschwiegnen Stein einzudrücken oder in das nüchterne Wort auszugiessen und den treuen Händen der Zeit zu vertrauen. Viel zu ungestüm, um durch dieses ruhige Mittel zu wandern, stürzt sich der göttliche Bildungstrieb oft unmittelbar auf die Gegenwart und auf das handelnde Leben und unternimmt, den formlosen Stoff der moralischen Welt umzubilden. Dringend spricht das Unglück seiner Gattung zu dem fühlenden Menschen, dringender ihre Entwürdigung, der Enthusiasmus entflammt sich, und das glühende Verlangen strebt in kraftvollen Seelen ungeduldig zur Tat. Aber befragte er sich auch, ob diese Unordnungen in der moralischen Welt seine Vernunft beleidigen oder nicht vielmehr seine Selbstliebe schmerzen? Weiss er es noch nicht, so wird er es an dem Eifer erkennen, womit er auf bestimmte und beschleunigte Wirkungen dringt. Der reine moralische Trieb ist aufs Unbedingte gerichtet, für ihn gibt es keine Zeit, und die Zukunft wird ihm zur Gegenwart, sobald sie sich aus der Gegenwart notwendig entwickeln muss. Vor einer Vernunft ohne Schranken ist die Richtung zugleich die Vollendung, und der Weg ist zurückgelegt, sobald er eingeschlagen ist.

7. Gib also, werde ich dem jungen Freund der Wahrheit und Schönheit zur Antwort geben, der von mir wissen will, wie er dem edeln Trieb in seiner Brust, bei allem Widerstande des Jahrhunderts, Genüge zu tun habe, gib der Welt, auf die du wirkst, die R i c h t u n g zum Guten, so wird der ruhige Rhythmus der Zeit die Entwicklung bringen. Diese Richtung hast du ihr gegeben, wenn du, lehrend, ihre Gedanken zum Notwendigen und Ewigen erhebst, wenn du, handelnd oder bildend, das Notwendige und Ewige in einen Gegenstand ihrer Triebe verwandelst. Fallen wird das Gebäude des Wahns und der Willkürlichkeit, fallen muss es, es ist schon gefallen, sobald du gewiss bist, dass es sich neigt; aber in dem innern, nicht bloss in dem äussern Menschen muss es sich neigen. In der schamhaften Stille deines Gemüts erziehe die siegende Wahrheit, stelle sie aus dir heraus in der Schönheit, dass

him express this ideal both in semblance and in truth, set the stamp of it upon the play of his imagination as upon the seriousness of his conduct, let him express it in all sensuous and spiritual forms, and silently project it into the infinity of time.

6. But not everyone whose soul glows with this ideal was granted either the creative tranquillity or the spirit of long patience required to imprint it upon the silent stone, or pour it into the sober mould of words, and so entrust it to the executory hands of time. Far too impetuous to proceed by such unobtrusive means, the divine impulse to form often hurls itself directly upon present-day reality and upon the life of action, and undertakes to fashion anew the formless material presented by the moral world. The misfortunes of the human race speak urgently to the man of feeling; its degradation more urgently still; enthusiasm is kindled, and in vigorous souls ardent longing drives impatiently on towards action. But did he ever ask himself whether those disorders in the moral world offend his reason, or whether they do not rather wound his self-love? If he does not yet know the answer, he will detect it by the zeal with which he insists upon specific and prompt results. The pure moral impulse is directed towards the Absolute. For such an impulse time does not exist, and the future turns into the present from the moment that it is seen to develop with inevitable Necessity out of the present. In the eyes of a Reason which knows no limits, the Direction is at once the Destination, and the Way is completed from the moment it is trodden.

7. To the young friend of truth and beauty who would inquire of me how, despite all the opposition of his century, he is to satisfy the noble impulses of his heart, I would make answer: Impart to the world you would influence a D i r e c t i o n towards the good, and the quiet rhythm of time will bring it to fulfilment. You will have given it this direction if, by your teaching, you have elevated its thoughts to the Necessary and the Eternal, if, by your actions and your creations, you have transformed the Necessary and the Eternal into an object of the heart's desire. The edifice of error and caprice will fall—it must fall, indeed it has already fallen—from the moment you are certain that it is on the point of giving way. But it is in man's inner being that it must give way, not just in the externals he presents to the world. It is in the modest sanctuary of your heart that you must rear victorious truth, and project it out of yourself

nicht bloss der Gedanke ihr huldige, sondern auch der Sinn ihre Erscheinung liebend ergreife. Und damit es dir nicht begegne, von der Wirklichkeit das Muster zu empfangen, das du ihr geben sollst, so wage dich nicht eher in ihre bedenkliche Gesellschaft, bis du eines idealischen Gefolges in deinem Herzen versichert bist. Lebe mit deinem Jahrhundert, aber sei nicht sein Geschöpf; leiste deinen Zeitgenossen, aber was sie bedürfen, nicht was sie loben. Ohne ihre Schuld geteilt zu haben, teile mit edler Resignation ihre Strafen und beuge dich mit Freiheit unter das Joch, das sie gleich schlecht entbehren und tragen. Durch den standhaften Mut, mit dem du ihr Glück verschmähest, wirst du ihnen beweisen, dass nicht deine Feigheit sich ihren Leiden unterwirft. Denke sie dir, wie sie sein sollten, wenn du auf sie zu wirken hast, aber denke sie dir, wie sie sind, wenn du für sie zu handeln versucht wirst. Ihren Beifall suche durch ihre Würde, aber auf ihren Unwert berechne ihr Glück, so wird dein eigener Adel dort den ihrigen aufwecken und ihre Un-würdigkeit hier deinen Zweck nicht vernichten. Der Ernst deiner Grundsätze wird sie von dir scheuchen, aber im Spiele ertragen sie sie noch; ihr Geschmack ist keuscher als ihr Herz, und hier musst du den scheuen Flüchtling ergreifen. Ihre Maximen wirst du um-sonst bestürmen, ihre Taten umsonst verdammen, aber an ihrem Müssiggange kannst du deine bildende Hand versuchen. Verjage die Willkür, die Frivolität, die Rohigkeit aus ihren Vergnügungen, so wirst du sie unvermerkt auch aus ihren Handlungen, endlich aus ihren Gesinnungen verbannen. Wo du sie findest, umgib sie mit edeln, mit grossen, mit geistreichen Formen, schliesse sie ringsum mit den Symbolen des Vortrefflichen ein, bis der Schein die Wirk-lichkeit und die Kunst die Natur überwindet.

in the form of beauty, so that not only thought can pay it homage, but sense, too, lay loving hold on its appearance. And lest you should find yourself receiving from the world as it is the model you yourself should be providing, do not venture into its equivocal company without first being sure that you bear within your own heart an escort from the world of the ideal. Live with your century; but do not be its creature. Work for your contemporaries; but create what they need, not what they praise. Without sharing their guilt, yet share with noble resignation in their punishment, and bow your head freely beneath the yoke which they find as difficult to dispense with as to bear. By the steadfast courage with which you disdain their good fortune, you will show them that it is not through cowardice that you consent to share their sufferings. Think of them as they ought to be, when called upon to influence them; think of them as they are, when tempted to act on their behalf. In seeking their approval appeal to what is best in them, but in devising their happiness recall them as they are at their worst; then your own nobility will awaken theirs, and their unworthiness not defeat your purpose. The seriousness of your principles will frighten them away, but in the play of your semblance they will be prepared to tolerate them; for their taste is purer than their heart, and it is here that you must lay hold of the timorous fugitive. In vain will you assail their precepts, in vain condemn their practice; but on their leisure hours you can try your shaping hand. Banish from their pleasures caprice, frivolity, and coarseness, and imperceptibly you will banish these from their actions and, eventually, from their inclinations too. Surround them, wherever you meet them, with the great and noble forms of genius, and encompass them about with the symbols of perfection, until Semblance conquer Reality, and Art triumph over Nature.

ZEHNTER BRIEF

1. Sie sind also mit mir darin einig und durch den Inhalt meiner vorigen Briefe überzeugt, dass sich der Mensch auf zwei entgegengesetzten Wegen von seiner Bestimmung entfernen könne, dass unser Zeitalter wirklich auf beiden Abwegen wandle und hier der Rohigkeit, dort der Erschlaffung und Verkehrtheit zum Raub geworden sei. Von dieser doppelten Verirrung soll es durch die Schönheit zurückgeführt werden. Wie kann aber die schöne Kultur beiden entgegengesetzten Gebrechen zugleich begegnen und zwei widersprechende Eigenschaften in sich vereinigen? Kann sie in dem Wilden die Natur in Fesseln legen und in dem Barbaren dieselbe in Freiheit setzen? Kann sie zugleich anspannen und auflösen — und wenn sie nicht wirklich beides leistet, wie kann ein so grosser Effekt, als die Ausbildung der Menschheit ist, vernünftigerweise von ihr erwartet werden?

2. Zwar hat man schon zum Überdruss die Behauptung hören müssen, dass das entwickelte Gefühl für Schönheit die Sitten verfeinere, so dass es hiezu keines neuen Beweises mehr zu bedürfen scheint. Man stützt sich auf die alltägliche Erfahrung, welche fast durchgängig mit einem gebildeten Geschmacke Klarheit des Verstandes, Regsamkeit des Gefühls, Liberalität und selbst Würde des Betragens, mit einem ungebildeten gewöhnlich das Gegenteil verbunden zeigt. Man beruft sich, zuversichtlich genug, auf das Beispiel der gesittetsten aller Nationen des Altertums, bei welcher das Schönheitsgefühl zugleich seine höchste Entwicklung erreichte, und auf das entgegengesetzte Beispiel jener teils wilden, teils barbarischen Völker, die ihre Unempfindlichkeit für das Schöne mit einem rohen oder doch austeren Charakter büssen. Nichtsdestoweniger fällt es zuweilen denkenden Köpfen ein, entweder das Faktum zu leugnen, oder doch die Rechtmässigkeit der daraus gezogenen Schlüsse zu bezweifeln. Sie denken nicht ganz so schlimm von jener Wildheit, die man den ungebildeten Völkern zum Vorwurf macht, und nicht ganz so vorteilhaft von dieser Verfeinerung, die man an den gebildeten preist. Schon im Altertum gab es Männer, welche die schöne Kultur für nichts weniger als eine Wohltat hielten und

TENTH LETTER

1. You are, then, in agreement with me, and persuaded by the content of my previous Letters, that man can deviate from his destiny in two quite different ways; that our own age is, in fact, moving along both these false roads, and has fallen a prey, on the one hand, to coarseness, on the other, to enervation and perversity. From this twofold straying it is to be brought back by means of beauty. But how can education through beauty counter both these opposite failings at one and the same time, and unite within itself two quite incompatible qualities? Can it enchain nature in the savage, and set it free in the barbarian? Can it at the same time tense and release? And if it does not really manage to do both, how can we reasonably expect it to effect anything so important as the education of mankind?

2. True, we are always being told, *ad nauseam*, that a developed feeling for beauty refines morals, so that this would not seem to stand in need of any further proof. People base this assumption on everyday experience, which almost always shows that clarity of mind, liveliness of feeling, graciousness, yes even dignity, of conduct, are linked with a cultivated taste, and their opposite for the most part with an uncultivated one. People invoke confidently enough the example of the most civilized of all the nations of antiquity, in whom the feeling for beauty at the same time reached its highest development, and the opposite example of those partly savage, partly barbaric, peoples, who paid for their insensitivity to beauty by a coarse, or at least austere, character. Nevertheless, it sometimes occurs to thinking minds either to deny this fact or at least to doubt the legitimacy of the conclusions drawn from it. They do not think quite so ill of that savagery with which primitive peoples are usually reproached, nor quite so well of that refinement for which the cultivated are commended. Even in antiquity there were men who were by no means so convinced that aesthetic culture

deswegen sehr geneigt waren, den Künsten der Einbildungskraft den Eintritt in ihre Republik zu verwehren.

3. Nicht von denjenigen rede ich, die bloss darum die Grazien schmähn, weil sie nie ihre Gunst erfuhren. Sie, die keinen andern Massstab des Wertes kennen als die Mühe der Erwerbung und den handgreiflichen Ertrag — wie sollten sie fähig sein, die stille Arbeit des Geschmacks an dem äussern und innern Menschen zu würdigen, und über den zufälligen Nachteilen der schönen Kultur nicht ihre wesentlichen Vorteile aus den Augen setzen? Der Mensch ohne Form verachtet alle Anmut im Vortrage als Bestechung, alle Feinheit im Umgang als Verstellung, alle Delikatesse und Grossheit im Betragen als Überspannung und Affektation. Er kann es dem Günstling der Grazien nicht vergeben, dass er als Gesellschafter alle Zirkel aufheitert, als Geschäftsmann alle Köpfe nach seinen Absichten lenkt, als Schriftsteller seinem ganzen Jahrhundert vielleicht seinen Geist aufdrückt, während dass Er, das Schlachtopfer des Fleisses, mit all seinem Wissen keine Aufmerksamkeit erzwingen, keinen Stein von der Stelle rücken kann. Da er jenem das genialische Geheimnis, angenehm zu sein, niemals abzulernen vermag, so bleibt ihm nichts anders übrig, als die Verkehrtheit der menschlichen Natur zu bejammern, die mehr dem Schein als dem Wesen huldigt.

4. Aber es gibt achtungswürdige Stimmen, die sich gegen die Wirkungen der Schönheit erklären und aus der Erfahrung mit furchtbaren Gründen dagegen gerüstet sind. „Es ist nicht zu leugnen", sagen sie, „die Reize des Schönen können in guten Händen zu löblichen Zwecken wirken, aber es widerspricht ihrem Wesen nicht, in schlimmen Händen gerade das Gegenteil zu tun und ihre seelenfesselnde Kraft für Irrtum und Unrecht zu verwenden. Eben deswegen, weil der Geschmack nur auf die Form und nie auf den Inhalt achtet, so gibt er dem Gemüt zuletzt die gefährliche Richtung, alle Realität überhaupt zu vernachlässigen und einer reizenden Einkleidung Wahrheit und Sittlichkeit aufzuopfern. Aller Sachunterschied der Dinge verliert sich, und es ist bloss die Erscheinung, die ihren Wert bestimmt. Wie viele Menschen von Fähigkeit", fahren sie fort, „werden nicht durch die verführerische Macht des Schönen von einer ernsten und anstrengenden Wirksamkeit abgezogen, oder wenigstens verleitet, sie oberflächlich zu behandeln! Wie mancher schwache Verstand wird bloss deswegen mit der bürgerlichen Einrichtung uneins, weil es der Phantasie der Poeten beliebte, eine

is a boon and a blessing, and were hence more than inclined to refuse the arts of the imagination admission to their Republic.

3.   I do not refer to those who despise the Graces because they have never experienced their favour. Those who know no other criterion of value than the effort of earning or the tangible profit, how should they be capable of appreciating the unobtrusive effect of taste on the outward appearance and on the mind and character of men? How can they help shutting their eyes to the essential advantages of an aesthetic education in view of its incidental disadvantages? A man who has himself no form will despise any grace of speech as bribery and corruption, any elegance in social intercourse as hypocrisy, any delicacy or distinction of bearing as exaggeration and affectation. He cannot forgive the darling of the Graces for brightening every circle by his company, for swaying all minds to his purpose in the world of affairs, for perhaps, through his writings, leaving the impress of his mind upon the whole century—whilst he, poor victim of sheer application, can with all his knowledge command no interest, nor move so much as a stone from its place. Since he cannot learn from his fortunate rival the blessed secret of pleasing, he has no choice but to bewail the perversity of human nature which honours the appearance rather than the substance.

4.   But there are voices worthy of respect raised against the effects of beauty, and armed against it with formidable arguments drawn from experience. 'It cannot be denied', they say, 'that the delights of the Beautiful can, in the right hands, be made to serve laudable ends. But it is by no means contrary to its nature for it to have, in the wrong hands, quite the opposite effect, and to put its soul-seducing power at the service of error and injustice. Just because taste is always concerned with form, and never with content, it finally induces in the mind a dangerous tendency to neglect reality altogether, and to sacrifice truth and morality to the alluring dress in which they appear. All substantial difference between things is lost, and appearance alone determines their worth. How many men of talent', they continue, 'are not deflected by the seductive power of beauty from serious and strenuous effort, or at least misled into treating it lightly? How many of feeble intelligence are not in conflict with the social order just because the fancy of poets was pleased

Welt aufzustellen, worin alles ganz anders erfolgt, wo keine Konvenienz die Meinungen bindet, keine Kunst die Natur unterdrückt. Welche gefährliche Dialektik haben die Leidenschaften nicht erlernt, seitdem sie in den Gemälden der Dichter mit den glänzendsten Farben prangen und im Kampf mit Gesetzen und Pflichten gewöhnlich das Feld behalten? Was hat wohl die Gesellschaft dabei gewonnen, dass jetzt die Schönheit dem Umgang Gesetze gibt, den sonst die Wahrheit regierte, und dass der äussere Eindruck die Achtung entscheidet, die nur an das Verdienst gefesselt sein sollte? Es ist wahr, man sieht jetzt alle Tugenden blühen, die einen gefälligen Effekt in der Erscheinung machen und einen Wert in der Gesellschaft verleihen, dafür aber auch alle Ausschweifungen herrschen und alle Laster im Schwange gehn, die sich mit einer schönen Hülle vertragen." In der Tat muss es Nachdenken erregen, dass man beinahe in jeder Epoche der Geschichte, wo die Künste blühen und der Geschmack regiert, die Menschheit gesunken findet und auch nicht ein einziges Beispiel aufweisen kann, dass ein hoher Grad und eine grosse Allgemeinheit ästhetischer Kultur bei einem Volke mit politischer Freiheit und bürgerlicher Tugend, dass schöne Sitten mit guten Sitten, und Politur des Betragens mit Wahrheit desselben Hand in Hand gegangen wäre.

5.   Solange A t h e n und S p a r t a ihre Unabhängigkeit behaupteten und Achtung für die Gesetze ihrer Verfassung zur Grundlage diente, war der Geschmack noch unreif, die Kunst noch in ihrer Kindheit, und es fehlte noch viel, dass die Schönheit die Gemüter beherrschte. Zwar hatte die Dichtkunst schon einen erhabenen Flug getan, aber nur mit den Schwingen des Genies, von dem wir wissen, dass es am nächsten an die Wildheit grenzt und ein Licht ist, das gern aus der Finsternis schimmert, welches also vielmehr gegen den Geschmack seines Zeitalters als für denselben zeugt. Als unter dem Perikles und Alexander das goldne Alter der Künste herbeikam und die Herrschaft des Geschmacks sich allgemeiner verbreitete, findet man Griechenlands Kraft und Freiheit nicht mehr: die Beredsamkeit verfälschte die Wahrheit, die Weisheit beleidigte in dem Mund eines Sokrates, und die Tugend in dem Leben eines Phocion. Die R ö m e r, wissen wir, mussten erst in den bürgerlichen Kriegen ihre Kraft erschöpfen und, durch morgenländische Üppigkeit entmannt, unter das Joch eines glücklichen Dynasten sich beugen, ehe wir die griechische Kunst über die

to present a world in which everything proceeds quite differently, in which no conventions fetter opinion, and no artifice suppresses nature? What dangerous dialectics have the passions not learned since, in the portrayals of the poets, they have been made to flaunt themselves in brilliant colours and, when in conflict with laws and duties, usually been left masters of the field? What has society profited from letting beauty prescribe the laws of social intercourse, which formerly were regulated by truth, or outward impression determine the respect which should attach to merit alone? It is true we now see all those virtues flourishing whose appearance creates a pleasing impression and confers social prestige; but, as against this, every kind of excess, too, is rampant, and every vice in vogue which is compatible with a fair exterior.' And indeed it must give pause for reflection that in almost every historical epoch in which the arts flourish, and taste prevails, we find humanity at a low ebb, and cannot point to a single instance of a high degree and wide diffusion of aesthetic culture going hand in hand with political freedom and civic virtue, fine manners with good morals, refinement of conduct with truth of conduct.

5. As long as Athens and Sparta maintained their independence, and respect for laws served as the basis of their constitution, taste was as yet immature, art still in its infancy, and beauty far from ruling over the hearts of men. It is true that the art of poetry had already soared to sublime heights; but only on the wings of that kind of genius which we know to be closely akin to the primitive, a light wont to shine in the darkness, and evidence, therefore, against the taste of the time rather than for it. When, under Pericles and Alexander, the Golden Age of the arts arrived, and the rule of taste extended its sway, the strength and freedom of Greece are no longer to be found. Rhetoric falsified truth, wisdom gave offence in the mouth of a Socrates, and virtue in the life of a Phocion. The Romans, as we know, had first to exhaust their strength in the civil wars and, enervated by oriental luxury, to bow beneath the yoke of a successful ruler, before Greek art can be seen triumphing over the rigidity of their character. Nor did the light of culture dawn

Rigidität ihres Charakters triumphieren sehen. Auch den A r a b e r n ging die Morgenröte der Kultur nicht eher auf, als bis die Energie ihres kriegerischen Geistes unter dem Zepter der Abbassiden erschlafft war. In dem neuern I t a l i e n zeigte sich die schöne Kunst nicht eher, als nachdem der herrliche Bund der Lombarden zerrissen war, Florenz sich den Municeern unterworfen und der Geist der Unabhängigkeit in allen jenen mutvollen Städten einer unrühmlichen Ergebung Platz gemacht hatte. Es ist beinahe überflüssig, noch an das Beispiel der neuern Nationen zu erinnern, deren Verfeinerung in demselben Verhältnisse zunahm, als ihre Selbständigkeit endigte. Wohin wir immer in der vergangenen Welt unsre Augen richten, da finden wir, dass Geschmack und Freiheit einander fliehen und dass die Schönheit nur auf den Untergang heroischer Tugenden ihre Herrschaft gründet.

6.   Und doch ist gerade diese Energie des Charakters, mit welcher die ästhetische Kultur gewöhnlich erkauft wird, die wirksamste Feder alles Grossen und Trefflichen im Menschen, deren Mangel kein anderer, wenn auch noch so grosser Vorzug ersetzen kann. Hält man sich also einzig nur an das, was die bisherigen Erfahrungen über den Einfluss der Schönheit lehren, so kann man in der Tat nicht sehr aufgemuntert sein, Gefühle auszubilden, die der wahren Kultur des Menschen so gefährlich sind; und lieber wird man, auf die Gefahr der Rohigkeit und Härte, die schmelzende Kraft der Schönheit entbehren als sich bei allen Vorteilen der Verfeinerung ihren erschlaffenden Wirkungen überliefert sehen. Aber vielleicht ist die E r f a h r u n g der Richterstuhl nicht, vor welchem sich eine Frage wie diese ausmachen lässt, und ehe man ihrem Zeugnis Gewicht einräumte, müsste erst ausser Zweifel gesetzt sein, dass es dieselbe Schönheit ist, von der wir reden und gegen welche jene Beispiele zeugen. Dies scheint aber einen Begriff der Schönheit vorauszusetzen, der eine andere Quelle hat als die Erfahrung, weil durch denselben erkannt werden soll, ob das, was in der Erfahrung schön heisst, mit Recht diesen Namen führe.

7.   Dieser reine V e r n u n f t b e g r i f f der Schönheit, wenn ein solcher sich aufzeigen liesse, müsste also — weil er aus keinem wirklichen Falle geschöpft werden kann, vielmehr unser Urteil über jeden wirklichen Fall erst berichtigt und leitet — auf dem Wege der Abstraktion gesucht und schon aus der Möglichkeit der sinnlich-vernünftigen Natur gefolgert werden können; mit einem Wort: die

among the A r a b s until the vigour of their warlike spirit had languished under the sceptre of the Abbassids. In modern I t a l y the fine arts did not appear until after the glorious Lombard League was destroyed, Florence subjected to the Medicis, and in all the vigorous City States the spirit of independence had made way for an inglorious submission. It is almost superfluous to recall the example of modern nations whose refinement increased as their independence declined. Wherever we turn our eyes in past history we find taste and freedom shunning each other, and beauty founding her sway solely upon the decline and fall of heroic virtues.

6. And yet it is precisely this energy of character, at whose expense aesthetic culture is commonly purchased, which is the mainspring of all that is great and excellent in man, and the lack of which no other advantage, however great, can repair. If, then, we only heed what past experience has to teach us about the influence of beauty, there is certainly no encouragement to develop feelings which are so much of a threat to the true civilization of man; and even at the risk of coarseness and harshness we shall prefer to dispense with the melting power of Beauty, rather than see ourselves, with all the advantages of refinement, delivered up to her enervating influence. But perhaps E x p e r i e n c e is not the judgement-seat before which such an issue as this can be decided. And before any weight can be attached to her evidence, it would first have to be established beyond all doubt that the beauty of which we are speaking, and the beauty against which those examples from history testify, are one and the same. But this seems to presuppose a concept of beauty derived from a source other than experience, since by means of it we are to decide whether that which in experience we call beautiful is justly entitled to the name.

7. This pure r a t i o n a l c o n c e p t of Beauty, if such could be found, would therefore—since it cannot be derived from any actual case, but rather itself corrects and regulates our judgement of every actual case—have to be discovered by a process of abstraction, and deduced from the sheer potentialities of our sensuo-rational nature. In a single word, Beauty would have to be shown to be a necessary

Schönheit musste sich als eine notwendige Bedingung der Menschheit aufzeigen lassen. Zu dem reinen Begriff der Menschheit müssen wir uns also nunmehr erheben, und da uns die Erfahrung nur einzelne Zustände einzelner Menschen, aber niemals die Menschheit zeigt, so müssen wir aus diesen ihren individuellen und wandelbaren Erscheinungsarten das Absolute und Bleibende zu entdecken und durch Wegwerfung aller zufälligen Schranken uns der notwendigen Bedingungen ihres Daseins zu bemächtigen suchen. Zwar wird uns dieser transcendentale Weg eine Zeitlang aus dem traulichen Kreis der Erscheinungen und aus der lebendigen Gegenwart der Dinge entfernen und auf dem nackten Gefild abgezogener Begriffe verweilen — aber wir streben ja nach einem festen Grund der Erkenntnis, den nichts mehr erschüttern soll, und wer sich über die Wirklichkeit nicht hinauswagt, der wird nie die Wahrheit erobern.

condition of Human Being. From now on, then, we must lift our thoughts to the pure concept of human nature; and since experience never shows us human nature as such, but only individual human beings in individual situations, we must endeavour to discover from all these individual and changing manifestations that which is absolute and unchanging, and, by the rejection of all contingent limitations, apprehend the necessary conditions of their existence. True, this transcendental way will lead us out of the familiar circle of phenomenal existence, away from the living presence of things, and cause us to tarry for a while upon the barren and naked land of abstractions. But we are, after all, struggling for a firm basis of knowledge which nothing shall shake. And he who never ventures beyond actuality will never win the prize of truth.

ELFTER BRIEF

1. WENN die Abstraktion so hoch, als sie immer kann, hinaufsteigt, so gelangt sie zu zwei letzten Begriffen, bei denen sie stille stehen und ihre Grenzen bekennen muss. Sie unterscheidet in dem Menschen etwas, das bleibt, und etwas, das sich unaufhörlich verändert. Das Bleibende nennt sie seine P e r s o n, das Wechselnde seinen Z u s t a n d.

2. Person und Zustand — das Selbst und seine Bestimmungen — die wir uns in dem notwendigen Wesen als Eins und dasselbe denken, sind ewig Zwei in dem endlichen. Bei aller Beharrung der Person wechselt der Zustand, bei allem Wechsel des Zustands beharret die Person. Wir gehen von der Ruhe zur Tätigkeit, vom Affekt zur Gleichgültigkeit, von der Übereinstimmung zum Widerspruch, aber w i r sind doch immer, und was unmittelbar aus u n s folgt, bleibt. In dem absoluten Subjekt allein beharren m i t der Persönlichkeit auch alle ihre Bestimmungen, weil sie a u s der Persönlichkeit fliessen. Alles, w a s die Gottheit ist, ist sie deswegen, w e i l sie ist; sie ist folglich alles auf ewig, weil sie ewig ist.

3. Da in dem Menschen, als endlichem Wesen, Person und Zustand verschieden sind, so kann sich weder der Zustand auf die Person, noch die Person auf den Zustand gründen. Wäre das letztere, so müsste die Person sich verändern; wäre das erstere, so müsste der Zustand beharren; also in jedem Fall entweder die Persönlichkeit oder die Endlichkeit aufhören. Nicht weil wir denken, wollen, empfinden, sind wir; nicht weil wir sind, denken, wollen, empfinden wir. Wir sind, weil wir sind; wir empfinden, denken und wollen, weil ausser uns noch etwas anderes ist.

4. Die Person also muss ihr eigener Grund sein, denn das Bleibende kann nicht aus der Veränderung fliessen; und so hätten wir denn fürs erste die Idee des absoluten, in sich selbst gegründeten Seins, d.i. die F r e i h e i t. Der Zustand muss einen Grund haben; er muss, da er nicht durch die Person, also nicht absolut ist, e r f o l g e n; und so hätten wir fürs zweite die Bedingung alles abhängigen Seins oder Werdens, die Z e i t. Die Zeit ist die

ELEVENTH LETTER

1. WHEN abstraction rises to the highest level it can possibly attain, it arrives at two ultimate concepts before which it must halt and recognize that here it has reached its limits. It distinguishes in man something that endures and something that constantly changes. That which endures it calls his P e r s o n, that which changes, his C o n d i t i o n.

2. Person and Condition—the self and its determining attributes —which in the Absolute Being we think of as one and the same, are in the finite being eternally two. Amid all persistence of the Person, the Condition changes; amid all the changes of Condition, the Person persists. We pass from rest to activity, from passion to indifference, from agreement to contradiction; but w e remain, and what proceeds directly from us remains too. In the Absolute Subject alone do all its determining Attributes persist w i t h the Personality, since all of them proceed f r o m the Personality. W h a t the Godhead is, and all that it is, it is just b e c a u s e it is. It is consequently everything for all eternity, because it is eternal.

3. Since in man, as finite being, Person and Condition are distinct, the Condition can neither be grounded upon the Person, nor the Person upon the Condition. Were the latter the case, the Person would have to change; were the former the case, the Condition would have to persist; hence, in each case, either the Personality or the Finiteness cease to be. Not because we think, will, or feel, do we exist; and not because we exist, do we think, will, or feel. We are because we are; we feel, think and will, because outside of ourselves something other than ourselves exists too.

4. The Person therefore must be its own ground; for what persists cannot proceed from what changes. And so we would, in the first place, have the idea of Absolute Being grounded upon itself, that is to say, F r e e d o m. The Condition, on the other hand, must have a ground other than itself; it must, since it does not owe its existence to the Person, i.e., is not absolute, p r o c e e d f r o m something. And so we would, in the second place, have the condition of all contingent being or becoming, that is to say, T i m e. 'Time is the

Bedingung alles Werdens ist ein identischer Satz, denn er sagt nichts anders als: die Folge ist die Bedingung, dass etwas erfolgt.

5. Die Person, die sich in dem ewig beharrenden ICH und nur in diesem offenbart, kann nicht werden, nicht anfangen in der Zeit, weil vielmehr umgekehrt die Zeit in ihr anfangen, weil dem Wechsel ein Beharrliches zum Grund liegen muss. Etwas muss sich verändern, wenn Veränderung sein soll; dieses Etwas kann also nicht selbst schon Veränderung sein. Indem wir sagen, die Blume blühet und verwelkt, machen wir die Blume zum Bleibenden in dieser Verwandlung und leihen ihr gleichsam eine Person, an der sich jene beiden Zustände offenbaren. Dass der Mensch erst wird, ist kein Einwurf, denn der Mensch ist nicht bloss Person überhaupt, sondern Person, die sich in einem bestimmten Zustand befindet. Aller Zustand aber, alles bestimmte Dasein entsteht in der Zeit, und so muss also der Mensch, als Phänomen, einen Anfang nehmen, obgleich die reine Intelligenz in ihm ewig ist. Ohne die Zeit, das heisst, ohne es zu werden, würde er nie ein bestimmtes Wesen sein; seine Persönlichkeit würde zwar in der Anlage, aber nicht in der Tat existieren. Nur durch die Folge seiner Vorstellungen wird das beharrliche Ich sich selbst zur Erscheinung.

6. Die Materie der Tätigkeit also, oder die Realität, welche die höchste Intelligenz aus sich selber schöpft, muss der Mensch erst empfangen, und zwar empfängt er dieselbe als etwas ausser ihm Befindliches im Raume, und als etwas in ihm Wechselndes in der Zeit, auf dem Wege der Wahrnehmung. Diesen in ihm wechselnden Stoff begleitet sein niemals wechselndes Ich — und in allem Wechsel beständig Er selbst zu bleiben, alle Wahrnehmungen zur Erfahrung, d. h. zur Einheit der Erkenntnis, und jede seiner Erscheinungsarten in der Zeit zum Gesetz für alle Zeiten zu machen, ist die Vorschrift, die durch seine vernünftige Natur ihm gegeben ist. Nur indem er sich verändert, existiert er; nur indem er unveränderlich bleibt, existiert er. Der Mensch, vorgestellt in seiner Vollendung, wäre demnach die beharrliche Einheit, die in den Fluten der Veränderung ewig dieselbe bleibt.

7. Ob nun gleich ein unendliches Wesen, eine Gottheit, nicht werden kann, so muss man doch eine Tendenz göttlich nennen, die das eigentlichste Merkmal der Gottheit, absolute Verkündigung des Vermögens (Wirklichkeit alles Möglichen) und absolute Einheit

condition of all becoming' is an identical proposition, for it does nothing but assert that 'succession is the condition of things succeeding one upon another'.

5. The Person, which manifests itself in the eternally persisting 'I', and only in this, cannot become, cannot have a beginning in time. The reverse is rather the case; time must have its beginning in the Person, since something constant must form the basis of change. For change to take place, there must be something which changes; this something cannot therefore itself be change. If we say 'the flower blooms and fades', we make the flower the constant in this transformation, and endow it, as it were, with a Person, in which these two conditions become manifest. To say that man has first to become, is no objection; for man is not just Person pure and simple, but Person situated in a particular Condition. Every Condition, however, every determinate existence, has its origins in time; and so man, as a phenomenal being, must also have a beginning, although the pure Intelligence within him is eternal. Without time, that is to say, without becoming, he would never be a determinate being; his Personality would indeed exist potentially, but not in fact. It is only through the succession of its perceptions that the enduring 'I' ever becomes aware of itself as a phenomenon.

6. The material of activity, therefore, or the reality which the Supreme Intelligence creates out of itself, man has first to r e c e i v e; and he does in fact receive it, by way of perception, as something existing outside of him in space, and as something changing within him in time. This changing material within him is accompanied by his never-changing 'I'—and to remain perpetually h i m s e l f throughout all change, to convert all that he apprehends into experience, i.e., to organize it into a unity which has significance, and to transform all his modes of existence in time into a law for all times: this is the injunction laid upon him by his rational nature. Only inasmuch as he changes does he e x i s t; only inasmuch as he remains unchangeable does h e exist. Man, imagined in his perfection, would therefore be the constant unity which remains eternally itself amidst the floods of change.

7. Now although an infinite being, a Godhead, cannot b e c o m e, we must surely call divine any tendency which has as its unending task the realization of that most characteristic attribute of Godhead, viz., absolute manifestation of potential (the actualization of all that

des Erscheinens (Notwendigkeit alles Wirklichen) zu ihrer unendlichen Aufgabe hat. Die Anlage zu der Gottheit trägt der Mensch unwidersprechlich in seiner Persönlichkeit in sich; der Weg zu der Gottheit, wenn man einen Weg nennen kann, was niemals zum Ziele führt, ist ihm aufgetan in den S i n n e n.

8. Seine Persönlichkeit, für sich allein und unabhängig von allem sinnlichen Stoffe betrachtet, ist bloss die Anlage zu einer möglichen unendlichen Äusserung; und solange er nicht anschaut und nicht empfindet, ist er noch weiter nichts als Form und leeres Vermögen. Seine Sinnlichkeit, für sich allein und abgesondert von aller Selbsttätigkeit des Geistes betrachtet, vermag weiter nichts, als dass sie ihn, der ohne sie bloss Form ist, zur Materie macht, aber keineswegs, dass sie die Materie mit ihm vereinigt. Solange er bloss empfindet, bloss begehrt und aus blosser Begierde wirkt, ist er noch weiter nichts als W e l t, wenn wir unter diesem Namen bloss den formlosen Inhalt der Zeit verstehen. Seine Sinnlichkeit ist es zwar allein, die sein Vermögen zur wirkenden Kraft macht, aber nur seine Persönlichkeit ist es, die sein Wirken zu dem seinigen macht. Um also nicht bloss Welt zu sein, muss er der Materie Form erteilen; um nicht bloss Form zu sein, muss er der Anlage, die er in sich trägt, Wirklichkeit geben. Er verwirklichet die Form, wenn er die Zeit erschafft und dem Beharrlichen die Veränderung, der ewigen Einheit seines Ichs die Mannigfaltigkeit der Welt gegenüber stellt; er formt die Materie, wenn er die Zeit wieder aufhebt, Beharrlichkeit im Wechsel behauptet und die Mannigfaltigkeit der Welt der Einheit seines Ichs unterwürfig macht.

9. Hieraus fliessen nun zwei entgegengesetzte Anforderungen an den Menschen, die zwei Fundamentalgesetze der sinnlich-vernünftigen Natur. Das erste dringt auf absolute R e a l i t ä t: er soll alles zur Welt machen, was bloss Form ist, und alle seine Anlagen zur Erscheinung bringen; das zweite dringt auf absolute F o r m a l i t ä t: er soll alles in sich vertilgen, was bloss Welt ist, und Übereinstimmung in alle seine Veränderungen bringen; mit andern Worten: er soll alles Innre veräussern und alles Äussere formen. Beide Aufgaben, in ihrer höchsten Erfüllung gedacht, führen zu dem Begriff der Gottheit zurücke, von dem ich ausgegangen bin.

is possible), and absolute unity of manifestation (the necessity of all that is made actual). A disposition to the divine man does indubitably carry within him, in his Personality; the way to the divine (if we can call a way that which never leads to the goal) is opened up to him through the S e n s e s.

8. His Personality, considered for itself alone, and independently of all sense-material, is merely the predisposition to a possible expression of his infinite Nature; and as long as he has neither perceptions nor sensations, he is nothing but form and empty potential. His Sensuous Nature, considered for itself alone, and apart from any spontaneous activity of the mind, can do no more than reduce him, who without it is nothing but form, into matter, but can in no wise bring it about that he becomes conjoined with matter. As long as he merely feels, merely desires and acts upon mere desire, he is as yet nothing but w o r l d, if by this term we understand nothing but the formless content of time. True, it is his Sensuous Nature alone which can turn this potential into actual power; but it is only his Personality which makes all his actual activity into something which is inalienably his own. In order, therefore, not to be mere world, he must impart form to matter; in order not to be mere form, he must give reality to the predisposition he carries within him. He gives reality to form when he brings time into being, when he confronts changelessness with change, the eternal unity of his own Self with the manifold variety of the World. He gives form to matter when he annuls time again, when he affirms persistence within change, and subjugates the manifold variety of the World to the unity of his own Self.

9. From this there proceed two contrary challenges to man, the two fundamental laws of his sensuo-rational nature. The first insists upon absolute r e a l i t y: he is to turn everything which is mere form into world, and make all his potentialities fully manifest. The second insists upon absolute f o r m a l i t y: he is to destroy everything in himself which is mere world, and bring harmony into all his changes. In other words, he is to externalize all that is within him, and give form to all that is outside him. Both these tasks, conceived in their highest fulfilment, lead us back to that concept of Godhead from which I started.

ZWÖLFTER BRIEF

1. ZUR Erfüllung dieser doppelten Aufgabe, das Notwendige i n
u n s zur Wirklichkeit zu bringen und das Wirkliche a u s s e r u n s
dem Gesetz der Notwendigkeit zu unterwerfen, werden wir durch
zwei entgegengesetzte Kräfte gedrungen, die man, weil sie uns
antreiben, ihr Objekt zu verwirklichen, ganz schicklich Triebe
nennt. Der erste dieser Triebe, den ich den s i n n l i c h e n nennen
will, geht aus von dem physischen Dasein des Menschen oder von
seiner sinnlichen Natur und ist beschäftigt, ihn in die Schranken
der Zeit zu setzen und zur Materie zu machen: nicht ihm Materie
zu geben, weil dazu schon eine freie Tätigkeit der Person gehört,
welche die Materie aufnimmt und von Sich, dem Beharrlichen,
unterscheidet. Materie aber heisst hier nichts als Veränderung oder
Realität, die die Zeit erfüllt; mithin fordert dieser Trieb, dass
Veränderung sei, dass die Zeit einen Inhalt habe. Dieser Zustand
der bloss erfüllten Zeit heisst Empfindung, und er ist es allein, durch
den sich das physische Dasein verkündigt.

2. Da alles, was in der Zeit ist, n a c h e i n a n d e r ist, so wird dadurch, dass etwas ist, alles andere ausgeschlossen. Indem man auf
einem Instrument einen Ton greift, ist unter allen Tönen, die es
möglicherweise angeben kann, nur dieser einzige wirklich; indem
der Mensch das Gegenwärtige empfindet, ist die ganze unendliche
Möglichkeit seiner Bestimmungen auf diese einzige Art des Daseins
beschränkt. Wo also dieser Trieb ausschliessend wirkt, da ist notwendig die höchste Begrenzung vorhanden; der Mensch ist in
diesem Zustande nichts als eine Grössen-Einheit, ein erfüllter
Moment der Zeit — oder vielmehr E r ist nicht, denn seine Persönlichkeit ist solange aufgehoben, als ihn die Empfindung beherrscht
und die Zeit mit sich fortreisst.*

* Die Sprache hat für diesen Zustand der Selbstlosigkeit unter der Herrschaft der
Empfindung den sehr treffenden Ausdruck: a u s s e r s i c h s e i n, das heisst, ausser
seinem Ich sein. Obgleich diese Redensart nur da stattfindet, wo die Empfindung zum
Affekt und dieser Zustand durch seine längere Dauer mehr bemerkbar wird, so ist doch
jeder ausser sich, solange er nur empfindet. Von diesem Zustande zur Besonnenheit
zurückkehren, nennt man ebenso richtig: i n s i c h g e h e n, das heisst, in sein Ich
zurückkehren, seine Person wieder herstellen. Von einem, der in Ohnmacht liegt,
sagt man nicht: er ist ausser sich, sondern: er ist v o n s i c h, d.h. er ist seinem Ich

TWELFTH LETTER

1. TOWARDS the accomplishment of this twofold task—of giving reality to the necessity w i t h i n, and subjecting to the law of necessity the reality w i t h o u t—we are impelled by two opposing forces which, since they drive us to the realization of their object, may aptly be termed drives. The first of these, which I will call the s e n s u o u s drive, proceeds from the physical existence of man, or his sensuous nature. Its business is to set him within the limits of time, and to turn him into matter—not to provide him with matter, since that, of course, would presuppose a free activity of the Person capable of receiving such matter, and distinguishing it from the Self as from that which persists. By matter in this context we understand nothing more than change, or reality which occupies time. Consequently this drive demands that there shall be change, that time shall have a content. This state, which is nothing but time occupied by content, is called sensation, and it is through this alone that physical existence makes itself known.

2. Since everything that exists in time exists as a s u c c e s s i o n, the very fact of something existing at all means that everything else is excluded. When we strike a note on an instrument, only this single note, of all those it is capable of emitting, is actually realized; when man is sensible of the present, the whole infinitude of his possible determinations is confined to this single mode of his being. Wherever, therefore, this drive functions exclusively, we inevitably find the highest degree of limitation. Man in this state is nothing but a unit of quantity, an occupied moment of time—or rather, h e is not at all, for his Personality is suspended as long as he is ruled by sensation, and swept along by the flux of time.*

* For this condition of self-loss under the dominion of feeling linguistic usage has the very appropriate expression: t o b e b e s i d e o n e s e l f, i.e., to be outside of one's own Self. Although this turn of phrase is only used when sensation is intensified into passion, and the condition becomes more marked by being prolonged, it can nevertheless be said that every one is beside himself as long as he does nothing but feel. To return from this condition to self-possession is termed, equally aptly: t o b e o n e s e l f a g a i n, i.e., to return into one's own Self, to restore one's Person. Of someone who has fainted, by contrast, we do not say that he is beside himself, but that he is a w a y f r o m h i m s e l f, i.e., he has been rapt away from his Self, whereas in the former case he is merely not

3. Soweit der Mensch endlich ist, erstreckt sich das Gebiet dieses Triebs; und da alle Form nur an einer Materie, alles Absolute nur durch das Medium der Schranken erscheint, so ist es freilich der sinnliche Trieb, an dem zuletzt die ganze Erscheinung der Menschheit befestiget ist. Aber, obgleich er allein die Anlagen der Menschheit weckt und entfaltet, so ist er es doch allein, der ihre Vollendung unmöglich macht. Mit unzerreissbaren Banden fesselt er den höher strebenden Geist an die Sinnenwelt, und von ihrer freiesten Wanderung ins Unendliche ruft er die Abstraktion in die Grenzen der Gegenwart zurücke. Der Gedanke zwar darf ihm augenblicklich entfliehen, und ein fester Wille setzt sich seinen Forderungen sieghaft entgegen; aber bald tritt die unterdrückte Natur wieder in ihre Rechte zurück, um auf Realität des Daseins, auf einen Inhalt unsrer Erkenntnisse und auf einen Zweck unsers Handelns zu dringen.

4. Der zweite jener Triebe, den man den Formtrieb nennen kann, geht aus von dem absoluten Dasein des Menschen oder von seiner vernünftigen Natur und ist bestrebt, ihn in Freiheit zu setzen, Harmonie in die Verschiedenheit seines Erscheinens zu bringen und bei allem Wechsel des Zustands seine Person zu behaupten. Da nun die letztere als absolute und unteilbare Einheit mit sich selbst nie im Widerspruch sein kann, da wir in alle Ewigkeit wir sind, so kann derjenige Trieb, der auf Behauptung der Persönlichkeit dringt, nie etwas anders fordern, als was er in alle Ewigkeit fordern muss; er entscheidet also für immer wie er für jetzt entscheidet, und gebietet für jetzt was er für immer gebietet. Er umfasst mithin die ganze Folge der Zeit, das ist soviel als: er hebt die Zeit, er hebt die Veränderung auf; er will, dass das Wirkliche notwendig und ewig, und dass das Ewige und Notwendige wirklich sei; mit andern Worten: er dringt auf Wahrheit und auf Recht.

5. Wenn der erste nur Fälle macht, so gibt der andre Gesetze — Gesetze für jedes Urteil, wenn es Erkenntnisse, Gesetze für jeden Willen, wenn es Taten betrifft. Es sei nun, dass wir einen Gegenstand erkennen, dass wir einem Zustande unsers Subjekts objektive Gültigkeit beilegen, oder dass wir aus Erkenntnissen handeln, dass wir das Objektive zum Bestimmungsgrund unsers Zustandes machen — in beiden Fällen reissen wir diesen Zustand

geraubt, da jener nur nicht in demselben ist. Daher ist derjenige, der aus einer Ohnmacht zurückkehrte, bloss bei sich, welches sehr gut mit dem Ausser sich sein bestehen kann.

3. The domain of this drive embraces the whole extent of man's finite being. And since form is never made manifest except in some material, nor the Absolute except through the medium of limitation, it is indeed to this sensuous drive that the whole of man's phenomenal existence is ultimately tied. But although it is this drive alone which awakens and develops the potentialities of man, it is also this drive alone which makes their complete fulfilment impossible. With indestructible chains it binds the ever-soaring spirit to the world of sense, and summons abstraction from its most unfettered excursions into the Infinite back to the limitations of the Present. Thought may indeed escape it for the moment, and a firm will triumphantly resist its demands; but suppressed nature soon resumes her rights, and presses for reality of existence, for some content to our knowing and some purpose for our doing.

4. The second of the two drives, which we may call the f o r m a l d r i v e, proceeds from the absolute existence of man, or from his rational nature, and is intent on giving him the freedom to bring harmony into the diversity of his manifestations, and to affirm his Person among all his changes of Condition. Since this Person, being an absolute and indivisible unity, can never be at variance with itself, since we are to all eternity we ourselves, that drive which insists on affirming the Personality can never demand anything but that which is binding upon it to all eternity; hence it decides for ever as it decides for this moment, and commands for this moment what it commands for ever. Consequently it embraces the whole sequence of time, which is as much as to say: it annuls time and annuls change. It wants the real to be necessary and eternal, and the eternal and the necessary to be real. In other words, it insists on truth and on the right.

5. If the first drive only furnishes c a s e s, this second one gives l a w s—laws for every judgement, where it is a question of knowledge, laws for every will, where it is a question of action. Whether it is a case of knowing an object, i.e., of attributing objective validity to a condition of our subject, or of acting upon knowledge, i.e., of making an objective principle the determining motive of our condition—in both cases we wrest this our condition from the jurisdiction

in his Self. Consequently, someone who has come out of a faint has merely c o m e t o h i m s e l f, which state is perfectly compatible with being beside oneself.

aus der Gerichtsbarkeit der Zeit und gestehen ihm Realität für alle Menschen und alle Zeiten, d.i. Allgemeinheit und Notwendigkeit zu. Das Gefühl kann bloss sagen: das ist wahr für dieses Subjekt und in diesem Moment, und ein anderer Moment, ein anderes Subjekt kann kommen, das die Aussage der gegenwärtigen Empfindung zurücknimmt. Aber wenn der Gedanke einmal ausspricht: das ist, so entscheidet er für immer und ewig, und die Gültigkeit seines Ausspruchs ist durch die Persönlichkeit selbst verbürgt, die allem Wechsel Trotz bietet. Die Neigung kann bloss sagen: das ist für dein Individuum und für dein jetziges Bedürfnis gut, aber dein Individuum und dein jetziges Bedürfnis wird die Veränderung mit sich fortreissen und, was du jetzt feurig begehrst, dereinst zum Gegenstand deines Abscheues machen. Wenn aber das moralische Gefühl sagt: das soll sein, so entscheidet es für immer und ewig — wenn du Wahrheit bekennst, weil sie Wahrheit ist, und Gerechtigkeit ausübst, weil sie Gerechtigkeit ist, so hast du einen einzelnen Fall zum Gesetz für alle Fälle gemacht, einen Moment in deinem Leben als Ewigkeit behandelt.

6. Wo also der Formtrieb die Herrschaft führt und das reine Objekt in uns handelt, da ist die höchste Erweiterung des Seins, da verschwinden alle Schranken, da hat sich der Mensch aus einer Grössen-Einheit, auf welche der dürftige Sinn ihn beschränkte, zu einer Ideen-Einheit erhoben, die das ganze Reich der Erscheinungen unter sich fasst. Wir sind bei dieser Operation nicht mehr in der Zeit, sondern die Zeit ist in uns mit ihrer ganzen nie endenden Reihe. Wir sind nicht mehr Individuen, sondern Gattung; das Urteil aller Geister ist durch das unsrige ausgesprochen, die Wahl aller Herzen ist repräsentiert durch unsre Tat.

of time, and endow it with reality for all men and all times, that is with universality and necessity. Feeling can only say: this is true for this individual and at this moment, and another moment, another individual, can come along and revoke assertions made thus under the impact of momentary sensation. But once thought pronounces: that is, it decides for ever and aye, and the validity of its verdict is guaranteed by the Personality itself, which defies all change. Inclination can only say: this is good for you as an individual and for your present need; but your individuality and your present need will be swept away by change, and what you now so ardently desire will one day become the object of your aversion. But once the moral feeling says: this shall be, it decides for ever and aye—once you confess truth because it is truth, and practise justice because it is justice, then you have made an individual case into a law for all cases, and treated one moment of your life as if it were eternity.

6. Where, then, the formal drive holds sway, and the pure object acts within us, we experience the greatest enlargement of being: all limitations disappear, and from the mere unit of quantity to which the poverty of his senses reduced him, man has raised himself to a unity of ideas embracing the whole realm of phenomena. During this operation we are no longer in time; time, with its whole never-ending succession, is in us. We are no longer individuals; we are species. The judgement of all minds is expressed through our own, the choice of all hearts is represented by our action.

DREIZEHNTER BRIEF

1. BEIM ersten Anblick scheint nichts einander mehr entgegen gesetzt zu sein als die Tendenzen dieser beiden Triebe, indem der eine auf Veränderung, der andre auf Unveränderlichkeit dringt. Und doch sind es diese beiden Triebe, die den Begriff der Menschheit erschöpfen, und ein dritter Grundtrieb, der beide vermitteln könnte, ist schlechterdings ein undenkbarer Begriff. Wie werden wir also die Einheit der menschlichen Natur wieder herstellen, die durch diese ursprüngliche und radikale Entgegensetzung völlig aufgehoben scheint?

2. Wahr ist es, ihre Tendenzen widersprechen sich, aber, was wohl zu bemerken ist, nicht in denselben Objekten, und was nicht aufeinander trifft, kann nicht gegeneinander stossen. Der sinnliche Trieb fordert zwar Veränderung, aber er fordert nicht, dass sie auch auf die Person und ihr Gebiet sich erstrecke, dass ein Wechsel der Grundsätze sei. Der Formtrieb dringt auf Einheit und Beharrlichkeit — aber er will nicht, dass mit der Person sich auch der Zustand fixiere, dass Identität der Empfindung sei. Sie sind einander also von Natur nicht entgegengesetzt, und wenn sie demohngeachtet so erscheinen, so sind sie es erst geworden durch eine freie Übertretung der Natur, indem sie sich selbst missverstehen und ihre Sphären verwirren.* Über diese zu wachen und

* 1. Sobald man einen ursprünglichen, mithin notwendigen Antagonism beider Triebe behauptet, so ist freilich kein anderes Mittel, die Einheit im Menschen zu erhalten, als dass man den sinnlichen Trieb dem vernünftigen unbedingt unterordnet. Daraus aber kann bloss Einförmigkeit, aber keine Harmonie entstehen, und der Mensch bleibt noch ewig fort geteilt. Die Unterordnung muss allerdings sein, aber wechselseitig: denn wenn gleich die Schranken nie das Absolute begründen können, also die Freiheit nie von der Zeit abhängen kann, so ist es ebenso gewiss, dass das Absolute durch sich selbst nie die Schranken begründen, dass der Zustand in der Zeit nicht von der Freiheit abhängen kann. Beide Prinzipien sind einander also zugleich subordiniert und coordiniert, d.h. sie stehen in Wechselwirkung: ohne Form keine Materie, ohne Materie keine Form. (Diesen Begriff der Wechselwirkung und die ganze Wichtigkeit desselben findet man vortrefflich auseinandergesetzt in Fichtes Grundlage der gesamten Wissenschaftslehre, Leipzig, 1794). Wie es mit der Person im Reich der Ideen stehe, wissen wir freilich nicht; aber dass sie, ohne Materie zu empfangen, in dem Reiche der Zeit sich nicht offenbaren könne, wissen wir gewiss; in diesem Reiche also wird die Materie nicht bloss unter der Form, sondern auch neben der Form und unabhängig von derselben etwas zu bestimmen haben. So notwendig es also ist, dass das Gefühl im Gebiet der Vernunft nichts entscheide, ebenso notwendig ist es, dass die Vernunft

THIRTEENTH LETTER

1. AT first sight nothing could seem more diametrically opposed than the tendencies of these two drives, the one pressing for change, the other for changelessness. And yet it is these two drives which, between them, exhaust our concept of humanity, and make a third fundamental drive which might possibly reconcile the two a completely unthinkable concept. How, then, are we to restore the unity of human nature which seems to be utterly destroyed by this primary and radical opposition?

2. It is true that their tendencies do indeed conflict with each other, but—and this is the point to note—not in the same objectives, and things which never make contact cannot collide. The sensuous drive does indeed demand change; but it does not demand the extension of this to the Person and its domain, does not demand a change of principles. The formal drive insists on unity and persistence—but it does not require the Condition to be stabilized as well as the Person, does not require identity of sensation. The two are, therefore, not by nature opposed; and if they nevertheless seem to be so, it is because they have become opposed through a wanton transgression of Nature, through mistaking their nature and function, and confusing their spheres of operation.* To watch over these,

---

* 1. Once you postulate a primary, and therefore necessary, antagonism between these two drives, there is, of course, no other means of maintaining unity in man than by unconditionally subordinating the sensuous drive to the rational. From this, however, only uniformity can result, never harmony, and man goes on for ever being divided. Subordination there must, of course, be; but it must be reciprocal. For even though it is true that limitation can never be the source of the Absolute, and hence freedom never be dependent upon time, it is no less certain that the Absolute can of itself never be the source of limitation, or a condition in time be dependent upon freedom. Both principles are, therefore, at once subordinated to each other and co-ordinated with each other, that is to say, they stand in reciprocal relation to one another: without form no matter, and without matter no form. (This concept of reciprocal action, and its fundamental importance, is admirably set forth in Fichte's *Fundaments of the Theory of Knowledge*, Leipzig, 1794). How things stand with the Person in the realm of ideas we frankly do not know; but that it can never become manifest in the realm of time without taking on matter, of that we are certain. In this realm, therefore, matter will have some say, and not merely in a role subordinate to form, but also co-ordinate with it and independently of it. Necessary as it may be, therefore, that feeling should have no say in the realm of reason, it is no less necessary that reason should not presume

einem jeden dieser beiden Triebe seine Grenzen zu sichern, ist die
Aufgabe der Kultur, die also beiden eine gleiche Gerechtigkeit
schuldig ist und nicht bloss den vernünftigen Trieb gegen den
sinnlichen, sondern auch diesen gegen jenen zu behaupten hat. Ihr
Geschäft ist also doppelt: erstlich: die Sinnlichkeit gegen die
Eingriffe der Freiheit zu verwahren; zweitens: die Persönlichkeit gegen die Macht der Empfindungen sicher zu stellen. Jenes
erreicht sie durch Ausbildung des Gefühlvermögens, dieses durch
Ausbildung des Vernunftvermögens.

3. Da die Welt ein Ausgedehntes in der Zeit, Veränderung, ist,
so wird die Vollkommenheit desjenigen Vermögens, welches den
Menschen mit der Welt in Verbindung setzt, grösstmöglichste
Veränderlichkeit und Extensität sein müssen. Da die Person das
Bestehende in der Veränderung ist, so wird die Vollkommenheit
desjenigen Vermögens, welches sich dem Wechsel entgegensetzen
soll, grösstmöglichste Selbständigkeit und Intensität sein müssen.
Je vielseitiger sich die Empfänglichkeit ausbildet, je beweglicher
dieselbe ist, und je mehr Fläche sie den Erscheinungen darbietet,
desto mehr Welt ergreift der Mensch, desto mehr Anlagen entwickelt er in sich; je mehr Kraft und Tiefe die Persönlichkeit, je
mehr Freiheit die Vernunft gewinnt, desto mehr Welt begreift
der Mensch, desto mehr Form schafft er ausser sich. Seine Kultur
wird also darin bestehen: erstlich: dem empfangenden Vermögen die vielfältigsten Berührungen mit der Welt zu verschaffen und
auf Seiten des Gefühls die Passivität aufs Höchste zu treiben;
zweitens: dem bestimmenden Vermögen die höchste Unabhängigkeit von dem empfangenden zu erwerben und auf Seiten der
Vernunft die Aktivität aufs Höchste zu treiben. Wo beide Eigenschaften sich vereinigen, da wird der Mensch mit der höchsten
Fülle von Dasein die höchste Selbständigkeit und Freiheit verbinden und, anstatt sich an die Welt zu verlieren, diese vielmehr

im Gebiet des Gefühls sich nichts zu bestimmen anmasse. Schon indem man jedem von
beiden ein Gebiet zuspricht, schliesst man das andere davon aus und setzt jedem eine
Grenze, die nicht anders als zum Nachteile beider überschritten werden kann.
2. In einer Transcendental-Philosophie, wo alles darauf ankommt, die Form von dem
Inhalt zu befreien und das Notwendige von allem Zufälligen rein zu erhalten, gewöhnt
man sich gar leicht, das Materielle sich bloss als Hindernis zu denken und die Sinnlichkeit, weil sie gerade bei diesem Geschäft im Wege steht, in einem notwendigen Widerspruch mit der Vernunft vorzustellen. Eine solche Vorstellungsart liegt zwar auf keine
Weise im Geiste des Kantischen Systems, aber im Buchstaben desselben könnte
sie gar wohl liegen.

and secure for each of these two drives its proper frontiers, is the task of c u l t u r e, which is, therefore, in duty bound to do justice to both drives equally: not simply to maintain the rational against the sensuous, but the sensuous against the rational too. Hence its business is twofold: f i r s t, to preserve the life of Sense against the encroachments of Freedom; and s e c o n d, to secure the Personality against the forces of Sensation. The former it achieves by developing our capacity for feeling, the latter by developing our capacity for reason.

3. Since the World is extension in time, i.e., change, the perfection of that faculty which connects man with the world will have to consist in maximum changeability and maximum extensity. Since the Person is persistence within change, the perfection of that faculty which is to oppose change will have to be maximum autonomy and maximum intensity. The more facets his Receptivity develops, the more labile it is, and the more surface it presents to phenomena, so much more world does man a p p r e h e n d, and all the more potentialities does he develop in himself. The more power and depth the Personality achieves, and the more freedom reason attains, so much more world does man c o m p r e h e n d, and all the more form does he create outside of himself. His education will therefore consist, f i r s t l y, in procuring for the receptive faculty the most manifold contacts with the world, and, within the purview of feeling, intensifying passivity to the utmost; s e c o n d l y, in securing for the determining faculty the highest degree of independence from the receptive, and, within the purview of reason, intensifying activity to the utmost. Where both these aptitudes are conjoined, man will combine the greatest fullness of existence with the highest autonomy and freedom, and instead of losing himself to the world, will rather

to have a say in the realm of feeling. Just by assigning to each of them its own sphere, we are by that very fact excluding the other from it, and setting bounds to each, bounds which can only be transgressed a t t h e r i s k o f d e t r i m e n t t o b o t h.

2. In the Transcendental method of philosophizing, where everything depends on clearing form of content, and obtaining Necessity in its pure state, free of all admixture with the contingent, one easily falls into thinking of material things as nothing but an obstacle, and of imagining that our sensuous nature, just because it happens to be a hindrance in t h i s operation, must of necessity be in conflict with reason. Such a way of thinking is, it is true, wholly alien to the s p i r i t of the Kantian system, but it may very well be found in the l e t t e r of it.

mit der ganzen Unendlichkeit ihrer Erscheinungen in sich ziehen
und der Einheit seiner Vernunft unterwerfen.

4. Dieses Verhältnis nun kann der Mensch u m k e h r e n und
dadurch auf eine zweifache Weise seine Bestimmung verfehlen. Er
kann die Intensität, welche die tätige Kraft erheischt, auf die leidende legen, durch den Stofftrieb dem Formtriebe vorgreifen und
das empfangende Vermögen zum bestimmenden machen. Er kann
die Extensität, welche der leidenden Kraft gebührt, der tätigen
zuteilen, durch den Formtrieb dem Stofftriebe vorgreifen und dem
empfangenden Vermögen das bestimmende unterschieben. In
dem ersten Fall wird er nie E r s e l b s t, in dem zweiten wird er
nie e t w a s a n d e r s sein, mithin eben darum in beiden Fällen
k e i n e s v o n b e i d e n, folglich — Null sein.*

*1. Der schlimme Einfluss einer überwiegenden Sensualität auf unser Denken und
Handeln fällt jedermann leicht in die Augen; nicht so leicht, ob er gleich ebenso häufig
vorkommt und ebenso wichtig ist, der nachteilige Einfluss einer überwiegenden
Rationalität auf unsre Erkenntnis und auf unser Betragen. Man erlaube mir daher aus
der grossen Menge der hieher gehörenden Fälle nur zwei in Erinnerung zu bringen,
welche den Schaden einer der Anschauung und Empfindung vorgreifenden Denk- und
Willenskraft ins Licht setzen können.

2. Eine der vornehmsten Ursachen, warum unsre Natur-Wissenschaften so langsame
Schritte machen, ist offenbar der allgemeine und kaum bezwingbare Hang zu teleolo-
gischen Urteilen, bei denen sich, sobald sie konstitutiv gebraucht werden, das bestimmende Vermögen dem empfangenden unterschiebt. Die Natur mag unsre Organe noch
so nachdrücklich und noch so vielfach berühren — alle ihre Mannigfaltigkeit ist verloren für uns, weil wir nichts in ihr suchen, als was wir in sie hineingelegt haben, weil
wir ihr nicht erlauben, sich g e g e n u n s h e r e i n zu bewegen, sondern vielmehr mit
ungeduldig vorgreifender Vernunft g e g e n s i e h i n a u s streben. Kommt alsdann in
Jahrhunderten einer, der sich ihr mit ruhigen, keuschen und offenen Sinnen naht und
deswegen auf eine Menge von Erscheinungen stösst, die wir bei unsrer Prävention
übersehen haben, so erstaunen wir höchlich darüber, dass so viele Augen bei so hellem
Tag nichts bemerkt haben sollen. Dieses voreilige Streben nach Harmonie, ehe man
die einzelnen Laute beisammen hat, die sie ausmachen sollen, diese gewalttätige Usurpation der Denkkraft in einem Gebiete, wo sie nicht unbedingt zu gebieten hat, ist der
Grund der Unfruchtbarkeit so vieler denkenden Köpfe für das Beste der Wissenschaft,
und es ist schwer zu sagen, ob die Sinnlichkeit, welche keine Form annimmt, oder die
Vernunft, welche keinen Inhalt abwartet, der Erweiterung unserer Kenntnisse mehr
geschadet haben.

3. Ebenso schwer dürfte es zu bestimmen sein, ob unsre praktische Philanthropie mehr
durch die Heftigkeit unsrer Begierden oder durch die Rigidität unsrer Grundsätze,
mehr durch den Egoism unsrer Sinne oder durch den Egoism unsrer Vernunft gestört
und erkältet wird. Um uns zu teilnehmenden, hilfreichen, tätigen Menschen zu machen,
müssen sich Gefühl und Charakter mit einander vereinigen, so wie, um uns Erfahrung
zu verschaffen, Offenheit des Sinnes mit Energie des Verstandes zusammentreffen muss.
Wie können wir, bei noch so lobenswürdigen Maximen, billig, gütig und menschlich
gegen andere sein, wenn uns das Vermögen fehlt, fremde Natur treu und wahr in uns
aufzunehmen, fremde Situationen uns anzueignen, fremde Gefühle zu den unsrigen

draw the latter into himself in all its infinitude of phenomena, and subject it to the unity of his reason.

4. But man can turn these relations u p s i d e   d o w n, and thus miss his destiny in two different ways. He can transfer the intensity required by the active function to the passive, let his sensuous drive encroach upon the formal, and make the receptive faculty do the work of the determining one. Or he can assign to the active function that extensity which is proper to the passive, let the formal drive encroach upon the sensuous, and substitute the determining faculty for the receptive one. In the first case he will never be h i m s e l f; in the second he will never be a n y t h i n g   e l s e; and for that very reason, therefore, he will in both cases be n e i t h e r   t h e   o n e   n o r t h e   o t h e r, consequently—a non-entity.*

*1. The pernicious effect, upon both thought and action, of an undue surrender to our sensual nature will be evident to all. Not quite so evident, although just as common, and no less important, is the nefarious influence exerted upon our knowledge and upon our conduct by a preponderance of rationality. Permit me therefore to recall, from the great number of relevant instances, just two which may serve to throw light upon the damage caused when the functions of thought and will encroach upon those of intuition and feeling.

2. One of the chief reasons why our natural sciences make such slow progress is obviously the universal, and almost uncontrollable, propensity to teleological judgements, in which, once they are used constitutively, the determining faculty is substituted for the receptive. However strong and however varied the impact made upon our organs by nature, all her manifold variety is then entirely lost upon us, because we are seeking nothing in her but what we have put into her; because, instead of letting her come i n   u p o n u s, we are thrusting ourselves o u t   u p o n   h e r with all the impatient anticipations of our reason. If, then, in the course of centuries, it should happen that a man tries to approach her with his sense-organs untroubled, innocent and wide open, and, thanks to this, should chance upon a multitude of phenomena which we, with our tendency to prejudge the issue, have overlooked, then we are mightily astonished that so many eyes in such broad daylight should have noticed nothing. This premature hankering after harmony before we have even got together the individual sounds which are to go to its making, this violent usurping of authority by ratiocination in a field where its right to give orders is by no means unconditional, is the reason why so many thinking minds fail to have any fruitful effect upon the advancement of science; and it would be difficult to say which has done more harm to the progress of knowledge: a sense-faculty unamenable to form, or a reasoning faculty which will not stay for a content.

3. It would be no less difficult to determine which does more to impede the practice of brotherly love: the violence of our passions, which disturbs it, or the rigidity of our principles, which chills it—the egotism of our senses or the egotism of our reason. If we are to become compassionate, helpful, effective human beings, feeling and character must unite, even as wide-open senses must combine with vigour of intellect if we are to acquire experience. How can we, however laudable our precepts, how can we be just, kindly, and human towards others, if we lack the power of receiving into ourselves, faithfully and truly, natures unlike ours, of feeling our way into the situation of others, of making other people's feelings our own? But in the education we receive, no less than

5. Wird nämlich der sinnliche Trieb bestimmend, macht der Sinn den Gesetzgeber, und unterdrückt die Welt die Person, so hört sie in demselben Verhältnisse auf, Objekt zu sein, als sie Macht wird. Sobald der Mensch nur Inhalt der Zeit ist, so ist Er nicht, und er h a t folglich auch keinen Inhalt. Mit seiner Persönlichkeit ist auch sein Zustand aufgehoben, weil beides Wechselbegriffe sind — weil die Veränderung ein Beharrliches und die begrenzte Realität eine unendliche fordert. Wird der Formtrieb empfangend, das heisst, kommt die Denkkraft der Empfindung zuvor und unterschiebt die Person sich der Welt, so hört sie in demselben Verhältnis auf, selbständige Kraft und Subjekt zu sein, als sie sich in den Platz des Objektes drängt, weil das Beharrliche die Veränderung, und die absolute Realität zu ihrer Verkündigung Schranken fordert. Sobald der Mensch nur Form i s t, so h a t er keine Form, und mit dem Zustand ist folglich auch die Person aufgehoben. Mit einem Wort: nur insofern er selbständig ist, ist Realität ausser ihm, ist er empfänglich; nur insofern er empfänglich ist, ist Realität in ihm, ist er eine denkende Kraft.

6. Beide Triebe haben also Einschränkung und, insofern sie als Energien gedacht werden, Abspannung nötig; jener, dass er sich

zu machen? Dieses Vermögen aber wird sowohl in der Erziehung, die wir empfangen, als in der, die wir selbst uns geben, in demselben Masse unterdrückt, als man die Macht der Begierden zu brechen und den Charakter durch Grundsätze zu befestigen sucht. Weil es Schwierigkeit kostet, bei aller Regsamkeit des Gefühls seinen Grundsätzen treu zu bleiben, so ergreift man das bequemere Mittel, durch Abstumpfung der Gefühle den Charakter sicher zu stellen; denn freilich ist es unendlich leichter, vor einem entwaffneten Gegner Ruhe zu haben, als einen mutigen und rüstigen Feind zu beherrschen. In dieser Operation besteht dann auch grösstenteils das, was man e i n e n M e n s c h e n f o r m i e r e n nennt; und zwar im besten Sinne des Worts, wo es Bearbeitung des innern, nicht bloss des äussern Menschen bedeutet. Ein so formierter Mensch wird freilich davor gesichert sein, rohe Natur zu sein und als solche zu erscheinen; er wird aber zugleich gegen alle Empfindungen der Natur durch Grundsätze geharnischt sein, und die Menschheit v o n a u s s e n wird ihm ebenso wenig als die Menschheit v o n i n n e n beikommen können.

4. Es ist ein sehr verderblicher Missbrauch, der von dem Ideal der Vollkommenheit gemacht wird, wenn man es bei der Beurteilung anderer Menschen und in den Fällen, wo man für sie wirken soll, in seiner ganzen Strenge zum Grund legt. Jenes wird zur Schwärmerei, dieses zur Härte und zur Kaltsinnigkeit führen. Man macht sich freilich seine gesellschaftlichen Pflichten ungemein leicht, wenn man dem w i r k l i c h e n Menschen, der unsre Hilfe auffordert, in Gedanken den I d e a l-Menschen unterschiebt, der sich wahrscheinlich selbst helfen könnte. Strenge gegen sich selbst, mit Weichheit gegen andre verbunden. macht den wahrhaft vortrefflichen Charakter aus. Aber meistens wird der gegen andere weiche Mensch es auch gegen sich selbst, und der gegen sich selbst strenge es auch gegen andere sein; weich gegen sich und streng gegen andre ist der verächtlichste Charakter.

5. For if the sensuous drive becomes the determining one, that is to say, if the senses assume the role of legislator and the world suppresses the Person, then the world ceases to be an object precisely to the extent that it becomes a force. From the moment that man is merely a content of time, h e ceases to exist, and h a s in consequence no content either. With his Personality his Condition, too, is annulled, because these two concepts are reciprocally related—because change demands a principle of permanence, and finite reality an infinite reality. If, on the other hand, the formal drive becomes receptive, that is to say, if thought forestalls feeling and the Person supplants the world, then the Person ceases to be autonomous force and subject precisely to the extent that it forces its way into the place of the object—because, in order to become manifest, the principle of permanence requires change, and absolute reality has need of limitation. From the moment that man i s only form, he ceases to h a v e a form; the annulling of his Condition, consequently, involves that of his Person too. In a single word, only inasmuch as he is autonomous, is there reality outside him and is he receptive to it; and only inasmuch as he is receptive, is there reality within him and is he a thinking force.

6. Both drives, therefore, need to have limits set to them and, inasmuch as they can be thought of as energies, need to be relaxed;

in that we give ourselves, this power gets repressed in exactly the measure that we seek to break the force of passions, and strengthen character by means of principles. Since it costs effort to remain true to one's principles when feeling is easily stirred, we take the easier way out and try to make character secure by blunting feeling; for it is, of course, infinitely easier to have peace and quiet from an adversary you have disarmed than to master a spirited and active foe. And this, for the most part, is the operation that is meant when people speak of f o r m i n g c h a r a c t e r; and that, even in the best sense of the word, where it implies the cultivation of the inner, and not merely of the outer, man. A man so formed will, without doubt, be immune from the danger of being crude nature or of appearing as such; but he will at the same time be armoured by principle against all natural feeling, and be equally inaccessible to the claims of humanity f r o m w i t h o u t as he is to those of humanity f r o m w i t h i n.

4. It is a most pernicious abuse of the ideal of perfection, to apply it in all its rigour, either in our judgements of other people, or in those cases where we have to act on their behalf. The former leads to sentimental idealism; the latter to hardness and coldness of heart. We certainly make our duty to society uncommonly easy for ourselves by mentally substituting for the a c t u a l man who claims our help the i d e a l man who could in all probability help himself. Severity with one's self combined with leniency towards others is a sign of the truly excellent character. But mostly the man who is lenient to others will also be lenient to himself; and he who is severe with himself will be the same with others. To be lenient to oneself and severe towards others is the most contemptible character of all.

nicht ins Gebiet der Gesetzgebung, dieser, dass er sich nicht ins Gebiet der Empfindung eindringe. Jene Abspannung des sinnlichen Triebes darf aber keineswegs die Wirkung eines physischen Unvermögens und einer Stumpfheit der Empfindungen sein, welche überall nur Verachtung verdient; sie muss eine Handlung der Freiheit, eine Tätigkeit der Person sein, die durch ihre moralische Intensität jene sinnliche mässigt und durch Beherrschung der Eindrücke ihnen an Tiefe nimmt, um ihnen an Fläche zu geben. Der Charakter muss dem Temperament seine Grenzen bestimmen, denn nur an den Geist darf der Sinn verlieren. Jene Abspannung des Formtriebs darf ebensowenig die Wirkung eines geistigen Unvermögens und einer Schlaffheit der Denk- oder Willenskräfte sein, welche die Menschheit erniedrigen würde. Fülle der Empfindungen muss ihre rühmliche Quelle sein; die Sinnlichkeit selbst muss mit siegender Kraft ihr Gebiet behaupten und der Gewalt widerstreben, die ihr der Geist durch seine vorgreifende Tätigkeit gerne zufügen möchte. Mit einem Wort: den Stofftrieb muss die Persönlichkeit, und den Formtrieb die Empfänglichkeit, oder die Natur, in seinen gehörigen Schranken halten.

the sense-drive so that it does not encroach upon the domain of law, the formal drive so that it does not encroach on that of feeling. But the relaxing of the sense-drive must in no wise be the result of physical impotence or blunted feeling, which never merits anything but contempt. It must be an act of free choice, an activity of the Person which, by its moral intensity, moderates that of the senses and, by mastering impressions, robs them of their depth only in order to give them increased surface. It is character which must set bounds to temperament, for it is only to profit the mind that sense may go short. In the same way the relaxing of the formal drive must not be the result of spiritual impotence or flabbiness of thought or will; for this would only degrade man. It must, if it is to be at all praiseworthy, spring from abundance of feeling and sensation. Sense herself must, with triumphant power, remain mistress of her own domain, and resist the violence which the mind, by its usurping tactics, would fain inflict upon her. In a single word: Personality must keep the sensuous drive within its proper bounds, and receptivity, or Nature, must do the same with the formal drive.

VIERZEHNTER BRIEF

1. WIR sind nunmehr zu dem Begriff einer solchen Wechselwirkung zwischen beiden Trieben geführt worden, wo die Wirksamkeit des einen die Wirksamkeit des andern zugleich begründet und
begrenzt, und wo jeder einzelne für sich gerade dadurch zu seiner
höchsten Verkündigung gelangt, dass der andere tätig ist.

2. Dieses Wechselverhältnis beider Triebe ist zwar bloss eine Aufgabe der Vernunft, die der Mensch nur in der Vollendung seines
Daseins ganz zu lösen im Stand ist. Es ist im eigentlichsten Sinne
des Worts die Idee seiner Menschheit, mithin ein Unendliches, dem er sich im Laufe der Zeit immer mehr nähern kann, aber
ohne es jemals zu erreichen. „Er soll nicht auf Kosten seiner Realität
nach Form, und nicht auf Kosten der Form nach Realität streben;
vielmehr soll er das absolute Sein durch ein bestimmtes und das
bestimmte Sein durch ein unendliches suchen. Er soll sich eine
Welt gegenüber stellen, weil er Person ist, und soll Person sein, weil
ihm eine Welt gegenüber steht. Er soll empfinden, weil er sich
bewusst ist, und soll sich bewusst sein, weil er empfindet." — Dass
er dieser Idee wirklich gemäss, folglich in voller Bedeutung des
Worts Mensch ist, kann er nie in Erfahrung bringen, solange er nur
Einen dieser beiden Triebe ausschliessend, oder nur Einen nach dem
Andern, befriedigt: denn solange er nur empfindet, bleibt ihm seine
Person oder seine absolute Existenz, und, solange er nur denkt,
bleibt ihm seine Existenz in der Zeit oder sein Zustand Geheimnis.
Gäbe es aber Fälle, wo er diese doppelte Erfahrung zugleich
machte, wo er sich zugleich seiner Freiheit bewusst würde und sein
Dasein empfände, wo er sich zugleich als Materie fühlte und als
Geist kennen lernte, so hätte er in diesen Fällen, und schlechterdings
nur in diesen, eine vollständige Anschauung seiner Menschheit, und
der Gegenstand, der diese Anschauung ihm verschaffte, würde ihm
zu einem Symbol seiner ausgeführten Bestimmung, folglich (weil diese nur in der Allheit der Zeit zu erreichen ist) zu
einer Darstellung des Unendlichen dienen.

3. Vorausgesetzt, dass Fälle dieser Art in der Erfahrung vor-

FOURTEENTH LETTER

1. WE have now been led to the notion of a reciprocal action between the two drives, reciprocal action of such a kind that the activity of the one both gives rise to, and sets limits to, the activity of the other, and in which each in itself achieves its highest manifestation precisely by reason of the other being active.

2. Such reciprocal relation between the two drives is, admittedly, but a task enjoined upon us by Reason, a problem which man is only capable of solving completely in the perfect consummation of his existence. It is, in the most precise sense of the word, the Idea of his Human Nature, hence something Infinite, to which in the course of time he can approximate ever more closely, but without ever being able to reach it. 'He is not to strive for form at the cost of reality, nor for reality at the cost of form; rather is he to seek absolute being by means of a determinate being, and a determinate being by means of infinite being. He is to set up a world over against himself because he is Person, and he is to be Person because a world stands over against him. He is to feel because he is conscious of himself, and be conscious of himself because he feels.'—That he does actually conform to this Idea, that he is consequently, in the fullest sense of the word, a human being, is never brought home to him as long as he satisfies only one of these two drives to the exclusion of the other, or only satisfies them one after the other. For as long as he only feels, his Person, or his absolute existence, remains a mystery to him; and as long as he only thinks, his existence in time, or his Condition, does likewise. Should there, however, be cases in which he were to have this twofold experience s i m u l t a n e o u s l y, in which he were to be at once conscious of his freedom and sensible of his existence, were, at one and the same time, to feel himself matter and come to know himself as mind, then he would in such cases, and in such cases only, have a complete intuition of his human nature, and the object which afforded him this vision would become for him a symbol of his a c c o m p l i s h e d   d e s t i n y and, in consequence (since that is only to be attained in the totality of time), serve him as a manifestation of the Infinite.

3. Assuming that cases of this sort could actually occur in

kommen können, so würden sie einen neuen Trieb in ihm aufwecken, der eben darum, weil die beiden andern in ihm zusammenwirken, einem jeden derselben, einzeln betrachtet, entgegengesetzt sein und mit Recht für einen neuen Trieb gelten würde. Der sinnliche Trieb will, dass Veränderung sei, dass die Zeit einen Inhalt habe; der Formtrieb will, dass die Zeit aufgehoben, dass keine Veränderung sei. Derjenige Trieb also, in welchem beide verbunden wirken (es sei mir einstweilen, bis ich diese Benennung gerechtfertigt haben werde, vergönnt, ihn S p i e l t r i e b zu nennen), der Spieltrieb also würde dahin gerichtet sein, die Zeit i n d e r Z e i t aufzuheben, Werden mit absolutem Sein, Veränderung mit Identität zu vereinbaren.

4.   Der sinnliche Trieb will bestimmt w e r d e n, er will sein Objekt empfangen; der Formtrieb will s e l b s t bestimmen, er will sein Objekt hervorbringen: der Spieltrieb wird also bestrebt sein, so zu empfangen, wie er selbst hervorgebracht hätte, und so hervorzubringen, wie der Sinn zu empfangen trachtet.

5.   Der sinnliche Trieb schliesst aus seinem Subjekt alle Selbsttätigkeit und Freiheit, der Formtrieb schliesst aus dem seinigen alle Abhängigkeit, alles Leiden aus. Ausschliessung der Freiheit ist aber physische, Ausschliessung des Leidens ist moralische Notwendigkeit. Beide Triebe nötigen also das Gemüt, jener durch Naturgesetze, dieser durch Gesetze der Vernunft. Der Spieltrieb also, als in welchem beide verbunden wirken, wird das Gemüt zugleich moralisch und physisch nötigen; er wird also, weil er alle Zufälligkeit aufhebt, auch alle Nötigung aufheben und den Menschen, sowohl physisch als moralisch, in Freiheit setzen. Wenn wir jemand mit Leidenschaft umfassen, der unsrer Verachtung würdig ist, so empfinden wir peinlich die N ö t i g u n g d e r N a t u r. Wenn wir gegen einen andern feindlich gesinnt sind, der uns Achtung abnötigt, so empfinden wir peinlich die N ö t i g u n g d e r V e r n u n f t. Sobald er aber zugleich unsre Neigung interessiert und unsre Achtung sich erworben, so verschwindet sowohl der Zwang der Empfindung als der Zwang der Vernunft, und wir fangen an, ihn zu lieben, d.h. zugleich mit unsrer Neigung und mit unsrer Achtung zu spielen.

6.   Indem uns ferner der sinnliche Trieb physisch, und der Formtrieb moralisch nötigt, so lässt jener unsre formale, dieser unsre

experience, they would awaken in him a new drive which, precisely because the other two drives co-operate within it, would be opposed to each of them considered separately and could justifiably count as a new drive. The sense-drive demands that there shall be change and that time shall have a content; the form-drive demands that time shall be annulled and that there shall be no change. That drive, therefore, in which both the others work in concert (permit me for the time being, until I have justified the term, to call it the p l a y - d r i v e), the play-drive, therefore, would be directed towards annulling time w i t h i n t i m e, reconciling becoming with absolute being and change with identity.

4. The sense-drive wants to b e determined, wants to receive its object; the form-drive wants i t s e l f to determine, wants to bring forth its object. The play-drive, therefore, will endeavour so to receive as if it had itself brought forth, and so to bring forth as the intuitive sense aspires to receive.

5. The sense-drive excludes from its subject all autonomy and freedom; the form-drive excludes from its subject all dependence, all passivity. Exclusion of freedom, however, implies physical necessity, exclusion of passivity moral necessity. Both drives, therefore, exert constraint upon the psyche; the former through the laws of nature, the latter through the laws of reason. The play-drive, in consequence, as the one in which both the others act in concert, will exert upon the psyche at once a moral and a physical constraint; it will, therefore, since it annuls all contingency, annul all constraint too, and set man free both physically and morally. When we embrace with passion someone who deserves our contempt, we are painfully aware of the c o m p u l s i o n o f n a t u r e. When we feel hostile towards another who compels our esteem, we are painfully aware of the c o m p u l s i o n o f r e a s o n. But once he has at the same time engaged our affection and won our esteem, then both the compulsion of feeling and the compulsion of reason disappear and we begin to love him, i.e., we begin to play with both our affection and our esteem.

6. Since, moreover, the sense-drive exerts a physical, the form-drive a moral constraint, the first will leave our formal, the second

materiale Beschaffenheit zufällig; das heisst, es ist zufällig, ob unsere Glückseligkeit mit unsrer Vollkommenheit, oder ob diese mit jener übereinstimmen werde. Der Spieltrieb also, in welchem beide vereinigt wirken, wird zugleich unsre formale und unsre materiale Beschaffenheit, zugleich unsre Vollkommenheit und unsre Glückseligkeit zufällig machen; er wird also, eben weil er b e i d e zufällig macht, und weil mit der Notwendigkeit auch die Zufälligkeit verschwindet, die Zufälligkeit in beiden wieder aufheben, mithin Form in die Materie und Realität in die Form bringen. In demselben Masse, als er den Empfindungen und Affekten ihren dynamischen Einfluss nimmt, wird er sie mit Ideen der Vernunft in Übereinstimmung bringen, und in demselben Masse, als er den Gesetzen der Vernunft ihre moralische Nötigung benimmt, wird er sie mit dem Interesse der Sinne versöhnen.

our material disposition at the mercy of the contingent; that is to say, it is a matter of chance whether our happiness will coincide with our perfection or our perfection with our happiness. The play-drive, in consequence, in which both work in concert, will make our formal as well as our material disposition, our perfection as well as our happiness, contingent. It will therefore, just because it makes b o t h contingent and because with all constraint all contingency too disappears, abolish contingency in both, and, as a result, introduce form into matter and reality into form. To the extent that it deprives feelings and passions of their dynamic power, it will bring them into harmony with the ideas of reason; and to the extent that it deprives the laws of reason of their moral compulsion, it will reconcile them with the interests of the senses.

FÜNFZEHNTER BRIEF

1. IMMER näher komm' ich dem Ziel, dem ich Sie auf einem wenig ermunternden Pfade entgegen führe. Lassen Sie es sich gefallen, mir noch einige Schritte weiter zu folgen, so wird ein desto freierer Gesichtskreis sich auftun und eine muntre Aussicht die Mühe des Wegs vielleicht belohnen.

2. Der Gegenstand des sinnlichen Triebes, in einem allgemeinen Begriff ausgedrückt, heisst L e b e n in weitester Bedeutung; ein Begriff, der alles materiale Sein und alle unmittelbare Gegenwart in den Sinnen bedeutet. Der Gegenstand des Formtriebes, in einem allgemeinen Begriff ausgedrückt, heisst G e s t a l t, sowohl in uneigentlicher als in eigentlicher Bedeutung; ein Begriff, der alle formalen Beschaffenheiten der Dinge und alle Beziehungen derselben auf die Denkkräfte unter sich fasst. Der Gegenstand des Spieltriebes, in einem allgemeinen Schema vorgestellt, wird also l e b e n d e G e s t a l t heissen können; ein Begriff, der allen ästhetischen Beschaffenheiten der Erscheinungen und mit einem Worte dem, was man in weitester Bedeutung S c h ö n h e i t nennt, zur Bezeichnung dient.

3. Durch diese Erklärung, wenn es eine wäre, wird die Schönheit weder auf das ganze Gebiet des Lebendigen ausgedehnt, noch bloss in dieses Gebiet eingeschlossen. Ein Marmorblock, obgleich er leblos ist und bleibt, kann darum nichtsdestoweniger lebende Gestalt durch den Architekt und Bildhauer werden; ein Mensch, wiewohl er lebt und Gestalt hat, ist darum noch lange keine lebende Gestalt. Dazu gehört, dass seine Gestalt Leben und sein Leben Gestalt sei. Solange wir über seine Gestalt bloss denken, ist sie leblos, blosse Abstraktion; solange wir sein Leben bloss fühlen, ist es gestaltlos, blosse Impression. Nur indem seine Form in unsrer Empfindung lebt und sein Leben in unserm Verstande sich formt, ist er lebende Gestalt, und dies wird überall der Fall sein, wo wir ihn als schön beurteilen.

4. Dadurch aber, dass wir die Bestandteile anzugeben wissen, die in ihrer Vereinigung die Schönheit hervorbringen, ist die Genesis derselben auf keine Weise noch erklärt; denn dazu würde erfordert,

FIFTEENTH LETTER

1. I AM drawing ever nearer the goal towards which I have been leading you by a not exactly encouraging path. If you will consent to follow me a few steps further along it, horizons all the wider will unfold and a pleasing prospect perhaps requite you for the labour of the journey.

2. The object of the sense-drive, expressed in a general concept, we call l i f e, in the widest sense of this term: a concept designating all material being and all that is immediately present to the senses. The object of the form-drive, expressed in a general concept, we call f o r m, both in the figurative and in the literal sense of this word: a concept which includes all the formal qualities of things and all the relations of these to our thinking faculties. The object of the play-drive, represented in a general schema, may therefore be called l i v i n g f o r m: a concept serving to designate all the aesthetic qualities of phenomena and, in a word, what in the widest sense of the term we call b e a u t y.

3. According to this explanation, if such it be, the term beauty is neither extended to cover the whole realm of living things nor is it merely confined to this realm. A block of marble, though it is and remains lifeless, can nevertheless, thanks to the architect or the sculptor, become living form; and a human being, though he may live and have form, is far from being on that account a living form. In order to be so, his form would have to be life, and his life form. As long as we merely think about his form, it is lifeless, a mere abstraction; as long as we merely feel his life, it is formless, a mere impression. Only when his form lives in our feeling and his life takes on form in our understanding, does he become living form; and this will always be the case whenever we adjudge him beautiful.

4. But because we know how to specify the elements which when combined produce beauty, this does not mean that its genesis has as yet in any way been explained; for that would require us to

dass man jene Vereinigung selbst begriffe, die uns, wie überhaupt alle Wechselwirkung zwischen dem Endlichen und Unendlichen, unerforschlich bleibt. Die Vernunft stellt aus transcendentalen Gründen die Forderung auf: es soll eine Gemeinschaft zwischen Formtrieb und Stofftrieb, das heisst, ein Spieltrieb sein, weil nur die Einheit der Realität mit der Form, der Zufälligkeit mit der Notwendigkeit, des Leidens mit der Freiheit den Begriff der Menschheit vollendet. Sie muss diese Forderung aufstellen, weil sie Vernunft ist — weil sie ihrem Wesen nach auf Vollendung und auf Wegräumung aller Schranken dringt, jede ausschliessende Tätigkeit des einen oder des andern Triebes aber die menschliche Natur unvollendet lässt und eine Schranke in derselben begründet. Sobald sie demnach den Ausspruch tut: es soll eine Menschheit existieren, so hat sie eben dadurch das Gesetz aufgestellt: es soll eine Schönheit sein. Die Erfahrung kann uns beantworten, o b eine Schönheit ist, und wir werden es wissen, sobald sie uns belehrt hat, ob eine Menschheit ist. Wie aber eine Schönheit sein kann, und wie eine Menschheit möglich ist, kann uns weder Vernunft noch Erfahrung lehren.

5.   Der Mensch, wissen wir, ist weder ausschliessend Materie, noch ist er ausschliessend Geist. Die Schönheit, als Konsummation seiner Menschheit, kann also weder ausschliessend blosses Leben sein, wie von scharfsinnigen Beobachtern, die sich zu genau an die Zeugnisse der Erfahrung hielten, behauptet worden ist, und wozu der Geschmack der Zeit sie gern herabziehen möchte; noch kann sie ausschliessend blosse Gestalt sein, wie von spekulativen Weltweisen, die sich zu weit von der Erfahrung entfernten, und von philosophierenden Künstlern, die sich in Erklärung derselben allzu sehr durch das Bedürfnis der Kunst leiten liessen, geurteilt worden ist:* sie ist das gemeinschaftliche Objekt beider Triebe, das heisst, des Spieltriebs. Diesen Namen rechtfertigt der Sprachgebrauch vollkommen, der alles das, was weder subjektiv noch objektiv zufällig ist und doch weder äusserlich noch innerlich nötigt, mit dem

---

* Zum blossen Leben macht die Schönheit B u r k e in seinen Philosophischen Untersuchungen über den Ursprung unsrer Begriffe vom Erhabenen und Schönen. Zur blossen Gestalt macht sie, soweit mir bekannt ist, jeder Anhänger des d o g m a t i s c h e n Systems, der über diesen Gegenstand je sein Bekenntnis ablegte: unter den Künstlern R a p h a e l M e n g s in seinen Gedanken über den Geschmack in der Malerei; andrer nicht zu gedenken. So wie in allem, hat auch in diesem Stück die k r i t i s c h e Philosophie den Weg eröffnet, die Empirie auf Prinzipien und die Spekulation zur Erfahrung zurückzuführen.

understand the actual manner of their combining, and this, like all reciprocal action between finite and infinite, remains for ever inaccessible to our probing. Reason, on transcendental grounds, makes the following demand: Let there be a bond of union between the form-drive and the material drive; that is to say, let there be a play-drive, since only the union of reality with form, contingency with necessity, passivity with freedom, makes the concept of human nature complete. Reason must make this demand because it is reason—because it is its nature to insist on perfection and on the abolition of all limitation, and because any exclusive activity on the part of either the one drive or the other leaves human nature incomplete and gives rise to some limitation within it. Consequently, as soon as reason utters the pronouncement: Let humanity exist, it has by that very pronouncement also promulgated the law: Let there be beauty. Experience can provide an answer to the question whether there is such a thing as beauty, and we shall know the answer once experience has taught us whether there is such a thing as humanity. But how there can be beauty, and how humanity is possible, neither reason nor experience can tell us.

5. Man, as we know, is neither exclusively matter nor exclusively mind. Beauty, as the consummation of his humanity, can therefore be neither exclusively life nor exclusively form. Not mere life, as acute observers, adhering too closely to the testimony of experience, have maintained, and to which the taste of our age would fain degrade it; not mere form, as it has been adjudged by philosophers whose speculations led them too far away from experience, or by artists who, philosophizing on beauty, let themselves be too exclusively guided by the needs of their craft.* It is the object common to both drives, that is to say, the object of the play-drive. This term is fully justified by linguistic usage, which is wont to designate as 'play' everything which is neither subjectively nor objectively contingent, and yet imposes no kind of constraint either from within

* Burke, in his *Philosophical Enquiry into the Origin of our Ideas of the Sublime and the Beautiful*, makes beauty into mere life. As far as I know, every adherent of dogmatic philosophy, who has ever confessed his belief on this subject, makes it into mere form: among artists, Raphael Mengs, in his *Reflections on Taste in Painting*, not to speak of others. In this, as in everything else, critical philosophy has opened up the way whereby empiricism can be led back to principles, and speculation back to experience.

Wort Spiel zu bezeichnen pflegt. Da sich das Gemüt bei Anschauung des Schönen in einer glücklichen Mitte zwischen dem Gesetz und Bedürfnis befindet, so ist es eben darum, weil es sich zwischen beiden teilt, dem Zwange sowohl des einen als des andern entzogen. Dem Stofftrieb wie dem Formtrieb ist es mit ihren Forderungen e r n s t, weil der eine sich, beim Erkennen, auf die Wirklichkeit, der andre auf die Notwendigkeit der Dinge bezieht; weil, beim Handeln, der erste auf Erhaltung des Lebens, der zweite auf Bewahrung der Würde, beide also auf Wahrheit und Vollkommenheit gerichtet sind. Aber das Leben wird gleichgültiger, sowie die Würde sich einmischt, und die Pflicht nötigt nicht mehr, sobald die Neigung zieht; ebenso nimmt das Gemüt die Wirklichkeit der Dinge, die materiale Wahrheit, freier und ruhiger auf, sobald solche der formalen Wahrheit, dem Gesetz der Notwendigkeit, begegnet, und fühlt sich durch Abstraktion nicht mehr angespannt, sobald die unmittelbare Anschauung sie begleiten kann. Mit einem Wort: indem es mit Ideen in Gemeinschaft kommt, verliert alles Wirkliche seinen Ernst, weil es k l e i n wird, und indem es mit der Empfindung zusammentrifft, legt das Notwendige den seinigen ab, weil es l e i c h t wird.

6. Wird aber, möchten Sie längst schon versucht gewesen sein mir entgegen zu setzen, wird nicht das Schöne dadurch, dass man es zum blossen Spiel macht, erniedrigt und den frivolen Gegenständen gleichgestellt, die von jeher im Besitz dieses Namens waren? Widerspricht es nicht dem Vernunftbegriff und der Würde der Schönheit, die doch als ein Instrument der Kultur betrachtet wird, sie auf ein b l o s s e s S p i e l einzuschränken, und widerspricht es nicht dem Erfahrungsbegriffe des Spiels, das mit Ausschliessung alles Geschmackes zusammen bestehen kann, es bloss auf Schönheit einzuschränken?

7. Aber was heisst denn ein b l o s s e s Spiel, nachdem wir wissen, dass unter allen Zuständen des Menschen gerade das Spiel und n u r das Spiel es ist, was ihn vollständig macht und seine doppelte Natur auf einmal entfaltet? Was Sie, nach Ihrer Vorstellung der Sache, E i n s c h r ä n k u n g nennen, das nenne ich, nach der meinen, die ich durch Beweise gerechtfertigt habe, E r w e i t e r u n g. Ich würde also vielmehr gerade umgekehrt sagen: mit dem Angenehmen, mit dem Guten, mit dem Vollkommenen ist es dem Menschen n u r ernst, aber mit der Schönheit spielt er.

or from without. Since, in contemplation of the beautiful, the psyche finds itself in a happy medium between the realm of law and the sphere of physical exigency, it is, precisely because it is divided between the two, removed from the constraint of the one as of the other. The material drive, like the formal drive, is wholly e a r n e s t in its demands; for, in the sphere of knowledge, the former is concerned with the reality, the latter with the necessity of things; while in the sphere of action, the first is directed towards the preservation of life, the second towards the maintenance of dignity: both, therefore, towards truth and towards perfection. But life becomes of less consequence once human dignity enters in, and duty ceases to be a constraint once inclination exerts its pull; similarly our psyche accepts the reality of things, or material truth, with greater freedom and serenity once this latter encounters formal truth, or the law of necessity, and no longer feels constrained by abstraction once this can be accompanied by the immediacy of intuition. In a word: by entering into association with ideas all reality loses its earnestness because it then becomes o f s m a l l a c c o u n t; and by coinciding with feeling necessity divests itself of its earnestness because it then becomes o f l i g h t w e i g h t.

6. But, you may long have been tempted to object, is beauty not degraded by being made to consist of mere play and reduced to the level of those frivolous things which have always borne this name? Does it not belie the rational concept as well as the dignity of beauty —which is, after all, here being considered as an instrument of culture—if we limit it to m e r e p l a y? And does it not belie the empirical concept of play—a concept which is, after all, entirely compatible with the exclusion of all taste—if we limit it merely to beauty?

7. But how can we speak of m e r e play, when we know that it is precisely play and play a l o n e, which of all man's states and conditions is the one which makes him whole and unfolds both sides of his nature at once? What you, according to your idea of the matter, call l i m i t a t i o n, I, according to mine—which I have justified by proof—call e x p a n s i o n. I, therefore, would prefer to put it exactly the opposite way round and say: the agreeable, the good, the perfect, with these man is m e r e l y in earnest; but with beauty

Freilich dürfen wir uns hier nicht an die Spiele erinnern, die in dem wirklichen Leben im Gange sind und die sich gewöhnlich nur auf sehr materielle Gegenstände richten; aber in dem wirklichen Leben würden wir auch die Schönheit vergebens suchen, von der hier die Rede ist. Die wirklich vorhandene Schönheit ist des wirklich vorhandenen Spieltriebes wert; aber durch das Ideal der Schönheit, welches die Vernunft aufstellt, ist auch ein Ideal des Spieltriebes aufgegeben, das der Mensch in allen seinen Spielen vor Augen haben soll.

8. Man wird niemals irren, wenn man das Schönheitsideal eines Menschen auf dem nämlichen Wege sucht, auf dem er seinen Spieltrieb befriedigt. Wenn sich die griechischen Völkerschaften in den Kampfspielen zu Olympia an den unblutigen Wettkämpfen der Kraft, der Schnelligkeit, der Gelenkigkeit und an dem edleren Wechselstreit der Talente ergötzen, und wenn das römische Volk an dem Todeskampf eines erlegten Gladiators oder seines libyschen Gegners sich labt, so wird es uns aus diesem einzigen Zuge begreiflich, warum wir die Idealgestalten einer Venus, einer Juno, eines Apolls nicht in Rom, sondern in Griechenland aufsuchen müssen.* Nun spricht aber die Vernunft: das Schöne soll nicht blosses Leben und nicht blosse Gestalt, sondern lebende Gestalt, das ist, Schönheit sein, indem sie ja dem Menschen das doppelte Gesetz der absoluten Formalität und der absoluten Realität diktiert. Mithin tut sie auch den Ausspruch: der Mensch soll mit der Schönheit n u r s p i e l e n, und er soll n u r m i t d e r S c h ö n h e i t spielen.

9. Denn, um es endlich auf einmal herauszusagen, der Mensch spielt nur, wo er in voller Bedeutung des Worts Mensch ist, und e r ist n u r d a g a n z M e n s c h, w o e r s p i e l t. Dieser Satz, der in diesem Augenblicke vielleicht paradox erscheint, wird eine grosse und tiefe Bedeutung erhalten, wenn wir erst dahin gekommen sein werden, ihn auf den doppelten Ernst der Pflicht und des Schicksals anzuwenden; er wird, ich verspreche es Ihnen, das ganze Gebäude der ästhetischen Kunst und der noch schwierigern

---

* Wenn man (um bei der neuern Welt stehen zu bleiben) die Wettrennen in London, die Stiergefechte in Madrid, die Spectacles in dem ehemaligen Paris, die Gondelrennen in Venedig, die Tierhatzen in Wien und das frohe schöne Leben des Corso in Rom gegeneinander hält, so kann es nicht schwer sein, den Geschmack dieser verschiedenen Völker gegeneinander zu nüancieren. Indessen zeigt sich unter den Volksspielen in diesen verschiedenen Ländern weit weniger Einförmigkeit als unter den Spielen der feinern Welt in eben diesen Ländern, welches leicht zu erklären ist.

he plays. True, we must not think here of the various forms of play which are in vogue in actual life, and are usually directed to very material objects. But then in actual life we should also seek in vain for the kind of beauty with which we are here concerned. The beauty we find in actual existence is precisely what the play-drive we find in actual existence deserves; but with the ideal of Beauty that is set up by Reason, an ideal of the play-drive, too, is enjoined upon man, which he must keep before his eyes in all his forms of play.

8.   We shall not go far wrong when trying to discover a man's ideal of beauty if we inquire how he satisfies his play-drive. If at the Olympic Games the peoples of Greece delighted in the bloodless combats of strength, speed, and agility, and in the nobler rivalry of talents, and if the Roman people regaled themselves with the death throes of a vanquished gladiator or of his Libyan opponent, we can, from this single trait, understand why we have to seek the ideal forms of a Venus, a Juno, an Apollo, not in Rome, but in Greece.* Reason, however, declares: The beautiful is to be neither mere life, nor mere form, but living form, i.e., Beauty; for it imposes upon man the double law of absolute formality and absolute reality. Consequently Reason also makes the pronouncement: With beauty man shall o n l y p l a y, and it is w i t h b e a u t y o n l y that he shall play.

9.   For, to mince matters no longer, man only plays when he is in the fullest sense of the word a human being, and h e i s o n l y f u l l y a h u m a n b e i n g w h e n h e p l a y s. This proposition, which at the moment may sound like a paradox, will take on both weight and depth of meaning once we have got as far as applying it to the two-fold earnestness of duty and of destiny. It will, I promise you, prove capable of bearing the whole edifice of the art of the beautiful, and

---

* If (to confine ourselves to the modern world) we compare horse-racing in London, bull-fights in Madrid, *spectacles* in the Paris of former days, the gondola races in Venice, animal-baiting in Vienna, and the gay attractive life of the Corso in Rome, it will not be difficult to determine the different nuances of taste among these different peoples. However, there is far less uniformity among the amusements of the common people in these different countries than there is among those of the refined classes in those same countries, a fact which it is easy to account for.

Lebenskunst tragen. Aber dieser Satz ist auch nur in der Wissenschaft unerwartet; längst schon lebte und wirkte er in der Kunst und in dem Gefühle der Griechen, ihrer vornehmsten Meister; nur dass sie in den Olympus versetzten, was auf der Erde sollte ausgeführt werden. Von der Wahrheit desselben geleitet, liessen sie sowohl den Ernst und die Arbeit, welche die Wangen der Sterblichen furchen, als die nichtige Lust, die das leere Angesicht glättet, aus der Stirne der seligen Götter verschwinden, gaben die ewig Zufriedenen von den Fesseln jedes Zweckes, jeder Pflicht, jeder Sorge frei und machten den Müssiggang und die Gleichgültigkeit zum beneideten Lose des Götterstandes: ein bloss menschlicherer Name für das freieste und erhabenste Sein. Sowohl der materielle Zwang der Naturgesetze als der geistige Zwang der Sittengesetze verlor sich in ihrem höhern Begriff von Notwendigkeit, der beide Welten zugleich umfasste, und aus der Einheit jener beiden Notwendigkeiten ging ihnen erst die wahre Freiheit hervor. Beseelt von diesem Geiste, löschten sie aus den Gesichtszügen ihres Ideals zugleich mit der Neigung auch alle Spuren des Willens aus, oder besser, sie machten beide unkenntlich, weil sie beide in dem innigsten Bund zu verknüpfen wussten. Es ist weder Anmut, noch ist es Würde, was aus dem herrlichen Antlitz einer Juno Ludovisi zu uns spricht; es ist keines von beiden, weil es beides zugleich ist. Indem der weibliche Gott unsre Anbetung heischt, entzündet das gottgleiche Weib unsre Liebe; aber indem wir uns der himmlischen Holdseligkeit aufgelöst hingeben, schreckt die himmlische Selbstgenügsamkeit uns zurück. In sich selbst ruhet und wohnt die ganze Gestalt, eine völlig geschlossene Schöpfung, und als wenn sie jenseits des Raumes wäre, ohne Nachgeben, ohne Widerstand; da ist keine Kraft, die mit Kräften kämpfte, keine Blösse, wo die Zeitlichkeit einbrechen könnte. Durch jenes unwiderstehlich ergriffen und angezogen, durch dieses in der Ferne gehalten, befinden wir uns zugleich in dem Zustand der höchsten Ruhe und der höchsten Bewegung, und es entsteht jene wunderbare Rührung, für welche der Verstand keinen Begriff und die Sprache keinen Namen hat.

of the still more difficult art of living. But it is, after all, only in philosophy that the proposition is unexpected; it was long ago alive and operative in the art and in the feeling of the Greeks, the most distinguished exponents of both; only they transferred to Olympus what was meant to be realized on earth. Guided by the truth of that same proposition, they banished from the brow of the blessed gods all the earnestness and effort which furrow the cheeks of mortals, no less than the empty pleasures which preserve the smoothness of a vacuous face; freed those ever-contented beings from the bonds inseparable from every purpose, every duty, every care, and made i d l e n e s s and i n d i f f e r e n c y the enviable portion of divinity— merely a more human name for the freest, most sublime state of being. Both the material constraint of natural laws and the spiritual constraint of moral laws were resolved in their higher concept of Necessity, which embraced both worlds at once; and it was only out of the perfect union of those two necessities that for them true Freedom could proceed. Inspired by this spirit, the Greeks effaced from the features of their ideal physiognomy, together with i n - c l i n a t i o n, every trace of v o l i t i o n too; or rather they made both indiscernible, for they knew how to fuse them in the most intimate union. It is not Grace, nor is it yet Dignity, which speaks to us from the superb countenance of a J u n o L u d o v i s i; it is neither the one nor the other because it is both at once. While the woman-god demands our veneration, the god-like woman kindles our love; but even as we abandon ourselves in ecstasy to her heavenly grace, her celestial self-sufficiency makes us recoil in terror. The whole figure reposes and dwells in itself, a creation completely self-contained, and, as if existing beyond space, neither yielding nor resisting; here is no force to contend with force, no frailty where temporality might break in. Irresistibly moved and drawn by those former qualities, kept at a distance by these latter, we find ourselves at one and the same time in a state of utter repose and supreme agitation, and there results that wondrous stirring of the heart for which mind has no concept nor speech any name.

SECHZEHNTER BRIEF

1. Aus der Wechselwirkung zwei entgegengesetzter Triebe und aus der Verbindung zwei entgegengesetzter Prinzipien haben wir das Schöne hervorgehen sehen, dessen höchstes Ideal also in dem möglichstvollkommensten Bunde und Gleichgewicht der Realität und der Form wird zu suchen sein. Dieses Gleichgewicht bleibt aber immer nur Idee, die von der Wirklichkeit nie ganz erreicht werden kann. In der Wirklichkeit wird immer ein Übergewicht des einen Elements über das andere übrig bleiben, und das Höchste, was die Erfahrung leistet, wird in einer Schwankung zwischen beiden Prinzipien bestehen, wo bald die Realität, bald die Form überwiegend ist. Die Schönheit in der Idee ist also ewig nur eine unteilbare einzige, weil es nur ein einziges Gleichgewicht geben kann; die Schönheit in der Erfahrung hingegen wird ewig eine doppelte sein, weil bei einer Schwankung das Gleichgewicht auf eine doppelte Art, nämlich diesseits und jenseits, kann übertreten werden.

2. Ich habe in einem der vorhergehenden Briefe bemerkt, auch lässt es sich aus dem Zusammenhange des Bisherigen mit strenger Notwendigkeit folgern, dass von dem Schönen zugleich eine auflösende und eine anspannende Wirkung zu erwarten sei: eine auflösende, um sowohl den sinnlichen Trieb als den Formtrieb in ihren Grenzen zu halten; eine anspannende, um beide in ihrer Kraft zu erhalten. Diese beiden Wirkungsarten der Schönheit sollen aber, der Idee nach, schlechterdings nur eine einzige sein. Sie soll auflösen, dadurch dass sie beide Naturen gleichförmig anspannt, und soll anspannen, dadurch dass sie beide Naturen gleichförmig auflöst. Dieses folgt schon aus dem Begriff einer Wechselwirkung, vermöge dessen beide Teile einander zugleich notwendig bedingen und durch einander bedingt werden, und deren reinstes Produkt die Schönheit ist. Aber die Erfahrung bietet uns kein Beispiel einer so vollkommenen Wechselwirkung dar, sondern hier wird jederzeit, mehr oder weniger, das Übergewicht einen Mangel und der Mangel ein Übergewicht begründen. Was also in dem Ideal-Schönen nur in der Vorstellung unterschieden wird, das

SIXTEENTH LETTER

1. WE have seen how beauty results from the reciprocal action of two opposed drives and from the uniting of two opposed principles. The highest ideal of beauty is, therefore, to be sought in the most perfect possible union and equilibrium of reality and form. This equilibrium, however, remains no more than an Idea, which can never be fully realized in actuality. For in actuality we shall always be left with a preponderance of the one element over the other, and the utmost that experience can achieve will consist of an oscillation between the two principles, in which now reality, now form, will predominate. Beauty as Idea, therefore, can never be other than one and indivisible, since there can never be more than one point of equilibrium; whereas beauty in experience will be eternally twofold, because oscillation can disturb the equilibrium in twofold fashion, inclining it now to the one side, now to the other.

2. I observed in one of the preceding Letters—and it follows with strict necessity from the foregoing argument—that we must expect from beauty at once a releasing and a tensing effect: a releasing effect in order to keep both the sense-drive and the form-drive within proper bounds; a tensing effect, in order to keep both at full strength. Ideally speaking, however, these two effects must be reducible to a single effect. Beauty is to release by tensing both natures uniformly, and to tense by releasing both natures uniformly. This already follows from the concept of a reciprocal action, by virtue of which both factors necessarily condition each other and are at the same time conditioned by each other, and the purest product of which is beauty. But experience offers us no single example of such perfect reciprocal action; for here it will always happen that, to a greater or lesser degree, a preponderance entails a deficiency, and a deficiency a preponderance. What, then, in the case of ideal beauty is but a distinction which is made in the mind, is in the

i s t in dem Schönen der Erfahrung der Existenz nach verschieden. Das Ideal-Schöne, obgleich unteilbar und einfach, zeigt in verschiedener Beziehung sowohl eine schmelzende als energische Eigenschaft; in der Erfahrung g i b t e s eine schmelzende und energische Schönheit. So ist es, und so wird es in allen den Fällen sein, wo das Absolute in die Schranken der Zeit gesetzt ist und Ideen der Vernunft in der Menschheit realisiert werden sollen. So denkt der reflektierende Mensch sich die Tugend, die Wahrheit, die Glückseligkeit; aber der handelnde Mensch wird bloss T u - g e n d e n üben, bloss W a h r h e i t e n fassen, bloss g l ü c k s e l i g e T a g e geniessen. Diese auf jene zurückzuführen — an die Stelle der Sitten die Sittlichkeit, an die Stelle der Kenntnisse die Erkenntnis, an die Stelle des Glückes die Glückseligkeit zu setzen, ist das Geschäft der physischen und moralischen Bildung; aus Schönheiten Schönheit zu machen, ist die Aufgabe der ästhetischen.

3.   Die energische Schönheit kann den Menschen ebenso wenig vor einem gewissen Überrest von Wildheit und Härte bewahren, als ihn die schmelzende vor einem gewissen Grade der Weichlichkeit und Entnervung schützt. Denn da die Wirkung der erstern ist, das Gemüt sowohl im Physischen als Moralischen anzuspannen und seine Schnellkraft zu vermehren, so geschieht es nur gar zu leicht, dass der Widerstand des Temperaments und Charakters die Empfänglichkeit für Eindrücke mindert, dass auch die zärtere Humanität eine Unterdrückung erfährt, die nur die rohe Natur treffen sollte, und dass die rohe Natur an einem Kraftgewinn teilnimmt, der nur der freien Person gelten sollte; daher findet man in den Zeitaltern der Kraft und der Fülle das wahrhaft Grosse der Vorstellung mit dem Gigantesken und Abenteuerlichen, und das Erhabene der Gesinnung mit den schauderhaftesten Ausbrüchen der Leidenschaft gepaart; daher wird man in den Zeitaltern der Regel und der Form die Natur ebenso oft unterdrückt als beherrscht, ebenso oft beleidigt als übertroffen finden. Und weil die Wirkung der schmelzenden Schönheit ist, das Gemüt im Moralischen wie im Physischen aufzulösen, so begegnet es ebenso leicht, dass mit der Gewalt der Begierden auch die Energie der Gefühle erstickt wird und dass auch der Charakter einen Kraftverlust teilt, der nur die Leidenschaft treffen sollte: daher wird man in den sogenannten verfeinerten Weltaltern Weichheit nicht selten in Weichlichkeit, Fläche in Flachheit, Korrektheit in Leerheit, Liberalität in

case of actual beauty a difference which exists in fact. Ideal Beauty, though one and indivisible, exhibits under different aspects a melting as well as an energizing attribute; but in experience there actually is a melting and an energizing type of beauty. So it is, and so it always will be, in all those cases where the Absolute is set within the limitations of time, and the ideas of Reason have to be realized in and through human action. Thus man, when he reflects, can conceive of Virtue, Truth, Happiness; but man, when he acts, can only practise virtues, comprehend truths, and enjoy happy hours. To refer these experiences back to those abstractions—to replace morals by Morality, happy events by Happiness, the facts of knowledge by Knowledge itself—that is the business of physical and moral education. To make Beauty out of a multiplicity of beautiful objects is the task of aesthetic education.

3. Energizing beauty can no more preserve man from a certain residue of savagery and hardness than melting beauty can protect him from a certain degree of effeminacy and enervation. For since the effect of the former is to brace his nature, both physical and moral, and to increase its elasticity and power of prompt reaction, it can happen all too easily that the increased resistance of temperament and character will bring about a decrease in receptivity to impressions; that our gentler humanity, too, will suffer the kind of repression which ought only to be directed at our brute nature, and our brute nature profit from an increase of strength which should only be available to our free Person. That is why in periods of vigour and exuberance we find true grandeur of conception coupled with the gigantic and the extravagant, sublimity of thought with the most frightening explosions of passion; that is why in epochs of discipline and form we find nature as often suppressed as mastered, as often outraged as transcended. And because the effect of melting beauty is to relax our nature, physical and moral, it happens no less easily that energy of feeling is stifled along with violence of appetite, and that character too shares the loss of power which should only overtake passion. That is why in so-called refined epochs, we see gentleness not infrequently degenerating into softness, plainness into platitude, correctness into emptiness, liberality into

Willkürlichkeit, Leichtigkeit in Frivolität, Ruhe in Apathie ausarten und die verächtlichste Karikatur zunächst an die herrlichste Menschlichkeit grenzen sehen. Für den Menschen unter dem Zwange entweder der Materie oder der Formen ist also die schmelzende Schönheit Bedürfnis; denn von Grösse und Kraft ist er längst gerührt, ehe er für Harmonie und Grazie anfängt empfindlich zu werden. Für den Menschen unter der Indulgenz des Geschmacks ist die energische Schönheit Bedürfnis; denn nur allzugern verscherzt er im Stand der Verfeinerung eine Kraft, die er aus dem Stand der Wildheit herüberbrachte.

4. Und nunmehr, glaube ich, wird jener Widerspruch erklärt und beantwortet sein, den man in den Urteilen der Menschen über den Einfluss des Schönen und in Würdigung der ästhetischen Kultur anzutreffen pflegt. Er ist erklärt, dieser Widerspruch, sobald man sich erinnert, dass es in der Erfahrung eine zweifache Schönheit gibt und dass beide Teile von der ganzen Gattung behaupten, was jeder nur von einer besondern Art derselben zu beweisen im Stande ist. Er ist gehoben, dieser Widerspruch, sobald man das doppelte Bedürfnis der Menschheit unterscheidet, dem jene doppelte Schönheit entspricht. Beide Teile werden also wahrscheinlich Recht behalten, wenn sie nur erst mit einander verständigt sind, welche Art der Schönheit und welche Form der Menschheit sie in Gedanken haben.

5. Ich werde daher im Fortgange meiner Untersuchungen den Weg, den die Natur in ästhetischer Hinsicht mit dem Menschen einschlägt, auch zu dem meinigen machen und mich von den Arten der Schönheit zu dem Gattungsbegriff derselben erheben. Ich werde die Wirkungen der schmelzenden Schönheit an dem angespannten Menschen und die Wirkungen der energischen an dem abgespannten prüfen, um zuletzt beide entgegengesetzten Arten der Schönheit in der Einheit des Ideal-Schönen auszulöschen, so wie jene zwei entgegengesetzten Formen der Menschheit in der Einheit des Ideal-Menschen untergehn.

arbitrariness, lightness of touch into frivolity, calmness into apathy, and the most despicable caricatures in closest proximity to the most splendid specimens of humanity. The man who lives under the constraint of either matter or forms is, therefore, in need of melting beauty; for he is moved by greatness and power long before he begins to be susceptible to harmony and grace. The man who lives under the indulgent sway of taste is in need of energizing beauty; for he is only too ready, once he has reached a state of sophisticated refinement, to trifle away the strength he brought with him from the state of savagery.

4. And now, I think, we have explained and resolved the discrepancy commonly met with in the judgements people make about the influence of beauty, and in the value they attach to aesthetic culture. The discrepancy is explained once we remember that, in experience, there are two types of beauty, and that both parties to the argument tend to make assertions about the whole genus which each of them is only in a position to prove about one particular species of it. And the discrepancy is resolved once we distinguish a twofold need in man to which that twofold beauty corresponds. Both parties will probably turn out to be right if they can only first agree among themselves which kind of beauty and which type of humanity each has in mind.

5. In the rest of my inquiry I shall, therefore, pursue the path which nature herself takes with man in matters aesthetic, and setting out from the two species of beauty move upwards to the generic concept of it. I shall examine the effects of melting beauty on those who are tensed, and the effects of energizing beauty on those who are relaxed, in order finally to dissolve both these contrary modes of beauty in the unity of Ideal Beauty, even as those two opposing types of human being are merged in the unity of Ideal Man.

SIEBZEHNTER BRIEF

1. So lange es bloss darauf ankam, die allgemeine Idee der Schönheit aus dem Begriffe der menschlichen Natur überhaupt abzuleiten, durften wir uns an keine andere Schranken der letztern erinnern, als die unmittelbar in dem Wesen derselben gegründet und von dem Begriffe der Endlichkeit unzertrennlich sind. Unbekümmert um die zufälligen Einschränkungen, die sie in der wirklichen Erscheinung erleiden möchte, schöpften wir den Begriff derselben unmittelbar aus der Vernunft, als der Quelle aller Notwendigkeit, und mit dem Ideale der Menschheit war zugleich auch das Ideal der Schönheit gegeben.

2. Jetzt aber steigen wir aus der Region der Ideen auf den Schauplatz der Wirklichkeit herab, um den Menschen in einem bestimmten Zustand, mithin unter Einschränkungen anzutreffen, die nicht ursprünglich aus seinem blossen Begriff, sondern aus äussern Umständen und aus einem zufälligen Gebrauch seiner Freiheit fliessen. Auf wie vielfache Weise aber auch die Idee der Menschheit in ihm eingeschränkt sein mag, so lehrt uns schon der blosse Inhalt derselben, dass im Ganzen nur zwei entgegengesetzte Abweichungen von derselben statthaben können. Liegt nämlich seine Vollkommenheit in der übereinstimmenden Energie seiner sinnlichen und geistigen Kräfte, so kann er diese Vollkommenheit nur entweder durch einen Mangel an Übereinstimmung oder durch einen Mangel an Energie verfehlen. Ehe wir also noch die Zeugnisse der Erfahrung darüber abgehört haben, sind wir schon im voraus durch blosse Vernunft gewiss, dass wir den wirklichen, folglich beschränkten Menschen entweder in einem Zustande der Anspannung oder in einem Zustande der Abspannung finden werden, je nachdem entweder die einseitige Tätigkeit einzelner Kräfte die Harmonie seines Wesens stört oder die Einheit seiner Natur sich auf die gleichförmige Erschlaffung seiner sinnlichen und geistigen Kräfte gründet. Beide entgegengesetzte Schranken werden, wie nun bewiesen werden soll, durch die Schönheit gehoben, die in dem angespannten Menschen die Harmonie, in dem abgespannten die Energie wieder herstellt und auf diese Art, ihrer Natur gemäss,

SEVENTEENTH LETTER

1. As long as it was simply a question of deriving the generic idea of beauty from the concept of human nature as such, there was no need to recall any limitations of this latter other than those which derive directly from the essence of it, and are inseparable from the concept of finiteness. Unconcerned with any of the contingent limitations to which human nature may in actual experience be subject, we derived our notion of it directly from Reason as the source of all Necessity, and with the Ideal of human nature the Ideal of beauty was automatically given too.

2. Now, by contrast, we descend from this region of Ideas on to the stage of reality, in order to encounter man in a definite and determinate state, that is to say, among limitations which are not inherent in the very notion of Man but derive from outward circumstance and from the contingent use of his freedom. Yet whatever diversity of limitation the Idea of human nature may undergo when made manifest in any particular human being, its components alone are enough to tell us that there are, broadly speaking, only two, contrasting, deviations from it that can possibly occur. For if man's perfection resides in the harmonious energy of his sensuous and spiritual powers, he can, in fact, only fall short of this perfection, either through lack of harmony or through lack of energy. So that even before we have heard the testimony of experience on this matter, we are already assured in advance by pure Reason that we shall find actual, consequently limited, man either in a state of tension or in a state of relaxation, according as the one-sided activity of certain of his powers is disturbing the harmony of his being, or the unity of his nature is founded upon the uniform enfeeblement of his sensuous and spiritual powers. Both these contrasting types of limitation are, as I now propose to show, removed by beauty, which restores harmony to him who is over-tensed, and energy to him who is relaxed, and thus, in accordance with its nature, brings

den eingeschränkten Zustand auf einen absoluten zurückführt und den Menschen zu einem in sich selbst vollendeten Ganzen macht.

3. Sie verleugnet also in der Wirklichkeit auf keine Weise den Begriff, den wir in der Spekulation von ihr fassten; nur dass sie hier ungleich weniger freie Hand hat als dort, wo wir sie auf den reinen Begriff der Menschheit anwenden durften. An dem Menschen, wie die Erfahrung ihn aufstellt, findet sie einen schon verdorbenen und widerstrebenden Stoff, der ihr gerade so viel von ihrer i d e a l e n Vollkommenheit raubt, als er von seiner i n d i v i d u a l e n Beschaffenheit einmischt. Sie wird daher in der Wirklichkeit überall nur als eine besondere und eingeschränkte Species, nie als reine Gattung sich zeigen; sie wird in angespannten Gemütern von ihrer Freiheit und Mannigfaltigkeit, sie wird in abgespannten von ihrer belebenden Kraft ablegen; uns aber, die wir nunmehr mit ihrem wahren Charakter vertrauter geworden sind, wird diese widersprechende Erscheinung nicht irre machen. Weit entfernt, mit dem grossen Haufen der Beurteiler aus einzelnen Erfahrungen ihren Begriff zu bestimmen und s i e für die Mängel verantwortlich zu machen, die der Mensch unter ihrem Einflusse zeigt, wissen wir vielmehr, dass es der Mensch ist, der die Unvollkommenheiten seines Individuums auf sie überträgt, der durch seine subjektive Begrenzung ihrer Vollendung unaufhörlich im Wege steht und ihr absolutes Ideal auf zwei eingeschränkte Formen der Erscheinung herabsetzt.

4. Die schmelzende Schönheit, wurde behauptet, sei für ein angespanntes Gemüt, und für ein abgespanntes die energische. Angespannt aber nenne ich den Menschen sowohl, wenn er sich unter dem Zwange von Empfindungen, als wenn er sich unter dem Zwange von Begriffen befindet. Jede a u s s c h l i e s s e n d e Herrschaft eines seiner beiden Grundtriebe ist für ihn ein Zustand des Zwanges und der Gewalt; und Freiheit liegt nur in der Zusammenwirkung seiner beiden Naturen. Der von Gefühlen einseitig beherrschte oder sinnlich angespannte Mensch wird also aufgelöst und in Freiheit gesetzt durch Form; der von Gesetzen einseitig beherrschte oder geistig angespannte Mensch wird aufgelöst und in Freiheit gesetzt durch Materie. Die schmelzende Schönheit, um dieser doppelten Aufgabe ein Genüge zu tun, wird sich also unter zwei verschiednen Gestalten zeigen. Sie wird e r s t l i c h als ruhige

the limited condition back to an absolute condition, and makes of man a whole perfect in itself.

3. Beauty in the world of reality thus in no way belies the idea we formed of it by way of speculation; only it has here far less of a free hand than it had there, where we were free to apply it to the pure concept of human nature. In man, as presented by experience, beauty encounters a material already vitiated and recalcitrant, which robs her of her i d e a l perfection precisely to the extent that it interposes its own i n d i v i d u a l characteristics. Beauty will, therefore, in actuality never show herself except as a particular and limited species, never as pure genus; she will in tense natures lay aside something of her freedom and variety, in relaxed natures something of her vivifying power. But we, who have by now become more familiar with her true nature, should not let ourselves be confused by such discrepancies in her appearance. Far from following the ordinary run of critics, who define the concept of beauty from their individual experience of it, and make h e r responsible for the imperfections displayed by man under her influence, we know that it is, on the contrary, man himself who transfers to her the imperfections of his own individuality, who by his subjective limitation perpetually stands in the way of her perfection, and reduces the absolute Ideal to two limited types of manifestation.

4. Melting beauty, so it was maintained, is for natures which are tense; energizing beauty for those which are relaxed. I call a man tense when he is under the compulsion of thought, no less than when he is under the compulsion of feeling. E x c l u s i v e domination by either of his two basic drives is for him a state of constraint and violence, and freedom lies only in the co-operation of both his natures. The man one-sidedly dominated by feeling, or the sensuously tensed man, will be released and set free by means of form; the man one-sidedly dominated by law, or the spiritually tensed man, will be released and set free by means of matter. In order to be adequate to this twofold task, melting beauty will therefore reveal herself under two different guises. F i r s t, as tranquil form, she will

Form das wilde Leben besänftigen und von Empfindungen zu Gedanken den Übergang bahnen; sie wird z w e i t e n s als lebendes Bild die abgezogene Form mit sinnlicher Kraft ausrüsten, den Begriff zur Anschauung und das Gesetz zum Gefühl zurückführen. Den ersten Dienst leistet sie dem Naturmenschen, den zweiten dem künstlichen Menschen. Aber weil sie in beiden Fällen über ihren Stoff nicht ganz frei gebietet, sondern von demjenigen abhängt, den ihr entweder die formlose Natur oder die naturwidrige Kunst darbietet, so wird sie in beiden Fällen noch Spuren ihres Ursprunges tragen und dort mehr in das materielle Leben, hier mehr in die blosse abgezogene Form sich verlieren.

5.   Um uns einen Begriff davon machen zu können, wie die Schönheit ein Mittel werden kann, jene doppelte Anspannung zu heben, müssen wir den Ursprung derselben in dem menschlichen Gemüt zu erforschen suchen. Entschliessen Sie sich also noch zu einem kurzen Aufenthalt im Gebiete der Spekulation, um es alsdann auf immer zu verlassen und mit desto sicherm Schritt auf dem Feld der Erfahrung fortzuschreiten.

assuage the violence of life, and pave the way which leads from sensation to thought. S e c o n d l y, as living image, she will arm abstract form with sensuous power, lead concept back to intuition, and law back to feeling. The first of these services she renders to natural man, the second to civilized man. But since in neither case does she have completely unconditional control over her human material, but is dependent on that offered her by either the form-lessness of nature or the unnaturalness of civilization, she will in both cases still bear traces of her origins, and tend to lose herself, in the one case, more in material life, in the other, more in pure and abstract form.

5. In order to get some idea of how beauty can become a means of putting an end to that twofold tension, we must endeavour to seek its origins in the human psyche. Resign yourself therefore to one more brief sojourn in the sphere of speculation, in order thereafter to leave it for good, and proceed, with steps made all the more sure, over the terrain of experience.

ACHTZEHNTER BRIEF

1. Durch die Schönheit wird der sinnliche Mensch zur Form und zum Denken geleitet; durch die Schönheit wird der geistige Mensch zur Materie zurückgeführt und der Sinnenwelt wiedergegeben.

2. Aus diesem scheint zu folgen, dass es zwischen Materie und Form, zwischen Leiden und Tätigkeit einen mittleren Zustand geben müsse, und dass uns die Schönheit in diesen mittleren Zustand versetze. Diesen Begriff bildet sich auch wirklich der grösste Teil der Menschen von der Schönheit, sobald er angefangen hat, über ihre Wirkungen zu reflektieren, und alle Erfahrungen weisen darauf hin. Auf der andern Seite aber ist nichts ungereimter und widersprechender als ein solcher Begriff, da der Abstand zwischen Materie und Form, zwischen Leiden und Tätigkeit, zwischen Empfinden und Denken unendlich ist und schlechterdings durch nichts kann vermittelt werden. Wie heben wir nun diesen Widerspruch? Die Schönheit verknüpft die zwei entgegengesetzten Zustände des Empfindens und des Denkens, und doch gibt es schlechterdings kein Mittleres zwischen beiden. Jenes ist durch Erfahrung, dieses ist unmittelbar durch Vernunft gewiss.

3. Dies ist der eigentliche Punkt, auf den zuletzt die ganze Frage über die Schönheit hinausläuft, und gelingt es uns, dieses Problem befriedigend aufzulösen, so haben wir zugleich den Faden gefunden, der uns durch das ganze Labyrinth der Ästhetik führt.

4. Es kommt aber hiebei auf zwei höchst verschiedene Operationen an, welche bei dieser Untersuchung einander notwendig unterstützen müssen. Die Schönheit, heisst es, verknüpft zwei Zustände mit einander, die einander entgegengesetzt sind und niemals Eins werden können. Von dieser Entgegensetzung müssen wir ausgehen; wir müssen sie in ihrer ganzen Reinheit und Strengigkeit auffassen und anerkennen, so dass beide Zustände sich auf das bestimmteste scheiden; sonst vermischen wir, aber vereinigen nicht. Zweitens heisst es: jene zwei entgegengesetzten Zustände verbindet die Schönheit und hebt also die Entgegensetzung auf. Weil aber beide Zustände einander ewig entgegengesetzt bleiben,

EIGHTEENTH LETTER

1. By means of beauty sensuous man is led to form and thought; by means of beauty spiritual man is brought back to matter and restored to the world of sense.

2. From this it seems to follow that there must be a state midway between matter and form, passivity and activity, and that it is into this m i d d l e state that beauty transports us. This is, indeed, the idea of beauty that most people form for themselves once they have begun to reflect upon her operations, and all experience points to the same conclusion. But, on the other hand, nothing is more absurd and contradictory than such an idea, since the distance between matter and form, passivity and activity, feeling and thought, is i n f i n i t e, and there exists nothing that can conceivably mediate between them. How, then, are we to resolve this contradiction? Beauty links the two opposite conditions of feeling and thinking; yet between these two there is absolutely no middle term. The former truth we know from Experience; the latter is given to us directly by Reason.

3. This precisely is the point on which the whole question of beauty must eventually turn. And if we succeed in solving this problem satisfactorily, we shall at the same time have found the thread which will guide us through the whole labyrinth of aesthetics.

4. But everything here depends on two completely distinct operations which, in the investigation we are about to undertake, must of necessity support one another. Beauty, it was said, unites two conditions w h i c h a r e d i a m e t r i c a l l y o p p o s e d and can never become One. It is from this opposition that we have to start; and we must first grasp it, and acknowledge it, in all its unmitigated rigour, so that these two conditions are distinguished with the utmost precision; otherwise we shall only succeed in confusing but never in uniting them. In the second place, it was said, beauty u n i t e s these two opposed conditions and thus destroys the opposition. Since, however, both conditions remain everlastingly opposed

so sind sie nicht anders zu verbinden, als indem sie aufgehoben werden. Unser zweites Geschäft ist also, diese Verbindung vollkommen zu machen, sie so rein und vollständig durchzuführen, dass beide Zustände in einem Dritten gänzlich verschwinden und keine Spur der Teilung in dem Ganzen zurückbleibt; sonst vereinzeln wir, aber vereinigen nicht. Alle Streitigkeiten, welche jemals in der philosophischen Welt über den Begriff der Schönheit geherrscht haben und zum Teil noch heutzutag herrschen, haben keinen andern Ursprung, als dass man die Untersuchung entweder nicht von einer gehörig strengen Unterscheidung anfing oder sie nicht bis zu einer völlig reinen Vereinigung durchführte. Diejenigen unter den Philosophen, welche sich bei der Reflexion über diesen Gegenstand der Leitung ihres Gefühls blindlings anvertrauen, können von der Schönheit keinen Begriff erlangen, weil sie in dem Total des sinnlichen Eindrucks nichts Einzelnes unterscheiden. Die andern, welche den Verstand ausschliessend zum Führer nehmen, können nie einen Begriff von der Schönheit erlangen, weil sie in dem Total derselben nie etwas anders als die Teile sehen und Geist und Materie auch in ihrer vollkommensten Einheit ihnen ewig geschieden bleiben. Die ersten fürchten, die Schönheit dynamisch, d. h. als wirkende Kraft aufzuheben, wenn sie trennen sollen, was im Gefühl doch verbunden ist; die andern fürchten, die Schönheit logisch, d. h. als Begriff aufzuheben, wenn sie zusammenfassen sollen, was im Verstand doch geschieden ist. Jene wollen die Schönheit auch ebenso denken, wie sie wirkt; diese wollen sie ebenso wirken lassen, wie sie gedacht wird. Beide müssen also die Wahrheit verfehlen: jene, weil sie es mit ihrem eingeschränkten Denkvermögen der unendlichen Natur nachtun; diese, weil sie die unendliche Natur nach ihren Denkgesetzen einschränken wollen. Die ersten fürchten, durch eine zu strenge Zergliederung der Schönheit von ihrer Freiheit zu rauben; die andern fürchten, durch eine zu kühne Vereinigung die Bestimmtheit ihres Begriffs zu zerstören. Jene bedenken aber nicht, dass die Freiheit, in welche sie mit allem Recht das Wesen der Schönheit setzen, nicht Gesetzlosigkeit, sondern Harmonie von Gesetzen, nicht Willkürlichkeit, sondern höchste innere Notwendigkeit ist; diese bedenken nicht, dass die Bestimmtheit, welche sie mit gleichem Recht von der Schönheit fordern, nicht in der Ausschliessung gewisser Realitäten, sondern in der absoluten Einschliessung aller besteht, dass sie also nicht Begrenzung, sondern Unendlichkeit ist. Wir werden

to each other, there is no other way of uniting them except by destroying them. Our second task, therefore, is to make this union complete; and to do it with such unmitigated thoroughness that both these conditions totally disappear in a third without leaving any trace of division behind in the new whole that has been made; otherwise we shall only succeed in distinguishing but never in uniting them. All the disputes about the concept of beauty which have ever prevailed in the world of philosophy, and to some extent still prevail today, have no other source than this: either the investigation did not start with a sufficiently strict distinction, or it was not carried through to a pure and complete synthesis. Those among the philosophers who, in reflecting on this matter, entrust themselves blindly to the guidance of their f e e l i n g, can arrive at no c o n c e p t of beauty, because in the totality of their sensuous impression of it they can distinguish no separate elements. Those others, who take intellect as their exclusive guide, can never arrive at any concept of b e a u t y, because in the totality which constitutes it they can discern nothing else but the parts, so that spirit and matter, even when most perfectly fused, remain for them eternally distinct. The former are afraid that by separating what in their feeling is, after all, one and indivisible, they will destroy the d y n a m i c of beauty, i.e., beauty as effective force. The latter are afraid that by subsuming under a single category what in their intellect is, after all, distinct, they will destroy the l o g i c of beauty, i.e., beauty as concept. The former would like to think beauty as it actually behaves; the latter would have it behave as it is actually thought. Both, therefore, are bound to miss the truth: the former because they would make the limitations of discursive understanding vie with the infinity of nature; the latter because they would limit the infinity of nature according to the laws of discursive understanding. The first are afraid that by a too rigorous dissection they will rob beauty of some measure of her freedom; the latter are afraid that by too audacious a synthesis they will destroy the precision of their concept. The former do not, however, reflect that the freedom, in which they rightly locate the essence of beauty, is not just lawlessness but rather harmony of laws, not arbitrariness but supreme inner necessity; the latter do not reflect that the exactitude which they, no less rightly, require of beauty, does not reside in the e x c l u s i o n o f c e r t a i n r e a l i-t i e s, but in the a b s o l u t e i n c l u s i o n o f a l l r e a l i t i e s; that it is, therefore, not limitation but infinity. We shall avoid the rocks

die Klippen vermeiden, an welchen beide gescheitert sind, wenn wir von den zwei Elementen beginnen, in welche die Schönheit sich vor dem Verstande teilt, aber uns alsdann auch zu der reinen ästhetischen Einheit erheben, durch die sie auf die Empfindung wirkt und in welcher jene beiden Zustände gänzlich verschwinden.*

* Einem aufmerksamen Leser wird sich bei der hier angestellten Vergleichung die Bemerkung dargeboten haben, dass die sensualen Ästhetiker, welche das Zeugnis der Empfindung mehr als das Raisonnement gelten lassen, sich der Tat nach weit weniger von der Wahrheit entfernen als ihre Gegner, obgleich sie der Einsicht nach es nicht mit diesen aufnehmen können; und dieses Verhältnis findet man überall zwischen der Natur und der Wissenschaft. Die Natur (der Sinn) vereinigt überall, der Verstand scheidet überall, aber die Vernunft vereinigt wieder; daher ist der Mensch, ehe er anfängt zu philosophieren, der Wahrheit näher als der Philosoph, der seine Untersuchung noch nicht geendigt hat. Man kann deswegen ohne alle weitere Prüfung ein Philosophem für irrig erklären, sobald dasselbe, dem Resultat nach, die gemeine Empfindung gegen sich hat; mit demselben Rechte aber kann man es für verdächtig halten, wenn es, der Form und Methode nach, die gemeine Empfindung auf seiner Seite hat. Mit dem letztern mag sich ein jeder Schriftsteller trösten, der eine philosophische Deduktion nicht, wie manche Leser zu erwarten scheinen, wie eine Unterhaltung am Kaminfeuer vortragen kann. Mit dem erstern mag man jeden zum Stillschweigen bringen, der auf Kosten des Menschenverstandes neue Systeme gründen will.

on which both have foundered if we start from the two elements into which beauty can be divided when considered by the intellect, but subsequently ascend to the pure aesthetic unity through which it works upon our feeling, and in which the two conditions previously described completely disappear.*

* It will have occurred to any attentive reader of the comparison I have just made that the s e n s a t i o n a l i s t aestheticians, who attach more weight to the testimony of feeling than to that of reasoning, are by no means so far removed from the truth i n p r a c t i c e as their opponents, although they are no match for them i n p e r s p i c a c i t y. And this is the relation we always find between nature and systematic thought. Nature (sense and intuition) always unites, Intellect always divides; but Reason unites once more. Before he begins to philosophize, therefore, man is nearer to truth than the philosopher who has not yet completed his investigation. Hence we can, without further examination, declare a philosophical argument to be false if, i n i t s r e s u l t s, it has the general feeling against it; but with equal justice we may consider it suspect if, in its form and method, it has this general feeling on its side. This latter consideration may serve to console any writer who finds himself unable to set forth a process of philosophical deduction, as many readers seem to expect, just as if it were a fireside chat; while with the former we may reduce to silence anyone who would fain found new systems at the expense of ordinary common sense.

NEUNZEHNTER BRIEF

1. Es lassen sich in dem Menschen überhaupt zwei verschiedene Zustände der passiven und aktiven Bestimmbarkeit und ebenso viele Zustände der passiven und aktiven Bestimmung unterscheiden. Die Erklärung dieses Satzes führt uns am kürzesten zum Ziel.

2. Der Zustand des menschlichen Geistes v o r aller Bestimmung, die ihm durch Eindrücke der Sinne gegeben wird, ist eine Bestimmbarkeit ohne Grenzen. Das Endlose des Raumes und der Zeit ist seiner Einbildungskraft zu freiem Gebrauch hingegeben, und weil, der Voraussetzung nach, in diesem weiten Reiche des Möglichen nichts gesetzt, folglich auch noch nichts ausgeschlossen ist, so kann man diesen Zustand der Bestimmungslosigkeit eine l e e r e U n e n d l i c h k e i t nennen, welches mit einer unendlichen Leere keineswegs zu verwechseln ist.

3. Jetzt soll sein Sinn gerührt werden, und aus der unendlichen Menge möglicher Bestimmungen soll eine Einzelne Wirklichkeit erhalten. Eine Vorstellung soll in ihm entstehen. Was in dem vorhergegangenen Zustand der blossen Bestimmbarkeit nichts als ein leeres Vermögen war, das wird jetzt zu einer wirkenden Kraft, das bekommt einen Inhalt; zugleich aber erhält es, als wirkende Kraft, eine Grenze, da es, als blosses Vermögen, unbegrenzt war. Realität ist also da, aber die Unendlichkeit ist verloren. Um eine Gestalt im Raum zu beschreiben, müssen wir den endlosen Raum b e g r e n z e n; um uns eine Veränderung in der Zeit vorzustellen, müssen wir das Zeitganze t e i l e n. Wir gelangen also nur durch Schranken zur Realität, nur durch N e g a t i o n oder Ausschliessung zur P o s i t i o n oder wirklichen Setzung, nur durch Aufhebung unsrer freien Bestimmbarkeit zur Bestimmung.

4. Aber aus einer blossen Ausschliessung würde in Ewigkeit keine Realität und aus einer blossen Sinnenempfindung in Ewigkeit keine Vorstellung werden, wenn nicht etwas vorhanden wäre, v o n w e l c h e m ausgeschlossen wird, wenn nicht durch eine absolute Tathandlung des Geistes die Negation auf etwas Positives bezogen und aus Nichtsetzung Entgegensetzung würde; diese Handlung des

NINETEENTH LETTER

1. WE can distinguish in man as such two different states of determinability, the one passive, the other active, and—corresponding to these—two states of passive and active determination. The explanation of this proposition will offer the shortest way of reaching our goal.

2. The condition of the human mind b e f o r e it is determined by sense-impressions at all, is one of unlimited determinability. The infinity of space and time is at the disposal of the imagination to do as it likes with. And since *ex hypothesi* nothing in this whole vast realm of the possible has yet been posited, and consequently nothing as yet excluded either, we may call this condition of complete absence of determination one of e m p t y i n f i n i t y—which is by no means to be confused with infinite emptiness.

3. Now comes the moment when sense is to be stirred, and out of the endless multiplicity of possible determinations one single one is to achieve actuality. A perception is to be born in him. What in the preceding state of mere determinability was nothing but empty potential, now becomes an effective force and acquires a content. At the same time, however, as effective force, it has limits set to it, whereas, as mere potential, it was entirely without limits. Thus reality has come into being; but infinity has been lost. In order to describe a figure in space we have to s e t l i m i t s to infinite space; in order to imagine a change in time, we have to d i v i d e u p the totality of time. Thus it is only through limits that we attain to reality, only through n e g a t i o n or exclusion that we arrive at p o s i t i o n or real affirmation, only through the surrender of our unconditional determinability that we achieve determination.

4. But mere exclusion would never in all eternity produce reality, nor mere sensation ever give birth to perception, unless something existed f r o m w h i c h to exclude, unless through some autonomous act of the mind the negating were referred to something positive, and from no-position op-position were to ensue. This activity of

Gemüts heisst urteilen oder denken, und das Resultat derselben der Gedanke.

5. Ehe wir im Raum einen Ort bestimmen, gibt es überhaupt keinen Raum für uns; aber ohne den absoluten Raum würden wir nimmermehr einen Ort bestimmen. Ebenso mit der Zeit. Ehe wir den Augenblick haben, gibt es überhaupt keine Zeit für uns; aber ohne die ewige Zeit würden wir nie eine Vorstellung des Augenblicks haben. Wir gelangen also freilich nur durch den Teil zum Ganzen, nur durch die Grenze zum Unbegrenzten; aber wir gelangen auch nur durch das Ganze zum Teil, nur durch das Unbegrenzte zur Grenze.

6. Wenn nun also von dem Schönen behauptet wird, dass es dem Menschen einen Übergang vom Empfinden zum Denken bahne, so ist dies keineswegs so zu verstehen, als ob durch das Schöne die Kluft könnte ausgefüllt werden, die das Empfinden vom Denken, die das Leiden von der Tätigkeit trennt; diese Kluft ist unendlich, und ohne Dazwischenkunft eines neuen und selbständigen Vermögens kann aus dem Einzelnen in Ewigkeit nichts Allgemeines, kann aus dem Zufälligen nichts Notwendiges werden. Der Gedanke ist die unmittelbare Handlung dieses absoluten Vermögens, welches zwar durch die Sinne veranlasst werden muss, sich zu äussern, in seiner Äusserung selbst aber so wenig von der Sinnlichkeit abhängt, dass es sich vielmehr nur durch Entgegensetzung gegen dieselbe verkündiget. Die Selbständigkeit, mit der es handelt, schliesst jede fremde Einwirkung aus; und nicht insofern sie beim Denken hilft (welches einen offenbaren Widerspruch enthält), bloss insofern sie den Denkkräften Freiheit verschafft, ihren eigenen Gesetzen gemäss sich zu äussern, kann die Schönheit ein Mittel werden, den Menschen von der Materie zur Form, von Empfindungen zu Gesetzen, von einem beschränkten zu einem absoluten Dasein zu führen.

7. Dies aber setzt voraus, dass die Freiheit der Denkkräfte gehemmt werden könne, welches mit dem Begriff eines selbständigen Vermögens zu streiten scheint. Ein Vermögen nämlich, welches von aussen nichts als den Stoff seines Wirkens empfängt, kann nur durch Entziehung des Stoffes, also nur negativ an seinem Wirken gehindert werden, und es heisst die Natur eines Geistes verkennen, wenn man den sinnlichen Passionen eine Macht beilegt, die Freiheit

the psyche we call judging or thinking; and the result of it we call
thought.

5.   Before we determine a point in space, space does not exist for
us; but without absolute space we should never be able to determine
a point at all. It is the same with time. Before we become aware of
the moment, time does not exist for us; but without infinite time
we should never have any awareness of the moment. We do then,
admittedly, only reach the whole through the part, the limitless only
through limitation; but it is no less true that we only reach the part
through the whole, and limitation only through the limitless.

6.   When, therefore, it is asserted of the beautiful that it provides
man with a transition from feeling to thinking, this must in no sense
be taken to mean that beauty could ever bridge the gulf separating
feeling from thinking, passivity from activity. This gulf is infinite,
and without the intervention of some new and independent faculty
we shall never in all eternity find a particular becoming a universal,
or the merely contingent turning into the necessary. Thought is
the spontaneous act of this absolute faculty. The senses, it is true,
have to provide the occasion for it to manifest itself; but in its actual
manifestation it is so little dependent upon the senses that, on the
contrary, it makes itself felt only when it is at odds with them. The
autonomy with which it operates excludes all outside influence; and
it is not by p r o v i d i n g a n a i d to thought (which would imply a
manifest contradiction), but merely by furnishing the thinking
faculty with the freedom to express itself according to its own laws,
that beauty can become a means of leading man from matter to
form, from feeling to law, from a limited to an absolute existence.

7.   But this presupposes that the freedom of the thinking powers
could be inhibited, which seems to contradict the notion of an
autonomous faculty. For a faculty receiving from without nothing
but the material on which to work can only be impeded in its
activity by the withdrawal of that material, i.e., only negatively;
and we misconstrue the very nature of mind if we attribute to
sensuous passions the power of being able to suppress the freedom

des Gemüts positiv unterdrücken zu können. Zwar stellt die Erfahrung Beispiele in Menge auf, wo die Vernunftkräfte in demselben Mass unterdrückt erscheinen, als die sinnlichen Kräfte feuriger wirken; aber anstatt jene Geistesschwäche von der Stärke des Affekts abzuleiten, muss man vielmehr diese überwiegende Stärke des Affekts durch jene Schwäche des Geistes erklären; denn die Sinne können nicht anders eine Macht gegen den Menschen vorstellen, als insofern der Geist frei unterlassen hat, sich als eine solche zu beweisen.

8. Indem ich aber durch diese Erklärung einem Einwurfe zu begegnen suche, habe ich mich, wie es scheint, in einen andern verwickelt und die Selbständigkeit des Gemüts nur auf Kosten seiner Einheit gerettet. Denn wie kann das Gemüt a u s s i c h s e l b s t zugleich Gründe der Nichttätigkeit und der Tätigkeit nehmen, wenn es nicht selbst geteilt, wenn es nicht sich selbst entgegengesetzt ist?

9. Hier müssen wir uns nun erinnern, dass wir den endlichen, nicht den unendlichen Geist vor uns haben. Der endliche Geist ist derjenige, der nicht anders als durch Leiden tätig wird, nur durch Schranken zum Absoluten gelangt, nur, insofern er Stoff empfängt, handelt und bildet. Ein solcher Geist wird also mit dem Triebe nach Form oder nach dem Absoluten einen Trieb nach Stoff oder nach Schranken verbinden, als welche die Bedingungen sind, ohne welche er den ersten Trieb weder haben noch befriedigen könnte. Inwiefern in demselben Wesen zwei so entgegengesetzte Tendenzen zusammen bestehen können, ist eine Aufgabe, die zwar den Metaphysiker, aber nicht den Transzendentalphilosophen in Verlegenheit setzen kann. Dieser gibt sich keineswegs dafür aus, die Möglichkeit der Dinge zu erklären, sondern begnügt sich, die Kenntnisse festzusetzen, aus welchen die Möglichkeit der Erfahrung begriffen wird. Und da nun Erfahrung ebenso wenig ohne jene Entgegensetzung im Gemüte als ohne die absolute Einheit desselben möglich wäre, so stellt er beide Begriffe mit vollkommner Befugnis als gleich notwendige Bedingungen der Erfahrung auf, ohne sich weiter um ihre Vereinbarkeit zu bekümmern. Diese Inwohnung zweier Grundtriebe widerspricht übrigens auf keine Weise der absoluten Einheit des Geistes, sobald man nur von beiden Trieben i h n s e l b s t unterscheidet. Beide Triebe existieren und wirken zwar i n i h m, aber Er selbst ist weder Materie noch Form, weder Sinnlichkeit

of the spirit positively. True, experience offers us examples in plenty of the forces of reason appearing to be suppressed in proportion as the forces of sense wax more ardent. But instead of attributing that weakness of the spirit to the strength of the passions, we ought rather to put this overwhelming strength of the passions down to that weakness of the spirit; for the senses can never set themselves up against man as a power, unless the spirit has of its own free will renounced all desire to prove itself such.

8. But in trying by this explanation to counter one objection, I seem to have involved myself in another, and rescued the autonomy of the psyche only at the cost of its unity. For how can the psyche produce o u t o f i t s e l f at one and the same time the motive for inactivity as well as activity, unless it is itself divided, unless it is at odds with itself?

9. At this point we must remind ourselves that we are dealing with a finite, not with an infinite, mind. The finite mind is that which cannot become active except through being passive, which only attains to the absolute by means of limitation, and only acts and fashions inasmuch as it receives material to fashion. Such a mind will accordingly combine with the drive towards form, or towards the absolute, a drive towards matter, or towards limitation, these latter being the conditions without which it could neither possess nor satisfy the first of these drives. How far two such opposed tendencies can co-exist in the same being is a problem which may well embarrass the metaphysician, but not the transcendental philosopher. The latter does not pretend to explain how things are possible, but contents himself with determining the kind of knowledge which enables us to understand how experience is possible. And since experience would be just as impossible without that opposition in the psyche as without the absolute unity of the psyche, he is perfectly justified in postulating both these concepts as equally necessary conditions of experience, without troubling himself further as to how they are to be reconciled. Moreover, the immanence in the mind of two fundamental drives in no way contradicts its absolute unity, as long as we make a distinction between these two drives and the m i n d i t s e l f. Both drives exist and operate w i t h i n i t; but the mind itself is neither matter nor form, neither sense nor reason—

noch Vernunft, welches diejenigen, die den menschlichen Geist nur da selbst handeln lassen, wo sein Verfahren mit der Vernunft übereinstimmt, und wo dieses der Vernunft widerspricht, ihn bloss für passiv erklären, nicht immer bedacht zu haben scheinen.

10. Jeder dieser beiden Grundtriebe strebt, sobald er zur Entwicklung gekommen, seiner Natur nach und notwendig nach Befriedigung; aber eben darum, weil beide notwendig und beide doch nach entgegengesetzten Objekten streben, so hebt diese doppelte Nötigung sich gegenseitig auf, und der Wille behauptet eine vollkommene Freiheit zwischen beiden. Der Wille ist es also, der sich gegen beide Triebe als eine Macht (als Grund der Wirklichkeit) verhält, aber keiner von beiden kann sich für sich selbst als eine Macht gegen den andern verhalten. Durch den positivsten Antrieb zur Gerechtigkeit, woran es ihm keineswegs mangelt, wird der Gewalttätige nicht von Unrecht abgehalten, und durch die lebhafteste Versuchung zum Genuss der Starkmütige nicht zum Bruch seiner Grundsätze gebracht. Es gibt in dem Menschen keine andere Macht als seinen Willen, und nur was den Menschen aufhebt, der Tod und jeder Raub des Bewusstseins, kann die innere Freiheit aufheben.

11. Eine Notwendigkeit ausser uns bestimmt unsern Zustand, unser Dasein in der Zeit vermittelst der Sinnenempfindung. Diese ist ganz unwillkürlich, und so, wie auf uns gewirkt wird, müssen wir leiden. Ebenso eröffnet eine Notwendigkeit in uns unsre Persönlichkeit, auf Veranlassung jener Sinnenempfindung und durch Entgegensetzung gegen dieselbe; denn das Selbstbewusstsein kann von dem Willen, der es voraussetzt, nicht abhängen. Diese ursprüngliche Verkündigung der Persönlichkeit ist nicht unser Verdienst, und der Mangel derselben nicht unser Fehler. Nur von demjenigen, der sich bewusst ist, wird Vernunft, das heisst absolute Konsequenz und Universalität des Bewusstseins gefordert; vorher ist er nicht Mensch, und kein Akt der Menschheit kann von ihm erwartet werden. So wenig nun der Metaphysiker sich die Schranken erklären kann, die der freie und selbständige Geist durch die Empfindung erleidet, so wenig begreift der Physiker die Unendlichkeit, die sich auf Veranlassung dieser Schranken in der Persönlichkeit offenbart. Weder Abstraktion noch Erfahrung leiten uns bis zu der Quelle zurück, aus der unsre Begriffe von Allgemeinheit und Notwendigkeit fliessen; ihre frühe Erscheinung in der Zeit

which fact does not always seem to have been taken into account
by those who will only allow the human mind to be active when its
operations are in accordance with reason, and declare it to be merely
passive when they are at odds with reason.

10.   Each of these two primary drives, from the time it is developed,
strives inevitably, and according to its nature, towards satisfaction;
but just because both are necessary, and yet strive towards opposite
ends, these two compulsions cancel each other out, and the will
maintains perfect freedom between them. It is, then, the will which
acts as a p o w e r (power being the ground of all reality) *vis-à-vis*
both drives; but neither of these can of itself act as a power against
the other. Thus, not even the most positive impulse towards justice,
in which he may well not be lacking, will turn the man of violence
from doing an injustice; and not even the liveliest temptation to
pleasure persuade the man of character to violate his principles.
There is in Man no other power than his will; and his inner freedom
can only be destroyed by that which destroys Man himself, namely
death or anything that robs him of consciousness.

11.   It is a necessity o u t s i d e o f u s which, through the medium
of sensation, determines our Condition, our existence in time. This
life of sensation is quite involuntary, and we have no option but to
submit to any impact that is made upon us. And it is no less a necessity w i t h i n u s which, at the instance of sensation and in opposition to it, awakens our Personality; for self-awareness cannot be
dependent upon the will which presupposes it. This original manifestation of Personality is not our merit; nor is the lack of it our
fault. Only of him who is conscious of himself can we demand
Reason, that is, absolute consistency and universality of consciousness; prior to that he is not a human being at all, and no act of
humanity can be expected of him. Even as the m e t a p h y s i c i s t
is unable to account for the limitations imposed upon the freedom
and autonomy of the mind by sensation, so the p h y s i c i s t is
unable to comprehend the infinity which, at the instigation of those
limitations, manifests itself within the Personality. Neither philosophical abstraction nor empirical method can ever take us back to
the source from which our concepts of Universality and Necessity
derive: their early manifestation in time veils it from the scrutiny

entzieht sie dem Beobachter und ihr übersinnlicher Ursprung dem metaphysischen Forscher. Aber genug, das Selbstbewusstsein ist da, und zugleich mit der unveränderlichen Einheit desselben ist das Gesetz der Einheit für alles, was f ü r d e n Menschen ist, und für alles, was d u r c h i h n werden soll, für sein Erkennen und Handeln aufgestellt. Unentfliehbar, unverfälschbar, unbegreiflich stellen die Begriffe von Wahrheit und Recht schon im Alter der Sinnlichkeit sich dar, und ohne dass man zu sagen wüsste, woher und wie es entstand, bemerkt man das Ewige in der Zeit und das Notwendige im Gefolge des Zufalls. So entspringen Empfindung und Selbstbewusstsein, völlig ohne Zutun des Subjekts, und beider Ursprung liegt ebensowohl jenseits unseres Willens, als er jenseits unseres Erkenntniskreises liegt.

12.   Sind aber beide wirklich, und hat der Mensch, vermittelst der Empfindung, die Erfahrung einer bestimmten Existenz, hat er durch das Selbstbewusstsein die Erfahrung seiner absoluten Existenz gemacht, so werden mit ihren Gegenständen auch seine beiden Grundtriebe rege. Der sinnliche Trieb erwacht mit der Erfahrung des Lebens (mit dem Anfang des Individuums), der vernünftige mit der Erfahrung des Gesetzes (mit dem Anfang der Persönlichkeit), und jetzt erst, nachdem beide zum Dasein gekommen, ist seine Menschheit aufgebaut. Bis dies geschehen ist, erfolgt alles in ihm nach dem Gesetz der Notwendigkeit; jetzt aber verlässt ihn die Hand der N a t u r, und es ist s e i n e Sache, die Menschheit zu behaupten, welche jene in ihm anlegte und eröffnete. Sobald nämlich zwei entgegengesetzte Grundtriebe in ihm tätig sind, so verlieren beide ihre Nötigung, und die Entgegensetzung zweier Notwendigkeiten gibt der F r e i h e i t den Ursprung.*

* Um aller Missdeutung vorzubeugen, bemerke ich, dass, so oft hier von Freiheit die Rede ist, nicht diejenige gemeint ist, die dem Menschen, als Intelligenz betrachtet, notwendig zukommt und ihm weder gegeben noch genommen werden kann, sondern diejenige, welche sich auf seine gemischte Natur gründet. Dadurch, dass der Mensch überhaupt nur vernünftig handelt, beweist er eine Freiheit der ersten Art; dadurch, dass er in den Schranken des Stoffes vernünftig und unter Gesetzen der Vernunft materiell handelt, beweist er eine Freiheit der zweiten Art. Man könnte die letztere schlechtweg durch eine natürliche Möglichkeit der erstern erklären.

of the empirical observer, their supersensuous origin from that of the metaphysical inquirer. But enough, self-consciousness is there; and once its immutable unity is established, there is also established a law of unity for everything which is there f o r man, and for everything which is to come about t h r o u g h h i m, i.e., for all his knowing and for all his doing. Ineluctable, incorruptible, incomprehensible, the concepts of Truth and Right make their appearance at an age when we are still little more than a bundle of sensations; and without being able to say whence or how it arose, we acquire an awareness of the Eternal in Time, and of Necessity in the sequence of Chance. Thus sensation and self-consciousness both arise entirely without any effort on our part, and the origin of both lies as much beyond the reach of our will as it is beyond the orbit of our understanding.

12.   But once they have come into being, once Man has, through the medium of sensation, acquired awareness of a determinate existence, once he has, through self-consciousness, acquired awareness of his absolute existence, then these two basic drives are quickened, together with their objects. The sensuous drive awakens with our experience of life (with the beginning of our individuality); the rational drive, with our experience of law (with the beginning of our personality); and only at this point, when both have come into existence, is the basis of man's humanity established. Until this has happened, everything in him takes place according to the law of Necessity. But now the hand of N a t u r e is withdrawn from him, and it is up to h i m to vindicate the humanity which she implanted and opened up within him. That is to say, as soon as two opposing fundamental drives are active within him, both lose their compulsion, and the opposition of two necessities gives rise to F r e e d o m.*

---

* To obviate any possible misunderstanding, I would observe that, whenever there is any mention of freedom here, I do not mean that freedom which necessarily appertains to man considered as intelligent being, and which can neither be given unto him nor taken from him, but only that freedom which is founded upon his mixed nature. By acting rationally at all man displays freedom of the first order; by acting rationally within the limits of matter, and materially under the laws of reason, he displays freedom of the second order. We might explain the latter quite simply as a natural possibility of the former.

ZWANZIGSTER BRIEF

1. Dass auf die Freiheit nicht gewirkt werden könne, ergibt sich schon aus ihrem blossen Begriff; dass aber die Freiheit selbst eine Wirkung der Natur (dieses Wort in seinem weitesten Sinne genommen), kein Werk des Menschen sei, dass sie also auch durch natürliche Mittel befördert und gehemmt werden könne, folgt gleich notwendig aus dem vorigen. Sie nimmt ihren Anfang erst, wenn der Mensch vollständig ist und seine beiden Grundtriebe sich entwickelt haben; sie muss also fehlen, so lang' er unvollständig und einer von beiden Trieben ausgeschlossen ist, und muss durch alles das, was ihm seine Vollständigkeit zurückgibt, wieder hergestellt werden können.

2. Nun lässt sich wirklich, sowohl in der ganzen Gattung als in dem einzelnen Menschen, ein Moment aufzeigen, in welchem der Mensch noch nicht vollständig und einer von beiden Trieben ausschliessend in ihm tätig ist. Wir wissen, dass er anfängt mit blossem Leben, um zu endigen mit Form; dass er früher Individuum als Person ist, dass er von den Schranken aus zur Unendlichkeit geht. Der sinnliche Trieb kommt also früher als der vernünftige zur Wirkung, weil die Empfindung dem Bewusstsein vorhergeht, und in dieser Priorität des sinnlichen Triebes finden wir den Aufschluss zu der ganzen Geschichte der menschlichen Freiheit.

3. Denn es gibt nun einen Moment, wo der Lebenstrieb, weil ihm der Formtrieb noch nicht entgegenwirkt, als Natur und als Notwendigkeit handelt; wo die Sinnlichkeit eine Macht ist, weil der Mensch noch nicht angefangen; denn in dem Menschen selbst kann es keine andere Macht als den Willen geben. Aber im Zustand des Denkens, zu welchem der Mensch jetzt übergehen soll, soll gerade umgekehrt die Vernunft eine Macht sein, und eine logische oder moralische Notwendigkeit soll an die Stelle jener physischen treten. Jene Macht der Empfindung muss also vernichtet werden, ehe das Gesetz dazu erhoben werden kann. Es ist also nicht damit getan, dass etwas anfange, was noch nicht war; es muss zuvor etwas aufhören, welches war. Der Mensch kann nicht unmittelbar vom Empfinden zum Denken übergehen; er muss einen Schritt zurücktun, weil nur, indem eine Determination wieder aufgehoben

TWENTIETH LETTER

1. THAT freedom cannot be affected by anything whatsoever follows from our very notion of freedom. But that f r e e d o m i s i t s e l f an effect of N a t u r e (this word taken in its widest sense) and not the work of Man, that it can, therefore, also be furthered or thwarted by natural means, follows no less inevitably from what has just been said. It arises only when man is a c o m p l e t e being, when b o t h his fundamental drives are fully developed; it will, therefore, be lacking as long as he is incomplete, as long as one of the two drives is excluded, and it should be capable of being restored by anything which gives him back his completeness.

2. Now we can, in fact, in the species as a whole as well as in the individual human being, point to a moment in which man is not yet complete, and in which one of his two drives is exclusively active within him. We know that he begins by being nothing but life, in order to end by becoming form; that he is an Individual before he is a Person, and that he proceeds from limitation to infinity. The sensuous drive, therefore, comes into operation earlier than the rational, because sensation precedes consciousness, and it is this p r i o r i t y of the sensuous drive which provides the clue to the whole history of human freedom.

3. For there is, after all, a moment in which the life-impulse, just because the form-impulse is not yet running counter to it, operates as nature and as necessity; a moment in which the life of sense is a power because man has not yet begun to be a human being; for in the human being proper there cannot exist any power other than the will. But in the state of reflection into which he is now to pass, it will be precisely the opposite: Reason is to be a power, and a logical or moral necessity to take the place of that physical necessity. Hence sensation as a power must first be destroyed before law can be enthroned as such. It is, therefore, not simply a matter of something beginning which was not there before; something which was there must first cease to be. Man cannot pass directly from feeling to thought; he must first t a k e o n e s t e p b a c k w a r d s, since only through one determination being annulled again can a contrary

wird, die entgegengesetzte eintreten kann. Er muss also, um Leiden mit Selbsttätigkeit, um eine passive Bestimmung mit einer aktiven zu vertauschen, augenblicklich von aller Bestimmung frei sein und einen Zustand der blossen Bestimmbarkeit durchlaufen. Mithin muss er auf gewisse Weise zu jenem negativen Zustand der blossen Bestimmungslosigkeit zurückkehren, in welchem er sich befand, ehe noch irgend etwas auf seinen Sinn einen Eindruck machte. Jener Zustand aber war an Inhalt völlig leer, und jetzt kommt es darauf an, eine gleiche Bestimmungslosigkeit und eine gleich unbegrenzte Bestimmbarkeit mit dem grösstmöglichen Gehalt zu vereinbaren, weil unmittelbar aus diesem Zustand etwas Positives erfolgen soll. Die Bestimmung, die er durch Sensation empfangen, muss also festgehalten werden, weil er die Realität nicht verlieren darf; zugleich aber muss sie, insofern sie Begrenzung ist, aufgehoben werden, weil eine unbegrenzte Bestimmbarkeit stattfinden soll. Die Aufgabe ist also, die Determination des Zustandes zugleich zu vernichten und beizubehalten, welches nur auf die einzige Art möglich ist, dass man ihr eine andere entgegensetzt. Die Schalen einer Wage stehen gleich, wenn sie leer sind; sie stehen aber auch gleich, wenn sie gleiche Gewichte enthalten.

4. Das Gemüt geht also von der Empfindung zum Gedanken durch eine mittlere Stimmung über, in welcher Sinnlichkeit und Vernunft zugleich tätig sind, eben deswegen aber ihre bestimmende Gewalt gegenseitig aufheben und durch eine Entgegensetzung eine Negation bewirken. Diese mittlere Stimmung, in welcher das Gemüt weder physisch noch moralisch genötigt und doch auf beide Art tätig ist, verdient vorzugsweise eine freie Stimmung zu heissen; und wenn man den Zustand sinnlicher Bestimmung den physischen, den Zustand vernünftiger Bestimmung aber den logischen und moralischen nennt, so muss man diesen Zustand der realen und aktiven Bestimmbarkeit den ästhetischen heissen.*

---

* Für Leser, denen die reine Bedeutung dieses durch Unwissenheit so sehr gemissbrauchten Wortes nicht ganz geläufig ist, mag folgendes zur Erklärung dienen. Alle Dinge, die irgend in der Erscheinung vorkommen können, lassen sich unter vier verschiedenen Beziehungen denken. Eine Sache kann sich unmittelbar auf unsern sinnlichen Dasein (unser Dasein und Wohlsein) beziehen: das ist ihre physische Beschaffenheit. Oder sie kann sich auf den Verstand beziehen und uns eine Erkenntnis verschaffen: das ist ihre logische Beschaffenheit. Oder sie kann sich auf unsern Willen beziehen und als ein Gegenstand der Wahl für ein vernünftiges Wesen betrachtet werden: das ist ihre moralische Beschaffenheit. Oder endlich, sie kann sich auf das

determination take its place. In order to exchange passivity for autonomy, a passive determination for an active one, man must therefore be momentarily f r e e of all determination whatsoever, and pass through a state of pure determinability. He must consequently, in a certain sense, return to that negative state of complete absence of determination in which he found himself before anything at all had made an impression upon his senses. But that former condition was completely devoid of content; and now it is a question of combining such sheer absence of determination, and an equally unlimited determinability, with the greatest possible content, since directly from this condition something positive is to result. The determination he has received through sensation must therefore be preserved, because there must be no loss of reality; but at the same time it must, inasmuch as it is limitation, be annulled, since an unlimited determinability is to come into existence. The problem is, therefore, at one and the same time to destroy and to maintain the determination of the condition—and this is possible in one way only: by confronting it with another determination. The scales of the balance stand level when they are empty; but they also stand level when they contain equal weights.

4. Our psyche passes, then, from sensation to thought *via* a middle disposition in which sense and reason are both active a t t h e s a m e t i m e. Precisely for this reason, however, they cancel each other out as determining forces, and bring about a negation by means of an opposition. This middle disposition, in which the psyche is subject neither to physical nor to moral constraint, and yet is active in both these ways, pre-eminently deserves to be called a free disposition; and if we are to call the condition of sensuous determination the physical, and the condition of rational determination the logical or moral, then we must call this condition of real and active determinability the a e s t h e t i c.*

---

* For readers not altogether familiar with the precise meaning of this word, which is so much abused through ignorance, the following may serve as an explanation. Every thing which is capable of phenomenal manifestation may be thought of under four different aspects. A thing can relate directly to our sensual condition (to our being and well-being): that is its p h y s i c a l character. Or it can relate to our intellect, and afford us knowledge: that is its l o g i c a l character. Or it can relate to our will, and be considered as an object of choice for a rational being: that is its m o r a l character. Or,

Ganze unsrer verschiedenen Kräfte beziehen, ohne für eine einzelne derselben ein bestimmtes Objekt zu sein: das ist ihre ä s t h e t i s c h e Beschaffenheit. Ein Mensch kann uns durch seine Dienstfertigkeit angenehm sein; er kann uns durch seine Unterhaltung zu denken geben; er kann uns durch seinen Charakter Achtung einflössen; endlich kann er uns aber auch, unabhängig von diesem allen, und ohne dass wir bei seiner Beurteilung weder auf irgend ein Gesetz, noch auf irgend einen Zweck Rücksicht nehmen, in der blossen Betrachtung und durch seine blosse Erscheinungsart gefallen. In dieser letztern Qualität beurteilen wir ihn ästhetisch. So gibt es eine Erziehung zur Gesundheit, eine Erziehung zur Einsicht, eine Erziehung zur Sittlichkeit, eine Erziehung zum Geschmack und zur Schönheit. Diese letztere hat zur Absicht, das Ganze unsrer sinnlichen und geistigen Kräfte in möglichster Harmonie auszubilden. Weil man indessen, von einem falschen Geschmack verführt und durch ein falsches Raisonnement noch mehr in diesem Irrtum befestigt, den Begriff des Willkürlichen in den Begriff des Ästhetischen gerne mit aufnimmt, so merke ich hier zum Überfluss noch an (obgleich diese Briefe über ästhetische Erziehung fast mit nichts anderm umgehen, als jenen Irrtum zu widerlegen), dass das Gemüt im ästhetischen Zustande zwar frei und im höchsten Grade frei von allem Zwang, aber keineswegs frei von Gesetzen handelt und dass diese ästhetische Freiheit sich von der logischen Notwendigkeit beim Denken und von der moralischen Notwendigkeit beim Wollen nur dadurch unterscheidet, dass die Gesetze, nach denen das Gemüt dabei verfährt, n i c h t v o r g e s t e l l t w e r d e n und, weil sie keinen Widerstand finden, nicht als Nötigung erscheinen.

finally, it can relate to the totality of our various functions without being a definite object for any single one of them: that is its a e s t h e t i c character. A man can please us through his readiness to oblige; he can, through his discourse, give us food for thought; he can, through his character, fill us with respect; but finally he can also, independently of all this, and without our taking into consideration in judging him any law or any purpose, please us simply as we contemplate him and by the sheer manner of his being. Under this last-named quality of being we are judging him aesthetically. Thus there is an education to health, an education to understanding, an education to morality, an education to taste and beauty. This last has as its aim the development of the whole complex of our sensual and spiritual powers in the greatest possible harmony. Because, however, misled by false notions of taste and confirmed still further in this error by false reasoning, people are inclined to include in the notion of the aesthetic the notion of the arbitrary too, I add here the superfluous comment (despite the fact that these Letters on Aesthetic Education are concerned with virtually nothing else but the refutation of that very error) that our psyche in the aesthetic state does indeed act freely, is in the highest degree free from all compulsion, but is in no wise free from laws; and that this aesthetic freedom is distinguishable from logical necessity in thinking, or moral necessity in willing, only by the fact that the laws according to which the psyche then behaves d o n o t b e c o m e a p p a r e n t a s s u c h, and since they encounter no resistance, never appear as a constraint.

EINUNDZWANZIGSTER BRIEF

1. Es gibt, wie ich am Anfange des vorigen Briefs bemerkte, einen doppelten Zustand der Bestimmbarkeit und einen doppelten Zustand der Bestimmung. Jetzt kann ich diesen Satz deutlich machen.

2. Das Gemüt ist bestimmbar, bloss insofern es überhaupt nicht bestimmt ist; es ist aber auch bestimmbar, insofern es nicht ausschliessend bestimmt, d. h. bei seiner Bestimmung nicht beschränkt ist. Jenes ist blosse Bestimmungslosigkeit (es ist ohne Schranken, weil es ohne Realität ist); dieses ist die ästhetische Bestimmbarkeit (es hat keine Schranken, weil es alle Realität vereinigt).

3. Das Gemüt ist bestimmt, insofern es überhaupt nur beschränkt ist; es ist aber auch bestimmt, insofern es sich selbst aus eigenem absoluten Vermögen beschränkt. In dem ersten Falle befindet es sich, wenn es empfindet; in dem zweiten, wenn es denkt. Was also das Denken in Rücksicht auf Bestimmung ist, das ist die ästhetische Verfassung in Rücksicht auf Bestimmbarkeit; jenes ist Beschränkung aus innrer unendlicher Kraft, diese ist eine Negation aus innrer unendlicher Fülle. So wie Empfinden und Denken einander in dem einzigen Punkt berühren, dass in beiden Zuständen das Gemüt determiniert, dass der Mensch ausschliessungsweise Etwas — entweder Individuum oder Person — ist, sonst aber sich ins Unendliche von einander entfernen: gerade so trifft die ästhetische Bestimmbarkeit mit der blossen Bestimmungslosigkeit in dem einzigen Punkt überein, dass beide jedes bestimmte Dasein ausschliessen, indem sie in allen übrigen Punkten wie Nichts und Alles, mithin unendlich verschieden sind. Wenn also die letztere, die Bestimmungslosigkeit aus Mangel, als eine leere Unendlichkeit vorgestellt wurde, so muss die ästhetische Bestimmungsfreiheit, welche das reale Gegenstück derselben ist, als eine erfüllte Unendlichkeit betrachtet werden; eine Vorstellung, welche mit demjenigen, was die vorhergehenden Untersuchungen lehren, aufs genaueste zusammentrifft.

4. In dem ästhetischen Zustande ist der Mensch also Null, insofern man auf ein einzelnes Resultat, nicht auf das ganze Vermögen achtet und den Mangel jeder besondern Determination in

TWENTY-FIRST LETTER

1. THERE is, as I observed at the beginning of the last Letter, a twofold condition of determinability and a twofold condition of determination. I can now clarify this statement.

2. The psyche may be said to be determinable simply because it is not determined at all; but it is also determinable inasmuch as it is determined in a way which does not exclude anything, i.e., when the determination it undergoes is of a kind which does not involve limitation. The former is mere indetermination (it is without limits, because it is without reality); the latter is aesthetic determinability (it has no limits, because it embraces all reality).

3. And the psyche may be said to be determined inasmuch as it is limited at all; but it is also determined inasmuch as it limits itself, by virtue of its own absolute power. It finds itself in the first of these two states whenever it feels; in the second, whenever it thinks. What thought is in respect of determination, therefore, the aesthetic disposition is in respect of determinability; the former is limitation by virtue of the infinite force within it, the latter is negation by virtue of the infinite abundance within it. Even as sensation and thought have one single point of contact—viz., that in both states the psyche is determined, and man is something, either individual or person, to the exclusion of all else—but in all other respects are poles apart: so, in like manner, aesthetic determinability has one single point of contact with mere indetermination—viz., that both exclude any determinate mode of existence—while in all other respects they are to each other as nothing is to everything, hence, utterly and entirely different. If, therefore, the latter—indetermination through sheer absence of determination—was thought of as an e m p t y i n f i n i t y, then aesthetic freedom of determination, which is its counterpart in reality, must be regarded as an i n f i n i t y f i l l e d w i t h c o n t e n t: an idea which accords completely with the results of the foregoing inquiry.

4. In the aesthetic state, then, man is N o u g h t, if we are thinking of any particular result rather than of the totality of his powers, and considering the absence in him of any specific determination. Hence

ihm in Betrachtung zieht. Daher muss man denjenigen vollkommen Recht geben, welche das Schöne und die Stimmung, in die es unser Gemüt versetzt, in Rücksicht auf E r k e n n t n i s und G e s i n-n u n g für völlig indifferent und unfruchtbar erklären. Sie haben vollkommen Recht, denn die Schönheit gibt schlechterdings kein einzelnes Resultat weder für den Verstand noch für den Willen, sie führt keinen einzelnen, weder intellektuellen noch moralischen Zweck aus, sie findet keine einzige Wahrheit, hilft uns keine einzige Pflicht erfüllen und ist, mit einem Worte, gleich ungeschickt, den Charakter zu gründen und den Kopf aufzuklären. Durch die ästhetische Kultur bleibt also der persönliche Wert eines Menschen, oder seine Würde, insofern diese nur von ihm selbst abhängen kann, noch völlig unbestimmt, und es ist weiter nichts erreicht, als dass es ihm nunmehr v o n N a t u r w e g e n möglich gemacht ist, aus sich selbst zu machen, was er will — dass ihm die Freiheit, zu sein, was er sein soll, vollkommen zurückgegeben ist.

5.   Eben dadurch aber ist etwas Unendliches erreicht. Denn sobald wir uns erinnern, dass ihm durch die einseitige Nötigung der Natur beim Empfinden und durch die ausschliessende Gesetzgebung der Vernunft beim Denken gerade diese Freiheit entzogen wurde, so müssen wir das Vermögen, welches ihm in der ästhetischen Stimmung zurückgegeben wird, als die höchste aller Schenkungen, als die Schenkung der Menschheit betrachten. Freilich besitzt er diese Menschheit der Anlage nach schon vor jedem bestimmten Zustand, in den er kommen kann; aber der Tat nach verliert er sie mit jedem bestimmten Zustand, in den er kommt, und sie muss ihm, wenn er zu einem entgegengesetzten soll übergehen können, jedesmal aufs neue durch das ästhetische Leben zurückgegeben werden.*

6.   Es ist also nicht bloss poetisch erlaubt, sondern auch philo-sophisch richtig, wenn man die Schönheit unsre zweite Schöpferin

* Zwar lässt die Schnelligkeit, mit welcher gewisse Charaktere von Empfindungen zu Gedanken und zu Entschliessungen übergehen, die ästhetische Stimmung, welche sie in dieser Zeit notwendig durchlaufen müssen, kaum oder gar nicht bemerkbar werden. Solche Gemüter können den Zustand der Bestimmungslosigkeit nicht lang' ertragen und dringen ungeduldig auf ein Resultat, welches sie in dem Zustand ästhetischer Unbe-grenztheit nicht finden. Dahingegen breitet sich bei andern, welche ihren Genuss mehr in das Gefühl d e s g a n z e n V e r m ö g e n s als einer e i n z e l n e n Handlung desselben setzen, der ästhetische Zustand in eine weit grössere Fläche aus. So sehr die ersten sich vor der Leerheit fürchten, so wenig können die letzten Beschränkung ertragen. Ich brauche kaum zu erinnern, dass die ersten fürs Detail und für subalterne Geschäfte, die letzten, vorausgesetzt dass sie mit diesem Vermögen zugleich Realität vereinigen, fürs Ganze und zu grossen Rollen geboren sind.

we must allow that those people are entirely right who declare beauty, and the mood it induces in us, to be completely indifferent and unfruitful as regards either k n o w l e d g e or c h a r a c t e r. They are entirely right; for beauty produces no particular result whatsoever, neither for the understanding nor for the will. It accomplishes no particular purpose, neither intellectual nor moral; it discovers no individual truth, helps us to perform no individual duty and is, in short, as unfitted to provide a firm basis for character as to enlighten the understanding. By means of aesthetic culture, therefore, the personal worth of a man, or his dignity, inasmuch as this can depend solely upon himself, remains completely indeterminate; and nothing more is achieved by it than that he is henceforth enabled b y t h e g r a c e o f N a t u r e to make of himself what he will—that the freedom to be what he ought to be is completely restored to him.

5. But precisely thereby something Infinite is achieved. For as soon as we recall that it was precisely of this freedom that he was deprived by the one-sided constraint of nature in the field of sensation and by the exclusive authority of reason in the realm of thought, then we are bound to consider the power which is restored to him in the aesthetic mode as the highest of all bounties, as the gift of humanity itself. True, he possesses this humanity *in potentia* before every determinate condition into which he can conceivably enter. But he loses it in practice with every determinate condition into which he does enter. And if he is to pass into a condition of an opposite nature, this humanity must be restored to him each time anew through the life of the aesthetic.*

6. It is, then, not just poetic licence but philosophical truth when we call beauty our second creatress. For although it only offers us

* Admittedly the rapidity with which certain types pass from sensation to thought or decision scarcely—if indeed at all—allows them to become aware of the aesthetic mode through which they must in that time necessarily pass. Such natures cannot for any length of time tolerate the state of indetermination, but press impatiently for some result which in the state of aesthetic limitlessness they cannot find. In others, by contrast, who find enjoyment more in the feeling of t o t a l c a p a c i t y than in any s i n g l e action, the aesthetic state tends to spread itself over a much wider area. Much as the former dread emptiness, just as little are the latter capable of tolerating limitation. I need scarcely say that the former are born for detail and subordinate occupations, the latter, provided they combine this capacity with a sense of reality, destined for wholeness and for great roles.

nennt. Denn ob sie uns gleich die Menschheit bloss möglich macht und es im übrigen unserm freien Willen anheimstellt, inwieweit wir sie wirklich machen wollen, so hat sie dieses ja mit unsrer ursprünglichen Schöpferin, der Natur, gemein, die uns gleichfalls nichts weiter als das Vermögen zur Menschheit erteilte, den Gebrauch desselben aber auf unsere eigene Willensbestimmung ankommen lässt.

the possibility of becoming human beings, and for the rest leaves it to our own free will to decide how far we wish to make this a reality, it does in this resemble our first creatress, Nature, which likewise conferred upon us nothing more than the power of becoming human, leaving the use and practice of that power to our own free will and decision.

ZWEIUNDZWANZIGSTER BRIEF

1. WENN also die ästhetische Stimmung des Gemüts in Einer Rücksicht als Null betrachtet werden muss, sobald man nämlich sein Augenmerk auf einzelne und bestimmte Wirkungen richtet, so ist sie in anderer Rücksicht wieder als ein Zustand der höchsten Realität anzusehen, insofern man dabei auf die Abwesenheit aller Schranken und auf die Summe der Kräfte achtet, die in derselben gemeinschaftlich tätig sind. Man kann also denjenigen ebenso wenig Unrecht geben, die den ästhetischen Zustand für den fruchtbarsten in Rücksicht auf Erkenntnis und Moralität erklären. Sie haben vollkommen Recht; denn eine Gemütsstimmung, welche das Ganze der Menschheit in sich begreift, muss notwendig auch jede einzelne Äusserung derselben, dem Vermögen nach, in sich schliessen; eine Gemütsstimmung, welche von dem Ganzen der menschlichen Natur alle Schranken entfernt, muss diese notwendig auch von jeder einzelnen Äusserung derselben entfernen. Eben deswegen, weil sie keine einzelne Funktion der Menschheit ausschliessend in Schutz nimmt, so ist sie einer jeden ohne Unterschied günstig, und sie begünstigt ja nur deswegen keine einzelne vorzugsweise, weil sie der Grund der Möglichkeit von allen ist. Alle andere Übungen geben dem Gemüt irgend ein besondres Geschick, aber setzen ihm dafür auch eine besondere Grenze; die ästhetische allein führt zum Unbegrenzten. Jeder andere Zustand, in den wir kommen können, weist uns auf einen vorhergehenden zurück und bedarf zu seiner Auflösung eines folgenden; nur der ästhetische ist ein Ganzes in sich selbst, da er alle Bedingungen seines Ursprungs und seiner Fortdauer in sich vereinigt. Hier allein fühlen wir uns wie aus der Zeit gerissen; und unsre Menschheit äussert sich mit einer Reinheit und Integrität, als hätte sie von der Einwirkung äussrer Kräfte noch keinen Abbruch erfahren.

2. Was unsern Sinnen in der unmittelbaren Empfindung schmeichelt, das öffnet unser weiches und bewegliches Gemüt jedem Eindruck, aber macht uns auch in demselben Grad zur Anstrengung weniger tüchtig. Was unsre Denkkräfte anspannt und zu abgezogenen Begriffen einladet, das stärkt unsern Geist zu jeder Art des Widerstandes, aber verhärtet ihn auch in demselben Verhältnis und

TWENTY-SECOND LETTER

1. IF, then, in o n e respect the aesthetic mode of the psyche is to be regarded as N o u g h t—once, that is, we have an eye to particular and definite effects—it is in another respect to be looked upon as a state o f S u p r e m e R e a l i t y, once we have due regard to the absence of all limitation and to the sum total of the powers which are conjointly active within it. One cannot, then, say that those people are wrong either who declare the aesthetic state to be the most fruitful of all in respect of knowledge and morality. They are entirely right; for a disposition of the psyche which contains within it the whole of human nature, must necessarily contain within it *in potentia* every individual manifestation of it too; and a disposition of the psyche which removes all limitations from the totality of human nature must necessarily remove them from every individual manifestation of it as well. Precisely on this account, because it takes under its protection no single one of man's faculties to the exclusion of the others, it favours each and all of them without distinction; and it favours no single one more than another for the simple reason that it is the ground of possibility of them all. Every other way of exercising its functions endows the psyche with some special aptitude—but only at the cost of some special limitation; the aesthetic alone leads to the absence of all limitation. Every other state into which we can enter refers us back to a preceding one, and requires for its termination a subsequent one; the aesthetic alone is a whole in itself, since it comprises within itself all the conditions of both its origin and its continuance. Here alone do we feel reft out of time, and our human nature expresses itself with a purity and i n t e g r i t y, as though it had as yet suffered no impairment through the intervention of external forces.

2.   That which flatters our senses in immediate sensation exposes our susceptible and labile psyche to every impression—but only by rendering us proportionately less fitted for exertion. That which tenses our intellectual powers and invites them to form abstract concepts, strengthens our mind for every sort of resistance—but only by hardening it and depriving us of sensibility in proportion

raubt uns ebenso viel an Empfänglichkeit, als es uns zu einer grössern Selbsttätigkeit verhilft. Eben deswegen führt auch das eine wie
das andre zuletzt notwendig zur Erschöpfung, weil der Stoff nicht
lange der bildenden Kraft, weil die Kraft nicht lange des bildsamen
Stoffes entraten kann. Haben wir uns hingegen dem Genuss echter
Schönheit dahingegeben, so sind wir in einem solchen Augenblick
unsrer leidenden und tätigen Kräfte in gleichem Grad Meister, und
mit gleicher Leichtigkeit werden wir uns zum Ernst und zum Spiele,
zur Ruhe und zur Bewegung, zur Nachgiebigkeit und zum Widerstand, zum abstrakten Denken und zur Anschauung wenden.

3.   Diese hohe Gleichmütigkeit und Freiheit des Geistes, mit
Kraft und Rüstigkeit verbunden, ist die Stimmung, in der uns ein
echtes Kunstwerk entlassen soll, und es gibt keinen sicherern Pro-
bierstein der wahren ästhetischen Güte. Finden wir uns nach einem
Genuss dieser Art zu irgend einer besondern Empfindungsweise
oder Handlungsweise vorzugsweise aufgelegt, zu einer andern hingegen ungeschickt und verdrossen, so dient dies zu einem un-
trüglichen Beweise, dass wir keine r e i n ä s t h e t i s c h e Wirkung
erfahren haben; es sei nun, dass es an dem Gegenstand oder an
unserer Empfindungsweise oder (wie fast immer der Fall ist) an
beiden zugleich gelegen habe.

4.   Da in der Wirklichkeit keine rein ästhetische Wirkung anzutreffen ist (denn der Mensch kann nie aus der Abhängigkeit der
Kräfte treten), so kann die Vortrefflichkeit eines Kunstwerks bloss
in seiner grössern Annäherung zu jenem Ideale ästhetischer Reinig-
keit bestehen, und bei aller Freiheit, zu der man es steigern mag,
werden wir es doch immer in einer besondern Stimmung und mit
einer eigentümlichen Richtung verlassen. Je allgemeiner nun die
Stimmung und je weniger eingeschränkt die Richtung ist, welche
unserm Gemüt durch eine bestimmte Gattung der Künste und
durch ein bestimmtes Produkt aus derselben gegeben wird, desto
edler ist jene Gattung und desto vortrefflicher ein solches Produkt.
Man kann dies mit Werken aus verschiedenen Künsten und mit
verschiedenen Werken der nämlichen Kunst versuchen. Wir verlassen eine schöne Musik mit reger Empfindung, ein schönes Gedicht mit belebter Einbildungskraft, ein schönes Bildwerk und
Gebäude mit aufgewecktem Verstand; wer uns aber unmittelbar
nach einem hohen musikalischen Genuss zu abgezogenem Denken
einladen, unmittelbar nach einem hohen poetischen Genuss in

as it fosters greater independence of action. Precisely because of this, the one no less than the other must lead to exhaustion, since material cannot for long dispense with shaping power, nor power with material to be shaped. If, by contrast, we have surrendered to the enjoyment of genuine beauty, we are at such a moment master in equal degree of our passive and of our active powers, and we shall with equal ease turn to seriousness or to play, to repose or to movement, to compliance or to resistance, to the discursions of abstract thought or to the direct contemplation of phenomena.

3. This lofty equanimity and freedom of the spirit, combined with power and vigour, is the mood in which a genuine work of art should release us, and there is no more certain touchstone of true aesthetic excellence. If, after enjoyment of this kind, we find ourselves disposed to prefer some one particular mode of feeling or action, but unfitted or disinclined for another, this may serve as infallible proof that we have not had a p u r e l y a e s t h e t i c experience—whether the cause lies in the object or in our own response or, as is almost always the case, in both at once.

4. Since in actuality no purely aesthetic effect is ever to be met with (for man can never escape his dependence upon conditioning forces), the excellence of a work of art can never consist in anything more than a high approximation to that ideal of aesthetic purity; and whatever the degree of freedom to which it may have been sublimated, we shall still leave it in a particular mood and with some definite bias. The more general the mood and the less limited the bias produced in us by any particular art, or by any particular product of the same, then the nobler that art and the more excellent that product will be. One can test this by considering works from different arts and different works from the same art. We leave a beautiful piece of music with our feeling excited, a beautiful poem with our imagination quickened, a beautiful sculpture or building with our understanding awakened. But should anyone invite us, immediately after a sublime musical experience, to abstract thought; or employ us, immediately after a sublime poetic experience, in

einem abgemessenen Geschäft des gemeinen Lebens gebrauchen, unmittelbar nach Betrachtung schöner Malereien und Bildhauerwerke unsre Einbildungskraft erhitzen und unser Gefühl überraschen wollte, der würde seine Zeit nicht gut wählen. Die Ursache ist, weil auch die geistreichste Musik d u r c h i h r e M a t e r i e noch immer in einer grössern Affinität zu den Sinnen steht, als die wahre ästhetische Freiheit duldet; weil auch das glücklichste Gedicht von dem willkürlichen und zufälligen Spiele der Imagination, a l s s e i n e s M e d i u m s, noch immer mehr partizipiert, als die innere Notwendigkeit des wahrhaft Schönen verstattet; weil auch das trefflichste Bildwerk, und dieses vielleicht am meisten, d u r c h d i e B e s t i m m t h e i t s e i n e s B e g r i f f s an die ernste Wissenschaft grenzt. Indessen verlieren sich diese besondren Affinitäten mit jedem höhern Grade, den ein Werk aus diesen drei Kunstgattungen erreicht, und es ist eine notwendige und natürliche Folge ihrer Vollendung, dass, ohne Verrückung ihrer objektiven Grenzen, die verschiedenen Künste i n i h r e r W i r k u n g a u f d a s G e m ü t einander immer ähnlicher werden. Die Musik in ihrer höchsten Veredlung muss Gestalt werden und mit der ruhigen Macht der Antike auf uns wirken; die bildende Kunst in ihrer höchsten Vollendung muss Musik werden und uns durch unmittelbare sinnliche Gegenwart rühren; die Poesie in ihrer vollkommensten Ausbildung muss uns, wie die Tonkunst, mächtig fassen, zugleich aber, wie die Plastik, mit ruhiger Klarheit umgeben. Darin eben zeigt sich der vollkommene Stil in jeglicher Kunst, dass er die spezifischen Schranken derselben zu entfernen weiss, ohne doch ihre spezifischen Vorzüge mit aufzuheben, und durch eine weise Benutzung ihrer Eigentümlichkeit ihr einen mehr allgemeinen Charakter erteilt.

5. Und nicht bloss die Schranken, welche der spezifische Charakter seiner Kunstgattung mit sich bringt, auch diejenigen, welche dem besondern Stoffe, den er bearbeitet, anhängig sind, muss der Künstler durch die Behandlung überwinden. In einem wahrhaft schönen Kunstwerk soll der Inhalt nichts, die Form aber alles tun; denn durch die Form allein wird auf das Ganze des Menschen, durch den Inhalt hingegen nur auf einzelne Kräfte gewirkt. Der Inhalt, wie erhaben und weitumfassend er auch sei, wirkt also jederzeit einschränkend auf den Geist, und nur von der Form ist wahre ästhetische Freiheit zu erwarten. Darin also besteht das eigentliche

some routine business of everyday life; or try, immediately after the contemplation of beautiful paintings or sculptures, to inflame our imagination or surprise our feeling—he would certainly be choosing the wrong moment. The reason for this is that even the most ethereal music has, by virtue of its material, an even greater affinity with the senses than true aesthetic freedom really allows; that even the most successful poem partakes more of the arbitrary and casual play of the imagination, as the medium through which it works, than the inner lawfulness of the truly beautiful really permits; that even the most excellent sculpture—the most excellent, perhaps, most of all—does, by virtue of its conceptual precision, border upon the austerity of science. Nevertheless, the greater the degree of excellence attained by a work in any of these three arts, the more these particular affinities will disappear; and it is an inevitable and natural consequence of their approach to perfection that the various arts, without any displacement of their objective frontiers, tend to become ever more like each other in their effect upon the psyche. Music, at its most sublime, must become sheer form and affect us with the serene power of antiquity. The plastic arts, at their most perfect, must become music and move us by the immediacy of their sensuous presence. Poetry, when most fully developed, must grip us powerfully as music does, but at the same time, like the plastic arts, surround us with serene clarity. This, precisely, is the mark of perfect style in each and every art: that it is able to remove the specific limitations of the art in question without thereby destroying its specific qualities, and through a wise use of its individual peculiarities, is able to confer upon it a more general character.

5.   And it is not just the limitations inherent in the specific character of a particular art that the artist must seek to overcome through his handling of it; it is also the limitations inherent in the particular subject-matter he is treating. In a truly successful work of art the contents should effect nothing, the form everything; for only through the form is the whole man affected, through the subject-matter, by contrast, only one or other of his functions. Subject-matter, then, however sublime and all-embracing it may be, always has a limiting effect upon the spirit, and it is only from form that true aesthetic freedom can be looked for. Herein, then, resides the real secret of

Kunstgeheimnis des Meisters, d a s s e r d e n S t o f f d u r c h d i e
F o r m v e r t i l g t; und je imposanter, anmassender, verführeri-
scher der Stoff an sich selbst ist, je eigenmächtiger derselbe mit
s e i n e r Wirkung sich vordrängt, oder je mehr der Betrachter
geneigt ist, sich unmittelbar mit dem Stoff einzulassen, desto
triumphierender ist die Kunst, welche jenen zurückzwingt und über
diesen die Herrschaft behauptet. Das Gemüt des Zuschauers und
Zuhörers muss völlig frei und unverletzt bleiben, es muss aus dem
Zauberkreise des Künstlers rein und vollkommen wie aus den
Händen des Schöpfers gehn. Der frivolste Gegenstand muss so
behandelt werden, dass wir aufgelegt bleiben, unmittelbar von demselben zu dem strengsten Ernste überzugehen. Der ernsteste Stoff
muss so behandelt werden, dass wir die Fähigkeit behalten, ihn
unmittelbar mit dem leichtesten Spiele zu vertauschen. Künste des
Affekts, dergleichen die Tragödie ist, sind kein Einwurf: denn
e r s t l i c h sind es keine ganz freien Künste, da sie unter der Dienstbarkeit eines besondern Zweckes (des Pathetischen) stehen; und
d a n n wird wohl kein wahrer Kunstkenner leugnen, dass Werke,
auch selbst aus dieser Klasse, um so vollkommener sind, je mehr
sie auch im höchsten Sturme des Affekts die Gemütsfreiheit schonen. Eine schöne Kunst der Leidenschaft gibt es; aber eine schöne
leidenschaftliche Kunst ist ein Widerspruch, denn der unausbleib-
liche Effekt des Schönen ist Freiheit von Leidenschaften. Nicht
weniger widersprechend ist der Begriff einer schönen lehrenden
(didaktischen) oder bessernden (moralischen) Kunst, denn nichts
streitet mehr mit dem Begriff der Schönheit, als dem Gemüt eine
bestimmte Tendenz zu geben.

6.   Nicht immer beweist es indessen eine Formlosigkeit in dem
Werke, wenn es bloss durch seinen Inhalt Effekt macht; es kann
ebenso oft von einem Mangel an Form in dem Beurteiler zeugen.
Ist dieser entweder zu gespannt oder zu schlaff, ist er gewohnt,
entweder bloss mit dem Verstand oder bloss mit den Sinnen aufzunehmen, so wird er sich auch bei dem glücklichsten Ganzen nur
an die Teile und bei der schönsten Form nur an die Materie halten.
Nur für das r o h e E l e m e n t empfänglich, muss er die ästhetische
Organisation eines Werks erst zerstören, ehe er einen Genuss daran
findet, und das Einzelne sorgfältig aufscharren, das der Meister mit
unendlicher Kunst in der Harmonie des Ganzen verschwinden
machte. Sein Interesse daran ist schlechterdings entweder moralisch

the master in any art: that he can make his form consume his material; and the more pretentious, the more seductive this material is in itself, the more it seeks to impose itself upon us, the more high-handedly it thrusts itself forward with effects of its own, or the more the beholder is inclined to get directly involved with it, then the more triumphant the art which forces it back and asserts its own kind of dominion over him. The psyche of the listener or spectator must remain completely free and inviolate; it must go forth from the magic circle of the artist pure and perfect as it came from the hands of the Creator. The most frivolous theme must be so treated that it leaves us ready to proceed directly from it to some matter of the utmost import; the most serious material must be so treated that we remain capable of exchanging it forthwith for the lightest play. Arts which affect the passions, such as tragedy, do not invalidate this: in the first place, they are not entirely free arts since they are enlisted in the service of a particular aim (that of pathos); and in the second, no true connoisseur of art will deny that works even of this class are the more perfect, the more they respect the freedom of the spirit even amid the most violent storms of passion. There does indeed exist a fine art of passion; but a fine passionate art is a contradiction in terms; for the unfailing effect of beauty is freedom from passion. No less self-contradictory is the notion of a fine art which teaches (didactic) or improves (moral); for nothing is more at variance with the concept of beauty than the notion of giving the psyche any definite bias.

6.   But it is by no means always a proof of formlessness in the work of art itself if it makes its effect solely through its contents; this may just as often be evidence of a lack of form in him who judges it. If he is either too tensed or too relaxed, if he is used to apprehending either exclusively with the intellect or exclusively with the senses, he will, even in the case of the most successfully realized whole, attend only to the parts, and in the presence of the most beauteous form respond only to the matter. Receptive only to the raw material, he has first to destroy the aesthetic organization of a work before he can take pleasure in it, and laboriously scratch away until he has uncovered all those individual details which the master, with infinite skill, had caused to disappear in the harmony of the whole. The interest he takes in it is quite simply either a moral or a

oder physisch; nur gerade, was es sein soll, ästhetisch ist es nicht. Solche Leser geniessen ein ernsthaftes und pathetisches Gedicht wie eine Predigt, und ein naives oder scherzhaftes wie ein berauschendes Getränk; und waren sie geschmacklos genug, von einer Tragödie und Epopöe, wenn es auch eine Messiade wäre, E r b a u u n g zu verlangen, so werden sie an einem anacreontischen oder catullischen Liede unfehlbar ein Ärgernis nehmen.

material interest; but what precisely it ought to be, namely aesthetic, that it certainly is not. Such readers will enjoy a serious and moving poem as though it were a sermon, a naïve or humorous one as though it were an intoxicating drink. And if they were sufficiently lacking in taste to demand edification of a tragedy or an epic—and were it about the Messiah himself—they will certainly not fail to take exception to a poem in the manner of Anacreon or Catullus.

DREIUNDZWANZIGSTER BRIEF

1. Ich nehme den Faden meiner Untersuchung wieder auf, den ich nur darum abgerissen habe, um von den aufgestellten Sätzen die Anwendung auf die ausübende Kunst und auf die Beurteilung ihrer Werke zu machen.

2. Der Übergang von dem leidenden Zustande des Empfindens zu dem tätigen des Denkens und Wollens geschieht also nicht anders als durch einen mittleren Zustand ästhetischer Freiheit, und obgleich dieser Zustand an sich selbst weder für unsere Einsichten noch Gesinnungen etwas entscheidet, mithin unsern intellektuellen und moralischen Wert ganz und gar problematisch lässt, so ist er doch die notwendige Bedingung, unter welcher allein wir zu einer Einsicht und zu einer Gesinnung gelangen können. Mit einem Wort: es gibt keinen andern Weg, den sinnlichen Menschen vernünftig zu machen, als dass man denselben zuvor ästhetisch macht.

3. Aber, möchten Sie mir einwenden, sollte diese Vermittlung durchaus unentbehrlich sein? Sollten Wahrheit und Pflicht nicht auch schon für sich allein und durch sich selbst bei dem sinnlichen Menschen Eingang finden können? Hierauf muss ich antworten: sie können nicht nur, sie sollen schlechterdings ihre bestimmende Kraft bloss sich selbst zu verdanken haben, und nichts würde meinen bisherigen Behauptungen widersprechender sein, als wenn sie das Ansehen hätten, die entgegengesetzte Meinung in Schutz zu nehmen. Es ist ausdrücklich bewiesen worden, dass die Schönheit kein Resultat weder für den Verstand noch den Willen gebe, dass sie sich in kein Geschäft weder des Denkens noch des Entschliessens mische, dass sie zu beiden bloss das Vermögen erteile, aber über den wirklichen Gebrauch dieses Vermögens durchaus nichts bestimme. Bei diesem fällt alle fremde Hilfe hinweg, und die reine logische Form, der Begriff, muss unmittelbar zu dem Verstand — die reine moralische Form, das Gesetz, unmittelbar zu dem Willen reden.

4. Aber dass sie dieses überhaupt nur könne — dass es überhaupt nur eine reine Form für den sinnlichen Menschen gebe, dies, behaupte ich, muss durch die ästhetische Stimmung des Gemüts erst möglich gemacht werden. Die Wahrheit ist nichts, was so wie die

TWENTY-THIRD LETTER

1. I TAKE up once more the thread of my inquiry, which I broke off only in order to apply to the practice of art, and the judgement of its works, the propositions previously established.

2. The transition from a passive state of feeling to an active state of thinking and willing cannot, then, take place except *via* a middle state of aesthetic freedom. And although this state can of itself decide nothing as regards either our insights or our convictions, thus leaving both our intellectual and our moral worth as yet entirely problematic, it is nevertheless the necessary pre-condition of our attaining to any insight or conviction at all. In a word, there is no other way of making sensuous man rational except by first making him aesthetic.

3. But, you will be tempted to object, can such mediation really be indispensable? Should truth and duty not be able, of and by themselves alone, to gain access to sensuous man? To which I must answer: they not only can, they positively must, owe their determining power to themselves alone; and nothing would be more at variance with my previous assertions than if they should seem to support the opposite view. It has been expressly proved that beauty can produce no result, neither for the understanding nor for the will; that it does not meddle in the business of either thinking or deciding; that it merely imparts the power to do both, but has no say whatsoever in the actual use of that power. In the actual use of it all other aid whatsoever is dispensed with; and the pure logical form, namely the concept, must speak directly to the understanding, the pure moral form, namely the law, directly to the will.

4. But for them to be able to do this at all, for such a thing as a pure form to exist for sensuous man at all, this, I insist, has first to be made possible by the aesthetic modulation of the psyche. Truth is not something which, like actuality or the physical existence of

M

Wirklichkeit oder das sinnliche Dasein der Dinge von aussen empfangen werden kann; sie ist etwas, das die Denkkraft selbsttätig und
in ihrer Freiheit hervorbringt, und diese Selbsttätigkeit, diese Freiheit ist es ja eben, was wir bei dem sinnlichen Menschen vermissen.
Der sinnliche Mensch ist schon (physisch) bestimmt und hat folglich
keine freie Bestimmbarkeit mehr: diese verlorne Bestimmbarkeit
muss er notwendig erst zurück erhalten, eh' er die leidende Bestimmung mit einer tätigen vertauschen kann. Er kann sie aber nicht
anders zurückerhalten, als entweder indem er die passive Bestimmung verliert, die er hatte, oder indem er die aktive schon
in sich enthält, zu welcher er übergehen soll. Verlöre er bloss
die passive Bestimmung, so würde er zugleich mit derselben auch
die Möglichkeit einer aktiven verlieren, weil der Gedanke einen
Körper braucht und die Form nur an einem Stoffe realisiert werden
kann. Er wird also die letztere schon in sich enthalten, er wird zugleich leidend und tätig bestimmt sein, das heisst, er wird ästhetisch
werden müssen.

5.　　Durch die ästhetische Gemütsstimmung wird also die Selbsttätigkeit der Vernunft schon auf dem Felde der Sinnlichkeit eröffnet, die Macht der Empfindung schon innerhalb ihrer eigenen
Grenzen gebrochen und der physische Mensch so weit veredelt,
dass nunmehr der geistige sich nach Gesetzen der Freiheit aus
demselben bloss zu entwickeln braucht. Der Schritt von dem ästhetischen Zustand zu dem logischen und moralischen (von der Schönheit zur Wahrheit und zur Pflicht) ist daher unendlich leichter, als
der Schritt von dem physischen Zustande zu dem ästhetischen (von
dem blossen blinden Leben zur Form) war. Jenen Schritt kann der
Mensch durch seine blosse Freiheit vollbringen, da er sich bloss zu
nehmen, und nicht zu geben, bloss seine Natur zu vereinzeln, nicht
zu erweitern braucht; der ästhetisch gestimmte Mensch wird allgemein gültig urteilen und allgemein gültig handeln, sobald er es
wollen wird. Den Schritt von der rohen Materie zur Schönheit, wo
eine ganz neue Tätigkeit in ihm eröffnet werden soll, muss die
Natur ihm erleichtern, und sein Wille kann über eine Stimmung
nichts gebieten, die ja dem Willen selbst erst das Dasein gibt. Um
den ästhetischen Menschen zur Einsicht und grossen Gesinnungen
zu führen, darf man ihm weiter nichts als wichtige Anlässe geben;
um von dem sinnlichen Menschen eben das zu erhalten, muss man
erst seine Natur verändern. Bei jenem braucht es oft nichts als die

things, can simply be received from without. It is something produced by our thinking faculty, autonomously and by virtue of its freedom. And it is precisely this autonomy, this freedom, which is lacking in sensuous man. Sensuous man is already (physically speaking) determined, and in consequence no longer possesses free determinability. This lost determinability he will first have to recover before he can exchange his passive determination for an active one. But he cannot recover it except by either losing the passive determination which he had, or by already possessing within himself the active determination towards which he is to proceed. Were he merely to lose the passive determination, he would at the same time lose the possibility of an active one, since thought needs a body, and form can only be realized in some material. He will, therefore, need to have the active determination already within him, need to be at one and the same time passively, and actively, determined; that is to say, he will have to become aesthetic.

5. Through the aesthetic modulation of the psyche, then, the autonomy of reason is already opened up within the domain of sense itself, the dominion of sensation already broken within its own frontiers, and physical man refined to the point where spiritual man only needs to start developing out of the physical according to the laws of freedom. The step from the aesthetic to the logical and moral state (i.e., from beauty to truth and duty) is hence infinitely easier than was the step from the physical state to the aesthetic (i.e., from merely blind living to form). The former step man can accomplish simply of his own free will, since it merely involves taking from himself, not giving to himself, fragmenting his nature, not enlarging it; the aesthetically tempered man will achieve universally valid judgements and universally valid actions, as soon as he has the will to do so. But the step from brute matter to beauty, in which a completely new kind of activity has to be opened up within him, must first be facilitated by the grace of Nature, for his will can exert no sort of compulsion upon a temper of mind which is, after all, the very means of bringing his will into existence. In order to lead aesthetic man to understanding and lofty sentiments, one need do no more than provide him with motives of sufficient weight. To obtain the same results from sensuous man we must first alter his very nature. Aesthetic man often needs no more than the

Aufforderung einer erhabenen Situation (die am unmittelbarsten auf das Willensvermögen wirkt), um ihn zum Held und zum Weisen zu machen; diesen muss man erst unter einen andern Himmel versetzen.

6. Es gehört also zu den wichtigsten Aufgaben der Kultur, den Menschen auch schon in seinem bloss physischen Leben der Form zu unterwerfen und ihn, so weit das Reich der Schönheit nur immer reichen kann, ästhetisch zu machen, weil nur aus dem ästhetischen, nicht aber aus dem physischen Zustande der moralische sich entwickeln kann. Soll der Mensch in jedem einzelnen Fall das Vermögen besitzen, sein Urteil und seinen Willen zum Urteil der Gattung zu machen, soll er aus jedem beschränkten Dasein den Durchgang zu einem unendlichen finden, aus jedem abhängigen Zustande zur Selbständigkeit und Freiheit den Aufschwung nehmen können, so muss dafür gesorgt werden, dass er in keinem Momente bloss Individuum sei und bloss dem Naturgesetz diene. Soll er fähig und fertig sein, aus dem engen Kreis der Naturzwecke sich zu Vernunftzwecken zu erheben, so muss er sich schon i n n e r h a l b   d e r   e r s t e r n für die letztern geübt und schon seine physische Bestimmung mit einer gewissen Freiheit der Geister, d. i. nach Gesetzen der Schönheit, ausgeführt haben.

7.   Und zwar kann er dieses, ohne dadurch im geringsten seinem physischen Zweck zu widersprechen. Die Anforderungen der Natur an ihn gehen bloss auf das, w a s   e r   w i r k t ,   a u f   d e n   I n h a l t seines Handelns; über die Art, w i e er wirkt, über die Form desselben, ist durch die Naturzwecke nichts bestimmt. Die Anforderungen der Vernunft hingegen sind streng auf die Form seiner Tätigkeit gerichtet. So notwendig es also für seine moralische Bestimmung ist, dass er rein moralisch sei, dass er eine absolute Selbsttätigkeit beweise, so gleichgültig ist es für seine physische Bestimmung, ob er rein physisch ist, ob er sich absolut leidend verhält. In Rücksicht auf diese letztere ist es also ganz in seine Willkür gestellt, ob er sie bloss als Sinnenwesen und als Naturkraft (als eine Kraft nämlich, welche nur wirkt, je nachdem sie erleidet), oder ob er sie zugleich als absolute Kraft, als Vernunftwesen ausführen will, und es dürfte wohl keine Frage sein, welches von beiden seiner Würde mehr entspricht. Vielmehr, so sehr es ihn erniedrigt und schändet, dasjenige aus sinnlichem Antriebe zu tun, wozu er sich aus reinen Motiven der Pflicht bestimmt haben sollte, so sehr ehrt und adelt es ihn, auch

challenge of a sublime situation (which is what acts most directly upon our will-power) to make of him a hero or a sage. Sensuous man must first be transported beneath another clime.

6.   It is, therefore, one of the most important tasks of education to subject man to form even in his purely physical life, and to make him aesthetic in every domain over which beauty is capable of extending her sway; since it is only out of the aesthetic, not out of the physical, state that the moral can develop. If man is, in every single case, to possess the power of enlarging his judgement and his will into the judgement of the species as a whole; if out of his limited existence he is to be able to find the path which will lead him through to an infinite existence, out of every dependent condition be able to wing his way towards autonomy and freedom: then we must see to it that he is in no single moment of his life a mere individual, and merely sub-servient to the law of nature. If he is to be fit and ready to raise him-self out of the restricted cycle of natural ends towards rational purposes, then he must already have prepared himself for the latter within the limits of the former, and have realized his physical destiny with a certain freedom of the spirit, that is, in accordance with the laws of beauty.

7.   And this he can indeed accomplish without in the least acting counter to his physical ends. The claims which nature makes upon him are directed merely to what he does, to the content of his actions; in the matter of how he does it, the form of his actions, the purposes of nature offer no directives whatsoever. The claims of reason, by contrast, are directed strictly towards the form of his activity. Necessary as it is, then, for his moral destiny that he should be purely moral, and display absolute autonomy, for his physical destiny it is a matter of complete indifference whether he is purely physical, and behaves with absolute passivity. In respect of the latter, it is left entirely to his own discretion whether he realizes it merely as sensuous being and natural force (i.e., as a force which only reacts as it is acted upon), or whether he will at the same time realize it as absolute force and rational being; and there should be no question as to which of these two ways is more in keeping with his human dignity. On the contrary, just as it debases and degrades him to do from physical impulse what he should have decided to do from pure motives of duty, so it dignifies and exalts him to strive for

da nach Gesetzmässigkeit, nach Harmonie, nach Unbeschränktheit zu streben, wo der gemeine Mensch nur sein erlaubtes Verlangen stillt.* Mit einem Wort: im Gebiete der Wahrheit und Moralität darf die Empfindung nichts zu bestimmen haben; aber im Bezirke der Glückseligkeit darf Form sein und darf der Spieltrieb gebieten.

8. Also hier schon, auf dem gleichgültigen Felde des physischen Lebens, muss der Mensch sein moralisches anfangen; noch in seinem Leiden muss er seine Selbsttätigkeit, noch innerhalb seiner sinnlichen Schranken seine Vernunftfreiheit beginnen. Schon seinen Neigungen muss er das Gesetz seines Willens auflegen; er muss,

* 1. Diese geistreiche und ästhetisch freie Behandlung gemeiner Wirklichkeit ist, wo man sie auch antrifft, das Kennzeichen einer e d e l n Seele. Edel ist überhaupt ein Gemüt zu nennen, welches die Gabe besitzt, auch das beschränkteste Geschäft und den kleinlichsten Gegenstand durch die Behandlungsweise in ein Unendliches zu verwandeln. Edel heisst jede Form, welche dem, was seiner Natur nach bloss d i e n t (blosses Mittel ist), das Gepräge der Selbständigkeit aufdrückt. Ein edler Geist begnügt sich nicht damit, selbst frei zu sein; er muss alles andere um sich her, auch das Leblose in Freiheit setzen. Schönheit aber ist der einzig mögliche Ausdruck der Freiheit in der Erscheinung. Der vorherrschende Ausdruck des V e r s t a n d e s in einem Gesicht, einem Kunstwerk u. dgl. kann daher niemals edel ausfallen, wie er denn auch niemals schön ist, weil er die Abhängigkeit (welche von der Zweckmässigkeit nicht zu trennen ist) heraushebt, anstatt sie zu verbergen.

2. Der Moralphilosoph lehrt uns zwar, dass man nie m e h r tun könne als seine Pflicht, und er hat vollkommen Recht, wenn er bloss die Beziehung meint, welche Handlungen auf das Moralgesetz haben. Aber bei Handlungen, welche sich bloss auf einen Zweck beziehen, ü b e r d i e s e n Z w e c k n o c h h i n a u s ins Übersinnliche gehen (welches hier nichts anders heissen kann als das Physische ästhetisch ausführen), heisst zugleich ü b e r d i e Pflicht h i n a u s gehen, indem diese nur vorschreiben kann, dass der W i l l e heilig sei, nicht dass auch schon die N a t u r sich geheiligt habe. Es gibt also zwar kein moralisches, aber es gibt ein ästhetisches Übertreffen der Pflicht; und ein solches Betragen heisst edel. Eben deswegen aber, weil bei dem Edeln immer ein Überfluss wahrgenommen wird, indem dasjenige auch einen freien formalen Wert besitzt, was bloss einen materialen zu haben brauchte, oder mit dem innern Wert, den es haben soll, noch einen äussern, der ihm fehlen dürfte, vereinigt, so haben manche ästhetischen Überfluss mit einem moralischen verwechselt und, von der Erscheinung des Edeln verführt, eine Willkür und Zufälligkeit in die Moralität selbst hineingetragen, wodurch sie ganz würde aufgehoben werden.

3. Von einem edeln Betragen ist ein erhabenes zu unterscheiden. Das erste geht über die sittliche Verbindlichkeit noch hinaus, aber nicht so das letztere, obgleich wir es ungleich höher als jenes achten. Wir achten es aber nicht deswegen, weil es den Vernunftbegriff seines Objekts (des Moralgesetzes), sondern weil es den Erfahrungsbegriff seines Subjekts (unsre Kenntnisse menschlicher Willensgüte und Willensstärke) übertrifft; so schätzen wir umgekehrt ein edles Betragen nicht darum, weil es die Natur des Subjekts überschreitet, aus der es vielmehr völlig zwanglos hervorfliessen muss, sondern weil es über die Natur seines Objekts (den physischen Zweck) hinaus in das Geisterreich schreitet. Dort, möchte man sagen, erstaunen wir über den Sieg, den der Gegenstand über den Menschen davonträgt; hier bewundern wir den Schwung, den der Mensch dem Gegenstande gibt.

order, harmony, and infinite freedom in those matters where the common man is content merely to satisfy his legitimate desires.* In a word: in the realm of truth and morality, feeling may have no say whatsoever; but in the sphere of being and well-being, form has every right to exist, and the play-drive every right to command.

8. It is here, then, in the indifferent sphere of physical life, that man must make a start upon his moral life; here, while he is still passive, already start to manifest his autonomy, and while still within the limitations of sense begin to make some show of rational freedom. The law of his will he must apply even to his inclinations; he must,

* 1. This genial and aesthetically free handling of common reality is, wherever it may be found, the mark of a n o b l e soul. In general we call noble any nature which possesses the gift of transforming, purely by its manner of handling it, even the most trifling occupation, or the most petty of objects, into something infinite. We call that form noble which impresses the stamp of autonomy upon anything which by its nature merely s e r v e s s o m e p u r p o s e (is a mere means). A noble nature is not content to be itself free; it must also set free everything around it, even the lifeless. Beauty, however, is the only way that freedom has of making itself manifest in appearance. That is why a face, a work of art, or the like, which expresses i n t e l l i g e n c e more than anything else, can never strike us as noble, any more than it is beautiful, since it emphasizes a relation of dependence (which is inseparable from purposefulness) instead of concealing it.

2. The moral philosopher does, it is true, teach us that man can never do m o r e than his duty; and he is perfectly right if he merely has in mind the relation between actions and the moral law. But in the case of actions which are merely end-serving, to e x c e e d the e n d, and pass beyond it into the supra-sensible (which in the present context can mean nothing more than carrying out the physical in an aesthetic manner), is in fact to e x c e e d d u t y, since duty can only prescribe that the w i l l be sacred, but not that n a t u r e i t s e l f shall have taken on sacral character. There is thus no possibility of a moral transcendence of duty; but there is such a thing as an aesthetic transcendence; and such conduct we call noble. But just because an element of supererogation can always be discerned in noble conduct—inasmuch as what was only required to have material value has acquired a free formal value, or, in other words, has combined with the inner value, which it ought to have, an outer value, which it could legitimately do without—for this reason many have confused aesthetic supererogation with moral, and, misled by the appearance of what is noble, have imported into morality an element of arbitrariness and contingency which would end in its entire destruction.

3. Noble conduct is to be distinguished from sublime conduct. The first transcends moral obligation; not so the latter, although we rate it incomparably higher. But we do not thus esteem it because it exceeds the rational concept of its object (i.e., the moral law), but because it exceeds the empirical concept of its subject (i.e., our experience of the goodness and strength of the human will). Conversely, we do not prize noble conduct because it surpasses the nature of its subject—on the contrary, it must flow freely and without constraint out of this—but because it surpasses the nature of its object (i.e., its physical end) and passes beyond this into the realm of spirit. In the first case, one might say, we marvel at the victory which the object achieves over man; in the latter we admire the *élan* which man imparts to the object.

wenn Sie mir den Ausdruck verstatten wollen, den Krieg gegen die Materie in ihre eigene Grenze spielen, damit er es überhoben sei, auf dem heiligen Boden der Freiheit gegen diesen furchtbaren Feind zu fechten; er muss lernen e d l e r begehren, damit er nicht nötig habe, e r h a b e n z u w o l l e n. Dieses wird geleistet durch ästhetische Kultur, welche alles das, worüber weder Naturgesetze die menschliche Willkür binden noch Vernunftgesetze, Gesetzen der Schönheit unterwirft und in der Form, die sie dem äussern Leben gibt, schon das innere eröffnet.

if you will permit me the expression, p l a y the war against Matter into the very territory of Matter itself, so that he may be spared having to fight this dread foe on the sacred soil of Freedom. He must learn to desire m o r e n o b l y, so that he may not need t o w i l l s u b l i m e l y. This is brought about by means of aesthetic education, which subjects to laws of beauty all those spheres of human behaviour in which neither natural laws, nor yet rational laws, are binding upon human caprice, and which, in the form it gives to outer life, already opens up the inner.

VIERUNDZWANZIGSTER BRIEF

1. Es lassen sich also drei verschiedene Momente oder Stufen der Entwicklung unterscheiden, die sowohl der einzelne Mensch als die ganze Gattung notwendig und in einer bestimmten Ordnung durchlaufen müssen, wenn sie den ganzen Kreis ihrer Bestimmung erfüllen sollen. Durch zufällige Ursachen, die entweder in dem Einfluss der äussern Dinge oder in der freien Willkür des Menschen liegen, können zwar die einzelnen Perioden bald verlängert, bald abgekürzt, aber keine kann ganz übersprungen, und auch die Ordnung, in welcher sie auf einander folgen, kann weder durch die Natur noch durch den Willen umgekehrt werden. Der Mensch in seinem p h y s i s c h e n Zustand erleidet bloss die Macht der Natur; er entledigt sich dieser Macht in dem ä s t h e t i s c h e n Zustand, und er beherrscht sie in dem m o r a l i s c h e n.

2. Was ist der Mensch, ehe die Schönheit die freie Lust ihm entlockt und die ruhige Form das wilde Leben besänftigt? Ewig einförmig in seinen Zwecken, ewig wechselnd in seinen Urteilen, selbstsüchtig, ohne Er selbst zu sein, ungebunden, ohne frei zu sein, Sklave, ohne einer Regel zu dienen. In dieser Epoche ist ihm die Welt bloss Schicksal, noch nicht Gegenstand; alles hat nur Existenz für ihn, insofern es ihm Existenz verschafft; was ihm weder gibt noch nimmt, ist ihm gar nicht vorhanden. Einzeln und abgeschnitten, wie er sich selbst in der Reihe der Wesen findet, steht jede Erscheinung vor ihm da. Alles, was ist, ist ihm durch das Machtwort des Augenblicks; jede Veränderung ist ihm eine ganz frische Schöpfung, weil mit dem Notwendigen i n i h m die Notwendigkeit a u s s e r i h m fehlt, welche die wechselnden Gestalten in ein Weltall zusammenbindet und, indem das Individuum flieht, das Gesetz auf dem Schauplatze festhält. Umsonst lässt die Natur ihre reiche Mannigfaltigkeit an seinen Sinnen vorübergehen; er sieht in ihrer herrlichen Fülle nichts als seine Beute, in ihrer Macht und Grösse nichts als seinen Feind. Entweder er stürzt auf die Gegenstände und will sie in sich reissen, in der Begierde; oder die Gegenstände dringen zerstörend auf ihn ein, und er stösst sie von sich, in der Verabscheuung. In beiden Fällen ist sein Verhältnis zur Sinnenwelt unmittelbare B e r ü h r u n g, und ewig von ihrem Andrang

TWENTY-FOURTH LETTER

1. WE can, then, distinguish three different moments or stages of development through which both the individual and the species as a whole must pass, inevitably and in a definite order, if they are to complete the full cycle of their destiny. Through contingent causes, deriving either from the influence of external circumstances or from the arbitrary caprice of man himself, these several periods may indeed be either lengthened or shortened, but no one of them can be left out altogether; nor can the order in which they follow upon each other be reversed, neither by the power of nature nor by that of the will. Man in his p h y s i c a l state merely suffers the dominion of nature; he emancipates himself from this dominion in the a e s t h e t i c state, and he acquires mastery over it in the m o r a l.

2. What is man before beauty cajoles from him a delight in things for their own sake, or the serenity of form tempers the savagery of life? A monotonous round of ends, a constant vacillation of judgements; self-seeking, and yet without a Self; lawless, yet without Freedom; a slave, yet to no Rule. At this stage the world is for him merely Fate, not yet Object; nothing exists for him except what furthers his own existence; that which neither gives to him, nor takes from him, is not there for him at all. Each phenomenon stands before him, isolated and cut off from all other things, even as he himself is isolated and unrelated in the great chain of being. All that exists, exists for him only at the behest of the moment; every change seems to him an entirely new creation, since with the lack of necessity within him there is none outside of him either, to connect the changing forms into a universe and, though individual phenomena pass away, to hold fast upon the stage of the world the unvarying law which informs them. In vain does nature let her rich variety pass before his senses; he sees in her splendid profusion nothing but his prey, in all her might and grandeur nothing but his foe. Either he hurls himself upon objects to devour them in an access of desire; or the objects press in upon him to destroy him, and he thrusts them away in horror. In either case his relation to the world of sense is that of immediate c o n t a c t; and eternally anguished by

geängstigt, rastlos von dem gebieterischen Bedürfnis gequält, findet
er nirgends Ruhe als in der Ermattung und nirgends Grenzen als
in der erschöpften Begier.

> Zwar die gewalt'ge Brust und der Titanen
> Kraftvolles Mark ist sein...
> Gewisses Erbteil; doch es schmiedete
> Der Gott um seine Stirn ein ehern Band.
> Rat, Mässigung und Weisheit und Geduld
> Verbarg er seinem scheuen düstern Blick.
> Es wird zur Wut ihm jegliche Begier,
> Und grenzenlos dringt seine Wut umher.
>
> *Iphigenie auf Tauris*

Mit s e i n e r Menschenwürde unbekannt, ist er weit entfernt, sie
in andern zu ehren, und der eignen wilden Gier sich bewusst, fürch-
tet er sie in jedem Geschöpf, das ihm ähnlich sieht. Nie erblickt
er andre in sich, nur sich in andern, und die Gesellschaft, anstatt
ihn zur Gattung auszudehnen, schliesst ihn nur enger und enger in
sein Individuum ein. In dieser dumpfen Beschränkung irrt er durch
das nachtvolle Leben, bis eine günstige Natur die Last des Stoffes
von seinen verfinsterten Sinnen wälzt, die Reflexion i h n s e l b s t
von den Dingen scheidet und im Widerscheine des Bewusstseins
sich endlich die Gegenstände zeigen.

3. Dieser Zustand roher Natur lässt sich freilich, so wie er hier
geschildert wird, bei keinem bestimmten Volk und Zeitalter nach-
weisen; er ist bloss Idee, aber eine Idee, mit der die Erfahrung in
einzelnen Zügen aufs genaueste zusammen stimmt. Der Mensch,
kann man sagen, war nie ganz in diesem tierischen Zustand, aber
er ist ihm auch nie ganz entflohen. Auch in den rohesten Subjekten
findet man unverkennbare Spuren von Vernunftfreiheit, so wie es
in den gebildetsten nicht an Momenten fehlt, die an jenen düstern
Naturstand erinnern. Es ist dem Menschen einmal eigen, das
Höchste und das Niedrigste in seiner Natur zu vereinigen, und
wenn seine W ü r d e auf einer strengen Unterscheidung des einen
von dem andern beruht, so beruht auf einer geschickten Aufhebung
dieses Unterschieds seine G l ü c k s e l i g k e i t. Die Kultur, welche
seine Würde mit seiner Glückseligkeit in Übereinstimmung bringen
soll, wird also für die höchste Reinheit jener beiden Prinzipien in
ihrer innigsten Vermischung zu sorgen haben.

its pressures, ceaselessly tortured by imperious needs, he finds rest nowhere but in exhaustion, and limits nowhere but in spent desire.

> His violent passions and the Titans'
> Vigorous marrow are his ...
> Certain heritage; yet round his brow
> Zeus forged a brazen band.
> Counsel and Patience, Wisdom, Moderation
> He shrouded from his fearful sullen glance.
> In him each passion grows to savage fury,
> And all uncheck'd his fury rages round.
>
> *Iphigenia in Tauris*

Unacquainted as yet with h i s   o w n human dignity, he is far from respecting it in others; and, conscious of his own savage greed, he fears it in every creature which resembles him. He never sees others in himself, but only himself in others; and communal life, far from enlarging him into a representative of the species, only confines him ever more narrowly within his own individuality. In this state of sullen limitation he gropes his way through the darkness of his life until a kindly nature shifts the burden of matter from his beclouded senses, and he learns through reflection to distinguish h i m s e l f from things, so that objects reveal themselves at last in the reflected light of consciousness.

3.   This state of brute nature is not, I admit, to be found exactly as I have presented it here among any particular people or in any particular age. It is purely an Idea; but an idea with which experience is, in certain particulars, in complete accord. Man, one may say, was never in such a completely animal condition; but he has, on the other hand, never entirely escaped from it. Even among the rudest of human creatures one finds unmistakable traces of rational freedom, just as among the most cultivated peoples there are moments in plenty which recall that dismal state of nature. It is, after all, peculiar to man that he unites in his nature the highest and the lowest; and if his m o r a l   d i g n i t y depends on his distinguishing strictly between the one and the other, h i s   h o p e   o f j o y   a n d   b l e s s e d n e s s depends on a due and proper reconciliation of the opposites he has distinguished. An education which is to bring his dignity into harmony with his happiness will, therefore, have to see to it that those two principles are maintained in their utmost purity even while they are being most intimately fused.

4. Die erste Erscheinung der Vernunft in dem Menschen ist darum noch nicht auch der Anfang seiner Menschheit. Diese wird erst durch seine Freiheit entschieden, und die Vernunft fängt erstlich damit an, seine sinnliche Abhängigkeit grenzenlos zu machen; ein Phänomen, das mir für seine Wichtigkeit und Allgemeinheit noch nicht gehörig entwickelt scheint. Die Vernunft, wissen wir, gibt sich in dem Menschen durch die Forderung des Absoluten (auf sich selbst Gegründeten und Notwendigen) zu erkennen, welche, da ihr in keinem einzelnen Zustand seines physischen Lebens Genüge geleistet werden kann, ihn das Physische ganz und gar zu verlassen und von einer beschränkten Wirklichkeit zu Ideen aufzusteigen nötigt. Aber obgleich der wahre Sinn jener Forderung ist, ihn den Schranken der Zeit zu entreissen und von der sinnlichen Welt zu einer Idealwelt empor zu führen, so kann sie doch durch eine (in dieser Epoche der herrschenden Sinnlichkeit kaum zu vermeidende) Missdeutung auf das physische Leben sich richten und den Menschen, anstatt ihn unabhängig zu machen, in die furchtbarste Knechtschaft stürzen.

5. Und so verhält es sich auch in der Tat. Auf den Flügeln der Einbildungskraft verlässt der Mensch die engen Schranken der Gegenwart, in welche die blosse Tierheit sich einschliesst, um vorwärts nach einer unbeschränkten Zukunft zu streben; aber indem vor seiner schwindelnden I m a g i n a t i o n das Unendliche aufgeht, hat sein Herz noch nicht aufgehört, im Einzelnen zu leben und dem Augenblick zu dienen. Mitten in seiner Tierheit überrascht ihn der Trieb zum Absoluten — und da in diesem dumpfen Zustande alle seine Bestrebungen bloss auf das Materielle und Zeitliche gehen und bloss auf sein Individuum sich begrenzen, so wird er durch jene Forderung bloss veranlasst, sein Individuum, anstatt von demselben zu abstrahieren, ins Endlose auszudehnen, anstatt nach Form nach einem unversiegenden Stoff, anstatt nach dem Unveränderlichen nach einer ewig dauernden Veränderung und nach einer absoluten Versicherung seines zeitlichen Daseins zu streben. Der nämliche Trieb, der ihn, auf sein Denken und Tun angewendet, zur Wahrheit und Moralität führen sollte, bringt jetzt, auf sein Leiden und Empfinden bezogen, nichts als ein unbegrenztes Verlangen, als ein absolutes Bedürfnis hervor. Die ersten Früchte, die er in dem Geisterreich erntet, sind also S o r g e und F u r c h t ; beides Wirkungen der Vernunft, nicht der Sinnlichkeit, aber einer

4. The first appearance of Reason in man does not necessarily imply that he has started to become truly human. This has to wait upon his Freedom; and the first thing reason does is to make him utterly dependent upon his senses—a phenomenon which, for all its universality and importance, has still, so it seems to me, never been properly explored. It is, as we know, through the demand for the Absolute (as that which is grounded upon itself and necessary) that Reason makes itself known in man. This demand, since it can never be wholly satisfied in any single condition of his physical life, forces him to leave the physical altogether, and ascend out of a limited reality into the realm of ideas. But although the true purport of such a demand is to wrest him from the bondage of time, and lead him upwards from the sensuous world towards an ideal world, it can, through a misunderstanding (almost unavoidable in this early epoch of prevailing materiality), be directed towards physical life, and instead of making man independent plunge him into the most terrifying servitude.

5. And this is what does in fact happen. On the wings of fancy, man leaves the narrow confines of the present in which mere animality stays bound, in order to strive towards an unlimited future. But while the infinite opens up before his reeling i m a g i n a t i o n, his heart has not yet ceased to live in the particular or to wait upon the moment. In the very midst of his animality the drive towards the Absolute catches him unawares—and since in this state of apathy all his endeavour is directed merely towards the material and the temporal, and limited exclusively to himself as individual, he will merely be induced by that demand to give his own individuality unlimited extension rather than to abstract from it altogether: will be led to strive, not after form, but after an unfailing supply of matter; not after changelessness, but after perpetually enduring change; and after the absolute assurance of his temporal existence. That very drive which, applied to his thinking and activity, was meant to lead him to truth and morality, brought now to bear upon his passivity and feeling, produces nothing but unlimited longing and absolute instinctual need. The first fruits which he reaps in the realm of spirit are, therefore, C a r e and F e a r; both of them products of reason, not of sense; but of a reason which mistakes its

Vernunft, die sich in ihrem Gegenstand vergreift und ihren Imperativ unmittelbar auf den Stoff anwendet. Früchte dieses Baumes sind alle unbedingte Glückseligkeitssysteme, sie mögen den heutigen Tag oder das ganze Leben oder, was sie um nichts ehrwürdiger macht, die ganze Ewigkeit zu ihrem Gegenstand haben. Eine grenzenlose Dauer des Daseins und Wohlseins, bloss um des Daseins und Wohlseins willen, ist bloss ein Ideal der Begierde, mithin eine Forderung, die nur von einer ins Absolute strebenden Tierheit kann aufgeworfen werden. Ohne also durch eine Vernunftäusserung dieser Art etwas für seine Menschheit zu gewinnen, verliert er dadurch bloss die glückliche Beschränktheit des Tiers, vor welchem er nun bloss den unbeneidenswerten Vorzug besitzt, über dem Streben in die Ferne den Besitz der Gegenwart zu verlieren, ohne doch in der ganzen grenzenlosen Ferne je etwas anders als die Gegenwart zu suchen.

6.   Aber wenn sich die Vernunft auch in ihrem Objekt nicht vergreift und in der Frage nicht irrt, so wird die Sinnlichkeit noch lange Zeit die Antwort verfälschen. Sobald der Mensch angefangen hat, seinen Verstand zu brauchen und die Erscheinungen umher nach Ursachen und Zwecken zu verknüpfen, so dringt die Vernunft, ihrem Begriffe gemäss, auf eine absolute Verknüpfung und auf einen unbedingten Grund. Um sich eine solche Forderung auch nur aufwerfen zu können, muss der Mensch über die Sinnlichkeit schon hinausgeschritten sein; aber eben dieser Forderung bedient sie sich, um den Flüchtling zurückzuholen. Hier wäre nämlich der Punkt, wo er die Sinnenwelt ganz und gar verlassen und zum reinen Ideenreich sich aufschwingen müsste; denn der Verstand bleibt ewig innerhalb des Bedingten stehen und frägt ewig fort, ohne je auf ein Letztes zu geraten. Da aber der Mensch, von dem hier geredet wird, einer solchen Abstraktion noch nicht fähig ist, so wird er, was er in seinem sinnlichen E r k e n n t n i s k r e i s e nicht findet und über denselben hinaus in der reinen Vernunft noch nicht sucht, unter demselben in seinem G e f ü h l k r e i s e suchen und dem Scheine nach finden. Die Sinnlichkeit zeigt ihm zwar nichts, was sein eigener Grund wäre und sich selbst das Gesetz gäbe; aber sie zeigt ihm etwas, was von keinem Grunde weiss und kein Gesetz achtet. Da er also den fragenden Verstand durch keinen letzten und innern Grund zur Ruhe bringen kann, so bringt er ihn durch den Begriff des G r u n d l o s e n wenigstens zum Schweigen und bleibt

object and applies its imperative directly to matter. Fruits of this same tree are all your systems of unqualified eudemonism, whether they have as their object the present day, or the whole of our life, or—and this by no means makes them any more worthy of respect— the whole of eternity. An unlimited perpetuation of being and well-being, merely for the sake of being and well-being, is an ideal which belongs to appetite alone, hence a demand that can only be made by an animality striving towards the Absolute. Thus, without gaining anything for his humanity through such manifestations of reason, man merely loses thereby the happy limitation of the animal, over which he now possesses none but the—far from enviable—advantage of having forfeited possession of the here and now in favour of longings for what is not, yet without seeking in all those limitless vistas anything but the here and now he already knows.

6. But even if Reason does not mistake its objective and confuse the question, Sense will for a long time falsify the answer. As soon as man has begun to use his intellect, and to connect the phenomena around him in the relation of cause and effect, Reason, in accordance with its very definition, presses for an absolute connexion and an unconditioned cause. In order to be able to postulate such a demand at all, man must already have taken a step beyond mere sense; but it is this very demand that Sense now makes use of to recall her truant child. This, strictly speaking, would be the point at which he ought to leave the world of sense altogether, and soar upwards to the realm of pure ideas; for the intellect remains eternally confined within the realm of the conditioned, and goes on eternally asking questions without ever lighting upon any ultimate answer. But since the man with whom we are here concerned is not yet capable of such abstraction, that which he cannot find in his s p h e r e o f e m p i r i c a l k n o w l e d g e, and does not yet seek beyond it in the sphere of pure Reason, he will seek beneath it in his s p h e r e o f f e e l i n g and, to all appearances, find it. True, this world of sense shows him nothing which might be its own cause and subject to none but its own law; but it does show him something which knows of no cause and obeys no law. Since, then, he cannot appease his inquiring intellect by evoking any ultimate and inward cause, he manages at least to silence it with the notion of n o - c a u s e, and

innerhalb der blinden Nötigung der Materie stehen, da er die erhabene Notwendigkeit der Vernunft noch nicht zu erfassen vermag. Weil die Sinnlichkeit keinen andern Z w e c k kennt als ihren Vorteil und sich durch keine andre U r s a c h e als den blinden Zufall getrieben fühlt, so macht er jenen zum Bestimmer seiner Handlungen und diesen zum Beherrscher der Welt.

7. Selbst das Heilige im Menschen, das Moralgesetz, kann bei seiner ersten Erscheinung in der Sinnlichkeit dieser Verfälschung nicht entgehen. Da es bloss verbietend und gegen das Interesse seiner sinnlichen Selbstliebe spricht, so muss es ihm so lange als etwas Auswärtiges erscheinen, als er noch nicht dahin gelangt ist, jene Selbstliebe als das Auswärtige und die Stimme der Vernunft als sein wahres Selbst anzusehen. Er empfindet also bloss die Fesseln, welche die letztere ihm anlegt, nicht die unendliche Befreiung, die sie ihm verschafft. Ohne die Würde des Gesetzgebers in sich zu ahnen, empfindet er bloss den Zwang und das ohnmächtige Widerstreben des Untertans. Weil der sinnliche Trieb dem moralischen in seiner Erfahrung v o r h e r g e h t, so gibt er dem Gesetz der Notwendigkeit einen Anfang in der Zeit, einen p o s i t i v e n Ursprung, und durch den unglückseligsten aller Irrtümer macht er das Unveränderliche und Ewige in Sich zu einem Accidens des Vergänglichen. Er überredet sich, die Begriffe von Recht und Unrecht als Statuten anzusehen, die durch einen Willen eingeführt wurden, nicht die an sich selbst und in alle Ewigkeit gültig sind. Wie er in Erklärung einzelner Naturphänomene über die N a t u r hinaus schreitet und ausserhalb derselben sucht, was nur in ihrer innern Gesetzmässigkeit kann gefunden werden, ebenso schreitet er in Erklärung des Sittlichen über die V e r n u n f t hinaus und verscherzt seine Menschheit, indem er auf diesem Weg eine Gottheit sucht. Kein Wunder, wenn eine Religion, die mit Wegwerfung seiner Menschheit erkauft wurde, sich einer solchen Abstammung würdig zeigt, wenn er Gesetze, die nicht v o n Ewigkeit her banden, auch nicht für unbedingt und i n alle Ewigkeit bindend hält. Er hat es nicht mit einem heiligen, bloss mit einem mächtigen Wesen zu tun. Der Geist seiner Gottesverehrung ist also Furcht, die ihn erniedrigt, nicht Ehrfurcht, die ihn in seiner eigenen Schätzung erhebt.

8. Obgleich diese mannigfaltigen Abweichungen des Menschen von dem Ideale seiner Bestimmung nicht alle in der nämlichen

remains within the blind compulsion of Matter since he is not yet capable of grasping the sublime necessity of Reason. Because the life of sense knows no p u r p o s e other than its own advantage, and feels driven by no c a u s e other than blind chance, he makes the former into the arbiter of his actions and the latter into the sovereign ruler of the world.

7. Even what is most sacred in man, the moral law, when it first makes its appearance in the life of sense, cannot escape such perversion. Since its voice is merely inhibitory, and against the interest of his animal self-love, it is bound to seem like something external to himself as long as he has not yet reached the point of regarding his self-love as the thing that is really external to him, and the voice of reason as his true self. Hence he merely feels the fetters which reason lays upon him, not the infinite liberation which she is capable of affording him. Without suspecting the dignity of the lawgiver within, he merely experiences its coercive force and feels the impotent resistance of a powerless subject. Because in his experience the sense-drive p r e c e d e s the moral, he assigns to the law of necessity a beginning in time too, a p o s i t i v e   o r i g i n, and through this most unfortunate of all errors makes the unchangeable and eternal in himself into an accidental product of the transient. He persuades himself into regarding the concepts of right and wrong as statutes introduced by some will, not as something valid in themselves for all eternity. Just as in the explanation of particular natural phenomena he goes beyond N a t u r e and seeks outside of it what can only be found in the laws inherent within it, so too, in the explanation of the moral world, he goes beyond R e a s o n and forfeits his humanity by seeking a Godhead along these same lines. No wonder that a religion bought by the debasement of his humanity proves itself worthy of such an origin, or that man considers laws which were not binding f r o m all eternity as not unconditional and not binding t o all eternity either. His concern is not with a holy, but merely with a powerful, Being. The spirit in which he worships God is therefore fear, which degrades him, not reverence, which exalts him in his own estimation.

8. Although these manifold aberrations from the ideal that man is meant to achieve cannot all take place in the same epoch—since in

Epoche statthaben können, indem derselbe von der Gedanken-
losigkeit zum Irrtum, von der Willenlosigkeit zur Willensverderbnis
mehrere Stufen zu durchwandern hat, so gehören doch alle zum
Gefolge des physischen Zustandes, weil in allen der Trieb des
Lebens über den Formtrieb den Meister spielt. Es sei nun, dass die
Vernunft in dem Menschen noch gar nicht gesprochen habe und
das Physische noch mit blinder Notwendigkeit über ihn herrsche;
oder dass sich die Vernunft noch nicht genug von den Sinnen gereinigt habe und das Moralische dem Physischen noch diene: so
ist in beiden Fällen das einzige in ihm gewalthabende Prinzip ein
materielles und der Mensch, wenigstens seiner letzten Tendenz
nach, ein sinnliches Wesen; mit dem einzigen Unterschied, dass er
in dem ersten Fall ein vernunftloses, in dem zweiten ein vernünftiges Tier ist. Er soll aber keines von beiden, er soll Mensch sein;
die Natur soll ihn nicht ausschliessend und die Vernunft soll ihn
nicht bedingt beherrschen. Beide Gesetzgebungen sollen vollkommen unabhängig von einander bestehen, und dennoch vollkommen
einig sein.

order to move from absence of thought to error of thought, from lack of will to perversion of will, he must pass through several stages—these deviations are nevertheless all attendant upon his physical condition, since in all of them the life-impulse plays the master over the form-impulse. Whether it, then, be that reason has not yet made its voice heard in man, and the physical still rules him with blind necessity; or that reason has not yet sufficiently purified itself of sense, and the moral is still at the service of the physical: in either case the sole principle prevailing within him is a material one, and man is, at least in his ultimate tendency, a creature of sense—with this sole difference, that in the first case he is an animal void of reason, in the second an animal endowed with reason. What he is meant to be, however, is neither of these; he is meant to be a human being. Nature is not meant to rule him exclusively, nor Reason to rule him conditionally. Both these systems of rule are meant to co-exist, in perfect independence of each other, and yet in perfect concord.

FÜNFUNDZWANZIGSTER BRIEF

1. SOLANGE der Mensch, in seinem ersten physischen Zustande, die Sinnenwelt bloss leidend in sich aufnimmt, bloss empfindet, ist er auch noch völlig Eins mit derselben, und eben weil er selbst bloss Welt ist, so ist für ihn noch keine Welt. Erst wenn er in seinem ästhetischen Stande sie ausser sich stellt oder b e t r a c h t e t, sondert sich seine Persönlichkeit von ihr ab, und es erscheint ihm eine Welt, weil er aufgehört hat, mit derselben Eins auszumachen.*

2. Die Betrachtung (Reflexion) ist das erste liberale Verhältnis des Menschen zu dem Weltall, das ihn umgibt. Wenn die Begierde ihren Gegenstand unmittelbar ergreift, so rückt die Betrachtung den ihrigen in die Ferne und macht ihn eben dadurch zu ihrem wahren und unverlierbaren Eigentum, dass sie ihn vor der Leidenschaft flüchtet. Die Notwendigkeit der Natur, die ihn im Zustand der blossen Empfindung mit ungeteilter Gewalt beherrschte, lässt bei der Reflexion von ihm ab, in den Sinnen erfolgt ein augenblicklicher Friede, die Zeit selbst, das ewig Wandelnde, steht still, indem des Bewusstseins zerstreute Strahlen sich sammeln, und ein Nachbild des Unendlichen, die F o r m, reflektiert sich auf dem vergänglichen Grunde. Sobald es Licht wird in dem Menschen, ist auch ausser ihm keine Nacht mehr; sobald es stille wird in ihm, legt sich auch der Sturm in dem Weltall, und die streitenden Kräfte der Natur finden Ruhe zwischen bleibenden Grenzen. Daher kein Wunder, wenn die uralten Dichtungen von dieser grossen Begebenheit im Innern des Menschen als von einer Revolution in der Aussenwelt

---

* Ich erinnere noch einmal, dass diese beiden Perioden zwar in der Idee notwendig von einander zu trennen sind, in der Erfahrung aber sich mehr oder weniger vermischen. Auch muss man nicht denken, als ob es eine Zeit gegeben habe, wo der Mensch nur in diesem physischen Stande sich befunden, und eine Zeit, wo er sich ganz von demselben losgemacht hätte. Sobald der Mensch einen G e g e n s t a n d s i e h t, so ist er schon nicht mehr in einem bloss physischen Zustand, und solang' er fortfahren wird, einen Gegenstand zu sehen, wird er auch jenem physischen Stand nicht entlaufen, weil er ja nur sehen kann, insofern er empfindet. Jene drei Momente, welche ich am Anfang des vierundzwanzigsten Briefs namhaft machte, sind also zwar, im ganzen betrachtet, drei verschiedene Epochen für die Entwicklung der ganzen Menschheit und für die ganze Entwicklung eines einzelnen Menschen; aber sie lassen sich auch bei jeder einzelnen Wahrnehmung eines Objekts unterscheiden und sind mit einem Wort die notwendigen Bedingungen jeder Erkenntnis, die wir durch die Sinne erhalten.

TWENTY-FIFTH LETTER

1. As long as man, in that first physical state, is merely a passive recipient of the world of sense, i.e., does no more than feel, he is still completely One with that world; and just because he is himself nothing but world, there exists for him as yet no world. Only when, at the aesthetic stage, he puts it outside himself, or c o n-templates it, does his personality differentiate itself from it, and a world becomes manifest to him because he has ceased to be One with it.*

2. Contemplation (or reflection) is the first liberal relation which man establishes with the universe around him. If desire seizes directly upon its object, contemplation removes its object to a distance, and makes it into a true and inalienable possession by putting it beyond the reach of passion. The necessity of nature, which in the stage of mere sensation ruled him with undivided authority, begins at the stage of reflection to relax its hold upon him. In his senses there results a momentary peace; time itself, the eternally moving, stands still; and, as the divergent rays of consciousness converge, there is reflected against a background of transcience an image of the infinite, namely f o r m. As soon as light dawns within man, there is no longer any night without; as soon as it grows still within him, the storm in the universe abates and the contending forces of nature come to rest between stable confines. Small wonder, then, that the most primitive poetry speaks of this great happening in the inner world of man as though it were

---

* I remind my readers once again that, necessary as it is to distinguish these two periods in theory, in practice they more or less merge one into the other. Nor must we imagine that there ever was a time when man found himself purely at the physical stage, or another when he had entirely freed himself from it. From the moment man s e e s a n o b j e c t, he is no longer in a merely physical state; and as long as he continues to see objects, he will not entirely have escaped from that physical stage; for only inasmuch as he has physical sensations is he able to see at all. In a general way, then, those three moments which I mentioned at the beginning of the twenty-fourth Letter may well be considered as three different epochs, if we are thinking either of the development of mankind as a whole, or of the whole development of a single individual; but they are also to be distinguished in each single act of perception, and are, in a word, the necessary conditions of all knowledge which comes to us through the senses.

reden und den Gedanken, der über die Zeitgesetze siegt, unter dem Bilde des Z e u s versinnlichen, der das Reich des Saturnus endigt.

3.   Aus einem Sklaven der Natur, solang' er sie bloss empfindet, wird der Mensch ihr Gesetzgeber, sobald er sie denkt. Die ihn vor-dem nur als M a c h t beherrschte, steht jetzt als O b j e k t vor sei-nem Blick. Was ihm Objekt ist, hat keine Gewalt über ihn, denn um Objekt zu sein, muss es die seinige erfahren. Soweit er der Materie Form gibt, und solange er sie gibt, ist er ihren Wirkungen unver-letzlich; denn einen Geist kann nichts verletzen, als was ihm die Freiheit raubt, und er beweist ja die seinige, indem er das Form-lose bildet. Nur wo die Masse schwer und gestaltlos herrscht und zwischen unsichern Grenzen die trüben Umrisse wanken, hat die Furcht ihren Sitz; jedem Schrecknis der Natur ist der Mensch überlegen, sobald er ihm Form zu geben und es in sein Objekt zu verwandeln weiss. So wie er anfängt, seine Selbständigkeit gegen die Natur als Erscheinung zu behaupten, so behauptet er auch gegen die Natur als Macht seine Würde, und mit edler Freiheit richtet er sich auf gegen seine Götter. Sie werfen die Gespensterlarven ab, womit sie seine Kindheit geängstigt hatten, und überraschen ihn mit seinem eigenen Bild, indem sie seine Vorstellung werden. Das göttliche Monstrum des Morgenländers, das mit der blinden Stärke des Raubtiers die Welt verwaltet, zieht sich in der griechischen Phantasie in den freundlichen Contour der Menschheit zusammen, das Reich der Titanen fällt, und die unendliche Kraft ist durch die unendliche Form gebändigt.

4.   Aber indem ich bloss einen Ausgang aus der materiellen Welt und einen Übergang in die Geisterwelt suchte, hat mich der freie Lauf meiner Einbildungskraft schon mitten in die letztere hinein-geführt. Die Schönheit, die wir suchen, liegt bereits hinter uns, und wir haben sie übersprungen, indem wir von dem blossen Leben unmittelbar zu der reinen Gestalt und zu dem reinen Objekt übergingen. Ein solcher Sprung ist nicht in der menschlichen Natur, und um gleichen Schritt mit dieser zu halten, werden wir zu der Sinnenwelt wieder umkehren müssen.

5.   Die Schönheit ist allerdings das Werk der freien Betrachtung, und wir treten mit ihr in die Welt der Ideen — aber was wohl zu

a revolution in the outer, and symbolizes thought triumphing over the laws of time by the image of Z e u s putting an end to the reign of Saturn.

3. From being a slave of nature, which he remains as long as he merely feels it, man becomes its lawgiver from the moment he begins to think it. That which hitherto merely dominated him as f o r c e, now stands before his eyes as o b j e c t. Whatsoever is object for him has no power over him; for in order to be object at all, it must be subjected to the power that is his. To the extent that he imparts form to matter, and for precisely as long as he imparts it, he is immune to its effects; for spirit cannot be injured by anything except that which robs it of its freedom, and man gives evidence of his freedom precisely by giving form to that which is formless. Only where sheer mass, ponderous and inchoate, holds sway, its murky contours shifting within uncertain boundaries, can fear find its seat; man is more than a match for any of nature's terrors once he knows how to give it form and convert it into an object of his contemplation. Once he begins to assert his independence in the face of nature as phenomenon, then he also asserts his dignity *vis-à-vis* nature as force, and with noble freedom rises in revolt against his ancient gods. Now they cast off those ghastly masks which were the anguish of his childhood and surprise him with his own image by revealing themselves as projections of his own mind. The monstrous divinity of the Oriental, which rules the world with the blind strength of a beast of prey, shrinks in the imagination of the Greeks into the friendly contours of a human being. The empire of the Titans falls, and infinite force is tamed by infinite form.

4. But whilst I was merely seeking a way out from the material world and a transition to the world of spirit, my imagination has run away with me and carried me into the very heart of this latter. Beauty, which is what we were out to seek, already lies behind us; we have o'erleapt it completely in passing from mere life directly to pure form and the pure object. But a sudden leap of this kind is contrary to human nature, and in order to keep step with this latter we shall have to turn back once more to the world of sense.

5. Beauty is, admittedly, the work of free contemplation, and with it we do indeed enter upon the world of ideas—but, it should be

bemerken ist, ohne darum die sinnliche Welt zu verlassen, wie bei Erkenntnis der Wahrheit geschieht. Diese ist das reine Produkt der Absonderung von allem, was materiell und zufällig ist, reines Objekt, in welchem keine Schranke des Subjekts zurückbleiben darf, reine Selbsttätigkeit ohne Beimischung eines Leidens. Zwar gibt es auch von der höchsten Abstraktion einen Rückweg zur Sinnlichkeit, denn der Gedanke rührt die innre Empfindung, und die Vorstellung logischer und moralischer Einheit geht in ein Gefühl sinnlicher Übereinstimmung über. Aber wenn wir uns an Erkenntnissen ergötzen, so unterscheiden wir sehr genau unsere Vorstellung von unserer Empfindung und sehen diese letztere als etwas Zufälliges an, was gar wohl wegbleiben könnte, ohne dass deswegen die Erkenntnis aufhörte und Wahrheit nicht Wahrheit wäre. Aber ein ganz vergebliches Unternehmen würde es sein, diese Beziehung auf das Empfindungsvermögen von der Vorstellung der Schönheit absondern zu wollen; daher wir nicht damit ausreichen, uns die eine als den Effekt der andern zu denken, sondern beide zugleich und wechselseitig als Effekt und als Ursache ansehen müssen. In unserm Vergnügen an Erkenntnissen unterscheiden wir ohne Mühe den Übergang von der Tätigkeit zum Leiden und bemerken deutlich, dass das erste vorüber ist, wenn das letztere eintritt. In unserm Wohlgefallen an der Schönheit hingegen lässt sich keine solche Succession zwischen der Tätigkeit und dem Leiden unterscheiden, und die Reflexion zerfliesst hier so vollkommen mit dem Gefühle, dass wir die Form unmittelbar zu empfinden glauben. Die Schönheit ist also zwar Gegenstand für uns, weil die Reflexion die Bedingung ist, unter der wir eine Empfindung von ihr haben; zugleich aber ist sie ein Zustand unsers Subjekts, weil das Gefühl die Bedingung ist, unter der wir eine Vorstellung von ihr haben. Sie ist also zwar Form, weil wir sie betrachten; zugleich aber ist sie Leben, weil wir sie fühlen. Mit einem Wort: sie ist zugleich unser Zustand und unsre Tat.

6. Und eben weil sie dieses beides zugleich ist, so dient sie uns also zu einem siegenden Beweis, dass das Leiden die Tätigkeit, dass die Materie die Form, dass die Beschränkung die Unendlichkeit keineswegs ausschliesse — dass mithin durch die notwendige physische Abhängigkeit des Menschen seine moralische Freiheit keineswegs aufgehoben werde. Sie beweist dieses, und, ich muss hinzusetzen, sie allein kann es uns beweisen. Denn da beim Genuss der

emphasized, without therefore leaving behind the world of sense, as is the case when we proceed to knowledge of truth. Truth is the pure product of abstracting from everything which is material and contingent; it is object, pure and unadulterated, in which none of the limitations of the subject may persist, pure autonomous activity without any admixture of passivity. True, even from the highest abstractions, there is a way back to sense; for thought affects our inner life of feeling, and the perception of logical and moral unity passes over into a feeling of sensuous congruence. But when we take such delight in intellectual knowledge, we distinguish very exactly between our perception and our feeling, and look upon the latter as something incidental, which could well be absent without the knowledge therefore ceasing to be knowledge or truth being any the less true. But it would be a vain undertaking to try to clear our perception of b e a u t y of these connexions with feeling—which is why it will not do to think of the one as the effect of the other, but is imperative to consider each as being, at the same time and reciprocally, both effect and cause. In the pleasure we take in know-ledge we distinguish without difficulty the t r a n s i t i o n from activity to passivity, and are clearly aware that the first is over when the latter begins. In the delight we take in beauty, by contrast, no such succession of activity and passivity can be discerned; reflection is here so completely interfused with feeling that we imagine that the form is directly apprehended by sense. Beauty, then, is indeed an o b j e c t for us, because reflection is the condition of our having any sensation of it; but it is at the same time a s t a t e o f t h e p e r c e i v i n g s u b j e c t, because feeling is a condition of our having any perception of it. Thus beauty is indeed form, because we contemplate it; but it is at the same time life, because we feel it. In a word: it is at once a state of our being and an activity we perform.

6. And just because it is both these things at once, beauty pro-vides us with triumphant proof that passivity by no means excludes activity, nor matter form, nor limitation infinity—that, in conse-quence, the moral freedom of man is by no means abrogated through his inevitable dependence upon physical things. Beauty is proof of this and, I must add, she a l o n e can furnish such proof. For since in the enjoyment of truth, or logical unity, feeling is not

Wahrheit oder der logischen Einheit die Empfindung mit dem Gedanken nicht notwendig eins ist, sondern auf denselben zufällig folgt, so kann uns dieselbe bloss beweisen, dass auf eine vernünftige Natur eine sinnliche folgen könne und umgekehrt; nicht, dass beide zusammen bestehen, nicht, dass sie wechselseitig auf einander wirken, nicht, dass sie absolut und notwendig zu vereinigen sind. Vielmehr müsste sich gerade umgekehrt aus dieser Ausschliessung des Gefühls, solange gedacht wird, und des Gedankens, solange empfunden wird, auf eine Unvereinbarkeit beider Naturen schliessen lassen, wie denn auch wirklich die Analysten keinen bessern Beweis für die Ausführbarkeit reiner Vernunft in der Menschheit anzuführen wissen als den, dass sie geboten ist. Da nun aber bei dem Genuss der Schönheit oder der ästhetischen Einheit eine wirkliche Vereinigung und Auswechslung der Materie mit der Form und des Leidens mit der Tätigkeit vor sich geht, so ist eben dadurch die Vereinbarkeit beider Naturen, die Ausführbarkeit des Unendlichen in der Endlichkeit, mithin die Möglichkeit der erhabensten Menschheit bewiesen.

7. Wir dürfen also nicht mehr verlegen sein, einen Übergang von der sinnlichen Abhängigkeit zu der moralischen Freiheit zu finden, nachdem durch die Schönheit der Fall gegeben ist, dass die letztere mit der erstern vollkommen zusammen bestehen könne, und dass der Mensch, um sich als Geist zu erweisen, der Materie nicht zu entfliehen brauche. Ist er aber schon in Gemeinschaft mit der Sinnlichkeit frei, wie das Faktum der Schönheit lehrt, und ist Freiheit etwas Absolutes und Übersinnliches, wie ihr Begriff notwendig mit sich bringt, so kann nicht mehr die Frage sein, wie er dazu gelange, sich von den Schranken zum Absoluten zu erheben, sich in seinem Denken und Wollen der Sinnlichkeit entgegenzusetzen, da dieses schon in der Schönheit geschehen ist. Es kann, mit einem Wort, nicht mehr die Frage sein, wie er von der Schönheit zur Wahrheit übergehe, die dem Vermögen nach schon in der ersten liegt, sondern wie er von einer gemeinen Wirklichkeit zu einer ästhetischen, wie er von blossen Lebensgefühlen zu Schönheitsgefühlen den Weg sich bahne.

inevitably and of necessity one with thought, but merely follows incidentally upon it, truth can only offer us proof that sensuousness can follow upon rationality, or vice versa; but not that both exist together, nor that they reciprocally work upon each other, nor that they are absolutely and of necessity to be united. On the contrary, from the fact that feeling is excluded as long as we are thinking, and thinking excluded as long as we are feeling, the i n c o m - p a t i b i l i t y of our two natures would have to be inferred; and, indeed, analytical philosophers are unable to adduce any better proof that pure reason can in practice be realized in human kind than that this is in fact enjoined upon them. But since in the enjoy- ment of beauty, or a e s t h e t i c u n i t y, an actual u n i o n and interchange between matter and form, passivity and activity, momentarily takes place, the c o m p a t i b i l i t y of our two natures, the practicability of the infinite being realized in the finite, hence the possibility of sublimest humanity, is thereby actually proven.

7. We need, then, no longer feel at a loss for a way which might lead us from our dependence upon sense towards moral freedom, since beauty offers us an instance of the latter being perfectly com- patible with the former, an instance of man not needing to flee matter in order to manifest himself as spirit. But if he is already free while still in association with sense, as the fact of beauty teaches, and if freedom is something absolute and supra-sensual, as the very notion of freedom necessarily implies, then there can no longer be any question of how he is to succeed in raising himself from the limited to the absolute, or of how, in his thinking and willing, he is to offer resistance to the life of sense, since this has already hap- pened in beauty. There can, in a single word, no longer be any question of how he is to pass from Beauty to Truth, since this latter is potentially contained in the former, but only a question of how he is to clear a way for himself from common reality to aesthetic reality, from mere life-serving feelings to feelings of beauty.

SECHSUNDZWANZIGSTER BRIEF

1. DA die ästhetische Stimmung des Gemüts, wie ich in den vorhergehenden Briefen entwickelt habe, der Freiheit erst die Entstehung gibt, so ist leicht einzusehen, dass sie nicht aus derselben entspringen und folglich keinen moralischen Ursprung haben könne. Ein Geschenk der Natur muss sie sein; die Gunst der Zufälle allein kann die Fesseln des physischen Standes lösen und den Wilden zur Schönheit führen.

2. Der Keim der letztern wird sich gleich wenig entwickeln, wo eine karge Natur den Menschen jeder Erquickung beraubt, und wo eine verschwenderische ihn von jeder eigenen Anstrengung losspricht — wo die stumpfe Sinnlichkeit kein Bedürfnis fühlt, und wo die heftige Begier keine Sättigung findet. Nicht da, wo der Mensch sich troglodytisch in Höhlen birgt, ewig einzeln ist und die Menschheit nie ausser sich findet, auch nicht da, wo er nomadisch in grossen Heermassen zieht, ewig nur Zahl ist und die Menschheit nie in sich findet — da allein, wo er in eigener Hütte still mit sich selbst und, sobald er heraustritt, mit dem ganzen Geschlechte spricht, wird sich ihre liebliche Knospe entfalten. Da wo ein leichter Äther die Sinne jeder leisen Berührung eröffnet und den üppigen Stoff eine energische Wärme beseelt — wo das Reich der blinden Masse schon in der leblosen Schöpfung gestürzt ist und die siegende Form auch die niedrigsten Naturen veredelt — dort in den fröhlichen Verhältnissen und in der gesegneten Zone, wo nur die Tätigkeit zum Genusse und nur der Genuss zur Tätigkeit führt, wo aus dem Leben selbst die heilige Ordnung quillt, und aus dem Gesetz der Ordnung sich nur Leben entwickelt — wo die Einbildungskraft der Wirklichkeit ewig entflieht und dennoch von der Einfalt der Natur nie verirret — hier allein werden sich Sinne und Geist, empfangende und bildende Kraft in dem glücklichen Gleichmass entwickeln, welches die Seele der Schönheit und die Bedingung der Menschheit ist.

3. Und was ist es für ein Phänomen, durch welches sich bei dem Wilden der Eintritt in die Menschheit verkündigt? So weit wir auch die Geschichte befragen, es ist dasselbe bei allen Völkerstämmen,

TWENTY-SIXTH LETTER

1. SINCE, as I have argued in the preceding Letters, it is the aesthetic mode of the psyche which first gives rise to freedom, it is obvious that it cannot itself derive from freedom and cannot, in consequence, be of moral origin. It must be a gift of nature; the favour of fortune alone can unloose the fetters of that first physical stage and lead the savage towards beauty.

2. The germ of beauty is as little likely to develop where nature in her niggardliness deprives man of quickening refreshment, as where in her bounty she relieves him of any exertion—alike where sense is too blunted to feel any need, as where violence of appetite is denied satisfaction. Not where man hides himself, a t r o g l o d y t e, in caves, eternally an isolated unit, never finding humanity o u t - s i d e h i m s e l f; nor yet there where, a n o m a d, he roams in vast hordes over the face of the earth, eternally but one of a number, never finding humanity w i t h i n h i m s e l f—but only there, where, in his own hut, he discourses silently with himself and, from the moment he steps out of it, with all the rest of his kind, only there will the tender blossom of beauty unfold. There, where a limpid atmosphere opens his senses to every delicate contact, and an energizing warmth animates the exuberance of matter—there where, even in inanimate nature, the sway of blind mass has been over-thrown, and form triumphant ennobles even the lowest orders of creation—there, amid the most joyous surroundings, and in that favoured zone where activity alone leads to enjoyment, and enjoy-ment alone to activity, where out of life itself the sanctity of order springs, and out of the law of order nothing but life can develop—where imagination ever flees actuality yet never strays from the simplicity of nature—here alone will sense and spirit, the receptive and the formative power, develop in that happy equilibrium which is the soul of beauty and the condition of all humanity.

3. And what are the outward and visible signs of the savage's entry upon humanity? If we inquire of history, however far back, we find that they are the same in all races which have emerged from

welche der Sklaverei des tierischen Standes entsprungen sind: die Freude am S c h e i n, die Neigung zum P u t z und zum S p i e l e.

4. Die höchste Stupidität und der höchste Verstand haben darin eine gewisse Affinität mit einander, dass beide nur das R e e l l e suchen und für den blossen Schein gänzlich unempfindlich sind. Nur durch die unmittelbare Gegenwart eines Objekts in den Sinnen wird jene aus ihrer Ruhe gerissen, und nur durch Zurückführung seiner Begriffe auf Tatsachen der Erfahrung wird der letztere zur Ruhe gebracht; mit einem Wort, die Dummheit kann sich nicht über die Wirklichkeit erheben und der Verstand nicht unter der Wahrheit stehen bleiben. Insofern also das Bedürfnis der Realität und die Anhänglichkeit an das Wirkliche blosse Folgen des Mangels sind, ist die Gleichgültigkeit gegen Realität und das Interesse am Schein eine wahre Erweiterung der Menschheit und ein entschiedener Schritt zur Kultur. Fürs erste zeugt es von einer äussern Freiheit: denn solange die Not gebietet und das Bedürfnis drängt, ist die Einbildungskraft mit strengen Fesseln an das Wirkliche gebunden; erst wenn das Bedürfnis gestillt ist, entwickelt sie ihr ungebundenes Vermögen. Es zeugt aber auch von einer innern Freiheit, weil es uns eine Kraft sehen lässt, die unabhängig von einem äussern Stoffe sich durch sich selbst in Bewegung setzt, und die Energie genug besitzt, die andringende Materie von sich zu halten. Die Realität der Dinge ist ihr (der Dinge) Werk; der Schein der Dinge ist des Menschen Werk, und ein Gemüt, das sich am Scheine weidet, ergötzt sich schon nicht mehr an dem, was es empfängt, sondern an dem, was es tut.

5. Es versteht sich von selbst, das hier nur von dem ästhetischen Schein die Rede ist, den man von der Wirklichkeit und Wahrheit unterscheidet, nicht von dem logischen, den man mit derselben verwechselt — den man folglich liebt, weil er Schein ist, und nicht, weil man ihn für etwas Besseres hält. Nur der erste ist Spiel, da der letzte bloss Betrug ist. Den Schein der ersten Art für etwas gelten lassen, kann der Wahrheit niemals Eintrag tun, weil man nie Gefahr läuft, ihn derselben unterzuschieben, was doch die einzige Art ist, wie der Wahrheit geschadet werden kann; ihn verachten, heisst alle schöne Kunst überhaupt verachten, deren Wesen der Schein ist. Indessen begegnet es dem Verstande zuweilen, seinen Eifer für Realität bis zu einer solchen Unduldsamkeit zu treiben und über die ganze Kunst des schönen Scheins, weil sie bloss Schein ist, ein

the slavery of the animal condition: delight in s e m b l a n c e, and a propensity to o r n a m e n t a t i o n and p l a y.

4. Supreme stupidity and supreme intelligence have a certain affinity with each other in that both of them seek only the r e a l and are completely insensitive to mere semblance. Only by objects which are actually present to the senses is stupidity jerked out of its quiescence; only when its concepts can be referred back to the facts of experience is intelligence to be pacified. In a word, stupidity cannot rise above actuality, and intelligence cannot stop short of truth. Inasmuch as need of reality and attachment to the actual are merely consequences of some deficiency, then indifference to reality and interest in semblance may be regarded as a genuine enlargement of humanity and a decisive step towards culture. In the first place, this affords evidence of outward freedom: for as long as necessity dictates, and need drives, imagination remains tied to reality with powerful bonds; only when wants are stilled does it develop its unlimited potential. But it affords evidence, too, of inner freedom, since it makes us aware of a power which is able to move of its own accord, independently of any material stimulus from without, and which is sufficiently in control of energy to hold at arm's length the importunate pressure of matter. The reality of things is the work of things themselves; the semblance of things is the work of man; and a nature which delights in semblance is no longer taking pleasure in what it receives, but in what it does.

5. It goes without saying that the only kind of semblance I am here concerned with is aesthetic semblance (which we distinguish from actuality and truth) and not logical semblance (which we confuse with these): semblance, therefore, which we love just because it is semblance, and not because we take it to be something better. Only the first is play, whereas the latter is mere deception. To attach value to semblance of the first kind can never be prejudicial to truth, because one is never in danger of substituting it for truth, which is after all the only way in which truth can ever be impaired. To despise it, is to despise the fine arts altogether, the very essence of which is semblance. All the same, it sometimes happens that intelligence will carry its zeal for reality to such a pitch of intolerance, that it pronounces a disparaging judgement upon the whole art of

wegwerfendes Urteil zu sprechen; dies begegnet aber dem Verstande nur alsdann, wenn er sich der obengedachten Affinität erinnert. Von den notwendigen Grenzen des schönen Scheins werde ich noch einmal insbesondere zu reden Veranlassung nehmen.

6. Die Natur selbst ist es, die den Menschen von der Realität zum Scheine emporhebt, indem sie ihn mit zwei Sinnen ausrüstete, die ihn bloss durch den Schein zur Erkenntnis des Wirklichen führen. In dem Auge und dem Ohr ist die andringende Materie schon hinweggewälzt von den Sinnen, und das Objekt entfernt sich von uns, das wir in den tierischen Sinnen unmittelbar berühren. Was wir durch das Auge s e h e n, ist von dem verschieden, was wir e m p - f i n d e n; denn der Verstand springt über das Licht hinaus zu den Gegenständen. Der Gegenstand des Takts ist eine Gewalt, die wir erleiden; der Gegenstand des Auges und des Ohrs ist eine Form, die wir erzeugen. Solange der Mensch noch ein Wilder ist, geniesst er bloss mit den Sinnen des Gefühls, denen die Sinne des Scheins in dieser Periode bloss dienen. Er erhebt sich entweder gar nicht zum Sehen, oder er befriedigt sich doch nicht mit demselben. Sobald er anfängt, mit dem Auge zu geniessen, und das Sehen für ihn einen selbständigen Wert erlangt, so ist er auch schon ästhetisch frei, und der Spieltrieb hat sich entfaltet.

7. Gleich, sowie der Spieltrieb sich regt, der am Scheine Gefallen findet, wird ihm auch der nachahmende Bildungstrieb folgen, der den Schein als etwas Selbständiges behandelt. Sobald der Mensch einmal so weit gekommen ist, den Schein von der Wirklichkeit, die Form von dem Körper zu unterscheiden, so ist er auch im Stande, sie von ihm abzusondern; denn das hat er schon getan, indem er sie unterscheidet. Das Vermögen zur nachahmenden Kunst ist also mit dem Vermögen zur Form überhaupt gegeben; der Drang zu derselben beruht auf einer andern Anlage, von der ich hier nicht zu handeln brauche. Wie frühe oder wie spät sich der ästhetische Kunsttrieb entwickeln soll, das wird bloss von dem Grade der Liebe abhängen, mit der der Mensch fähig ist, sich bei dem blossen Schein zu verweilen.

8. Da alles wirkliche Dasein von der Natur als einer fremden Macht, aller Schein aber ursprünglich von dem Menschen als vorstellendem Subjekte, sich herschreibt, so bedient er sich bloss seines absoluten Eigentumsrechts, wenn er den Schein von dem Wesen

aesthetic semblance just because it is semblance. But this only happens to intelligence when it recalls the above mentioned affinity. Of the necessary limits of aesthetic semblance I shall treat separately on some other occasion.

6. It is nature herself which raises man from reality to semblance, by furnishing him with two senses which lead him to knowledge of the real world through semblance alone. In the case of the eye and the ear, she herself has driven importunate matter back from the organs of sense, and the object, with which in the case of our more animal senses we have direct contact, is set at a distance from us. What we actually s e e with the eye is something different from the s e n s a t i o n   w e   r e c e i v e; for the mind leaps out across light to objects. The object of touch is a force to which we are subjected; the object of eye and ear a form that we engender. As long as man is still a savage he enjoys by means of these tactile senses alone, and at this stage the senses of semblance are merely the servants of these. Either he does not rise to the level of seeing at all, or he is at all events not satisfied with it. Once he does begin to enjoy through the eye, and seeing acquires for him a value of its own, he is already aesthetically free and the play-drive has started to develop.

7. And as soon as the play-drive begins to stir, with its pleasure in semblance, it will be followed by the shaping spirit of imitation, which treats semblance as something autonomous. Once man has got to the point of distinguishing semblance from reality, form from body, he is also in a position to abstract the one from the other, and has indeed already done so by the very fact of distinguishing between them. The capacity for imitative art is thus given with the capacity for form in general; the urge towards it rests upon a quite different endowment which I need not discuss here. Whether the artistic impulse is to develop early or late, will depend solely upon the degree of loving attachment with which man is capable of abiding with sheer semblance.

8. Since all actual existence derives from nature considered as alien force, whereas all semblance originates in man considered as perceiving subject, he is only availing himself of the undisputed rights of ownership when he reclaims Semblance from Substance,

zurücknimmt und mit demselben nach eignen Gesetzen schaltet.
Mit ungebundener Freiheit kann er, was die Natur trennte, zu-
sammenfügen, sobald er es nur irgend zusammendenken kann, und
trennen, was die Natur verknüpfte, sobald er es nur in seinem Verstande absondern kann. Nichts darf ihm hier heilig sein als sein
eigenes Gesetz, sobald er nur die Markung in Acht nimmt, welche
s e i n Gebiet von dem Dasein der Dinge oder dem Naturgebiete
scheidet.

9. Dieses menschliche Herrscherrecht übt er aus in der K u n s t
d e s S c h e i n s, und je strenger er hier das Mein und Dein von
einander sondert, je sorgfältiger er die Gestalt von dem Wesen
trennt, und je mehr Selbständigkeit er derselben zu geben weiss,
desto mehr wird er nicht bloss das Reich der Schönheit erweitern,
sondern selbst die Grenzen der Wahrheit bewahren; denn er kann
den Schein nicht von der Wirklichkeit reinigen, ohne zugleich die
Wirklichkeit von dem Schein frei zu machen.

10. Aber er besitzt dieses souveräne Recht schlechterdings auch
nur in der W e l t d e s S c h e i n s, in dem wesenlosen Reich der
Einbildungskraft, und nur, solang' er sich im Theoretischen ge-
wissenhaft enthält, Existenz davon auszusagen, und solang' er im
Praktischen darauf Verzicht tut, Existenz dadurch zu erteilen. Sie
sehen hieraus, dass der Dichter auf gleiche Weise aus seinen Grenzen tritt, wenn er seinem Ideal Existenz beilegt, und wenn er eine
bestimmte Existenz damit bezweckt. Denn beides kann er nicht
anders zu Stande bringen, als indem er entweder sein Dichterrecht
überschreitet, durch das Ideal in das Gebiet der Erfahrung greift
und durch die blosse Möglichkeit wirkliches Dasein zu bestimmen
sich anmasst, oder indem er sein Dichterrecht aufgibt, die Erfahrung
in das Gebiet des Ideals greifen lässt und die Möglichkeit auf die
Bedingungen der Wirklichkeit einschränkt.

11. Nur soweit er a u f r i c h t i g ist (sich von allem Anspruch auf
Realität ausdrücklich lossagt), und nur soweit er s e l b s t ä n d i g
ist (allen Beistand der Realität entbehrt), ist der Schein ästhetisch.
Sobald er falsch ist und Realität heuchelt, und sobald er unrein
und der Realität zu seiner Wirkung bedürftig ist, ist er nichts als
ein niedriges Werkzeug zu materiellen Zwecken und kann nichts
für die Freiheit des Geistes beweisen. Übrigens ist es gar nicht

and deals with it according to laws of his own. With unrestricted freedom he is able, can he but imagine them together, actually to join together things which nature put asunder; and, conversely, to separate, can he but abstract them in his mind, things which nature has joined together. Nothing need here be sacred to him except his own law, if he but observes the demarcation separating his territory from the actual existence of things, that is to say from the realm of nature.

9.   This sovereign human right he exercises in the art of semblance; and the more strictly he here distinguishes between mine and thine, the more scrupulously he separates form from substance, and the more complete the autonomy he is able to give to the former, then the more he will not only extend the realm of beauty, but actually preserve intact the frontiers of truth. For he cannot keep semblance clear of actuality without at the same time setting actuality free from semblance.

10.   But it is in the world of semblance alone that he possesses this sovereign right, in the insubstantial realm of the imagination; and he possesses it there only as long as he scrupulously refrains from predicating real existence of it in theory, and as long as he renounces all idea of imparting real existence through it in practice. From this you see that the poet transgresses his proper limits, alike when he attributes existence to his ideal world, as when he aims at bringing about some determinate existence by means of it. For he can bring neither of these things to pass without either exceeding his rights as a poet (encroaching with his ideal upon the territory of experience, and presuming to determine actual existence by means of what is merely possible) or surrendering his rights as a poet (allowing experience to encroach upon the territory of the ideal, and restricting the possible to the conditions of the actual).

11.   Only inasmuch as it is honest (expressly renounces all claims to reality), and only inasmuch as it is autonomous (dispenses with all support from reality), is semblance aesthetic. From the moment it is dishonest, and simulates reality, or from the moment it is impure, and has need of reality to make its effect, it is nothing but a base instrument for material ends, and affords no evidence whatsoever of any freedom of the spirit. This does not,

nötig, dass der Gegenstand, an dem wir den schönen Schein finden,
ohne Realität sei, wenn nur unser Urteil darüber auf diese Realität
keine Rücksicht nimmt; denn soweit es diese Rücksicht nimmt, ist
es kein ästhetisches. Eine lebende weibliche Schönheit wird uns
freilich ebenso gut und noch ein wenig besser als eine ebenso schöne,
bloss gemalte, gefallen; aber insoweit sie uns besser gefällt als die
letztere, gefällt sie nicht mehr als selbständiger Schein, gefällt sie
nicht mehr dem reinen ästhetischen Gefühl: diesem darf auch das
Lebendige nur als Erscheinung, auch das Wirkliche nur als Idee
gefallen; aber freilich erfordert es noch einen ungleich höheren
Grad der schönen Kultur, in dem Lebendigen selbst nur den reinen
Schein zu empfinden, als das Leben an dem Schein zu entbehren.

12. Bei welchem einzelnen Menschen oder ganzen Volk man den
aufrichtigen und selbständigen Schein findet, da darf man auf Geist
und Geschmack und jede damit verwandte Trefflichkeit schliessen
— da wird man das Ideal, das wirkliche Leben regieren, die Ehre
über den Besitz, den Gedanken über den Genuss, den Traum der
Unsterblichkeit über die Existenz triumphieren sehen. Da wird die
öffentliche Stimme das einzig Furchtbare sein, und ein Olivenkranz
höher als ein Purpurkleid ehren. Zum falschen und bedürftigen
Schein nimmt nur die Ohnmacht und die Verkehrtheit ihre Zu-
flucht, und einzelne Menschen sowohl als ganze Völker, welche entweder „der Realität durch den Schein oder dem (ästhetischen)
Schein durch Realität nachhelfen" — beides ist gerne verbunden —
beweisen zugleich ihren moralischen Unwert und ihr ästhetisches
Unvermögen.

13. Auf die Frage „In wie weit darf Schein in der
moralischen Welt sein?" ist also die Antwort so kurz als
bündig diese: In so weit es ästhetischer Schein ist, d. h.
Schein, der weder Realität vertreten will, noch von derselben vertreten zu werden braucht. Der ästhetische Schein kann der Wahrheit
der Sitten niemals gefährlich werden, und wo man es anders findet,
da wird sich ohne Schwierigkeit zeigen lassen, dass der Schein nicht
ästhetisch war. Nur ein Fremdling im schönen Umgang z. B. wird
Versicherungen der Höflichkeit, die eine allgemeine Form ist, als
Merkmale persönlicher Zuneigung aufnehmen und, wenn er ge-
täuscht wird, über Verstellung klagen. Aber auch nur ein Stümper
im schönen Umgang wird, um höflich zu sein, die Falschheit zu
Hilfe rufen und schmeicheln, um gefällig zu sein. Dem ersten fehlt

of course, imply that an object in which we discover aesthetic semblance must be devoid of reality; all that is required is that our judgement of it should take no account of that reality; for inasmuch as it does take account of it, it is not an aesthetic judgement. The beauty of a living woman will please us as well, or even a little better, than a mere painting of one equally beautiful; but inasmuch as the living beauty pleases better than the painted, she is no longer pleasing us as autonomous semblance, no longer pleasing the purely aesthetic sense; for the appeal to this sense, even by living things, must be through sheer appearance, even by real things, purely in virtue of their existence as idea. But it does, admittedly, require an incomparably higher degree of aesthetic culture to perceive nothing but sheer semblance in what is actually alive, than it does to dispense with the element of life in sheer semblance.

12.   In whatever individual or whole people we find this honest and autonomous kind of semblance, we may assume both understanding and taste, and every kindred excellence. There we shall see actual life governed by the ideal, honour triumphant over possessions, thought over enjoyment, dreams of immortality over existence. There public opinion will be the only thing to be feared, and an olive wreath bestow greater honour than a purple robe. Only impotence and perversity will have recourse to dishonest and dependent semblance; and single individuals, as well as whole peoples, who either 'eke out reality with semblance, or (aesthetic) semblance with reality'—the two often go together—give evidence alike of their moral worthlessness and of their aesthetic incapacity.

13.   To the question 'How far can semblance legiti-mately exist in the moral world?' the answer is then, briefly and simply, this: To the extent that it is aesthetic semblance; that is to say, semblance which neither seeks to represent reality nor needs to be represented by it. Aesthetic semblance can never be a threat to the truth of morals; and where it might seem to be otherwise, it can be shown without difficulty that the semblance was not aesthetic. Only a stranger to polite society, for example, will take the protestations of courtesy, which are common form, for tokens of personal regard, and when deceived complain of dissimulation. But only a bungler in polite society will, for the sake of courtesy, call deceit to his aid, and produce flattery in order

noch der Sinn für den selbständigen Schein, daher kann er demselben nur durch die Wahrheit Bedeutung geben; dem zweiten fehlt es an Realität, und er möchte sie gern durch den Schein ersetzen.

14. Nichts ist gewöhnlicher, als von gewissen trivialen Kritikern des Zeitalters die Klage zu vernehmen, dass alle Solidität aus der Welt verschwunden sei und das Wesen über dem Schein vernachlässigt werde. Obgleich ich mich gar nicht berufen fühle, das Zeitalter gegen diesen Vorwurf zu rechtfertigen, so geht doch schon aus der weiten Ausdehnung, welche diese strengen Sittenrichter ihrer Anklage geben, sattsam hervor, dass sie dem Zeitalter nicht bloss den falschen, sondern auch den aufrichtigen Schein verargen; und sogar die Ausnahmen, welche sie noch etwa zu Gunsten der Schönheit machen, gehen mehr auf den bedürftigen als auf den selbständigen Schein. Sie greifen nicht bloss die betrügerische Schminke an, welche die Wahrheit verbirgt, welche die Wirklichkeit zu vertreten sich anmasst; sie ereifern sich auch gegen den wohltätigen Schein, der die Leerheit ausfüllt und die Armseligkeit zudeckt — auch gegen den idealischen, der eine gemeine Wirklichkeit veredelt. Die Falschheit der Sitten beleidigt mit Recht ihr strenges Wahrheitsgefühl; nur schade, dass sie zu dieser Falschheit auch schon die Höflichkeit rechnen. Es missfällt ihnen, dass äusserer Flitterglanz so oft das wahre Verdienst verdunkelt; aber es verdriesst sie nicht weniger, dass man auch Schein vom Verdienste fordert und dem innern Gehalte die gefällige Form nicht erlässt. Sie vermissen das Herzliche, Kernhafte und Gediegene der vorigen Zeiten, aber sie möchten auch das Eckigte und Derbe der ersten Sitten, das Schwerfällige der alten Formen, und den ehemaligen gotischen Überfluss wieder eingeführt sehen. Sie beweisen durch Urteile dieser Art dem Stoff an sich selbst eine Achtung, die der Menschheit nicht würdig ist, welche vielmehr das Materielle nur insoferne schätzen soll, als es Gestalt zu empfangen und das Reich der Ideen zu verbreiten im Stande ist. Auf solche Stimmen braucht also der Geschmack des Jahrhunderts nicht sehr zu hören, wenn er nur sonst vor einer bessern Instanz besteht. Nicht dass wir einen Wert auf den ästhetischen Schein legen (wir tun dies noch lange nicht genug), sondern dass wir es noch nicht bis zu dem reinen Schein gebracht haben, dass wir das Dasein noch nicht genug von der Erscheinung geschieden und dadurch beider Grenzen auf ewig

to please. The first still lacks all sense of autonomous semblance; hence he can only lend it significance by endowing it with some content of truth. The second is himself lacking in reality and would fain, therefore, replace it by semblance.

14. Nothing is more common than to hear certain shallow critics of our age voicing the complaint that the solid virtues have disappeared from the face of the world, and that Being is neglected for the sake of Seeming. Though I feel no call to defend our age against such accusations, it is obvious enough from the sweeping way in which these severe moralizers tend to generalize their indictment, that they reproach the age not only for dishonest but for honest semblance too. And even the exceptions they might possibly be prepared to make for the sake of beauty refer rather to dependent, than to autonomous, semblance. They do not merely attack the lying colours which mask the face of truth and are bold enough to masquerade as reality; they also inveigh against that beneficent semblance with which we fill out our emptiness and cover up our wretchedness, and against that ideal semblance which ennobles the reality of common day. The hypocrisy of our morals rightly offends their strict sense of truth; it is only regrettable that, in their eyes, politeness too should count as hypocrisy. They dislike the superficial glitter which so often eclipses true merit; but it irks them no less that we should require genuine merit to have style, and refuse to absolve inward substance from having a pleasing outward form. They regret the sincerity, soundness, and solidity of former times; but they would like to see reintroduced with these the uncouthness and bluntness of primitive manners, the heavy awkwardness of ancient forms, and the lost exuberance of a Gothick Age. With judgements of this kind they show a respect for s u b s t a n c e a s s u c h which is unworthy of man, who is meant to value matter only to the extent that it is capable of taking on form and extending the realm of ideas. To such voices, therefore, the taste of our century need pay no undue heed, so long as it can stand its ground before a higher tribunal. What a more rigoristic judge of beauty could well reproach us with, is not that we attach value to aesthetic semblance (we do not attach nearly enough), but that we have not yet attained to the level of pure semblance at all, that we have not sufficiently distinguished existence from appearance, and thereby

gesichert haben, dies ist es, was uns ein rigoristischer Richter der Schönheit zum Vorwurf machen kann. Diesen Vorwurf werden wir solang' verdienen, als wir das Schöne der lebendigen Natur nicht geniessen können, ohne es zu begehren, das Schöne der nachahmenden Kunst nicht bewundern können, ohne nach einem Zwecke zu fragen — als wir der Einbildungskraft noch keine eigene absolute Gesetzgebung zugestehn und durch die Achtung, die wir ihren Werken erzeigen, sie auf ihre Würde hinweisen.

made the frontiers of each secure for ever. We shall deserve this reproach as long as we cannot enjoy the beauty of living nature without coveting it, or admire the beauty of imitative art without inquiring after its purpose—as long as we still refuse Imagination any absolute legislative rights of her own, and, by the kind of respect we accord to her works, go on referring her instead to the dignity of her office.

SIEBENUNDZWANZIGSTER BRIEF

1. FÜRCHTEN Sie nichts für Realität und Wahrheit, wenn der hohe Begriff, den ich in dem vorhergehenden Briefe von dem ästhetischen Schein aufstellte, allgemein werden sollte. Er wird nicht allgemein werden, so lange der Mensch noch ungebildet genug ist, um einen Missbrauch davon machen zu können; und würde er allgemein, so könnte dies nur durch eine Kultur bewirkt werden, die zugleich jeden Missbrauch unmöglich machte. Dem selbständigen Schein nachzustreben, erfordert mehr Abstraktionsvermögen, mehr Freiheit des Herzens, mehr Energie des Willens, als der Mensch nötig hat, um sich auf die Realität einzuschränken, und er muss diese schon hinter sich haben, wenn er bei jenem anlangen will. Wie übel würde er sich also raten, wenn er den Weg zum Ideale einschlagen wollte, um sich den Weg zur Wirklichkeit zu ersparen! Von dem Schein, so wie er hier genommen wird, möchten wir also für die Wirklichkeit nicht viel zu besorgen haben; desto mehr dürfte aber von der Wirklichkeit für den Schein zu befürchten sein. An das Materielle gefesselt, lässt der Mensch diesen lange Zeit bloss seinen Zwecken dienen, ehe er ihm in der Kunst des Ideals eine eigene Persönlichkeit zugesteht. Zu dem letztern bedarf es einer totalen Revolution in seiner ganzen Empfindungsweise, ohne welche er auch nicht einmal a u f d e m W e g e zum Ideal sich befinden würde. Wo wir also Spuren einer uninteressierten freien Schätzung des reinen Scheins entdecken, da können wir auf eine solche Umwälzung seiner Natur und den eigentlichen Anfang der Menschheit in ihm schliessen. Spuren dieser Art finden sich aber wirklich schon in den ersten rohen Versuchen, die er zur V e r s c h ö n e r u n g seines Daseins macht, selbst auf die Gefahr macht, dass er es dem sinnlichen Gehalt nach dadurch verschlechtern sollte. Sobald er überhaupt nur anfängt, dem Stoff die Gestalt vorzuziehen und an den Schein (den er aber dafür erkennen muss) Realität zu wagen, so ist sein tierischer Kreis aufgetan, und er befindet sich auf einer Bahn, die nicht endet.

2. Mit dem allein nicht zufrieden, was der Natur genügt und was das Bedürfnis fordert, verlangt er Überfluss; anfangs zwar bloss einen Überfluss d e s S t o f f e s, um der Begier ihre Schranken zu

TWENTY-SEVENTH LETTER

1. YOU need have no fear for either reality or truth if the lofty conception of aesthetic semblance which I put forward in the last Letter were to become universal. It will not become universal as long as man is still uncultivated enough to be in a position to misuse it; and should it become universal, this could only be brought about by the kind of culture which would automatically make any misuse of it impossible. To strive after autonomous semblance demands higher powers of abstraction, greater freedom of heart, more energy of will, than man ever needs when he confines himself to reality; and he must already have left this reality behind if he would arrive at that kind of semblance. How ill-advised he would be, then, to take the path towards the ideal in order to save himself the way to the real! From semblance as here understood we should thus have little cause to fear for reality; all the more to be feared, I would suggest, is the threat from reality to semblance. Chained as he is to the material world, man subordinates semblance to ends of his own long before he allows it autonomous existence in the ideal realm of art. For this latter to happen a complete revolution in his whole way of feeling is required, without which he would not even find himself o n t h e w a y to the ideal. Wherever, then, we find traces of a disinterested and unconditional appreciation of pure semblance, we may infer that a revolution of this order has taken place in his nature, and that he has started to become truly human. Traces of this kind are, however, actually to be found even in his first crude attempts at e m b e l l i s h i n g his existence, attempts made even at the risk of possibly worsening it from the material point of view. As soon as ever he starts preferring form to substance, and jeopardizing reality for the sake of semblance (which he must, however, recognize as such), a breach has been effected in the cycle of his animal behaviour, and he finds himself set upon a′ path to which there is no end.

2. Not just content with what satisfies nature, and meets his instinctual needs, he demands something over and above this: to begin with, admittedly, only a superfluity of m a t e r i a l t h i n g s,

verbergen, um den Genuss über das gegenwärtige Bedürfnis hinaus
zu versichern; bald aber einen Überfluss an dem Stoffe, eine
ästhetische Zugabe, um auch dem Formtrieb genug zu tun, um den
Genuss über jedes Bedürfnis hinaus zu erweitern. Indem er bloss
für einen künftigen Gebrauch Vorräte sammelt und in der Ein-
bildung dieselben vorausgeniesst, so überschreitet er zwar den
jetzigen Augenblick, aber ohne die Zeit überhaupt zu überschreiten;
er geniesst mehr, aber er geniesst nicht anders. Indem er aber
zugleich die Gestalt in seinen Genuss zieht und auf die Formen der
Gegenstände merkt, die seine Begierden befriedigen, hat er seinen
Genuss nicht bloss dem Umfang und dem Grad nach erhöht, sondern auch der Art nach veredelt.

3. Zwar hat die Natur auch schon dem Vernunftlosen über die
Notdurft gegeben und in das dunkle tierische Leben einen Schimmer von Freiheit gestreut. Wenn den Löwen kein Hunger nagt und
kein Raubtier zum Kampf herausfordert, so erschafft sich die müs-
sige Stärke selbst einen Gegenstand; mit mutvollem Gebrüll erfüllt
er die hallende Wüste, und in zwecklosem Aufwand geniesst sich
die üppige Kraft. Mit frohem Leben schwärmt das Insekt in dem
Sonnenstrahl; auch ist es sicherlich nicht der Schrei der Begierde,
den wir in dem melodischen Schlag des Singvogels hören. Unleug-
bar ist in diesen Bewegungen Freiheit, aber nicht Freiheit von dem
Bedürfnis überhaupt, bloss von einem bestimmten, von einem
äussern Bedürfnis. Das Tier arbeitet, wenn ein Mangel die
Triebfeder seiner Tätigkeit ist, und es spielt, wenn der Reichtum
der Kraft diese Triebfeder ist, wenn das überflüssige Leben sich
selbst zur Tätigkeit stachelt. Selbst in der unbeseelten Natur zeigt
sich ein solcher Luxus der Kräfte und eine Laxität der Bestimmung,
die man in jenem materiellen Sinn gar wohl Spiel nennen könnte.
Der Baum treibt unzählige Keime, die unentwickelt verderben, und
streckt weit mehr Wurzeln, Zweige und Blätter nach Nahrung aus,
als zu Erhaltung seines Individuums und seiner Gattung verwendet
werden. Was er von seiner verschwenderischen Fülle ungebraucht
und ungenossen dem Elementarreich zurückgibt, das darf das
Lebendige in fröhlicher Bewegung verschwelgen. So gibt uns die
Natur schon in ihrem materiellen Reich ein Vorspiel des Unbegrenzten und hebt hier schon zum Teil die Fesseln auf, deren
sie sich im Reich der Form ganz und gar entledigt. Von dem Zwang
des Bedürfnisses oder dem physischen Ernste nimmt sie

in order to conceal from appetite the fact that it has limits, and ensure enjoyment beyond the satisfaction of immediate needs; soon, however, a superfluity in m a t e r i a l t h i n g s, an aesthetic surplus, in order to satisfy the formal impulse too, and extend enjoyment beyond the satisfaction of every need. By merely gathering supplies around him for future use, and enjoying them in anticipation, he does, it is true, transcend the present moment—but without transcending time altogether. He enjoys m o r e, but he does not enjoy d i f f e r e n t l y. But when he also lets form enter into his enjoyment, and begins to notice the outward appearance of the things which satisfy his desires, then he has not merely enhanced his enjoyment in scope and degree, but also ennobled it in kind.

3. It is true that Nature has given even to creatures without reason more than the bare necessities of existence, and shed a glimmer of freedom even into the darkness of animal life. When the lion is not gnawed by hunger, nor provoked to battle by any beast of prey, his idle strength creates an object for itself: he fills the echoing desert with a roaring that speaks defiance, and his exuberant energy enjoys its *self* in purposeless display. With what enjoyment of life do insects swarm in the sunbeam; and it is certainly not the cry of desire that we hear in the melodious warbling of the songbird. Without doubt there is freedom in these activities; but not freedom from compulsion altogether, merely from a certain kind of compulsion, compulsion from without. An animal may be said to be at w o r k, when the stimulus to activity is some lack; it may be said to be at p l a y, when the stimulus is sheer plenitude of vitality, when superabundance of life is its own incentive to action. Even inanimate nature exhibits a similar luxuriance of forces, coupled with a laxity of determination which, in that material sense, might well be called play. The tree puts forth innumerable buds which perish without ever unfolding, and sends out far more roots, branches, and leaves in search of nourishment than are ever used for the sustaining of itself or its species. Such portion of its prodigal profusion as it returns, unused and unenjoyed, to the elements, is the overplus which living things are entitled to squander in a movement of carefree joy. Thus does Nature, even in her material kingdom, offer us a prelude of the Illimitable, and even here remove i n p a r t the chains which, in the realm of form, she casts away entirely. From the compulsion of want, or p h y s i c a l

durch den Zwang des Überflusses oder das p h y s i s c h e S p i e l
den Übergang zum ästhetischen Spiele, und ehe sie sich in der
hohen Freiheit des Schönen über die Fessel jedes Zweckes erhebt,
nähert sie sich dieser Unabhängigkeit wenigstens von ferne schon
in der f r e i e n B e w e g u n g, die sich selbst Zweck und Mittel ist.

4. Wie die körperlichen Werkzeuge, so hat in dem Menschen auch
die Einbildungskraft ihre freie Bewegung und ihr materielles Spiel,
in welchem sie, ohne alle Beziehung auf Gestalt, bloss ihrer Eigen-
macht und Fessellosigkeit sich freut. Insofern sich noch gar nichts
von Form in diese Phantasiespiele mischt und eine ungezwungene
Folge von Bildern den ganzen Reiz derselben ausmacht, gehören
sie, obgleich sie dem Menschen allein zukommen können, bloss zu
seinem animalischen Leben und beweisen bloss seine Befreiung von
jedem äussern sinnlichen Zwang, ohne noch auf eine selbständige
bildende Kraft in ihm schliessen zu lassen.* Von diesem Spiel d e r
f r e i e n I d e e n f o l g e, welches noch ganz materieller Art ist und
aus blossen Naturgesetzen sich erklärt, macht endlich die Einbildungskraft in dem Versuch e i n e r f r e i e n F o r m den Sprung
zum ästhetischen Spiele. Einen Sprung muss man es nennen, weil
sich eine ganz neue Kraft hier in Handlung setzt; denn hier zum
erstenmal mischt sich der gesetzgebende Geist in die Handlungen
eines blinden Instinktes, unterwirft das willkürliche Verfahren der
Einbildungskraft seiner unveränderlichen ewigen Einheit, legt seine
Selbständigkeit in das Wandelbare und seine Unendlichkeit in das
Sinnliche. Aber solange die rohe Natur noch zu mächtig ist, die kein
anderes Gesetz kennt, als rastlos von Veränderung zu Veränderung
fortzueilen, wird sie durch ihre unstete Willkür jener Notwendigkeit, durch ihre Unruhe jener Stetigkeit, durch ihre Bedürftigkeit

* Die mehresten Spiele, welche im gemeinen Leben im Gange sind, beruhen entweder
ganz und gar auf diesem Gefühle der freien Ideenfolge, oder entlehnen doch ihren
grössten Reiz von demselben. So wenig es aber auch an sich selbst für eine höhere Natur
beweist, und so gerne sich gerade die schlaffesten Seelen diesem freien Bilderstrome zu
überlassen pflegen, so ist doch eben diese Unabhängigkeit der Phantasie von äussern
Eindrücken wenigstens die negative Bedingung ihres schöpferischen Vermögens. Nur
indem sie sich von der Wirklichkeit losreisst, erhebt sich die bildende Kraft zum Ideale,
und ehe die Imagination in ihrer produktiven Qualität nach eignen Gesetzen handeln
kann, muss sie sich schon bei ihrem reproduktiven Verfahren von fremden Gesetzen frei
gemacht haben. Freilich ist von der blossen Gesetzlosigkeit zu einer selbständigen innern Gesetzgebung noch ein sehr grosser Schritt zu tun, und eine ganz neue Kraft, das
Vermögen der Ideen, muss hier ins Spiel gemischt werden — aber diese Kraft kann sich
nunmehr auch mit mehrerer Leichtigkeit entwickeln, da die Sinne ihr nicht entgegen-
wirken und das Unbestimmte wenigstens negativ an das Unendliche grenzt.

earnestness, she makes the transition via the compulsion of superfluity, or p h y s i c a l p l a y, to aesthetic play; and before she soars, in the sublime freedom of beauty, beyond the fetters of ends and purposes altogether, she makes some approach to this independence, at least from afar, in that kind of f r e e a c t i v i t y which is at once its own end and its own means.

4. Like the bodily organs in man, his imagination, too, has its free movement and its material play, an activity in which, without any reference to form, it simply delights in its own absolute and unfettered power. Inasmuch as form does not yet enter this fantasy play at all, its whole charm residing in a free association of images, such play—although the prerogative of man alone—belongs merely to his animal life, and simply affords evidence of his liberation from all external physical compulsion, without as yet warranting the inference that there is any autonomous shaping power within him.* From this play o f f r e e l y a s s o c i a t e d i d e a s, which is still of a wholly material kind, and to be explained by purely natural laws, the imagination, in its attempt at a f r e e f o r m, finally makes the leap to aesthetic play. A leap it must be called, since a completely new power now goes into action; for here, for the first time, mind takes a hand as lawgiver in the operations of blind instinct, subjects the arbitrary activity of the imagination to its own immutable and eternal unity, introduces its own autonomy into the transient, and its own infinity into the life of sense. But as long as brute nature still has too much power, knowing no other law but restless hastening from change to change, it will oppose to that necessity of the spirit its own unstable caprice, to that stability its own unrest, to

* Most of the imaginative play which goes on in everyday life is either entirely based on this feeling for free association of ideas, or at any rate derives therefrom its greatest charm. This may not in itself be proof of a higher nature, and it may well be that it is just the most flaccid natures who tend to surrender to such unimpeded flow of images; it is nevertheless this very independence of the fantasy from external stimuli, which constitutes at least the negative condition of its creative power. Only by tearing itself free from reality does the formative power raise itself up to the ideal; and before the imagination, in its productive capacity, can act according to its own laws, it must first, in its reproductive procedures, have freed itself from alien laws. From mere lawlessness to autonomous law-giving from within, there is, admittedly, still a big step to be taken; and a completely new power, the faculty for ideas, must first be brought into play. But this power, too, can now develop with greater ease, since the senses are not working against it, and the indefinite does, at least negatively, border upon the infinite.

jener Selbständigkeit, durch ihre Ungenügsamkeit jener erhabenen Einfalt entgegenstreben. Der ästhetische Spieltrieb wird also in seinen ersten Versuchen noch kaum zu erkennen sein, da der sinnliche mit seiner eigensinnigen Laune und seiner wilden Begierde unaufhörlich dazwischentritt. Daher sehen wir den rohen Geschmack das Neue und Überraschende, das Bunte, Abenteuerliche und Bizarre, das Heftige und Wilde zuerst ergreifen und vor nichts so sehr als vor der Einfalt und Ruhe fliehen. Er bildet groteske Gestalten, liebt rasche Übergänge, üppige Formen, grelle Kontraste, schreiende Lichter, einen pathetischen Gesang. Schön heisst ihm in dieser Epoche bloss, was ihn aufregt, was ihm Stoff gibt — aber aufregt zu einem selbsttätigen Widerstand, aber Stoff gibt f ü r e i n m ö g l i c h e s B i l d e n, denn sonst würde es selbst ihm nicht das Schöne sein. Mit der Form seiner Urteile ist also eine merkwürdige Veränderung vorgegangen; er sucht diese Gegenstände nicht, weil sie ihm etwas zu erleiden, sondern weil sie ihm zu handeln geben; sie gefallen ihm nicht, weil sie einem Bedürfnis begegnen, sondern weil sie einem Gesetze Genüge leisten, welches, obgleich noch leise, in seinem Busen spricht.

5.   Bald ist er nicht mehr damit zufrieden, dass ihm die Dinge gefallen; er will selbst gefallen, anfangs zwar nur durch das, was s e i n ist, endlich durch das, was e r ist. Was er besitzt, was er hervorbringt, darf nicht mehr bloss die Spuren der Dienstbarkeit, die ängstliche Form seines Zwecks an sich tragen; neben dem Dienst, zu dem es da ist, muss es zugleich den geistreichen Verstand, der es dachte, die liebende Hand, die es ausführte, den heitern und freien Geist, der es wählte und aufstellte, widerscheinen. Jetzt sucht sich der alte Germanier glänzendere Tierfelle, prächtigere Geweihe, zierlichere Trinkhörner aus, und der Kaledonier wählt die nettesten Muscheln für seine Feste. Selbst die Waffen dürfen jetzt nicht mehr bloss Gegenstände des Schreckens, sondern auch des Wohlgefallens sein, und das kunstreiche Wehrgehänge will nicht weniger bemerkt sein als des Schwertes tötende Schneide. Nicht zufrieden, einen ästhetischen Überfluss in das Notwendige zu bringen, reisst sich der freiere Spieltrieb endlich ganz von den Fesseln der Notdurft los, und das Schöne wird für sich allein ein Objekt seines Strebens. Er s c h m ü c k t sich. Die freie Lust wird in die Zahl seiner Bedürfnisse aufgenommen, und das Unnötige ist bald der beste Teil seiner Freuden.

that autonomy its own subservience, to that sublime self-sufficiency its own insatiable discontent. The aesthetic play-drive, therefore, will in its first attempts be scarcely recognizable, since the physical play-drive, with its wilful moods and its unruly appetites, constantly gets in the way. Hence we see uncultivated taste first seizing upon what is new and startling—on the colourful, fantastic, and bizarre, the violent and the savage—and shunning nothing so much as tranquil simplicity. It fashions grotesque shapes, loves swift transitions, exuberant forms, glaring contrasts, garish lights, and a song full of feeling. At this stage what man calls beautiful is only what excites him, what offers him material—but excites him to a resistance involving autonomous activity, but offers him material f o r p o s s i b l e s h a p i n g. Otherwise it would not be beauty—even for him. The form of his judgements has thus undergone an astonishing change: he seeks these objects, not because they give him something to enjoy passively, but because they provide an incentive to respond actively. They please him, not because they meet a need, but because they satisfy a law which speaks, though softly as yet, within his breast.

5. Soon he is no longer content that things should please him; he himself wants to please. At first, indeed, only through that which is h i s; finally through that which h e is. The things he possesses, the things he produces, may no longer bear upon them the marks of their use, their form no longer be merely a timid expression of their function; in addition to the service they exist to render, they must at the same time reflect the genial mind which conceived them, the loving hand which wrought them, the serene and liberal spirit which chose and displayed them. Now the ancient German goes in search of glossier skins, statelier antlers, more elaborate drinking horns; and the Caledonian selects for his feasts the prettiest shells. Even weapons may no longer be mere objects of terror; they must be objects of delight as well, and the cunningly ornamented sword-belt claims no less attention than the deadly blade of the sword. Not content with introducing aesthetic superfluity into objects of necessity, the play-drive as it becomes ever freer finally tears itself away from the fetters of utility altogether, and beauty in and for itself alone begins to be an object of his striving. Man a d o r n s himself. Disinterested and undirected pleasure is now numbered among the necessities of existence, and what is in fact unnecessary soon becomes the best part of his delight.

6. So wie sich ihm von aussen her, in seiner Wohnung, seinem Hausgeräte, seiner Bekleidung allmählich die Form nähert, so fängt sie endlich an, von ihm selbst Besitz zu nehmen und anfangs bloss den äussern, zuletzt auch den innern Menschen zu verwandeln. Der gesetzlose Sprung der Freude wird zum Tanz, die ungestalte Geste zu einer anmutigen harmonischen Gebärdensprache; die verworrenen Laute der Empfindung entfalten sich, fangen an, dem Takt zu gehorchen und sich zum Gesange zu biegen. Wenn das trojanische Heer mit gellendem Geschrei gleich einem Zug von Kranichen ins Schlachtfeld heranstürmt, so nähert sich das griechische demselben still und mit edlem Schritt. Dort sehen wir bloss den Übermut blinder Kräfte, hier den Sieg der Form und die simple Majestät des Gesetzes.

7. Eine schönere Notwendigkeit kettet jetzt die Geschlechter zusammen, und der Herzen Anteil hilft das Bündnis bewahren, das die Begierde nur launisch und wandelbar knüpft. Aus ihren düstern Fesseln entlassen, ergreift das ruhigere Auge die Gestalt, die Seele schaut in die Seele, und aus einem eigennützigen Tausche der Lust wird ein grossmütiger Wechsel der Neigung. Die Begierde erweitert und erhebt sich zur Liebe, so wie die Menschheit in ihrem Gegenstand aufgeht, und der niedrige Vorteil über den Sinn wird verschmäht, um über den Willen einen edleren Sieg zu erkämpfen. Das Bedürfnis zu gefallen unterwirft den Mächtigen des Geschmackes zartem Gericht; die Lust kann er rauben, aber die Liebe muss eine Gabe sein. Um diesen höhern Preis kann er nur durch Form, nicht durch Materie ringen. Er muss aufhören, das Gefühl als Kraft zu berühren, und als Erscheinung dem Verstand gegenüber stehn; er muss Freiheit lassen, weil er der Freiheit gefallen will. So wie die Schönheit den Streit der Naturen in seinem einfachsten und reinsten Exempel, in dem ewigen Gegensatz der Geschlechter löst, so löst sie ihn — oder zielt wenigstens dahin, ihn auch in dem verwickelten Ganzen der Gesellschaft zu lösen und nach dem Muster des freien Bundes, den sie dort zwischen der männlichen Kraft und der weiblichen Milde knüpft, alles Sanfte und Heftige in der moralischen Welt zu versöhnen. Jetzt wird die Schwäche heilig, und die nicht gebändigte Stärke entehrt; das Unrecht der Natur wird durch die Grossmut ritterlicher Sitten verbessert. Den keine Gewalt erschrecken darf, entwaffnet die holde Röte der Scham, und Tränen ersticken eine Rache, die kein Blut löschen konnte. Selbst der Hass merkt auf der Ehre zarte Stimme, das

6. And as form gradually comes upon him from without—in his dwelling, his household goods, and his apparel—so finally it begins to take possession of him himself, transforming at first only the outer, but ultimately the inner, man too. Uncoordinated leaps of joy turn into dance, the unformed movements of the body into the graceful and harmonious language of gesture; the confused and indistinct cries of feeling become articulate, begin to obey the laws of rhythm, and to take on the contours of song. If the Trojan host storms on to the battlefield with piercing shrieks like a flock of cranes, the Greek army approaches it in silence, with noble and measured tread. In the former case we see only the exuberance of blind forces; in the latter, the triumph of form and the simple majesty of law.

7. Now compulsion of a lovelier kind binds the sexes together, and a communion of hearts helps sustain a connexion but intermittently established by the fickle caprice of desire. Released from its dark bondage, the eye, less troubled now by passion, can apprehend the form of the beloved; soul looks deep into soul, and out of a selfish exchange of lust there grows a generous interchange of affection. Desire widens, and is exalted into love, once humanity has dawned in its object; and a base advantage over sense is now disdained for the sake of a nobler victory over will. The need to please subjects the all-conquering male to the gentle tribunal of taste; lust he can steal, but love must come as a gift. For this loftier prize he can only contend by virtue of form, never by virtue of matter. From being a force impinging upon feeling, he must become a form confronting the mind; he must be willing to concede freedom, because it is freedom he wishes to please. And even as beauty resolves the conflict between opposing natures in this simplest and clearest paradigm, the eternal antagonism of the sexes, so too does it resolve it—or at least aims at resolving it—in the complex whole of society, endeavouring to reconcile the gentle with the violent in the moral world after the pattern of the free union it there contrives between the strength of man and the gentleness of woman. Now weakness becomes sacred, and unbridled strength dishonourable; the injustice of nature is rectified by the magnanimity of the chivalric code. He whom no violence may alarm is disarmed by the tender blush of modesty, and tears stifle a revenge which no blood was able to assuage. Even hatred pays heed to the gentle voice

Schwert des Überwinders verschont den entwaffneten Feind, und ein gastlicher Herd raucht dem Fremdling an der gefürchteten Küste, wo ihn sonst nur der Mord empfing.

8. Mitten in dem furchtbaren Reich der Kräfte und mitten in dem heiligen Reich der Gesetze baut der ästhetische Bildungstrieb unvermerkt an einem dritten, fröhlichen Reiche des Spiels und des Scheins, worin er dem Menschen die Fesseln aller Verhältnisse abnimmt und ihn von allem, was Zwang heisst, sowohl im Physischen als im Moralischen entbindet.

9. Wenn in dem d y n a m i s c h e n Staat der Rechte der Mensch dem Menschen als Kraft begegnet und sein Wirken beschränkt — wenn er sich ihm in dem e t h i s c h e n Staat der Pflichten mit der Majestät des Gesetzes entgegenstellt und sein Wollen fesselt, so darf er ihm im Kreise des schönen Umgangs, in dem ä s t h e t i - s c h e n Staat, nur als Gestalt erscheinen, nur als Objekt des freien Spiels gegenüber stehen. F r e i h e i t z u g e b e n d u r c h F r e i h e i t ist das Grundgesetz dieses Reichs.

10. Der dynamische Staat kann die Gesellschaft bloss möglich machen, indem er die Natur durch Natur bezähmt; der ethische Staat kann sie bloss (moralisch) notwendig machen, indem er den einzelnen Willen dem allgemeinen unterwirft; der ästhetische Staat allein kann sie wirklich machen, weil er den Willen des Ganzen durch die Natur des Individuums vollzieht. Wenn schon das Bedürfnis den Menschen in die Gesellschaft nötigt und die Vernunft gesellige Grundsätze in ihm pflanzt, so kann die Schönheit allein ihm einen g e s e l l i g e n C h a r a k t e r erteilen. Der Geschmack allein bringt Harmonie in die Gesellschaft, weil er Harmonie in dem Individuum stiftet. Alle andre Formen der Vorstellung trennen den Menschen, weil sie sich ausschliessend entweder auf den sinnlichen oder auf den geistigen Teil seines Wesens gründen; nur die schöne Vorstellung macht ein Ganzes aus ihm, weil seine beiden Naturen dazu zusammenstimmen müssen. Alle andere Formen der Mitteilung trennen die Gesellschaft, weil sie sich ausschliessend entweder auf die Privatempfänglichkeit oder auf die Privatfertigkeit der einzelnen Glieder, also auf das Unterscheidende zwischen Menschen und Menschen beziehen; nur die schöne Mitteilung vereinigt die Gesellschaft, weil sie sich auf das Gemeinsame aller bezieht. Die Freuden der Sinne geniessen wir bloss als Individuen, ohne

of honour; the sword of the victor spares the disarmed foe, and a friendly hearth sends forth welcoming smoke to greet the stranger on that dread shore where of old only murder lay in wait for him.

8. In the midst of the fearful kingdom of forces, and in the midst of the sacred kingdom of laws, the aesthetic impulse to form is at work, unnoticed, on the building of a third joyous kingdom of play and of semblance, in which man is relieved of the shackles of circumstance, and released from all that might be called constraint, alike in the physical and in the moral sphere.

9. If in the d y n a m i c State of rights it is as force that one man encounters another, and imposes limits upon his activities; if in the e t h i c a l State of duties Man sets himself over against man with all the majesty of the law, and puts a curb upon his desires: in those circles where conduct is governed by beauty, in the a e s t h e t i c State, none may appear to the other except as form, or confront him except as an object of free play. T o b e s t o w f r e e d o m b y m e a n s o f f r e e d o m is the fundamental law of this kingdom.

10. The dynamic State can merely make society possible, by letting one nature be curbed by another; the ethical State can merely make it (morally) necessary, by subjecting the individual will to the general; the aesthetic State alone can make it real, because it consummates the will of the whole through the nature of the individual. Though it may be his needs which drive man into society, and reason which implants within him the principles of social behaviour, beauty alone can confer upon him a s o c i a l c h a r a c t e r. Taste alone brings harmony into society, because it fosters harmony in the individual. All other forms of perception divide man, because they are founded exclusively either upon the sensuous or upon the spiritual part of his being; only the aesthetic mode of perception makes of him a whole, because both his natures must be in harmony if he is to achieve it. All other forms of communication divide society, because they relate exclusively either to the private receptivity or to the private proficiency of its individual members, hence to that which distinguishes man from man; only the aesthetic mode of communication unites society, because it relates to that which is common to all. The pleasures of the senses we enjoy merely as individuals, without the genus which is immanent

dass die Gattung, die in uns wohnt, daran Anteil nähme; wir können also unsre sinnlichen Freuden nicht zu allgemeinen erweitern, weil wir unser Individuum nicht allgemein machen können. Die Freuden der Erkenntnis geniessen wir bloss als Gattung, und indem wir jede Spur des Individuums sorgfältig aus unserm Urteil entfernen; wir können also unsre Vernunftfreuden nicht allgemein machen, weil wir die Spuren des Individuums aus dem Urteile anderer nicht so wie aus dem unsrigen ausschliessen können. Das Schöne allein geniessen wir als Individuum und als Gattung zugleich, d. h. als Repräsentanten der Gattung. Das sinnliche Gute kann nur Einen Glücklichen machen, da es sich auf Zueignung gründet, welche immer eine Ausschliessung mit sich führt; es kann diesen Einen auch nur einseitig glücklich machen, weil die Persönlichkeit nicht daran teilnimmt. Das absolut Gute kann nur unter Bedingungen glücklich machen, die allgemein nicht vorauszusetzen sind; denn die Wahrheit ist nur der Preis der Verleugnung, und an den reinen Willen glaubt nur ein reines Herz. Die Schönheit allein beglückt alle Welt, und jedes Wesen vergisst seiner Schranken, so lang' es ihren Zauber erfährt.

11.   Kein Vorzug, keine Alleinherrschaft wird geduldet, soweit der Geschmack regiert und das Reich des schönen Scheins sich verbreitet. Dieses Reich erstreckt sich aufwärts, bis wo die Vernunft mit unbedingter Notwendigkeit herrscht und alle Materie aufhört; es erstreckt sich niederwärts, bis wo der Naturtrieb mit blinder Nötigung waltet und die Form noch nicht anfängt; ja selbst auf diesen äussersten Grenzen, wo die gesetzgebende Macht ihm genommen ist, lässt sich der Geschmack doch die vollziehende nicht entreissen. Die ungesellige Begierde muss ihrer Selbstsucht entsagen und das Angenehme, welches sonst nur die Sinne lockt, das Netz der Anmut auch über die Geister auswerfen. Der Notwendigkeit strenge Stimme, die Pflicht, muss ihre vorwerfende Formel verändern, die nur der Widerstand rechtfertigt, und die willige Natur durch ein edleres Zutrauen ehren. Aus den Mysterien der Wissenschaft führt der Geschmack die Erkenntnis unter den offenen Himmel des Gemeinsinns heraus, und verwandelt das Eigentum der Schulen in ein Gemeingut der ganzen menschlichen Gesellschaft. In seinem Gebiete muss auch der mächtigste Genius sich seiner Hoheit begeben und zu dem Kindersinn vertraulich herniedersteigen. Die Kraft muss sich binden lassen durch die Huldgöttinnen,

within us having any share in them at all; hence we cannot make the pleasures of sense universal, because we are unable to universalize our own individuality. The pleasures of knowledge we enjoy merely as genus, and by carefully removing from our judgement all trace of individuality; hence we cannot make the pleasures of reason universal, because we cannot eliminate traces of individuality from the judgements of others as we can from our own. Beauty alone do we enjoy at once as individual and as genus, i.e., as r e p r e s e n t a t i v e s of the human genus. The good of the Senses can only make o n e man happy, since it is founded on appropriation, and this always involves exclusion; and it can only make this o n e man one-sidedly happy, since his Personality has no part in it. Absolute good can only bring happiness under conditions which we cannot presume to be universal; for truth is the prize of abnegation alone, and only the pure in heart believe in the pure will. Beauty alone makes the whole world happy, and each and every being forgets its limitations while under its spell.

11.   No privilege, no autocracy of any kind, is tolerated where taste rules, and the realm of aesthetic semblance extends its sway. This realm stretches upwards to the point where reason governs with unconditioned necessity, and all that is mere matter ceases to be. It stretches downwards to the point where natural impulse reigns with blind compulsion, and form has not yet begun to appear. And even at these furthermost confines, where taste is deprived of all legislative power, it still does not allow the executive power to be wrested from it. A-social appetite must renounce its self-seeking, and the Agreeable, whose normal function is to seduce the senses, must cast toils of Grace over the mind as well. Duty, stern voice of Necessity, must moderate the censorious tone of its precepts —a tone only justified by the resistance they encounter—and show greater respect for Nature through a nobler confidence in her willingness to obey them. From within the Mysteries of Science, taste leads knowledge out into the broad daylight of Common Sense, and transforms a monopoly of the Schools into the common possession of Human Society as a whole. In the kingdom of taste even the mightiest genius must divest itself of its majesty, and stoop in all humility to the mind of a little child. Strength must allow itself to be bound by the Graces, and the lion have its defiance

und der trotzige Löwe dem Zaum eines Amors gehorchen. Dafür breitet er über das physische Bedürfnis, das in seiner nackten Gestalt die Würde freier Geister beleidigt, seinen mildernden Schleier aus und verbirgt uns die entehrende Verwandtschaft mit dem Stoff in einem lieblichen Blendwerk von Freiheit. Beflügelt durch ihn entschwingt sich auch die kriechende Lohnkunst dem Staube, und die Fesseln der Leibeigenschaft fallen, von seinem Stabe berührt, von dem Leblosen wie von dem Lebendigen ab. In dem ästhetischen Staate ist alles — auch das dienende Werkzeug ein freier Bürger, der mit dem edelsten gleiche Rechte hat, und der Verstand, der die duldende Masse unter seine Zwecke gewalttätig beugt, muss sie hier um ihre Beistimmung fragen. Hier also, in dem Reiche des ästhetischen Scheins, wird das Ideal der Gleichheit erfüllt, welches der Schwärmer so gern auch dem Wesen nach realisiert sehen möchte; und wenn es wahr ist, dass der schöne Ton in der Nähe des Thrones am frühesten und am vollkommensten reift, so müsste man auch hier die gütige Schickung erkennen, die den Menschen oft nur deswegen in der Wirklichkeit einzuschränken scheint, um ihn in eine idealische Welt zu treiben.

12.   Existiert aber auch ein solcher Staat des schönen Scheins, und wo ist er zu finden? Dem Bedürfnis nach existiert er in jeder feingestimmten Seele; der Tat nach möchte man ihn wohl nur, wie die reine Kirche und die reine Republik, in einigen wenigen auserlesenen Zirkeln finden, wo nicht die geistlose Nachahmung fremder Sitten, sondern eigne schöne Natur das Betragen lenkt, wo der Mensch durch die verwickeltsten Verhältnisse mit kühner Einfalt und ruhiger Unschuld geht und weder nötig hat, fremde Freiheit zu kränken, um die seinige zu behaupten, noch seine Würde wegzuwerfen, um Anmut zu zeigen.

curbed by the bridle of a Cupid. In return, taste throws a veil
of decorum over those physical desires which, in their naked form,
affront the dignity of free beings; and, by a delightful illusion of
freedom, conceals from us our degrading kinship with matter. On
the wings of taste even that art which must cringe for payment can
lift itself out of the dust; and, at the touch of her wand, the fetters
of serfdom fall away from the lifeless and the living alike. In the
Aesthetic State everything—even the tool which serves—is a free
citizen, having equal rights with the noblest; and the mind, which
would force the patient mass beneath the yoke of its purposes, must
here first obtain its assent. Here, therefore, in the realm of Aesthetic
Semblance, we find that ideal of equality fulfilled which the
Enthusiast would fain see realized in substance. And if it is true
that it is in the proximity of thrones that fine breeding comes
most quickly and most perfectly to maturity, would one not have
to recognize in this, as in much else, a kindly dispensation which
often seems to be imposing limits upon man in the real world,
only in order to spur him on to realization in an ideal world?

12. But does such a State of Aesthetic Semblance really exist?
And if so, where is it to be found? As a need, it exists in every
finely attuned soul; as a realized fact, we are likely to find it, like
the pure Church and the pure Republic, only in some few chosen
circles, where conduct is governed, not by some soulless imitation
of the manners and morals of others, but by the aesthetic nature
we have made our own; where men make their way, with undismayed
simplicity and tranquil innocence, through even the most involved
and complex situations, free alike of the compulsion to infringe the
freedom of others in order to assert their own, as of the necessity
to shed their Dignity in order to manifest Grace.

COMMENTARY

Roman numerals refer to the Letter, Arabic to the paragraph within the Letter. 'Note' refers to our notes in the Commentary; 'fn.' to Schiller's footnotes, or to the footnotes in our Introduction. Captions from Schiller's footnotes are preceded by an asterisk.

Title-page: the motto, from *Julie ou la Nouvelle Héloïse* (III. 7), appears only in the *Horen* version (cf. p. lvii above). Schiller wrote to his wife, 20.ix.1794: 'Don't forget to bring me Sévigné, the Héloïse and the Rollin'—all three presumably for use in the final revision of his *Aesthetic Letters*. The other references are to Madame de Sévigné's famous letters, fascinating gazettes of the times and models of style, and to Charles Rollin's *Histoire ancienne* (1730–8) and/or *Histoire romaine* (1738). The two latter were the standard reference books on ancient history in the eighteenth century: Rousseau made use of them for his *Premier Discours*, and Burke, while a student at Trinity College, Dublin, asked for one or other of them as a prize (letter of 4.vii.1745; *Correspondence*, ed. cit., p. 52).

LETTER I

I. I. *in the form of a series of letters*: the main emphasis in the German sentence is surely, despite the spaced type, on the form in which the results of the inquiry are to be submitted, rather than on the nature of the inquiry itself. The imagined situation is evoked quite clearly by the first two paragraphs, even if we did not know the history of the Letters' inception: release from any obligation to present his results in the shape of a formal treatise and according to the recognized procedures of philosophy. It is, however, clearly confirmed by external evidence. On 9.ii.1793 Schiller had written to his patron, the Duke of Augustenburg, asking if he might first submit his ideas on the Philosophy of Beauty in a series of letters before offering them to the public: 'Diese freiere Form wird dem Vortrage derselben mehr Individualität und Leben, und der Gedanke, dass ich mit Ihnen rede und von Ihnen beurteilt werde, mir selbst ein höheres Interesse an meiner Materie geben' (Jonas, iii. 250). This 'real' epistolary situation is then retained in the fictional form of the finished treatise.

I. 2. *scholastic*: a rendering of *schulgerecht* which seems justified by Schiller's own use of the word *scholastisch* at the same time and in a related context: 'As far as is practicable we shall endeavour to free the results of knowledge from their scholastic form . . . and make them available to the Common Sense' (*Ankündigung der Horen*; SA xvi. 152). 'Scholastic' here, then, in its wider sense of 'pertaining to formal methods of philosophy', and not specifically to those of the medieval schoolmen. Cf. Kant's insistence, in his Preface to the second edition (1794) of *Die Religion innerhalb der Grenzen der blossen Vernunft* (a work which greatly impressed Schiller), that the technical terms from his two *Critiques* were here 'nur der Schule wegen gebraucht', and that to understand the substance of this treatise nothing more was needed than the Common Moral Sense.

rich experience of the world: Schiller was painfully aware of the self-generative nature of his ideas, especially by contrast with Goethe's. Cf. one of the letters with which he inaugurated their friendship, 31.viii.1794:

You must not expect of me any very rich material in the way of ideas; that is what I shall find in you. My need, and my endeavour, is to make much out of little, and should you ever become aware of the poverty in me of all that is usually called acquired knowledge, you will perhaps conclude that I have in some respects not been altogether unsuccessful. Since the circle of my ideas is smaller, I can range through it more quickly and more often, and for that very reason put my poor stock of ready cash to better use, and generate through form a manifold variety which, as regards content, is entirely lacking. You make it your endeavour to simplify your vast world of ideas; I seek to lend variety to my few possessions. You are sovereign over an entire kingdom; I only over a somewhat numerous family of concepts which I would fain expand into a little cosmos.

I. 4. *Practical part of the Kantian system*: i.e. the second of Kant's *Critiques*, concerned with ethics, the *Critique of Practical Reason* (1788).

immemorial pronouncements: *Aussprüche* seems to make as good, if not better, sense than *Ansprüche* (claims), the emendation introduced by Körner (see p. 336 below). As on other occasions, he was perhaps trying to make Schiller more of a Kantian than in fact he was. The contrast here, surely, is not between the claims of Reason and their technical formulation, but between technical and non-technical modes of utterance: Kant in his Ethics had expressed in the technical terms of his philosophy what from time immemorial had been voiced in the language of conscience and common sense. Cf. Note to *scholastic* (I. 2 above) and Schiller's letter to Goethe, 28.x.1794:

It gives me no cause for fear that the law of change, from which neither human nor divine works are exempt, will destroy the *form* of this [the Kantian] philosophy, too, as it will that of any other. But the *foundations* of this philosophy will have no need to fear such a fate; for as long as the human race has existed, and as long as there has been Reason at all, they have been tacitly acknowledged and, on the whole, followed in practice. (Our italics.)

Common Reason: see Glossary under *Gemeinsinn*.

at years of discretion: an echo of Kant's famous description of Enlightenment, in his *Beantwortung der Frage: Was ist Aufklärung?* (1784), as 'man's emergence from a tutelage which he has brought upon himself'. Cf. VIII. 5 and IX. 4 for other echoes.

For alas! intellect: for similar expressions of Schiller's ambivalent attitude to the 'destructive' procedures of the analytical understanding see his contemporary letters to Goethe; e.g. 23.viii.1794: 'for alas! we can only know that which we separate', and 7.i.1795, where he contrasts the world of poetry with that of philosophy—the former so serene, so living, harmonious, and human, the other severe, rigid, abstract, and unnatural—and goes on to claim that he, in his own philosophical writings, has

remained as true to nature as is consonant with the conception of analysis; perhaps, indeed, truer than our Kantians would consider either permissible or possible. And yet in spite of this I feel no less sharply the infinite gap between living and thinking about living—and in such melancholy moments cannot refrain from interpreting as a defect of my nature what in happier hours I must merely regard as a natural peculiarity of the thing [i.e. of analytical philosophy]. Still, so much is certain: the poet is the only true *human being*, and the best of philosophers by contrast a mere caricature.

But where lesser men would have foundered on the obvious tension, Schiller managed to resolve the opposition between philosophic abstraction and poetic imagination. As he claimed in a letter to Goethe, 16.x.1795, he had, for the writing of his philosophic poems, been forced to keep both these powers at full stretch, and only by a constant movement within himself been able to maintain the two heterogeneous elements 'in einer Art von Solution'.

Like the analytical chemist: *Scheidekünstler* was the ordinary word for chemist in the eighteenth century (see Glossary under *Kunst*). Cf. the discussion on its appropriateness in Goethe's *Wahlverwandtschaften*, I. 4 (JA xxi. 40 f.).

the workings of spontaneous Nature: i.e. nature both within and without (see Glossary under *Natur* and *Sinn*). It is the spontaneous operations of moral conduct, i.e. nature within, that the philosopher is here said to analyse, in much the same way as the chemist subjects to his analytical techniques the wholes which physical nature presents.

torment of his own techniques: *Kunst* here (see Glossary) is not, as it is often taken to be, an objective but a subjective genitive. Böhm (op. cit., pp. 7 f.) makes great play with Schiller's antagonism to philosophy at this point. But it was a question of ambivalence, not antagonism. Contrast his strictures on armchair-philosophers in XVIII. 4fn. and his letter to Goethe, 9.ii.1798, in which he castigates those who try to synthesize in philosophy where synthesis is out of place:

You and I, and other good people, know very well that man . . . always acts as a whole, and that Nature proceeds by way of synthesis. But it would never occur to us to deny on that account the need for analysis and distinctions in philosophy . . . any more than we should attack the chemist for destroying nature's syntheses. But this Herr Schlosser [Goethe's brother-in-law, who had just published a second attack on Kant] and his like want to sniff and fumble their way through metaphysics. They insist on knowing everything by way of synthesis. This apparent richness, however, merely conceals the most wretched and platitudinous emptiness. The affectation of these gentlemen for keeping man in a permanent state of totality, for spiritualizing the physical and humanizing the spiritual is, I fear, nothing but a miserable attempt to ensure the survival of their own wretched Self in all its obscurantism.

I. 5. *the essential amalgam*: mindful of the contemporary Xenion *Das Amalgama* (SA ii. 96)—'Alles mischt die Natur so einzig und innig . . .'—we have preferred this to 'union' or 'combination'. The whole train of thought is reminiscent of Mephisto's 'debunking' of the philosophy of the Schools, the 'Gedanken-fabrik':

> Wer will was Lebendigs erkennen und beschreiben,
> Sucht erst den Geist heraus zu treiben,
> Dann hat er die Teile in seiner Hand,
> Fehlt leider! nur das geistige Band.
>
> (*Faust, Ein Fragment*, 1790, 415 ff.)

For a similar thought cf. XV. 4.

LETTER II

II. 1. *to be achieved by the art of man*: for our justification of this rendering see above p. lxiv and Glossary under *Kunst*.

II. 2. *in a century other than my own*: this unreserved commitment to his own age is in no way invalidated by his letter to Reichardt of 3.viii.1795, with its half-ironic disclaimer of any accurate knowledge of the events in France 'be-cause . . . it is in the most literal sense true that I do not really "live" in my own century'. Cf. Geneviève Bianquis, 'Schiller et Reichardt', *EG* xiv (1959), 327. For a more complete statement of his attitude see the earlier letter to F. H. Jacobi of 25.i.1795, enclosing the first number of the *Horen*:

> We intend to be, *in the body*, citizens of our own age, and to remain so, since this may not be otherwise; but in other respects, and *in the spirit*, it is the privilege and the duty of the philosopher, as it is of the poet, to belong to no people and to no age, but to be, in the literal sense of the word, the con-temporary of all times ['der Zeitgenosse aller Zeiten'].

II. 3. *art of the Ideal*: cf. XXVII. 1 and Glossary under both *Idee* and *Kunst*. The important thing is not to take this term as referring to any particular *kind* or *quality* of art. It is, as the subsequent context suggests, rather Fine Art *per se* as distinct from artefacts serving practical purposes; art for its own sake, then, one might almost say, but only in the sense that release from all other purposes enables it to have expressive function, to become the vehicle of ideas, and so take its place alongside other manifestations of the symbolizing processes of mind.

The spirit of philosophical inquiry: something wider than philosophy in the technical sense is to be understood here; rather the empirical, scientific, analysis of things as fostered by the *philosophes* throughout the century. D'Alembert himself, an ardent advocate of Newtonian method, had stated in his preamble to the *Encyclopédie* (1751) that the empirical spirit had created an atmosphere in which the arts of the imagination could not possibly flourish.

II. 4. *the political scene*: cf. pp. xv ff. above.

this great action: the imagery of this whole Letter is clearly legal, but (by contrast with IX. 3) concerned with natural law, *ius naturale*, not with *lex civilis*, or positive law. It is the law innate in man, *in corde scripta*, the light of natural reason by which he discerns good and evil. In the eighteenth century it was normally equated with natural rights, the *ius gentium*. Cf. W. Witte, 'Goethe and *ius naturale*', *PEGS* xxii (1953).

II. 5. *liberal citizen of the world*: echoing the term *Weltbürgersinn* which his patron had applied to himself in his first letter to Schiller of 27.xi.1791.

leave the decision: *heimstellen* for *anheimstellen*.

LETTER III

III. 1. *as a free intelligence*: the *Horen* reads 'als freie Spontaneität'. The relevant meaning of 'spontaneity' would seem to be 'activity in the absence of any external stimulus'. Cf. I. 4, where we have translated 'das Werk der freiwilligen Natur' as 'the workings of spontaneous Nature'. For other instances of man considered as *Intelligenz* see XI. 5 and XIX. 12fn.

III. 2. *finds himself—in the State*: i.e. in the political State as it has grown up through force of circumstances, what Schiller will call the *Notstaat*, or *Naturstaat*, by contrast with the *Vernunftstaat*, a body politic evolved through the deliberations of Reason. We have consistently used 'State', with capital, to render *Staat*, reserving 'state' for *Stand*.

upon sexual love: cf. XXVII. 7, where erotic love is given as an example of the transformation of blind instinct by means of the aesthetic. Burke, *On the Sublime*, i. 10 (which Schiller, of course, knew) had similarly distinguished two elements in erotic love: sexual passion and love of beauty, the second, as he pointed out, being a social phenomenon.

a state of nature: the argument is based on Rousseau's distinction between 'l'homme de la nature' and 'l'homme de l'homme' (Vaughan, op. cit. ii. 138, fn. 3), man in his natural state and man as man has made him. But, as Rousseau explicitly stated (*De l'inégalité*; Vaughan, op. cit. i. 141), this 'state of nature' is not to be thought of as an historical reality; rather as one of those 'raisonnements hypothétiques et conditionnels, plus propres à éclaircir la nature des choses qu'à en montrer la véritable origine, et semblables à ceux que font tous les jours nos physiciens sur la formation du monde'. And Schiller makes it equally clear, in other terms, that he is not using the mode of historical description for historical purposes either (cf. p. xlvi above). Questions of historical accuracy are therefore beside the point. In fact, two 'states of nature' (*Naturstand*) are here distinguished: only the one, a not very pleasant one—Hobbes's *bellum omnium contra omnes* (cf. Schiller's letter to Schütz, 30.ix.1794)—is presented as historical reality; the other is frankly stated to be a construct of Reason—an idealized state of nature in which each man lives solely for and by himself (cf. Vaughan, op. cit. i. 9 f.). The point to notice, however, is that even the

former, though apparently more realistic, is a construct too, not to be taken—
and not really intended by Schiller to be taken (as XXIV. 3 will confirm)—as
a 'state' which existed at some time in the early history of man, but rather as a
hypothesis which is indispensable in political thinking. For when he implies
that of course there never was a moment when man voluntarily relinquished a
state of individual freedom for a state of social contracts, that in fact man was
pressured by force of circumstance and natural need (cf. XXVII. 10) into the
State as we know it (*Notstaat, Naturstaat*), he is not making a factual assertion
at all. He is, as it were, saying: Whatever historical research may reveal about
the origins of society and the State can in no way invalidate those procedures of
Reason by means of which men endeavour to transform the political structures
which have arisen by chance into political structures based on principle. Reasoning about principles is bound to turn on the voluntary surrender of individual
liberty, and in historico-mythical terms this may well present itself as the
emergence from an idealized 'state of nature'.

for a state of social contracts: not, as other English translations have it, exchanging a state of bondage, or contract, for one of independence. This is to
mistake not only the German construction but the point of the whole passage.
Schiller is concerned with rational man's—in his view, legitimate—rationalization of how he found himself in the political State, viz., by a voluntary and
reasoned surrender of his individual liberty. Cf. p. lxiii above.

in him as Person: *Person* will be a technical term from XI onwards, but even
thereafter Schiller does not strictly distinguish between *Person* and *Persönlichkeit*.

III. 3. *from forces and not from laws*: 'laws' here, of course, 'moral' laws and not
either 'natural' or 'positive' laws. Cf. Note to II. 4.

III. 4. *When the craftsman has a timepiece*: on *Künstler* see Glossary. Kant, in
his *Critique of Judgement*, i, § 43(3), is still debating whether a watchmaker is
an artist (*Künstler*) or a craftsman (*Handwerker*), and it is perhaps not idle to
remind ourselves that Rousseau, his revered master, was the son of a watchmaker. The craft of clocks, esp. astronomical clocks, had reached a high peak
in the Württemberg of Schiller's day, and the precision instruments invented
by the Swabian theosophist, Pastor J. M. Hahn (1758–1819), were famous
(cf. Goethe's letter to Lavater, 19.ii.1781). The image of the clock or watch had
been current in philosophy since Leibniz had compared the Universe to a clock
set going by its Creator, and the perfection of the structure of a watch and its
relation to beauty had been discussed by Burke (*On the Sublime*, iii. 7). He concluded that, for all the perfection of its parts and their fitness to the whole, yet
it is not beautiful—whereas its engraved case may be so, since in beauty 'the
effect is previous to any knowledge of the use' (ed. cit., p. 108).

III. 5. *because it never becomes manifest*: 'moral character' here, not of course in
the sense of some realized and recognizable pattern of moral behaviour, but
rather of that aspect of Man which is 'free' (see Glossary under *Freiheit* [2]),
pure spirit, as opposed to his animal nature, or that aspect of him which is

contingent and conditioned. The former, according to Schiller (XXIII. 7fn.
§ 1), has no way of actually becoming manifest except through beauty which,
in its fusion of sense and spirit, is at once symbol of the unity of human nature
and 'triumphant proof' (XXV. 6) that it is possible to restore such unity through
reconciling those two opposed aspects. If freedom, or the 'moral character' in
this sense, is here said to be inaccessible to the legislator because it never
becomes manifest, it will, as is clear from IX. 3, still remain outside his jurisdiction when it does become manifest in art and beauty, or when, under the
educative influence of these, it is realized in the freedom of 'noble' conduct.
The point is thus central to Schiller's argument: that a community of truly free
men, however favourable the political and social conditions, can only be brought
about through the education of the individual. The culmination of his argument
from the point of view of the individual will be the analysis of noble, i.e.
aesthetic, conduct, at the end of XXIII; from the point of view of the community it will be the unwritten law 'Freiheit zu geben durch Freiheit' towards
the end of XXVII.

LETTER IV

IV. 1. *Absolute Being*: on the several names used by Schiller for God, or the
Highest Being, see pp. cxxii ff. above.

IV. 2. *the archetype of a human being*: for the justification of our translation of
rein and *ideal* here, and in the rest of this paragraph, see Glossary under *Idee*.

*fn. Fichte, *Lectures on the Vocation of a Scholar*: in the first of these (1794)
Fichte had demanded that man's essential nature ought to reveal itself in his
outward life, shine forth in all his thoughts, desires, and deeds, and become his
unvarying and unalterable character. Schiller will draw on this work again in
Letters XI and XIV. In view of our remarks in the Glossary on the ambiguity
of *Bestimmung*, it is worth noting that Fichte's chief work, *Die Bestimmung
des Menschen*, has been published in English as both *The Vocation of Man* and
The Destination of Man.

IV. 3. *the complete anthropological view*: *anthropologisch* here, as the contrast
with *moralisch* implies, in its widest sense of the science of man, a physical and
social, as well as a rational, being. Schiller was clearly drawing on his friend
Humboldt's *Plan einer vergleichenden Anthropologie* which, though not actually
printed until many years after Humboldt's death, must have been the subject
of discussion between them during its inception, 1795-7 (cf. R. Leroux,
L'Anthropologie comparée de Guillaume de Humboldt. Publications de la Faculté
des Lettres de l'Université de Strasbourg, 135, Paris, 1958). The contrast
between the two views, the one-sidedly moral and the complete anthropological,
is exemplified by Kant's rigoristic definition of a strictly moral act and the
ethical ideal of the harmony of the whole personality as set forth by, say,
Shaftesbury.

IV. 4. *but the eye which would seek to protect the freedom of the material*: the first mention in this treatise of the basic concept of aesthetic semblance, or illusion, which in XXVI. 5 will be carefully distinguished from other kinds of illusion, or mere deception. The intellect of course knows that physical material has no freedom; but an eye prepared to accept aesthetic semblance as a valid mode of perception will demand the *appearance* of freedom through the artist's treatment of it. Cf. IX. 4, where an eye predisposed to such semblance is said to go on finding significant beauty in religious objects even when it can no longer accord them the assent of religious credence.

a show of yielding: the distinction is subtle but important. Schiller is not, despite some appearance to the contrary, saying the opposite of those artists who have insisted on respect for the material medium, even on its power to inspire (for a persuasive account of this position see Epstein's *Let there be Sculpture*, London, 1940, ch. xviii). Nor is he denying that the sheer physical properties of a given material (clay, stone, wood) may affect the range of what an artist can do with it. What he *is* saying is that it is not by mere respect for its physical properties that he achieves that perfect marriage of mind and medium which so delights us in the work of the master. Within the limits imposed by its physical properties, the artist does what he likes with his medium. His creative act consists precisely in so adapting it to his own aesthetic ends that he *seems* to have been doing nothing but obey its own laws. In other words, he creates the *appearance* of freedom ('Freiheit in der Erscheinung')—the theme of Schiller's *Kallias oder über die Schönheit* (cf. pp. xxvii f. above and Glossary under *Freiheit* and *Materie*). The educationist and politician, by contrast, must show a real, not a seeming, respect for the—human—material they are shaping.

becomes identical with the medium: man as 'medium', or 'material', an image which recurs in XVII. 3 and 4, and XXVII. 11. The thought is echoed in Goethe's distich (first printed in Schiller's *Musenalmanach für das Jahr 1797*, p. 28, and subsequently in Goethe's poetical works as no. 70 of *Vier Jahreszeiten*, JA i. 243):

> Wer ist das würdigste Glied des Staats? Ein wackerer Bürger;
> Unter jeglicher Form bleibt er der edelste Stoff.

IV. 5. *the State will be merely the interpreter*: this doctrine of the State and its function presupposes a notion of 'positive' freedom. Cf. pp. xvi, cxi above. Those interested in Schiller's debt to Rousseau should compare, at this point, *Le Contrat social*, i. 6 ('Du pacte social'; Vaughan, op. cit. ii. 32 f.), and ii. 4 ('Des bornes du pouvoir souverain'; ibid. 43 f.).

IV. 6. *as savage . . . or as barbarian*: a distinction, fundamental to these Letters (cf. V. 3; X. 1 and 2), which Schiller had already made in his Jena lectures (SA xii. 334), although in *Die Künstler* (111 and 165) the terms still seem to be synonymous. Under the influence of the eighteenth-century cult of 'the noble savage', he rates the 'Wilde' higher than the 'Barbar'. For the psychological insight which informs his evaluation see XIII. 4fn. §§ 3–4, where he castigates an education which seeks to instil principles without seeing to it that they are founded on fully developed and differentiated feelings. This, he implies, is the way to produce a race of barbarians, people who are always, whenever the rigidity of their principles cracks under pressure, threatened by an upsurge of the repressed feelings which have been left to their own primitive devices. Cf. Boucher, loc. cit., and, for a similar thought, Hölderlin's denunciation, in identical terms, of the Germans as 'Barbaren von Alters her, durch Fleiss und Wissenschaft und selbst durch Religion barbarischer geworden' (*Hyperion*, ii. 2; ed. cit. ii. 282).

IV. 7. *Wholeness of character*: with the loan-word *Totalität* Schiller announces his main theme. Cf. *Integrität* in XXII. 1, where he clinches this argument.

LETTER V

V. 2. *over there*, and *over here*: there is neither lexical nor historical support for 'on all sides', as some translators have it. What Schiller had in mind was the American Revolution on the other side of the Atlantic and the French Revolution on this. The reversal of the normal order, *diesseits und jenseits*, reflects the chronological sequence.

generation unprepared to receive it: cf. the Xenion *Der Zeitpunkt*, first printed in Schiller's *Musenalmanach für das Jahr 1797* (SA ii. 96; JA iv. 158):

Eine grosse Epoche hat das Jahrhundert geboren,
    Aber der grosse Moment findet ein kleines Geschlecht.

For a like formulation of an earlier, but in some respects similar, historical situation cf. *Der Dreissigjährige Krieg* (SA xv. 96): 'Der grosse Zeitpunkt fand nur mittelmässige Geister auf der Bühne, und unbenutzt blieb das entscheidende Moment, weil es den Mutigen an Macht, den Mächtigen an Einsicht, Mut und Entschlossenheit fehlte.' The picture of contemporary society which Schiller draws in these Letters, though obviously a response to the disillusionment which followed upon the French Revolution, is not solely, or even chiefly, orientated towards France. Hölderlin was to make its reference to Germany explicit (cf. Note to VI. 7). And it is just as obviously inspired by Rousseau's indictment of the evils of civilization as a whole. Its relevance has increased rather than diminished since it was written.

V. 3. *a return to the savage state*: not, as Snell has it, 'barbarity'. Schiller is pursuing the distinction established in IV. 6 between 'Wilder' and 'Barbar', and 'Verwilderung' obviously belongs to the former, not the latter.

V. 4. *gravity and cohesion*: we have added 'mechanical' and 'organic' here in order to bring out the implied contrast between the State conceived as mere physical mechanism and the State conceived as living organism. The forces of gravity and cohesion belong to the Newtonian world-picture of mechanical forces; the formative drive (*nisus formativus* was a term used by the contemporary biologist, Blumenbach) reflects the interest of the late eighteenth century in the newer sciences of living things. These contrasting images occur again in connexion with the organization of States in VI. 7. They had already been used by Schiller in connexion with human beauty and grace in *Anmut und Würde*

(SA xi. 207): 'But the universal forces of nature, as is well known, are engaged in perpetual warfare with the particular, or organic, forces, and even the most intricately organized form is still subject to the laws of gravity and cohesion.'

the kingdom of the elements: whether Schiller is thinking of the four elements of ancient philosophy—earth, water, air, and fire—or of the presumably simple substances of pre-scientific chemistry—water, air, oil, salt, earth, &c.—is immaterial (though Lavoisier's death on the scaffold in 1794 may well have recalled the latter). The point of the analogy is the return of society to non-organized forms of existence, and here, as in XXVII. 3, *Elementarreich* is being contrasted with organic life.

V. 5. *culture itself is its source*: the allusion is of course to the *Premier Discours*, *Sur les sciences et les arts*. At the end of it Rousseau, somewhat paradoxically, reached the conclusion that if carried on by men of virtue, and protected by enlightened princes, science and art could bring both virtue and happiness. It was an ideal Schiller saw to some extent realized in classical Weimar. His reference to the fructifying influence of court life on culture in XXVII. 11, thus has a real, as well as a literary, source.

which of the ancient or modern philosophers: the reviewer of the *Horen* in the *Allgemeine Literaturzeitung* (Jena, 31.i.1795), C. G. Schütz, took it to be a modern one: 'Hier können wir nachhelfen: es war Moses Mendelssohn' (cf. Fambach, op. cit., p. 108). The ancient one was, of course, Plato (whom Mendelssohn had recently made popular in Germany with his *Phaedon*, 1767): 'Are we not to say that those natures which are most nobly endowed, become, if they receive a bad upbringing, superlatively evil?' (*Republic*, vi. 491 E). The editor in the Loeb Classics offers parallels from several authors (together with the tag 'corruptio optimi pessima')—not, however, from Aristotle (*Nic. Eth.* viii. 10. 2) whom Snell (op. cit., p. 36) takes to be the source.

creature of Civilization: not, as some translators have it, 'art scholar' or 'disciple of art'. It is a subjective genitive, parallel to 'the child of nature'. Throughout this Letter, Schiller is concerned with the effects of our so-called civilization, and this is another instance of *Kunst* being used in a far wider sense than 'fine art'. *Sohn* is again contrasted with *Zögling* in IX. 4; *Naturmensch* with *künstlicher Mensch* in XVII. 4.

bolster up depravity: the convolution of the rhetorical figure tends to obscure the acuity of this statement of the principle of 'rationalization': purely intellectual enlightenment simply provides us with reasons for justifying what we want, feel, or believe; encourages the use of intelligence for purposes not reasonable or, as Schiller would say, not in accordance with Reason. This attack on Enlightenment in the narrower sense is part of the strategy designed to achieve Enlightenment of the whole personality, including the irrational functions of the psyche.

to take over her principles: i.e. where we should be natural, we are prudes, while in our personal and social morality the law of the jungle often prevails.

The sham propriety of our manners: cf. *Über das Pathetische* (SA xi. 247): 'Die Decenz verfälscht überall, auch wenn sie an ihrer rechten Stelle ist, den Ausdruck der Natur, und doch fordert diesen die Kunst unnachlasslich.' *Decenz* was a favourite word of Schiller's somewhat strait-laced wife, the aristocratic Lotte; he sometimes even referred to her in jest as 'die Decenz' (cf. Jonas, iii. 489).

of the enthusiast: 'enthusiast' here, of course, in its eighteenth-century sense of 'one who indulges in ill-regulated and inappropriate exaltation'. Shaftesbury had condemned it in *A Letter Concerning Enthusiasm*, and that most popular of *Popularphilosophen*, Christian Garve, made a distinction between *Enthusiasmus* (*Begeisterung*) and *Schwärmerei*:

> Jene exaltiert nur die Begierden, erhöht die Hoffnungen, verschönert das wirklich Vorhandne. Diese aber schafft neue Gegenstände; sie gibt dem ein Dasein und eine Gestalt, was nirgend ist. Die Begeisterung schränkt sich auf Empfindungen und Begierden ein; die Schwärmerei schiebt uns Erdichtungen als wirkliche Kenntnisse unter. ('Über die Schwärmerei'. *Versuche*. 5. Theil, Breslau, 1802, p. 342)

What *Schwärmergeist* meant to Schiller is clear enough from IX. 5 and XIII. 4fn. §4. Cf. his distich *Der Philosoph und der Schwärmer* (SA ii. 131):

> Jener steht auf der Erde, doch schauet das Auge zum Himmel;
> Dieser, die Augen im Kot, recket die Beine hinauf.

LETTER VI

VI. 1. *by the use of Reason*: a key-sentence in the argument, and a reflection in miniature of the prevailing 'circularity' in the structure of Schiller's thinking (cf. pp. xlix–li above).

VI. 2. *the natural humanity of the Greeks*: Schiller's idealized view of the Greeks here is clearly based on Winckelmann whom he had recently been reading. But cf. X. 5, which is much closer to the notes and emendations he made to his friend Wilhelm von Humboldt's essay *Über das Studium des Altertums, und des griechischen insbesondere* (1793):

> Greek civilization was purely *aesthetic*; and that, I think, would have to be the point of departure in any attempt to explain this phenomenon. Nor must one forget that in the political sphere too the Greeks never managed to get beyond the youthful stage, and it is very much open to question whether they would have deserved a like commendation had they ever come to political manhood. (Cited Walzel, SA xii. 361)

VI. 3. *no dissension had as yet*: this contrast between the wholeness of the Greeks and the fragmentation of modern man no doubt does, as Walzel suggests, owe much to Herder's *Vom Erkennen und Empfinden der menschlichen Seele* (1778; ed. cit. viii. 217 ff.; cf. Note to VI. 7). But as Green (op. cit., p. 8) observes, the theme of vanished Grecian grandeur was a cliché even in 1749; it was only that 'Rousseau's genius for language endowed it with the quality of a new and original emotion'. And, of course, the notion that faculties now distinct had originally been one is as old as Quintilian (whom Schiller had recently been reading; cf. above pp. lxxiii f.).

coquetted with wit: 'wit', here, not in the broad sense in which the early eighteenth century often used it, viz. almost as a synonym for 'genius', but rather in the sense of the French *esprit* or, as Dryden defined it, 'sharpness of conceit'.

project . . . into the divinities of its glorious pantheon: the underlying image here seems to be optical, as it certainly is in XXV. 2 and 3, where the psychological implications of projection are also brought out.

in no single one of their deities: a similar thought in Goethe's *Römische Elegien*, I. xi, printed in the same number of the *Horen* as Letters XVII–XXVII. Cf. Humphry Trevelyan, *Goethe and the Greeks*, Cambridge, 1941, p. 173: 'All [the Greek gods] were *Abweichungen*, variations, from the basic idea; yet behind each variation, as the Greeks portrayed it, the norm of the *Urmensch* was visible.'

VI. 6. *It was civilization itself*: yet another allusion to Rousseau's *Premier Discours*, on the deleterious effects of the arts and sciences, as the next three paragraphs are an allusion to his second, on the deleterious effect of government based on blind need and force. In § 10 Schiller then develops the psychical consequences of this twofold pressure, from within and from without. If his indebtedness is obvious, so is the Schillerian slant he gives it: the dramatist in him is everywhere apparent, in the compression and conflict, and in the spectacular confrontations of the faculties of the human mind.

VI. 7. *crude and clumsy mechanism*: for related images of the State cf. above V. 4.

into nothing but a fragment: the reader may like to compare this analysis with the passage from Herder's *Vom Erkennen und Empfinden der menschlichen Seele* referred to in the Note to VI. 3 above:

> Since, together with classes, ranks, and occupations, the human faculties too, alas, have got separated . . . since diplomas, appointments, and letters of privilege make every Tom, Dick, and Harry into all that an ape could possibly want; since, then, *the one* does nothing *but think*—he doesn't use his eyes or explore or feel or act, but just keeps on calling out, like the caged bird who couldn't learn to talk: 'I'm thinking!'—while another is supposed to be able to *act and plan* without using his head at all: No single member partakes of the whole any more. . . . (ed. cit. viii. 217)

and with Hölderlin's famous lament at the end of *Hyperion* (1799) which may well have been, in part at least, inspired by Schiller:

> These are hard words, and yet I say them, because they are the truth. I can think of no people more dissociated than the Germans. Craftsmen are to be seen, but no human beings; thinkers, but no human beings; priests, but no human beings; masters and men, young people and those of mature years, but no human beings; is it not like a field of battle, where hands and arms and other limbs lie scattered in pieces, while the spilt blood of life seeps away into the sand? (ed. cit. ii. 283)

It is also interesting to compare the different emphasis in Rousseau. Whereas for all three German writers the contrast is between fragmentation and the whole man, for Rousseau, in the *Premier Discours*, it had been between specialist and citizen: 'Nous avons des Physiciens, des Géometres, des Chymistes, des Astronomes, des Poëtes, des Musiciens, des Peintres; nous n'avons plus de citoyens' (ed. cit., p. 150).

putting the stamp of humanity: for this secularized use of the term *ausprägen* see Note to IX. 5.

by means of a formulary: *Formular*, like *Formel* below (VI. 10 and XXVII. 11), is pejorative, a prescriptive rule imposed from without. Both are contrasted with *Form*, a free spontaneous development from within.

VI. 8. *Cytherean . . . Uranian, Venus*: i.e. the Venus who presides over profane, and the Venus who presides over sacred, love; the implication being that things of the spirit are likely to absorb more of a man's energies than a passing *amour*.

VI. 9. *into a state of primitive morality*: the function of the German adjective *moralisch* here is not descriptive. Like *schön* in *schöne Kunst*, it has the force of a substantive in the genitive. Again the argument follows Rousseau's description of the degeneration of government into despotism in his *De l'inégalité*.

VI. 10. *The practical spirit, by contrast*: more than just 'the spirit of business', as some translators have it. Opposed, as it is, to the spirit of speculation, it must include all the human offices and occupations set out in §§ 6–8.

depends for its intensity . . . for its scope: in XIII. 3 Schiller will pursue this thought, analysing the relation of 'intensity' to 'extensity' in the education of a 'complete' personality.

VI. 11. *exact discursive understanding*: Schiller is clearly operating with the Leibniz/Wolffian dichotomy between 'klare und deutliche Begriffe' (*notio clara* and *notio distincta*), the first given to us immediately, by sense-perception or intuition, the second, mediately, by analytical reflection upon these. For Coleridge's preoccupation with this distinction see his notes and marginalia on Wolff's *Logic* (*Notebooks*, ed. cit. i. 902 and note). Schiller probably has in mind, too, the eighteenth-century version of the 'Querelle des anciens et des modernes', that passionate debate concerning the 'priority' of scientific discoveries: Were the vaunted achievements of the moderns not illusory? Had not the ancients discovered it all before them? The solution implied here is that the question of priority is inapposite: the knowledge is, in a sense, the same; but it is also completely new, because it has been arrived at by different methods of thinking.

This degree the Greeks had attained: the Greeks, according to Schiller (and many others before and since), were not yet victims of the dichotomy discussed in the previous Note. For them an 'idea' was something *seen*, at once with the eye and with the mind's eye—the word εἶδος is cognate with both 'to see' and 'to know' (cf. Glossary under *Anschauung*). In marginal notes which he made on Wilhelm von Humboldt's essay cited above (see Note to VI. 2 and Walzel,

SA xii. 363) Schiller applied these distinctions between ways of knowing to stages in the development of culture:

> Are not those three stages which we can distinguish in all empirical knowledge likely to hold approximately for the general development of human culture?
> 1. The object stands before us as a whole, but confused and fluid.
> 2. We separate particular characteristics and distinguish; our knowledge is now *distinct*, but isolated and limited.
> 3. We unite what we have separated, and the whole stands before us again, no longer confused, however, but illuminated from all sides.
> The Greeks found themselves in the first of these three phases. We find ourselves in the second. The third, therefore, we may still hope for, and when it comes we shall no longer yearn for the Greeks to return.

With these three phases or periods cf. XXIV. 1; XXV. 1fn.

VI. 12. *into conflict with the truth of things*: the recent discovery that air and water are not, as had hitherto been supposed, elements, but compounds, or Lavoisier's demonstration by experiment of Newton's idea that coal and diamonds, though in appearance so different, are substantially the same, would be cases in point. What for centuries had been thought to be thus and thus, was now, by means of a highly specialized analytical understanding, shown to be otherwise, and the 'common' sense thereby forced to exchange a simpler 'truth' for a more complex one.

By pure thought usurping: for a similar statement about the way the various faculties depend on each other and help each other out, see Goethe's letter to Maria Paulowna of 3.i.1817, cited p. xxx above.

imagination allows her caprice: see Glossary under *Einbildungskraft* (2) and pp. lxv f. above. Imagination is here, as elsewhere (cf. XXIV. 5 and 6), presented as a two-edged sword. It is the generative, but also the 'blind', function of the mind, throwing up not only the myths by which men live, but the problems which challenge science and philosophy to resolve them; not only the visions of the poet, but the superstitions of the common man; enabling the artist to dissolve and dissipate the known order of the world in order to re-create it after his own fashion, but also generating those hypostasizations and personifications which can obstruct the progress of thought for generations. Even in the poet, according to Schiller, it has to be bridled by Reason. Cf. Coleridge (*Notebooks*, ed. cit. ii. 2355): 'Idly talk they who speak of Poets as mere Indulgers of Fancy, Imagination, Superstition, &c. . . . They are . . . they that combine them with *reason* and order, the true Protoplasts, Gods of Love who tame the Chaos.'

compel Reason to rise: *sie* could be either subject or object; but the sense seems to require it to be subject, since Reason is the faculty most likely to invoke the law of Necessity. If it is taken as object, the final *sie* of the paragraph would, presumably, have to refer to *Willkür*, and Reason would then be forcing Imagination to invoke the law of Necessity against her own caprice—a not impossible, but less likely, reading. To refer this final *sie* to *Weltordnung*, as Snell does, seems less likely still.

VI. 13. *in the individuals called to perform such feats*: not, as some translators have it, 'in the various branches of knowledge'. *Subjekt*, in German, can never mean 'a particular department of art or science', as 'subject' can in English. Cf. also XII. 5; XIII. 5.

armed their eyes with a glass: a metaphor from the physical sciences: *mit bewaffnetem Auge* means 'to aid the eye with a glass'.

innocent of preconceptions and faithful to the object: admittedly a paraphrase of 'with true and chaste sense'. But the emphasis is on the fidelity to the object which may be achieved by the 'innocent eye'. Schiller has Goethe in mind (cf. XIII. 4fn. § 2): in his letter of 23.viii.1794 he had written of Goethe's 'beobachtender Blick, der so still und rein auf den Dingen ruht', and gone on to advocate, in terms identical with those used here, that the speculative type of mind (his own) should attempt to supplement its own natural tendencies by seeking experience 'mit keuschem und treuem Sinn', the intuitive type (Goethe's) by penetrating through the manifold of phenomena to the laws informing them. The two may then hope to meet half way. The tone here is much more resigned and pessimistic—more like that of the letter of 7.i.1795, which we have cited as a gloss to one of our Notes to I. 4.

safeguards against error: the implication is presumably as follows: Whereas among the Greeks poetry and philosophy were one, among the Moderns philosophy has become increasingly analytical, involving less intuition and imagination; hence the philosopher, as human being, is 'martyred' to the specialization of a single faculty. For Schiller the culmination of this trend was Kant's 'critical' philosophy. For us, it might be linguistic philosophy; while existential philosophy (the German brand at least, which expressly seeks to 'render' existence directly) might be thought of as a reaction against it. The current interest of *Existenzphilosophen* in the pre-Socratics is no accident; according to Heidegger, the analytical tendency had already set in with Plato.

VI. 14. *harmonious play of the limbs*: dance was for Schiller the very image of dynamic form, a symbol both of the unceasing movement in macrocosm and microcosm, and of the 'law', or 'rule', which nevertheless obtains in the movements of the mind of man no less than in the harmony of the spheres. Coleridge was fascinated by this image: he copied out, supplementing with an English paraphrase, most of Schiller's poem *Der Tanz* (*Notebooks*, ed. cit. ii. 2363), and used the encounters and partings of the couples in the figure-dance as a simile for 'those conceits of words which are analogous to sudden fleeting affinities of mind . . .' (ibid. 2396; cf. 3220 and note thereto).

only the equal tempering: like all his contemporaries, Schiller too (see the setting of the first chapter of his *Geisterseher*) was interested in 'heavenly alchemy' (i.e. a symbolic interpretation of alchemical operations in terms of the processes of the psyche), and *Temperatur* is here used in its original meaning of the 'mixture of elements in due proportion'. But musical associations should probably not be ruled out either: *gleichförmige Temperatur* also means 'equal temperament', and the implied dance-image in the previous sentence would support this. *Temperament* in XIII. 6, by contrast, which could have the same meaning as *Temperatur*, appears to be used in the sense of '*natural* disposition', or 'habits of mind depending upon, or connected with, physical constitution', a meaning going back to the medieval notion of the four cardinal humours of the body.

in blissful indolence: as is evident from VIII. 6, IX. 7, and XV. 9, it is not *Müssiggang* in itself that is being condemned. Aristotle in his *Politics* had made a distinction between rest (recovery from occupation) and leisure (when the free man may do things for their own sake). And it was no doubt this element of creative purposelessness which made Hobbes refer to leisure as the 'mother of philosophy'. In the 'Idylle über den Müssiggang' (an episode in his novel *Lucinde*, 1799) Friedrich Schlegel took up Schiller's idea that leisure is necessary for the development of a complete human being.

VI. 15. *destined to miss himself*: one of Schiller's most eloquent passages—though easy to parody! Goethe, willing and loyal co-worker for aesthetic education though he was, pokes gentle fun at the cult of personality in a well-known poem of his *West-östlicher Divan* ('Volk und Knecht und Überwinder'; JA v. 76), in which the couplet 'Jedes Leben sei zu führen, / Wenn man sich nicht selbst vermisst' (You may lead what life you like, provided you don't miss yourself) seems like an echo of Schiller's words here.

restore by means of a higher Art: the circular, or rather spiral, movement of the thought is reflected in the qualified repetition of the same word, *Kunst*: the remedy is to be sought in a modification of that which caused the disaster (cf. above p. xlix). We might compare the content given to this same form of argument by a modern educationist, Sir Eric Ashby, in a lecture delivered at the Congress of European Vice-Chancellors (Dijon, September 1959): 'Science and invention have contributed to [the destruction of European civilization]; but in science and invention lies one hope for its repair' (*Le Figaro*, 10.ix.1959).

LETTER VII

VII. 2. *lower organisms . . . physical man*: this, like much else in these Letters, reflects the intense interest of the later eighteenth century in the biological sciences, inspired of course by Buffon, whose great *Histoire naturelle* in 36 vols. (which was appearing at intervals, 1749–88) had made evolution and the mutability of species familiar conceptions among the enlightened public. Walzel (SA xii. 365) refers us to Herder's *Ideen zur Philosophie der Geschichte der Menschheit*, x. 1; ed. cit. xiii. 396 ff.

The gift of liberal principles: the kind of passage which, quoted out of context, could give rise to the view that Schiller was a reactionary in politics: Men are not to be entrusted with freedom until they are fit to use it. The pragmatic Englishman, for whom politics is the art of the possible, not of the ideal, is tempted to ask, as Kant had asked (cf. above p. xviii): How then are they ever to become free? But Schiller asks this question himself in IX. 1. Cf. § 3 of this same Letter, where he concedes that, pending the proper education of humanity, isolated attempts at political liberty and social reform may well succeed.

independence and individuality: not, as the first translator has it, 'possession'. Schiller first wrote *Eigentümlichkeit*. In the eighteenth century the two words were still interchangeable.

VII. 3. *honour humanity in the negro*: no doubt a reference to the recently inaugurated campaign for the abolition of the slave trade by Wilberforce and others. Schiller, with his future tense, may have been over-optimistic about the long-term results of that campaign, but can he be charged with undue pessimism in his prophecy that Europe would yet see the triumph of abstraction, or the tyranny of 'l'homme machine'?

Philosophy now lend her name: Voltaire, Diderot, Frederick the Great had all protested against the retrogression to a dogmatic mode of thinking represented by the scientism of such *philosophes* as d'Holbach and La Mettrie, with their insistence on materialism and determinism.

LETTER VIII

VIII. 1. *this, the most important good of all*: i.e. political freedom, which was referred to in II. 1 as 'das vollkommenste aller Kunstwerke'.

VIII. 2. *No more than the son of Saturn in the Iliad*: i.e. Zeus, who sat inactive on the mountain tops watching the Greeks and the Trojans do battle (*Iliad*, viii. 41 ff.). Achilles, 'seed of Zeus', having received divine armour from Hephaestos, decided the issue by slaying Hector. A mythological exemplification of Schiller's main thesis: Reason cannot of itself achieve practical results, but only by taking on flesh, becoming allied with the sensuous. Or, as Schiller puts it in the next paragraph: 'If Truth is to be victorious in her conflict with forces, she herself must first become a *force*.'

VIII. 4. *empirical science*: *Erfahrung* here signifies knowledge obtained by way of observation and experiment (cf. French *expérience*, i.e. 'experiment') as distinct from philosophical speculation.

Our Age is Enlightened: cf. Goethe's equally ironic dismissal of the witches in the 'Walpurgisnacht' (written between 1797 and 1805):

Verschwindet doch! Wir haben ja aufgeklärt! (*Faust I*, 4159)

VIII. 5. *sapere aude*: (Horace, *Epistles*, i. 2). Richard Bentley, in the Preface to his famous edition of Horace (1711–13), had made use of the phrase to exhort editors of texts to think for themselves: 'Noli itaque Librarios solos venerare; sed per te sapere aude' (Don't make a fetish of tradition; dare to have a mind of your own). The tag was in general use amongst German *Aufklärer* as early as 1736, when it served as the motto for one of the many philosophic societies inspired by Wolff, that of the Alethophiles, or Lovers of Truth, in Berlin. By the end of the century it had become the maxim of the *Aufklärung*, and Kant in his well-known pamphlet *Was ist Aufklärung?* had interpreted it as 'Habe Mut, dich deines eigenen Verstandes zu bedienen!' A comparative analysis of Kant's treatment of the theme and Schiller's by Meyer (loc. cit., pp. 315 ff.) brings out certain differences between a poet's use of language and a philosopher's. But Schiller's version enables him to contrast wisdom with intellectual enlightenment, thus maintaining the distinction made in medieval theology between *scientia* and *sapientia* (cf. E. F. Rice, *The Renaissance Idea of Wisdom*, Cambridge, Mass., 1958), to play on the myth of Minerva and on the meaning of the word 'philosophy', and thus to come round, at the end of this Letter, to the formulation of the essential circularity of his thesis, which, at the beginning of Letter IX, he will openly acknowledge. But cf. also p. xcvi above.

VIII. 6. *from the head of Jupiter*: a favourite myth, used also in *Anmut und Würde* and in the poems *Die Künstler* and *Das Glück*:

> Wie die erste Minerva, so tritt, mit der Aegis gerüstet,
> Aus des Donnerers Haupt jeder Gedanke des Lichts.
>
> (SA i. 124)

by him who gave philosophy her name: according to Cicero (*Tusculanae Disputationes*, v. iii), this was Pythagoras.

LETTER IX

IX. 1. *to argue in a circle*: with our translation of this first sentence we have committed Schiller to a purely logical statement. But it is by no means certain that he is not referring to the circularity inherent in the process of education as well as to the apparently vicious circle of his own argument. Certainly the paradoxes presented in the last two paragraphs of Letter VIII refer unambiguously to the former; those presented here, in the first paragraph of Letter IX, by contrast, unambiguously to the latter. But, on second thoughts, perhaps not so unambiguously as all that! Is 'soll' to be taken as 'is said to' or as 'is to'? Probably as both. By choosing the latter we have endeavoured to restore to Schiller's language something of that characteristic openness of reference— logical, ontological, and also psychological—of which we have deprived it by plumping for '*argue in* a circle' in the preceding sentence.

open up living springs: this notion of 'opening' (though not always of 'springs' —in XIX. 12 it will be of the 'humanity' which Nature implanted in Man, and in XXIII. 5 of 'a completely new kind of activity' within him) is to be found in various religions (thus Zen Buddhism speaks of the 'opening' of *satori*, or 'realization'); and it is of course the assumption, tacit or expressed, underlying such psychoanalytical procedures as Jung's. The main feature of it is that Man's realization, or salvation, is to be brought about, not by the introduction *into* him of something new, but by the opening up of something already present within him.

IX. 3. *from all positive constraint*: 'positive' here, as in VI. 9 and XXIV. 7, in the sense of laws or conventions established by man (by contrast with the natural law of II. 4; see Note). Cf. *Position* and *Positiv* in XIX. 3 and 4, where the context is philosophical.

creative minds . . . prevailing taste: lit. 'and for creative taste to accept the law from critical taste'. But in English, nowadays at least, this would sound as though art alone were implied, whereas it is clear from the context that Schiller means it to refer to science and philosophy too.

IX. 4. *if he is at the same time its ward*: not 'disciple', as some translate it. It is important to remain within the semantic range of 'tutelage', 'dependence', 'guardianship'; for Schiller is still thinking, as he was in VIII. 5, of Kant's definition of *Aufklärung*. See Note to I. 4.

under a distant Grecian sky: again reminiscent of the letter to Goethe of 23.viii.1794, discussed in Note to VI. 13. Cf., too, that of 20.x.1794 and Goethe's answer of the 26th.

like Agamemnon's son: Orestes, come to avenge his father.

to cleanse and to purify it: cf. Coleridge (*Notebooks*, ed. cit. ii. 2355): 'They [the poets] are the Bridlers by Delight, the Purifiers ....'

the pure aether of his genius: in view of the nefarious effects which the concept of the daemonic has had upon German life and thought, it seemed wiser to avoid the word altogether. Schiller is using both words in their Greek sense, and *dämonisch* is simply a transliteration of the Greek word for genius, a being of a nature intermediate between that of gods and men, and providing the connecting link between them. It is because genius is of this order that it is able to produce *our* 'second creatress', as beauty will be called in XXI. 6. 'Aether' in ancient cosmology denoted an element filling all space beyond the sphere of the moon (Newton still postulated 'an aetherial medium, much of the same constitution with air, but far rarer, subtiler, and more strongly elastic'; cf. Nicolson, op. cit. [1], p. 65). It was from this rarefied upper atmosphere that inspiration was thought to proceed. John Cowper Powys (*Homer and the Aether*, London, 1959), in retelling *The Iliad*, revived this tradition, making of the aether a deity who acted as Homer's inspirational assistant, 'the Immortal One, beyond all gods and men'. Schiller follows the ancient tradition more closely in his original letter to the Duke of Augustenburg, 13.vii.1793: 'Aus dem göttlichen Teil unsers Wesens, aus dem ewig reinen Aether idealischer Menschheit strömt der lautere Quell der Schönheit herab, unangesteckt von dem Geist des Zeitalters . . .' (Jonas, iii. 338). His immediate source may well have been Herder's *Ideen zur Philosophie der Geschichte der Menschheit*, v. 2:

In den tiefsten Abgründen des Werdens, wo wir keimendes Leben sehen, werden wir das unerforschte und so wirksame Element gewahr, das wir mit den unvollkommenen Namen Licht, Aether, Lebenswärme benennen und das vielleicht das Sensorium des Allerschaffenden ist, dadurch er alles belebet, alles erwärmet. (ed. cit. xiii. 175)

Hölderlin, whose poem *An den Aether* first appeared in Schiller's *Musenalmanach* for 1798, was surely aware of this passage in the *Aesthetic Letters*, though Seebass (Hölderlin, *Werke*, ed. cit. ii. 474) suggests Heinse's *Ardinghello* (1787) as the strongest influence.

Truth lives on in the illusion of Art: see Glossary under *Täuschung*, and p. 340 below.

from this copy, or after-image: the German equivalent of Aristotle's 'mimesis' was, and still is, *Nachahmung*. If Schiller prefers *Nachbild* here, it is surely in order to play on *Urbild*. But *Nachbild* also has the meaning of 'after-image'. Schiller's interest in optics had been rekindled by Goethe (cf. letter of 16.ix.1794; Jonas, iv. 18), and an optical interpretation is supported by the immediately following image of the poet intercepting the rays of truth as in the burning-glass of his symbol. By the choice of this word, then, he obtains a double contrast: 1. in terms of aesthetics, between original and imitation; 2. in terms of optics, between the image originally cast on the retina by an object actually present, and the image which the eye produces in the absence of any object, and which is, therefore, in some sense an illusion, a virtual image. This passage might, then, be regarded as an anticipation of the concept of *Schein* developed in Letter XXVI (cf. esp. XXVI. 6 and Notes thereto).

dews of night . . . in the valley: an image which will recur in *Wilhelm Tell* (and in modified form in the *Braut von Messina*, 2582 ff.), where the implication is that the Swiss had attained to 'the peaks of humanity':

(Walther Fürst) Sorgt nicht, die Nacht weicht langsam aus den Tälern.
                 (*Alle haben unwillkürlich die Hüte abgenommen und betrachten
                 mit stiller Sammlung die Morgenröte.*)
(Rösselmann)   Bei diesem Licht, das uns zuerst begrüsst
                 Von allen Völkern, die tief unter uns
                 Schwer atmend wohnen in dem Qualm der Städte,
                 Lasst uns den Eid des neuen Bundes schwören.

                                                              (1443 ff.)

This play might itself be regarded as an example of the poet's 'interception of the rays of truth' through his art; for it represents a realization in dramatic form of that aesthetic State which Schiller will evoke in XXVII (cf. Willoughby, loc. cit., p. 172; Martini, loc. cit., pp. 117 f.).

IX. 5. *downwards towards Fortune*: *Glück* here has all the ambiguity of Schiller's poem of that title (cf. above, pp. xli f.), and the translator has to choose between 'happiness' and 'fortune'. 'Fortuna' was a favourite emblem of the Renaissance. Personifying the apparently random operations of fate, it was opposed to 'virtù' (sometimes *Tugend*, here *Würde*), signifying the energies of the individual genius. Both notions will occur again in these Letters: in X. 3 (where 'Günstling der Grazien' is opposed to 'das Schlachtopfer des Fleisses') and in XIX. 11; XXI. 4; XXIII. 5; XXVI. 1, in all of which the idea of 'grace' or 'fortune' is, implicitly or explicitly, opposed to that of 'merit'.

the impatient spirit of enthusiasm: because of the immediately following contrast between the Absolute and Time, *Schwärmer* here has more obviously religious overtones than in V. 5 (see Note). Common to both religious exaltation and the over-zealous social reformer is the 'impatient spirit' (contrasted, in § 6 below, with the true artist's 'spirit of long patience'), which would translate the Ideal directly into practice (cf. XIII. 4fn. § 4; XXVII. 11). It is in this sense that Lessing (*Die Erziehung des Menschengeschlechts*, §§ 87–90) uses *Schwärmer* of the mystics of the thirteenth and fourteenth centuries, who would not bide their time for 'die Zeit eines "neuen ewigen Evangeliums"', but were always predicting its imminent arrival. The most famous of them, Joachim di Fiore, had foretold that the year 1260 would usher it in (cf. Note to XXVII. 8). The prototype of the *Schwärmer* in German eighteenth-century literature is, according to Schiller himself (SA xii. 213 ff.), Goethe's Werther, an 'enthusiast' in every sphere: religion, society, morals, art, love. On enthusiasm as 'a chapter in the history of religion with special reference to the seventeenth and eighteenth centuries' see R. A. Knox, op. cit.

actual . . . Ideal . . . possible . . . necessary: an old truth in Kantian terms (see Glossary under *Idee* and *Notwendigkeit*). The artist is by no means a wholly free agent; he is subject, not only to the limitations of his medium, but to the contingencies of time, place, and his own personality. Yet out of these limited possibilities he is able to create a form which is significant (*Ideal*), an image expressive of universals (*Notwendigkeit*). But he can only do this if he renounces all attempts, either to copy actuality, or to modify it directly. For the same thought, in somewhat different terms, see XXVI. 10.

set the stamp of it upon: *prägen, ausprägen* (is there any significance in the change from complex to simplex and back again?) are words heavy with both secular and sacred significations (on their use in the language of Pietism see Langen's *Wortschatz*, ed. cit.). According to the medieval doctrine of 'signatura' all created things are signed, or 'stamped', by the Creator. This is the mark of their inherent nature, which resists the ravages of time, and persists through all change and transformation—'Geprägte Form, die lebend sich entwickelt' (Goethe, *Urworte. Orphisch*). By analogy, works made by man also bear the signature of their originator. Hence the ancient belief in the power inherent in incised stones, or gems. These were the subject of a sharp controversy between Lessing and C. A. Klotz (author of *Über den Nutzen und Gebrauch der alten geschnittenen Steine und ihrer Abdrücke*, 1768), and there were many famous collections in Germany. One of these, inherited by the Princess Gallitzin from the philosopher Hemsterhuis, was lent to Goethe for a number of years and aroused great interest in Weimar circles (evidence of Schiller's earlier interest in gems in his letter of 14.iii.1790). In this passage the artist, as a 'second creator', is being urged to incise his signature, not only on the 'playful semblance' of the products of his imagination, but also on the 'serious reality' of his thoughts and deeds. The distinction between *Spiel* and *Ernst* will not be explicitly drawn until XV.

IX. 6. *executory hands of time*: we have taken *treu* in the more technical sense, as it appears, for instance, in *Treuhänder*, i.e. 'executor'.

the Way: there can be no doubt of the religious overtones here (cf. XI. 7), certainly Western—Christ is 'the Way, the Truth, and the Life' (John xiv. 6); most probably Eastern too—the original meaning of *Tao* (variously translated by Western scholars as 'Way', 'Meaning', 'Providence', or even 'God') is that of a 'track which, though fixed itself, leads from the beginning directly to the goal' (*The Secret of the Golden Flower*, ed. cit., p. 12; cf. p. 94).

IX. 7. *To the young friend of truth and beauty*: presumably in the tradition of Letters to a Young Poet, of which Wieland's was the most recent in German literature. But Goethe was to write one, and Rilke and Hofmannsthal continued the tradition down to our own day. As a literary form it goes back to the rhetorical exercises of the Greeks and Romans.

an object of the heart's desire: a paraphrase, but a justifiable one. The artist's duty is to transform the great ideas and ideals into objects which not only convince men's minds, but are able to activate their 'drives' (cf. VIII. 3 and Glossary under *Trieb*).

Live with your century: cf. II. 2 and Note.

think of them as they are: cf. XIII. 4fn. § 4 for an even more forthright statement on the inappropriate use of ideals.

their taste is purer than their heart: another variant of the thesis as stated in II. 5: in order to reach either *true* freedom or *true* morality man must take the indirect way, via Beauty. He may respond to the symbols of art where he would resist a direct appeal to his moral sense.

on their leisure hours: cf. VI. 14 and XV. 9.

LETTER X

X. 1. *savage . . . barbarian*: the distinction made in IV. 6.

X. 2. *graciousness, yes even dignity, of conduct*: *Liberalität* here, as the juxtaposition with *Würde* suggests, is almost synonymous with *Anmut*. See Glossary under *Freiheit*.

sometimes occurs to thinking minds: here, as in § 4, the reference is clearly to Rousseau; not only to his *Premier Discours*, but to his *Lettre sur les spectacles*, with which Schiller had already come to terms in his *Schaubühne als moralische Anstalt betrachtet* (1784), where the theatre is defended as the first school of humanity.

admission to their Republic: the allusion is obviously to Plato.

X. 3. *has himself no form*: cf. XXII. 6 and XXVI. 13.

darling of the Graces: Schiller's poem *Das Glück* could be read as an answer to the opinions quoted here. Cf. Note to IX. 5.

X. 4. *dangerous tendency to neglect reality*: Schiller will offer his own answers to such criticism in XXVI. 13, after he has established his distinction between true and false semblance. See Notes thereto.

X. 5. *closely akin to the primitive*: a reference to Hamann's view of poetry as 'the mother-tongue of the human race', and to Herder's vindication of Homer and 'the poetry of primitive peoples'.

virtue in the life of a Phocion: Athenian general and statesman at the time of Alexander of Macedon. As a fervent advocate of peace with the Macedonians, he was executed in 318 B.C. for alleged subservience to the conquerors. He became a model for the idealists among the French revolutionaries: Brissot, the Girondin, 'burned to resemble Phocion'. Schiller knew of him from Plutarch's *Lives*.

the Abbassids: the ruling family of Baghdad. They took their name from Abbas, uncle of Mohammed. It was under the caliphate of Harun al Rashid (786–809), of *Arabian Nights* fame, that Islamic civilization, during a period of comparative peace, reached its zenith.

the glorious Lombard League: originally formed by the North-Italian cities, with Milan at their head, to defend civil liberties against Frederick Barbarossa. In the course of the thirteenth and fourteenth centuries these voluntarily surrendered their liberties to local despots. It was under the Medici, especially Lorenzo il Magnifico (1449–92), that Florence enjoyed the most glorious period of her cultural history.

X. 6. *energy of character . . . commonly purchased*: cf. XXII. 3, where this problem is solved by including 'Kraft und Rüstigkeit' among the essential attributes of the condition in which a genuine work of art should leave us.

the melting power of Beauty: a foreshadowing of the distinction made in XVI. 2 between 'melting' and 'energetic' beauty.

perhaps Experience is not the judgement-seat: *Erfahrung* here includes not only the 'experience' of history, but empirical method in general (cf. Note to VIII. 4). This is now rejected in favour of the 'transcendental' method proposed in the next paragraph.

X. 7. *This pure rational concept of Beauty*: the same train of thought in a letter to Körner, 25.x.1794. The disagreements about beauty and its effects, which abound among like-minded people, usually arise from their tacit assumption that there is such a thing as an empirical concept of beauty, which they expect to find exhibited in certain phenomena. But, Schiller goes on—following Kant (*Critique of Judgement*, i, § 19) who was himself following the Scotsman, Home (*Elements of Criticism*, 1762, ch. xxv; cf. Meredith, op. cit., p. 257)—beauty is not an empirical concept at all, but an 'imperative', i.e. something which it is enjoined upon a sensuo-rational being to achieve, but which, in actual experience, never can be achieved. He concludes with a difficult sentence, but one which is crucial for his critical position: 'It is a purely subjective matter whether we do in fact experience something beautiful as beautiful; but that is what, objectively speaking, it is enjoined upon us to do.' In other words, his 'transcendental' insistence on an objective Idea of Beauty does not exclude a 'psychological' acceptance of empirical and subjective variations, whether in art or in the beholder (cf. XVI. 4)—which is of course why Jung could find in Schiller's writings an anticipation of his own psychological types.

this transcendental way: further remarks on [Kant's] 'transcendental', 'critical' philosophy in XIII. 2fn. § 2; XV. 5fn.; XIX. 9.

cause us to tarry for a while: *verweilen* here is transitive. An even clearer instance of this now obsolete use in a letter to the Duke of Augustenburg of 21.xi.1793: 'er verweilt sie [seine Leser] länger, als es dem Sinne gefallen kann, bei dem zwangvollen Zustand der Abstraktion . . .' (Jonas, iii. 396).

LETTER XI

Schiller was well aware of the 'allzugrosse Trockenheit' of both this Letter and the next, but thought he had remedied it somewhat by frequent references to concrete experience (letter to Körner, 19.i.1795). The reader may well feel that these are still too few. But it would be a pity if the metaphysical abstractions, derived in part from Fichte, were to obscure for him the important psychological and pedagogic truths they contain. What Schiller is here concerned to do, is to establish the philosophical foundations of the educational 'programme' that he will announce in XIII. 3, with its demand for equal attention to 'extensity' and 'intensity'. Without opportunity for manifold contacts with the world, for a variety of manifestations (*Zustände*), personality will remain meagre and impoverished; but without a point at which all these manifestations meet, an identity which persists through all changes, and is able to make sense of all its encounters, personality will not develop at all. When Schiller speaks of making a unity out of experience, or of turning world into form, he means much the same as T. S. Eliot, when he points a contrast between the 'continual impact of external events' and knowledge of 'the meaning of happening' (*The Family Reunion*, i. 1 and ii. 3); or as Goethe, when he observes that those who are always extolling the virtues of experience overlook the fact that 'experience' is only the half of Experience—the other half being the understanding of its significance (*Maximen und Reflexionen*; JA xxxv. 319).

XI. 1. *Person . . . Condition*: Kant (*Kritik der praktischen Vernunft*, pt. i, bk. i, ch. 3) defined *Persönlichkeit* as 'die Freiheit und Unabhängigkeit von dem Mechanismus der ganzen Natur'. Schiller, for whom the two terms appear to be synonymous (see XI. 2 ff.), had equated *Person* with 'das freie Prinzipium im Menschen' in *Anmut und Würde* (SA xi. 194) and opposed it to *Zustand* in *Über das Pathetische* (SA xi. 264). He then found new support for the distinction in Fichte's *Vorlesungen* (referred to in IV. 2fn.) and in his *Wissenschaftslehre* (referred to in XIII. 2fn. § 1).

XI. 3. *We are because we are*: Fichte's anti-Cartesian 'ich bin schlechthin, weil ich bin'. Schiller is again making use, for his own purposes, of Fichte's *Grundlage der gesamten Wissenschaftslehre* (1794, p. 12; ed. cit. i. 98 f.).

XI. 5. *To say . . . is no objection*: an anticipation of the kind of objection which might be raised by, say, an existentialist, for whom existence precedes essence.

man, as a phenomenal being: see Glossary under *Schein*.

pure Intelligence . . . is eternal: cf. III. 1 and Note; XIX. 12fn.

XI. 6. *Only inasmuch as he changes does he exist*: at the instance of his friend Körner, Schiller replaced an original 'is' here by 'exist', in order to avoid possible objections by Kantians that he was confusing the phenomenal with the noumenal realm. Though he obviously thought that the context would have made it clear in any case: 'Denn wenn ich sage: "der *Mensch ist* nur, insofern er sich verändert", so kann der strengste Kantische Rigorist nichts dagegen haben, da der *Mensch* ja schon kein Noumenon mehr ist' (to Körner, 19.i.1795). On *Rigorist* see Note to XXVI. 14.

XI. 9. *from which I started*: Schiller is not, as Böhm (op. cit., p. 39) with undue literal-mindedness assumes, referring to the point of departure of his argument in this Letter, which is indeed the concept of Man, but to the most basic of all his philosophical assumptions, the notion of an Absolute Being on which all else depends.

LETTER XII

XII. 1. *not to provide him with matter*: as was stressed in XI. 6, the *material* of experience does not come from within man at all, but from the world outside him. Hence it cannot be the function of his sensuous drive to supply it. Its function is to impel him towards existence in time, towards change and becoming. And this, as Schiller makes clear in this same paragraph, is what is meant by 'turning him into matter'.

XII. 2*fn. *linguistic usage*: more tentatively than some modern philosophers, Schiller ventures to point a relation between linguistic usage and the thesis he is defending (cf., too, XV. 5). But he is content with noting the way that language reflects the state of affairs he is describing—i.e. linguistic usage is only adduced as supporting evidence; he does not make it a starting-point from which to derive a thesis. The impossibility of rendering these linguistic forms in another language shows his wisdom in not making it the mainstay of his argument. While the English 'beside oneself' evokes a not dissimilar image to *ausser sich sein*, 'to be oneself again' bears no formal resemblance to *in sich gehen*.

XII. 5. *once thought pronounces*: one expects *Vernunft* (Pure Reason), and not *Gedanke*. We know, and Schiller knew, that 'thought' can be as subjective as 'feeling', and in the very next Letter (XIII. 4fn. § 3) he will dilate on the 'egotism of our reason' and the danger of 'rigid principles', stressing the importance of feeling and the education of feeling. But here, in this Letter, his concern is to throw into as sharp relief as possible the two opposed aspects of human nature which it will thereafter be his aim to reconcile. What is important to him is the opposition, not the terms in which it is stated at any one point, and we have to learn in what sense to take any particular term from the one with which it is immediately contrasted and from the series in which it finds itself. *Gedanke* here, then—though not always—belongs in the series: objective, universal, eternal, necessary, law, truth, justice, form; *Gefühl*, to which it is opposed, in the series: subjective, individual, arbitrary, momentary, matter. But when preceded by *moralisch* a sentence or two further on, *Gefühl* moves over into the other camp, and takes over the functions of *Vernunft* or *Wille*.

XII. 6. *the pure object*: *rein* here in the Kantian sense of 'frei von allem Erfahrungsstoff, von der Empfindung, vom Sinnlichen überhaupt'. Cf. IV. 2, where Schiller spoke of the 'reinen idealischen Menschen' which each individual carries within him, and to which he subsequently refers as 'die rein objektive Menschheit' (IV. 5).

unit of quantity . . . unity of ideas: we have taken advantage of the fact that *Einheit* has both meanings in order to play on words in a way which is in tune with Schiller's thought. For his dislike of the merely quantitative is apparent throughout. The mathematical imagery is reminiscent of Rousseau's *Émile, ou de l'éducation* (1762):

> L'homme naturel est tout pour lui; il est l'unité numérique, l'entier absolu, qui n'a de rapport qu'à lui-même ou à son semblable. L'homme civil n'est qu'une unité fractionnaire qui tient au dénominateur, et dont la valeur est dans son rapport avec l'entier qui est le Corps social. (Vaughan, op. cit. ii. 145)

But Rousseau's contrast between 'l'homme naturel' and 'l'homme civil' is here transposed by Schiller into psychological terms (cf. VI. 7 and Note): into a contrast between man who remains a mere number as long as he is the slave of each successive impression and man who becomes a significant unity by integrating these fragmentary impressions into the context of humanity as a whole.

LETTER XIII

XIII. 2. *not by nature opposed*: an excellent example of Schiller's 'Socratic' tactics. He constantly dramatizes his argument by an implied dialogue situation, in which the antagonist usually states the case as it appears to be (as he has just done in § 1), while the protagonist retaliates by breaking down appearances to uncover the state of affairs as Schiller thinks it really is. His own considered opinion appears in XIX. 12fn.; XXIV. 8; XXV. 6—and in the footnote to this paragraph: the conflict between man's two natures is not primary, but has arisen in the course of history through the misuse and misdirection of them. One ought to say, in the course of Western history. For the two illustrations given in the footnote to § 4 of this Letter are peculiar to the West: the kind of science which presumes to control Nature through prediction; and our puritanical 'philanthropy', which so often allows the rigour of moral judgements to usurp the role of charity.

a wanton transgression of Nature: not, as earlier translators have it, a 'willing' transgression. This is an instance of 'Freiheit der Willkür'. See Glossary under *Freiheit* (1), and Wilkinson, loc. cit. (3), pp. 58, 70.

*fn. § 1. only uniformity can result: note the sharp contrast between 'uniformity' and 'harmony'. Cf. above pp. lxxxiii ff..

the task of culture: *Kultur* here in its dynamic sense of 'cultivating', 'developing' (see introduction to Glossary). We have rendered it by 'education' in § 3 of this Letter because of the requirements of English usage.

the encroachments of Freedom: *Freiheit* here, by contrast with *frei* just above, is on the side of *Vernunft*, *Person*, &c., of *Wille*, as opposed to *Willkür*. See Glossary under *Freiheit* (2).

XIII. 3. *maximum extensity*: '*Extensity*. The quality of having (a certain) extension; in Psychology of the breadth of sensation, as opposed to *intensity*' (*OED*). De Quincey, in the analysis of 'Superficial Knowledge' (*London Magazine*, July 1824) which, as he maintained, was written before he had read Schiller, used the antonyms 'extension' and 'intension' to contrast the spread and the specialization of knowledge in the modern world. Schiller, of course, is not treating of knowledge alone, but of the development of the whole psyche.

His education will therefore consist: from the educationist's point of view, one of the most important paragraphs in the whole treatise, analysing as it does the relation between the principles of 'extensity' and 'intensity'. Everything turns on the proper integration of two contrary processes—linguistically reflected in the cognates *ergreift*/*begreift*—on the interrelation of *ap*prehending and *com*-prehending. The task of the educator is thus always a dual one: 1. to ensure an adequate supply of the material of experience, to develop the power of being open to it, and foster a many-faceted and labile receptivity; 2. to ensure the development of an organizing power, which can make sense of all that is received, and assimilate it into a continuing identity. Only thus shall we educate personalities which are both well-defined and many-sided, at once flexible and strong. If, until a generation or two ago, education still tended to neglect 'extensity'—very much in the way Schiller deplores in the footnote to the next paragraph—it has of recent years, in an otherwise healthy reaction, tended to lose sight of the need for 'intensity'; for this, as the whole Letter makes clear, is obviously not to be equated with specialization.

XIII. 4. *miss his destiny*: cf. VI. 15: 'can any human being be destined to miss himself?' *Bestimmung* is never easy to render. Leroux has *destinée* here, though *destination* elsewhere. All three English translators have 'destination'. *Bestimmung*, however, includes both (see Glossary).

a non-entity: we have here borrowed Snell's felicitous rendering of *Null*, which at this point is unambiguously pejorative—by contrast with XXI. 4, where its association with the Infinite, and with 'an Infinity filled with content', gives it positive value.

*fn. § 2. *once they are used constitutively*: according to Kant, the principles of teleological judgements (i.e. the assumption of an end or purpose in the universe) are only to be used regulatively: their sole function is to guide the mind in its investigation of the objects of the world of sensible experience, not to enable it to discover anything about the supra-sensible. Constitutive principles, by contrast, are 'principles capable of giving us knowledge of things in themselves'. Hence teleological judgements, if used constitutively, will purport to throw light on the Creator through scrutinizing His handiwork with reference to His purpose. Such preconceptions were bound to impede the progress of free inquiry, and Goethe (see next Note) could not praise Kant highly enough for having banished teleological judgements from science. He nevertheless realized, and many modern biologists have come to agree, that, as a regulative principle, some refined form of teleology is indispensable in the science of growing things—if only for linguistic reasons: it is difficult to devise statements about growth, i.e. an irreversible process, without implying an end, if not a purpose.

**with his sense-organs untroubled*: a similar phrase in VI. 13 (see Note thereto), where the allusion was also, though less obviously, to Goethe's morphological approach to the study of nature. In his essays on scientific method he never tired of exploring the relation of theory to observation, recognizing that theory is at once indispensable and a constant source of danger, and that the only safe-guard against its inappropriate intrusions is constant inspection of our own mental procedures. Goethe himself was concerned to cultivate *Anschauung* (see Glossary, also under *Sinn*). Schiller is here making *amende honorable* for his attack on 'überwiegende Sensualität' in *Anmut und Würde* which Goethe had taken amiss. In his zeal he now offers this energetic critique of 'überwiegende Rationalität'.

our tendency to prejudge the issue: Prävention, from the French *prévention*, 'bias, prejudice, prepossessions, opinions which precede examination, tendency to prejudge the issue'.

fn. § 3. the practice of brotherly love: 'philanthropy' was still, in the eighteenth century, used in its original Greek sense, 'love of men'. An interesting example is the 'philanthropine' school which Goethe's *Jugendfreund*, Basedow, founded at Dessau in 1774 'for the education of children by his "natural system", in the principles of philanthropy, natural religion, &c.' (*OED*). It is clear from the rest of this footnote that Schiller, who refers to such institutions in *Die Schaubühne als eine moralische Anstalt betrachtet* (SA xi. 98), has something far wider in mind than 'works of charity and benevolence', which is what the word has come to mean since the middle of the nineteenth century.

a spirited and active foe: the same image in *Anmut und Würde* (SA xi. 218), though the thought is by no means identical (cf. above p. lxxxiii).

fn. § 4. act on their behalf: cf. IX. 7: 'Think of them as they ought to be, when called upon to influence them; think of them as they are, when tempted to act on their behalf.'

sentimental idealism: we rendered *Schwärmer* by 'enthusiast' in our Note to V. 5. But the present context warrants the inclusion of the word 'idealism'.

XIII. 6. *set bounds to temperament*: *Temperament* here (by contrast with XVI. 3) is opposed to *Charakter*: the former signifying 'natural' disposition, or habits of mind connected with physical constitution, the latter, disposition achieved through the exercise of reason and will.

LETTER XIV

XIV. 1. *gives rise to*: this translation of *begründen* is supported by XI. 3, where it was expressly stated that 'the Condition can neither be grounded upon the Person, nor the Person upon the Condition', and by XII. 3, where the preposition *an* (first occurrence) makes it clear that the relation of *Stofftrieb* to *Formtrieb* is not one of cause and effect, but rather of medium and occasion.

its highest manifestation: *Verkündigung*, lit. 'proclamation', 'announcement', 'annunciation'. And, indeed, the association with 'Mariä Verkündigung' is inescapable, especially as the 'vision of our human nature and symbol of our accomplished destiny' (§ 2), viz. beauty, is compounded of sense and spirit, matter and mind.

XIV. 2. *a task enjoined upon us by Reason*: as distinct from anything given to us by experience. Schiller obviously has in mind the Kantian distinction, between *gegeben* and *aufgegeben* (*Critique of Pure Reason*: 'The Antinomy of Pure Reason', sect. 8; ed. cit., p. 449). As the verb *lösen* implies, *Aufgabe* has here the double meaning of a task (to be carried out) and a problem (to be solved).

'*He is not to strive for form* . . .': with the quotation marks Schiller indicates that he is making another allusion to 'his friend Fichte', again to the *Lectures on the Vocation of a Scholar* referred to in IV. 2fn.

a symbol of his accomplished destiny: the first stage of the quest which was defined in III. 5 has now been reached. What was there postulated as 'a third character which . . . might on the contrary serve as a pledge in the sensible world of a morality as yet unseen' will be brought about by the play-drive evolved in the rest of this Letter. The symbol sought will, in Letter XV, turn out to be the objective correlative of this drive, viz. 'living form', or Beauty.

XIV. 3. *could justifiably count as a new drive*: the apparent inconsistency has often been pointed out. In XIII. 1 Schiller stated that 'these two drives . . . between them exhaust our concept of humanity', and that 'a third *fundamental drive* . . . is completely unthinkable'. But we have here yet another example of Schiller's dramatic strategy (cf. XIII. 2 and Note). And psychologically speaking there is no problem. For the *Spieltrieb* is not presented as fundamental—it is not even called a *Grundtrieb*—but is brought into being through the interaction of the other two. In other words, it is a question of a qualitative, or formal, not of a substantial, change in behaviour. Cf. above pp. xciii ff.

XIV. 4. *as the intuitive sense aspires to receive*: a difficult passage, as conflicting translations show. The sentence lacks the symmetry we have come to expect: in the two parallel *wie*-clauses, we find pronoun and noun, instead of either two nouns or two pronouns. Leroux seems to have felt this, since in the first he translates 'er selbst' as if it read 'der Formtrieb selbst', thus tacitly restoring what might seem to be a missing leg of the chiasmus. And the Bohn translator restores it more drastically still by simply rendering 'der Sinn' as 'it'. But, it should be noted, the verbs in the two *wie*-clauses are not parallel either—the first is in the subjunctive, the second in the indicative; and *wie* does not mean the same thing in each—in the first it is used in the now obsolete sense of 'as if'.

But if the sentence is asymmetrical, the thought is not. *Both* the basic drives are at work in the play-drive—but not both *aspects* of each (since each is being conditioned by the other). Hence the play-drive partakes of the spontaneous activity of the *Formtrieb*, of its power *itself* to bring forth (this is reflected linguistically by the transference of *selbst* from *Formtrieb* to *Spieltrieb*); but it does not share its determining function, its tendency to impose laws. And it partakes of the receptivity of the *sinnlicher Trieb*, of that openness to impressions which sense shares with intuition (for the full meaning of *Sinn* see Glossary); but it does not share its passivity, its readiness to *be* determined. Each of its basic activities in fact takes on the modality of the other: its receptivity is not passive but creative—it receives as if it had itself brought forth; and its creativity is not purposefully end-directed, but receptive—more like the activity we associate with intuition and 'wide-open senses' (XIII. 4fn. § 2), in short, with what is commonly called 'inspiration'. Whatever we may think of Schiller's argument here, his conclusions are perfectly familiar to us in such oxymora as Wordsworth's 'wise passiveness', Keats's 'negative capability' or Coleridge's 'willing suspension of disbelief'; in the common contention that aesthetic contemplation is a form of creativity (cf. XXV. 2 and Note); in the frequently reported tricks and devices of creative minds (and not of artists alone) for suspending the directive drives of the conscious mind in order to give the results of less conscious creative processes a chance to 'present themselves' (Schiller is said to have had recourse to the sniffing of rotten apples for this purpose! Cf. Goethe to Eckermann, 7.x.1827).

XIV. 5. The play on words in this paragraph—*Notwendigkeit, nötigen, Nötigung*; *Achtung, Verachtung*—is impossible to render in English. It is intimately bound up with the thought, and offers a reflection in language of that 'playing' with psychical forces which forms the climax of the paragraph.

LETTER XV

XV. 2. *in a general schema*: Schiller is obviously borrowing a term from Kant (*Critique of Pure Reason*, I. ii, sect. 1, bk. ii, ch. 1: 'The Schematism of the Pure Concepts of Understanding'; ed. cit., p. 181 f.) and adapting it to his own purposes. In order to explain how the *a priori* concepts of the Understanding, which are the necessary conditions of our knowledge of objects, can ever be applied to intuitions of particular cases, we need, according to Kant, a third thing which is in some respects homogeneous with those concepts, in others with the phenomena themselves. This mediating representation (*vermittelnde Vorstellung*), which must be in one respect intellectual, in another sensible, Kant calls 'the transcendental schema', and insists that it is always the product of the imagination. Schiller's aesthetic schema, *lebende Gestalt*, obviously fulfils these conditions.

XV. 3. *though it is and remains lifeless*: cf. Schiller's letter to Körner, 28.ii.1793: 'In a work of art, form is mere appearance; that is to say, the marble *seems* a human being, but in fact it remains marble' (Jonas, iii. 294).

though he may live and have form: 'living form' is here contrasted with life, on the one hand, and with form, on the other. Cf. XXVII. 9, where *Gestalt* alone will do duty for *lebende Gestalt*. See Glossary under *Gestalt*.

XV. 4. *the actual manner of their combining*: cf. the similar thought at the end of I. 5.

XV. 5. *our age would fain degrade it*: an age of debased tastes and ideals, whose literary movements and styles—Storm and Stress, the tragedies of common life, the popular melodramas of contemporary playwrights such as Kotzebue and Iffland—had confused life and art, either by trying to make art reflect life as closely as possible, or by trying to make it influence life directly.

by the needs of their craft: for the justification of our translation here see Glossary under *Kunst*.

*footnote: the illustrations do not correspond exactly to the four distinctions in the text. Burke is obviously one of the 'acute observers' who make beauty into mere life, and Schiller no doubt had in mind a passage such as the following:

And, since it is no creature of our reason, since it strikes us without any reference to use . . . we must conclude that beauty is, for the greater part, some quality in bodies, acting mechanically upon the human mind by the intervention of the senses. (*On the Sublime*, iii. 12)

No example is offered of the 'taste of our age' which would fain degrade beauty into mere life, though no doubt many would spring to the mind of his contemporaries, and we have suggested some in our Note above. Nor is any particular speculative, or dogmatic, philosopher mentioned by name. Mengs is, presumably, meant to serve not just (as Böhm, op. cit., p. 50, assumes) as an example of a dogmatic philosopher—though Schiller's colon might easily lead one to think so—but of an artist who, in his philosophizing about art, reduces beauty to mere form through excessive interest in technique. The final reference to 'critical' philosophy is of course to Kant's, an echo of the closing words of his *Critique of Pure Reason*.

*of dogmatic philosophy: Kant designated as 'dogmatic' all those systems of philosophy which speculated about the nature of things; whereas he, in his own 'critical' philosophy, was concerned only to examine the competence of the human mind to *know* about the nature of things.

*Raphael Mengs: 1728–99, head of the Vatican School, and generally acclaimed as the representative painter in the neo-classical style. His *Parnassus*, in the Villa Albani in Rome, seemed to Winckelmann to be of a perfection surpassing even that of Raphael, and Goethe admired it too. He also confessed (*Italienische Reise*, Rom, I. iii. 1788) to having received 'glückliche Erleuchtungen', not least about colour, from Mengs's *Gedanken über die Schönheit und über den Geschmack in der Malerei* (1762), 'which to many seem obscure'—as, indeed, they did to Casanova who complained in his *Memoirs* of their unbearable metaphysical platitudinizing.

in contemplation of the beautiful: 'des Schönen' here, rather than 'der Schönheit', presumably because the reference is to empirical, rather than ideal, beauty. Cf. § 8 below where the two terms are explicitly opposed in the same sentence.

wholly earnest in its demands: *Ernst* and *Spiel*, terms frequently used by Goethe and Schiller to express the contrast between life and art. Cf. the schema at the end of *Der Sammler und die Seinigen* (JA xxxiii. 204) and the end of the Prologue to *Wallensteins Lager*.

life becomes of less consequence: for the range of meaning of 'life' in this context, i.e. life-serving activities in the biological sense, see Schiller's own definition in § 2 of this Letter.

once human dignity enters in: not, as some translators have it, 'blends with it' or 'is mixed up with it'. It is not here a question of life and dignity being united or fused; rather of the urgency of our life-preserving impulses being reduced by the appearance on the scene of the larger questions of human value. Nor is it a matter of duty being at odds with inclination; rather of the asperities of duty being softened once inclination endorses our decision. What has to be rendered is the reciprocal tempering of each drive by the other, expressed throughout this sustained period, in the form of chiasmus within chiasmus (see below, p. 348 f.). 'Life' and 'inclination' both appertain to the material, 'dignity' and 'duty' to the formal, drive. If, in the first half of this chiasmus, the intervention by dignity reduces the importunacy of life, in the second half, it is life (in the form of inclination) which reduces the constraint of dignity (in the form of duty).

XV. 7. *but with beauty he plays*: Schiller is here developing Kant's distinction between three delights: that of the good, the beautiful, and the agreeable (*Critique of Judgement*, i, § 5). In the *Horen* Schiller had an amusing and illuminating footnote to this: 'Es giebt ein Charten*spiel* und giebt ein Trauer*spiel*; aber offenbar ist das Chartenspiel viel zu *ernsthaft* für diesen Nahmen.' Schiller is not often ironical; but with this heavy irony he both brings out what he means by play and has a dig at the obsessive earnestness of contemporary card-playing (he spoke from experience; like Lessing, he had a passion for cards and would play from afternoon until two or three in the morning, having dinner served at the card-table!). Tragedy—as the German word implies—is play, despite the weightiness of its matter and import (cf. XXII. 5 and Note); card-playing, by contrast, is *far* too serious an activity to merit the name!—not only because of the practical nature of its end (financial gain), but because of the player's emotional identification with this end.

XV. 8. *Libyan opponent*: i.e. the lion. Schiller may have known the story of Androcles and the Lion as told by Aulus Gellius, v. 14. But he is probably just referring to the Roman *venationes* in general, the hunting and killing of animals in public display.

footnote: Dubos (*Réflexions critiques sur la poésie et la peinture*, 1719) had cited gladiatorial combats and bull-fights as examples of the sources of such painful but delightful emotions. Burke (*On the Sublime*, i. 7 f.) seems to be following him when he discusses how pain can be a source of delight. Schiller, by contrast, cites these same combats in order to prevent the reader confusing such 'games' with aesthetic play as he understands it. Even in his earlier essays on tragedy, *Über den Grund des Vergnügens an tragischen Gegenständen* (1791) and *Über die tragische Kunst* (1792), he had been groping for a better explanation of our delight in tragedy than the 'mixed feelings'—pleasure-pain theory—of Dubos and Mendelssohn.

horse-racing in London: horse-racing seems first to have developed in an organized form during the reign of Henry VIII. By the middle of the eighteenth century, under the authority of the Jockey Club (1750), it had become a major popular sport.

bull-fights in Madrid: according to Ignacio Olagüe (*This is Spain*. Trsl. W. Starkie, London, 1954, pp. 106 f.), the Spanish bull-fight, which Schiller here dismisses as popular entertainment of a wholly non-aesthetic kind, had, under the influence of the dance, become 'a noble ritualistic spectacle. . . . . The *corrida* came to resemble more and more a ballet, and the style of each pass, the gestures, the dignity and elegance of the man as compared with the noble ferocity of the animal, all increased the aesthetic beauty of the spectacle.' In XXVII. 6 Schiller will himself give several examples of such aesthetic transformation.

*spectacles in the Paris of former days: scarcely the *soties* or *farces* of the fifteenth century; more likely the parodies and burlesques of the *théâtre de la foire* in the eighteenth or, perhaps more generally still, any of the various entertainments provided for the populace in pre-Revolutionary days.

*gondola races in Venice: a fashionable rendezvous of high society in the eighteenth century, and a favourite haunt of Schiller's own Duke, Karl Eugen, especially at Carnival time, Venice forms the background of Schiller's novel, *Der Geisterseher*.

*animal-baiting in Vienna: Tierhatz can mean either 'baiting' or 'coursing'. Dr. Burney's detailed and horrific account of the savage and ferocious '*combats*, as they are called, or baiting of wild beasts' in the Vienna of the 1770's (op. cit. ii. 112 f.) suggests that Schiller means the former. This is confirmed by Hugo von Hofmannsthal's description of *Tierhetzen* in his essay 'Unsere Fremdwörter' (*Gesammelte Werke*, 1952; *Prosa*, iii. 201): 'In diesen wurde zuerst mit der Meute gegen Stiere, Bären usw. gearbeitet; die Glanznummer zum Schluss war aber, dass ein besonders hervorragender Fanghund den Bären oder den Eber *solo* fing.'

*life of the Corso in Rome: the main street where the Romans promenaded on Sundays and holidays, and scene of the Carnival, 'ein Fest, das dem Volke eigentlich nicht gegeben wird, sondern das sich das Volk selbst gibt' (JA xxvii. 195). Schiller may well have been acquainted with this description, for although the *Italienische Reise* itself did not appear until 1829, Goethe had published *Das römische Karneval* in book form (with coloured plates) in 1789, and again in his *Neue Schriften* of 1792.

XV. 9. *only fully a human being when he plays*: the application of this paradoxical-sounding proposition to 'the twofold earnestness of duty and of destiny' will be made in the last few Letters, esp. XXIII. 7 and XXVII. 8–12. It is not quite such an audacious statement as it sounds out of context, or even in its immediate context here. The reader has been prepared for 'the weight and depth of meaning' that Schiller promises to uncover by XIV. 5, where the play-drive was linked not only with human freedom but with human love.

only in philosophy: 'philosophy' here—in its original sense of the systematic treatment of a subject, scientific investigation of any kind—in order to avoid the inevitable misunderstandings to which 'science' would give rise.

the most distinguished exponents of both: something of a crux. Does *ihrer* refer to *Kunst* alone, or to both *Kunst* and *Gefühl*? The English translators are divided, and Leroux refers it to the Greeks: 'chez les plus distingués d'entre leurs maîtres'. If we refer it to both 'art' and 'feeling', it is because they are parallel to *ästhetische Kunst* and *Lebenskunst* in the preceding sentence, and it was of *both* these that the Greeks were, in the eyes of the eighteenth century, the most distinguished masters.

idleness and indifferency: we have chosen the less familiar word in the hope of avoiding such common connotations of 'indifference' as apathy, unconcern, absence of feeling. The emphasis here is rather on the absence of bias or favour, on indetermination of the will (there is a close connexion with the notion of *Bestimmbarkeit* which will be developed in XIX), on substantial equivalence of opposites. The 'point of indifference' in magnetism might be relevant: 'the middle zone of a magnet where the attractive powers of the two ends neutralize each other' (*OED*). The term actually occurs in Burke (though not surely in the sense assigned to the occurrence in *OED*, viz. 'unconcern', 'apathy'): 'The human mind is often, and I think it is for the most part, in a state neither of pain nor pleasure, which I call a state of indifference' (*On the Sublime*, i. 2). Readers may like to compare a similar use of the term by Paul Valéry ('Poésie et pensée abstraite', *Variété*, v. 136): 'chacune [spécialisation successive] est un écart de l'état purement disponible et superficiellement accordé avec le milieu extérieur, qui est l'état moyen de notre être, l'état d'indifférence des échanges.' This 'idleness', 'equivalence', 'indifference', or 'happy medium' (as it was called in § 5 of this Letter) is not only 'the enviable portion of the gods', but, as is clear from VI. 14 and IX. 7, the goal of complete human beings and, at the same time, a pre-condition of their reaching it.

Necessity . . . true Freedom: cf. XIX. 12 and, for a Pietistic equivalent of the thought, Oetinger's *Biblisches Wörterbuch*, ed. cit., p. 347: 'Notwendigkeit und Freiheit läuft in Gott zusammen.'

Juno Ludovisi: like Lessing, Herder, and Goethe before him, Schiller had been stimulated by the famous *Antikensammlung* in Mannheim to a passionate vindication of Greek art. The *Brief eines reisenden Dänen*, published in his *Thalia* in 1785, declares his belief—in terms clearly borrowed from Winckelmann—that the Greeks had expressed the innate harmony of their lives in the noble simplicity of their sculpture: 'Der Mensch brachte hier etwas zustande, das mehr ist, als er selbst war, das an etwas Grösseres erinnert, als seine Gattung.' The *Götter Griechenlands* (1788), in which he went on to contrast the harmonious synthesis of spirit and matter in the Greek world with the one-sided materialism of the moderns (cf. J. G. Robertson, *The Gods of Greece in German Poetry*, Taylorian Lecture, Oxford, 1924), is the poetic counterpart of his denunciation of modern 'fragmentation' in the *Aesthetic Letters*. If Schiller here chooses Juno Ludovisi as his illustration rather than any of the statues in the Mannheim collection, it was no doubt under the recent influence of Goethe, who had come under the spell of this colossal bust during his Roman sojourn, and taken great pains to install a cast of this, his first Roman 'sweetheart', as he called her, in his rooms: 'Keine Worte geben eine Ahnung davon. Es ist wie ein Gesang Homers' (*Italienische Reise*; JA xxvi. 179). On leaving Rome he bequeathed it to Angelika Kauffmann, and it was not until 1823 that he received a replica of it from Staatsrat Schultz which he set up in the 'Juno-Zimmer' of his house in Weimar. Whether the bust is in fact of Juno at all has been questioned by archeologists in recent years: it is now thought to be the head of a statue commissioned by the emperor Claudius in honour of his mother, Antonia Augusta (cf. *Goethes Werke*, Hamb. Ausg., Bd. xi, hrsg. von Herbert von Einem, p. 616).

heavenly grace: yet another example of the confluence of Greek and Christian traditions in these Letters. *Holdselig* is the word by which Luther (*Sendbrief vom Dolmetschen*) replaced the Catholic 'vol Gnaden' in the 'Hail Mary'. *Schrecken*, by contrast, was a common German rendering of one of the two concomitants of Aristotle's catharsis.

as if existing beyond space: hence not subject to physical laws such as those governing mass and motion (i.e. 'neither yielding nor resisting'). The seeming transcendence of these, Schiller had argued in his *Kallias* letters (23.ii.1793; Jonas, iii. 270 f.), was the prime attribute of beauty. Among the examples he gave were a bird in flight, seemingly defying the law of gravity, and a vase so fashioned that it gives the semblance of soaring, though in physical fact it is actually obeying the laws of mass.

LETTER XVI

XVI. 2. *in one of the preceding Letters*: i.e. in X. 1; but also in XIII. 6, at least by implication.

tense by releasing both natures uniformly: at this point Leroux, without any indication that it comes from an earlier version, inserts the following sentence from the *Horen*: 'By activating the material drive at the same time as the formal drive, it has set limits to both; by letting each hold the other within bounds, it has given to both the freedom proper to each.'

enjoy happy hours: 'happy days' has become too trivialized. And it is really irrelevant which noun is used as long as it evokes a plurality of experienced happiness to oppose to the abstraction, in the singular, of *Glückseligkeit*. The reader may think that in the next series of antitheses we have tried to go one better than the original by making the third of them into a plural–singular opposition as well. But this was due, not to any wish to improve on the symmetry of Schiller's style, but simply to the absence in English of a pair of words related as *Glück* is to *Glückseligkeit*. Our justification for translating *Glück* by a plural, is that by virtue of its associations with 'luck' or 'chance' it implies a plurality of occasions when one has been favoured by fortune, whereas *Glückseligkeit* is an abstraction connoting a certain state of being.

XVI. 3. *Energizing beauty . . . melting beauty*: Kant (*Critique of Judgement*, i, § 29) had made a distinction between affections of the strenuous and affections of the languid type (*animus strenuus* and *animus languidus*). The terms themselves may have been suggested by Burke's enumeration of the 'qualities' of Beauty (*On the Sublime*, iii. 18): 'Thirdly, to have a variety in the direction of the parts; but fourthly, to have those parts not angular, but *melted* as it were into each other. Fifthly, to be of a delicate frame, without any remarkable appearance of *strength*' (our italics). In *Anmut und Würde* Schiller had already distinguished between 'architectonic' and 'gracious' beauty, the one characteristically masculine, the other feminine, and had given poetic expression to this idea in his *Würde der Frauen* (1795) and *Die Geschlechter* (1796). Wilhelm von Humboldt took up the idea in his essay *Über die männliche und weibliche Form* (*Horen* 1795), where he proclaimed that ideal beauty, being the external appearance of complete humanity, could only reside in the organized equilibrium of the masculine and feminine elements in man. Cf. Leroux, 'L'esthétique sexuée de Guillaume de Humboldt', ed. cit., p. 261. Schiller makes great play with the terms *energisch* and *schmelzend* in *Naive und sentimentalische Dichtung*.

elasticity and power of prompt reaction: an expanded translation, in order to indicate which meanings of 'elastic' are appropriate here. As the verb *anspannen* suggests, the underlying image is that of a bow, taut, ready to let fly, yet able to resume its own form once response to a stimulus has been made. The contrast is with utter lability, with such openness to impressions that inherent form is constantly being threatened with disruption by incoming stimuli.

plainness into platitude: Körner (letter of 11.i.1795), indifferent to the alliteration and surely also to the sense, urged Schiller to replace *Fläche* by *Deutlichkeit*.

XVI. 4. *the discrepancy commonly met with*: cf. X. 7; XVII. 3, and Schiller's letter to Körner of 25.x.1794:

> Davon bin ich nun überzeugt, dass alle Misshelligkeiten, die zwischen uns und unsers Gleichen, die doch sonst im Empfinden und in Grundsätzen so ziemlich einig sind, darüber entstehen, bloss davon herrühren, dass wir einen empirischen Begriff von Schönheit zum Grunde legen, der doch nicht vorhanden ist.

about one particular species of it: *Species* was the word Schiller originally used. At Körner's instance (cf. his letter to Schiller of 11.i.1795) he changed it to *Art* here, though he keeps it elsewhere, e.g. in XVII. 3.

XVI. 5. *the effects of energizing beauty*: this second part of the intention was not carried out in this treatise (cf. above p. lviii), and in the *Horen*, Letters XVII–XXVII actually bore the sub-title: 'Die schmelzende Schönheit'. When he later removed it, Schiller also deleted *schmelzend* in XVIII. 1, but did nothing to iron out the obvious inconsistency between XVIII. 1 and XVII. 4. Strangely, in view of his subsequent statement to Körner (letter of 21.ix.1795) that Letters XVIII–XXIII—and especially the 'very important eighteenth'—were impeccably argued.

LETTER XVII

XVII. 2. *or through lack of energy*: the problem raised in Letter X, though not solved until XXII. 3. Cf. p. lv above and Note to X. 6.

a whole perfect in itself: the *Horen* had a footnote here acknowledging a debt to K. Th. von Dalberg's *Grundsätze der Aesthetik* (1791), which had similarly distinguished two basic principles of beauty: Grace (*Anmut*) and Power (*Kraft*). Dalberg was the elder brother of the Mannheim *Theaterintendant* who had been instrumental in producing Schiller's *Räuber*.

XVII. 3. *less of a free hand*: a good example of Schiller's tendency to hypostasize, and even personify, abstractions.

its own individual characteristics: not 'his', as Weiss has it. In this, as in the next, paragraph (where for clarity's sake we have inserted 'human') man is thought of as the material which beauty is to shape, even as in IV. 4 he was the *Stoff* of the pedagogic or political *Künstler*.

the ordinary run of critics: cf. XVI. 4 on 'the discrepancy commonly met with in judgements . . . about beauty', and our Note thereto.

XVII. 4. *under the compulsion of thought*: 'the compulsion of concepts' seemed to us impossible; and to have translated by 'the compulsion of ideas' would have raised the irrelevant issue of *Idee* being a technical term in Kant's philosophy (see Glossary under *Idee*). 'Thought' has the advantage of including the process as well as the products (thinking as well as thoughts), which accords very well with Schiller's meaning.

the unnaturalness of civilization: 'art' will not do as a rendering of *Kunst* here (see Glossary). It is the old distinction between *Wilder* and *Barbar* which is being invoked again. Cf. IV. 6 and Note.

pure and abstract form: the *Horen* had here the single adjective *rein*—our justification for rendering *bloss* by 'pure'.

LETTER XVIII

According to Schiller (letter to Körner, 21.ix.1795), this is one of the most important Letters for the understanding of his thesis, analysing as it does the two basic, and basically opposed, approaches to the problem of beauty, and proposing his own resolution of the conflict between them. In a much earlier letter to Körner, 25.i.1793, he had actually distinguished three possible ways of explaining beauty: the *sinnlich-subjectiv* (Burke among others); the *subjectiv-rational* (Kant); the *rational-objectiv* (Baumgarten, Mendelssohn, and the whole tribe of 'beauty=perfection' types). The fourth way, his own, was to be the *sinnlich-objectiv*.

XVIII. 1. *By means of beauty*: in this short paragraph the theme of *Die Künstler* is epitomized in abstract terms.

XVIII. 2. *this middle state*: a notion dear to Schiller from the beginning (cf. above pp. xxxiii f.). As early as 1784, in *Die Schaubühne als eine moralische Anstalt betrachtet*, he uses the term 'mittlerer Zustand' to designate that equilibrium between our sensuous and our rational nature which it is the function of dramatic art, as a mode of beauty, to restore:

> Unsre Natur . . . verlangte einen mittleren Zustand, der beide widersprechende Enden vereinigte, die harte Spannung zu sanfter Harmonie herabstimmte und den wechselsweisen Übergang eines Zustandes in den andern erleichterte. Diesen Nutzen leistet überhaupt nun der ästhetische Sinn oder das Gefühl für das Schöne. (SA xi. 89)

XVIII. 3. *the whole labyrinth of aesthetics*: Schiller here puts his finger on the central, and still unsolved, problem of aesthetics. *Labyrinth*, a word frequently used by German writers of the late eighteenth century, is derived from the language of Pietism: once the guiding thread is found, it will lead through the labyrinthine confusion of this mortal life to the secret knowledge, the hidden mystery, the esoteric truth (cf. Edna Purdie, 'Some Word-Associations in the Writings of Hamann and Herder' in *German Studies presented to Leonard Ashley Willoughby*, Oxford, 1952, pp. 151 ff.). Goethe, in whose poetry the word frequently occurs, uses it in his *Geschichte der Farbenlehre* (JA xl. 204) to much the same purpose as Schiller here: 'wenn man . . . ein solches Schema vor Augen hat . . . so wird man, wie an einem guten Leitfaden, sich durch die labyrinthischen Schicksale manches Menschenlebens hindurchfinden'.

XVIII. 4. *except by destroying them*: for this dialectical notion of 'preserving by means of destroying' see Glossary under *aufheben*.

to the guidance of their feeling: this first category would also include those critics of art who cry 'murder to dissect', and—in the hope of preserving intact the beautiful object and their own aesthetic experience of it—rely on evocation rather than analysis. Logically, of course, they should have recourse to silence. For, as Goethe put it (JA xxxv. 303), 'Die wahre Vermittlerin ist die Kunst. Über Kunst sprechen, heisst die Vermittlerin vermitteln wollen.' Yet, he hastened to add, much that is valuable has nevertheless been said by those who venture to talk about art: 'und doch ist uns daher viel Köstliches erfolgt'. The other category would include those whose passion for clear distinctions is such that, like Kant, they seek a 'pure' example of the concept of beauty in a form such as the arabesque. Since its impact on the life of feeling is negligible, this is in no danger of raising precisely those problems in aesthetics which are so difficult of solution (cf. above pp. xxiv f.). In a letter to Goethe of 7.vii.1797, Schiller deplores the recent attempts of 'analytical philosophers' to distinguish a 'pure' concept of beauty. It has, he maintains, led them to empty the word of content and turn it into a meaningless sound.

the limitations of discursive understanding: i.e. the limitations inherent in discursive understanding in general, not in that of any particular philosophers. The possessive adjective here, as in the next part of the sentence, has disparaging, rather than proprietary, function.

the freedom . . . is not just lawlessness: Schiller, in this sentence, touches on a central, and seemingly insoluble, problem of aesthetics (he will take it up again in XX. 4fn.): How is it that a work of art can mean many things to many people, and yet does not mean anything and everything we would like it to mean? That it can be pregnant with meanings still to be discovered, and yet, by its form, exert such control that there are some things it cannot possibly mean? How is it that we can speak of a 'better' or a 'worse' reading of a work of art, or of one which is beside the point? How is it that we feel the poet uses language with an exactitude not even dreamed of by other men, and yet produces thereby a structure which can articulate the feeling of such a variety of men? What are we to make of this paradox of inexhaustible meaning on the one hand, and utterly precise articulation on the other? The problem is explored at greater length, and in less abstract terms, in *Über Matthissons Gedichte* (SA xvi. 253 ff.): 'Es findet sich alsdann, dass beide Forderungen einander nicht nur nicht aufheben, sondern vielmehr in sich enthalten, und dass die höchste Freiheit gerade nur durch die höchste Bestimmtheit möglich ist.' In other words, the poet has to reckon with the free association of the imagination, which is differently conditioned in different individuals, and likes nothing better than to pursue unhindered its own spontaneous promptings. To deprive it of this would be to deprive it of the freedom and activity by which alone it can respond to poetry at all; but only through his intuitive grasp of the laws underlying all such individual variety of association can the poet hope to make his work universally expressive.

the two conditions previously described: i.e. in XVII. 2.

*fn. *the sensationalist aestheticians*: among these Schiller would, presumably, have reckoned Burke (cf. XV. 5fn. and Note), for whom the senses were, as they had been for Locke, 'the great originals of all our ideas, and consequently of all our pleasures' (*On the Sublime*, ed. cit., p. 23). And he probably had Diderot in mind too. In his letter to Goethe of 7.viii.1797, he explains his objections to aestheticians who, like Diderot, 'hit the truth with their feeling, but often lose it again through their reasoning'. Perceiving the beneficial effect of art, they seek the explanation in its content, thus subordinating the aesthetic to the moral or didactic. 'It is', he concludes, 'one of the advantages of our recent philosophy to have provided the perfect formula for expressing the subjective effect of the aesthetic without destroying its essentially aesthetic character.'

**sense and intuition*: the addition of *Sinn* in brackets is a neat reminder that Schiller is under no illusion that the wholes presented by nature are 'given', but knows very well that they are construed by us. See Glossary under *Sinn* and *Natur*.

*a fireside chat: probably an answer to the objections of readers of the *Horen* that the *Aesthetic Letters* were too difficult! Goethe and Schiller summed up the reception of the first volume of the Journal (which also contained the *Römische Elegien*) in one of their earliest *Xenien*:

Horen. Erster Jahrgang.
Einige wandeln zu ernst, die andern schreiten verwegen,
Wenige gehen den Schritt, wie ihn das Publikum hält.
(SA ii. 118)

With the view expressed in this footnote compare Schiller's essay on the necessary limitations of the use of fine writing, *Von den notwendigen Grenzen des Schönen besonders im Vortrag philosophischer Wahrheiten* (*Horen*, 1795, St. ix; cf. Note to XXVI. 5).

LETTER XIX

XIX. 3. *A perception is to be born in him*: not, surely, as one translator has it, 'conception'. *Vorstellung* includes a wider range of mental activity—from the involuntary, and seemingly simple, act of sense-perception to the more conscious thinking and judging which is involved when we entertain mental images and notions.

position or real affirmation: '*Position: Setzung, Bejahung, Behauptung, Voraussetzung, Annahme.* Jede Setzung besteht in einem Urteilsakte, durch welchen etwas als gültig, wahr, seiend, objektiv, wirklich . . . bestimmt wird' (Eisler, op. cit. [1], II. 126, 360).

XIX. 6. *at odds with them*: in other words, we only become aware of how much 'thought' is involved in sense-perception, when some mistake in interpreting the data presented to our sense-organs brings us up short and causes us to re-interpret. The eighteenth century was fascinated by such problems, and today numbers of experiments have been devised by psychologists and physiologists (cf. Johnson Abercrombie, op. cit.) to throw into relief just how much our visual perceptions are determined by all the assumptions and expectations, conscious and unconscious, that we bring to the act of construing the images which fall upon the retina. For a related thought see VI. 12 and our Note thereto.

not by providing an aid to thought: for similar safeguards, designed to ensure the autonomy of the intellectual and the moral spheres *vis-à-vis* possible encroachments on the part of the aesthetic, cf. XXIII. 7 and fn.

XIX. 9. *except through being passive*: i.e. except through suffering the impact of stimuli from the outside world.

the metaphysician, but not the transcendental philosopher: this paragraph (as far as 'how they are to be reconciled') was quoted, without acknowledgement, by Kant in a posthumous work ('Übergang von den metaphysischen Anfangsgründen der Naturwissenschaften zur Physik'; *Ges. Schriften*, Akademie-Ausg., Berlin, 1902–55, xxi. 76) to support his own argument concerning the limits of transcendental philosophy and the consequences of transgressing them. Cf. K. Vorländer in *Philos. Monatshefte*, xxx (1894), 57 ff. and E. Adickes, *Kantstudien*, 50, Berlin, 1920, p. 743.

XIX. 10. *no other power than his will*: cf. the opening paragraph of *Über das Erhabene* (1801): ' "Kein Mensch muss müssen" sagt der Jude Nathan zum Derwisch' (i.e. in Lessing's *Nathan der Weise*). Schiller continues:

> This saying is true in a wider sense than we are usually prepared to allow. The Will is the racial characteristic of Man, and Reason itself is simply the eternal rule which governs it. The whole of Nature acts in accordance with Reason; Man's prerogative is that he does so with full consciousness and intention. All other things in Nature are under compulsion; Man alone is the Being which wills. (SA xii. 264)

XIX. 11. *metaphysicist . . . physicist*: ordinary English usage would require 'metaphysician'. But in order to preserve Schiller's verbal contrast we have coined 'metaphysicist'. 'Physicist' here is to be understood in the widest possible sense: not only one who studies the physical universe, but also one who holds, as a philosophical doctrine, that all the phenomena of this universe, including mental life itself, are to be explained by reference to physical or material forces.

For further views on these two extremes, and on the 'rational empiricism' which was the only philosophical and scientific doctrine to which Goethe and Schiller inclined, see their correspondence in January 1798, and especially Goethe to Schiller on the 6th:

> It always seems to me that if the one party never manages to arrive at mind from outside inwards, the other will never reach the concept of bodies from inside outwards, and that one had, therefore, far better remain in the state of philosophical innocence (Schelling's *Ideen*, p. xvi) and make the best possible use of one's undivided existence, until the philosophers are agreed among themselves how that which they have separated is ever to be put together again.

Cf. Goethe's essays *Der Versuch als Vermittler von Objekt und Subjekt* and *Erfahrung und Wissenschaft*, which he sent to Schiller just at this time, and which are discussed at length in their letters of the 12th and the 19th.

Ineluctable, incorruptible, incomprehensible: the *Horen* clinches this 'Trinity' with the explanatory phrase 'eine Theophanie, wenn es jemals eine gab' (a theophany if ever there was one). 'Theophany', a festival held at Delphi in which the images of the gods were shown to the people; in the wider sense, a manifestation of God in human or divine form. A distich with this title appeared in the *Horen* for 1795 (SA i. 152):

> Zeigt sich der Glückliche mir, ich vergesse die Götter des Himmels;
> Aber sie stehn vor mir, wenn ich den Leidenden seh'.

XIX. 12. *according to the law of Necessity*: 'Necessity' is here unpolarized: it includes both the necessities mentioned at the beginning of §11. 'Nature' in the next sentence is also unpolarized—it is NATUR 'in the widest sense of the word' (XX. 1). See Glossary under both terms. At the end of this paragraph *Notwendigkeit* is then polarized again: for man experiences in terms of opposites what to an infinite mind (§9) are not opposites at all. But if, through a wise and courageous use of the self-awareness and freedom which NATURE has implanted in him, he succeeds in reuniting the two opposed necessities in the larger concept of NECESSITY, then he will indeed have achieved true FREEDOM—Necessity will, as it were, have turned into its opposite. He will have fulfilled his specifically human Destiny, as set forth in III. 1, and have rivalled the achievements of the Greeks (XV. 9).

LETTER XX

XX. 2. *this priority of the sensuous drive*: 'priority' in time, it should be stressed, not in the scale of values (for a further reference to the chronological priority of the sense-drive, both in the life of the individual and the race, see XXIV. 7). This, the key-sentence of the whole treatise, should make us adjust our image of an 'idealist' Schiller (cf. above pp. xc ff.). This has long stood in need of adjustment, and was recently shifted into new, and somewhat startling, focus by Käte Hamburger in 'Schiller und Sartre', loc. cit.

XX. 3. *Man cannot pass directly from feeling to thought*: was this a commonplace
of eighteenth-century psychology? See, f.i., Burke's letter of 28.xii.1745
(*Correspondence*, ed. cit., p. 59): 'Sorrow is a passion and a strong one and must
not immediately be oppose'd by a direct Contrary which is reason the product
of a Calm and undisturbed mind.' This 'doctrine of Indirection', or the 'Indirect Method' of educating either ourselves or others (cf. Hourd, op. cit.,
pp. 19, 119 ff.), has antecedents in the mysticism of both East and West. Is
this yet another instance of Schiller adapting such lore to his own purposes
(cf. above pp. lxxxi ff.), or had the 'secularization' in this case been done for
him? See, f.i., Lessing on the 'indirections' of Providence (*Erziehung des
Menschengeschlechts*, § 91): 'Let me not despair of Thee, even if Thy steps
should seem to me to go backwards!—It is not true that the shortest line is
always a straight line.'

through a state of pure determinability: in the *Horen* this difficult notion was
amplified thus: 'weil man, um von Minus zu Plus fortzuschreiten, durch Null
den Weg nehmen muss'.

But that former condition: i.e. the condition described in XIX. 2.

XX. 4 *fn. *word . . . abused through ignorance*: see Glossary under *ästhetisch*.

**under four different aspects*: there is an obvious similarity, though not an exact
correspondence, between these four ways of looking at a thing and Aristotle's
four causes: the material, the efficient, the final, and the formal.

**simply as we contemplate him*: an entry in Ottilie's 'Commonplace Book' in the
Wahlverwandtschaften (ii. 2) may serve as a gloss to this passage:

'Sometimes in the presence of a human being we commune with him as
though he were a picture. He need not even speak to us or look at us or concern himself with us at all; we look at him, we savour our relation to him, our
relation to him can actually grow without his doing anything about it, without
his having any idea that he is affecting us as if he were merely a painting.'

**in no wise free from laws*: cf. 'the freedom, in which they rightly locate the
essence of beauty, is not just lawlessness, but rather harmony of laws . . .'
(XVIII. 4).

LETTER XXI

XXI. 1. *at the beginning of the last Letter*: he means the last but one.

XXI. 2. *which does not exclude*: this actually refers back beyond Letter XIX to
the end of XVIII.

XXI. 3. *an empty infinity*: a term already used in XIX. 2. The notion is poetically
symbolized by Goethe in the endless wastes through which Faust (6239 ff.)
must pass on his way to the 'Mothers', who are themselves, by contrast, the
ground of all potentiality, hence 'an infinity filled with content'.

with the results of the foregoing inquiry: a note in the *Horen* at this point
referred the reader back to Letters XIV and XV.

XXI. 4. *man is Nought*: 'nought' here, by contrast with XIII. 4 where we translated *Null* by 'non-entity', because of the need for a double association: 1. the 'nothing' that man is in the aesthetic state in respect of any specific result; 2. the numerical contrast, i.e. zero, or cipher, with the 'infinity' referred to at the beginning of the next paragraph. These two numbers, nought and infinity, provide Schiller with a perfect symbol for his present argument of the *coincidentia oppositorum*: they are opposite extremes; yet in the circle (cf. Foss, op. cit., and Nicolson, op. cit. [2]) which can symbolize both, extremes meet, even as in one respect the 'emptiness' of sheer indetermination coincides with the 'fullness' of aesthetic determinability (XXI. 3). Moreover, zero and infinity, though not classifiable except as numbers, have a character entirely different from all other numbers. They thus afford an analogy with the dual character of the aesthetic mode: this latter shares in the contingency of all things manifest in time and space; but it also, as will be stressed in XXII. 1, partakes of the timeless and the universal. Again, there are analogies with the mysticism of both East and West. The Pietistic term *Nichts* was applied both to Man and to God, the first representing the nullity of all things earthly, the latter, that transcendence of Self which should be the Goal of all man's earthly striving. Quirinus Kuhlmann, in his *Kühlpsalter* (1684), actually opposed to this *Nichts* the neologism *Ichts* (Langen's *Wortschatz*, ed. cit., p. 413). Cf. the *Todo y nada* of St. John of the Cross (Maritain, *The Degrees of Knowledge*, London, 1937, pp. 431 f.); or—for an Eastern formulation: 'Zen "Nothing" is a complete nothing, entirely nothing, an utter void which is the source of infinite possibilities' (D. T. Suzuki, *The Middle Way. Journal of the Buddhist Society*, London, xxxiv [1959], 50).

unfruitful as regards either knowledge or character: in XXII. 1 Schiller will say that the opposite is also true (cf. III. 1 and IV. 1, which at first sight also present a contradiction). But this, as he makes clear, is no mere paradox: it all depends on whether we are thinking of particular results, either in knowledge or in conduct, or of an effect upon the total psyche. Cf. Maritain (*Art and Scholasticism*, ed. cit., p. 125):

> It is thereby clear . . . how the beautiful can be such a marvellous *tonic* for the mind without developing in the least its power of abstraction or reasoning, and that the perception of the beautiful is accompanied by that curious feeling of intellectual fullness through which we seem to be swollen with a superior knowledge of the object contemplated though it leaves us powerless to express and possess it by our ideas or make it the object of scientific analysis. So music perhaps more than any other art gives us an enjoyment of being, but does not give us *knowledge* of being.

no individual duty: this is the passage that Ruskin objected to as a 'gross and inconceivable falsity' (*Modern Painters*, pt. III, sec. i, ch. 15, § 9). He may have been misled by the rendering 'no *single* duty' in the translation he was probably using (Weiss). But he was clearly not very familiar with the *Aesthetic Letters*— he assigns to them (ibid., ch. 7, § 6fn.) a discussion of the Laocoon statue which is actually in *Über das Pathetische*. And surely the very next paragraph, to say nothing of the first paragraph of the next Letter, should have made clear beyond all doubt the extent and nature of the benefits that Schiller does in fact expect from beauty.

by the grace of Nature: admittedly an interpreting translation of 'von Natur wegen'—but surely warranted, both here and in XXIII. 5, by the thought in XIX. 11, where the 'annunciation' of personality and self-awareness is said not to be our merit, and in XXVI. 1, where the aesthetic tempering of the psyche is said to be a 'Geschenk der Natur' and dependent on the 'Gunst der Zufälle'.

XXI. 5 *fn. *press impatiently for some result*: cf. Keats's famous definition of that 'Negative Capability' which he thought essential to a 'Man of Achievement', viz. the power of 'being in uncertainties, Mysteries, doubts, without any irritable reaching after fact and reason' (letter of 21.xii.1817).

for great roles: though Schiller is here thinking primarily of the stage of the world, the word 'role' inevitably calls up the theatre; and the indecision and uncommittedness in which many of Schiller's dramatic characters find themselves, e.g. Fiesco, Posa, Elisabeth, has been associated with this state of aesthetic indeterminacy (Graham, loc. cit. [3]). The one who might be said to 'combine this capacity with a sense of reality' is Wilhelm Tell (cf. Martini, loc. cit., p. 114).

XXI. 6. *our second creatress*: cf. Shaftesbury's 'Philosophical Rhapsody' (*Characteristicks*, ed. cit. ii. 345): 'O mighty *Nature*! Wise Substitute of *Providence*! impower'd *Creatress*! O Thou impowering DEITY, Supreme Creator! Thee I invoke and Thee alone adore . . .'. Schiller owed his introduction to Shaftesbury and his Scottish interpreters, Hutcheson and Ferguson, to his teacher at the *Akademie*, Professor Abel, though he did not actually read him until after 27.xi.1788, when he wrote in a letter to Caroline von Beulwitz: 'Den Shaftesbury freue ich mich einmal zu geniessen, vielleicht ist das ein Geschäft für den Sommer.' But by 1793 he knew him well enough to borrow from him his conception of 'moral grace'. The concept of 'die schöne Seele' elaborated in *Anmut und Würde* has been described as an attempt to defend Shaftesbury's ideal of harmony against Kant's ethical rigorism (E. Cassirer, 'Schiller und Shaftesbury', loc. cit., p. 51).

LETTER XXII

XXII. 1. *that those people are wrong either*: the contrast is with the views set forth in XXI. 4.

integrity: according to the Schoolmen, one of the three requisites of beauty. St. Thomas (*Summum Theologiae*, i, q. 39, a. 8) equates it with perfection (cf. Maritain, op. cit., p. 123). It represents here the fulfilment of the demand for 'Totalität des Charakters' made in IV. 7.

XXII. 2. *only by hardening it*: a return, in different terms, to the train of thought in XIII. 4fn. §3. Another example of the circular movement of the thought in this treatise.

XXII. 3. *the mood in which a genuine work of art should release us*: this is Schiller's answer to the problem raised in X. 6.

XXII. 4. *to which it may have been sublimated*: it might seem not altogether wise to translate *steigern* by a word which is now widely known and used as a technical term of Freudian psychology. But the range of meaning of the two words coincides perfectly. For *steigern* does not only mean 'raise', 'exalt', 'elevate to a higher state', but also 'refine', 'concentrate', 'rarefy'. Both the English and the German word had chemical and alchemical associations—Goethe on occasion used *steigern* as a near-synonym of *cohobieren* ('cohobate'), another word from that same sphere (cf. Wilkinson, ' "Tasso — ein gesteigerter Werther" in the Light of Goethe's Principle of *Steigerung*', *MLR* xliv [1949], 305 ff.). And on reflection the reader may agree that the Freudian connotations are by no means inappropriate in a passage whose tenor is the alchemy of art: the transmutation of materials into form through the shaping power of the artist, and the transmutation of feeling through form in aesthetic contemplation.

The reason for this is: the point of this passage is that each of the arts has some characteristic 'disadvantage' which the artist must seek to overcome, and which genius will even manage to turn to account. The subsequent corollary, that the greater the work the less we shall be aware of the peculiarities of the art to which it belongs (undoubtedly the fountain-head of Pater's famous remarks on the relations between the arts at the beginning of 'The School of Giorgione') must be read with care. The qualifying clauses—'without any displacement of their objective frontiers' and 'without thereby destroying the specific qualities of the art in question'—are crucial. It would be unthinkable for Schiller to go back behind the distinctions established by Lessing in *Laokoon*—even though, like others of his contemporaries, he might have seen the need for modifying them. Here is no plea for either descriptive poetry or painting in music—or for that reunion of all the branches of art advocated by the German Romantics. And if poetry is to 'grip us powerfully as music does', this is not to be done through making it *sound* more musical, by so-called word-music. Nor, as Schiller's qualifying clauses make clear, are we simply to be *reminded* of one art when enjoying another. What the artist is exhorted to do (or, rather, what it is said that great art does) is not to try to copy the modes or media of the other arts, but rather to transmute, through his mastery of the modes and media of his *own* art, the effects which are natural to it into effects which are merely *natural* to theirs, but only become *his* by virtue of his genius.

music . . . by virtue of its material: Schiller's friend Körner wrote an essay on the aesthetics of music (*Horen*, 1795, St. v). Schiller's remarks here, as well as the more extensive account in his review *Über Matthissons Gedichte* (1794), are the fruit of discussions with both Körner and Goethe. The essence of their position is that music is the language *par excellence* for articulating the dynamics of the inner life without the intermediary of either concepts or images (a clear statement of this in Goethe's letter to A. Schöpke, 16.ii.1818). Hence it is often said to be the 'purest' of the art-forms. But as Schiller points out here, and as Goethe was to confirm out of his own immediate experience in his correspondence with the composer, Zelter (24.viii.1823), the impact of the *medium* of music is far from 'pure': it assaults the senses, the nerves, the bodily rhythms directly, and in aesthetic experience this has to be, if not exactly overcome, then transmuted by composer and listener alike.

the arbitrary and casual play of the imagination: Schiller again comes back to a problem he had dealt with at length in *Über Matthissons Gedichte* (cf. Note to XVIII. 4): The poet has the dual task of leaving the reader's imagination free (otherwise he will fail to evoke the spontaneous *activity* which is a characteristic of aesthetic response) and at the same time of controlling it (otherwise he will fail in that other function of all art, which is to articulate a *particular* structure of feeling). Since words have reference, and evoke different associations in different people, the poet can only to a certain extent, by means of an inner logic of associations and by the 'numbers' of his verse (relations of sound, rhyme, metre, &c.), exert the kind of control which will call forth maximum richness of relevant associations while exluding irrelevant ones. As Elizabeth Sewell has illuminatingly shown (*The Structure of Poetry*, London, 1951), a Rimbaud who (to transpose her arguments into Schiller's terms) simply exploits 'the arbitrary and casual play of the imagination', or a Mallarmé who simply exploits the possibilities of an 'inner logic', are two extremes who pass eventually beyond the high seas where great poetry sails into the backwaters of the purely private or the totally incommunicable.

as the medium through which it works: note the distinction between *Materie* and *Medium* here. *Medium*, as we have pointed out in the Glossary, was on occasion used by Schiller to signify the poet's medium, i.e. language (*Worte*). But here, where it is in apposition to 'imagination', it quite obviously signifies 'medium' in the sense of an 'intervening substance through which . . . impressions are conveyed', or even the 'enveloping . . . "element" in which an organism lives' (*OED*). In other words, imagination is here seen as the mediating substance through which the abstract signs of language must pass if they are to address themselves to feeling, as the psychic 'element' in which poetry lives, moves and has its being. Cf. *Über Matthissons Gedichte* (SA xvi. 252 ff.) and *Kallias* letters (Jonas, iii. 299).

sculpture . . . by virtue of its conceptual precision: sculpture and, even more, architecture ('Bildwerk und Gebäude') are dependent upon physical laws to the point where they presuppose in the artist (though not in the beholder) an exact conceptual, even mathematical, knowledge of what can and cannot be done with the medium. In Leonardo's words, science is the frame within which art moves. Cf. Schiller's distinction, in a letter to Körner of 3.ii.1794 (Jonas, iii. 420), between the technical and the aesthetic laws of art which, as he insists, must not be confused though they are obviously related. The point here is that unless the artist is able to impart to this physical exactitude an illusion of aesthetic freedom, these arts will tend to invite a response which may well be scientific rather than aesthetic.

The plastic arts . . . must become music: if the complex coexistence and succession of sounds in music is to be so ordered that it creates the impression of a form in space, as clear in its outlines as a piece of sculpture, the plastic arts, on their side, must so transcend their physical immobility as to create an illusion of flow and rhythm and succession. It was in this sense that Goethe could concur in the Romantic view of architecture as 'frozen music'. Behind all this we still feel the influence of Winckelmann's belief in the primacy of the plastic arts. But we feel, too, how this belief is being transcended even as it is accepted, so that the passage reflects an allegiance to classicism which is vibrant with anticipations of the Romantics' adoration of music.

Poetry, when most fully developed: Schiller will take up this point again in *Über naive und sentimentalische Dichtung* (SA xii. 209), distinguishing between 'musical' poetry, which aims at representing a state of feeling, and 'plastic' poetry, which aims at reproducing an object of the external world.

XXII. 5. *the contents should effect nothing, the form everything*: cf. the complementary statement in *Über Matthissons Gedichte* (SA xvi. 252) which makes the same point from the angle of the creative process: 'Es ist, wie man weiss, niemals der *Stoff*, sondern bloss die *Behandlungsweise*, was den Künstler und Dichter macht.' Neither statement, it should be noted, reflects an empty formalism, a belief that the forms of art should be without import. See Glossary under *Inhalt*, &c.

make his form consume his material: we have preferred to render *vertilgen* in this way rather than by 'abolish', 'annihilate', 'destroy' or *détruire*, as other translators variously have it. It is true that Schiller often does conceive of the process of artistic creation as a struggle between the artist's impulse to shape his often recalcitrant *Stoff* (whether in the sense of medium or of subject-matter)—e.g. in his *Kallias* letters (to Körner, 28.ii.1793; Jonas, iii. 294): 'Also ist es die *Form*, welche in der Kunstdarstellung den Stoff besiegt haben muss.' But he sometimes has less drastic formulations of the same thought—e.g. in his *Ästhetische Vorlesungen* (SA xii. 349): 'der Stoff muss sich in der Form . . . verlieren'; or, in the next paragraph of this same Letter: 'das Einzelne [des rohen Elements] . . ., das der Meister mit unendlicher Kunst in der Harmonie des Ganzen verschwinden machte'. And the manner of the 'vanquishing' or 'destroying' is, surely, that of assimilation rather than of total annihilation. As in organic transformation, the raw material is broken down during the process and subordinated to a different principle of organization, serving a different end. The elements of the subject-matter do, in a sense, disappear; but they reappear in the completed work, though in totally different form. Cf. his essay, *Über den Gebrauch des Chors in der Tragödie* (SA xvi. 124 f.).

seeks to impose itself upon us: we have tried to give the full force of the adjective *imposant* by enlarging it into a clause—which meant transposing the order of Schiller's adjectives. All three suggest improper assault upon the mind and heart of the beholder.

which forces it back: the passage is something of a crux and is discussed on p. 341 below. Everything depends on whether *jenen* is to be referred to its immediate grammatical antecedent, *Betrachter*, or to the several earlier occurrences of *Stoff*, one of which is typographically emphasized. Either makes sense; for what is at stake here is the 'psychical' distance (cf. Bullough, op. cit.) which has to be maintained between the subject-matter of a work of art and its beholder if the aesthetic freedom of his psyche is to be ensured. And on balance it does not seem to matter which of these two poles is to be 'forced back' from the other. In favour of an interpretation which 'forces back the beholder' and 'asserts dominion over the material' is the apparent self-contradiction which results from the opposite solution: i.e. between asserting dominion over the beholder and the demand of the next sentence that 'his mind must be left completely free and inviolate'. But 'perforce to freedom' is characteristic of Schiller's philosophy of education, perhaps even inherent in education itself (cf. above pp. cx f.); and all things considered the sense of the whole paragraph, with its stress on the *power* of form to make the psyche free, seems to favour 'forcing back the *material*' and 'asserting dominion over the *beholder*'. Certainly the antithesis between 'sich *vor*drängen' and '*zurück*zwingen' supports this: since the former is explicitly used of *Stoff*, the latter must presumably refer to this too.

its own kind of dominion over him: not, as Snell has it, 'over form' since the word *Form* is feminine.

the most serious material: it is clear from this and the following paragraph that Schiller would include under this head even the most 'sublime subject-matter', e.g. religious themes. Goethe continued to hold this, their joint conviction, to the end of his life, and his conversation with Eckermann of 2.v.1824 offers an illuminating gloss to this Letter:

'Religion', said Goethe, 'stands in precisely the same relation to art as any other of man's higher interests. It is to be considered simply as material, having equal rights with all other kinds of material drawn from life. Nor are belief and disbelief the appropriate organs for apprehending a work of art. For this quite different powers and abilities are required, and art must form and fashion for those organs with which we do in fact apprehend it. If it does not, it fails in its purpose, and passes us by without having achieved the effect peculiar and proper to it.'

such as tragedy: on the subject of tragedy Schiller is, as always, strangely uncertain and ambiguous—perhaps because it was the art he chiefly practised, and he was too involved in the outcome. His essays on tragedy fluctuate constantly between the aesthetic and the moral point of view in a way that this Letter does not; and in a well-known passage of *Naïve and Sentimental Poetry* he lands himself in the untenable position of acclaiming comedy as a higher form of art than tragedy on the grounds that, the theme being so slight, the art which sustains it must be all the greater. He might just as well have argued that tragedy is a higher form because there the artist has a more recalcitrant material to cope with—i.e. one more likely to make a direct assault upon feeling and the moral sense. This is in fact the position he reaches at the end of this paragraph, but only after having first denied that tragedy is a 'free' art. For a different view from ours see Miller (op. cit., pp. 113 f.) who, however, introduces an unnecessary ambiguity into Schiller's argument by rendering *Gemütsfreiheit* as 'freedom of mind' and referring it to the moral freedom of the tragic protagonist. The context makes it quite clear that it means (aesthetic) freedom of the whole psyche and refers unambiguously to the spectator.

even amid the most violent storms of passion: an ideal admired by Schiller even in the storm and stress of his youth. It was with similar words that—following Plato—he described the serenity of spirit consequent upon virtue in an oration delivered at the Carlsschule, 10.i.1780: '. . . Ruhe der Seele in allen Stürmen des Schicksals, Stärke des Geists in allen Auftritten des Jammers . . .' (SA xi. 16 f.).

is freedom from passion: this, Schiller's firmly held conviction about the effect proper to art, has often been criticized; for it seems to run counter to all our preconceptions that the function of art is to move. It can, for instance, lead F. Usinger (loc. cit., p. 10) to state that for Schiller passion never 'penetrates as an element into art', and even to deny him the insight that supreme art 'can only proceed from the highest passion of all, namely the passion for form'. This is astonishing; for the chief distinction made by Schiller in *Über Bürgers Gedichte* was precisely between the poet's passion for form, as the true source of his poetic power, and the passions presented in his poetry (SA xvi. 239 f.). Only when the former triumphs over the latter, does he achieve that freedom from passion which can enable him to make the presentation of passion meaningful to others. If there Schiller had tackled the problem from the angle of the creative artist, here he considers it from that of the recipient. Here is no plea for disengagement or detachment *vis-à-vis* art. If we are to be free of the *dominion* of passion, it is in order that we may have insight into the nature and structure of passion: hence his distinction between 'a fine art of passion' and 'a fine passionate art'. If the whole effect of art must derive from the form, this is not in order that we may coolly admire from a distance some 'merely' aesthetically satisfying relations, but that, being kept by the form at some 'distance' from a merely personal-practical involvement with the materials out of which it was made, we shall come closer to the more universal import of which it has become the vehicle; in order that, being released by the artist from the compulsion of our stock responses, we shall be open to significances we might otherwise have missed.

XXII. 6. *a lack of form in him who judges it*: this turn from the work of art to the recipient is wholly characteristic of Schiller's aesthetics. His concern is always with a relation between subject and object; and though in discussion of it he may start now with the one pole, now with the other, his constant aim is to do justice to both and preserve the sense of their relation.

attend only to the parts: lines to be pondered by all advocates of critical analysis! Not that Schiller would have condemned the enterprise itself—far from it. One has only to think of his own close analysis of the poems of either Bürger or Matthisson.

and were it about the Messiah himself: in his distich from the *Anthologie* of 1782 entitled *Die Messiade* (SA ii. 50) Schiller had applied the term exclusively to Klopstock's famous poem *Der Messias* (1748). But *Messiade* was the ordinary name for an epic treatment of the life and sufferings of the Messiah.

in the manner of . . . Catullus: no doubt an oblique reference to the triumph of form over subject-matter in Goethe's *Roman Elegies*. If transposed into the measures of Byron's *Don Juan*, Goethe told Eckermann some thirty years later (25.ii.1824), their themes could scarcely fail to give offence; as it was, the classical distichs lent distinction to their eroticism. Is Schiller not perhaps echoing Catullus himself, who had similarly protested against taking the statements in his verse for affirmation of fact? He rebukes (*Poems*, xvi) those 'who have supposed me to be immodest on account of my verses, because they are rather voluptuous. For though the sacred poet ought to be chaste himself, his verses need not be so.'

> Nam castum esse decet pium poetam
> Ipsum, versiculos nihil necesse est.

Cf. Schiller's letter to Goethe of 1.iii.1795, in which he criticizes Jacobi's objections to the alleged immorality of *Wilhelm Meisters Lehrjahre* by applying the distinctions between subject-matter and treatment established in this Letter.

LETTER XXIII

XXIII. 1. *the thread of my inquiry*: which, according to Walzel (SA xii. 373), he had broken off at the end of XVI. But this can scarcely be so. For there is mention of a 'middle' mode or condition—the theme he now takes up again— not only in XVIII. 2, but even as late as XX. 4. The point at which he broke off his argument to apply his theories 'to the practice of art and the judgement of its works' was actually XXII. 4. The turn of the argument at the end of XVI, by contrast, represented, not a change from theory to practice, but a descent from the 'singleness' of beauty on the plane of Idea to its twofold manifestation on the plane of experience.

the practice of art: such passive, or middle, use of the present participle—in which the activity of the verbal adjective is transferred to the noun it qualifies although the association between the two ideas is in fact of a much looser kind— was common in the older language and is not unknown as a syntactical curiosity in modern German: *schwindelnde Höhe*, *liegende Stellung*. Cf. 'falling sickness', or *thé dansant*.

XXIII. 2. *a middle state of aesthetic freedom*: for the persistence of this notion in Schiller's thought see Note to XVIII. 2.

first making him aesthetic: Schiller comes back yet again, after further argument and demonstration, to his main theme, first announced in II. 5.

XXIII. 4. *need to have the active determination*: it seemed necessary to repeat the antecedent, since 'die letztere' does not, as Leroux assumes, refer to 'Form', the feminine noun which immediately precedes it, but, as the repetition of the verb 'sich enthalten' implies, to the second of the two 'Bestimmungen' with which the whole paragraph is concerned.

XXIII. 5. *refined to the point*: we have preferred 'refined' to 'ennobled' here because the hidden metaphor is almost certainly alchemical, or metallurgical, or both (cf. Glossary under *Idee, Ideal*, &c.).

taking from himself: 'sich' is not, as Snell assumes, accusative, but dative. This we can only know from the total argument. Only in the 'indeterminate', aesthetic, state is man *whole*; in all other, 'determinate', states he is limited and —inasmuch as one faculty or function predominates—one-sided, hence less than complete. To move, therefore, from the aesthetic to any specific activity involves a 'retrenchment', or reduction, of the personality; while to move in the opposite direction implies an expansion or enlargement (*Erweiterung* is the word used in XV. 7 and XXVI. 4).

completely new kind of activity: Cf. Note to IX. 1.

by the grace of Nature: for the justification of this interpreting translation see Note to XXI. 4.

beneath another clime: again Schiller's letters to Goethe at the end of August 1794 provide the gloss. It is not possible to transport every northerner to those southern climes where both sides of his nature can unfold in harmony; but, Schiller there maintains, a similar result may be attained through conscious effort, and Goethe affords the proof.

XXIII. 7 *fn. § 1. *freedom . . . manifest in appearance*: this is Schiller's famous definition of beauty from the *Kallias* letters. Cf. Notes to III. 5, XV. 5, Glossary under *Freiheit*, and pp. xxvii f. above.

*fn. § 2. *moral transcendence . . . aesthetic transcendence*: cf. the Schoolmen's distinction between the universal rules of moral science, whose ends and direction are fixed, and Prudence, or the art of carrying these out in particular circumstances:

> It goes without saying that as far as the precepts of the moral law are concerned, all cases are identical *in this sense*, that such precepts ought always to be obeyed. But there are individual differences in moral cases as to the *modalities* of the conduct to be observed in conformity with the said precepts. (Maritain, op. cit., pp. 14, 118)

What Schiller calls 'aesthetic transcendence of duty' might be termed one of the modalities of right conduct.

many have confused: Schiller here anticipates the major confusion of aestheticism. Those who would see him as a progenitor of such aesthetic cults as that led by Stefan George—the glorification of Beauty or Greatness regardless of whether it is evil—might ponder such pronouncements as 'misled by the appearance of what is noble, they have imported into morality an element of arbitrariness and contingency which would end in its utter destruction'. Another instance of how much would be missed by neglecting Schiller's footnotes!

XXIII. 7. *sphere of being and well-being*: we have preferred this paraphrase to 'happiness', since *Glückseligkeit* here, where it is more or less co-extensive with 'das physische Leben', approximates to the meaning in XXIV. 5, where *Glückseligkeitssysteme* will be defined as the 'unlimited perpetuation of being and well-being merely for the sake of being and well-being'. In XXIV. 3, by contrast, *Glückseligkeit*, though still opposed to *Würde*, i.e. to the moral aspect of man, has a positive spiritual content, since it rests on the reconciliation of the 'highest' and the 'lowest' in man. On this principle of the narrower and wider connotations of the same key-word in Schiller's usage see pp. lxxxv ff. above.

XXIII. 8. *make a start upon his moral life*: yet another example of that apparent circularity to which Schiller himself drew attention at the beginning of Letter IX. It is in order to prepare himself for his moral life that man is to make his physical life aesthetic; yet the means by which he is to achieve this aesthetic transformation are themselves 'moral', i.e. reason and the will. To borrow his own words from IV. 4, 'the end here turns back upon itself and reappears in the means'. As we have argued in the Introduction, pp. liii f. (see also our next Note), this is no mere terminological confusion. For Schiller's use of the same concept (Reason, Freedom, the Moral, &c.) in a narrow and a wider sense, reflects a reality in the growth of the psyche: the *germ* of moral freedom is indeed implanted in man; the problem for the educationist is how to foster its full realization.

The law of his will . . . even to his inclinations: this, according to Wernly (op. cit., p. 199), means that man is to demonstrate his moral freedom by *imposing* his will upon his inclinations. In other words, she takes it as an instance of the Kantian conflict between Duty and Inclination. Admittedly the image of *war* might seem to support her interpretation; but surely the substitution of *play* for the usual *wage*—a substitution to which Schiller himself draws attention —should have warned her that he has something quite different in mind. What he is here suggesting is not that our physical life should be lived in a moral way, by applying to it our fully developed powers of rationality and free choice (a misunderstanding which Böhm's ambiguous formulation [op. cit., p. 94] might also be held to foster); rather that the full and proper development of those powers can only be brought about by encouraging and nurturing their very earliest manifestations, viz. love of play, and a delight in form and semblance. These aesthetic phenomena are to be regarded as the germ of rational and moral conduct for the reasons given by Schiller in the preceding paragraph: it is, from Nature's point of view, a matter of complete indifference how we perform those acts which preserve life and perpetuate the species; but in seeing that one and the same act can be performed in more than one way we manifest that power of abstracting form from substance which is the basis of all reasoning; and in preferring one of these ways rather than another we demonstrate that power of free choice which is the basis of the moral will.

desire more nobly . . . will sublimely: the difference between noble (see Glossary under *edel*) and sublime conduct is elaborated in the difficult, but crucially important, last paragraph of the footnote to §7. It really turns on a double distinction: between harmony and conflict and between character and conduct. A 'noble soul' (in *Anmut und Würde* it was termed a 'beautiful soul') is, for Schiller, a man essentially at one with himself, 'free' because all his functions are working in harmony, and because moral conduct has become so much second nature that in all normal situations of daily life he can be relied upon to behave in accordance with duty without any conflict of moral decision. Sublime *conduct*, by contrast—for sublimity manifests itself in situations of crisis, and would, in the nature of the case, rarely if ever be sustainable long enough for us to speak of a sublime character or 'soul'—is conduct in which a man achieves the seemingly impossible by, as we say, 'rising above himself', i.e. by a victory over his life-serving and self-preserving impulses. The deed he performs, however, does not, as Schiller is at pains to emphasize, transcend the moral law (i.e. the object), but rather *our experience* of human behaviour (i.e. the subject): he does not do more than duty in fact demands, but more than we have come to expect human beings to do.

already opens up the inner: for the notion of 'opening up' cf. VIII. 7, XIX. 12 and Note to IX. 1. The idea that outward forms, though not the *cause* of the 'inner alchemy', are its essential prerequisites, is a common feature of religious, especially mystical, directives for the disciplining of the soul. It is also the assumption underlying certain schools of acting—the reverse, in fact, of the method which says: 'get the feeling and the form will follow'. Schiller, by contrast, says: 'perform the right motions and gestures, and the feeling will follow'. He knows very well, and makes it clear in various places, that outward form can never take the place of the inner (any more than the practice of religious forms necessarily brings about a change of heart), and is not to be confused with it. But he knows, too, that it nevertheless has its part to play as one means, and an important means, in education.

LETTER XXIV

XXIV. 2. *delight in things for their own sake*: for a justification of this rendering of *frei* see Glossary under *Freiheit* (3). And because of its association with this kind of freedom, we have preferred 'delight' as a rendering of *Lust*, in order to distinguish this, aesthetic, pleasure from the gratification of appetite and affection, or the merely Agreeable: 'das Angenehme, welches sonst nur die Sinne lockt' (XXVII. 11). In XXVII. 7, by contrast, where *Lust* (without adjective) is equated with *Begierde*, and opposed to *Neigung* and *Liebe*, it seemed better to render it by 'lust'.

unvarying law which informs them: an interpretation rather than a translation, but warranted by the importance, as well as the condensation, of the thought. In describing this emergence from the primitive state of what Lévy-Bruhl (*Primitive Mentality*, London, 1923) was to call *participation mystique*, Schiller is also saying something valid about the perceptual process, indeed about the learning process in general: without some schema in the mind we are unable to 'discover' order and sense in the phenomena we perceive, unable even to perceive them as distinct phenomena at all. The fact that a rigid schema of preconceptions can also prevent us seeing (literally and figuratively) by inclining us 'to prejudge the issue' (the point Schiller made in XIII. 4fn. § 2), does not alter the fact that some schema of expectations is indispensable. The process of learning to distinguish the *forms* of plants from the *chaos* of vegetable growth is nowhere more vividly—or more movingly—expressed than in Goethe's poem *Die Metamorphose der Pflanzen* (1798).

but in spent desire: in XXVII. 1 Schiller will return, in so many words, to this recurrent 'cycle of animal behaviour', a notion which had recently found poetic expression in the chiasmus with which Goethe let Faust express his disgust at Mephistopheles' efforts to reduce him to a mere animal:

> So tauml' ich von Begierde zu Genuss,
> Und im Genuss verschmacht' ich nach Begierde.
> (*Faust, Ein Fragment*, 1790, 1922 f.)

The reader may like to compare—and contrast—Schiller's evocation of the 'dumpfer Zustand' of primitive man with Rousseau's description of 'l'homme sauvage' in *De l'inégalité*:

L'homme sauvage, livré par la nature au seul instinct, . . . commencera donc par les fonctions purement animales. Apercevoir et sentir sera son premier état, qui lui sera commun avec tous les animaux; vouloir et ne pas vouloir, désirer et craindre, seront les premières et presque les seules opérations de son âme, jusqu'à ce que de nouvelles circonstances y causent de nouveaux développements. . . . Le spectacle de la nature lui devient indifférent à force de lui devenir familier . . . il n'a pas l'esprit de s'étonner des plus grandes merveilles. . . . Son âme, que rien n'agite, se livre au seul sentiment de son existence actuelle, sans aucune idée de l'avenir. (Vaughan, op. cit. i. 150 f.)

and with Lessing's evocation, in *Hamburgische Dramaturgie*, 70, of what life would be like were it not for the abstractive and selective powers of the mind:

Dieses Vermögen üben wir in allen Augenblicken des Lebens; ohne dasselbe würde es für uns gar kein Leben geben; wir würden vor allzu verschiedenen Empfindungen nichts empfinden; wir würden ein beständiger Raub des gegenwärtigen Eindruckes sein; wir würden träumen, ohne zu wissen, was wir träumten.

His violent passions: the lines from Goethe's *Iphigenie* (i. 3) are slightly adapted by Schiller to fit his own context. In letters to Goethe and Körner, both of 12.ix.1794, he had praised very warmly the translation of William Taylor of Norwich, done 'with such felicity that it reads like an original, and retains completely the Goethean character'. Readers may like to judge for themselves:

His sons and grandsons heir'd the mighty breast
and curbless strength of Titan's progeny;
but fate with iron bandage from their eyes
hid wisdom, patience, prudence, moderation.
Their wishes rul'd with boundless violence.

(*Iphigenia in Tauris, a Tragedy written originally in German by
J. W. von Goethe*, London, 1793, p. 22)

In this state of sullen limitation: neither 'sullen' nor 'sombre' is quite right for *dumpf*. But what is? Schiller is still moving in the atmosphere of *Iphigenie*, and *dumpf*, one of Goethe's favourite words, has here and in § 5 below almost as many kinds of association—aural, visual, vegetative, psychical—as it had for him. Its synaesthetic quality was there clearly apparent in Orest's description of the 'night' in which he would fain hide his dreadful deed:

Ins klanglos-dumpfe Höhlenreich der Nacht. (iii. 1)

The contrast between light and darkness, which prevails throughout this paragraph, no doubt controls the associations of *dumpf* to some extent. But aural associations—'lack of resonance'—would not be inappropriate either: Iphigenie, in her desperate opening monologue, had spoken of the 'dumpfe Töne' of the unfeeling waves, and gone on to contrast the death in life she now endures with the 'selbstbewusstes Leben' (i. 2) to which every man—and woman—has a right. It is such awakening out of blind, hollow, vegetable existence to the light of self-consciousness which is Schiller's chief concern here.

in the reflected light of consciousness: by contrast with XVIII. 2 and 4, where the meaning of *reflektieren* and *Reflexion* was simply that of 'pondering', the connexion of *Reflexion* with light and mirror ('he never sees others in himself but only himself in others') is here explicitly established. This brings out, as Schiller intends it should, the continual reciprocity between self and world in the development of any knowledge, whether of ourselves or of the world. In XXV. 2 *Reflexion* in this sense will appear as a synonym of *Betrachtung*, and be called 'the first *liberal* relation of man to the universe'—liberal, because it is the first relation in which he is actively involved in construing objects instead of passively suffering the impact of natural events and processes. The connexion with the notion of aesthetic distance, and its natural basis in the organs of sight and hearing, in XXVI. 6 is also relevant.

XXIV. 3. *joy and blessedness . . . opposites he has distinguished*: we would justify this, at first sight somewhat free, translation on the following grounds:

1. it preserves the relation between *Unterscheidung*, with its almost verbal activity, and *Unterschied*, the product of that activity;
2. with 'reconciliation', it makes some attempt at rendering the double meaning of *Aufhebung* (see Glossary); it would be contrary to Schiller's entire thesis to translate by 'obliteration of the difference', since both man's natures are to be present, in all their characteristic activity, in the harmony which he envisages;
3. it draws attention to the manifold associations which are co-present in *Glückseligkeit*: (*a*) the 'well-being' of XXIII. 7 (see our Note thereto), though at a level which embraces spirit as well as sense; (*b*) the grace, or favour, of the gods implicit in the word *Glück* (see Note to IX. 5); (*c*) the biblical associations of joy, blessedness, and the peace of God implicit in *Seligkeit*.

In a marginal note (cited K. Coburn, *The Philosophical Lectures*, London, 1949, p. 409) Coleridge criticized Tennemann's 'arbitrary rendering of the Socratic *Eupraxy* and Godlikeness by Glück-seligkeit, i.e. Happiness': he would have had him dispense with the *Glück*—the '*Hap*', as he characteristically puts it! But does *Glückseligkeit* not in fact render very adequately indeed the 'four perfectly distinct states' of happiness which Coleridge himself was at such pains to distinguish (ibid., p. 141)? On his interest in the related distinction between 'being' and 'doing', and his indebtedness to Schiller in this respect, see notes to entries 1705 and 3131 [9]–[12] in Coleridge's *Notebooks*, ed. cit. i and ii. This related distinction is, of course, also implicit (cf. XXIII. 8 and Note) in what Schiller is saying here: the contrast between *Würde* and *Glückseligkeit* implies a contrast between isolated moral *deeds* performed *à contre-cœur* and the 'spontaneously' outflowing activity of a moral *being*. We may perhaps see here yet another instance of secularization: of the Protestant-Pietist insistence that, to find favour in the eyes of the Lord, good works must spring from a joyful and willing heart.

XXIV. 4. *wait upon his Freedom*: cf. the definition of freedom in XIX. 12fn. and Glossary. Schiller's distinction between Reason and Freedom here receives its most interesting application with his insistence that 'the first thing reason does is to make man utterly dependent upon his senses'. It is important to insist on this distinction since Böhm (op. cit., p. 97) can sum up these paragraphs as 'a chapter on the vagaries of Freedom when it became operative at too early an "epoch"'—despite the fact that Schiller has just said that it is of the vagaries of *Reason* he is now going to treat, and that man's true humanity will have to wait upon his Freedom. Nor is Schiller here talking about 'das ästhetisch Falsche', as Böhm—presumably out of his mistaken conviction that 'the aesthetic' is to be equated with *Einbildungskraft* and *Imagination*—sees fit to assert. Cf. pp. lxv f. above.

utterly dependent upon his senses: again, as in XIII. 4fn. §§ 3-4, an attack on the more narrowly rationalistic aspects of the *Aufklärung*. But Schiller's target is also those aspects of religion which have either contributed towards the repression of the senses and the passions or, paradoxically, strengthened man's dependence upon these by depicting his salvation in terms of them, or painting his heaven as an endless extension of his earthly, physical, happiness. And it cannot too often be stressed that the very attack on the historical Enlightenment —or rather on certain of its less fortunate aspects—was undertaken for the sake of greater Enlightenment, in the conviction that man has to 'fall away from Nature by the abuse of Reason before he can return to her by the use of Reason' (VI. 1).

in this early epoch: we have inserted 'early' in order to guard against the assumption shared by previous translators that 'in dieser Epoche' refers to Schiller's own age. The perspective of this whole Letter is historical, even if mythico-historical: as was stated in its opening paragraph, it deals with successive phases in the development of the individual and the race.

XXIV. 5. *what does in fact happen*: in other words, Reason, in mistaking its proper object, does what all doctrines of eudaemonism do—provides a rationalization of man's instinctual desires.

Care and Fear . . . products of reason: *Furcht* here not, presumably, to be taken as the terror aroused by some danger or threat presenting itself directly to instinct and sense; rather as imagined contingencies, remote in space and time, the Unknown, even Unthinkable, about which man can feel anguish only because Reason has afforded him intimations of something beyond the Here and Now. Among the obvious negative results of such intimations must be reckoned awareness of Death and of the possible annihilation of the Self. This kind of fear is accompanied, or even preceded, by a general undifferentiated state of apprehension, *Sorge*, which, knowing no particular object for its anxiety, is ready to seize on any of those which Reason so promptly contrives as a plausible explanation. Nowhere have the operations of Care been more terrifyingly evoked than in Faust's visitation by Frau Sorge at the end of Part II. To her tremendous question: 'Hast du die Sorge nie gekannt?' he offers an account of a life lived largely as a series of responses to the stimulus of the moment (11433-40). Again it is instructive to look back at what may well be the germ of such reflections in Rousseau's *De l'inégalité*:

Les seuls maux qu'il craigne sont la douleur et la faim. Je dis la douleur, et non la mort; car jamais l'animal ne saura ce que c'est que mourir; et la connaissance de la mort et de ses terreurs est une des premières acquisitions que l'homme ait faites en s'éloignant de la condition animale. (Vaughan, op. cit. i. 151)

We might also look forwards to Kierkegaard's doctrine of *Angst*, which was in part provoked by the alleged optimism of Weimar aestheticism. Yet compare the following lines from Schiller's poem *Das Ideal und das Leben* (which had, strangely at first sight, originally been entitled *Das Reich der Schatten* and then *Das Reich der Formen*):

> Werft die Angst des Irdischen von euch,
> Fliehet aus dem engen dumpfen Leben . . .

and Wilhelm von Humboldt's comment (letter of 21.viii.1795): '"Die Angst des Irdischen" ist ein prächtig gewählter Ausdruck. Kein anderes Wort könnte alles, was Sie hier sagen wollen, so treu und unmittelbar ans Gefühl legen.'

XXIV. 6. *with the notion of no-cause*: Schiller is here working strictly within Kantian thought and terminology. The Understanding (*Verstand*) assumes that all objects of experience, whether natural events or human actions, depend on something else, on a determining antecedent; and if it ever entertains anything beyond this infinite regress it can only arrive at the notion of absence of cause, or, as we have translated, 'no-cause'. Reason (*Vernunft*), by contrast, makes the assumption that it is its business to postulate a first condition which is itself unconditioned, i.e. it infers that the totality of conditions cannot be given unless there is a first member of the series which does not belong to it, in other words, a Final Cause.

XXIV. 7. *accidental product of the transient*: *accidens*, in Logic, an attribute which is not part of the essence, which does not arise from the nature of the thing, but from some external circumstance; e.g. water is heated *per accidens*, fire burns *per se*. As Schiller argued in XIX. 11, our concepts of Universality and Necessity, of Eternity, Truth and Right—i.e. 'the unchangeable and eternal within us'—make their appearance without our being able to say whence or how they arose; their origin is veiled alike from empirical investigation and from metaphysical inquiry.

fear . . . not reverence: unfortunately the play on words, 'Furcht . . . Ehrfurcht', cannot be rendered in English. Goethe was to elaborate the distinction in the Pedagogic Province of *Wilhelm Meisters Wanderjahre* (ii. 1). Both authors are concerned to argue that, despite the common root of the German words, awe and reverence, properties of the spirit of man, do not develop out of fear.

XXIV. 8. *an animal endowed with reason*: it will be evident that the 'mixture' of reason and animality implied in the term 'vernünftiges Tier' is not at all what Schiller understands by the 'mixed nature' on which alone, as he explained in XIX. 12fn., true human freedom must be based (cf. Glossary under *Freiheit* [3]). In the one case, the two aspects of man's nature merely coexist; in the other, they are integrated into a whole by means of reciprocal subordination. An analogy would be the difference between a 'mechanical mixture' and a 'chemical compound'. What Schiller is here concerned with is the age-old distinction between intellect and Wisdom, or rationality and Reason.

he is meant to be a human being: this sounds the keynote of the *Aufklärung*, whether it is expressed in Lessing's terms: 'Denn g'nug, es ist ein Mensch' (*Nathan*, i. 2); or in Mozart's (Schikaneder's): 'Er ist ein Prinz. Noch mehr — er ist Mensch' (*Zauberflöte*, ii. 1); or in Goethe's: 'Hier bin ich Mensch, hier darf ich's sein!' (*Faust* I, 940). Schiller had declared his adherence to this conviction as early as 1784 in his Mannheim *Rede*: the aim of the theatre is to produce integrated human beings, to teach them 'ein *Mensch* zu sein' (SA xi. 100). For further evidence concerning the central place of this conviction in eighteenth-century thought see Usinger, *Du bist ein Mensch!* ed. cit. (1941).

LETTER XXV

XXV. 1. *does no more than feel*: see Glossary under *Empfindung*.

*fn. *these two periods*: i.e. the first two of the three mentioned in XXIV. 1. Schiller is now concerned with directing attention to the transition from the first to the second phase, i.e. from the physical to the aesthetic, since, as he said in XXIII. 5, this is a far more difficult transition to make than that from the second to the third, i.e. from the aesthetic to the moral.

**From the moment man sees*: he is then no longer in a purely physical state, because in order to arrive at visual percepts he is, in fact, construing the purely physical data—the images which fall on the retina—is, however unconsciously, involved in thought processes such as inference. For an elaboration of this point see XXVI. 6 and Note thereto. It seemed essential to translate *empfindet* by 'has physical sensations', rather than by 'feels', in order to bring out the point that it would be inaccurate to speak of man seeing at all once he has ceased to receive stimuli through the organs of sense.

**in each single act of perception*: it is important to note that Schiller is not here talking about the act of aesthetic judgement, but about the act of visual perception, i.e. the apprehension of *any* object, not just of a beautiful object. This act may be thought of as having three aspects (not of course distinguished in succession), which correspond to the physical, the aesthetic, and the moral:

1. we receive, without even knowing or feeling it, the physical stimulus; the image falls on the retina;
2. we interpret this as an object distinct from ourselves, 'out there', to be looked at;
3. we place it in a context of meanings and values, i.e. we perform an act of judgement.

XXV. 2. *Contemplation (or reflection)*: the meaning of 'reflection' in this sense was already established in XXIV. 2 (see Note). In one of his *Kallias* letters (to Körner, 8.ii.1793; Jonas, iii. 241) Schiller distinguished *betrachten* from *beobachten* ('to observe'): When we perceive (*vorstellen*) objects in order to know them, then we may be said to observe them; when we let ourselves be invited by things themselves to perceive them, we may be said to contemplate them.

Thus in contemplation of anything we are at once passive and active: passive inasmuch as we are receptive to the impression it makes, active inasmuch as we subject this impression to the forms of reason (cf. XIV. 4 and Note). This is why, in XXV. 5 below, Schiller will call beauty 'the work of free contemplation': it involves our active participation, but also demands that we surrender to its power, thus uniting both aspects of our nature, the passive and the active.

and, as the divergent rays of consciousness converge: the underlying image is that of a burning-glass, a favourite one in an age fascinated by optics (cf. Note to XXVI. 6). The young Goethe had used it (*Aus Goethes Brieftasche*, 1775; JA xxxvi. 116) to express the symbolizing power of art-forms (cf. IX. 4 and Note); the young Schiller (*Philosophische Briefe*, 1786; SA xi. 127) to express the relation between God and Nature, between the Oneness of Ineffable Light and the manifold play of colour resulting from its refraction through the prism of the finite world. For both, the optical interest was interfused with potent memories, both Classical and Biblical: of Plato's cave and the mystic symbol of Pythagoras; of God's first miracle, the creation of light; and of his last, the creation of the light of man's reason, of the *lumen animae*, as St. Augustine called it (cf. Nicolson, op. cit. [1], p. 37). Both were to immortalize in verse what they felt about this inexhaustible symbol: Goethe in his *Faust* (4727),

Am farbigen Abglanz haben wir das Leben;

Schiller in the last lines of his *Künstler*,

Wie sich in sieben milden Strahlen
Der weisse Schimmer lieblich bricht,
Wie sieben Regenbogenstrahlen
Zerrinnen in das weisse Licht —
So spielt in tausendfacher Klarheit
Bezaubernd um den trunknen Blick,
So fliesst in Einen Bund der Wahrheit,
In Einen Strom des Lichts zurück!

the most primitive poetry: presumably a reference to Hesiod's *Works and Days* or, more probably, to the *Theogony* by one of his imitators. This latter is a mythological history and genealogy of the gods, beginning with the primordial Chaos, followed by Uranus, and leading up to the advent of Zeus. Schiller might well have seen in it an allegory of the emergence of order out of chaos through the instrumentality of form.

an end to the reign of Saturn: one of the most puzzling of the deities of classical antiquity, Saturn seems to have been associated with quite contrary things, e.g. day *and* night, light *and* darkness. According to the more common tradition, the reign of Saturn was the equivalent of the Golden Age—*Saturno rege*— a time of peace and plenty and innocent happiness, and the passing of his reign thus a variant of Paradise Lost. Cf. Virgil, *Eclogues*, iv. 6 f.:

Iam redit et Virgo, redeunt Saturnia regna;
Iam nova progenies cœlo demittitur alto.

In this sense Schiller had used it in his essay *Über Matthissons Gedichte* (SA xvi. 269), making it synonymous with 'Simplizität der Natur', and was to use it again in his poem *Die vier Weltalter* (1802): 'Erst regierte Saturnus schlicht und gerecht. ... Da lebten die Hirten, ein harmlos Geschlecht...' (SA i. 14). This is, however, obviously not the sense here, where the advent of peace and light is due to the triumph of Zeus over Saturn. Schiller is clearly thinking of a tradition in which Saturn, via his Greek name Kronos, was confused with Chronos, i.e. Time (as Goethe confuses him in his poem *An Schwager Kronos*).

XXV. 3. *before his eyes as object*: see Glossary under *Gegenstand*, *Objekt*. We can see no point in reintroducing before *Blick*, as other editors have done (see below pp. 335 f.), the adjective *richtend* which Schiller himself dropped when he revised the *Horen*. As we have pointed out in our Note to XXV. 1fn., an element of judgement is indeed involved in each act of perception. But to introduce the notion of *judging* an object (by following this reading Snell, f.i., is forced to translate by 'the judgement of his glance') just at this point, where everything turns on the *distinguishing* of an object out of a confused flux of impacts, is surely misleading. It deflects attention from the involuntary and unconscious judgement involved in perception itself to the conscious and deliberate judgements made subsequent to perception.

sheer mass, ponderous and inchoate: for the distinction between *Masse* and *Materie* see Glossary. The chief point of interest in this paragraph is the idea of involuntary projection of unconscious fears on to the outer world. And by the swift transition from the brute, formless, aspect of matter to the nameless fears in the mind of man, these latter are no less firmly assigned to man's 'physical' nature than will be his fantasies in XXVII. 4, where it is explicitly stated that the 'free association of ideas' belongs purely to his 'animal' life. An excellent illustration of Schiller's point, and one he may well have had in mind, is provided by the change which had been wrought by Rousseau in the contemporary attitude to mountains. Through his passionate evocation of their natural perfection he had replaced fear of their sheer mass and height by an awed delight in their sublime forms (cf. Green, op. cit., p. 14).

as projections of his own mind: cf. VI. 3 and Note. The close connexion of Schiller's psychological and epistemological speculations with optics is apparent from the beginning of this Letter, and will continue until XXVI. 6 (cf. Note thereto).

monstrous divinity of the Oriental: cf. *Die Sendung Moses* (1790; SA xiii. 54) in which Schiller discusses certain 'hieroglyphische Götterbilder' of the Egyptian Mysteries which were compounded of a variety of animal shapes. In order to symbolize the Highest Being, they would devise an 'Emblem der Stärke', such as the lion or the bull—or the Sphinx which united in itself 'etwas von dem mächtigsten Vogel oder dem Adler, von dem mächtigsten wilden Tier oder dem Löwen, von dem mächtigsten zahmen Tier oder dem Stier, und endlich von dem mächtigsten aller Tiere, dem Menschen'. On his own admission, Schiller was drawing his information from *Die hebräischen Mysterien oder die älteste religiöse Freymaurerey* by Br. Decius (pseudonym for his colleague at Jena, the philosopher, Karl Reinhold), Leipzig, 1788. Interest in hieroglyphs and emblems was still very great in the eighteenth century; witness such famous collections as that of the Dutchman Romeyn de Hooghe, translated into German by S. J. Baumgarten (brother of the founder of Aesthetics): *Hieroglyphica oder*

Denkbilder der alten Völker . . . , Amsterdam, 1744. In his acceptance of an anthropomorphic conception of deity as a step towards *Humanität*, Schiller was clearly following Winckelmann (cf. Hatfield, loc. cit.).

XXV. 5. *when we proceed to knowledge of truth*: Schiller's sharp distinction between truth and beauty might, at first sight, seem like a contradiction of Boileau's 'rien n'est beau que le vrai', or of Shaftesbury's 'All Beauty is Truth' (*Characteristicks*, ed. cit. i. 142)—immortalized by Keats, in the form of a quotation, at the end of his *Ode on a Grecian Urn*: '"Beauty is truth, truth beauty"'. But Schiller knew very well, and in fact says so here, that truth *can* be viewed as beauty; even as elsewhere (§ 7 below and IX. 4) he makes it abundantly clear that beauty can prepare the way for truth precisely because truth is implicit within it. Indeed a couple of years after the publication of this treatise, in a mood of exasperation at the way the word 'beauty' was being emptied of content, he even went so far as to propose, in a letter to Goethe (7. vii.1797), that he would be glad to see it replaced by 'truth'—which does not, of course, mean that he would seriously have repudiated the kind of distinction he is concerned to make here.

or truth being any the less true: in the *Horen* the following sentence elaborated this point: 'This [Truth] remains what it is even if it were to have no effect upon sense whatsoever, even if there were no senses at all; and in our concept of the Godhead we do in fact allow Truth to remain and all sense-experience to cease.'

the transition from activity to passivity: is Schiller being sufficiently accurate here? The transition he has in mind is not, surely, from activity to sheer passivity, but from sheer activity to that *blend* of passivity and activity which is for him the mark of aesthetic contemplation. But his main point—that there *is* a transition in all intellectual inquiry which affords aesthetic delight, a transition from the activity of discovering to the delight in either the process or the results of discovery—is surely valid. Valid, too, his point that the truth of the discovery —its 'logische Einheit' as he will call it in the next paragraph—remains, whether it affords us aesthetic pleasure or not. A mathematical solution may be perfectly valid whether it is 'elegant' or not; a work of art has no validity apart from its beauty. This is an important, if not perhaps the chief, distinction between the beauty of mathematics and the beauty of art.

XXV. 6. *feeling is excluded as long as we are thinking*: Schiller is not—despite appearances—denying the psychological fact of the reciprocal involvement of feeling and thinking. He has, after all, just conceded it in so many words in § 5 ('denn der Gedanke rührt die innre Empfindung . . .'), and his whole treatise is testimony to his agreement with Rousseau's observation in *De l'inégalité*: 'Quoi qu'en disent les moralistes, l'entendement humain doit beaucoup aux passions, qui, d'un commun aveu, lui doivent beaucoup aussi' (Vaughan, op. cit. i. 150); testimony to his conviction that truly effective thinking can only develop with, and through, feeling and sense. But—like Rousseau—he is a moralist no less than a psychologist, concerned with what ought to be, no less than with what is; and what he is here concerned with is the *imperative* to exclude from our thinking the bias and prejudice of feeling, not the possibility of our ever being able to do this in fact. The imperative of beauty, by contrast, is the perfect fusion of thought and feeling, and it is the contrast between these two imperatives—that of the thinker and that of the artist—that Schiller is wholly intent on bringing out.

analytical philosophers are unable: the reference is to Kant's argument for a moral law. This is not something which simply *is*, any more than God is (the traditional logical arguments for whose existence he had been at pains to demolish), rather something that ought to be; not something given to man (*gegeben*), rather something which it is enjoined upon him (*aufgegeben*) to establish and to obey (cf. Note to XIV. 2). It is on account of such arguments that he has been accused of bringing God and Conscience back into philosophy by the back door—a view which the lightly ironical tone of Schiller's turn of phrase here might seem to support. It did not fall within the purview of Kant's 'transcendental' philosophy to inquire how, or whether, man is able to satisfy the demands of this categorical imperative (cf. XIX. 9). Schiller's whole concern, however, is precisely with the 'practicability' of doing so, and his answer is that beauty, by its union of the seemingly opposed aspects of human nature, offers 'proof and pledge', not only that it ought to be done, but that it can be done.

momentarily takes place: to do justice to the possible presence of Swabian overtones of *augenblicklich* in *wirklich* (as in *Fiesco*, ii. 17; see A. Heintze, *Deutscher Sprachhort*, Leipzig, 1900).

XXV. 7. *since this has already happened in beauty*: illogical only if we suppose Schiller to have defined beauty as a fusion of similars rather than as a reconciliation of contraries, as an easy and innocuous harmony, rather than an equilibrium of forces, normally resistant, but now held together in vibrant and fruitful tension.

LETTER XXVI

XXVI. 2. *a troglodyte, in caves*: a favourite symbol for primitive man since Montesquieu's ironical account in the *Lettres persanes* (1721) of how they were destroyed by abandoning themselves to their natural instincts. Troglodyte, nomad, and other images in this Letter also occur in Schiller's poem *Das Eleusische Fest*, composed between 1795 and 1798 (SA i. 170).

discourses silently with himself: 'spricht' governs 'mit sich selbst' as well as 'mit dem ganzen Geschlechte', and there is no need to supply a second verb— 'dwells', or *vit*, as some earlier translators do. Indeed to do this destroys Schiller's characteristic distribution of emphasis between individual and community even in the matter of speech and communication. By linking the aesthetic, and the birth of consciousness and self-consciousness, with language, Schiller is wholly in tune with his age—with the conviction, whether expressed by Hobbes or Condillac, Rousseau or Herder, that the faculty of speech is not only that which distinguishes man from animals, but the very condition of his becoming human at all. Cf. Clark, op. cit., p. 132.

the sway of blind mass: cf. Glossary under *Materie* and Note to XXV. 3. This is yet another reference, as in XXIII. 5 (see Note thereto) to the climate of Greece. One might paraphrase as follows: The limpidity of the atmosphere (*Aether*, here, not metaphorical, as in IX. 4) and the quality of the light throw the contours of things into relief so that we forget their sheer corporeal mass, their obedience to the mere physical law of gravity, and become aware of them as forms which delight the eye. In a footnote in the *Horen*, Schiller at this point had referred his readers to the thirteenth Book of Herder's *Ideen zur Philosophie der Geschichte der Menschheit*, where 'die veranlassenden Ursachen der griechischen Geistesbildung' were discussed.

XXVI. 4. *consequences of some deficiency*: in the *Horen* this was preceded by a sentence indicating the nature of the deficiency Schiller had in mind: 'What in the case of [stupidity] results from lack of imagination, is in the case of [intelligence] due to complete suppression of the same.' Thus, whatever the difference in cause, the net result is the same—deficiency of imagination; and inasmuch as imagination plays a prime role in the acceptance of aesthetic semblance, it is obvious that from this point of view 'indifference to reality and interest in semblance' may be regarded as a plus, as 'a genuine enlargement' of the personality.

genuine enlargement of humanity: cf. XV. 7, XXIII. 5 and Note.

XXVI. 5. *not logical semblance*: 'logical' here—in the Kantian rather than the Aristotelian sense—as defined by Schiller in XX. 4fn. and further elucidated in XXV. 5: a thing is in a logical relation to us when it has reference to our intellect and furnishes us with knowledge. A 'logical illusion' would furnish us with false information about either actuality or truth; 'aesthetic illusion' lays no claim to give information, true or false, about either. This is Schiller's version of a traditional argument to refute the charge that poetry is the mother of lies; in the words of Sir Philip Sidney's *Defence of Poesie*: '[The Poet] nothing affirmeth, and therefore never lieth.'

take it to be something better: i.e. not because we mistake it for either reality or truth. The thought-sequence is as follows:

1. a clearing up of the possible confusion between aesthetic semblance and other kinds of illusion;
2. only the former do we love, just because it *is* illusion and not, as is the case with other kinds of illusion, because we mistake it for something better than illusion;
3. provided that we are ourselves under no illusion about the fact that it is an illusion, and love it with our eyes open, so to speak, there can be no harm in attaching value to it; for to do so can in no way invalidate truth or reality, since it does not even try to compete with these.

To translate 'für etwas gelten lassen' by 'faire passer pour une réalité', as Leroux does, is to return to the first stage of the argument—the clearing up of confusion—when Schiller has already passed to the third—the problem of value-judgement.

when it recalls the above mentioned affinity: a difficult passage—so difficult that

Goedeke in his critical edition was actually prepared to reverse Schiller's meaning by the addition of *nicht* before *erinnert* (ed. cit. x. 371fn.) on the grounds that it seems highly improbable that intellect would reject aesthetic semblance precisely when it was reminded of its own affinity with stupidity! Subsequent German editors have not adopted the suggested emendation. But in offering more or less acceptable paraphrases of the sentence as it stands—e.g. 'wenn er sich der obengedachten Affinität erinnert' = 'wenn er nur das Reelle sucht' (Walzel); = 'wenn er seiner Verwandtschaft mit der Dummheit gemäss handelt' (Bellermann/Kaiser); = 'er verfährt, wenn auch unbewusst, so, wie diese Affinität es ihm eingibt' (Boxberger)—none has seen fit to explain how *sich erinnern* can be made to bear such interpretation. We tentatively suggest the following:

1. in spite of Schiller's general tendency to personify mental functions, it is important here *not* to endow *Verstand* with consciousness and unconsciousness, or with feelings of superiority and shame;
2. what is being recalled is not that *with which* there is affinity, viz. stupidity, but rather the common bond which makes for affinity, viz. the attachment to palpable reality—in this case as the touchstone for verifying theories or ideas.

Questions of psychological probability such as Goedeke entertained would not then arise, and *sich erinnert*, instead of evoking the highly personal process of 'calling to mind', have the force of 'is reminiscent of'. Readers must judge for themselves whether the ambiguity of our English 'recalls' improves the situation.

on some other occasion: Schiller did so later in 1795, in two essays—*Von den notwendigen Grenzen des Schönen* (*Horen*, St. ix) and *Über die Gefahr ästhetischer Sitten* (*Horen*, St. xi)—which finally appeared together in his *Kleinere prosaische Schriften* under the single title *Über die notwendigen Grenzen beim Gebrauch schöner Formen* (SA xii. 121). See also Note to XXVI. 13.

XXVI. 6. *In the case of the eye and the ear*: there is a long tradition behind this distinction between the organs of sight and hearing and 'our more animal senses'. Harris made use of it at the beginning of his second *Treatise* ('Concerning Music, Painting, and Poetry', 1744), and Home, with whom Schiller was familiar, gave it classical expression in the Introduction to his *Elements of Criticism* (1762):

In touching, tasting, and smelling, we are conscious of the impression. Not so in seeing and hearing. When I behold a tree, I am not sensible of the impression made upon my eye; nor of the impression made upon my ear, when I listen to a song.

And the connexion between art and sight had, of course, been firmly established in Aquinas's definition of beauty as *id quod visum placet* (cf. Maritain, op. cit., p. 124). It is characteristic of Schiller's thought to seek in the natural order of things the physical substructure of man's higher activities—he will do so in Letter XXVII with both play and love (cf. above p. xciii); and so he here discovers the physical basis (he means it as more than mere analogy) of the aesthetic phenomena of 'semblance' and 'distance' in optical illusions and in the actual distance of objects from the organs of sense in visual and aural perception. It is a subject which he could have found discussed at length in vol. ii of J. H. Lambert's *Neues Organon* (1764) which he certainly knew. Cf. Waldeck, loc. cit., p. 33.

different from the sensation we receive: Leroux takes *empfinden* to be the sense of touch—'ce que notre œil voit, se distingue de ce que le toucher sent'. On various grounds we take it to refer to the process of visual perception:

1. the sequence of the immediate argument. The contrast between eye and ear, on the one hand, and our more animal senses, on the other, having been established, Schiller proceeds to break down into its two component aspects the complex process of perception in those 'higher' senses by reference to the eye alone; only thereafter does he return to the contrast between the animal senses (touch doing duty for the rest) and eye and ear;
2. the analogous use of *empfinden* and *sehen* in XXV. 1fn. (see Note thereto): 'weil er ja nur sehen kann, insofern er empfindet';
3. the passionate interest of the whole century in precisely this problem of sight. Whether in the speculations of a Locke or a Berkeley, or in the empirical confirmation of these provided by optics and surgery (one thinks of the far-famed operation performed by Cheselden on a boy blind from birth), or in the psychological explorations of Condillac and Diderot—the figure of the blind man, and its implications for the way we actually see, haunts the intellectual scene down to the end of the century and beyond (cf. Nicolson, op. cit. [1], p. 84). The lesson it brought home was most succinctly summed up by Voltaire in his *Éléments de la philosophie de Newton* (ii. 7, § 19): 'We learn to see just as we learn to speak and read . . . the quick and almost uniform judgements which all our minds form at a certain age with regard to distances, magnitudes, and positions, make us think that we need only open our eyes in order to see things as we actually do perceive them. This is an illusion.' In other words: involuntary and unconscious though it may be, complex mental activity is involved in construing the physical datum into a visual percept.

If Schiller sees an element of illusion (*Schein*) in the process of seeing and hearing which, at the level of ordinary perception, anticipates the semblance of art and beauty at the level of aesthetic perception, he is still thinking of Optics. For the image perceived, by contrast with the physical datum, was thought of as in some sense illusory or 'virtual', a term used of the apparent image—e.g. of an object under water—resulting from the effect of reflection or refraction upon rays of light.

XXVI. 7. *abstract the one from the other*: we, like Snell, take *sie* to refer to *Form* (and/or *Wirklichkeit*); *ihm* to *Körper* (and/or *Schein*), and not, as Leroux's translation—'de les séparer de lui'—might suggest, to *Mensch*. It is, of course, true (cf. G. O. Curme, *A Grammar of the German Language*, 1952², p. 187) that the dative of the personal pronoun was still on occasion used reflexively in the classical period (as it still is today in the popular speech of southern Germany). And both interpretations make good sense. Leroux's points back to the preceding paragraphs, where Schiller is still concerned, as he was in Letter XXV, with the role played by optical and aesthetic semblance in the differentiation of subject from object, self from world. This was still, at the level of visual and aural perception, the theme of XXVI. 6. But with the beginning of XXVI. 7, he moves on to the related problem of art as an independent sphere. And our interpretation (which would seem to be supported by stanza 10 of *Die Künstler*) points forward to §§ 8–10, where he is concerned to define the conditions and frontiers of this realm. Here the distinction between subject and object is taken for granted, and it is a question of establishing man's power, right—and duty— to reclaim from objects an attribute with which his own mind has endowed them, viz. semblance, and to treat it with sovereign freedom. In this operation— which is the prerequisite of artefacts being made for contemplation as well as use, or (and this is the crux) for contemplation alone—it is imperative that form be kept clearly distinct from substance, semblance from reality. This paragraph is, in fact, the first of those establishing the autonomy of the world of semblance, or the Third Kingdom of XXVII. 8, not the last of those establishing the independence of objects from the perceiving subject.

the urge towards it: again Schiller makes it clear that this treatise is not meant to be a complete aesthetic. If at the end of XXVI. 5 he announced his intention of treating elsewhere of the limitations of the aesthetic, he here denies the need to offer in this context an account of the making of art. What is relevant to his present thesis is not the basis of artistic endowment in the sense of a talent for working in a particular medium, nor yet those impulses to compensation or sublimation with which Freud was to concern himself, but only the power to distinguish semblance from substance, and to abide with it in contentment, but also without confusion.

XXVI. 8. *can he but imagine them together*: a defence of the artist's right to create his own semblance, a world apart, with its own laws, independent of the laws of external nature—whether he elongates the necks of his human figures, or paints his horses blue, or distorts the laws of perspective, or in the words of Oscar Wilde (*The Decay of Lying*) 'bids the almond tree blossom in winter and sends snow upon the ripe cornfield'. All this is a matter of indifference, as long as—the proviso of the next sentence is all-important—he firmly marks off his work of art from the continuum of ordinary reality, offering it frankly as an analogue, a parallel symbolic language, and not as a copy which invites compara- tive evaluation with reality, or sets itself up as a means for changing the face of reality.

XXVI. 10. *exceeding . . . or surrendering his rights as a poet*: i.e. without falling into the twin heresies of didacticism or naturalism. At first sight this might seem like a total recoil from his younger self, from the ardent revolutionary who had hoped that his *Robbers* might help to make the roads safer, and held up the mirror to contemporary society in his 'tragedy of common life', *Kabale und Liebe*. And, indeed, the history of art and art-theory reveals a constant oscilla- tion—a movement towards naturalism being followed by a recoil towards formalism, a plea for art for art's sake by a cry for social 'engagement'. Yet it would be wrong to construe either the art or the aesthetics of Weimar Classicism as a move towards disengagement or detachment. It was rather a move towards 'Indirection': art was to play, in the life of both individual and society, a role no less vital than the *Stürmer und Dränger* had envisaged. It was now realized, however, that this can never be achieved by direct action upon particular thoughts and deeds, but only, as is made clear in Letters XXI and XXII, by imperceptibly affecting the totality of our human nature.

XXVI. 11. *inasmuch as it is honest*: cf. the end of the Prologue to *Wallensteins Lager*, where Schiller admonishes his audience in this sense:

Ja danket ihr's [der Muse], dass sie das düstre Bild
Der Wahrheit in das heitre Reich der Kunst
Hinüberspielt, die Täuschung, die sie schafft,
Aufrichtig selbst zerstört und ihren Schein
Der Wahrheit nicht betrüglich unterschiebt;
Ernst ist das Leben, heiter ist die Kunst.

pleases better than the painted: Schiller had long been interested in such inappropriate responses to works of art. Following Lessing in the opening scenes of *Emilia Galotti*, he too had presented the problem in both dramatic (*Fiesco*, ii. 17) and fictional form (*Der Geisterseher*; SA ii. 328 f.).

through sheer appearance: Erscheinung here, as in § 14 below, in the sense of form apprehended by both the outward and the inner eye, and divested of all practical, scientific, moral connexions, as of all appeals to desire or possessiveness; almost, then, though not quite, synonymous with *Schein* (see Glossary).

in virtue of their existence as idea: Idee, here, not in the sense of either Platonic 'idea' or pure mental abstraction, but rather of an image presented to the mind. Schiller is thinking of the artist's power to detach things from their normal anchorage in reality, and treat them as symbols which derive their meaning to a large extent from their relation to other such symbols in the total organization of his work.

to dispense with the element of life in sheer semblance: does this mean: 1. to dispense with life in art that hasn't got it, i.e. learn to appreciate art so abstract that it is not reminiscent of life at all—in which case it may well be a dig at Kant's elevation of an arabesque above the beauty of the human form (cf. letter to Körner, 25.i.1793; Jonas, iii. 238); or 2. to dispense with life in art that *has* got it, i.e. learn to abstract from the 'life' of even the most representational art, and appreciate it as pure semblance? Or does it mean both?

XXVI. 12. *dishonest and dependent semblance*: not 'necessitous' (Snell) or *mesquine* (Leroux). One has to infer the sense of *bedürftig* here (it has several meanings) by reference to the beginning of both this paragraph and the previous one. Obviously the two adjectives here are the opposites of 'aufrichtig' and 'selbständig'.

eke out reality with semblance: Schiller seems to have in mind the degeneracy of an effete society such as that of the later Roman Empire or the sophisticated world of his own day. 'Eking out semblance with reality', on the other hand, might be illustrated, in life, by such insistence on 'sincerity' as he will criticize in § 14 below; in art, by any such devices as the unities of time and place, which in the theory of French classicism had the express aim of giving events on the stage a greater semblance of reality.

XXVI. 13. *To the extent that it is aesthetic semblance*: as in XXI. 4—where he was concerned to bring out precisely what the aesthetic can do, and all that it can do, by insisting on what it cannot hope, and should not attempt, to do—so here, in the tricky field of the interrelations between the aesthetic and the moral, Schiller's method of safeguarding the autonomy and values of any one sphere or mode of existence by firmly defining its limits, appears to full advantage and is entirely vindicated. His prime concern may be the rights and privileges of the aesthetic mode; but, as he expressly stated in XXVI. 9, it is by keeping strictly within his own frontiers that the artist may best help to secure those of truth and morality as well. The violation of frontiers which Schiller had in mind may well have been those of a Nero (he was mentioned by name in IX. 4) or a Cesare Borgia, whose concern with the *manner* of a deed left them indifferent to its moral content (Nero fiddles whilst Rome burns and, on being forced to commit suicide, can only exclaim: 'What an artist is dying!'). But it is also appropriate to think forward to the German Romantics' deliberate attempts to 'confuse' art and life, to the 'mourir en beauté' of a Baudelaire, the immoralist aestheticism of a Stefan George, or to Oscar Wilde's *Picture of Dorian Gray* which may be read as the culmination of such trends—or perhaps as their cautionary tale.

Only a stranger to polite society: cf. 'dass jetzt die Schönheit dem Umgang Gesetze gibt . . .' (X. 4). Schiller intended to write a treatise on the aesthetics of social forms: 'Ich habe nämlich den Versuch gemacht, in einem Aufsatze über den *ästhetischen Umgang* den Grundsatz der Schönheit auf die Gesellschaft anzuwenden, und den Umgang als ein Objekt der schönen Kunst zu betrachten' (to Garve, 1.x.1794). He is probably referring to his essay *Über den moralischen Nutzen ästhetischer Sitten* (*Horen*, 1796, St. iii; SA xii. 150), perhaps also to his earlier one, *Über die Gefahr ästhetischer Sitten* (see Note to XXVI. 5). The gist of what he had to say appears in the last two paragraphs of this Letter. Clearly Schiller was writing in a tradition, to which the *Letters of Lord Chesterfield to his Son* belong, and which goes back to Castiglione's *Il libro del Cortegiano*, and beyond to Cicero's *De Officiis*.

complain of dissimulation: this whole paragraph was originally a footnote and has the character of a casual rejoinder to a forerunner—in fact to the 'thinking minds' and 'voices worthy of respect' referred to in X. 2 (see Note) and X. 4. It is no doubt a dig at Rousseau's condemnation of polite society in the first pages of the *Premier Discours* (which had as a motto 'Decipimur specie recti'; Horace, *Poetics*, 25):

. . . cette douceur de caractère et cette urbanité de mœurs qui rendent parmi vous le commerce si liant et si facile; en un mot, les apparences de toutes les vertus sans en avoir aucune. . . . Plus d'amitiés sincères; plus d'estime réelle; plus de confiance fondée. (ed. cit., pp. 102–6)

XXVI. 14. *beneficent semblance* . . . *ideal semblance*: what would happen if our life were totally divested of such semblance is ruthlessly described in Schiller's *Poesie des Lebens*, a poem which he characterized in a letter to Goethe (12.vi.1795) as 'a bridge' from metaphysics to poetry:

> 'Wer möchte sich an Schattenbildern weiden,
> Die mit erborgtem Schein das Wesen überkleiden,
> Mit trügrischem Besitz die Hoffnung hintergehn?
> Entblösst muss ich die Wahrheit sehn. . . .'
> So rufst du aus und blickst, mein strenger Freund,
> Aus der Erfahrung sicherm Porte
> Verwerfend hin auf alles, was nur scheint. . . .
>
> (SA i. 215)

require genuine merit to have style: for our justification of this rendering of *Schein* see Glossary.

the lost exuberance of a Gothick Age: we have endeavoured by our 'ck' to obviate associations with a specific architectural style, and evoke instead an eighteenth-century attitude of mind. Lessing, for example (in the Preface to his *Briefe antiquarischen Inhalts*), identifies 'gotische Höflichkeit' with 'der schleichende, süsse Komplimentierton'. And in spite of the attempted rehabilitation of Gothic architecture by Herder and Goethe in the seventies, 'Gothic' was still synonymous, even for Herder himself (cf. W. D. Robson Scott, 'Goethe and the Gothic Revival', *PEGS* xxv [1956], 95), with *barbarisch, überladen, geschmacklos, abenteuerlich, dunkel, fratzenhaft*. It was with a disparaging reference to the 'gothic' quality of his early work that Schiller had—in language reminiscent of Voltaire's ambivalent attitude to Shakespeare—announced his conversion to the 'classical' dramatic tradition:

> die gothische Vermischung von Komischem und Tragischem, die allzu-freihe Darstellung einiger mächtigen Narrenarten, und die zerstreuende Mannigfaltigkeit des Details. . . . (Letter to Reinwald, 27.iii.1783)

And it is perhaps indicative of a continuing ambivalence that, within a couple of months of the appearance of this Letter, XXVI, he should have printed, in the same Journal (*Horen*, St. viii), an essay (by Lazarus Bendavid) on the comparative merits of Greek and Gothic architecture.

a more rigoristic judge: Snell's 'puritanical' will scarcely do—though Schiller's term does indeed derive from a religious context. He had been reading (letter to Körner, 28.ii.1793) Kant's *Religion innerhalb der Grenzen der blossen Vernunft* (1793; *Ges. Schriften*, Akademie-Ausg., Berlin, 1902–55, vi. 22), and had found there the secularized meaning of the Catholic term *Rigorist*: one who in doubtful cases of conscience holds that the stricter course is always to be followed. The opposite term, also found in Kant's treatise, is *Latitudinarier*, and Schiller used both terms in *Anmut und Würde* (SA xi. 217).

without coveting it: a commonplace of aesthetic thought even before Kant formulated it as 'disinterested pleasure'. Goethe had expressed it through the image of the stars when he wished to assure his beloved that he would plague her no longer with his desire: 'Ich seh dich eben künftig wie man *Sterne* sieht! Denk das durch' (letter to Frau von Stein, variously dated mid-April and early

September, 1776); and he later gave it poetic expression in his poem *Trost in Tränen*:

> Die Sterne, die begehrt man nicht,
> Man freut sich ihrer Pracht.

referring her instead to the dignity of her office: Bohn, Snell, and even Leroux, apparently assume that the negatives of the earlier part of the sentence govern this last verb as well, for they make it mean 'fail to show her the dignity that is due'—perhaps because they read *hinweisen auf* as though it were *erweisen*, perhaps because they approach the sentence with preconceptions about the dignity and sublimity of the Imagination. In our view, Schiller is not here concerned with any *lack* of respect shown to works of imagination, but only with the wrong *kind* of respect. He is still pursuing the thought of §§ 9–11: the confusion of territories, or modes of experience. By according inappropriate respect to works of art, treating them, f.i., as though they were a 'Sermon in Stones' (it was no accident that Ruskin objected to XXI. 4), we implicitly assign to the artistic imagination a status it ought not to have, and make demands upon it that it cannot possibly fulfil. We thereby implicitly invite it to encroach upon the territory of morality and perform a moral office, instead of recognizing it for what it is—a gratuitous offering of grace abounding.

LETTER XXVII

XXVII. 1. *in order to save himself the way to the real*: a dig at those—e.g. the critics of *schöner Schein* dealt with in XXVI. 4, 5, and 14—who imply that the artist and the aesthete live in an ivory tower.

the cycle of his animal behaviour: cf. XXIV. 2 and Note.

XXVII. 2. *superfluity of material things*: the distinction between *of* and *in* (below) is crucial, and wholly characteristic of Schiller's assumptions and method. The first stirrings of the aesthetic impulse have often been associated with superfluity: the idea may well go back to Democritus, and his conviction that the arts are not the result of necessity but of superabundance; they do not, f.i., find a place in the Platonic commonwealth until the state of necessity has turned into a state of plenty or luxury (cf. T. B. L. Webster, 'Greek Theories of Art and Literature down to 400 B.C.', *The Classical Quarterly*, xxxiii [1939], 166 ff.). Schiller, however, makes a sharp distinction between quantitative and qualitative superfluity—'he enjoys *more*, but he does not enjoy *differently*'—and for him, only the latter is at once source and sign of the aesthetic. For it is only qualitative superfluity that engages the mind and the imagination. Too much food will make a man—or an animal—sick; but food dressed in a style over and above what is necessary for the mere satisfaction of hunger is the foundation of the culinary arts. Yet quantitative superfluity, we should not forget, Schiller regards as an indispensable step on the way, even as physical play—as he will emphasize in § 3 below—is the indispensable natural prerequisite of aesthetic play. There is an exact analogy in the three stages he distinguishes in each case:

COMMENTARY 291

§ 2	§ 3
1. bare satisfaction of instinctual needs	physical earnestness
2. material superfluity	physical play
3. aesthetic superfluity	aesthetic play

the fact that it has limits: this obviously cannot mean the temporary assuagement of any particular desire—by contrast with XXIV. 2, in which the recurrent cycle of desire and assuagement was, in fact, evoked. For what could be more calculated to bring home to man—by satiety, or even nausea—that desires have limits, than a material superfluity of whatever kind? Schiller must mean man's appetitive nature in general. And since he holds that man is more than a creature of appetite, he inevitably holds too that this latter must have limits. The diametrically opposite view is that of the advertising industry, which works, presumably, on the assumption that an unending supply of varied and novel consumer goods will stimulate appetite indefinitely.

enjoying them in anticipation: those editors are right who emend *dieselbe* to *dieselben* (see below p. 336); for the antecedent is 'Vorräte', not 'ästhetische Zugabe'. With this first *indem*-clause Schiller offers an example of 'Überfluss *des* Stoffes'; with the next he will elaborate 'Überfluss *an dem* Stoffe'.

XXVII. 3. *for itself* . . . *enjoys its self*: we have split the second 'itself' into two words, and italicized 'self' in order to draw attention to the point Schiller is making: the lion's energy, instead of having an object other than itself to enjoy, becomes its *own* object of enjoyment. The internalization of the object of the lion's interest is reflected linguistically in the change (which cannot be rendered in English) from *sich* (dative), i.e. indirect object, to *sich* (accusative), i.e. direct object.

warbling of the song-bird: cf. the famous line from Goethe's ballad *Der Sänger*: 'Ich singe, wie der Vogel singt . . .'. Though Goethe, of course, knew as well as Schiller that art, however spontaneous, is not the product of the 'physical' play-impulse. It is his fictional bard, not he, who makes the simple identification with the bird.

freedom from . . . *compulsion from without*: this rendering of *Bedürfnis* seems to us justified by 'Befreiung von jedem äussern sinnlichen Zwang' in § 4 below.

luxuriance . . . *laxity*: we have tried to reproduce the play on sound and sense—perhaps at the cost of immediate clarity. But in any case the reader has to recall at this point Letters XIX ff., where *Bestimmung* was developed as a technical term. 'Coupled with indeterminacy of ends and purposes' might have been a clearer, if less close, rendering.

innumerable buds . . . *to the elements*: this thought had already appeared in a philosophical dialogue which Schiller intended for his novel *Der Geisterseher* (1789; cf. SA i. 322): 'Wie viele Keime und Embryonen, die sie [die Natur] mit so viel Kunst und Sorgfalt zum künftigen Leben zusammensetzte, werden wieder in das Elementarreich aufgelöst, ohne je zur Entwicklung zu gedeihen.' It will recur, like so many of his philosophical thoughts, in the *Votiftafeln*, as the central distich of *Die verschiedene Bestimmung* (1797):

Tausend Keime zerstreuet der Herbst, doch bringet kaum einer
Früchte, zum Element kehren die meisten zurück.
(SA i. 141)

XXVII. 4. *his imagination, too, has* . . . *its material play*: the point of interest
here is that the difference between material, or physical, play and aesthetic play
is not simply identical with the difference between physical and mental activity.
The free association of images, or ideas, as Schiller variously calls them in this
paragraph (for 'material ideas' see Glossary under *Idee* 1 [*d*]), the day-dreaming
of those indolent souls referred to in his footnote, though obviously a mental
activity, constitutes for him material, not aesthetic, play. However unimpeded
its flow, and however beautiful the material it throws up, it is yet a feature of
man's 'animal' life. It proceeds under its own momentum, and is, in Freudian
terms, id-propelled. Aesthetic play, by contrast, involves a 'leap' to the 'shaping
power' of the imagination. This free, formative, activity is characteristic of the
artist (though not of him alone; it is also at work in aesthetic contemplation
and in the aesthetic conduct of life altogether). It is 'free' in the positive sense
—as distinct from the negative sense in 'freie Ideenfolge' and 'freier Bilder-
strom' (cf. Glossary under *Freiheit* 1)—because it is disciplined, informed by
laws which are none the less present because we remain unaware of them
(cf. XX. 4fn.).

*fn. *the negative condition of its creative power*: what makes the free association
of ideas important for aesthetic creativity is its independence of immediate
external stimulus (cf. § 3 above, where animals were said to be 'at play' in the
absence of any stimulus from without). Schiller here calls such independence
the 'negative' condition of creativity. In a letter to Körner of 1.xii.1788 he had
shown just how much it was also an *indispensable* condition; and it is not surprising that Freud, having had his attention drawn to that letter, should have
incorporated it into the second edition (1909) of his *Interpretation of Dreams*
(*Complete Psychological Works*, iv. 103), and referred to it again in his 'Note on
the Prehistory of the Technique of Analysis' (1920; ibid. xviii. 264). We give
the crux of it here in our own translation:

> The ground of your complaint seems to me to lie in the constraint imposed
> by your understanding upon your imagination. At this point I must throw
> out an idea, and bring it home by means of an image. It seems not to be a
> good thing, and prejudicial to the creative work of the psyche, if the under-
> standing submits the onrush of ideas to over-sharp scrutiny at the very gates,
> as it were. An idea considered in isolation may seem very unimportant or very
> extravagant; but it will perhaps gain weight from another which follows hard
> upon it; and perhaps, in a certain conjunction with other ideas, which in
> themselves seem no less insipid, turn out to be a very serviceable link [in the
> imaginative chain]: the understanding cannot judge of any of this unless
> it holds it fast long enough to view it in conjunction with these other ideas. In
> the creative mind, by contrast, so it seems to me, the understanding has with-
> drawn its sentinels from the gates, the ideas rush in *pêle-mêle*, and only then
> does it scrutinize and review the whole company of them.—You critics, or
> whatever you may like to call yourselves, are ashamed of, or fear, those

fleeting moments of inspired frenzy which are characteristic of truly creative minds, and the longer or shorter duration of which distinguishes the thinking artist from the mere dreamer. Hence your complaints of barrenness; it is because you reject too soon and discriminate too severely.

The modern reader may well be nonplussed at the qualification of 'artist' by 'thinking'. He has, after all, just been told that it is the too prompt intervention by the understanding (*Verstand*) which distinguishes the critic from the artist, only to be suddenly confronted with the seeming paradox that it is the activity of thought (*Denken*) which distinguishes the artist from the dreamer. But, of course, *Verstand* here is not coextensive with *Denken*; the former is confined to the analytical processes of mind, the latter includes the synthetic processes as well; and it is central to Schiller's view of art that it is essentially a product of the reflective mind, of what Herder had called *Besonnenheit*. The material for it may be thrown up by the unconscious, the conception of the form itself be the product of but half-conscious processes; yet by the very act of articulating it, and making it communicable, the artist transforms the unconscious into the conscious, and thereby fulfils his peculiarly artistic function: 'Das Bewusstlose mit dem Besonnenen vereinigt macht den poetischen Künstler aus' (letter to Goethe of 27.iii.1801; cf. Goethe's reply of 3.iv.1801, and his well-known analysis of the essential aspects of art and artistic creation in his *Noten und Abhandlungen zum Divan*; JA v. 212).

faculty for ideas: *Idee*, here, not in the same sense as in *Ideenfolge* above, where it was more or less synonymous with 'image' (cf. Glossary under *Idee* 1 [*d*]). The crucial difference is the 'leap' to a 'free form' referred to in § 4 itself (see our Note below); and in view of the fact that the Greek ἰδέα meant perceived by the eye as well as by the mind's eye, a more illuminating rendering might well have been 'the faculty for forms'.

since the senses are not working against it: the life of dream and day-dream is notoriously free of the demands and controls which govern our 'waking' life, our reality-oriented, purposeful activity. However much the images of this phantasy-life may derive from the life of sense, the senses themselves, as the gateway to the outer world, may be said to be in abeyance when we dream. The 'determinations' come solely from within; those from without are suspended. Schiller's point is that this suspension of *external* control makes room for the intervention of a new kind of control, the formative power of the mind, though it does not of necessity produce it. He pursues the thought into the play on '*in*definite' and '*in*finite'. The two are by no means synonymous; but the former may be thought of as the negative precondition of the latter (cf. XIX. 4 and XXI. 3). We have noted before (XXVII. 2 and p. xciii above) the all-pervading presence in Schiller's thought of the idea that the higher activities of man are superstructures erected on a ground provided by nature.

finally makes the leap: a book such as H. S. Reimarus's *Allgemeine Betrachtungen über die Triebe der Tiere, hauptsächlich über ihre Kunsttriebe* (1760) must have played its part in provoking speculations as to whether, in similar actions performed by beasts and men, the means are analogous or different only in degree. It certainly provoked Coleridge to the comment: 'The sameness of the end, and the equal fitness of the means, proves no identity of means' (*Notebooks*, ed. cit. ii. 2320). Schiller obviously thinks it more than mere analogy; but not simply a difference of degree either; rather a qualitative change, a *Steigerung* (see above p. xciv).

its own subservience: our rendering of *Bedürftigkeit* seemed justified by its occurrence in XXVI. 11, where its meaning when used as an antonym of *Selbständigkeit* emerged clearly from the context.

sublime self-sufficiency . . . insatiable discontent: unlike the rest of the series, these do not, at first sight, seem to be true opposites. But we have to think of such primary meanings of *Einfalt* as 'singleness', 'wholeness', 'all of one piece', hence almost 'self-sufficient'; in fact, all the qualities which, in XV. 9, were ascribed to the Juno Ludovisi.

what man calls beautiful: imperceptibly, and somewhat confusingly (since, grammatically speaking, the pronoun *ihm* could still refer to 'der rohe Geschmack'), Schiller has reintroduced the main subject of the paragraph, viz. 'der Mensch' (last mentioned in the second sentence). We infer this because even poetic licence could scarcely (in the last line) ascribe a 'Busen' to the 'Geschmack'!

XXVII. 5. *the ancient German . . . and the Caledonian*: P. H. Mallet's *Monumens de la mythologie et de la poésie des Celtes et particulièrement des anciens Scandinaves* (1756) had fostered the common confusion between German and Celt. It was Thomas Percy who made the much-needed distinction between them in the Preface to his translation (1770) of that same author's *Introduction à l'histoire de Dannemarc*. In the literary field, Mallet's work prepared the way for Macpherson's successful, and fruitful, hoax, *The Works of Ossian, the son of Fingal* (1765).

XXVII. 6. *turn into dance*: as we have already pointed out in the Introduction, and in a Note to VI. 14, dance was for Schiller a symbol of ordered freedom, and we find this same thought in his poem *Der Tanz* (1795):

. . . Es ist des Wohllauts mächtige Gottheit,
Die zum geselligen Tanz ordnet den tobenden Sprung. . . .

to take on the contours of song: a translation which seems justified by XXII. 4: 'Music, at its most sublime, must become sheer form and affect us with the serene power of antiquity.'

with noble and measured tread: cf. *Iliad*, iii. 1–9, and Lessing's comment thereon in *Laokoon*, i. 1:

If Homer lets the Trojans march into battle with wild cries, the Greeks on the other hand in determined silence, critics and commentators have not been slow to note that the poet intended by this to describe the former as barbarians, but the latter as civilized people.

'Ich lese jetzt fast nichts als Homer', Schiller reported to Körner, 20.viii.1788. He knew him at that time from Voss's translation of the *Odyssey* (1781) and

Fr. L. von Stolberg's prose version of the *Iliad* (1778). Voss's *Iliad* was not published until 1793. The relevant passage runs there as follows:

> Aber nachdem sich geordnet ein jegliches Volk mit den Führern,
> Zogen die Troer in Lärm und Geschrei einher, gleich wie die Vögel:
> So wie Geschrei hertönt von Kranichen unter dem Himmel,
> Welche, nachdem sie dem Winter entflohn und unendlichem Regen,
> Laut mit Geschrei hinziehn an Okeanos' strömende Fluten,
> Kleiner Pygmäen Geschlecht mit Mord und Verderben bedrohend,
> Und aus dämmernder Luft zum schrecklichen Kampfe herannahn.
> Jene wandelten still, die mutbeseelten Achaier,
> All' im Herzen gefasst, zu verteidigen einer den andern.

XXVII. 7. *compulsion of a lovelier kind*: English usage would seem to rule out 'necessity' here; though the change referred to is of course, as in XV. 9, that fusion of two 'necessities'—that of nature with that of reason—in a higher Necessity which is perfect Freedom.

a nobler victory over will: this might sound as though the highest form of love were for Schiller a battle of wills—until we remember that for him, as for Kant, *der Wille* is not 'life-force', 'power-impulse', 'the will to live', or any such Schopenhauer-inspired concept, but 'Reason in action', the highest of which man is capable. A victory over the will of the beloved means therefore, in this context, winning her free consent, in other words, her love as defined in XIV. 5: the fusion of inclination and esteem, the reconciliation of the compulsion of feeling with the compulsion of reason. Cf. also III. 2 and Note.

form confronting the mind: for our justification of 'form' here see Glossary under *Schein* &c.

the magnanimity of the chivalric code: cf. III. 2. The *Minnesang*, rediscovered by Bodmer (*Proben der alten schwäbischen Poesie des 13. Jahrhunderts*, 1748) was generally considered, in the wake of Herder, as *Volksdichtung*; not indeed in the sense that the later Romantics were to conceive this, as a product of 'das dichtende Volk', but rather as Schiller was to characterize it in *Über naive und sentimentalische Dichtung* (SA xii. 235fn.): a product of 'truly naïve poets' who treated of the relation between the sexes with greater delicacy than the Ancients, yet without any of the rarefied idealizations of 'sentimental' poets. But by 1803, perhaps under the influence of his growing estrangement from Romanticism, Schiller seems to have changed his mind. In a conversation with Falk (*Schillers Gespräche*, ed. cit., Nr. 400), he dismissed Tieck's *Minnelieder*, which had just appeared, in no uncertain terms:

> Welch eine Armut von Ideen, die diesen Minneliedern zum Grunde liegt! Ein Garten, ein Baum, eine Hecke, ein Wald und ein Liebchen; ganz recht! das sind ungefähr die Gegenstände alle, die in dem Kopfe eines Sperlings Platz haben! Und die Blumen die duften, und die Früchte die reifen, und ein Zweig, worauf ein Vogel im Sonnenschein sitzt und singt, und der Frühling der kommt, und der Winter der geht, und nichts, was dableibt — als die Langeweile.

where of old only murder lay in wait: Schiller may well be thinking of Goethe's

Iphigenie again, and of the law which obtained in Tauris until the Greek heroine arrived there. For the same thought see his poem *Das Eleusische Fest*:

> Weh dem Fremdling, den die Wogen
> Warfen an den Unglücksstrand!
> (SA i. 170)

XXVII. 8. *In the midst of the fearful kingdom of forces*: here is Schiller's solution to the problem posed in III. 4: How is society to be reformed without the violent destruction of the 'natural' State?

a third joyous kingdom: an obvious allusion to the Third Kingdom, or Third Age, dreamed of by mystics since Joachim di Fiore (cf. Note to IX. 5), and already 'secularized' by Lessing in *The Education of the Human Race*, §§ 81–91: 'It will certainly come, that time of a "new, eternal Gospel" which is promised us even in the Books of the New Testament.' Lessing's view of Utopia is, like Schiller's, forward-looking, a new Jerusalem rather than a Garden of Eden or a Golden Age, Elysium rather than Arcadia. It is the secularization of the promise of Christianity, which is itself regarded as but a stage on the way. Ibsen gave the thought dramatic expression in that eloquent passage of *Emperor and Galilean* in which Julian the Apostate proclaims—much as Schiller had done in these Letters—the advent of a Third Kingdom based on joy and beauty, love and justice, and good fellowship among men. But though, according to Friedrich Schlegel, nothing Lessing ever wrote was 'as precious as these few words', they were not without long-term repercussions of a more sinister kind. Like Schiller himself in that posthumous draft for an ode (1797) entitled by his modern editors 'Deutsche Grösse', Romantics such as Fichte, Schleiermacher, Adam Müller, seized on the idea of an a-political 'kingdom' as an invitation to Germans to assume cultural and moral leadership of the world. 'Our call is to civilize the earth', Novalis proclaimed; and even Hölderlin, for all his famous invective (cited in Note to IV. 6), contributed with his dream of an ideal 'Germania' to that Germanic myth which, once it had passed through the curious amalgam of pessimism and defiance generated by a Wagner, a Nietzsche, or a Spengler, was ready to bear whatever political and racial implications were projected upon it. It was given programmatic expression in *Das Dritte Reich* (1923) of Moeller van den Bruck, with its proclamation of 'das tausendjährige Reich' which Hitler attempted to realize. Cf. the various essays on Romantic *Germanentum* in *The German Mind and Outlook*, ed. G. P. Gooch, London, 1945, and L. A. Willoughby, 'The Romantic Background of Hitlerism' in *The Contemporary Review*, cxliv, 1933.

XXVII. 9. *the dynamic State of rights*: not, as at least one critic seems to think (Luise Gilde, *Friedrich von Schillers Geschichtsphilosophie*, London, 1959, i. 209), a State of legal or moral rights. The parallels of the immediate context make it abundantly clear that 'der dynamische Staat' is synonymous with 'das furchtbare Reich der Kräfte' of § 8. It is the *Naturstaat* of III. 2, based on force (*dynamisch* is used here in its primary, Greek, sense) because each member of it is interested only in asserting or maintaining his rights, and not in performing his duties.

bestow freedom by means of freedom: Schiller had elaborated this thought in his reflections on the aesthetics of social conduct ('Schönheit des Umgangs') in his *Kallias* letters (to Körner, 23.ii.1793; Jonas, iii. 285):

The first law of good breeding (des guten Tones) is: *Show respect for the freedom of others*; the second: *Show forth freedom in yourself.* Prompt and punctilius observance of these two is an unendingly difficult problem; but good breeding demands it without remission, and its achievement alone makes the perfect gentleman (den vollendeten Weltmann).

XXVII. 10. *we enjoy merely as individuals*: to agree that the world of sense-perception is a private world need not, it should be noted, commit us to the solipsistic view that there is no external world capable of being inferred.

without the genus which is immanent within us: cf. 'Every individual human being . . . carries within him, potentially and prescriptively, an ideal man' (IV. 2). In the draft of an undispatched letter to Fichte of 3.viii.1795, Schiller himself used the Latin term in a similar context: 'Diese Darstellung meiner ganzen Natur auch in trockenen Materien [i.e. in purely intellectual matters], wo der Mensch sonst nur als Genus zu sprechen pflegt . . . '. Cf. letter to Körner of 10.xi.1794, where he uses the derivative *generalisiert* in the same sense.

we cannot make the pleasures of reason universal: according to Kant (*Critique of Pure Reason*, but recapitulated in *Critique of Judgement*, i, § 21; cf. Meredith, op. cit., p. 257), cognitions, or logical judgements, unlike sense-perceptions, are universally valid, and admit of being universally communicated, because there exists a necessary relation between the faculties of cognition which must be the same in every subject which judges the same object. Schiller, however, is here talking of the *pleasure* attendant upon such cognitions; and though I myself, when delighting in knowledge or truth, may be able to transcend the adventitious aspects of my own individuality and delight in them as pure *genus*, I cannot be sure that others will do the same. Hence this pleasure is no more universalizable than the pleasures of sense, though for a different reason. Whatever we may think of Schiller's argument here, the important point is surely his contention that a true appreciation of beauty—as the only kind of communication and pleasure which *is* universalizable—is not to be achieved by leaving behind one's own individuality, but only by extending it and, as it were, purifying it. We tacitly acknowledge the truth of this when we speak of more than one good reading of the same symphony, or of several valid interpretations of one and the same poem. Such expression of individual variety does not preclude being true to the aesthetic object, and may well, so long as it fulfils this latter requirement, prove convincing and illuminating to those with a different, but not incompatible, interpretation.

which we cannot presume to be universal: what Schiller is here implying, and rightly, is that other ways to salvation—the way of the saint, the mystic, the recluse—call for a special vocation. The way of the aesthetic alone is suited to each and all of us in virtue of our common human nature.

XXVII. 11. *legislative power . . . executive power*: this distinction (of which the rest of the paragraph furnishes illustrations) springs from Schiller's basic conviction that things must be kept distinct and yet related—but, above all, never confused! Taste, i.e. 'the aesthetic'—as he has argued throughout, but especially in XXIII. 7 and footnote—must never supply the *directives* for moral choice; but it can legitimately modify the *manner* of acting on a moral decision. At the other extreme, it obviously cannot run counter to Nature's laws and purposes; but it can legitimately ensure that these are carried out with charm and grace. Within its own sphere, of course, i.e. chiefly in the sphere of art, taste both makes the laws and carries them out.

Duty, stern voice of Necessity: cf. the famous passage from *Anmut und Würde* (SA xi. 218) in which Schiller summed up his attitude to the matter and manner of Kant's Moral Philosophy:

> In Kant's Moral Philosophy the idea of *Duty* is presented with such an uncompromising rigour that all the Graces are repelled, and a feeble intelligence might easily be tempted to seek moral perfection by way of a gloomy monkish asceticism. However much the great philosopher might seek to preserve his work from such a misconception, which of all possible misconceptions must most have outraged his serene and liberal mind, yet it seems to me that he himself gave strong grounds for it by the strict and harsh opposition of the two principles which affect the will of man (although in view of what he intended this was perhaps unavoidable).

As the last sentence of § 12 below implies, this earlier essay must have been very much in his thoughts as he brought his *Aesthetic Letters* to a conclusion.

the censorious tone of its precepts: *Formel* here, as in VI. 10, and like *Formular* in VI. 7, evokes from Schiller a comminatory tone. In every case it means a collection of set forms according to which something is to be done. In accordance with Schiller's intention, here and throughout, we have attempted in our translation, by the use of 'tone' and 'precept', to distinguish the moral law itself from any particular formulation of it.

confidence in her willingness to obey them: 'Nature' here, of course, in the sense (Glossary, *Natur* 3 [*c*]) of that aspect of man which is the opposite of his 'Freedom'. Schiller's basic assumption, the theme of his whole treatise, is that it is possible so to educate human 'nature' that it willingly conforms with its 'moral' destiny. Hence our paraphrastic rendering of 'die willige Natur'.

From within the Mysteries of Science: 'mystery' here primarily in the sense of a trade, craft or guild: from the Old French *mestier*, Lat. *ministerium*; also used of medicine and alchemy. But Schiller is without doubt also playing on the other meaning (the two have always been confused): from Lat. *mysterium*, or 'secret'; particularly of religious rites and esoteric lore, or of cults, such as freemasonry. This unveiling of the secrets of science and philosophy was one of Schiller's chief educational aims as expressed in his 'Öffentliche Ankündigung' to the *Horen* (SA xvi. 152): 'So weit es tunlich ist, wird man die Resultate der Wissenschaft von ihrer scholastischen Form zu befreien und in einer reizenden, wenigstens einfachen, Hülle dem Gemeinsinn verständlich zu machen suchen.' *Wissenschaft*, like the Latin *scientia*, has never been restricted (as 'science' is nowadays in English) to the natural sciences. For the full range of meaning of this word see VI. 6 and 7; XIII. 4fn. § 2; XV. 9 and Note.

lion . . . curbed by the bridle of a Cupid: an allusion to a favourite emblem of the seventeenth century (cf. Mario Praz, *Studies in Seventeenth-Century Imagery*, London, 1939, i. 80, 87, 114). On Schiller's interest in emblems see Note to XXV. 3. According to Boxberger (*Schillers Werke*, ed. cit., p. 316) Lessing—who inevitably deprecated such allegorizing types of pictorial art, *muta poesis*, or 'stumme Gedichte' as he called them in his *Materialien zum 'Laokoon'*, 3, 1—had drawn attention to this very motif of Cupid bridling the Lion on an incised gem of classical antiquity (cf. Note to IX. 5). But the motif was also common in Christian art, for it could easily be 'accommodated' to the Biblical text 'and a little child shall lead them' (Isa. xi. 6); and there is a well-known picture of Titian representing the Child of Love standing on the lion (though there is no bridle). In Schiller, too, as we have so often had occasion to note, there is a confluence of Christian and Classical—though the spirit is different. Whereas in Christian art classical motifs and themes merely have the role of 'anticipations' of the higher truths of Christian doctrine, for the humanists of the eighteenth century the two traditions represent different expressions of the same fundamental truth. Goethe, in his *Novelle*, was to make wonderfully poetic use of the lion and child motif, in order, as he put it to Eckermann (18.i.1827), 'zu zeigen, wie das Unbändige, Unüberwindliche oft besser durch Liebe und Frömmigkeit als durch Gewalt bezwungen werde . . .'.

even that art which must cringe for payment: i.e. art dependent upon patronage. A burning question of the age, especially in Germany, with its numerous courts, and treated by all three great dramatists: Lessing in *Emilia Galotti*, Schiller in *Fiesco*, Goethe in *Torquato Tasso*. In the Aesthetic State, even a relation so fraught with possible humiliations and embarrassment would undergo a qualitative transformation—as indeed it had done in the classic case of Goethe and his Duke. Cf. Note to V. 5.

the tool which serves . . . the patient mass: both 'tool' and 'mass' are to be taken in the literal as well as the metaphorical sense. Snell's translation 'multitude' unfortunately confines it to the latter. But Schiller is here condensing the whole of IV. 4, and the four kinds of *Künstler* mentioned there—the *mechanische*, the *schöne*, the *pädagogische*, and the *politische*—into a single metaphor. In the Aesthetic State, the way in which the political artist handles people will be no different from that in which the 'fine' artist handles his medium. Whatever pejorative implications may have attached to 'feigns' in that earlier context (cf. Note thereto) should have been dispelled by Schiller's subsequent exploration of the concepts of play and semblance.

a free citizen: in his *Kallias* letters (23.ii.1793; Jonas, iii. 280) Schiller had elaborated this thought, and drawn an interesting contrast between his Aesthetic State (or 'world', as he there called it) and Plato's Republic:

> In der ästhetischen Welt ist jedes Naturwesen ein freier Bürger, der mit dem Edelsten gleiche Rechte hat, und *nicht einmal um des Ganzen willen* darf *gezwungen* werden, sondern zu allem schlechterdings *consentiren* muss. In dieser ästhetischen Welt, die eine ganz andere ist, als die vollkommenste

Platonische Republik, fordert auch der Rock, den ich auf dem Leibe trage,
Respekt von mir für seine Freiheit. . . .

Schiller goes on to stress there, as here, the complete reciprocity involved in
this ideal of freedom.

which the Enthusiast would fain see realized: on this 'impatient spirit of enthusiasm' see V. 5; IX. 5 and Notes thereto.

XXVII. 12. *State of Aesthetic Semblance*: in the *Horen* this last paragraph was
a footnote, and in the concluding part of it, which he did not later reprint,
Schiller undertook to furnish a Constitution for the Aesthetic State:

Since no good State should be without its *Constitution*, it is legitimate to
require one for the Aesthetic State too. No such is as yet known to me, and
I may therefore venture to hope that a first attempt at one, which I have
destined for this Journal, will be received with indulgence.

with undismayed simplicity and tranquil innocence: as Hatfield, loc. cit., p. 25,
points out, this is a highly characteristic Schillerian variation of Winckelmann's
famous formula of Greek beauty, 'edle Einfalt und stille Grösse'.

through even the most involved and complex situations: the perfect image for
such subtle and intricate forms of social intercourse—which are essentially
forms in movement—was, according to Schiller, an English figure-dance (letter
to Körner, 23.ii.1793; Jonas, iii. 285):

I can think of no more fitting image for the ideal of social conduct than an
English dance, composed of many complicated figures and perfectly executed.
A spectator in the gallery sees innumerable movements intersecting in the
most chaotic fashion, changing direction swiftly and without rhyme or reason,
yet *never colliding*. Everything is so ordered that the one has already yielded
his place when the other arrives; it is all so skilfully, and yet so artlessly,
integrated into a form, that each seems only to be following his own inclination, yet without ever getting in the way of anybody else. It is the most perfectly appropriate symbol of the assertion of one's own freedom and regard
for the freedom of others.

shed their Dignity in order to manifest Grace: as we implied in a Note to § 11
above, these last words of the *Aesthetic Letters* recall the essence of Schiller's
earlier treatise, *Über Anmut und Würde*. At this point he achieves a reconciliation of the two principles which he had there been at such pains to distinguish—
looked at in one way, the reconciliation of feminine and masculine into the idea
of perfect humanity (cf. Note to XVI. 3). But, it should never be forgotten, no
one of Schiller's syntheses is to be regarded as final and static. With his treatise
On the Sublime he will again offer a rehabilitation of *Würde* in its own right. And,
as we have argued in our Introduction (pp. lxxxvi ff. above), such subjective ambivalence as this may betray finds an objective correlative in the state of human
affairs: Schiller's changing hierarchy of values is warranted by the changing perspective of different situations and different contexts of experience.

GLOSSARY

If an author can be got at by means of a lexicon, Goethe once said,[1] he can't be worth very much. And we are under no illusions that even a glossary such as this, which is tailored to an individual work, can relieve us of the obligation to interpret for ourselves. 'The reader', Schiller told Körner when he complained of insufficient definition of terms, 'is meant to *think*; and if he can't find the key to difficult passages in the context of the whole, then there's no helping him.'[2] Yet their limitations granted, lexical aids are not to be despised. And they can be found, with varying degrees of usefulness, in the dictionaries and lexica cited in our Bibliography—Rudolph, Wernly, Eisler—in the Notes and Glosses of Buchwald, Lutz and Sayce, in Meredith's edition of the *Critique of Judgement*, in the 'Vocabulary of Terminology' appended to the translation of the *Aesthetic Letters* in Bohn's Library, in the 'terminological' Preface which the publisher of the first English translation felt moved to write before letting it loose on the British public, in order, as he put it, 'to avoid clouding the subject with unnecessary ambiguity'.

Ours differs from these chiefly because it has been shaped out of a conviction (elaborated above p. lxxiii) that the 'ambiguity' may well have point: that there is a case for treating Schiller's philosophical terminology, at any rate in this particular work, very much as one might treat that of a longer philosophical poem,[3] not resenting the fact that more than one of the distinguishable meanings of a word may be present in any single occurrence, and that its precise connotations at any one point are determined as much by its relations to other words, in both the immediate and the wider context, as they are by definition, whether explicit or implicit.[4] Hence just as in our translation we found it not so much impossible, as actually undesirable, to decide on a single English equivalent for any one term and then use it consistently throughout, so in our glossary we found it inappropriate to distinguish the relevant meanings of a word and then, in the interests of a static but deceptive clarity, force all occurrences of it into that classification. Our aim has been rather to strike a balance between the purely descriptive method, which treats every linguistic event as unique, and the abstracting, generalizing procedures of dictionary-making. Operating with

---

[1] *Maximen und Reflexionen* (ed. Günther Müller, Stuttgart, 1943), Nr. 771.

[2] Letter of 10.xi.1794.

[3] Which is not to say that the treatise is to be regarded as such, or that the language in other respects functions as poetry (cf. above pp. xcix ff.). It is one thing to claim that the 'Vieldeutigkeit' of Schiller's philosophical terms has point; quite another to conclude, as Sayce (loc. cit., p. 176) does, that this is adequately described as 'dichterische Bedeutungsfülle'.

[4] In fact the number of definitions that Schiller himself gives is surprisingly large: *ästhetisch* is defined XX. 4fn.; *Bestimmung*, XIX. 1–3; *Empfindung*, XII. 1; *Freiheit*, XIX. 12fn.; *Gestalt*, XV. 2; *Materie*, XII. 1; *Naturstaat*, III. 3; *Person*, XI. 1; *Schein*, XXVI. 5; *Spiel*, XIV. 3 and XV. 8; *Trieb*, VIII. 3 and XII. 1; *Welt*, XI. 8; *Zustand*, XI. 1.

an implicit scheme of sense-spheres,[1] we have grouped together in clusters words which, whether cognate or not, are related by likeness (e.g. *Ideal, edel*) or sometimes even by contrast (e.g. *Inhalt, Gehalt*), and tried to display something of the range of meaning of the whole cluster, the nature of the interdependence of the words within it, and the occasional change of direction in the meaning of any one of them.

The occurrence of the same word in more than one cluster (e.g. *Form, Stoff, Schein*) is thus no accident; it is indicative of overlapping areas of meaning. Nor is a certain repetition in our treatment of such words as *Bestimmung, Freiheit, Natur, Notwendigkeit*; it was precisely our object to bring out, by our arrangement of the occurrences cited, the recurrent pattern in Schiller's labile use of language, thus revealing the characteristic dynamic of his thought.

Our choice of words for glossing may occasion surprise. Why have we included the apparently trivial *bloss* and *gemein*, and omitted such imposing vocables as *Vernunft* and *Verstand*? Or words which have played an important part in the history of ideas, such as *Menschheit, Bildung*, and *Kultur*? Or such peculiar Schillerian concepts as *Spiel, Person*, and *Zustand*?

The first are omitted because Schiller is not concerned with establishing, let alone modifying, Kantian distinctions, but only with deploying the resultant psychical entities in the interests of his own, totally different, strategy. On the rare occasions when the distinction between them is of prime importance, as in VI.12 and XXIV.6, it becomes abundantly plain from the context; and there was indeed, as he told Körner (10.xi.1794), no need for him to recapitulate Kant's arguments even had there been room. Should the modern reader feel the need for further elucidation he may consult the *Kant-Lexikon*, as he may consult any dictionary for such sporadically occurring philosophic terms as *Ausdehnung, Position*, or *Grund*.

Nor is there anything particularly Schillerian about his use of *Menschheit*. He does not, like Herder,[2] employ the foreign term *Humanität* in order to make a distinction between what man is by nature and what he may by effort become (at least not in this treatise: at its single occurrence in XVI. 3—'die zärtere Humanität'—it obviously connotes one aspect of human nature only, and not its totality). He prefers—and this is wholly characteristic, since according to him (XIV. 2) what man by effort becomes is essentially an unfolding or fostering of what he by nature is—to employ the same word for both. Thus *Menschheit* may mean the quality of being human, the human race, or the 'idea' of human nature as the goal to which man, individually and collectively, should aspire. In some occurrences of the word more than one of these senses may be co-present (e.g. X. 7; XIII. 4fn. § 3; XV. 4-5), and the translator's chief problem is to reconcile the claims of such ambiguity with those of English usage. Again, the problem raised by *Kultur* turns not so much on the distinction—which has since become notorious[3]—between 'culture' and 'civilization', although in the first nine Letters, which are under the sign of Rousseau, the word is pre-

---

[1] Cf. J. Schwietering, 'On Dictionary-Making', *GLL* iv, 1950–1.

[2] Clark, op. cit., p. 314. Cf. Edna Purdie, 'Some Renderings of *Humanitas* in German in the Eighteenth Century' in *Memorial Essays to Fritz Saxl*, London, 1957.

[3] Cf. P. Hartog, '"Kultur" as a Symbol in Peace and in War', *Sociological Review*, xxx, 1938.

dominantly used in this latter sense. It turns rather on the fact that it is less
often used of the static result of cultivating, i.e. the state of culture of an individual or people, than of the process of cultivating, i.e. it usually has the full
dynamic force of the -*ung* suffix in its near synonyms *Erziehung* and *Bildung*,[1]
and the most appropriate rendering is often 'education' (e.g. IX. 1; XIII. 3;
XXIV. 3).

Finally, it would have been wasteful to gloss concepts especially evolved by
Schiller for the purpose of this thesis, and fully discussed in the course of his
argument. Our selection of terms has in fact been dictated by what one might
call their nuisance-value; i.e. we chose those which have proved tiresome either
to us or—to judge from their repeated misinterpretation—to other Schiller
scholars. The last impression we would wish to give is that the glossary we have
made is either exhaustive or definitive. It is intended as a working, and provisional, guide to this particular work, the product of a highly individual mind
writing in a particular place, at a particular time, and with a particular object
in view. It is meant above all to provoke the active reader to discussion and
dissent; or perhaps even—more constructively still—some future scholar to the
programming of a computer.

adeln : *see* IDEE.

Affekt : *see* EMPFINDUNG.

Anschauung : a word for which it is impossible to find a single English
equivalent. It may signify:

1. the abstractions made, habitually and unconsciously, by our organs of
   sense, the forms of direct perception (XI. 8; XIII. 4fn. § 1), hence close
   to *Empfindung*, though by no means synonymous with it;
2. the intuitive or synthesizing, as opposed to the abstracting and analytical,
   operations of the mind (XV. 5, second occurrence; XXII. 2);
3. contemplation, which includes both the activities referred to under 1 and
   2 (XV. 5, first occurrence);
4. a mode of apprehending phenomena which assimilates into the above
   synthesizing operations of mind knowledge obtained by its analytical processes; or, in the words of Agnes Arber (*The Natural Philosophy of Plant
   Form*, Cambridge, 1950, p. 209), combines 'the immediacy of *knowledge of*
   with the mediate character of *knowledge about*'. There must be overtones
   of this meaning in XIII. 4fn. §§ 1 and 2, where Schiller obviously has
   Goethe's natural science in mind.

ästhetisch : this still 'much abused word' is defined by Schiller himself (though
not until XX. 4, and then in a footnote) and, though one might object to his
definition, it is misplaced to judge his thesis (as do, f.i., Jung and Böhm) by
criteria derived from other meanings which have imperceptibly accrued, or been
explicitly attributed, to the word, or even from such as might properly seem
to belong to it by virtue of its etymology. Derived from the Greek αἴσθησις,

[1] Cf. F. Rauhut, 'Die Herkunft der Worte und Begriffe *Kultur, Civilisation* und
Bildung', *GRM* xxxiv, 1953.

'perception by the senses, esp. by feeling, but also by seeing, hearing, etc.', the Latin *aesthetica* was made by Baumgarten (1750) into the name of a new 'science': the science of what were usually referred to as the 'inferior' faculties of the mind, imagination and intuition, and of their products, art and poetry. Kant, in his *Critique of Pure Reason* (1781, i, § 1fn.), protested against such 'misuse', and would have had the word restricted, in accordance with its etymology, to the science which treats of the conditions of sense-perception. But in his *Critique of Judgement* (1790, i, § 49) he had clearly become reconciled to the new dispensation. Many have thought that Baumgarten was simply giving a new name to an old thing, viz. Rhetoric and Poetics. In fact, by according recognition to the rational study of phenomena which rationalistic philosophers had thought too 'dark' and 'confused' to be susceptible of rational exploration, he was claiming dignity for what had been thought common. And by sharply defining the frontiers of his new 'science', he was at once detaching art and beauty from those branches of philosophy with which they had traditionally been associated—logic, ethics, and metaphysics—and ensuring that it should not trespass on their domains (cf. Nivelle, op. cit., p. 68).

It is evident that Schiller's definition owes much to such distinctions, even though he himself is distinguishing between different ways of being related to things, or different modes of awareness, and not between different branches of philosophy. It is important to note that he does not attribute the power of apprehending beauty to any particular faculty or faculties; hence in his usage, 'aesthetic' does not refer exclusively to sense-perception, feeling, or even—as Böhm, f.i., seems to assume—to imagination. It is rather a distinctive modality of the *whole* being. Nor, as is clear from subsequent Letters, is the object of this mode of awareness confined to any particular class or classes of phenomena. Anything, from the most obscure organic feeling to the most abstract intellectual or moral operation, can become the object of aesthetic appreciation. Defending his use of technical terms, he writes to Garve (25.i.1795) that, though he has no great love for such words as *ästhetisch*, he is convinced that greater precision of thought is nevertheless to be gained by their gradual introduction: 'so halte ich es für einen Gewinn, solche Worte allmählich mehr in Umlauf zu bringen, weil dadurch die Bestimmtheit im Denken notwendig befördert werden muss'. Yet it is consistent with his flexible attitude to words and their meanings that less than a year later, in an epigram entitled *Der Genius mit der umgekehrten Fackel* (SA ii. 91), he should use *ästhetisch* in a wholly untechnical, almost modern, sense of 'false refinement':

Lieblich sieht er zwar aus mit seiner erloschenen Fackel;
Aber, ihr Herren, der Tod ist so ästhetisch doch nicht.

aufheben : two of the lexical meanings are relevant: 1. 'reserve', 'preserve', 'save'; 2. 'annul', 'destroy', 'abolish'. In most occurrences (I. 5; XIII. 1; XIV. 3; XX. 3 and 4; XXIII. 7fn. § 2) only the second is involved. In XVIII. 4 (first and second occurrences, but *not* the third and fourth) Schiller develops a process of the destruction of opposites, and their union in a new synthesis, to the point where *aufheben* is used in a double sense: 'to abolish *and* preserve' or 'preserve by destruction' (*Aufhebung* is also used thus in XXIV. 3). This dialectical concept had already made its appearance, though without the actual occurrence of the word *aufheben*, in XV. 9: 'they made both [opposites] indiscernible, for they knew how to fuse them in the most intimate union'. In this double sense (cf. Lutz, op. cit., p. 197) *aufheben* was to become a key-term of Hegel's dialectical method: 'Das *Aufheben* stellt seine wahrhafte gedoppelte Bedeutung dar . . . es ist ein *Negiren* und ein *Aufbewahren* zugleich . . .' (*Phänomenologie des Geistes*, A, ii: 'Die Wahrnehmung'). It seems likely, in view of his expressed admiration for Schiller's treatise, that it was from XVIII. 4 that he took it. According to Snell (ed. cit., p. 88fn.), Goethe sometimes uses *Aufhebung* to mean 'disappearance in a higher import'; but he gives no instance, and neither Grimm nor Fischer (*Goethe-Wortschatz*) records one.

Bedürfnis : *see* NOTWENDIGKEIT.

Begriff : *see* IDEE.

Bestimmung, Bestimmbarkeit, Bestimmungslosigkeit, Stimmung : a group of cognate words which is central to Schiller's argument. *Bestimmung* is used in two distinct senses, both of which create difficulties for the translator, and both of which have religious undertones:

1. 'destination'—though this only renders the future orientation; whereas the German word implies not only the goal to which man is called but also the way he is designed for such a goal, i.e. his 'true' nature. This double orientation is clearly apparent in the definition of woman's lot assigned by Goethe to his Dorothea: 'Dienen lerne beizeiten das Weib nach ihrer Bestimmung' (*Hermann und Dorothea*, vii. 114; the latest translator has here plumped for 'calling'). On the relation between the double orientation of this word and the 'circular' form of Schiller's argument see above, p.xcviii. When the reciprocal relation between 'design' and 'destination' is implied, there would be a case for rendering *Bestimmung* by 'destiny' (e.g. III. 2; X. 1; XIII. 4; XXIII. 7) though we have not always done so;

2. 'determination'. In this sense *Bestimmung* occurs chiefly from XIX onwards, and Schiller points to the obvious translation by equating it with the foreign word *Determination* (XX. 3; XXI. 4; cf. his comments on Körner's essay on music, NA xxii. 294). The disadvantages of this rendering for the English reader are obvious; for the commonest meaning of 'determination', i.e. resoluteness, firmness or fixity of purpose, is never relevant. Most relevant are the following: (*a*) delimitation, definition; (*b*) the making of something more definite by the addition of attributes; (*c*) the ascertaining of the position of anything; (*d*) decisive or determining bias. This whole range of meanings should be present to the reader at many occurrences of both noun and verb (e.g. XXVII. 3, 'Laxität der Bestimmung')—though obviously not in all: 'etwas zu bestimmen haben' (XIII. 2fn. § 1) simply means 'to have a say in'.

The condition preceding any *Bestimmung* in this second sense is *Bestimmbarkeit* (XIX. 2), a state of unlimited potentiality, of pure determinability. This may be due either to the entire absence of determination, to *Bestimmungslosigkeit* (XIX. 2), in which case it implies emptiness and passivity, or to the presence of contending determinations of equal force (XX. 3 and 4), in which case it implies a state of perfect equilibrium, active and full of content. It is to this latter kind of *Bestimmbarkeit* that man is briefly restored in the aesthetic mode. In a sense, this is of course only one among man's possible *Bestimmungen*, provoked by an object which 'determines' him to this rather than to any other mode of response. But since this particular 'determination' is a state characterized by utter determinability, or *disponibilité*, Schiller reserves for it the word *Stimmung* (XX. 4, 'mittlere Stimmung') with its musical associations of tuning and tempering. We have, when the context seemed to require it, rendered this by 'disposition' or 'mode', both of which are, however, too static. In XXIII. 5, where it appears together with 'der ästhetisch gestimmte Mensch', we have tried to bring out the verbal quality of the German noun by 'modulation'. Cf. XXVII. 12, where we have rendered 'feingestimmte Seele' by 'finely attuned soul'.

bloss : according to Böhm (op. cit., p. 122), the importance of this ubiquitous little word cannot be overestimated—though failure to catch one of its varying inflections may well have been partly responsible for his own misreading (ibid., p. 44) of the first sentence of XIV. 2, where *bloss* means 'purely' without any dismissive connotations whatsoever (the implication being that what is 'neither more nor less than' a task set us by Pure Reason can, like any other Idea, never be fully realized in experience; cf. above p. lxiv). In other words, the meaning is by no means always 'merely' in the now prevalent sense of 'nothing more than', but sometimes approximates to the older sense of 'nothing less than, entire, sheer, perfect', and quite often means simply 'without admixture'. Thus 'nach blossen Naturgesetzen' in III. 2 *may* have derogatory connotations—though Schiller's attitude to nature in this treatise is rarely disparaging—but 'blosse Gesetzmässigkeit' in III. 3 cannot possibly have. It cannot mean 'nothing more than *Gesetzmässigkeit*', but only '*Gesetzmässigkeit* itself, unmixed with anything else' (hence our translation: 'for whom the only Law should be to act in conformity with law'). Again, when he asserts that 'logischer Schein' is 'bloss Betrug', or criticizes those who reject art 'weil sie bloss Schein ist' (XXVI. 5), the inflexion is clearly pejorative. But when he writes that the awakening of the artistic impulse in man will depend on his capacity 'sich bei dem blossen Schein zu verweilen' (XXVI. 7), it is the very opposite, and 'sheer' would seem the appropriate rendering.

edel : *see* IDEE.

Einbildungskraft (Phantasie, Imagination) : according to Wernly (op. cit., p. 139), the three terms are used more or less interchangeably throughout Schiller's aesthetic writings. Two distinguishable meanings of *Einbildungskraft* were available:

1. deriving from England, the power of producing images, and identified by eighteenth-century writers with the inventive or poetic power, the aesthetic sense;
2. deriving from Kant's philosophy, the faculty which achieves the co-operation of intuition and understanding. Without it no knowledge is possible, since it alone performs the synthesis of the representations given to us in intuition (*Anschauung*); but it cannot of itself produce knowledge, since it depends on the laws of the understanding to transform the material

it presents in images into 'clear and distinct' notions. Being, as Kant puts it, the 'blind' function of the psyche, of which we are scarcely ever conscious, *Einbildungskraft* is not to be confused with *Vorstellungskraft*, the power of perceiving and conceiving. Cf. VI. 10, where the distinction between them is apparent.

With few exceptions (II. 3; X. 2; XXVI. 14 are the most obvious ones) the word is here used in the second of these two senses. This can be disconcerting to the English reader with his reminiscences of Shaftesbury and Coleridge, of the 'plastic' power, or the 'shaping' spirit, of imagination. He automatically expects it to be a power self-controlled and self-controlling, whereas in Schiller's usage other faculties of the mind (*Verstand*, *Vernunft*) are required to keep it in order. Otherwise—whether in science, philosophy, or practical life—it is capable of going off the rails and doing more harm than good (VI. 6 and 12; XXIV. 5). For the 'shaping power' of the artist to come into play, the imagination must, according to Schiller (XXVII. 4 and fn.), first have made the 'leap' from the involuntary production of images, or freely associated ideas, to the freedom of aesthetic play. Unless this distinction is made clear, it is a distortion of Schiller's thought to equate aesthetic semblance with imagination, or aesthetic education with 'Kultur der Phantasie' (see above pp. lxv f.).

Empfindung, Gefühl, Affekt : for Kant, *Empfindung* could be either objective or subjective. The green colour of the meadows, as the perception (*Wahrnehmung*) of an object of sense, belongs to the former; i.e. objective sensation has to do with the sensible qualities of objects. The pleasantness of the meadows, on the other hand, as a subjective sensation in which no representation (*Vorstellung*) of the object is involved, belongs to the latter; i.e. subjective sensation is not concerned with the properties of objects at all, but with the feelings aroused thereby in the subject. Hence Kant said that he would reserve for this latter the familiar name *Gefühl* (*Critique of Judgement*, i, § 3).

Schiller is less interested in this kind of verbal distinction. He uses the word *Empfindung* for both the above kinds of sensation (actually equating it with the foreign word *Sensation* in XX. 3), and *Gefühl* often seems to be interchangeable with it (e.g. XIII. 2 and 3). His chief concern is with the process whereby man passes from a state of non-differentiation—whether epistemological or psychological—of subject and object (what Lévy-Bruhl was to call *participation mystique*) to a state of intense awareness of the distinctness, yet interrelatedness, of self and world. *Empfindung* is therefore defined by him (XII. 1) as 'a state of merely occupied time', and 'the sole medium through which physical existence makes itself known'. It is equated with passivity (XIX. 6), with involuntariness (XIX. 11), is often prefixed by a derogatory *nur* or *bloss* (XXV. 1–3 and fn.), and is opposed to *sehen* (XXVI. 6), to *Vorstellung* (XIX. 3 and 4; XXV. 3), to *Betrachtung* and *Objekt* (XXV. 2 and 3; see Notes thereto). Its range of meaning is thus wide enough to include both the sensation-aspect of sense-perception (XXV. 1fn.; XXVI. 6) and the unconscious projection of fantasies on to the outside world (XXV. 3), and it is clearly impossible to render it consistently by a single English word throughout. We have variously translated it by 'sensation' ('to be sensible of'), and 'feeling', but never, as Snell does—often most misleadingly—by 'perception' ('to perceive').

Gefühl has an equally wide, though different, range of meaning—from the tactile senses (XXVI. 6) to the bodily life of felt thought (XXV. 7)—and is by no means always replaceable by *Empfindung*. In both I. 4 and XII. 5, whether prefixed by *moralisch* or not, it clearly signifies the 'faculty of primary moral truths' (see GEMEIN); and though in the latter context it is opposed to *Gedanke* and *Gesetz* (since it represents an individual judgement without universal validity) it obviously involves an activity of the mind (by contrast with the mindless passivity of *Empfindung*), as indeed it does when prefixed by *natürlich* in I. 4, where it is more or less synonymous with 'intuition' (see SINN).

Affekt, as is clear from XII. 2fn., connotes an intensified form of *Empfindung*— in XIV. 6 both are opposed to *Vernunft*. We could have translated it by 'affect' ('desire, passion, opposed to reason, 1619', *OED*); but since this now unfamiliar word has been reintroduced as a technical term in psychology, we have preferred 'passion'—encouraged by the equation of *Affekt* with *Passion* in XIX. 7. 'Künste des Affekts' (XXII. 5) are those arts, e.g. tragedy, which take human passions as their theme, and are therefore in danger of affecting the beholder directly through their *Stoff* or *Inhalt* (XXII. 6), through what Schiller and Goethe often referred to as their 'materielles' or 'pathologisches Interesse'. Cf. *Über naive und sentimentalische Dichtung* (SA xii. 195), where it is said that in much satire it is 'dieses materielle Interesse . . . was uns in Affekt versetzt', and a letter to Körner of 3.ii.1794 (Jonas, iii. 422), in which the 'Künste des Affekts' are distinguished from the 'schönen Künsten in strengster Bedeutung'.

Erscheinung : *see* SCHEIN.

Form (Formel, Formular), Gestalt : as the adoption of the German word in psychology and related fields would seem to imply, English has no adequate means of making a distinction between *Gestalt* and *Form*, and for purposes of a bilingual edition, where the original is conveniently to hand as a check, we have not attempted to make one. 'Shape', the rendering proposed by earlier translators (and followed, somewhat surprisingly, by aestheticians such as Ogden, Richards, and Wood, op. cit., p. 82), evokes—in modern English at least—predominantly visual properties, and scarcely does justice to the comprehensiveness of Schiller's own definition in XV. 2, where *Gestalt*—to be taken, as he insists, 'in the figurative and in the literal sense of the word'—is said to be a concept comprising '*all* the formal qualities of things' (and, incidentally, 'all the relations of these to our thinking faculties'—a notion of form which clearly anticipates the 'relational' preoccupations of current theories of perception and aesthetic judgement, whether emanating from the Gestalt School or not; cf. above p. xii). Obviously in those contexts where *Gestalt* is not used in this pregnant sense, as a technical term, but simply means visible appearance or outward form (e.g. XVII. 4; XXVII. 4 and 11), we have not hesitated to use 'shape'—or 'guise' or 'form', as English usage seemed to require.

The fact that *Gestalt* is said to be the 'object' of the *Formtrieb* (XV. 2) might seem to suggest that there is no difference at all between the meaning of the two words—that they stand in much the same relation as *Stoff* does to the corresponding loan-word, *Materie*, terms which are interchangeable in practically every context. But this is not quite the case: *Form* can usually do duty for *Gestalt*, but the converse is not true. Thus 'gestaltlose Masse' in IV. 4 could perfectly well be replaced by 'formlose Masse'; but one could scarcely substitute 'die Gestalt seiner Zwecke' for 'die Form seiner Zwecke' in that same paragraph. Again, it is of the 'technische Form'—not *Gestalt*—of the ideas of Kant's philosophy that Schiller speaks in I. 4; while in XXVI. 14, though he might well have replaced *Gestalt* by *Form* at the point where he talks of matter taking on form, he could scarcely have replaced *Form* by *Gestalt* at the point where the pleasing forms of social intercourse are being contrasted with the genuine sincerity of moral conduct—any more than he could in XXVI. 13, where protestations of politeness are said to be an 'allgemeine Form'. In other words, *Gestalt* always connotes formal relations as they are perceived in some actual phenomenon, which is what one would expect in view of its other meaning, succinctly defined by Goethe in the Preface to his *Morphologie* (JA xxxix. 251):

> For the whole complex of existence of an actual being German has the word *Gestalt*. With this [past participial and collective] expression we abstract from the labile flux around us, and assume that anything that belongs together as a whole is a stabile (*festgestellt*) and detached entity of permanently fixed character.

Cf. W. Köhler (*Gestalt Psychology*, London, 1930, p. 148):

> The noun 'Gestalt' has two meanings; besides the connotation of 'shape' or 'form' as a *property* of things, it has the meaning of a concrete individual and characteristic entity, existing as something detached and *having* a shape or form as one of its attributes.

Form, by contrast, often tends in the direction of *Idee*, and connotes formal relations after they have been abstracted from particular phenomena, or as they are conceived in the mind prior to their embodiment in some medium. Thus in XVIII. 1 and 2 *Form* is presented as the product of 'Denken'; in XXIII. 3 we find the 'reine logische Form' (i.e. concept) and 'reine moralische Form' (i.e. law) opposed, by implication, to the fusion of mind and medium which constitutes aesthetic form; while in VI. 10 it is clearly assigned to the 'Ideenreich' (as it is also, if less obviously, in XIII. 2fn. § 1). Even in IV. 7, where 'die siegende Form' is opposed, on the one hand, to the rigid uniformity of law, on the other, to the sheer confusion of life; or XXIII. 6, where one of the major tasks of education is said to be the subjection of man to *Form* 'even in his purely physical life'; or XXV. 2, where *Form* is termed 'an image of the infinite reflected against the background of transience'—in all of which *Form* is deliberately being presented as an interpenetration of sense and spirit, it yet implies such a high degree of abstraction from, and generalization about, concrete particulars that in no single one of these cases could it be replaced by *Gestalt* (any more than this would be used of the form of the sonnet in general, whereas either *Gestalt* or *Form* could be used of the form of any one sonnet in particular). When abstraction reaches such a pitch that a form has become devoid of life and significance, *Form* turns into *Formel* (VI. 10; XXVII. 11) or *Formular* (VI. 7); and we have an interesting example of Schiller's acute awareness that things have an uncanny way of turning into their opposite in XXVI. 14, where undue attachment to forms which have become petrified, and hence devoid of life and spirit, is said to constitute a material rather than a formal response. Cf. XXVII. 4, where *Idee*, in the context of the free association of ideas (sense 1 [*d*]), also goes over to the side of *Materie*.

This distinction made, a warning is in place: even the perception of a concrete particular involves, as Goethe pointed out in the passage quoted above, some considerable degree of abstraction—which is why, in XXVI. 14, the imparting of *Gestalt* to *Stoff* is said to extend 'das Reich der Ideen'. Nor, conversely, should we assume that *all* the higher abstractions connoted by *Form* are divorced from the activities of living phenomena. When, as in X. 3 ('der Mensch ohne Form'), or XXII. 6 ('ein Mangel an Form in dem Beurteiler'), the word is used of a characteristic style of behaviour, this abstraction from a succession of events in time is yet so bound up with the events themselves—with a man's appearance, gestures, speech, and deeds—that though recognizable it is not formulable as law, rule, or precept.

In aesthetic contexts 'form' should, strictly speaking, always be prefixed by 'living', in accordance with the schema arrived at in XV. 2, where the 'object' of the *Spieltrieb* was said to be 'lebende Gestalt'. Schiller is, however, quite likely to let the adjective drop even in such decisive contexts as XXVII. 9, where it is said that in the Aesthetic State none may confront another except 'als Gestalt . . . nur als Objekt des freien Spiels'. He clearly counts on our recalling XV. 3, where he had insisted that 'a human being, though he may live and have form, is far from being on that account a living form'. *Lebend* in this schema does not, incidentally, perform the same function as in 'lebende weibliche Schönheit' (XXVI. 11), where it is an attribute of the beautiful woman (even as *siegend* is an attribute of *Form* in IV. 7). Nor is the difference simply that between a literal and a figurative attribute. What we are here confronted with is not a simple attribute at all, but rather (as XV. 3 makes abundantly clear) a compressed chiasmus of great complexity. Not only is life to become form and form become life, but—since Schiller's whole aesthetic is conceived in relational terms—this is to be brought about through these two opposed aspects of the aesthetic object entering into chiastic relation with two opposed faculties of the perceiving subject: life, which we normally only feel, is to take on form in our thought; form, which we normally only think, is to become alive in our feeling. In other words, if we expand *this* verbal adjective into a subordinate clause (cf. Note to XXIII. 1), we get not only 'form which is (metaphorically speaking) alive, i.e. offers a semblance (*Schein*) of life', but also 'form which is expressive of, or articulates, the life we feel'. This felt life—not the ostensible 'contents' of the representational arts—is, according to Schiller and Goethe, the true content (*Gehalt*) of all art. Failure to grasp this is, in part at least, responsible for the common, but wholly groundless, assertion (e.g. Wernly, op. cit., pp. 33, 36, 74, 88) that in their usage *Gestalt* (or *Form*) sometimes has the meaning of *Gehalt* (or *Inhalt*), and for the logically untenable conclusion that in a work of art form *is* content. See also INHALT, &c.

Formtrieb : *see* TRIEB.

Freiheit (frei), Liberalität, Willkür : *Freiheit* is one of the words that Schiller himself defines for purposes of his argument in this particular treatise (XIX. 12fn.). But, as Goethe observed (to Eckermann, 18. i. 1827), the idea of freedom in Schiller's works underwent as many changes as did Schiller himself, and in this one alone he uses the word in roughly three distinct senses:

1. *physical freedom*, freedom from alien compulsion, freedom to do what one wants—Kant's 'Freiheit der Willkür'. In this, negative, sense *Freiheit* is close to *Willkür*—arbitrary caprice, licence (VII. 2), which is *blind* (III. 2) and *unstet* (XXVII. 4)—though rarely identical with it. Hence 'freie Willkür' (XXIV. 1) is not caprice which has become less arbitrary because modified by Reason, but *Willkür* which has been given its head; 'freie Übertretung der Natur' (XIII. 2), not the fine disregard of nature by free will, but a 'wanton transgression of Nature'; 'freie Ideenfolge' (XXVII. 4), not a product of the shaping imagination, but involuntary, uncontrolled free association of ideas, opposed in the same sentence to 'freie Form', where *frei* is used in senses 2 and 3 below;

2. *moral freedom*, freedom of the spirit. Absolute freedom from all conditions whatsoever is the prerogative of Absolute Being (XI. 4). Man, however, is very much a conditioned being, conditioned both bodily and mentally, both from within and from without. Yet he is at the same time capable of rising above this conditioned existence by sharing, as a moral being, in 'das freie Ganze', the unconditioned Whole (VI. 10), by countering 'what is' by 'what ought to be', and exercising freedom of choice (III. 2). In Lessing's words, 'kein Mensch muss müssen', in Kant's 'Bestimme Dich aus Dir selbst'—of which Schiller wrote (to Körner, 18.ii.1793): 'Es ist gewiss von *keinem* Sterblichen Menschen kein grösseres Wort noch gesprochen worden, als dieses Kantische, was zugleich der Inhalt seiner ganzen Philosophie ist' (Jonas, iii. 255). In this sense, Freedom belongs on the side of Pure Reason and the Pure Will, and is completely opposed to *Willkür* (III. 5).

Of the conflicts involved in such transcendence of Nature by Freedom, of the resultant Dignity and Sublimity, Schiller treated elsewhere in his theoretical works (cf. above p. lx; in the *Aesthetic Letters* only in XXIII. 7, 8, and fn. For his whole aim in *this* treatise is to teach, not the transcendence of one of our natures by the other, but precisely the reconciliation of the two. Hence he here uses *Freiheit* predominantly in a third sense, which may well be called

3. *anthropological freedom*, or freedom of the whole man (cf. IV. 3 and Note). If for an Absolute Being perfect freedom consists in freedom from all conditions, for Man perfect freedom can only consist in the acceptance of conditions (XV. 9, and see NOTWENDIGKEIT), in achieving the co-operation of his conditioned nature (XVII. 4), in acting rationally within the limits of a creature of sense, and sensuously as a creature who is also subject to the laws of reason (XIX. 12fn.). Such co-operation of his two natures is by no means the same as their mere co-existence; in other words, highly developed rationality is perfectly compatible with mere animality. On the distinction between a 'vernünftiges Tier' and a human being who has achieved true freedom, see XXIV. 8.

Freedom in this third sense does not make its appearance with the first dawn of reason in man (XXIV. 4); and it is to be distinguished from 'the freedom which belongs to man in his capacity as intelligent being and which can neither be given unto him nor taken from him' (XIX. 12fn.). Nature, too (writ large, see NATUR and above pp. lii f.), partakes of freedom in this widest sense: in IV. 6 man is urged to make friends with her by honouring her *Freiheit* and curbing only her *Willkür*. Hence what is perhaps the key-sentence of the whole treatise: in this [chronological] priority of our sensual nature is to be found the key to the whole history of human freedom (XX. 2). It is only because Nature, in the widest sense of the term, partakes of freedom that the germ of it is there in man from the start. It is at once part of his natural equipment—'eine Wirkung der Natur . . . kein Werk des Menschen' (XX. 1)—and that which it is enjoined upon him to achieve (XIX. 12).

It is freedom of this third kind, based on his 'gemischte Natur' (XIX. 12fn.), that is briefly vouchsafed to man in the aesthetic mode, which is at once the symbol of the co-operation of his two natures (XIV. 2) and the pledge that such co-operation is indeed his true *Bestimmung* (XXV. 6). Hence the central role that is assigned to it in education (II. 5; XXI. 4–6); hence its elevation to end as well as means. For Schiller, aesthetic freedom—contrary to popular, and even to much critical, opinion—is the very opposite of *Willkür*; it is informed by laws, even though these are not apparent as such (XX. 4fn.). In XXIV. 2, there-fore, *frei*, though qualifying *Lust*, which elsewhere has derogatory connotations (XXVII. 7), must be taken in sense 3 above and not in sense 1 (hence our translation: 'a delight in things for their own sake'). The famous definition of Beauty from the *Kallias* letters, 'Freiheit in der Erscheinung', only occurs once in this treatise, and then in a footnote (XXIII. 7), though it is, of course, implicit in the whole argument (see pp. xxvii f. above and Note to III. 5).

When Schiller speaks of freedom in the political sphere, he uses it in all three of the above senses: 1. freedom from interference with the activities of the individual (VII. 2, 3; X. 5); 2. willing obedience to laws he has willingly imposed upon himself (VI. 7); 3. freedom which springs from the whole per-sonality (II. 5; IV. 7). In XXVII. 9, the climax of these Letters, all senses of 'freedom' are present in the sentence which epitomizes his whole thesis: 'Freiheit zu geben durch Freiheit ist das Grundgesetz dieses [ästhetischen] Reichs'.

Liberalität is almost synonymous with 'freedom' in sense 3: in XVI. 3 it is opposed to *Willkürlichkeit* in art. Even in II. 5 'liberaler Weltbürger' (applied to Schiller's patron, the Duke of Augustenburg) means open-minded, free from narrow prejudice in general, rather than favourable to reforms of any particular kind. In X. 2 'Liberalität . . . des Betragens' is clearly synonymous with sense 3 above, complete harmony of sense and spirit, and might best be trans-lated as 'graciousness'. In XXV. 2, where reflexion is termed 'das erste liberale Verhältnis des Menschen zu dem Weltall', it clearly connotes the freedom which results from, and in turn fosters, the differentiation of self from world.

Gefühl : *see* EMPFINDUNG.

Gegenstand, Objekt : from about the end of the seventeenth century, *Gegen-stand*—having, like the English 'object', meant 'opposed or hostile stance'—

superseded *Gegenwurf* as the German equivalent of Latin *objectum*. In this sense, of 'a thing thrown before, or over against, the mind' (a meaning first made current by Wolff), Schiller uses both *Objekt* and its 'contrafact', *Gegenstand*, in connexion with one of his central arguments (viz. the differentiation of a perceiving subject and a perceived object out of a postulated unity of mere sensation) in XXV. 3, where the *Objekt* perceived is opposed to the *Macht* which merely impinges, and in XXV. 1fn., where the *Gegenstand* actually seen is opposed to the sense-data of visual perception. In XXIII. 7fn. § 1 ('Geschäft und . . . Gegenstand') the sense is the same, though the implicit metaphor is not exploited. In all such cases we have translated by 'object'—except in II. 5 and XXII. 5, where *Gegenstand* is synonymous with *Stoff* (see INHALT, &c.), and English usage requires 'subject', 'theme', or 'topic'.

In some occurrences (XIII. 2; XXIV. 6) the 'thing thrown over against the mind' is also something to be aimed at; i.e. the object of cognition also has strong conative attachments, is a goal or objective, by which latter term we have then translated it. In others (IX. 7; XXIV. 5) it is difficult to know which of these two senses predominates, and we have then preferred 'object' which may signify either or both.

In one or two cases (XII. 6; XXIII. 7fn. § 3) *Objekt* (like *objektiv* in IV. 5) is used in the Kantian sense of 'the Idea of something unconditioned', conceivable in the realm of Truth by the Pure, in the realm of Morality by the Practical, Reason.

Gehalt : *see* INHALT.

Geist (Geister, geistreich, geistlos), Gemüt : both words are notoriously difficult to render into English (though no more than 'mind' into German). In Schiller's usage *Gemüt* is normally—as it had been for the *Aufklärung* and for Kant—the wider concept, connoting the totality of the forces or functions of the psyche. It comprises both feeling and thought, sensation and reason (XIX. 4; XX. 4; XXI. 3), the sense-drive and the formal drive (XIV. 5), manifests both passivity and activity (XIX. 8), is capable of being determined physically, morally, and aesthetically (XIX. 7; XX. 4; XXII. 1). In all these cases—except in XIX. 7, where English usage seemed to call for 'freedom of the spirit'—we have translated by 'psyche'.

Geist, by contrast, is normally used for the active principle of the psyche, which works on the material passively received by the senses to produce thought (XIX. 4), and is opposed to the sensuous passions (XIX. 7—'die Natur eines Geistes', where *eines* has the force of the definite article). In such cases, and in all those where *Geist* is opposed to *Materie* (e.g. XV. 5), English usage would seem to demand 'mind'. But it would scarcely tolerate 'mental' for the corresponding adjective *geistig*, and we have preferred 'spiritual' (XV. 9; XVII. 4; XVIII. 1; XXIII. 5). With the plural *Geister*, Schiller is following an older usage, still persisting in the eighteenth century, which reflects the belief that certain substances or fluids, having their seat in the nerves and the blood, mediate between the bodily and the spiritual nature of man. He was particularly partial to it in his youth when, as a medical student, he was exploring the 'Zusammenhang der tierischen Natur des Menschen mit seiner geistigen'; but it also occurs in his plays: 'Noch sind Sie ausser Fassung. Sammeln Sie / Erst Ihre

Geister . . .' (*Don Carlos*, iv. 19; cf. Goethe, *Briefe aus der Schweiz*, JA xxv. 158: 'sonst wäre es besser, meine Geister ruhen zu lassen'). At no point in these Letters did it seem appropriate to use 'spirits' in the plural (though it is still in common use in such locutions as 'high spirits'). In II. 3 we used 'minds'; in XXIII. 6 and 7fn. § 3, 'spirit'.

The use of *Geist* in aesthetic contexts also presents its own problems. In the *Critique of Judgement* (i, § 49) Kant had used *Geist*, in an aesthetic sense, to signify:

1. the principle which, animating the mind, brings about an indefinite harmony of the mental powers, their free play in an internal, purely formal, purposiveness;

2. that indeterminate quality which gives 'life' to a work of art, a story, a conversation, or even a woman—Shaftesbury's *je ne scay quoy* (*Characteristicks*, ed. cit. i. 332; cf. Meredith, op. cit., p. 289; H. W. Cassirer, op. cit., p. 278 f.).

In the first of these senses it is used by Schiller in XVIII. 4 and XXII. 3, and is probably best rendered by 'spirit'; in the second sense it occurs in the adjectives *geistlos* (XXVII. 12), which seemed best rendered by 'soulless', and *geistreich* (XXIII. 7fn. § 1), where we have hazarded 'genial'. In XXII. 4, 'auch die geistreichste Musik', we have plumped for 'aetherial'—with some misgivings, although 'Aether' *was* the realm from which, in ancient times, inspiration was thought to proceed (cf. Note to IX. 4). The important thing is not to think of the modern meaning of *geistreich*, 'witty', but rather of the eighteenth-century meaning of 'wit' which was almost synonymous with 'genius'.

In one crucial context, where he is arguing that the presence of two opposing drives in the psyche involves no denial of its unity (XIX. 8 and 9), Schiller extends the concept of *Geist* until it is co-terminous with *Gemüt*, making this the occasion for registering his protest against those who will only allow mind to be actively involved when its operations are in accordance with Reason, and declare it to be merely passive when they are at odds with it. Some might wish to see in such enlargement of the concept an anticipation of Hegel's elevation of *Geist*—'Es gibt nichts Höheres als den Geist, nichts, das würdiger wäre, sein Gegenstand zu sein' (*Vorlesungen über die Philosophie der Weltgeschichte*, i, B(*a*); *Sämtliche Werke*, hrsg. Lasson u. Hoffmeister, xviii. A, p. 73)—to that position of prime importance which it subsequently occupied in the history of German thought right down to Thomas Mann. Others, however, observing that Schiller is not here concerned with the evaluation of this (or any other) faculty, but only with its extension to include irrational mental processes, will be more inclined to discern an early stage in that direction of thought which will lead ultimately to Freud. In the above context (XIX. 8 and 9), where the synonymization of the two terms is highly significant, we have preserved the distinction between 'psyche' and 'mind'; in XXIII. 7fn. § 1, by contrast, where it has no discernible significance, we have translated both words by 'nature'.

Gemein, Gemeinsinn : in a letter to Goethe (24.xi.1797) Schiller equated *das Gemeine* with *das Platte* ('the banal'); and in the opening sentences of his *Gedanken über den Gebrauch des Gemeinen und Niedrigen in der Kunst* he called *gemein* 'everything which does not speak to the mind, and makes no appeal except to the senses' (SA xii. 283). But, like the English 'common', *gemein* had then—and still has today in such phrases as *das gemeine Wesen* ('the common weal') or *Gemeingeist* ('public spirit')—the meaning of 'general', 'universal', *allgemein*, and as with *bloss* one has to be on one's guard against attributing pejorative meaning where none was intended. It is not always easy to decide. In Wallenstein's famous monologue (*Wallensteins Tod*, i. 4),

> Das ganz
> Gemeine ist's, das ewig Gestrige,
> Was immer war und immer wiederkehrt
> Und morgen gilt, weil's heute hat gegolten!
> Denn aus Gemeinem ist der Mensch gemacht,
> Und die Gewohnheit nennt er seine Amme . . .

it is clearly the ordinary, everyday events of life, our common humanity, that is meant. And is this not also the case in the often misunderstood lines of Goethe's famous tribute to Schiller?

> Und hinter ihm, in wesenlosem Scheine,
> Lag, was uns alle bändigt, das Gemeine.
> (JA i. 283)

Goethe's remarks to Eckermann (11.ix.1828) suggest that it is. Outside of poetry the exact shade of meaning is not so easy to determine; but it should not be automatically assumed that even in such phrases as *gemeine Wirklichkeit* or *gemeine Sinnlichkeit* the implications are necessarily derogatory, though they often may be. In III. 2 and IX. 3 they obviously are.

Gemeinsinn (see also SINN) is wholly free from any such pejorative implications. It nevertheless comprises two distinguishable meanings, either of which may predominate in a given context:

1. the 'faculty of primary truths', which is 'common' in the sense that it is the common bond, originally between the five senses, later between the various faculties, Kant's 'effect resulting from the free play of our cognitive faculties' (*Critique of Judgement*, i, § 20). This is the predominant sense in VI. 12, where the extreme specialization of the individual faculties—no single one of which is itself capable of grasping truth—forces the unifying, the 'common', sense to penetrate deeper into the nature of things than it would otherwise have done. Cf. letter to the Duke of Augustenburg (21.xi.1793; Jonas, iii. 396) in which Schiller opposes this *Gemeinsinn* to 'logischer Verstand', and equates it with 'a kind of tact'—an operation of the understanding, it is true, but one which remains unaware of the principles which guide it. For this notion Schiller was no doubt as much indebted to Oetinger's 'common human organ for feeling or perceiving Truth, Wisdom, Goodness, &c.' (see C. A. Auberlen, *Die Theosophie F. C. Oetingers*, Tübingen, 1847, p. 54 f.) as to the 'inward light'—which is 'a gift of nature' and 'has the light of truth in itself'—of the Scottish philosopher, Thomas Reid, whom, paradoxically enough, Schiller's teacher, Abel, had introduced to his pupils at the Carlsschule with the avowed aim of counteracting such 'unenlightened' thinking as Pietism;

2. the sense which is 'common' to all mankind, which has accrued from the

experience and wisdom of countless generations, general sagacity. This is clearly the predominant meaning in XXVII. 11, where the technical, and therefore in some sense esoteric, knowledge of science and philosophy is to be brought out into the open, made available to the *Gemeinsinn*, and transformed into a common possession (*Gemeingut*) of the whole community. This was the express aim of Schiller's Journal *Die Horen* (cf. p. xix above).

In this second meaning, 'common sense' derived from England— from Locke via the Moral Weeklies; and a journal with this title was actually published in London in 1737, arousing the mockery of Lady Mary Montagu, who retorted with the *Nonsense of Common Sense*. The meaning of the term was still being debated in 1790 in an article in the *Deutsche Monatsschrift*, i. 61, where *Gemeinsinn* was equated with 'gesunder Menschenverstand' (the justification of our translation of this latter term in XVIII. 4fn.). Though the notion obviously lent itself to trivialization, it yet epitomized the 'democratic' educational ideals of the Enlightenment; and thinkers such as Schiller and Coleridge, who were uncompromisingly insistent on the need for rigorous analysis and strict distinctions, not only took it as their own proud aim to 'combine and harmonize Philosophy and Common Sense' (see above p. ciii) but were convinced that their severance would be disastrous both for philosophy (here in the widest sense, to include 'science') and for mankind. This is supported by what Schiller says in I. 4, about 'gemeine Vernunft'. Equated with 'moralischer Instinkt' and opposed to the technicalities of Ethics, it clearly signifies the organ of primary *moral* truths, thus representing the ethical counterpart of *Gemeinsinn* (cf. above p. civ).

Gemüt : *see* GEIST.

Gesinnung : *see* SINN.

Gestalt : *see* FORM.

Idee, Ideal, edel, veredeln, adeln : although the words in the first half of this list are obviously not cognate with those in the second, there is a case for thus grouping them in order to bring out certain connexions and distinctions in Schiller's usage.

Idee is used

1. in a more general sense as synonym, or near synonym, of (*a*) *Gedanke*, thought (XV. 5); (*b*) *Begriff*, notion, conception, concept (IV. 5; XI. 4); (*c*) *Vorstellung*, any product of mental activity existing in the mind as an object of knowledge (XXVI. 11); (*d*) *Bild*, image, phantasy (XXVII. 4), 'material idea', as Schiller, following Descartes, Wolff, and Baumgarten, had termed it in his Carlsschule dissertation (cf. Wernly, op. cit., p. 41 f.— though surely she should have included 'freie Ideenfolge' in XXVII. 4 under this rubric and not under *Gedanke*). The wide range of meaning of *Idee* in this more general sense is exhibited in XXVII. 4fn. (cf. Note). In XXV. 1fn. we thought it appropriate to render 'in der Idee' by 'in theory', although a case could be made out for including this occurrence under sense 2;

2. in the more philosophical sense of (*a*) the Kantian *Vernunftbegriff*, a concept of Reason (III. 4; XIV. 2; XVII. 2—'die Idee der Menschheit'; cf. X. 7—'der reine Begriff der Menschheit'); (*b*) something more akin to the Platonic *noumenon* (XXV. 5; XXVI. 14).

Ideal is primarily the adjective to *Idee*, and has the same connotation when used substantivally, i.e. relating to ideas, having existence only as idea. Admittedly the notion of perfection cannot be ruled out ('Ideal der Begierde' f.i., in XXIV. 5, definitely carries such connotations), but it is by no means as much to the fore as Schiller scholarship has been inclined to assume. In XVII. 1 'Ideal der Schönheit' is obviously equated with 'Idee der Schönheit'; and in IV. 2 'reiner idealischer Mensch' is no less obviously the idea, or archetype, of a human being. Similarly in XXIV. 4 'Idealwelt' is not primarily an ideal world, but the world of ideas as opposed to the world of sense; 'Kunst des Ideals' (II. 3; XXVII. 1), not an ideal kind of art, but art which is a vehicle of significance as distinct from artefacts serving some practical end (see KUNST); 'idealischer Schein' (XXVI. 14), not some ideal kind of semblance, but simply semblance which is accepted as such by the mind and not confused with *Wirklichkeit*. In IX. 5, where the artist is exhorted to achieve 'das Ideal' through a 'synthesis of the possible with the necessary', *Ideal* clearly signifies an analogue, perhaps the only possible analogue in the phenomenal world, of the *noumenon*, a reflection of the *Idee* in the perceptible forms and symbols of art.

Nor should *idealisieren*, or *veredeln*, a central notion of Schiller's aesthetics since his review of Bürger's *Gedichte*, be primarily associated with standards of excellence, and certainly not of moral excellence. It was to avoid such possible confusion that he told Körner (in an enclosure to his letter of 10.iii.1795; NA xxii. 293) that it would be better to avoid *veredeln* in this sense altogether, since 'the word always has a suggestion of improvement, moral elevation, and the Devil idealized would have to be morally *worse* than he would otherwise be', would have to represent the very *Idee*, or quintessence, of devilry. 'Idealisierkunst', as he had termed it in *Über Bürgers Gedichte*, is thus the act of raising the individual to the typical and so endowing it with universal significance. In the *Aesthetic Letters*, however, Schiller still uses *veredeln* very much in this sense: e.g. IV. 2, where the connexion with *Idee* is most clearly established; XXVI. 14, where the connexion is maintained by the adjective *idealisch*; and XXVII. 2, where the notion of a quantitative change passing over into a qualitative one clearly recalls those underlying metallurgical and alchemical implications of *veredeln* (cf. IV. 2; XXIII. 5 and Note) which made it possible for it to be used not only as a synonym of *idealisieren* but also of *steigern*, as *Veredlung* actually is in XXII. 4 (see Note). All these affiliations are present in the use of *edel* (*adeln*) in XXIII. 7, 8, and fn., and are of crucial importance in the distinction there made between noble and sublime conduct.

Imagination: *see* EINBILDUNGSKRAFT.

Inhalt (Gegenstand), Stoff (Materie), Gehalt: the first four of these words occur together in a passage (XXII. 5–6) which has given rise to considerable controversy (see Wernly, op. cit., p. 81 f.). Had Schiller safeguarded himself by including the fifth at this point too, there might have been less.

The offending propositions, which may well at first sight seem to make him an advocate of 'pure' form devoid of all 'content', are the following:

> In a truly successful work of art the *Inhalt* should effect nothing, the *Form* everything. . . . Hence the secret of artistic creation resides in the artist's power to make his *Form* consume his *Stoff*.

From an understandable desire to defend him against a charge which is alien to the whole temper of his aesthetics, scholars (e.g. Wernly, ibid.) have even gone to the length of insisting that *Stoff* in the second of the above propositions must on no account be identified with *Inhalt*, otherwise Schiller would have to be taken as saying that as long as the form is beautiful the *Inhalt* is a matter of indifference. But this is more or less what he *is* saying, unpalatable as it may at first sound. The weakness of this line of defence is that it shies away from the implications of the first proposition, ignores the 'hence' which links it to the second, and mistakes the whole tenor of the argument in these two paragraphs. Indeed in the treatise as a whole. For all the intervening Letters have been designed to show that the objections to art and beauty raised in Letter X, by 'voices worthy of respect', are without foundation. Plausible as it may sound (Schiller has in effect been arguing) to say that attention to *Form* at the expense of *Inhalt* is likely to foster a dangerous tendency to neglect reality altogether (X. 4), it is in fact only through such disregard of mere *Inhalt*, and response to the *Form* as a whole, that we can ever hope to have access to the real, the living, significance of a work of art.

True, *Inhalt* is not exactly a synonym of *Stoff*; but it connotes the same thing looked at from a different angle. *Stoff* (*Materie*) here (and in IX. 4, both occurrences), by contrast with the examples cited under MATERIE, MATERIAL, &c. (*and* by contrast with a deceptively similar-sounding passage of the *Kallias* letters; Jonas, iii. 294), does not mean the artist's medium but his subject-matter (there can be no doubt about this, if only for the reason that the adjective *ernst* would scarcely be applicable to the medium of any of the arts). To use the same word for both can on occasion give rise to confusion; but it has the advantage of lumping together as 'raw material' *all* the things which the artist takes ready-made from the world around him: not just clay or stone, paint and canvas, tones or language, but the forms of perception and experience—objects, persons, scenes and events—even cultural forms derived from myth, philosophy, or 'the most serious material', such as religion (cf. Note to XXII. 5) or the forms of the moral world (IX. 6), even artistic forms themselves and the work of bygone artists. All of this comes to him from outside—'Den Stoff', as Goethe wrote, 'gibt ihm die Welt nur allzu freigebig' (*Noten und Abhandlungen zum Divan*; JA v. 212). All of it, however highly formed in itself, is mere grist to his artistic mill. Or, as Schiller put it in no. 19 of his *Votivtafeln*:

> Selbst Gebildetes ist Stoff nur dem bildenden Geist

(not, as E. v. d. Hellen emends in SA i. 144 and 323, 'Selbstgebildetes' in one word; cf. Wilkinson, loc. cit. [3], pp. 52 f.). All of it is transmuted by the artist into the form of his own work (it is not the case that some aspects of it are turned into the form of the work, while others remain its content—a common misconception). All of it is 'consumed by his form', i.e. broken down and subjected to a totally different principle of organization; so that, although still present in the new form, none of it should be functioning, or making its effect, in the identical form it had before it underwent its present artistic metamorphosis (the analogy is clearly with the assimilative processes of living organisms, and implies the concept of a hierarchy of forms in which the lower are constantly being assimilated into the higher).

If we are capable of responding to the totality of the form the artist has made, then we have access to the 'meaning' inherent in it, a meaning which is different from any or all of the meanings of the various materials which have gone to its making. For this 'meaning', which is implicit in the form of a work of art, and never to be explicated out of it by formulation in any other terms, Goethe and Schiller usually reserved the term *Gehalt*—in many ways a happy choice, partly because of the collective force of the prefix *Ge-*, partly because one of its significations (e.g. in connexion with precious metals) is not just 'what a thing contains', but 'what a thing contains of real value' (perhaps the best English rendering is S. Langer's 'import'; op. cit., p. 31). In their view this 'import' is something possessed by all the arts, whether representational (referential) or not. Cf. Goethe's aphorism on music: in this art there is 'no *Stoff* to be discounted, it is all *Form* and *Gehalt*' (*Maximen und Reflexionen*; JA xxxv. 313); cf., too, Schiller's letter to Goethe, 7. ii.1797, in which he says that only what he calls *Gehalt*, never *Stoff*, is compatible with *Form*, or his statements in *Über naive und sentimentalische Dichtung* (SA xii. 225) that in the 'naïve' pastoral the *Gehalt* is already implicit in the form, and that all poetry must have 'einen unendlichen Gehalt', without which it would not be poetry. It is unfortunate that in the *Aesthetic Letters* he never uses *Gehalt* in this sense, of the 'import' of a finished work of art—though the schema 'lebende Gestalt' (see under FORM) implies clearly enough what he conceived it to be; viz. the inner life of feeling and thought which can find expression in no other way (cf. Goethe in *Noten und Abhandlungen zum Divan*; JA v. 212: 'der Gehalt entspringt freiwillig aus der Fülle seines Innern'). And in XXVI. 14 Schiller uses it analogously, in the context of aesthetic behaviour, of the inner reality of feeling behind the pleasing forms of social intercourse.

Whereas *Gehalt* is the unitary import of a unitary form, *Inhalt* has something of the multiplicity of the materials out of which this latter was made (hence the appropriateness of rendering it by the plural 'contents'; cf. Wilkinson, '"Form" and "Content" in the Aesthetics of German Classicism', ed. cit., p. 18). As XXII. 6 makes clear, even if the artist has been successful in integrating all the elements of his *Stoff* into his form, there will always be minds (which is what makes censorship so irrelevant to art) which will insist, for one reason or another, on reducing it to the discrete materials with which the artist began, on responding to details or to fragments of meaning, and on regarding these as its true 'contents'. In other words, *Inhalt* is that which, unlike *Gehalt*, can be abstracted from any representational work of art, and expressed in other terms.

Stoff, then, may be used of both the formative process and the finished form; *Inhalt* only of the latter, since contents imply a form which contains them. *Inhalt*, in the second of the two paragraphs under discussion, belongs unmistakably in the series: *Teile, Materie, rohes Element, das Einzelne*; in both it is unmistakably 'on the side of' *Stoff/Gegenstand* (as it is, too, in the letters to Körner of

25.v.1792 and 28.xi.1796), and opposed to 'whole', 'aesthetic organization', *Form (Gestalt)* and, by implication, to *Gehalt*—even if this word itself does not actually appear. Failure to recognize this, and an inclination to insist that *Inhalt* and *Gehalt* are synonyms—Wernly (op. cit., pp. 85 f.) baldly asserts as much without offering a shred of evidence to prove it—is responsible for the dilemma in which many German scholars find themselves when faced with Schiller's statement that in art 'the *Inhalt* must effect nothing, the form everything'. They feel that they are left with empty forms on their hands—but the difficulty is of their making rather than his, for all his terminological inexactitude.

Gegenstand, which may be used of both the creative process and aesthetic appreciation, connotes that coherent selection of materials which beckons the artist for treatment because it seems a potentially suitable vehicle for the feeling he wants to express. From the point of view of the beholder, it is an abstraction from the *Inhalt*. In aesthetic contexts it is rarely appropriate to translate it by 'object', but rather by 'subject' or 'theme'. In non-aesthetic contexts, none of these words presents a problem: in II. 5 *Gegenstand* and *Materie* are respectively the subject and theme of Schiller's own treatise; in XI. 8 and XII. 1 the *Inhalt* of time is defined as a formless succession of change.

Kunst, Künstler : in the eighteenth century what we call the Fine Arts were not yet clearly distinguished from
  1. the seven liberal arts of the medieval schools—an 'artist' was originally a master of arts, one skilled in those learned arts which included not only music but astronomy, mathematics, and philosophy too;
  2. craft, business, or profession—it was only gradually that the difference between 'artist' and 'artisan' evolved. In Leonardo's day, for example, the painter was just beginning to be accounted an artist, and to look down on the sculptor who still remained an artisan.

It was not until the 1762 edition of the Dictionary of the French Academy that the word 'artist' appeared in its modern meaning (for an account of its development see Maritain, op. cit., p. 120 f.), and in Germany the meaning of *Kunst* and *Künstler* remained fluid until after the end of the century. Cognate with *können*, they long retained their connexion with 'know-how', skill, especially mechanical skill (cf. Schiller's ironical comment, in a letter to Heinrich Meyer of 5.ii.1795, on a recent definition of *Kunst* which had come his way: 'Jetzt weiss ich endlich, was die *Kunst* ist. "Die Kunst ist diejenige mechanische Handgeschicklichkeit, durch welche vermittelst gewisser Werkzeuge ein natürlicher Körper zur Waare gemacht wird"'). Adelung in 1796 was still confining *Künstler* 'in the narrower sense' to those who practised 'die schönen Künste [an obvious *calque* of *les beaux-arts*] . . . wie die Maler, Baumeister, Tanzmeister, usf. . . . Nur von Dichtern und Rednern ist es ungewöhnlich.' By 1808 Campe can record its occasional application to poets too.

Hence even as late as 1795, and in a treatise actually dealing with aesthetics, Schiller may well feel no need to qualify these words when he uses them in non-aesthetic contexts: e.g. *Künstler* of a watchmaker (III. 4) or *Kunst* of technical procedures (e.g. those of philosophy, as in I. 4)—a meaning still evident in *Kunstwort*, 'technical term' (cf. his letter to Garve of 25.i.1795, where even though it is the word *ästhetisch* itself which is under discussion, the

Kunst in *Kunstwörter* has no reference to the subject-matter in hand, but simply specifies the artificial nature of the words necessary for any technical discussion). On other occasions, however, he does feel the need to qualify: either by a genitive—*Staatskünstler* (IV. 4)—or by an adjective—*mechanisch, pädagogisch, politisch* (IV. 4), *nachahmend* (XXVI. 7). There is a similar fluctuation when he uses *Kunst* and *Künstler* in their modern, specifically aesthetic, sense. He often —but by no means always—qualifies them: either by a following genitive—*die Kunst des Scheins* (XXVI. 9) or *des schönen Scheins* (XXVI. 5)—or by a preceding adjective—*schöne Kunst* (XXII. 5; XXVI. 5), *ästhetische Kunst* (XV. 9), *der schöne Künstler* (IV. 4)—where the adjective has, of course, genitive function, and must under no circumstances be translated as though it meant a beautiful kind of art—or a beautiful artist!—but as 'art' *tout court*, or as 'the art of the beautiful' (cf. letter to Körner, 3.ii.1794; Jonas, iii. 421, where he explicitly states that *schöne Kunst* is a 'Species' of the 'Gattung' *Kunst*).

Following Rousseau's contrast between *l'art* and *la nature*, Schiller also uses *Kunst* in the sense of 'civilization'. Thus in IV. 6 it is not art that the savage despises, but civilization; in X. 4, not art that suppresses nature, but artifice; in V. 5, not with 'the disciple of Art' (Snell) that the child of nature is being contrasted, but with the product of civilization (cf. in XVII. 4 the contrast between *Naturmensch* and *künstlicher Mensch*); while, again in XVII. 4, 'naturwidrige Kunst' is not an art which offends against nature, but the unnaturalness of civilization.

Inevitably it is often difficult to determine the exact range of meaning in a given occurrence. When in II. 1 the construction of true political freedom is referred to as 'das vollkommenste aller Kunstwerke', the predominant meaning is 'artefact', although obviously in a treatise which is to culminate in the idea of the aesthetic State aesthetic overtones cannot be ruled out (any more than they can in the preface to *Fiesco*, where Schiller defined his hero as 'ein Opfer der Kunst und Kabale'; SA xvi. 42). To allow such overtones is, however, very different from insisting (as does Böhm, op. cit., p. 8) that political freedom is already, at this stage of the argument, being referred to as an aesthetic pheno-menon. Again, in XV. 5—'das Bedürfnis der Kunst'—the context obviously *is* that of aesthetic objects. Yet the meaning which is uppermost is not that of beauty, but of craft, skill, or technique, and to render it as the 'needs of art' would make utter nonsense of the passage. Finally, the last sentence of Letter VI offers an excellent example of the word being used in two distinct senses which are nevertheless related to each other in a way which epitomizes the form and content of the whole treatise: 'it must be open to us to restore by means of a higher Art [i.e. the art of the beautiful] the totality of our nature which the arts themselves [in Rousseau's sense of civilization] have destroyed'. Cf. above, pp. xlix, li, lxxxvi and Note to VI. 15.

Liberalität : *see* FREIHEIT.

Masse : *see* MATERIE.

Materie (Material, Masse), Stoff, Medium : in non-aesthetic contexts the loan-word *Materie* (more rarely *Material*, on one occasion, XXVI. 14, *das Materielle*) is used more or less interchangeably with *Stoff* to mean 'matter',

'material' (e.g. VI. 3; XIII. 2fn. § 1; XIV. 2; XXIII. 5; XXV. 7; XXVII. 11).
In XII. 1 Schiller extends the term to mean 'change, or reality which occupies time'. When he particularly wishes to stress the brute nature of matter, inchoate, inert, 'blind', obedient only to physical laws, he tends to use *Masse* (e.g. IV. 4; XXV. 3; XXVI. 2; XXVII. 11, and see Note). In such, more or less philo-sophical, contexts, where *Materie* (or *Stoff*) is opposed to *Geist*, *Vernunft*, *Idee*, *Form*, or *Gestalt*, it is best rendered by 'matter', 'mass', or 'substance'. In IV. 1, however, 'die Materie seines Wollens', we have preferred 'content', though the phrase no doubt implies the material on which the will works, as well as the content of a particular act of will.

In aesthetic contexts, *Stoff*—a key-concept in the aesthetics of Schiller and Goethe—more often means the 'subject-matter' of the representational arts, and in this sense it is discussed, together with *Materie* which occasionally replaces it, under *Inhalt*. It is also, however—and in this treatise several times—used as a synonym of *Materie* in the sense of the artist's 'medium', the material of clay, stone, paint, tones, or words, which the artist fashions and shapes into an expressive form. All four words, *Stoff*, *Masse*, *Materie*, *Material*, are used in this sense, in IV. 4, of the physical material on which builder and sculptor work and, by analogy, of the human material of educationist and statesman. This is also the meaning of *Stoff* in IX. 6, and of *Materie* (of music) in XXII. 4. *Medium* in this latter context (see Note thereto), being in apposition to *Imagina-tion*, can scarcely mean 'medium' in the sense of the poet's material of language (though Schiller sometimes did use it in this sense, e.g. in his *Ästhetische Vorlesungen*, SA xii. 351, and in his *Kallias* letters, Jonas, iii. 297: 'Das Medium des Dichters sind Worte'). It is rather 'medium' in the sense of 'intervening mental substance', the faculty of the psyche through which poetry must pass in order to address itself to feeling.

The difficulties of interpreting these words are displayed in II. 3, where, although the context is aesthetic, 'Notdurft der Materie' does not signify the exigencies of the artist's medium in particular, but of matter in general; and in XVII. 4, where *Materie*, though opposed to *Form* in an aesthetic context, means neither the medium of art nor its subject-matter, but rather its sensuous aspect in general. *Stoff* in this same paragraph, by contrast, *does* mean the artist's medium, though only metaphorically: human beings are thought of, much as in IV. 4, as the material which Beauty, personified as artist, fashions and forms. For the way that 'forms', if we allow them to petrify, can as it were turn into matter (XXVI. 14) see FORM.

Medium : *see* MATERIE.

Natur : nowhere is the confusion of Schiller's terminology more apparent— or more irritating! The senses available to him, both secular and sacred, were many. It could, and can, mean: the essential qualities of a thing or person (as in XVII. 2, 'ihrer Natur gemäss'; XIX. 10, 'seiner Natur nach'—a use which presents no problems and will not be discussed); the phenomena of the outside world and the power thought to operate these (often personified; the stock image, 'Mother Nature', does not actually occur, but 'die weise Natur' of I. 4 implies it—though the 'freiwillige Natur' in the same paragraph, *pace* Lutz, op. cit., p. 218, does not); inherent or innate disposition (nature as opposed to nurture); the natural order and course of things established in the world by the Creator; the light of Reason implanted in the mind of man. It can connote not only man's corrupt and sinful state, our 'fallen' nature, but also our holy and divine qualities, our 'true' nature; yet the 'natural' man is one who, however much he may have 'improved' his natural endowments, including Reason, still remains 'unrenewed' by Faith and by Grace. To such dictionary and biblical meanings must be added: that staple resource of eighteenth-century thinkers, the Rousseauean hypothesis of a primitive 'order', or Nature, to which 'return' must be made (a secular exploitation of the 'Fall'); Nature as opposed to Freedom in the Kantian dichotomy; the Goethean notion of an all-unifying Nature which embraces the polarities experienced by man. A genetic examination of Schiller's use of the word (cf. David, loc. cit., pp. 3 ff.) undoubtedly reveals some tension between the Kantian, dualistic, and the Goethean, unitary–polar, view. But a structural approach to its use in this treatise suggests less confusion of thought than appears on the surface. And some of it disappears if, instead of listing observed uses of the word as discrete meanings, we relate them to the movement of Schiller's thought as displayed in the behaviour of such words as *Vernunft, Freiheit, Notwendigkeit*, and *Bestimmung*; if we allow for his characteristic strategy of presenting a paradox as though it were insoluble, only thereafter to resolve it; and if we realize that he is at least as much preoccupied with the subject–object dichotomy, i.e. with various ways of knowing, as with the Nature–Freedom dichotomy, i.e. with the problem of willing. The following arrangement of 'meanings' may help to bring out the order inherent in his use of this word; it does not claim to dispose of every inconsistency, or of the— perhaps intentional—ambiguity in some occurrences (e.g. I. 4 and IV. 4).

 1. *NATUR*, in 'the widest sense of the word' (XX. 1), as the source of all things: of man's moral, no less than of his animal, nature, of his self-awareness as of his determinedness (XIX. 11 and 12), of his freedom (XX. 1), even of that aesthetic mode which is to enable him to make the transition from 'blind' living to moral freedom (XXIII. 5; XXVI. 1), and which, though said to be a 'leap' (XXVII. 4), is not represented as a leap made outside of nature in this sense.

Normally, however, man experiences this unity as twofold: as an opposition between (*a*) self and world, subject and object; (*b*) that aspect of the self which is subject to the same laws as the rest of nature and that aspect which feels free. And so we have:

 2. *Natur* as that which stands over against us, and to which we are related in various ways:

  (*a*) as power, or force, which is merely felt (XXIV. 1);

  (*b*) as a multiplicity of forms (XXV. 2 and 3), construed involuntarily, and for the most part unconsciously, by the synthesizing processes of sense-perception and intuition. So involuntary is the process, so involved the relation between inner world and outer (cf. XXV. 1–3 and Notes), that these forms seem 'given' by nature, not something we have produced ourselves at all. Hence the possibility of equating *Natur* with *Sinn* (see thereunder and Note to XVIII. 4fn.). Hence the legitimacy (*pace* David, loc. cit., p. 21) of speaking, on the one hand, of 'formless' nature (XVII. 4), on the other, of the 'forms' *in* nature (XXVI. 2): the former reminds us of the unconscious mental activity involved in the construing of nature's forms; the latter of that consensus of perception which enables us to treat them, in fact and in language, as though they were 'given'. In this sense, *Natur* is indeed equated with multiplicity (IV. 3 and 7), but also with wholeness; for it is, at this stage, a multiplicity of *wholes* (XIII. 4fn. § 2) by contrast with (*a*) above, where it was a multiplicity of meaningless *impacts*;

(*c*) as something to be used—in IV. 4, as synonym of the builder's and sculptor's material medium (contrasted with the human 'nature' which is the material of educationist and statesman);

(*d*) as the results of the processes of the analytical understanding, which breaks down the wholes presented by *Natur/Sinn*—including the moral (I. 4) and aesthetic (XVI. 5) phenomena thrown up spontaneously by the mind of man—in order to discover the relations between them and the laws that govern them (I. 4; VI. 12; XIII. 4fn. § 2; XVI. 5; XVIII. 4fn.);

(*e*) as the meaningful unity glimpsed by the unifying tendencies of Pure Reason (XVIII. 4fn.)—not to be confused with the scientific laws discovered by the analytical understanding which, however universal, are always necessarily provisional (XXIV. 6). Such unifying tendencies, when they mistake their proper object and sphere, can actually impede the progress of science (XIII. 4fn. § 2) and lead man astray both in the moral and the religious sphere (XXIV. 4–8). Rightly used they enable man to comprehend *NATUR* in sense 1 above and his own place within it.

There is thus no inconsistency (David, loc. cit., p. 14) between IV. 3, where the multiplicity of *Natur* is opposed to the unity of *Vernunft*, and VI. 5, where the unifying tendency of *Natur* is opposed to the separating operations of *Verstand*. Both statements are in complete accord with XVIII. 4fn., where it is said that 'die Natur (der Sinn) vereinigt überall, der Verstand scheidet überall; aber die Vernunft vereinigt wieder'.

A similar 'circularity' is apparent in the use of

3. *Natur* in the sense of man's own, 'human', nature. Here, again, Reason enables him to conceive this as a totality, as

(*a*) *menschliche Natur* in the widest sense, a primary unity ordained by *NATUR* in sense 1 above (XIII. 1, 2, and fn.). Like the 'Naturstand in der Idee' of III. 2, this unified conception is but a model which can serve him as guide in his efforts at right living. In actual experience, however, it presents itself as twofold, as a

(*b*) *gemischte*, a *sinnlich-vernünftige*, *Natur* (XIX. 12fn.; X. 7). It is important to realize that the 'Abfallen von der Natur' of VI. 1 does not, for Schiller, lie in this awareness of duality—to be human at all is to be thus 'mixed', compound of sense and spirit. It lies in achieving the wrong kind of *Mischung*, of mismanaging the relations between the two aspects of his Nature or, as they are variously called (XVI. 2; XVII. 4), his 'two natures':

(c) his *sinnliche Natur*; not to be equated with physical, as opposed to mental, behaviour—it includes, for example, free association of ideas (XXVII. 4) and the kind of political activity which led him into the *Naturstaat* (III. 3); nor with mere crude instinct—it is the source of natural feeling, of *Empfänglichkeit*, our 'zärtere Humanität', no less than of 'rohe Natur' (XIII. 4fn. § 3; XVI. 3). It is rather involuntary life, 'blind', uninformed by the self-awareness and freedom which characterizes

(d) his *vernünftige (sittliche) Natur*, or *Persönlichkeit* (XIX. 11). But even the freedom and awareness of this latter can be misused (XIII. 4fn. § 1, and 5). Regarding his *sinnliche Natur* as an obstacle to greater intellectual insights, or as a break upon his moral freedom, he may treat it as a 'lower' nature, and in curbing its arbitrary caprice (IV. 6) curtail its legitimate activities too.

Each of our two natures is thus in constant danger of transgressing the limits set them by *NATUR* (in sense 1 above), of confusing their proper objectives and spheres of operation (XIII. 2). Such mismanagement can result in: (1) failure to develop some of our manifold potentialities—in which case we have 'verstümmelte Natur' (VI. 14); (2) failure to rise to the challenge of our 'higher' nature (sense 3 [d])—in which case we have 'rohe Natur' (XVI. 3; XXIV. 3) or the 'wilde Ungebundenheit des Naturstands' (VII. 3); (3) tyrannous repression of our 'lower' nature by our 'higher'—in which case we have 'Unnatur' (V. 5; = the *Barbar* of IV. 6); (4) the varied and complex rationalizations of instinctual needs and desires alluded to in V. 5, and described in XXIV. 4–7—in which case we have the unfortunate 'mixture' termed by Schiller 'ein vernünftiges Tier' (XXIV. 8). The kind of *Mischung* we are, however, meant to achieve is

(e) *Menschliche Natur*, again a totality, but one which differs in significant ways from sense 3 (a): it is not an undifferentiated unity, but a cooperation of opposites (XVII. 4); not a static condition, but a dynamic process of reciprocal subordination (XIII–XV; XVI. 1; XIX. 12fn.); not a mere idea conceived as a normative model, but an ideal which is achievable if rarely achieved. The prime example of its realization in history was the civilization of the Greeks (VI. 2; XV. 9). Yet from the vantage point of our modern differentiation even their achievement is to be regarded as merely a stage on the way to the ideal, a 'Maximum' of 'edle Natur' certainly (VI. 11; IX. 4), and one which, at that 'naïve' level of human consciousness, has never been surpassed; yet, from our point of view, still 'blosse Natur' (VI. 2 and Note). For *NATURE'S* purposes (VI. 11 and 15) continually present man with new challenges —but also, through the gift of Reason, with the power of meeting them if he so wills (XIX. 12), and with the necessary support whilst he struggles to do so (hence the reference to the 'ladder of Nature' in III. 3). The limits she seems to have set him (VI. 13) are sometimes there only for him to transcend. To have to learn when he may legitimately transcend, and when he must not on any account transgress, them, is an inevitable result of his being part, even if a special part, of the natural order.

It is evident from the above that for Schiller *NATUR* lacks neither form (XXVI. 2) nor even freedom (IV. 6)—and certainly not Reason (see *Über das Erhabene*: 'Vernünftig handelt die ganze Natur...'; SA xii. 264). What she lacks is consciousness. Hence man can transcend her, by retracing in full consciousness the steps she took on his behalf—which power enables him to regard even *NATUR* (III. 1, first occurrence) as 'blosse Natur' (III. 1, second occurrence). But he can also feel the need to emulate her, to make his own, moral, behaviour approximate to the certainty of her laws (IV. 1), to perform moral deeds spontaneously rather than by reflective effort, thus transforming right doing into right being, making of virtue, as linguistic usage has it, a 'second' nature. The contradiction which Lutz (op. cit., pp. 169 ff.) discerns between these two Letters—III and IV—has been dealt with on pp. xlvi ff. above, as has also his contention (ibid., pp. 179 f.) that Schiller confuses a normative *Ur*=*Naturstaat* with a positive *Naturstaat*. But it may be well to reiterate here that the first of these is attributed to him gratuitously by Lutz. Schiller himself operates with only one *Naturstaat*, defined in III. 3, and used in this single sense throughout. It is the term *Naturstand* that has to do double duty, the whys and wherefores of which Schiller, following Rousseau closely, makes clear in III. 2 (see Note).

Notwendigkeit, Nötigung, Not(durft), Bedürfnis: the meaning of *Notwendigkeit* is as wide as that of English 'necessity', ranging from something indispensable (a need), through something unavoidable (the constraining power of circumstances), to a compulsion having its basis in the natural constitution of things, especially when such compulsion is conceived as a law prevailing throughout the universe and within the sphere of human action. In distinguishing between different kinds of necessity—*physische, moralische* (III. 1), *logische* (XX. 3), *schönere* (XXVII. 7), 'Notwendigkeit der Geister' (II. 3), 'eine Notwendigkeit ausser uns ... eine Notwendigkeit in uns' (XIX. 11)—Schiller is following normal practice (cf. *OED*: 'absolute, conditional, logical, moral, natural, philosophical, physical necessity'), and many of the difficulties connected with his use of this word disappear once we have grasped the general structure of his thought. Thus in III. 1 we are confronted with what seems like a very simple opposition between *physische Notwendigkeit*, 'ein Werk der Not', and *moralische Notwendigkeit*, 'ein Werk [des Menschen] freier Wahl'. By XIV. 5, however, it has been disclosed that this power of 'free' choice, by virtue of which man is able to transcend the constraint of natural necessity, is itself a kind of constraint (*Nötigung, Zwang*); and by XV. 9 his true freedom, freedom from the constraint of either of these necessities, will be said to result, not from the presence within him of one principle alone (the *freie Intelligenz* of III. 1), but only from the reconciliation, in a 'higher concept of Necessity', of the *two* necessities to which he is heir: the one *outside* him, in which, however, as a creature subject to natural laws, he also shares, i.e. physical necessity; and the one *inside* him, which distinguishes him from the rest of nature, i.e. moral necessity (XIX. 11; XXIV. 2). The use of this word thus reflects the characteristically 'circular' movement of Schiller's thought (see pp. li ff. above): the perfect *coincidence* of physical and moral necessity can only be imagined in an Absolute Being (IV. 1)—referred to in XI. 2 as 'das notwendige Wesen'; man, as a finite being, must always experience necessity as twofold; yet it is given to him, through an effort of understanding and will, to see both moral laws and natural laws as aspects of the greater 'lawfulness' of the whole universe (XII. 5; XIX. 11), thus approximating, in the only way open to a finite being, to that single Necessity which was said to be characteristic of Absolute Being. Like *Natur* and *Freiheit*, this word is used, with and without qualification, in both a narrower and a wider sense—'Gesetz der Notwendigkeit' in XIX. 12 is, f.i., unpolarized, despite appearances to the contrary—and its development is intimately linked with the widening of the concept of Nature and the probing of the concept of Freedom. Whereas in III. 1 it seemed that physical necessity alone was a product of nature, and of 'der blossen Natur' at that, by XIX. 12 we see that Nature—now 'in the widest sense of this word' (XX. 1)—is the source of moral necessity too. She it is who makes man what he is, a 'freie Intelligenz' as well as a creature of sense, thus implanting in him the *possibility* of becoming fully and truly free by reconciling both (XIX. 12fn.), but leaving to him the decision whether he will carry out this task or not.

Yet difficulties remain, chiefly because *Notwendigkeit* tends to be weighted with lofty and sublime connotations in a way that *Not* and *Nötigung* are not. Whereas in XIV. 5 the only difference between them is that *Notwendigkeit* represents more of an abstraction, while *Nötigung* evokes the actual process of constraining, in other instances (e.g. XXIV. 6) we find them opposed to each other as 'high' and 'low'—'erhabene Notwendigkeit der Vernunft', 'blinde Nötigung der Materie'. Where this happens *without* qualification, it is from the series in which the word finds itself that we have to infer its connotations. In XV. 5 particularly, but also in other places (II. 3; IX. 7; XIX. 11; XXVII. 4 and 7), we find *Notwendigkeit* on the 'side' of *Pflicht*, *Würde*, *Gesetz*, *Form*, *Idee*, or *Freiheit*, and opposed to *Wirklichkeit*, *Leben*, *Neigung*, *Zufall*, *Willkür*, *Notdurft der Materie*, or *Bedürfnis*.

But this last word, *Bedürfnis*, is not wholly without lability either. Though not confined to purely physical needs—the *freie Ideenfolge* of XXVII. 4 is a *Bedürfnis*, and those aspects of art which have to do with medium and technique constitute the 'Bedürfnis der Kunst' (XV. 5)—it normally belongs to the realm of nature, as opposed to the realm of spirit: it is a near-synonym of *Not* (XXVI. 4), of *Notdurft* (XXVII. 3), and is opposed to *Gesetz* (XV. 5; XXVII. 4); it was the 'Zwang des Bedürfnisses' which drove man into society and the *Naturstaat* (III. 2; XXVII. 3 and 10). Yet even as early as II. 5, it is clear that it can be used of man's higher spiritual needs too (Kant had spoken of faith in God as 'ein Bedürfnis der Vernunft'; cf. Eisler, op. cit. [2], pp. 57, 206), or rather of the needs of his nature as a whole, the Whole which comprises both nature and spirit (see NATUR and GEMÜT). In one instance, illuminating for Schiller's whole method (XXVII. 5), we can actually watch this word moving from one camp into the other: 'Die freie Lust [see FREIHEIT] wird in die Zahl seiner Bedürfnisse aufgenommen', i.e. what was completely unnecessary to the natural man, viz. the aesthetic mode, turns into one of the deepest needs of his *whole* nature.

Objekt : *see* GEGENSTAND.

Phantasie : *see* EINBILDUNGSKRAFT.

Schein, Erscheinung, Täuschung : the word which Schiller elevated to the role of master-concept in his aesthetic 'system' is more ambiguous than most. *Scheinen* not only has two quite distinct meanings, 'to shine' and 'to appear or seem', but the second of these is of the very essence of ambiguity: a thing may appear to be what it in fact is, or seem to be what it is not. It is thus a highly appropriate word to express that highly ambiguous and illusive phenomenon, beauty, which even as a very young man Goethe had thought fit to characterize as *schielend* ('squinting'; letter to Friederike Oeser, 13.ii.1769). And in the eighteenth century, both in and out of aesthetic contexts, *Schein* was variously identified with both *Erscheinung* ('appearance') and *Täuschung* ('deception', or 'illusion'). Thus Sulzer treats *Schein* and *Täuschung* as synonymous, while Mendelssohn sometimes makes *Schein* into a near-synonym of *Erscheinung* (cf. Wernly, op. cit., p. 124). Kant, on the other hand, insists on a strict distinction between these two, using the latter as the German equivalent of the Greek 'phenomenon'—a thing manifest in sensible experience and opposed to 'noumenon', an underlying suprasensible reality, or, in terms of his own 'critical' philosophy, 'our perception of an object according to the forms of our mind and sense-organs, not as it is in itself'—and reserving *Schein* for that which leads us to take a false judgement of something for truth. Thus for him, too, *Schein* savours of deception, and in his *Critique of Judgement*, he uses the concept, as Herder had done in his *Plastik* (ed. cit. viii. 10 ff.), to distinguish painting from sculpture and architecture. The two latter are arts of sensuous truth, the former of sensuous semblance (*Schein*); for although all three use figures in space for the expression of ideas, architecture and sculpture make them discernible to both sight and touch, whereas painting makes them discernible to sight alone, i.e. it only gives the *semblance* of bodily extension (cf. Meredith, op. cit., pp. 186–92).

Schiller, by contrast, applies the concept of *Schein* to all the arts without discrimination, and uses it to distinguish art from reality. But his application of it is even wider: he makes it into an indispensable characteristic of all phenomena whatsoever—whether natural or human, whether objects or persons, events or behaviour—when viewed under their aesthetic aspect. The chief distinction he is concerned to make—and he makes it with emphasis and care in Letter XXVI—is between such aesthetic semblance and any kind of deception (*Betrug*). And even then he does not insist on different terms, but is content to point the distinction by varying the adjective: *logischer Schein*, *ästhetischer Schein* (XXVI. 5). Nor, having so painstakingly divested *ästhetischer Schein* of all taint of deception, and established its 'honesty' and 'independence' (XXVI. 11), does he thereafter eschew the traditional *Täuschung* in aesthetic contexts: he had used it thus in IX. 4, and he will do so again in a *locus classicus* of his aesthetic *credo* at the end of the Prologue to *Wallenstein*. We find a similar indifference to verbal distinctions in his occasional identification of *Schein* and *Erscheinung*. The aesthetic connotations of the latter are established in XX. 4fn. (second occurrence); and in XXVI. 11 and 14 the two words become almost synonymous. But not quite; and the translator would be ill advised (*pace* Snell) to choose the same English word for both. For *Erscheinung* in the aesthetic sense is the brief abstraction of the sheer appearance of something which is still firmly anchored by its material and purposive attachments in 'existence' or 'reality'; whereas *Schein* only *has* existence at all in the world of forms, Ideas, or 'shades' (the earlier title of Schiller's poem *Das Ideal und das Leben* was *Das Reich der Schatten*), independently of all material or 'existential' purposes and functions whatsoever. *Schein* thus implies greater autonomy (XXVI. 7). It is also, in one sense, the wider concept in that it includes the whole realm of art-objects as well as the aesthetic 'appearance' of other phenomena. We have usually translated it by 'semblance', reserving 'appearance' for *Erscheinung*. Though in neither case have we found it possible, or even desirable, to be consistent. On one occasion—'Schein vom Verdienste fordern' (XXVI. 14)—the only possible rendering seemed to be 'style' (in the sense of *OED* iii. 23: 'manner of executing a task or performing an action, etc.'). On another—'er muss aufhören, das Gefühl als Kraft zu berühren, und als Erscheinung dem Verstand gegenüber stehn' (XXVII. 7)—encouraged by the parallel antithesis *Form/Materie*, we decided on 'form'.

Both *Schein* and *Erscheinung* also occur in their ordinary, non-aesthetic, meaning. In I. 2 'den Schein eines Verdienstes' means nothing more than 'the appearance of merit'—by contrast with 'Schein vom Verdienste fordern' in XXVI. 14, where it is (*pace* Wernly, op. cit., p. 121) pregnant with highly aesthetic connotations. Cf. 'mit welchem Scheine von Ehrwürdigkeit' (III. 2) and 'dem Scheine nach' (XXIV. 6), in both of which the word is used in its non-technical sense. So, too, with *Erscheinung*: in X. 4, where a decadent age is castigated for judging by appearances, the implication is derogatory and only partially aesthetic—by contrast with XXVI. 11 and 14, where, although opposed to similar concepts, e.g. *Wesen*, *Dasein*, *Realität*, *Gehalt*, no derogation is implied since such abstraction of sheer appearance is there presented as a step on the way to the autonomy of pure semblance (cf. the precisely parallel ambivalence in the meaning of *Schein* in these same two Letters).

Erscheinung also occurs in its philosophical sense of 'phenomenon' (*Phänomen* itself is actually used in XI. 5), and it is important not to confuse this with its aesthetic use, as does Wernly (ibid., p. 117) in XII. 6, where 'das Reich der Erscheinungen' obviously means 'the realm of phenomena' and has nothing to do with *aesthetic* appearances. If we assume aesthetic connotations in XV. 2, as she also suggests, the result is sheer tautology.

Sinn, Sinnlichkeit, innerer Sinn, Gesinnung : *Sinn* itself has two main meanings:

1. 'organ of sense' (XIX. 2 and 3). As a medium of sensation and a source of appetite the senses are obviously connected with *Empfindung* (XXIII. 7; XXV. 1) and with *Gefühl* (XXIV. 6); but as our means of perception (*Vorstellung*, XIX. 3) they are also connected with knowledge; and 'sinnlicher Erkenntniskreis' (XXIV. 6) has nothing to do with 'sensuality', or even 'sensuousness', but means simply the 'sphere of empirical knowledge', i.e. knowledge derived through the senses (though not through the action of the senses alone), the only kind of *knowledge* available to man, who remains *Sinnenwesen* however much he may be *Vernunftwesen* too (XXIII. 7). *Sinnlichkeit* thus covers not only the life of sensation and appetite, but also the passive aspects of perceiving and knowing, together with the 'blinde', 'dumpfe', 'düstere' aspects of willing and doing (XXIII. 5; XXIV. 2 and 3);

2. the involuntary process of mental synthesis which organizes the data provided by the senses into the primary forms which we apprehend. In this sense, Schiller identifies it with *Natur* (XVIII. 4fn.) and opposes the unifying activity of both to the 'separating', analytical operations of *Verstand*. This is also the meaning in I. 4, where *Sinn*, prefixed by *innerer*, is opposed to *Verstand*, which is only able to understand the wholes presented to it directly by *Sinn* through breaking them down into their component parts. Here, too, *Sinn* is approximated to *Gefühl*; but whereas in XXIV. 6 it was *Gefühl* which pulled *Sinn* in the direction of passive sensation, here we have *Sinn* pulling *Gefühl* over in the direction of a mode of knowing, however diffused and vague this mode may be.

In a letter to the Duke of Augustenburg (21.xi.1793) Schiller stressed the point that *Sinn* cannot itself do the thinking, and so take the place of *Verstand*:

> Nicht als ob der Sinn jemals denken könnte; der Verstand wirkt hier ebenso gut, als bei dem schulgerechten Denker, nur dass die Regeln, nach denen er verfährt, nicht im Bewusstsein festgehalten werden, und dass wir in einem solchen Fall nicht die Verstandesoperation selbst, nur ihre Wirkung auf unsern Zustand durch ein Gefühl der Lust oder Unlust erfahren. Ehe das Gemüt sich Zeit nimmt, sein eigener Zuschauer zu sein, und von seinem Verfahren sich Rechenschaft zu geben, wird der innere Sinn affiziert, die Handlung geht in Leiden, der Gedanke in eine Empfindung über.
>
> (Jonas, iii. 396)

Readers may like to compare Coleridge on the 'Inner Sense' (*Biographia Literaria*, ch. xii; cf. I. A. Richards's comments in *Coleridge on Imagination*, London, 1934, pp. 44 f.) and Goethe's poem (*West-östlicher Divan*; JA v. 94) 'In tausend Formen magst du dich verstecken', in which the full meaning of *Sinn*, and its connexion with both feeling *and* knowing, is abundantly clear:

> Was ich mit äusserm Sinn, mit innerm kenne,
> Du Allbelehrende, kenn' ich durch dich.

In XIV. 4 (see Note) *Sinn* probably has both the above meanings; as it may well have in XIII. 4fn. §2, even though it is in the plural ('mit ruhigen, keuschen und offenen Sinnen'); for in his letter to Goethe (23.viii.1794) Schiller used an almost identical phrase with *Sinn* in the singular ('mit keuschem und treuem Sinn').

It is evident that in its fullest sense *Sinn* embraces the concept of *Sinnlichkeit*, but goes beyond it into the realms of moral feeling and judgement; and it is here that it links up with *Gesinnung*, a difficult word to translate, but important because it forms the feeling-bridge between knowing and doing. We have rendered it in one place (V. 5) by 'feeling and character', in another (XXIII. 2) by 'convictions', and in XXIII. 5 by 'sentiments'. For *Gesinnungen* are insights which have become so much part of the personality that they provide the springboard of action. They can be opposed to 'mere' intellectual enlightenment (with derogatory implications, as in V. 5) or to 'sheer' intellectual insight (with no derogatory implications, as in XXI. 4 or XXIII. 2).

Spieltrieb : *see* TRIEB.

Stimmung : *see* BESTIMMUNG.

Stoff : *see* MATERIE and INHALT.

Stofftrieb : *see* TRIEB.

Täuschung : *see* SCHEIN.

Trieb (Stofftrieb, Formtrieb, Spieltrieb) : according to Freud ('The Question of Lay Analysis', *Complete Psychological Works*, xx. 200), *Trieb* is a word which is the envy of other languages. Recalling that Schiller (in his poem, *Die Weltweisen*) had said that it was hunger and love that made the world go round, he went on to define *Triebe* as 'bodily needs inasmuch as they represent an incentive to mental activity'. Schiller himself used the word in a much wider sense, and it affords an excellent example of the way he will adapt to his own purposes, as a technical term (XII. 1), a word in common use, while still continuing to employ it in its ordinary, not clearly defined, sense. *Trieb* ('drive') was commonly used for the instincts of both man and beast (hunger, sex, &c.); but also for such higher activities as man's creativity (as in IX. 6, 'der göttliche Bildungstrieb'), or his intellectual, social, and moral strivings (as in V. 5, 'Trieb nach Verbesserung'; or IX. 6, 'der reine moralische Trieb'). Doubts as to the propriety of its use in certain contexts were, however, not uncommon. Goethe, f.i., in urbane dissent from Kant (*Critique of Judgement*, ii, § 81), objected to the extension of the term *Bildungstrieb* to inanimate nature by the contemporary biologist, Blumenbach, because of the implied 'anthropomorphization' of the processes of formation and metamorphosis (*Zur Botanik. Bildungstrieb*; JA xxxix. 335). And Schiller himself clearly had qualms about extending *Trieb* upwards, as it were, and using it 'of the urge to obey a law as well as of the urge to satisfy a need'. In a footnote to XII. 1 in the *Horen* (not included in his revised version) he justified his decision to do so on the grounds that, whenever we have to act on the imperatives of Pure Reason in a particular situation, then duties have to be transformed into drives. His decision to use the single term thus reflects the general psychological orientation of his moral philosophy—his desire to find a bridge from theoretical to practical enlightenment (IX. 1), from knowledge of general moral truths to the power to perform particular moral deeds; in short, his thesis, as defined in VIII. 3, that Truth will have to find a Drive to be her champion 'for drives are the only motive forces in the sensible world'. But it also reflects his own abiding conviction, and that of his century, that there is an intimate connexion between our spiritual and our animal nature—a conviction apparent in the rational controversies which challenged established doctrine by trying to prove that animals might well have souls, as in the attempts of empirical observers to discern in their behaviour anticipations of the higher activities of man (cf. Note to XXVII. 4).

The inevitable ambiguity which his decision involved is amply displayed in IV.1, i.e. long before he defines his own terms. And its disadvantages are attested by subsequent misunderstandings of his *Spieltrieb* (cf. p. clxxxvi, above). Körner (letter of 11.i.1795) drew his attention to the undesirability of a word which had such 'unedle Nebenideen'—it was, for instance, commonly used of gambling, of the 'Leidenschaft für das Lotteriewesen'. But Schiller preferred to retain it—even acknowledging the connexion with card-playing in an ironical footnote of the *Horen* (cf. Note to XV. 7)—precisely because of its connexions with ordinary language and ordinary activities, hoping to offset the inevitable disadvantages by the care he expended on distinguishing between such a 'physical', or 'material', play-drive and his own 'aesthetic' play-drive (XV. 5 f.; XXVII. 3 f.), a care which reflects his equally strong conviction that, for all the continuity between our animal and our spiritual nature, the difference is one of kind and not merely one of degree. And there is clear evidence, in such qualifications as 'inasmuch as they [*Stofftrieb* and *Formtrieb*] can be thought of as energies' (XIII. 6), or in his use of the more neutral *Tendenz* and *Prinzip* as variants of *Trieb* (XIX. 9; XXIV. 8), that he was fully aware that the borrowings we make from the physical sphere—'force', 'energy', 'drive'—to explain the dynamics of the psychical, are always in the nature of metaphor.

Where *Trieb* is used in Schiller's own technical sense, we have usually translated by 'drive'—though in the case of 'Trieb des Lebens' (XXIV. 8; not, incidentally, synonymous with the self-preservative instinct, though connected with it) euphony forbade it. Elsewhere we have variously rendered it by 'instinct' (V. 4), 'impulse' (IV. 1), and in one case (IX. 7, second occurrence), by 'desire'. The attentive reader will realize that no particular significance is to be attached to the variation of *sinnlicher Trieb* by *Stofftrieb* (in the *Horen* it had been *Sachtrieb*), or of *Formtrieb* by *vernünftiger Trieb*, and we have not always observed the distinction.

veredeln : *see* IDEE.

Vorstellung : *see* EINBILDUNGSKRAFT, EMPFINDUNG, IDEE, SINN.

Willkür : *see* FREIHEIT.

APPENDIXES

APPENDIX I

THE TEXT AND ITS STORY

IN May 1791 Schiller was granted a pension by a Danish admirer, Prince Friedrich Christian, Duke of Schleswig-Holstein-Augustenburg, to enable him, freed from the cares and worries of an unsalaried professorship, to pursue his historical and philosophical studies. In the course of 1793 he addressed to his patron—as a kind of progress report before casting his ideas into publishable form (cf. letter of 9.ii.1793)—a series of letters embodying his views on the problems brought to a head by the recent crisis of civilization, the French Revolution, and his own proposals for solving them by means of aesthetic education. The originals of these particular letters were destroyed by fire in January 1794. But the existence of the correspondence was well known, and in April 1875 the Oxford professor Max Müller, who had been in touch with the Duke's grandson, was able to publish a number of other letters from it in the *Deutsche Rundschau* (i. 7),[1] at the same time expressing the hope that further items might eventually turn up. This hope was fulfilled in the very next year, when no less than six of the 1793 letters actually came to light in the form of copies which had been made for circulation among the Duke's friends. They were published in the same Journal (ii. 7–9, 11) by A. L. J. Michelsen, and promptly compared with the *Letters on Aesthetic Education* by L. Urlichs (ibid. ii. 12). In 1884 the two 'versions', as they have often been called, were subjected to philological examination[2] by Karl Breul (*ZfdA* xxviii).

But to call Schiller's letters to the Duke a 'version' of his treatise is misleading. He certainly used his own drafts of them as a basis. But he more than doubled the length; and he organized them, according to a completely new plan, into a new whole (cf. letter to the Duke of 20.i.1795) which differs markedly from the 'real' letters even in those parts which cover roughly the same ground. This recasting took longer than he had anticipated, and the first instalment, Letters I–IX, was not ready for press until towards the end of 1794. It appeared as the second figure in 'the dance of *The Graces*' (as he put it to Goethe in his letter of 20.x.1794), i.e., in his newly founded Journal, *Die Horen*, in January 1795. Letters

---

[1] Cf. *The Life and Letters of the Rt. Hon*[ble] *Friedrich Max Müller*, ed. by his Wife. London, 1902, i. 503.

[2] According to Lutz (op. cit., p. 3), too narrowly 'philological'—though a little more attention to the meaning and function of 'words' might have provided a firmer foundation for his own radical and sweeping conclusions.

X–XVI followed in the February number; but XVII–XXVII had to wait until the vi. *Stück* in June of that year. Some five years later Schiller undertook a revision of the treatise for his *Kleinere prosaische Schriften: Aus mehrern Zeitschriften vom Verfasser selbst gesammelt und verbessert.* It consisted chiefly of pruning, especially in the footnotes, the shifting of a couple of important passages from footnote to text (XXVI. 5 and 13; XXVII. 12), the removal of the sub-title of the third instalment—'Die schmelzende Schönheit'—and of the motto from Rousseau which had introduced the first instalment. This revised version appeared in vol. iii (1801) sandwiched between his essays *Über das Erhabene* (hitherto unpublished) and *Über das Pathetische*, a clear indication of the context in which he intended it to be read (cf. above p. lx).

Editors thus had a choice of two versions—though more than one text of each version. Schiller's friend Körner took the second version for vol. viii. 1 (1813) of the first edition of the Collected Works. So did Joachim Meyer for the Collected Works of 1844 and 1860. Reinhold Köhler, by contrast, in vol. x (1871) of Goedeke's Historisch-kritische Ausgabe, chose to reprint the *Horen* version, correcting obvious misprints, collating it with the 1801 version and its reprint (editorially labelled B and b), with Körner's edition (K) and the two by Meyer (W and M), thus providing a full critical apparatus. All subsequent editors have reverted to the revised version of 1801. But it is not always easy to see just what their editorial policy has otherwise been, since they rarely indicate which text they have taken as their basis, or where and why they have departed from it.[1] Thus Walzel, editor of the authoritative Säkular-Ausgabe (xii, 1905), introduces in XV. 4, without comment, the phrase 'weil sie Vernunft ist' which Schiller dropped when he revised the *Horen* version and which was not reintroduced in K, W, or M; in XXV. 3, presumably following W and M, he restores the adjective *richtenden* before *Blick*, which Schiller, and Körner following him, had dropped; on the other hand, in I. 4—supported presumably by the recently published copies of Schiller's letters to the Duke (see Jonas, iii. 328)—he adopts Körner's emendation of *Aussprüche* to *Ansprüche* which both W and M had rejected. Leroux, who in his bilingual edition might seem to be following Walzel, since he tacitly accepts all three of the above readings, unaccountably includes in XVI. 2 three lines from the *Horen* which are not to be found in any other edition. And when the most recent English translator, Snell, declares (op. cit., pp. 19 f.) that he has followed the 'text' of the 1801 edition and 'from the *Graces* version retained only the motto from Rousseau', he can only be referring in a general way to

---

[1] The editors of NA xx, which appeared after we had prepared our own text, will presumably do so in the companion volume, xxi, which is not yet available as this goes to press.

the 1801 *version*; for the text he is following is obviously a modern edition
of it which includes some of the above insertions from the *Horen* too—
though not apparently Walzel's, since in I. 4 he writes 'utterances', presumably translating *Aussprüche*, while in XXIV. 4 he is either reading
ernstlich for *erstlich*, or else using a text such as Benno von Wiese's paper-
back (1948) which is marred by this as well as other unfortunate misprints and omissions.

We have taken as a basis the 1801 version revised by Schiller himself—
as being the 'Ausgabe letzter Hand'—preferring the reprint b because it
corrected many of the misprints of B (e.g., *nun* as against B's *nur* in the
first line of XX. 3; *Genüge leisten* as against *Genüge leiden*, XXVII. 4;
Trinkhörner as against *Trinkkörner*, XXVII. 5; *Beistimmung* as against
Bestimmung, XXVII. 11). In common with other editors, we have corrected the obvious misprints which remained, e.g., 'die Freiheit ihres
Geistes' (I. 3), 'die alles verneinende Natur' (VI. 5) and the *Verwirrung*
of X. 1, which Körner missed, though it had actually been listed as a
misprint in the *Horen* itself, and the sense obviously requires *Verirrung*.
From the *Horen* version we have restored the motto on the title-page—
not without misgivings, for although the first nine Letters are quite
obviously under the sign of Rousseau, the relation between 'la raison'
and 'le sentiment' is ultimately revealed as far more complex than this
motto perhaps suggests (cf. above p. liv). Otherwise we have restored
from it only the single phrase 'weil sie Vernunft ist' in XV. 4; we agree
that it clarifies the sense. To restore *richtenden* before *Blick* (XXV. 3), on
the other hand,[1] tends, we think, to obscure it, and for the reasons given
in our Note thereto. And, unlike many modern editors, we think Körner's
mind was moving on the wrong lines when in I. 4 (see our Note thereto)
he emended *Aussprüche*, of both the *Horen* and the 1801 version, to
Ansprüche (though he left *Ausspruch* [*der Vernunft*] in XV. 4); but we
have adopted his emendation of *musste* to *müsste* (XXIV. 6), which was
accepted by Goedeke though not by Walzel. We see no reason either to
follow Goedeke's suggestion and add a *nicht* at the end of XXVI. 5. On
the other hand we think it imperative, despite the evidence of all Schiller's
texts (or of Körner), to follow nineteenth-century editors (including
Walzel, though not Goedeke) and correct *dieselbe* to *dieselben* in XXVII. 2
(see Note).[2]

In order to remove unnecessary obstacles to understanding we have
normally modernized punctuation and spelling—though not in those cases
where Schiller's own seemed to act as pointers to his meaning. If we have
retained *auf Seiten, im Stande*, &c., it is because it is not always easy to
see whether he is using the noun in 'verblasster Bedeutung' or in its full

---

[1] As NA xx does too.
[2] In VII. 2 Goedeke errs in assigning the reading *Elementarstreit* to b.

and literal sense. And in the case of an author so preoccupied with reconciling antagonisms within the psyche, it often seemed appropriate to retain his separation of the prefix in such verbs as *entgegensetzen*. For similar reasons we have followed his predilection for capitals and spaced type to emphasize the meaning of words or the relation between them. And, despite Schiller's insistence to his publisher that for *Die Horen* 'deutsche Schrift der lateinischen vorzuziehen sei',[1] we ourselves have preferred the Latin type of his 1801 edition. Finally we thought it expedient to number the paragraphs within each Letter in order to facilitate reference to other editions and to our own Commentary and Glossary.

[1] Letter to Cotta, 2.x.1794.

APPENDIX II

TRANSLATORS AND TRANSLATION

Eine schlechte Übersetzung ist die schlechteste aller
Schlechtigkeiten, und eine gute Übersetzung kostet Zeit.

SCHILLER to KÖRNER, 4.X.1792

THE first English rendering of any part of the *Aesthetic Letters* seems to
have been the extracts from Letter VI which De Quincey appended to
his article on 'Superficial Knowledge' in the *London Magazine* of July
1824.[1] Seven years later Carlyle included a passage from XXIV. 5 in his
essay on Schiller in *Fraser's Magazine*.[2] Both make reasonably good sense,
as do the substantial quotations in H. G. Baynes's version of Jung's
Psychological Types,[3] E. F. Carritt's admittedly free renderings of snippets
from various Letters in his *Philosophies of Beauty*,[4] or Jane Bannard
Greene's new, and on the whole admirable, translation of five of the
Letters in a recent Schiller anthology.[5] And all these translators have
felicitous turns of phrase. Only closer inspection reveals to what extent
Schiller's language defeated them at times—even though they were free
to select their passages and to omit such difficulties as proved recalcitrant.
Thus Baynes[6] can miss the point by taking *welche* to be object instead of
subject in VI. 8, or obscure the sustained, and significant, imagery of a
passage by translating *zusammenziehen* as 'knit together' and *Kraft* by
'gift' in VI. 13; Carlyle replaces the Kantian exactitude of 'ihren Imperativ
unmittelbar auf den Stoff anwendet' by the vague generality 'mistook its
mode of application' (XXIV. 5); while De Quincey's expansion of 'die
Totalität der Gattung zusammen zu lesen' into 'spell out . . . the representative *word* (as it were) of the total species' (VI. 3) was misplaced
ingenuity, necessitated only by his having taken *lesen* in its more obvious
sense of 'to read', ignoring its primary, and here certainly predominant,
sense of 'gather together' or 'glean'.

Faced with the obligation of completeness, and some semblance of
fidelity to the letter, both the first English translators of the whole work—
Weiss (1844) and the anonymous translator in Bohn's Standard Library
(1875)—went sadly astray, the second in particular rarely deviating into

---

[1] *Collected Writings*, ed. D. Masson, x. 452 ff. Cf. P. Michelsen, loc. cit.
[2] *Critical and Miscellaneous Essays*, 1869, iii. 117.
[3] Ed. cit., pp. 87–163.
[4] Ed. cit., pp. 125–7.
[5] By Ungar; see Bibliography under 'Translations'.
[6] Jung, op. cit. (1), pp. 91, 96.

sense, and omitting all Schiller's footnotes into the bargain. An American translator, Charles J. Hempel, had meanwhile produced not only a more readable but a more accurate rendering (1861). He at least usually got his grammar right, and showed some grasp of Schiller's aesthetic theories— though for a 'medical' man (he was the translator, editor, or author of several works on the science of homoeopathy) he has some curious lapses when coping with Schiller's use of contemporary science. For a fourth English version we had to wait until the middle of this century—until Herbert Read's enthusiastic praise of the *Aesthetic Letters*[1] inspired Reginald Snell to undertake the task anew (1954). In the meantime the Strasbourg Germanist, Robert Leroux, had produced an admirable French version for his bilingual edition of 1943. The *Schiller-Bibliographie* of Vulpius lists further translations: three in Spanish, three in Japanese, and one each in Italian, Czech, Swedish, and Hebrew, all of them published between 1915 and 1954. We are not competent to pronounce on the merits or demerits of any of these.

Snell's translation is a great improvement on those of his English predecessors. He has avoided their grosser errors; but errors still remain. His version certainly contains nothing so incongruous as Weiss's rendering of Schiller's definition of aesthetic semblance (XXVI. 11): 'Nur so weit er aufrichtig ist . . . ist der Schein ästhetisch', which became 'Show is aesthetic . . . only so far as it is upright'! Nor anything which betrays such an ingenuously ingenious use of the dictionary (or was he using a French translation?) as Bohn's 'The way to divinity . . . is open to him in every *direction*' as a rendering of 'Der Weg zu der Gottheit . . . ist ihm aufgetan in den *Sinnen*' (XI. 7). But there are mistakes of gender in Snell (*das Band* treated as though it were masculine in XXIV. 2); and of case ('den das Bedürfnis der Geschlechtsliebe aufdrückte' becomes 'which the needs of sexual love imprinted on him' in III. 2); there is also confusion of near-homonyms (*wagt* read as *wägt* in III. 3, first occurrence), of subject and object (as in XII. 1, where *welche* is taken to be accusative), of subjective and objective genitive (as in I. 4, where 'the torture of Art' —Hempel made the same mistake—suggests that art is the *object* of torture, whereas 'die Marter der Kunst' really means that artificial techniques are the *source* of torture, i.e., that nature and human nature are put on the rack by chemist and philosopher); there is misprision of idiomatic constructions—'ihn an etwas anweisen' becomes 'assigns something to him' instead of 'refers him to something' (III. 3); *dazu* in XXVII. 10 is taken to refer to a specific antecedent ('schöne Vorstellung') instead of to the general end or purpose defined in the previous clause.

Because of Schiller's heavily pronominal style—he is addicted to sustained periods containing a series of parallel and antithetical clauses—

<hr />

[1] In *Education through Art*, ed. cit., p. 278.

the problem of finding the right antecedent to an often confusing number of personal and demonstrative pronouns is a recurrent one. It is fatally easy to refer them to the wrong one. Nor is it always a simple question of grammar. If Snell refers *jenen* to *Sinnlichkeit* (XXIV. 6) or *diesen* to *Form* (XXII. 5), these are plain grammatical mistakes. But in XV. 5 we have to go back nine lines to find the right antecedent for *sie*, which is *Schönheit* and not any of the other five intervening feminine nouns (to which antecedent Snell's 'them' is supposed to refer is not clear); and in XXIII. 4 *die letztere* refers not, as Leroux assumes, to the immediately preceding feminine noun, *Form*, but to the second of the two *Bestimmungen* with which the whole paragraph is concerned, and if the thought is to be brought out clearly, the translator has here no option but to repeat the noun.

An altogether different kind of error, and one common to most translators, derives from the fact that although we tend, and with justification, to speak in general terms of 'knowing a language', there are in any one language as many 'languages' to know as there have been periods in which to write, subjects to be written about, even authors to write about them. The eighteenth century, often and rightly referred to as the beginning of our own age, is at the same time strangely remote from us. The French Revolution was destructive of the past not only in the social and political spheres, and Schiller could still take for granted in his readers a prompt response to traditions which have long been inaccessible to us except through an effort of the historical imagination. Thus when Schiller opposes *Täuschung* to *Wahrheit* in an aesthetic context (IX. 4), his contemporaries would immediately recognize the age-old theory of art as illusion; and, though they might also hear echoes of innumerable controversies about the relation of Art to Lying, it would not have occurred to them to imagine, as Snell does, that Schiller was here maintaining that 'truth lives on in the midst of *deception*' or, as Leroux has it, 'dans l'illusion des hommes', or even, as Hempel suggests, 'in fiction'. At all costs the translator must avoid any derogatory turn of phrase which would make this one sentence at odds with the tenor of the whole paragraph, indeed of the whole treatise. The ambiguity of language in this period, which saw the beginnings of a need for technical terms in many different spheres, raises enormous problems of interpretation. And nowhere more than in the field of aesthetics. Many of these have been discussed in the Glossary under *Kunst*, which affords an excellent example of the lability a word displays when it is already in the process of being specified but still retains its more general meaning too. The 'indetermination' of this noun in turn affects the adjective *schön*. This is rarely, if ever in this treatise, used to distinguish one kind of art from another—e.g., beautiful art from, say, 'characteristic' or grotesque art—but always to distinguish artefacts whose function is aesthetic from other products of man's skill and ingenuity. Even in XXII. 5 the locution 'in einem wahrhaft schönen Kunstwerk' is not quite as simple as it sounds: for the question there raised is not the *degree* of beauty in what we nowadays would call 'a work of art', but rather the *threshold* of beauty, i.e., whether an artefact has achieved the status of an aesthetic object at all; and 'successful' is perhaps the least misleading translation of *schön* here—though 'aesthetic' would be the most exact, did it not to modern ears result in a kind of tautology. Frequently the function of this adjective is that of a noun in the genitive, most obviously when it precedes *Künstler*. But not always: 'Die schöne Mitteilung' in XXVII. 10 is obviously not a finely phrased *communiqué*. But neither is it, as Snell translates, 'the communication of the Beautiful'. It is rather 'the aesthetic mode of communication'.

But, as we have said, it is not just a question of knowing 'the language' of this particular period; it is also a question of knowing the particular field of ideas and the prevailing climate of thought. Neither Hempel nor Leroux, for instance—not even Carritt who enjoys the freedom of paraphrase—brings out the notion of 'distance' which is inherent in Schiller's account of the secret of artistic creation and the nature of aesthetic effect in XXII. 5. A general awareness of his characteristic modification of the classical rule of *éloignement* into a psychological principle would surely have prevented them from translating *zurückzwingen* as 'subdue', *endiguer*, or 'master'. For what is involved here is the 'forcing back' of the raw material, or subject-matter, of art, its removal to a distance, so that it no longer impinges too violently on the beholder, or tempts him to become directly involved with it. Of course over-awareness of such general implications can, paradoxically enough, also lead to a misreading of the text. Thus E. M. Wilkinson,[1] in her eagerness to bring out this notion of distance, falsely accused Leroux of getting his antecedents mixed, and herself offered an alternative translation in which, by referring *jenen* to *Betrachter* and *diesen* to *Stoff*, the beholder was forced back instead of the subject-matter—a solution which is possible as regards grammar, and just possible as regards sense, but totally unnecessary. For whether it is the material that is 'forced back', or the beholder, amounts to much the same thing as far as Schiller's theory of distance is concerned. What has to be ensured is the freedom of the psyche. And the possibility of ensuring it—as Schiller makes abundantly clear—will always be dependent upon *two* factors: an artist's power to assimilate even the most seductive or intractable theme into his form; but also—and this is something not entirely within the control of even the most supreme master— the tendency of some particular beholder to become involved with a certain theme in a way which is not aesthetic.

Thus, however much the translator may know about the background, the controlling principle must always be the letter of the text before him.

[1] Loc. cit. (3), pp. 49–51.

Or rather, it is a question of reciprocal control: general awareness of ideas must be controlled by fidelity to linguistic particulars—but also vice versa. In XXVI. 7, for example, the tenor of the preceding Letters ought to be sufficient to tell us that 'das Vermögen zur Form überhaupt' cannot just be the power of *producing* forms as 'mise en forme' (Leroux) implies, but must include, if not primarily refer to, the power of *perceiving* them. Here, one might say, there is no need to 'go outside the text'—so long as one is alive to a sufficiently wide sense-unit. But in some cases nothing less than the context of the whole century must be brought to bear. In XXVI. 14 (see our Note thereto), would not less un-Schillerian, less essentially romantic, preconceptions about the dignity of Imagination, and the high seriousness of Art, have saved both Snell and Leroux from the temptation to reverse Schiller's sense at the end of the paragraph? And to introduce an irrelevant 'dwells' when translating 'wo er in eigener Hütte still mit sich selbst und, sobald er heraustritt, mit dem ganzen Geschlechte spricht', as they do in XXVI. 2, is to ignore the eighteenth century's conviction that, since language is the mark of man, the growth of self-awareness will inevitably depend on his power to commune, with himself no less than with others. Again, no eighteenth-century reader would have missed—and the translator must not miss it either—the significance of either noun in 'Zögling der Kunst' (V. 5), i.e., the ward, or creature, of civilization, not 'the disciple of Art' (Snell). Both here and in IX. 4 we are within the orbit of Kant's definition of *Aufklärung* as 'emancipation from a tutelage that man has brought upon himself', and in neither case is the notion of disciple appropriate, though in the first of these passages we ourselves thought it undesirable to preserve the legal associations by translating as 'ward'. And familiarity with Rousseau's political theory would certainly prevent any such solecism as both Snell and Greene perpetrate in III. 2, when they let 'natural man' exchange a state of 'social contracts' for a state of freedom instead of vice versa. Even Hempel, who gets the grammar right here, obscures the allusion to Rousseau by translating *Verträge* as 'a compact'.

Yet though all translators be traitors, translation—as Joseph Needham recently observed[1]—has at least the merit of forcing decisions about meaning, provisional though they may have to be.[2] It compels the solution of problems of which the native scholar, his linguistic sensibility dulled by long familiarity with normal usage, may be entirely oblivious. Whether, or how, a native scholar understands the difficulties of a text such as this, can only be inferred from the occasional emendation, comment or

[1] *Science and Civilisation in China*, iii, Cambridge, 1959, p. xlv.

[2] The uncompromising tone in which we have argued for our own decisions, either here or in our Commentary, does not reflect any doubts we may have about their inevitably provisional nature. It springs from our belief that the likeliest way to provoke fruitful dissension is through an unambiguous statement of one's present conviction.

paraphrase, perhaps even from faulty proof-reading. The result in this case is not without comfort for translators. If they on occasion get their antecedents mixed, so after all did Böhm (op. cit., p. 30): it is presumably because he referred *jene* to *Philosophen* and *diese* to *Künstler* at the end of IX. 3 (instead of *jene* to 'die Philosophen wie die Künstler' and *diese* to 'Wahrheit und Schönheit') that he was able to accuse Schiller of ejecting science from his ideal of culture.[1] And if both Snell and Leroux find it necessary at one point (XXVI. 14) to reverse Schiller's meaning by the tacit introduction of a superfluous negative, so after all did the great Goedeke (op. cit. x. 371) in another paragraph of the same Letter (XXVI. 5). Lutz does not inspire confidence in his powers of interpreting linguistic structures when he reverses Schiller's meaning by paraphrasing *absondern* (III. 5: 'Es käme also darauf an, von dem physischen Charakter die Willkür und von dem moralischen die Freiheit abzusondern . . .') first by *ausschalten* (op. cit., p. 170) and then by *unterdrücken* (ibid., p. 172). Had he taken as his context a large enough unit of utterance,[2] he might have recalled XXV. 5, where *Absonderung* is clearly a synonym of *Abstraktion*, and the latent image quite unmistakably the chemical-alchemical process of extraction, by distillation or other means.[3] Urlichs (*Deutsche Rundschau*, ii. 12, p. 378) was so bemused by his discovery that much of Schiller's prose in this treatise falls naturally into distichs that, in his attempt to exhibit this, he could perpetrate such senseless misquotations as 'zeigen sich die Philosophen um den [instead of 'wie die'] Künstler geschäftig' (IX. 3) and 'seinen Stoff kann die Laune entbehren', instead of 'entehren' (IX. 4); while Ernst Müller could pass such obvious misprints as 'die alles verneinende Natur' (VI. 5) and *Entwurf* instead of *Einwurf* (XIX. 8).

* * *

But perhaps where we differ most from our predecessors is in our conviction that only by close adherence to the intricacies of Schiller's rhetorical style can his meaning be fully conveyed. It is in our view misguided to aim at a 'plain prose' version in the hope of thereby uncovering his essential 'message'—breaking down the complex structure of his sustained periods into simpler units, conscientiously eschewing German inversion in favour of 'normal' English word-order, ignoring his figures and configurations. Our own guiding principle has been to press the likeness to the original as far as it will go without flagrantly offending against English usage. We have done this not in order to give some superficial impression of our author's style, nor yet because of any cherished theories

---

[1] Or did he not grasp that science and philosophy are here synonymous?

[2] Cf. L. W. Forster's Introduction to *Aspects of Translation* (*Studies in Communication*, 2), London, 1958, pp. 11 ff.

[3] For further discussion of these, and other, misreadings by Lutz and Böhm see pp. xlv ff. and lxii ff. above.

concerning the superior merits of a 'contemporary', as opposed to a 'modern', translation. We have done it primarily and above all because in these Letters the manner is of the essence of the matter, and their form a function of their aim; because in this particular treatise at any rate—whether it is true of Schiller's other treatises would be a matter for investigation—the rhetorical figures, far from being the 'merely stylized exercises in declamation' that Friedrich Schlegel dubbed them,[1] are a vitally determining factor in the establishment of meaning, to a certain extent even the vehicle of meaning.

But the retention of this rhetorical style also has practical advantages for the translator. Consider, for instance, the problem of the relation between the pronouns, or the possessive adjectives, and their antecedents which proved such a stumbling-block to some of our predecessors. The English translator, deprived of the advantage of gender, is often hard put to it to make this relation unambiguously clear, even if he has understood it. We ourselves have had recourse to various devices. Wherever possible we avoided repetition of the noun, since this would have made Schiller's style sound more heavily substantival than it really is. We preferred to exploit the possibilities of 'she' and 'her'—even at the risk of seeming to endorse Schiller's tendency to anthropomorphize Nature or to personify such abstractions as Truth, Beauty, and Freedom. Nor did we hesitate to turn a singular into a plural in the interests of clarity. Thus in V. 4 we are well aware that it is of human nature that Schiller speaks, and not of human beings—'darf man ihn [den Staat] tadeln, dass er die Würde der menschlichen Natur aus den Augen setzte, solange es noch galt, ihre Existenz zu verteidigen?' But to translate by '*its* existence' might well imply that the State's concern was for its own survival (in earlier translations that is just what it did sound like), whereas 'their' makes it clear that it was for the survival of its citizens. We also followed Schiller's lead in employing visual aids: our spaced type corresponds exactly to his; but our use of capitals—except in the case of 'State', where we have throughout reserved the capital for the political entity—is governed solely by *ad hoc* requirements of emphasis and clarity, and to the casual reader may well seem arbitrary. But when all else failed, our retention of Schiller's highly symmetrical sentence-patterns—which exercise far stricter syntactical and formal control over the relations between the sense-units than we are accustomed to in prose today—often enabled us to point the correct antecedent in an unambiguous way.

Like any other philosophical text, Schiller's makes conflicting claims upon the translator. Is he to aim at a 'philosophical' translation, which shall bring over the subtleties of the argument even at the cost of stylistic awkwardness? Or at a 'literary' translation which shall read well even at

---

[1] In a letter to his brother, 17.viii.1795.

the cost of philosophical exactitude? We ourselves have opted now for the one, now for the other. But our decisions have not been quite as pragmatic and unprincipled as might at first sight appear. If we have not been consistent in our rendering of Kantian terms, it is not primarily because we were prepared to sacrifice philosophy to English usage. It is because, as we have explained in our Introduction, Schiller's strategy with the terms and concepts he borrows is quite different from the strategy of the author from whom he borrows them. When translating Kant himself it is imperative to reflect the distinctions he made because his chief aim was the making of such distinctions. Thus Meredith,[1] having decided on 'soul' for *Geist*, had no choice but to find another word for *Seele* even if it was something as clumsy as 'psychic substance'. Whereas we could legitimately feel free to vary the translation of either of these two words, using 'mind' not only for *Geist*, but also for *Seele*, *Verstand*—and in VI. 3 (because of the contrast with 'matter') even for *Vernunft*—though on the rare occasions when the Kantian distinction between *Vernunft* and *Verstand* is crucial (VI. 12; XXIV. 6) we have naturally been careful to preserve it. And in XXIII. 7fn. § 1 we had no compunction in rendering both *Gemüt* and *Geist* by 'nature' (cf. Glossary under *Geist*). We are convinced that such a policy rarely does violence to Schiller's intention, since his main concern is with the relations between the two 'sides' of the psyche, and not with the Kantian distinctions between the 'faculties' which inhabit either 'side'. In his usage the terms on either side are more or less interchangeable; the one important thing is not to get those of the one series mixed with those of the other—as Leroux does in XIV. 6, when he inadvertently replaces 'material' by 'moral', or as Snell does in XII. 1, when he reverses the roles of *Person* and *Materie*. On the contrary, we are convinced that, in the case of these Kantian terms, a rigorous consistency might itself do violence to Schiller's intention, by restricting the wide range of meaning he is prepared to allow to some of them. Thus Snell errs not so much by his choice of 'perception' for *Empfindung*, as by his persistent use of it throughout, even in contexts where it is positively misleading.

There are, of course, cases where we *have* let the claims of English usage influence us towards a 'literary' translation at the cost of philosophical exactitude. Our occasional translation of *Seelenkraft* (or *Denkkraft*) by 'faculty' instead of 'force', for instance, might seem to commit Schiller to a static 'faculty-psychology' to which he certainly would not have subscribed. In other cases we feel that our preference for the 'literary' solution has involved no loss of philosophical precision. Thus, to have rendered 'glückselige Tage' by 'happy days' (XVI. 2) would have been insufferable in view of the present triviality of this phrase. 'Happy

[1] Op. cit., p. 289.

hours' certainly represents a departure from the letter; but not from the spirit of the passage. For what Schiller is here concerned with is not the size of the time-unit, but only the contrast between a plurality of experienced 'happinesses' and the singular abstraction, Happiness. The claims of philosophy are met if the translator preserves intact his series of concrete plurals and singular abstracts. Within each contrasting pair of the series, however, he may legitimately allow the claims of 'literary' translation to become paramount. In the case of 'der innere Mensch' the choice was not so clear! To have risked a facetious response was out of the question. In XIII. 4fn. § 3 there was less chance of this happening because 'inner' is separated from 'man' by an adjectival phrase. Elsewhere we had recourse to paraphrase—'inwardly' (IV. 5), 'within' (VI. 7), 'mind and character' (X. 3). We don't *think* that we have thereby forfeited a hypostasization which is central to Schiller's thought—as we certainly should have done had we paraphrased out of existence his 'ideal man, which every human being carries within him' (IV. 2)—but we can't be sure.

But sometimes it is absolutely imperative to keep the same term consistently throughout, and even to risk a measure of quaintness in the translation in order to show how Schiller's thought is organized round certain key-concepts.[1] This is the case with *Person* and *Zustand* (the latter we should sometimes have liked to translate by 'attribute'; but the theological overtones would have been stronger than is warranted, and the grammatical associations unwarranted altogether). And it is certainly the case with *Stofftrieb*, *Formtrieb*, *Spieltrieb*. Either 'play-impulse' or 'play-instinct' might have sounded more euphonious than 'play-drive'. But an impulse is something momentary and fleeting; and both 'impulse' and 'instinct' are reminiscent of biological play-theories quite different from Schiller's own.

And there are other conflicting claims that this text makes upon the translator, claims which sometimes cut across the above conflict between 'philosophy' and English usage. More than most philosophers, Schiller often exploits his linguistic medium in a way that only poets are wont to do. Must the translator then be content with rendering the discursive meaning of the statements? Or should he try to render, or at least evoke, significances opened up by purely formal relations? Occasionally he can do both: the significant play on *ergreift/begreift* in XIII. 3, for instance, can be exactly paralleled by 'apprehend'/'comprehend'. The advisability of retaining the sound-look relation in *Luxus/Laxität* in XXVII. 3 is far more debatable. It certainly suggests possible, and fascinating, connexions between superabundance, on the one hand, and lack of specific

---

[1] Cf. D. J. Furley, 'Translation from Greek Philosophy' in *Aspects of Translation*, ed. cit., p. 54.

purpose, on the other. But Schiller's more obviously exact meaning might have been more unambiguously conveyed by paraphrasing *Laxität* as 'indeterminacy of ends and purposes'. In the case of the cognate pair *Vernunft/Vernünftelei* in VI. 1, there was no doubt about the choice to be made. The retention of the formal relation is imperative since it reflects in embryo the most characteristic movement of Schiller's thought in this treatise: the notion of returning to an original state of grace by the right use of that *same* faculty, the wrong use of which caused us to fall away from it. To play on the *use* and *abuse* of reason brings this out better, we think, than any of the dictionary meanings of *Vernünftelei*—'sophistry', 'subtilization', or 'over-subtle reasoning'.

Perhaps the quality most required in translating a text such as this is agility of recall. The mind has to be here, there, and everywhere, simultaneously taking the single word as unit and the whole work as unit, trying to do justice to the details of particular formal relations and to the essentially circular movement of the larger structure, alive to the hidden metaphors at particular points and to the all-pervading influence of a certain type of imagery. Thus in XXII. 4 the translator must be alive to the alchemical-chemical connexion between *steigern* and *Veredlung*, even though these two words are separated by almost a page of print; he must also be prepared to bring out the connexion between them, even though the word 'sublimate' may pull the reader up short. Nowhere is such agile recall more necessary than in the last Letter, where the language itself, and increasingly towards the end, becomes a kind of *Steigerung* or intensification of what has gone before. Schiller here relies on the mere mention of a single word or concept to evoke trains of thought and sets of associations which have been fully established in earlier Letters. And at this point, where we have sometimes ventured elucidatory paraphrase, we may perhaps justly be charged with having exceeded the translators' task, which is to be as clear as the original—but no clearer.

APPENDIX III

VISUAL AIDS

I

OUR first illustration is intended to exhibit three things: (1) the perfect symmetry of Schiller's periods even at their most sustained and most complex (discussed in our Introduction, pp. lxviii ff. above); (2) the bringing into being by deductive argument, and by the rhetorical figures of antithesis and chiasmus, a 'third thing', the *Spieltrieb*, which, though not an independent basic drive, does actually manifest itself in experience through a qualitative change in all our being and doing (cf. above, pp. lxx, xcvi); (3) the importance of the rhetoric and symmetry in determining the meaning of difficult passages.

Dem Stofftrieb wie dem Formtrieb ist es mit ihren Forderungen ernst, weil der eine sich, beim Erkennen, auf die Wirklichkeit, der andre auf die Notwendigkeit der Dinge bezieht; weil, beim Handeln, der erste auf Erhaltung des Lebens, der zweite auf Bewahrung der Würde, beide also auf Wahrheit und Vollkommenheit gerichtet sind. *Aber das Leben wird gleichgültiger, sowie die Würde sich einmischt, und die Pflicht nötigt nicht mehr, sobald die Neigung zieht*; ebenso nimmt das Gemüt die Wirklichkeit der Dinge, die materiale Wahrheit, freier und ruhiger auf, sobald solche der formalen Wahrheit, dem Gesetz der Notwendigkeit, begegnet, und fühlt sich durch Abstraktion nicht mehr angespannt, sobald die unmittelbare Anschauung sie begleiten kann. Mit einem Wort: indem es mit Ideen in Gemeinschaft kommt, verliert alles Wirkliche seinen Ernst, weil es klein wird, und indem es mit der Empfindung zusammentrifft, legt das Notwendige den seinigen ab, weil es leicht wird.

(XV. 5; our italics)

In the above passage there are some twenty-five substantival entities, all referring to the activities or objectives of the psyche; *Gemüt*, as the total psyche, subsumes them all; the rest, as our first diagram shows, are arranged strictly in pairs. Concepts which are only implicitly there are shown in square brackets: thus *Spiel*, which is the result of one aspect of our existence (*das Wirkliche*) becoming *klein*, and the other (*das Notwendige*) becoming *leicht*. What Schiller does is, first of all, to present the normal state of the psyche when it is involved in wholly 'serious' activity, whether this be intellectual or practical. Then, with the sentence beginning 'Aber das Leben . . .', he begins to let the two sides of our nature interact and temper each other, first in the mode of doing, then in the mode of knowing.

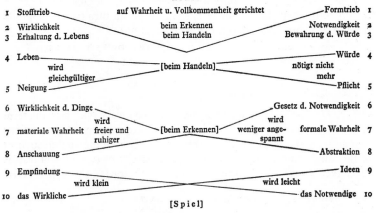

In the next diagram we have tried to make the symmetry of this same period more visual still by reducing the concepts to a kind of notation. S stands for *Stofftrieb* and all the concepts which belong to that 'side' (cf. above, p. lxviii), F for *Formtrieb* and all the concepts belonging to the other 'side'. Nouns in apposition are shown in lower case. Concepts which are only implicitly there, are again shown in square brackets.

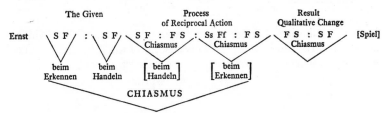

The sentence which is italicized in the above passage is one that has given rise to conflicting translations and interpretation. These diagrams, together with the Note in our Commentary, should show how we arrived at our own.

II

The following triangles are an attempt to represent visually the different types of synthesis employed by Schiller and the relation between them (cf. the discussion in our Introduction, pp. lxxxv ff., above).

Type I. In this, familiar, type the term at the apex is different from either of those at the base or contains them both:

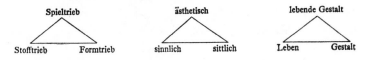

Type II. Here a single concept is polarized by qualifying adjectives. A feature of this type is that the term at the apex can turn into its opposite (as in XV. 9 and XIX. 12; cf. our Notes thereto).

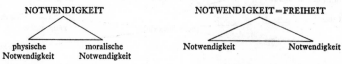

Type III. In this type, which we have termed binary synthesis, the term at the apex is the same as one of those at the base, but is printed in capitals to indicate that it is a higher concept, embracing both the limited concept of the same name and its opposite. The mark of this type of synthesis is that either of the terms at the base can move to the top (cf. above, p. lxxxvi).

The following are examples of this same type of synthesis in Goethe's thought:

With the following diagram we have tried to illustrate what Schiller appears to have had in mind with his concept of the progressive refinement, or ennoblement (*Veredlung*), of the psyche (cf. above, p. lxxxviii).

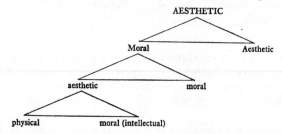

But it is important to realize that a horizontal extension is also necessary: the aesthetic and the moral (intellectual) can so interact that now the Aesthetic, now the Moral, goes to the apex of the triangle.

APPENDIX IV

ON THE IMPULSE TO INTRODUCE REDUNDANT NEGATIVES INTO LETTER XXVI

WE have stated in 'The Text and its Story' (above, p. 336; cf. also 'Translators and Translation', p. 343) that we saw no reason to adopt Goedeke's proposed emendation to the last sentence but one of XXVI. 5. A sixteen-year old *Gymnasiast* had pointed out that the sense required the addition of a *nicht*, and in a signed footnote (because the editor of that particular volume of the *Sämmtliche Schriften*, Reinhold Köhler, did not agree?) Goedeke declared that in any edition for popular use he would certainly incorporate the negative. In our Note to XXVI. 5 we have explained why we think Schiller's text makes sense without it; and if we revert to the point again here it is because vol. xx of the *Nationalausgabe* has meanwhile appeared with this emendation, though without—in either apparatus or commentary (vol. xxi)—offering reasons for its adoption or, as far as we can discover, making any reference to its source.

By a curious coincidence, as we pointed out some years ago,[1] both the latest English and the latest French translator felt a similar need to reverse Schiller's sense in another paragraph of that very same letter, XXVI. 14. Again we have given our reasons for diverging from their decision in our Commentary; and the purpose of this further Appendix is not to reiterate the details of either argument, but to suggest that the coincidence is perhaps not so curious after all, and turns on very large issues indeed.

For in both cases the impulse to reverse the sense of his text is provoked by Schiller's concept of *Schein*. In XXVI. 5 the point at issue is the relation of semblance to reality, in XXVI. 14 the relation of semblance to reality and morality. Why, from three different directions—German, French, English—and quite independently, this impulse to reverse the sense on this particular issue? Surely because it is felt, more or less obscurely, that to assign to aesthetic semblance the status, value, and function that Schiller's text actually does, is on the one hand to degrade truth and morality, on the other to degrade art itself. But Schiller's strategy here, as elsewhere (and he states it quite explicitly in XXVI. 9 and 14), is to ensure the value of all three by making the strictest possible distinctions about the nature and function of semblance. Only if it is clearly and sharply distinguished from the real, the true, and the moral, accorded its own particular function and its own *kind* of respect, can

---

[1] Wilkinson, loc. cit. (3), p. 52. In the English version of that article Köhler was mistakenly saddled with responsibility for the proposed emendation.

the distinctive value of any of these intimately related areas of experience be preserved. Once we start denigrating aesthetic semblance because it is neither palpably real nor demonstrably true (the *only* point of affinity between extreme stupidity and extreme intelligence is, as he claims in XXVI. 4–5, a tendency to do this) we risk losing precisely what art—and all that art—can give us. But once we start stepping up our expectations in the wrong direction, demanding of art what only truth or morality can provide, we lose all that it can give us too (XXVI. 14). And in either case, Schiller is arguing, it is not only art and aesthetic semblance that suffer, but the values with which they are confused. And in either case, of course, ourselves.

He hoped by his arguments to put an end to some of this confusion. It was a vain hope. The pendulum has gone on—and still goes on—swinging between either/or under various names: didacticism or aestheticism; naturalism or art for art's sake; social commitment or the symbolism of *poésie pure*; between those, whether of existentialist or Marxist persuasion, who are for art which is directly *engagé* and those who are for art which achieves its end via distance and the indirect method. The problem is a perennial one because it is a real one. Because art is, rightly, felt to be at the heart of life; and yet—and no less rightly—felt to be useless, without purpose, indifferent, purely gratuitous play and delight. Schiller's concern was precisely to relate these two intuitively right 'feelings' in a way that made logical sense. His arguments about semblance in Letter XXVI are in perfect—even verbal—accord with those about play, or about the art and feeling of the Greeks, in Letter XV. If the former are rejected, the latter must be too. As a practising artist he is naturally for semblance. As a thinker he is for it too; but only in the framework of the careful qualifications and distinctions with which, out of an artist's bitter experience, he hedges it around. In one of his original letters to his patron[1] he had bracketed art and taste together with religion—not because he intended the former to be a surrogate of the latter, but because, as he said, they were both far too easily and too often made a surrogate for true virtue. What he is against is surrogates of any kind. Just as he is against transgression of frontiers, confusion of functions. To reverse his meaning in a Letter which turns on nothing else but the issue of keeping distinct things which are easily confounded, yet intimately related, is not only to offend his spirit; it is to try to 'sell' his doctrine by leaving out its central tenet. It is all very well to speak of the heritage and challenge of his theory of aesthetic education. But it stands or falls by his concepts of play and semblance. If we try to put it into practice without these, we have only ourselves to blame if it fails.

[1] 3.xii.1793; Jonas, iii. 409.

BIBLIOGRAPHY

THE appearance of two exhaustive *Schiller-Bibliographien*, by Vulpius (1893–1958) and by Raabe and Bode (1959–61), relieves the scholar of a great burden of compilation. The material they contain is supplemented by Pick's Bibliography of Schiller in England (1787–1960). We, therefore, have confined ourselves to listing such works as are mentioned in our text or seemed specially relevant to the subject and period. Within each section, the items are arranged alphabetically according to author or editor.

I. WORKS OF REFERENCE

A. BIBLIOGRAPHIES OF SCHILLER

Rechenschaftsberichte des schwäbischen Schillervereins. Marbach u. Stuttgart, 1895–1939.
Schiller. Ein Verzeichnis der neueren und der wichtigsten älteren Ausgaben, Biographien, Würdigungen und Inszenierungen mit Einführung in Schillers Hauptwerke. V.E.B. Verlag f. Buch- u. Bibliothekswesen, Leipzig, 1956.
Friedrich Schiller 1759–1959. Deutscher Kulturbund, Berlin, 1959.
FAMBACH, O.: *Schiller und sein Kreis in der Kritik ihrer Zeit*. Die wesentlichen Rezensionen aus d. periodischen Literatur bis zu Schillers Tod, begl. v. Schillers u. seiner Freunde Äusserungen zu deren Gehalt. Anh.: *Bibliographie der Schiller-Kritik bis zu Schillers Tod*. Berlin, 1957. (*Ein Jahrhundert deutscher Literaturkritik 1750–1850*. Bd. ii.)
PAULSEN, W.: 'Friedrich Schiller 1955–1959. Ein Literaturbericht.' *Jb. d. deutschen Schillergesellschaft*, vi, 1962.
PICK, R.: *Schiller in England 1787–1960*. A Bibliography compiled by the staff of the Institute of Germanic Languages and Literatures, University of London. *PEGS* xxx, 1961.
RAABE, P. u. BODE, INGRID: 'Schiller-Bibliographie 1959–1961.' *Jb. d. deutschen Schillergesellschaft*, vi, 1962.
VULPIUS, W.: *Schiller Bibliographie 1893–1958*. Weimar, 1959.

B. DICTIONARIES AND LEXICA

ADELUNG, J. C.: *Versuch eines vollständigen grammatisch-kritischen Wörterbuches der Hochdeutschen Mundart*. Leipzig, 1774–86; 1793–1801².
CAMPE, J. H.: *Wörterbuch zur Erklärung und Verdeutschung der unserer Sprache aufgedrungenen fremden Ausdrücke*. Berlin, 1801.
DE BRIE, G. A.: *Bibliographia Philosophica 1934–1945*. Bruxelles, 1950. i: *Bibliographia Historiae Philosophiae*.
EISLER, R.:
  (1) *Wörterbuch der philosophischen Begriffe*. Historisch-quellenmässig bearb. v. R. Eisler. Berlin, 1904².
  (2) *Kant-Lexikon*. Berlin, 1930².

LANGEN, A.: *Der Wortschatz des deutschen Pietismus.* Tübingen, 1954.

OETINGER, F. C.: *Des Württembergischen Prälaten Fr. Chr. Oetinger Biblisches Wörterbuch dem Teller'schen Wörterbuch und Anderer falschen Schrifterklärungen entgegengesetzt.* 1776. Neu hrsg. v. J. Hamberger. Stuttgart, 1849.

RUDOLPH, L.: *Schiller-Lexicon. Erläuterndes Wörterbuch zu Schillers Dichterwerken.* Unter Mitwirkung v. K. Goldbeck. Berlin, 1869.

WERNLY, JULIA: *Prolegomena zu einem Lexikon der ästhetisch-ethischen Terminologie Friedrich Schillers.* Leipzig, 1909. (Untersuchungen zur neueren Sprach- u. Literatur-Geschichte, N.F. iv.)

II. PRIMARY SOURCES

A. SCHILLER

1. Collected Works

BLUMENTHAL u. WIESE v.: *Schillers Werke.* Nationalausgabe. Begr. v. J. Petersen u. H. Schneider. Hrsg. v. Lieselotte Blumenthal u. B. v. Wiese. Weimar, 1943– [in progress].

GOEDEKE: *Schillers sämmtliche Schriften.* Historisch-kritische Ausgabe. Hrsg. v. K. Goedeke. Stuttgart, 1867–76.

HELLEN V. D.: *Schillers Sämtliche Werke.* Säkular-Ausgabe. Hrsg. v. E. v. d. Hellen. Stuttgart u. Berlin, [1904–5].

2. Selected Editions of the Ästhetische Briefe *containing Introduction and/or Notes*

ABUSCH, A.: *Philosophische Schriften. Schillers Gesammelte Werke* (Textrevision u. Erläuterung v. C. Noch). Berlin. Bd. viii, 1954–5.

BOXBERGER, R.: *Kleinere Philosophische Schriften. Schillers Werke,* xii. 1. Kürschners *Deutsche National-Literatur.* Berlin u. Stuttgart. Bd. cxxix. 1, [n.d.].

HÖFER, C.: *Über die ästhetische Erziehung des Menschen. Schillers Sämtliche Werke.* Hrsg. v. O. Güntter u. G. Witkowski. Leipzig. Bd. xviii, 1910.

KAISER, P.: *Philosophische Schriften. Schillers Werke.* Hrsg. v. L. Bellermann. Leipzig u. Wien, 1895–7 (Meyers Klassiker Ausgaben). Bd. viii.

KÖHLER, R.: *Ästhetische Schriften.* Goedekes Historisch-kritische Ausgabe. Bd. x, 1871. [A critical edition of the first version of the *Aesthetic Letters* from *Die Horen,* 1795.]

KÜHNEMANN, E.: *Schillers Philosophische Schriften und Gedichte.* ⟨Auswahl⟩. Zur Einführung in seine Weltanschauung. Leipzig, 1922³.

MÜLLER, E.: *Schillers Ausgewählte Werke.* Stuttgart, 1954–5². Bd. v.

WALZEL, O.: *Philosophische Schriften.* Säkular-Ausgabe. Bd. xii [1904–5]. [A critical edition of the revised version of the *Aesthetic Letters* from the *Kleinere prosaische Schriften.* 1801. Bd. iii.]

WIESE, B. v.: *Friedrich Schiller, Über die ästhetische Erziehung des Menschen.* Mit einem Nachwort. Krefeld, 1948.

WIESE, B. v. u. KOOPMANN, H.: *Philosophische Schriften,* i. Nationalausgabe. Bd. xx, 1962; apparatus and commentary in *Philosophische Schriften,* ii. Bd. xxi, 1963. [A critical edition of the revised version of the *Aesthetic Letters* from the *Kleinere prosaische Schriften.* 1801. Bd. iii.]

3. *Translations of the* Aesthetic Letters

ANON.: *Essays aesthetical and philosophical; including the dissertation on the 'Connexion between the animal and the spiritual in Man'.* Newly trsl. from the German. Bohn's Standard Library, London, 1875 [frequently reprinted]. Also included by N. H. Dole in *Aesthetical and philosophical essays by Friedrich Schiller* (Boston, London, 1902, 1915) and by C. W. Eliot in *Literary and Philosophical Essays.* The Harvard Classics, vol. xxxii, New York, 1910.

HEMPEL, CH. J.: *Aesthetical Writings* in *Schiller's Complete Works.* Ed. [with careful revisions and new translations] by Ch. J. Hempel, M.D. Philadelphia, 1861, 1870.

LEROUX, R.: *Lettres sur l'éducation esthétique de l'homme.* Collection Bilingue des Classiques Étrangers. Éditions Montaigne. Paris, 1943.

SNELL, R.: *On the Aesthetic Education of Man. In a Series of Letters.* With an Introduction. London, 1954. Reprinted in Rare Masterpieces of Philosophy and Science. Ed. Dr. W. Stark. New Haven, 1954.

WEISS, J.: *Philosophical and Aesthetic Letters.* Preface by J. Chapman. London, The Catholic Series, 1844. Republished in 1845 by J. Chapman, and also by H. Bohn [not to be confused with the anonymous translation in Bohn's Standard Library above].

For particulars of translations into Italian, Swedish, Czech, Hebrew, Spanish (3), Japanese (3), see Vulpius, op. cit., p. 112.

Recent translations of selected letters are also available in:

CARRITT, E. F.: *Philosophies of Beauty, from Socrates to Robert Bridges.* Being the Sources of Aesthetic Theory. Oxford, 1931, pp. 125 ff.

UNGAR, F.: *Friedrich Schiller.* An Anthology for Our Time. In new English translations and the original German. New York, 1959, pp. 340 ff. [Trsl. by Jane Bannard Greene.]

4. *Letters and Conversations*

BLUMENTHAL, LIESELOTTE: *Schillers Briefe 1798–1800.* Nationalausgabe. Bd. xxx, 1961.

GARLAND, H. B.: *Friedrich Schiller, Ausgewählte Briefe.* Manchester, 1959.

GEIGER, L.: *Briefwechsel zwischen Schiller und Körner.* Stuttgart, [1892–6].

GRÄF, H. G. u. LEITZMANN, A.: *Der Briefwechsel zwischen Schiller und Goethe.* Leipzig, 1912.

JONAS, F.: *Schillers Briefe.* Kritische Gesamtausgabe. Stuttgart, 1892–6. Register bearb. v. A. Leitzmann, 1896.

LEITZMANN, A.: *Briefwechsel zwischen Schiller und Wilhelm von Humboldt.* Stuttgart, 1900³.

MICHELSEN, A. L. J.: *Briefe von Schiller an Herzog Friedrich Christian von Schleswig-Holstein-Augustenburg über ästhetische Erziehung.* In ihrem ungedruckten Urtexte. Berlin, 1876. [Reprint from *Deutsche Rundschau,* ii. 7–9, 11.]

MÜLLER, F. MAX: *Schillers Briefwechsel mit dem Herzog Friedrich Christian von Schleswig-Holstein-Augustenburg.* Eingel. u. hrsg. v. F. Max Müller, Professor in Oxford. Berlin, 1875. [Reprint from *Deutsche Rundschau,* i. 7. Further letters, ibid. (1881), viii. 1.]

2 A 2

MÜLLER-SEIDEL, W.: *Schillers Briefe 1772–1785*. Nationalausgabe. Bd. xxiii, 1956.

PETERSEN, J.: *Schillers Gespräche*. Leipzig, 1911. Abbreviated from: *Schillers Persönlichkeit*. Urteile d. Zeitgenossen u. Dokumente. Gesammelt v. M. Hecker u. J. Petersen. Weimar, 1904–9.

SCHULZ, G.: *Schillers Briefe 1794–1795*. Nationalausgabe. Bd. xxvii, 1958.

SCHULZ, HANS: *Schiller und der Herzog von Augustenburg in Briefen*. Mit Erläuterungen. Jena, 1905.

SIMPSON, L.: *Correspondence of Schiller with Körner*. Comprising Sketches and Anecdotes of Goethe, the Schlegels, Wieland, and other Contemporaries. With biographical sketches and notes. London, 1849.

URLICHS, C. L.: *Briefe an Schiller*. Stuttgart, 1877.

B. SCHILLER'S CONTEMPORARIES

ANON.: 'Kritischer Versuch über das Wort *Aufklärung* zur endlichen Beilegung der darüber geführten Streitigkeiten.' *Deutsche Monatsschrift* [Berlin], 1790. Heft 3, pp. 11 ff., 205 ff.

Ausstellung 'Die Hohe Carlsschule'. Württembergisches Landesmuseum Stuttgart. 4. November 1959 bis 31. Januar 1960.

BURKE, E.:
(1) *A Philosophical Enquiry into the Origin of our Ideas of the Sublime and Beautiful* [1757]. Ed. J. T. Boulton. London, 1958. [Trsl. by C. Garve as *Burkes philosophische Untersuchung über den Ursprung unsrer Begriffe vom Erhabnen und Schönen*. Nach d. 5. englischen Ausg. Riga, 1773.]
(2) *The Correspondence of Edmund Burke*. Ed. T. W. Copeland. Cambridge, 1958. Vol. i: April 1744–June 1768.

BURNEY, CH.: *Dr. Burney's Musical Tours in Europe*. Vol. ii: An Eighteenth-Century Musical Tour in Central Europe and the Netherlands [1772]. Ed. P. A. Scholes. London, 1959.

COLERIDGE, S. T.: *The Notebooks*. Ed. Kathleen Coburn. London, 1957– [in progress]. Vol. i: 1794–1804; vol. ii: 1804–8.

COOPER, A. A. [LORD SHAFTESBURY]: *Characteristicks of Men, Manners, Opinions, Times, &c.* London, 1711.

DALBERG, K. TH. V.: *Grundsätze der Ästhetik*. Erfurt, 1791.

ECKERMANN, J. P.: *Gespräche mit Goethe in den letzten Jahren seines Lebens* [1823–32]. 3 Bde. Leipzig u. Magdeburg, 1836–48.

FICHTE, J. G.: *Sämmtliche Werke*. Hrsg. v. J. H. Fichte. Berlin, 1845–6.

GOETHE, J. W. v.: *Sämtliche Werke*. Jubiläums-Ausgabe. Hrsg. v. E. v. d. Hellen. Stuttgart u. Berlin, 1902–7. Registerband, 1912.

HARRIS, J.:
(1) *Three Treatises*. London, 1744.
(2) *Hermes: Or a Philosophical Inquiry concerning Language and Universal Grammar*. London, 1751.

HERDER, J. G.: *Sämmtliche Werke*. Hrsg. v. B. Suphan. Berlin, 1877–1913.

HEYDENREICH, C. H.: *System der Ästhetik*. Erster Bd. Leipzig, 1790 [no more published].

HÖLDERLIN, F.: *Sämtliche Werke*. Historisch-kritische Ausgabe. Begonnen durch N. v. Hellingrath, fortgef. durch F. Seebass u. L. v. Pigenot. Berlin, 1943[3].

HOME, H. [LORD KAMES]: *Elements of Criticism.* Edinburgh, 1762.

HUMBOLDT, WILHELM V.:
(1) *Über Schiller und den Gang seiner Geistesentwicklung.* Stuttgart u. Tübingen, 1830. [Being the Preface to the first edition of the *Briefwechsel*, reprinted many times.]
(2) *Ansichten über Ästhetik und Literatur von Wilhelm von Humboldt. Seine Briefe an Christian Gottfried Körner. 1793–1830.* Hrsg. v. F. Jonas. Berlin, 1880.

KAMES: *see* HOME.

KANT, IMMANUEL:
(1) 'Beantwortung der Frage: Was ist Aufklärung?' *Berlinische Monatsschrift*, Dezember, 1784.
(2) *Critique of Practical Reason,* and other works on the theory of ethics. Trsl. by T. K. Abbott. London, 1879[2].
(3) *Critique of Aesthetic Judgement.* Trsl. with Seven Introductory Essays, Notes, &c., by J. C. Meredith. Oxford, 1911.
(4) *Critique of Pure Reason.* Trsl. by N. Kemp Smith. London, 1958.

LAMBERT, J. H.: *Neues Organon oder Gedanken über die Erforschung und Bezeichnung des Wahren und dessen Unterscheidung vom Irrthum und Schein.* Leipzig, 1764.

LESSING, G. E.: *Sämtliche Schriften.* Hrsg. v. K. Lachmann. 3. Aufl. besorgt durch F. Muncker. Stuttgart, 1886–1924.

MENDELSSOHN, MOSES: *Gesammelte Schriften.* Hrsg. v. G. B. Mendelssohn. Leipzig, 1843–5.

MEREDITH: *see* KANT (3).

ROUSSEAU, J.-J.:
(1) *Discours sur les sciences et les arts* [1750]. Édition critique par G. R. Havens. New York, London, 1946.
(2) *The Political Writings.* Ed. C. E. Vaughan. Cambridge, 1915.

SHAFTESBURY: *see* COOPER.

SULZER, J. G.: *Allgemeine Theorie der schönen Künste in einzeln, nach alphabetischer Ordnung der Kunstwörter auf einander folgenden Artikeln abgehandelt.* Leipzig, 1778[2].

USINGER, F. [Ed.]: *Du bist ein Mensch! Worte der Erkenntnis und Besinnung von G. Chr. Lichtenberg, H. P. Sturz und J. H. Merck.* Offenbach a. Main, [1941].

VAUGHAN: *see* ROUSSEAU (2).

[WIDMANN, M.]: *Wer sind die Aufklärer? Beantwortet nach dem ganzen Alphabeth.* Zweyte verbesserte Aufl. Augsburg, 1787.

III. CRITICAL LITERATURE

A. ON SCHILLER

ABUSCH, A.: 'Die Briefe über die ästhetische Erziehung des Menschen' in *Schiller in unserer Zeit.* Beiträge zum Schiller-Jahr 1955. Hrsg. v. Schiller Komitee. Weimar, 1955.

BAUMECKER, G.:
   (1) *Schillers Schönheitslehre.* Heidelberg, 1937.
   (2) *Schiller und die französische Revolution.* Berlin, 1939.
BEGENAU, S. H.: *Schiller zu Fragen der Ästhetik.* Einl., Kommentar u. Ausw. Dresden, 1953. (Studienmaterial zur Kunstdiskussion f. d. künstlerischen Lehranstalten d. Deutschen Demokratischen Republik, ii. 8.)
BERGER, K.: *Die Entwicklung von Schillers Ästhetik.* Weimar, 1894.
BOCK, E.: *Über das Verhältnis von Ethik und Ästhetik in Schillers Philosophischen Schriften.* Diss. Leipzig, 1958.
BÖHM, W.: *Schillers Briefe über die ästhetische Erziehung.* Halle/Saale, 1927.
BOUCHER, M.: 'Le "sauvage" et le "barbare" dans les *Lettres sur l'Éducation esthétique*.' *EG* xiv, 1959.
BREUL, K.: 'Schiller Studien i: Die ursprüngliche und die umgearbeitete Fassung der Briefe über ästhetische Erziehung.' *ZfdA* xxviii, 1884.
BUCHWALD, R.: *Schiller.* Leipzig u. Wiesbaden, 1956².
CASSIRER, E.:
   (1) 'Die Methodik des Idealismus in Schillers philosophischen Schriften' in *Idee und Gestalt.* Berlin, 1924².
   (2) 'Schiller und Shaftesbury.' *PEGS* xi, 1935.
CYSARZ, H.: *Schiller.* Halle, 1934.
DAVID, C.: 'La notion de "nature" chez Schiller.' *PEGS* xxix, 1960.
EGGLI, E.: *Schiller et le romantisme français.* Paris, 1927.
EMMELMANN, M.: 'Schillers Briefe "Über die ästhetische Erziehung des Menschen" in ihrer systematischen Bedeutung — mit einer Einleitung über die Entwicklung des Erziehungsgedankens bei Schiller.' *Sokrates. Zeitschrift f. d. Gymnasialwesen,* lxviii [N.F. ii]. Berlin, 1914.
GARLAND, H. B.: *Schiller.* London, 1949.
GERHARD, MELITTA:
   (1) *Schiller.* Bern, 1950.
   (2) 'Schillers Lehre von der erzieherischen Bedeutung des "Spiels".' *GQ* xxxii, 1959.
GNEISSE, K.: *Schillers Lehre von der ästhetischen Wahrnehmung.* Berlin, 1893.
GRAHAM, ILSE A.:
   (1) *Schiller's View of Tragedy in the Light of his General Aesthetics.* Unpubl. Diss. London, 1951.
   (2) 'Schillers *Wilhelm Tell*: Dankgesang eines Genesenden.' *Neophilologus,* xliv, 1960.
   (3) 'The Structure of the Personality in Schiller's Tragic Poetry' in *Schiller Bicentenary Lectures.* Ed. F. Norman. London, 1960.
GROSSMANN, W.: 'The Idea of Cultural Evolution in Schiller's *Aesthetic Education*.' *GR* xxxiv, 1959.
HAMBURGER, KÄTE: 'Schiller und Sartre. Ein Versuch zum Idealismus-Problem Schillers.' *Jb. d. deutschen Schillergesellschaft,* iii, 1959.
HARNACK, O.: *Die klassische Ästhetik der Deutschen.* Würdigung d. kunsttheoretischen Arbeiten Schillers, Goethes u. ihrer Freunde. Leipzig, 1892.
HATFIELD, H.: 'Schiller, Winckelmann and the Myth of Greece' in *Schiller 1759/1959.* Ed. J. R. Frey. Illinois Studies in Language and Literature, xlvi. Urbana, 1959.

HEADSTROM, B. R.: 'The Aesthetic Writings of Schiller.' *Open Court* [Chicago], xliii, 1929.

HELL, V.: 'Esthétique et philosophie de l'art: Éléments d'une théorie classique d'après la correspondance de Schiller.' *EG* xiv, 1959.

HERTEL, H.: 'Schillers und Kants Wertung von Genesis 3.' *Theologische Blätter* [Leipzig], xx, 1941.

JOLLES, M.: 'Toter Buchstabe und lebendiger Geist. Schillers Stellung zur Sprache.' *Deutsche Beiträge zur geistigen Überlieferung* [Chicago], iv: Friedrich Schiller 1759–1959. Bern, 1961.

KAUFMANN, F. W.: *Schiller, Poet of Philosophical Idealism.* Oberlin, Ohio, 1942.

KERKHOFF, EMMY: 'Schiller's Theorie van het schoone.' *Algemeen Nederlands Tijdschrift vor Wijsbegeerte en Psychologie*, xxxiv, 1941.

KERRY, S. S.:
(1) 'The Artist's Intuition in Schiller's Aesthetic Philosophy.' *PEGS* xxviii, 1959.
(2) *Schiller's Writings on Aesthetics.* Manchester, 1961.

KÜHNEMANN, E.: *Kants und Schillers Begründung der Ästhetik.* München, 1895.

LATZEL, S.: 'Die ästhetische Vernunft. Bemerkungen zu Schillers *Kallias* mit Bezug auf die Ästhetik des 18. Jahrhunderts.' *Literaturwissenschaftliches Jb. im Auftrage der Görres-Gesellschaft*, ii, 1961.

LEROUX, R.:
(1) 'Schiller, théoricien de l'État.' *RG* xxviii, 1937.
(2) 'L'idéologie politique dans *Guillaume Tell*.' *EG* x, 1955.
(3) 'Les spéculations philosophiques de Schiller jugées par G. Humboldt.' *EG* xiv, 1959.

LOHNER, E.: 'Schillers Begriff des Scheins und die moderne Lyrik.' *Deutsche Beiträge zur geistigen Überlieferung* [Chicago], iv: Friedrich Schiller 1759–1959. Bern, 1961.

LOSSOW, H.: *Schiller und Fichte in ihren persönlichen Beziehungen und in ihrer Bedeutung für die Grundlegung der Ästhetik.* Diss. Breslau. Dresden, 1935.

LUKÁCS, G.:
(1) 'Schillers Theorie der modernen Literatur' in *Goethe und seine Zeit.* Bern, 1947.
(2) 'Zur Ästhetik Schillers' in *Beiträge zur Geschichte der Ästhetik.* Berlin, 1954.

LUTZ, H.: *Schillers Anschauungen von Kultur und Natur.* Germanische Studien, lx. Berlin, 1928.

MAINLAND, W. F. [Ed.]: *Schiller's 'Über naive und sentimentalische Dichtung'.* Oxford, 1951.

MANN, THOMAS: *Versuch über Schiller.* Seinem Andenken zum 150. Todestage in Liebe gewidmet. Berlin, Frankfurt/M., 1955. [Trsl. by R. and C. Winston in *Last Essays*, London, 1959.]

MARTINI, F.: 'Wilhelm Tell, der ästhetische Staat und der ästhetische Mensch.' *Der Deutschunterricht*, xii, 1960.

MEYER, H.: 'Schillers philosophische Rhetorik.' *Euph* liii, 1959. [Reprinted in *Zarte Empirie. Studien zur Literaturgeschichte.* Stuttgart, 1963.]

MICHELSEN, P.: 'Thomas de Quincey und Schiller.' *GLL* ix, 1956.

MILLER, R. D.: *Schiller and the Ideal of Freedom.* A Study of Schiller's Philosophical Works with Chapters on Kant. Harrogate, 1959.

MINDER, R.: 'Schiller et les Pères "Souabes". Remarques à propos des *Räuber.*' *EG* x, 1955.

MÜLLER, J.: 'Schiller als Kunsttheoretiker.' *Urania,* 1955, Heft 5.

OTOKOZAWA, T.: 'Schillers Ästhetik.' *Jb. d. Goethe Gesellschaft in Japan,* i, 1959.

RAABE, A.: *Idealistischer Realismus.* Eine genetische Analyse d. Gedankenwelt Friedrich Schillers. Bonn, 1962.

RASCH, W.: 'Schein, Spiel und Kunst in der Anschauung Schillers.' *Wirkendes Wort,* x, 1960.

REISS, H. S.: 'The Concept of the Aesthetic State in the Work of Schiller and Novalis.' *PEGS* xxvi, 1957.

ROHRMOSER, G.: 'Zum Problem der ästhetischen Versöhnung. Schiller und Hegel.' *Euph* liii, 1959.

RÖHRS, H.: 'Schillers Philosophie des Schönen.' *Euph* l, 1956.

RÜDIGER, H.: 'Schiller und das Pastorale.' *Euph* liii, 1959.

SAYCE, OLIVE: 'Das Problem der Vieldeutigkeit in Schillers ästhetischer Terminologie.' *Jb. d. deutschen Schillergesellschaft,* vi, 1962.

SCHUCHARD, G. C. L.: 'Fausts "Vorschau" im Lichte von Schillers ästhetischen Briefen.' *JEGP* xlviii, 1949.

SCHÜTZ, O.: *Schillers Theorie des Schönen: eine kritische Betrachtung.* Schlehdorf, Obb., 1951.

SPRANGER, E.: 'Schillers Geistesart gespiegelt in seinen philosophischen Schriften und Gedichten.' *Abhandl. d. Preuss. Akad. d. Wissensch.,* Berlin, 1941.

STAHL, E. L.: *Friedrich Schiller's Drama: Theory and Practice.* Oxford, 1954.

STORZ, G.: *Der Dichter Friedrich Schiller.* Stuttgart, 1959.

TENENBAUM, A.: *Kants Ästhetik und ihr Einfluss auf Schiller.* Diss. Berlin, 1933.

ULRICH, J.: 'Goethes Einfluss auf die Entwicklung des Schillerschen Schönheitsbegriffes.' *Jb. d. Goethe-Gesellschaft,* xx, 1934.

USINGER, F.: 'Friedrich Schiller und die Idee des Schönen.' *Abhandl. d. Klasse d. Lit. Akad. d. Wissensch. u. d. Lit.,* i. Wiesbaden, 1955.

VORLÄNDER, K.: *Kant, Schiller, Goethe.* Leipzig, 1923².

WAIS, K.: 'Schillers Wirkungsgeschichte im Ausland' in *An den Grenzen der Nationalliteraturen.* Berlin, 1958.

WALDECK, MARIE-LUISE: 'Shadows, reflections, mirror-images and virtual "objects" in *Die Künstler* and their relation to Schiller's concept of "Schein".' *MLR* lviii, 1963.

WEIRICH, R.: *Schillers Auffassung von der Kunst als einer erziehenden Macht und ihre Bedeutung für die französische Literatur des 19. und 20. Jahrhunderts.* Diss. München. Würzburg, 1936.

WENZEL, H.: *Das Problem des Scheins in der Ästhetik.* Schillers 'Ästhetische Briefe'. Diss. Köln, 1961.

WIESE, B. v.: *Friedrich Schiller.* Stuttgart, 1959.

WILKINSON, ELIZABETH M.:
    (1) 'Schiller's Concept of *Schein* in the Light of recent Aesthetics.' *GQ* xxviii, 1955.

(2) 'Über den Begriff der künstlerischen Distanz. Von Schiller und Wordsworth bis zur Gegenwart.' *Deutsche Beiträge zur geistigen Überlieferung* [Chicago], iii. Bern, 1957.

(3) 'Reflections after Translating Schiller's *Letters on the Aesthetic Education of Man*' in *Schiller Bicentenary Lectures*. Ed. F. Norman. London, 1960. [Trsl. as 'Zur Sprache und Struktur der ästhetischen Briefe.' *Akzente*, 1959, Heft 5.]

(4) 'Schiller und die Idee der Aufklärung.' *Jb. d. deutschen Schillergesellschaft*, iv, 1960.

(5) *Schiller: Poet or Philosopher?* Special Taylorian Lecture. Oxford, 1961.

WILLOUGHBY, L. A.: 'Schiller on Man's Education to Freedom through Knowledge.' *GR* xxix, 1954.

WITTE, W.:

(1) *Schiller.* Oxford, 1949.

(2) 'Law and the Social Order in Schiller's Thought.' *MLR* l, 1955.

(3) 'Schiller: Reflections on a Bicentenary.' *PEGS* xxviii, 1959.

B. GENERAL

ALEXANDER, S.: *Beauty and other Forms of Value.* London, 1933.

ARIS, R.: *History of Political Thought in Germany from 1789 to 1815.* London, 1936.

BABBITT, I.: *On Being Creative, and other Essays.* London, Cambridge, Mass., 1932.

BEARDSLEY, M. C.: *Aesthetics. Problems in the Philosophy of Criticism.* New York, 1958.

BETTERIDGE, H. T.: 'Fichte's Political Ideas: a Retrospect.' *GLL* i, 1937.

BIANQUIS, GENEVIÈVE: 'Les écrivains allemands et la Révolution française.' *Revue des Cours et Conférences*, xl, 1939.

BOSANQUET, B.: *A History of Aesthetic.* London, 1892.

BOUCHER, M.: *La Révolution de 1789 vue par les écrivains allemands ses contemporains.* Paris, 1954.

BRUFORD, W. H.: *Culture and Society in Classical Weimar 1775–1806.* Cambridge, 1962.

BULLOUGH, E.: *Aesthetics.* Lectures and Essays. Ed. Elizabeth M. Wilkinson. London, 1957.

CARRITT, E. F.: *Philosophies of Beauty, from Socrates to Robert Bridges.* Being the Sources of Aesthetic Theory. Oxford, 1931.

CASSIRER, E.: *The Philosophy of the Enlightenment.* Princeton, 1951.

CASSIRER, H. W.: *A Commentary on Kant's 'Critique of Judgment'.* London, 1938.

CLARK, R. T.: *Herder: His Life and Thought.* Berkeley, Los Angeles, 1955.

COBBAN, A.: *In Search of Humanity.* The Rôle of the Enlightenment in Modern History. London, 1960.

COURTHOPE, W. J.: *Life in Poetry: Law in Taste.* Two Series of Lectures delivered in Oxford, 1895–1900. London, 1901.

DEMETZ, P.: *Marx, Engels und die Dichter.* Stuttgart, 1959.

DROZ, J.: *L'Allemagne et la Révolution française.* Paris, 1949.

362   BIBLIOGRAPHY

ELTON, W. [Ed.]: *Aesthetics and Language*. Oxford, 1954.
FOSS, M.: *The Idea of Perfection in the Western World*. Princeton, 1946.
FRANKEL, CH.: *The Case for Modern Man*. New York, 1957.
GILBERT, KATHARINE & KUHN, H.: *A History of Aesthetics*. New York, 1956².
GOMBRICH, E. H.:
    (1) '*Icones Symbolicae:* The Visual Image in Neo-Platonic Thought.'
        Journal of the Warburg and Courtauld Institutes, xi, 1948.
    (2) *Art and Illusion*. New York, 1960.
GOOCH, G. P.:
    (1) *Germany and the French Revolution*. London, 1920.
    (2) 'The Political Background of Goethe's Life.' *PEGS* iii, 1926.
    (3) *Studies in German History*. London, 1948.
GREEN, F. C.: *Rousseau and the Idea of Progress*. Zaharoff Lecture for 1950.
    Oxford, 1950.
HAMPSHIRE, S.:
    (1) 'The Conflict between Art and Politics.' *The Listener*, lxiv, no. 1646,
        1960.
    (2) 'A Ruinous Conflict.' *New Statesman and Nation*, lxiii, no. 1625, 1962.
HOURD, MARJORIE L.: *The Education of the Poetic Spirit*. London, 1949.
HUIZINGA, J.: *Homo Ludens*. A Study of the Play Element in Culture. Trsl. by
    R. F. C. Hull. London, 1949.
JOHNSON ABERCROMBIE, M. L.: *The Anatomy of Judgment*. An Investigation
    into the Processes of Perception and Reasoning. London, 1960.
JOUVENEL, B. DE: *Sovereignty*. An Inquiry into the Political Good. Trsl. by J. F.
    Huntington. Cambridge, 1957.
JUNG, C. G.:
    (1) *Psychological Types*. Trsl. by H. Godwin Baynes. London, 1923.
    (2) *The Integration of the Personality*. Trsl. by S. M. Dell. London, 1940.
KENNICK, W. E.: 'Does Traditional Aesthetics Rest on a Mistake?' *Mind*, lxvii,
    1958.
KNOX, I.: *The Aesthetic Theories of Kant, Hegel and Schopenhauer*. New York,
    1936.
KNOX, R. A.: *Enthusiasm*. A Chapter in the History of Religion, with special
    reference to the seventeenth and eighteenth centuries. Oxford, 1950.
KRONER, R.: *Kant's Weltanschauung*. Trsl. by J. E. Smith. With revisions by the
    author. Chicago, 1956.
KÜHNE, O.: 'Schöne Kunst und Lebenskunst.' *Zeitschrift f. Ästhetik u.
    allgemeine Kunstwissenschaft*, xxxvi, 1942.
LANGER, SUSANNE K.: *Feeling and Form*. New York, London, 1953.
LEHMANN, A. G.: *The Symbolist Aesthetic in France, 1885-1895*. Oxford,
    1950.
LEROUX, R.:
    (1) *Guillaume de Humboldt*. Publications de la Faculté des Lettres de l'Uni-
        versité de Strasbourg, lix. Paris, 1932.
    (2) 'L'esthétique sexuée de Guillaume de Humboldt.' *EG* iii, 1948.
MARITAIN, J.: *Art and Scholasticism*. Trsl. by J. F. Scanlan. London, 1946.
MEREDITH: *see* KANT (3).
MORGENSTERN, L.: *Esthétiques d'Orient et d'Occident*. Paris, 1937.

NICOLSON, MARJORIE H.:
(1) *Newton Demands the Muse.* Newton's 'Opticks' and the Eighteenth-Century Poets. History of Ideas Series, ii. Princeton, 1946.
(2) *The Breaking of the Circle.* Evanston, 1950.
NIVELLE, A.: *Les Théories esthétiques en Allemagne de Baumgarten à Kant.* Bibliothèque de la Faculté de Philosophie et Lettres de l'Université de Liège, cxxxiv. Paris, 1955.
NOLTE, F. O.: *Art and Reality.* Lancaster, Pa., 1942.
OGDEN, C. K., RICHARDS, I. A., & WOOD, J.: *The Foundations of Aesthetics.* London, 1922.
OGDEN, R. M.: *Psychology and Education.* London, 1926.
PARKER, DE WITT H.: *The Analysis of Art.* New Haven, 1926.
PASCAL, R.: '"Bildung" and the Division of Labour' in *German Studies presented to W. H. Bruford.* London, 1962.
PASSMORE, J. A.: 'The Dreariness of Aesthetics.' *Mind,* lx, 1951. [Reprinted in *Aesthetics and Language.* Ed. W. Elton. Oxford, 1954.]
RADHAKRISHNAN, S.: *Eastern Religions and Western Thought.* Oxford, 1939.
RAUHUT, F.: 'Die Herkunft der Worte und Begriffe *Kultur, Civilisation* und *Bildung.*' *GRM* xxxiv, 1953.
READ, H.:
(1) *Education through Art.* London, 1943.
(2) 'The Third Realm of Education.' The Burton Lecture. In *The Creative Arts in American Education.* Cambridge, Mass., 1960.
ROSENBLATT, LOUISE: *L'idée de l'art pour l'art dans la littérature anglaise pendant la période victorienne.* Bibliothèque de la Revue de Littérature Comparée, lxx. Paris, 1931.
RÜSTOW, A.: *Ortsbestimmung der Gegenwart.* Bd. ii: *Weg der Freiheit.* Zürich, 1952.
The Secret of the Golden Flower: A Chinese Book of Life. Trsl. and explained by R. Wilhelm with a European Commentary by C. G. Jung. Trsl. into English by C. F. Baynes. London, 1931.
SPARSHOTT, F. E.: *The Structure of Aesthetics.* Toronto, 1963.
STERN, A.: *Der Einfluss der französischen Revolution auf das deutsche Geistesleben.* Stuttgart, Berlin, 1928.
SUZUKI, D. T.: *Essays in Zen Buddhism.* 3 vols. London, 1927–1934.
TUBACH, F. C.: 'Perfectibilité: der zweite Diskurs Rousseaus und die deutsche Aufklärung.' *EG* xv, 1960.
VAUGHAN: see ROUSSEAU (2).
WEITZ, M.: *Philosophy of the Arts.* Cambridge, Mass., 1950.
WEITZ, M. [Ed.]: *Problems in Aesthetics.* An Introductory Book of Readings. New York, 1959.
WELLEK, R.: *A History of Modern Criticism: 1750–1950.* In Four Volumes. New Haven, 1955– [in progress]: i. The Later Eighteenth Century; ii. The Romantic Age.
WHYTE, L. L.: *The Unconscious before Freud.* A history of the evolution of human awareness. New York, 1960.
WILKINSON, ELIZABETH M.:
(1) *Johann Elias Schlegel: A German Pioneer in Aesthetics.* Oxford, 1945.

(2) '"Form" and "Content" in the Aesthetics of German Classicism' in *Stil- und Formprobleme in der Literatur*. Heidelberg, 1959.

WILLIAMS, R.: *Culture and Society, 1780–1950*. London, 1958.

WOLLHEIM, R.: 'Art and Illusion.' *British Journal of Aesthetics*, iii, 1963.

WÜRZBACH, F.: *Die zwei Grundtypen des Menschen. Der 'grosse Kopf' und der 'Günstling der Natur'*. Reutlingen, Leipzig, 1941².

ADDENDA

KOMMERELL, M.: 'Schiller als Psychologe' in *Geist und Buchstabe der Dichtung*. Frankfurt/M., 1940.

HAMBURGER, KÄTE: 'Schillers Fragment "Der Menschenfeind" und die Idee der Kalokagathie.' *Deutsche Vierteljahrsschrift*, xxx, 1956.

WIESE, B. V.: 'Die Utopie des Ästhetischen bei Schiller' in *Gratulatio. Festschrift für Christian Wegner*. Hamburg, 1963.

SCHAPER EVA: 'Friedrich Schiller: Adventures of a Kantian.' *British Journal of Aesthetics*, iv, 1964.

IVES, MARGARET C.: *An Examination of Schiller's Concept of Harmony*. With special reference to the use of the word 'Harmonie' in the philosophical writings. Unpubl. Diss. London, 1964.

ELLIS, J. M.: *Schiller's 'Kalliasbriefe'*. A critical re-examination of the text and of traditional methods of interpreting Schiller's Aesthetics. Unpubl. Diss. London, 1965.

INDEX

Numerals in italics denote entries in the Bibliography